Studies in Diplomacy and International Relations

Series Editors
Donna Lee
Keele University
Keele, UK

Paul Sharp
College of Liberal Arts
University of Minnesota
Duluth, USA

Marcus Holmes
College of William & Mary
Williamsburg, USA

Founded over two decades ago by Geoff Berridge, the *Studies in Diplomacy and International Relations* (*SDIR*) series aims to publish the best new scholarship interrogating and demonstrating the central role of diplomacy in contemporary international relations. We are proud to continue this tradition by publishing diverse and cutting-edge research from a global community of scholars that investigates diplomatic theory and practice, the diplomacy of sustainability and climate change, trade, economic and business diplomacy, international negotiations, the diplomacy of global health, the constitution and effects of great power politics, global communications, and public diplomacy, among other topics. *SDIR* seeks to publish work that will be of interest to communities of scholars, practitioners of diplomacy, and policymakers alike.

For an informal discussion for a book in the series, please contact one of the series editors Donna Lee (d.lee@keele.ac.uk), Paul Sharp (psharp@d.umn.edu), or Marcus Holmes (mholmes@wm.edu).

This series is indexed in Scopus.

Paul Webster Hare
Juan Luis Manfredi-Sánchez
Kenneth Weisbrode
Editors

The Palgrave Handbook of Diplomatic Reform and Innovation

palgrave
macmillan

Editors
Paul Webster Hare
Boston University
Boston, MA, USA

Kenneth Weisbrode
Bilkent University
Ankara, Turkey

Juan Luis Manfredi-Sánchez
School of Foreign Service
Georgetown University
Washington, D.C., USA

ISSN 2731-3921 ISSN 2731-393X (electronic)
Studies in Diplomacy and International Relations
ISBN 978-3-031-10970-6 ISBN 978-3-031-10971-3 (eBook)
https://doi.org/10.1007/978-3-031-10971-3

© The Editor(s) (if applicable) and The Author(s), under exclusive licence to Springer Nature Switzerland AG 2023
This work is subject to copyright. All rights are solely and exclusively licensed by the Publisher, whether the whole or part of the material is concerned, specifically the rights of translation, reprinting, reuse of illustrations, recitation, broadcasting, reproduction on microfilms or in any other physical way, and transmission or information storage and retrieval, electronic adaptation, computer software, or by similar or dissimilar methodology now known or hereafter developed.
The use of general descriptive names, registered names, trademarks, service marks, etc. in this publication does not imply, even in the absence of a specific statement, that such names are exempt from the relevant protective laws and regulations and therefore free for general use.
The publisher, the authors, and the editors are safe to assume that the advice and information in this book are believed to be true and accurate at the date of publication. Neither the publisher nor the authors or the editors give a warranty, expressed or implied, with respect to the material contained herein or for any errors or omissions that may have been made. The publisher remains neutral with regard to jurisdictional claims in published maps and institutional affiliations.

Cover illustration: © olrat/istock
Broken Chair is a symbol of both fragility and strength, precariousness and stability, brutality and dignity. Originally conceived by Handicap International-Humanity & Inclusion with the aim of urging States to ban anti-personnel mines (in 1997) and cluster munitions (in 2008), Broken Chair now embodies the fight against explosive weapons and the violence inflicted on populations during armed conflicts. Created by Daniel Berset, at the request of the organization, and installed in front of the United Nations, the monument is a challenge to the international community. It reminds it of its obligations to respect international humanitarian law and to protect civilians.

This Palgrave Macmillan imprint is published by the registered company Springer Nature Switzerland AG.
The registered company address is: Gewerbestrasse 11, 6330 Cham, Switzerland

Contents

Part I Introduction 1

1 Diplomacy the Neglected Global Issue: Why Diplomacy
   Needs to Catch Up with the World 3
   Paul Webster Hare

Part II State of Diplomacy 21

2 The Closing of the Diplomatic Mind 23
   Kenneth Weisbrode

3 A Diplomatic Taxonomy for the New World Disorder 41
   Chas W. Freeman Jr.

4 Knowledge Diplomacy: A Conceptual Analysis 59
   Jane Knight

5 Why Reforms Are Needed in Bilateral Diplomacy: A Global
   South Perspective 81
   Kishan S. Rana

Part III Politicization of Diplomacy — 109

6 Diplomats and Politicization — 111
   Pauline Kerr

7 Digital Diplomacy and International Society in the Age of Populism — 143
   Onur Erpul

8 Withering Ministry of Foreign Affairs: Evidence from China — 167
   Qingmin Zhang and Lize Yang

9 South Africa and Its Foreign Alignment and Practice: From Hope to Dashed Expectations — 193
   Anthony James Leon

Part IV Reforming Institutions — 211

10 From Great Expectations to Dwindling Status: Brazilian Diplomacy's Response to Post-Cold War Upheavals — 213
    Rogério de Souza Farias and Antônio Carlos Lessa

11 Crisis Prevention and Stabilization Made in Germany: Meeting the Demands of Modern Diplomacy? — 235
    Sarah Bressan

12 Integrated Statecraft and Australia's Diplomacy — 251
    Tom Barber and Melissa Conley Tyler ⓘ

13 African Union Reform: Challenges and Opportunities — 277
    Emmanuel Balogun and Anna Kapambwe Mwaba

14 What Motivates South Korea's Diplomatic Reform and Innovation? — 295
    HwaJung Kim

15 The Transformations of French Diplomacy — 315
    Maxime Lefebvre

Part V	Digital Revolution and Diplomatic Reform	321
16	**Digital Diplomacy in the Time of the Coronavirus Pandemic: Lessons and Recommendations** Corneliu Bjola and Michaela Coplen	323
17	**Exploring the Usefulness of Artificial Intelligence for Diplomatic Negotiations: Two Case Studies** Volker Stanzel	343
18	**Beyond Meeting and Tweeting: The Next Challenges for Innovation in Diplomacy** Tom Fletcher	367
19	**Disinformation and Diplomacy** Juan Luis Manfredi-Sánchez 🆔 and Zhao Alexandre Huang 🆔	375
20	**Digitalizing South American MFAs: Reform and Resistance** Jorge Heine and Daniel Aguirre 🆔	397
Part VI	Multilateral Diplomacy and Innovation	417
21	**Toward a More Credible Multilateralism at the United Nations: A Few Practical Steps** Bénédicte Frankinet	419
22	**A New Logic of Multilateralism on Demand** Akiko Fukushima	435
23	**About Spheres of Influence** Chas W. Freeman Jr.	455
24	**Regional Diplomacy and Its Variations: Change and Innovation** Rajiv Bhatia and Kishan S. Rana	481
25	**Why Collective Diplomacy Needs to Embrace Innovation** Martin Wählisch	505

26 Innovating International Cooperation for Development: A New Model for Partnerships Between Developed and Middle-Income Countries 521
José Antonio Zabalgoitia and Antonio Tenorio

27 The UAE's Innovative Diplomacy: How the Abraham Accords Changed (or Did Not Change) Emirati Foreign Policy 543
William Guéraiche

28 Small States: From Intuitive to Smart Diplomacy 559
Vesko Garčević

29 Urban Diplomacy: How Cities Will Leverage Multilateralism 581
Juan Luis Manfredi-Sánchez ⓘ

30 Reforming Global Health Diplomacy in the Wake of COVID-19 601
Mark C. Storella

31 The Reform of Humanitarian Diplomacy 629
Gregory Simons and Anna A. Velikaya

32 Geoeconomic Diplomacy: Reforming the Instrumentalization of Economic Interdependencies and Power 649
Kim B. Olsen

33 Science Diplomacy with Diplomatic Relations to Facilitate Common-Interest Building 673
Paul Arthur Berkman

34 Climate Diplomacy for a 1.5 Degree World 691
Olivia Rumble and Andrew Gilder

35 Global Diplomacy and Multi-stakeholderism: Does the Promise of the 2030 Agenda Hold? 703
Felicitas Fritzsche and Karin Bäckstrand

36 Conclusions 731
Paul Webster Hare

Index 737

Notes on Contributors

Daniel Aguirre is Professor at Arizona State University in Phoenix. Previously he lectured at Universidad de Chile's Instituto de Estudios Internacionales and other universities in Chile. He has also guest lectured at Universidad de la Sabana of Colombia and Universidad Nacional de Costa Rica, among other universities in the region. His research on Latin American public diplomacy has been published in high-profile journals and book volumes in both English and Spanish. He received a Master of Arts in International Studies from the University of Miami and holds a PhD in Communication from Pontificia Universidad Católica de Chile. He is an active member of the International Studies Association within both the International Communication and Diplomatic Studies sections. He can be followed on Twitter @agzocar.

Karin Bäckstrand is Professor of Environmental Social Science in the Department of Political Science at Stockholm University and researcher at the Institute for Future Studies. Her research revolves around the democratic legitimacy of global environmental politics, non-state actors in climate change governance, and the role of public–private partnerships in the 2030 Agenda.

Emmanuel Balogun is Assistant Professor of Political Science and Faculty Affiliate in Black Studies at Skidmore College. He is the author of *Region-Building in West Africa: Convergence and Agency in ECOWAS* (2022); an International Affairs Fellow at the Council on Foreign Relations; and a policy advisor with the U.S. Department of State in the Bureau of African Affairs. He was also the inaugural Diversity, Equity, and Inclusion fellow for Bridging the Gap. He has a PhD in Political Science and International Relations from the University of Delaware.

Tom Barber is Program Officer at the Asia-Pacific Development, Diplomacy & Defence Dialogue (AP4D), a new initiative that provides a platform for constructive dialogue, fresh ideas, and future-focused debate on Australia's role in the Asia-Pacific region.

Paul Arthur Berkman is a science diplomat, polar explorer, and global thought leader applying international, interdisciplinary, and inclusive processes with informed decision-making to balance national interests and common interests for the benefit of all on Earth across generations. He co-convened and chaired the Antarctic Treaty Summit in Washington, D.C., producing the first book on Science Diplomacy as well as a Congressional Resolution adopted with unanimous consent by the U.S. House of Representatives and U.S. Senate. Among other events, he also co-convened and chaired the first dialogue between the North Atlantic Treaty Organization and Russia regarding security in the Arctic.

Rajiv Bhatia is Distinguished Fellow, Foreign Studies Program at Gateway House, Mumbai. During a 37-year career in the Indian Foreign Service, he served as Ambassador to Myanmar and Mexico and as High Commissioner to Kenya, South Africa, and Lesotho. He dealt with a part of South Asia, while posted as Joint Secretary in the Ministry of External Affairs. He is a member of the Confederation of Indian Industry's International Advisory Council, Trade Policy Council, and Africa Committee. He is the Chair of the Federation of Indian Chambers of Commerce and Industry's Task Force on Blue Economy, and served as Chair of Core Group of Experts on the Bay of Bengal Initiative for Multi-Sectoral Technical and Economic Cooperation. He is a founding member of the Kalinga International Foundation and a member of the governing council of Asian Confluence. As Director General of the Indian Council of World Affairs from 2012 to 2015, he played a key role in strengthening India's Track-II research and outreach activities.

Corneliu Bjola is Associate Professor of Diplomatic Studies at the University of Oxford and Head of the Oxford Digital Diplomacy Research Group. He has published extensively on issues related to the impact of digital technology on the conduct of diplomacy, with a recent focus on public diplomacy, international negotiations, and methods for countering digital propaganda. His recent co-edited volume *Digital Diplomacy and International Organizations: Autonomy, Legitimacy and Contestation* (2020) examines the broader ramifications of digital technologies for the internal dynamics, multilateral policies, and strategic engagements of international organizations.

Sarah Bressan is Research Fellow at the Global Public Policy Institute in Berlin. Her work focuses on international security, political violence, conflict prevention, and the role of data, technology, foresight, and evaluation methods in German and European foreign policy. She was editor-in-chief of the PeaceLab Blog, the German government's debate platform on peacebuilding and conflict prevention, and has worked on academia-policy exchange and diplomatic training programs at Freie Universität Berlin, the German Federal Foreign Office, and the UN Office of the High Commissioner for Human Rights.

Melissa Conley Tyler, FAIIA, is Program Lead at the Asia-Pacific Development, Diplomacy & Defence Dialogue (AP4D), a new initiative that provides a platform for constructive dialogue, fresh ideas, and future-focused debate on Australia's role in the Asia-Pacific region.

Michaela Coplen is a DPhil candidate in the Department of Politics and International Relations at the University of Oxford. A Marshall Scholar, Coplen received her MPhil in International Relations from the University of Oxford and her BA from Vassar College.

Onur Erpul is Postdoctoral Fellow at the Center for Foreign Policy and Peace Research, Ihsan Doğramacı Peace Foundation. He is also an adjunct instructor in the Department of International Relations at Middle East Technical University. Erpul's publications have appeared in *International Theory*, *Foreign Policy Analysis*, *Southeast European and Black Sea Studies*, and *E-IR*.

Rogério de Souza Farias works for the Brazilian Ministry of Economy and is Professor of International Relations at the University of Brasília.

Tom Fletcher, CMG, is Principal of Hertford College, Oxford. He is a former British ambassador and foreign policy adviser to three prime ministers, and visiting professor at New York University. He is the author of the bestselling *The Naked Diplomat* (2016) and *Ten Survival Skills for a World in Flux* (2022).

Bénédicte Frankinet is a former Belgian diplomat. She was Minister-Counsellor at the Belgian Embassy in Paris and then Ambassador in Zimbabwe (1999–2003), also accredited in Zambia, Malawi, and Mozambique. From 2003 to 2008 she was Director of the United Nations Service at the Ministry of Foreign Affairs, after which she served as Ambassador to Israel (2008–13). Finally, she was Permanent Representative of Belgium to the United Nations in New York from 2013 to 2016, before acting as Special Envoy charged with heading Belgium's successful campaign for a non-permanent seat on the United Nations Security Council.

Chas W. Freeman Jr. is Visiting Scholar at Brown University's Watson Institute for International and Public Affairs. He is the former U.S. Assistant Secretary of Defense for International Security Affairs (1993–94), Ambassador to Saudi Arabia (1989–92), Principal Deputy Assistant Secretary of State for African Affairs (1986–89), and Chargé d'affaires at Bangkok (1984–86) and Beijing (1981–84). He was the principal American interpreter during Richard Nixon's path-breaking 1972 visit to Beijing. He is a graduate of Yale University and Harvard Law School who studied at the Universidad Nacional Autónoma de México and the 國立臺中教育大學 (Taichung National Normal University).

Felicitas Fritzsche is a PhD candidate in the Department of Political Science at Stockholm University as part of the Transformative Partnerships 2030 project. Her research focuses on global governance and multi-stakeholder partnerships. She has previously worked in the German public sector on the United Nations and development cooperation.

Akiko Fukushima is Senior Fellow at The Tokyo Foundation for Policy Research and a non-resident fellow of the Lowy Institute. She has a Master's degree in International Economy and International Relations from the Paul H. Nitze School of Advanced International Studies at Johns Hopkins University and a PhD in International Public Policy from Osaka University. She has previously been Director of Policy Studies at the National Institute for Research Advancement, Senior Fellow at the Japan Foundation, and Professor at Aoyama Gakuin University. She is a member of the International Advisory Board of *The Hague Journal of Diplomacy*. She has also been a visiting professor at the University of British Columbia and was a member of Prime Minister Abe's Advisory Panel on National Security and Defence Capabilities.

Vesko Garčević is Professor of the Practice of International Relations at the Frederic S. Pardee School of Global Studies at Boston University. He served as the Ambassador of Montenegro to NATO and to the Organization for Security and Co-operation in Europe (OSCE). He was also Montenegrin Ambassador to Austria, Belgium, Luxembourg, and the Netherlands. During his diplomatic career he held important positions at the challenging political time of the dissolution of the Socialist Federal Republic of Yugoslavia and democratic transition of Montenegro. After Montenegro regained independence in 2006, he served as the first Montenegrin Ambassador to Austria and the OSCE.

Andrew Gilder is South Africa's leading private sector environmental, climate change, and carbon markets lawyer. He is a director of Climate Legal, with more than 19 years' legal practice experience specializing in climate change (mitigation and adaptation), climate finance and development, carbon markets, carbon tax, environmental and energy law, policy, and governance. He has practical experience which spans a range of African jurisdictions, including advice to public and private sectors on water law and governance, the development and implementation of climate change, climate finance, carbon markets, carbon tax, environmental and energy law, policy, and governance, as well as regulatory and transactional advice.

William Guéraiche is Associate Professor at the University of Wollongong Dubai where he is also the director of the Master of International Relations. He successively taught at the American University of Dubai and the American University of Emirates. His book *The UAE: Geopolitics, Modernity and Tradition* (2017) examined the geopolitical issues in the Emirates. In his latest edited volume on traditional and non-traditional issues, *Facets of Security in the United Arab Emirates* (2022), he explores topics such as cybersecurity, demographics and community security, and the securitization of COVID-19.

Paul Webster Hare was a British diplomat for 30 years and the British ambassador to Cuba from 2001 to 2004. He is Senior Lecturer in International Relations at the Frederick S. Pardee School of Global Studies at Boston University. Hare graduated with First Class Honors in Politics and Economics from the University of Oxford in 1972 and from the College of Law in London in 1976. He worked for five years in the private sector, in law and investment banking, before entering the British Diplomatic Service. He served overseas at the UK Representation to the EU in Brussels, Portugal, New York, and Venezuela as Deputy Head of Mission. He was Head of the Foreign Office's Non-Proliferation Department and the first Project Director for the UK's presence at the Shanghai World Expo in 2010. Hare is a Fellow of the Weatherhead Center for International Affairs at Harvard University and served as president of the British Baseball Federation from 2000 to 2001. He was designated a Lieutenant of the Royal Victorian Order by Her Majesty Queen Elizabeth II. His novel *Moncada: A Cuban Story*, set in modern Cuba, was published in 2010. His book *Making Diplomacy Work: Intelligent Innovation for the Modern World* was published in 2015.

Jorge Heine is Research Professor at the Frederick S. Pardee School of Global Studies at Boston University. He is also a lawyer, IR scholar, and diplomat with a special interest in the international politics of the Global South. He has served as ambassador of Chile to China (2014–17), to India (2003–7), and to South Africa (1994–99), and as a Cabinet Minister in the Chilean Government. A past Vice-President of the International Political Science Association, he was Centre for International Governance Innovation (CIGI) Professor of Global Governance at the Balsillie School of International Affairs, Wilfrid Laurier University, from 2007 to 2017, and a Distinguished Fellow at CIGI. He has been a Guggenheim Fellow; a Visiting Fellow at St Antony's College, Oxford University; a United Nations Research Fellow at the Economic Commission for Latin America and the Caribbean; Visiting Professor of Political Science at the University of Konstanz; and the Pablo Neruda Visiting Professor of Latin American Studies at the University of Paris.

Zhao Alexandre Huang is Associate Professor of Communication at the Université Paris Nanterre. He works at the DICEN-IDF laboratory. He studies institutional practices, political and public communication strategies, and the formation of strategic narratives in the practice of public diplomacy. His research interests include public diplomacy, strategic communication, public relations, social media, and China's propaganda and international communication.

Pauline Kerr is Fellow Emerita at The Australian National University. She teaches in the Master of Diplomacy program and researches practices and theories of diplomacy, mostly in the Asia-Pacific region. Her recent research includes "China's Diplomacy: Towards ASEAN Way Norms in the South China Sea," *The Hague Journal of Diplomacy* 16, no. 2–3 (2021): 1–29, and *The SAGE Handbook of Diplomacy* (2016), edited by C. Constantinou, P. Kerr, and P. Sharp.

HwaJung Kim is Research Professor at the Institute of International Area Studies, Graduate School of International Studies (GSIS), Ewha Womans University, having been selected by the National Research Foundation in mid-2021. Previously, she worked at Ewha GSIS as an invited professor (2020–21) after completing a postdoctoral fellowship awarded by the National Research Foundation at the Institute of International Affairs, Seoul National University (2017–19).

Jane Knight is Professor at the University of Toronto. She is a scholar of the international, intercultural, and global dimensions of international higher education and more recently of international relations. Her work in over 75 countries brings a comparative, development, and international perspective to her research, teaching, and policy work. She sits on the advisory boards of several international organizations, universities, and journals and is the author of numerous publications. She holds a PhD in Higher Education and a PhD in Political Science, and is the recipient of several international awards including two honorary doctorates.

Maxime Lefebvre is Professor of Diplomacy and Geopolitics at the ESCP Business School. He is also a former French Ambassador.

Anthony James Leon served from 2009 until 2012 as South African Ambassador Extraordinary and Plenipotentiary to Argentina, Uruguay, and Paraguay. Previously he led the Democratic Alliance in South Africa and was Leader of the Official Oppositions in Parliament. He is a qualified attorney and lectured in Law at the University of Witwatersrand, Johannesburg. He was awarded fellowships to the Institute of Politics, John F. Kennedy School of Government, Harvard University (2007), Cato Institute, Washington, D.C. (2008), and Stellenbosch Institute for Advanced Studies (2013). He has authored five books, including *The Accidental Ambassador: From Parliament to Patagonia* (Pan Macmillan 2013) and *Future Tense: Reflections on my Troubled Land South Africa* (2021).

Antônio Carlos Lessa is Full Professor of International Relations at the University of Brasília, Brazil, and a researcher for the National Council for Scientific and Technological Development.

Juan Luis Manfredi-Sánchez is Prince of Asturias Distinguished Visiting Professor at the School of Foreign Service, Georgetown University, and Full Professor at University of Castilla-La Mancha, Spain. He writes on public diplomacy and propaganda, international relations and diplomacy, communication and technology, as well as political risk and the liberal order.

Anna Kapambwe Mwaba is Assistant Professor of Government and Faculty Affiliate in African Studies at Smith College. Mwaba was a McPherson/Eveillard Postdoctoral Fellow in Government from 2019 to 2021. She received her Doctorate in Political Science from the University of Florida, Gainesville, with concentrations in Comparative Politics and International Relations. Her research focuses on the role of African international and regional organizations in election observation and democracy promotion in Southern Africa.

Kim B. Olsen is a diplomatic practitioner and analyst who has published widely on sanctions, geoeconomics, and EU foreign and security policy. A former Senior Adviser to the Danish Ministry of Foreign Affairs, he is affiliated with the Danish Institute for International Studies and the German Council on Foreign Relations.

Kishan S. Rana joined the Indian Foreign Service in 1960. He served at the Indian Embassy, Beijing (1963–65, 1970–72); worked on China at the Ministry of External Affairs (1965–67, 1972–73); was Ambassador and High Commissioner: Algeria, Czechoslovakia, Kenya, Mauritius, and Germany; and consul general in San Francisco. He served on the staff of Prime Minister Indira Gandhi (1981–82). He has written 12 books, and about 300 articles and book reviews for academic and other journals. He is also Professor Emeritus at the DiploFoundation.

Olivia Rumble is Director of Climate Legal and Adjunct Senior Lecturer in Environmental Law at the University of Cape Town (UCT), and a visiting law lecturer at UCT's African Climate and Development Initiative. She has extensive expertise in climate change law, particularly on the African continent, and she regularly advises and writes on climate change law, carbon tax, carbon markets, climate finance, climate change loss and damage, and related legal and policy developments. She co-led the drafting team for the South African Climate Change Bill, 2018, and has worked and extensively written on climate change legislative developments at the national level.

Gregory Simons is Associate Professor at the Institute for Russian and Eurasian Studies at Uppsala University in Sweden and a lecturer in the Department of Communication Science at Turiba University in Riga, Latvia. He has a PhD from the University of Canterbury in New Zealand and his research interests include changing political dynamics and relationships, mass media, public diplomacy, political marketing, crisis management communications, media and armed conflict, and the Russian Orthodox Church. He also researches the relationships and connections between information, politics, and armed conflict more broadly, such as the Global War on Terror and Arab Spring.

Volker Stanzel is a former German diplomat who worked as Political Director and Ambassador to both China and Japan. Since retiring, he has been teaching in Germany, the United States, and Japan, and works at the German Institute for International and Security Affairs in Berlin.

Mark C. Storella is Professor of the Practice at the Frederick S. Pardee School of Global Studies at Boston University. As a longtime career U.S. diplomat, Storella served as U.S. Ambassador to Zambia, Deputy Assistant Secretary of

State, and Dean of the State Department leadership school. He has published articles on regional diplomacy, multilateral diplomacy, and health diplomacy.

Antonio Tenorio is Head of the Department of Cooperation in Innovation, Science, and Technology at the Mexican Embassy in the Netherlands and professor at the Universidad Iberoamericana in Mexico City. He is a leading specialist on issues of digital society, cultural change, global identities, and hybrid cultures. He graduated with honors as a sociologist at the National Autonomous University of Mexico. He holds a graduate degree in Modern Language and Culture and Public Policy. He has served previously as Cultural Attaché at the Embassy of Mexico in Chile and Attaché for Cultural, Academic, and Scientific Cooperation at the Embassy of Mexico in Colombia.

Anna A. Velikaya is Lecturer at the Russian Presidential Academy of National Economy and Public Administration, and is also affiliated with Turība University in Riga, Latvia. She has a PhD from MGIMO University. She is the co-editor of *Russia's Public Diplomacy* (Palgrave Macmillan, 2019). Her research interests include public and cultural diplomacy, nation-branding, and Eurasian and Central Asian states.

Martin Wählisch leads the Innovation Cell in the Policy and Mediation Division of the UN Department of Political and Peacebuilding Affairs, an interdisciplinary team dedicated to exploring, piloting, and scaling new technologies, tools, and practices in conflict prevention, mediation, and peacebuilding. He holds a PhD in International Law and recently published the edited volume *Rethinking Peace Mediation: Challenges of Contemporary Peacemaking Practice* (2021).

Kenneth Weisbrode is Assistant Professor of History at Bilkent University; co-founder of the Network for the New Diplomatic History (https://newdiplomatichistory.org); and co-editor of its journal, *Diplomatica* (Brill).

Lize Yang is Assistant Professor at the School of International Relations of Sun Yat-Sen University, with research and teaching interests in diplomatic studies, international financial institutions, and China's foreign policy. He obtained his PhD from the School of International Studies of Peking University. His research has appeared in *Global Policy*, *World Economics and Politics*, and *Foreign Affairs Review*.

José Antonio Zabalgoitia is Mexican Ambassador to the Kingdom of the Netherlands and Permanent Representative to the Organisation for the Prohibition of Chemical Weapons. He has been the Deputy Head of Mission in the Embassy to the United States (2017–19), Consul General in Miami

(2013–17), Director General for Western Hemisphere Multilateral and Regional Organizations (2008–13), Chief of Staff to the Secretary of Foreign Relations (2006–8), Director General for Latin America and the Caribbean (2001–4), and the Ambassador to Bolivia (2004–6). He holds a degree in International Relations from El Colegio de México (1980–85) and graduate degrees in International Relations from the London School of Economics and Political Science (1987), in Communication and Political Management from Universidad Complutense (1999), and in Peace Studies from Oslo University (1987). He is also one of the first two civilians to graduate from the National Defense College, Mexico's top military education program (1989).

Qingmin Zhang is Professor and Chair of the Department of Diplomacy, School of International Studies, Peking University. He teaches and conducts research on diplomatic studies and theory of foreign policy analysis, with an empirical focus on China. He has published seven books, including *Contemporary China's Diplomacy* (Beijing: China International Press, 2020) and *Foreign Policy Analysis* (Beijing: Peking University Press, 2019), and translated three books from English to Chinese, including *Diplomacy in a Globalizing World: Theories and Practice* (Shanghai: Shanghai People's Press, 2020). He has also contributed many book chapters and articles to scholarly journals, including *The Hague Journal of Diplomacy*, the *Journal of Contemporary China*, the *Chinese Journal of International Politics*, and the *Journal of Chinese Political Science*, as well as to major international studies in leading Chinese journals.

List of Figures

Fig. 7.1	Estimated marginal means of likes (Turkish Minister of Foreign Affairs, 9.2016–12.2020)	155
Fig. 7.2	Estimated marginal means of likes (Turkish Ministry of Foreign Affairs, 9.2016–12.2020)	155
Fig. 7.3	Estimated marginal means of likes (Turkish Embassy, Washington, D.C.), 9.2016–12.2020)	156
Fig. 7.4	Estimated marginal means of likes (Serdar Kılıç, Turkish Ambassador, Washington, D.C.), 9.2016–12.2020)	156
Fig. 7.5	Estimated marginal means of likes (Recep Tayyip Erdoğan)	157
Fig. 8.1	Statistical graph of the quantity of information blind spots by the spokesperson of the MFA (2002–19)	172
Fig. 8.2	Proportion graph of distribution of information blind spots by the spokesperson of the MFA (2002–19)	173
Fig. 16.1	Crisis communication approaches: adapt, improvise, and ignore	328
Fig. 16.2	Showcasing international collaboration	331
Fig. 16.3	Showcasing international collaboration	333
Fig. 16.4	Countering versus promoting disinformation	335
Fig. 16.5	Thinking outside the box	338
Fig. 20.1	Institutional Twitter followers in 2020 versus 2015. Source: The authors	411
Fig. 20.2	Follower growth of institutional accounts on Twitter. Source: The authors	411
Fig. 26.1	Middle-income countries' share of total ODA 2000–20. Source: OECD 2022	523
Fig. 26.2	Select middle-income countries' share of total ODA 2000–20. Source: OECD 2022	524
Fig. 26.3	Select middle-income countries' share of total ODA and of ODA to middle-income countries 2000–20. Source: OECD 2022	525

Fig. 26.4	Optimus4 helix cycle	537
Fig. 26.5	Partners. Four strategic lines and two cross-cutting areas. Source: Sistema de Naciones Unidas México 2020	538
Fig. 33.1	Balancing national interests and common interests on a planetary scale began during the twentieth century, illustrated with international environmental treaties to address sustainability questions at local-global levels. Adapted from Berkman (2002), including legal establishment of areas beyond national jurisdictions (yellow), international spaces (Kish 1973; Berkman et al. 2011; Berkman 2020a) to build common interests and minimize risks of conflict over jurisdictional boundaries across the Earth on a planetary scale (Berkman 2009)	674
Fig. 33.2	**a–d** Globally interconnected civilization time scales revealed by exponential changes with **(a)** climate and human-population size over decades to centuries in view of global events; **(b)** high-technology change over years to decades illustrated by "Moore's Law" with transistors on a chip; **(c)** global pandemic over months to years with COVID-19 cases; and **(d)** social-media interactions over minutes to months, illustrated by 2014–15 tweets about "Black Lives Matter." Adapted from Berkman (2020b), which has references to data sources with elaboration	677
Fig. 33.3	Spectrum of jurisdictions on Earth, illustrated by megacities with capacities of states at subnational levels, representing an inclusive framework for humankind to address impacts, issues, and resources in our globally interconnected civilization (Fig. 33.1) with diplomacy across diverse time scales (Fig. 33.2a–d). Adapted from Berkman et al. (2022a)	679
Fig. 33.4	Short- to long-term features of diplomatic relations, highlighting exponential change across an inflection point toward logistic (S-shaped, sigmoid) change, as described by numbers (N) changing per unit of time (t). Diplomatic relations are required before-through-after inflection points with scalability across embedded time scales in our globally interconnected civilization (Fig. 33.2a–d). Adapted from Berkman (2020b, 2020c)	681
Fig. 33.5	Informed decisions operate across a "continuum of urgencies," illustrated for peoples, nations, and our world from security to sustainability time scales (Figs. 33.1, 33.2, 33.3, and 33.4). Negotiation strategies that contribute to the decision-making with diplomatic agents (Boxes 33.1 and 33.3) also exist short term in view of conflicts to resolve and long term in view of common interests to build—balancing societal, economic, and environmental considerations across generations. Adapted from	

	Vienna Dialogue Team (2017); Young et al. (2020); Berkman et al. (2022a)	683
Fig. 33.6	Pyramid of informed decision-making with science diplomacy to apply, train, and refine across a "continuum of urgencies" (Vienna Dialogue Team 2017), characterizing the scope of an informed decision (Fig. 33.5) as the apex goal of an holistic process that begins at the stage of questions to build common interests among allies and adversaries alike. Enhancing research capacities is a positive feedback that results from common-interest building. Adapted from Berkman et al. (2022a)	684

List of Tables

Table 4.1	Conceptual framework for IHERI in a knowledge diplomacy approach	67
Table 4.2	PAU: application of key elements of knowledge diplomacy conceptual framework	74
Table 4.3	Differences between the role of IHERI in knowledge diplomacy and soft power approaches	75
Table 4.4	Proposed conceptual framework for IHERI in a soft power approach	76
Table 7.1	Breakdown of tweets by numbers (n English tweets = 3976, Turkish tweets = 5089, total n = 9056)	161
Table 7.2	Estimated marginal means	162
Table 20.1	Platform use for digital diplomacy 2021	402
Table 20.2	Presidents during two waves of digital diplomacy	408
Table 26.1	Size of economies	527
Table 26.2	Inequality	529
Table 26.3	Public expenditure	531
Table 26.4	Education rankings	533
Table 26.5	Investment	534
Table 29.1	City diplomacy (Acuto et al. 2018)	588
Table 29.2	Urban diplomacy	589

Part I

Introduction

1

Diplomacy the Neglected Global Issue: Why Diplomacy Needs to Catch Up with the World

Paul Webster Hare

Introduction

This book seeks to demonstrate that diplomacy is a neglected global issue. The ways it is conducted need more attention because, as a public good, it is central to how the world solves problems and avoids conflict. Diplomacy seeks to smooth edges of disputes and promote agreements for the mutual interest of states. It does this, in Ernest Satow's classic definition, by "the application of intelligence and tact to the conduct of official relations between the governments of independent states and between governments and international organizations" (Satow 2009 [1917]).

The book was conceived before the COVID pandemic and the war in Ukraine. It began as a brainstorming session among mainly practitioners of diplomacy on what they saw as obstacles to making diplomacy more effective. It was not crisis-driven but by a recognition that collective diplomacy is seldom considered by states as a topic for reform.

The group agreed that diplomacy is not currently treated as a public good that needs nurturing. The reasons are not difficult to identify. There is no set of global lobbying organizations such as on climate and environmental issues. There has been no Third World War leading to a redesign of diplomatic institutions. There has been no sustainable partnership between global business

P. W. Hare (✉)
Boston University, Boston, MA, USA

interests and foundations for a collaboration between states and non-states on ideas for reform. Few of the major technology companies see the future of diplomacy as linked with their continued development and growth. It is true that the United Nations has from time to time urged a new look at topics such as Security Council reform. But it has not created sustained momentum to recraft the Charter of the United Nations which was written for a different era—the era of the immediate aftermath of the Second World War and before the Internet. And the last salient reason is that world leaders generally have little time or interest in refining an activity which has no domestic dividend and may be viewed as a wasteful diversion of resources away from what are seen as foreign policy priorities. For reform and innovation to be achieved there needs to be a procedural imperative.

Once a book project developed, the group of interlocutors decided to invite a wide-ranging international group of experts—scholars and practitioners, and some a bit of both—to focus on areas where diplomacy could reform and innovate its practice. Several authors have drawn on their personal experiences. The result is a mixed anthology of a reexamination of diplomatic principles and practice, with the focus being on avenues for changes in and improvement of policies. The purpose was to enhance the chances of making diplomacy more effective and reaffirm the mutual benefit to all states. The authors are citizens of some 30 different countries. We (the editors) did not intend the list of countries to be exclusive and hope the essays will stimulate discussion of and ideas on better diplomacy in many others. All the authors in the project agree that the practice of both bilateral and multilateral diplomacy needs to be readdressed. The intended audience of this book comprises those interested in studying diplomacy in international relations, how it affects the solutions that are achieved, and how its failures affect the evolution of the planet. More generally it is hoped that representatives of states will recognize that diplomatic procedures should be adjusted according to the circumstances of today. Many of the authors address how the practice of diplomacy needs to catch up with contemporary power distribution and technology.

One of the challenges of addressing the issue of diplomacy is to define what the activity is. It has increasingly been replaced as a term by such concepts of "governance" in which diplomacy is a constant component; and the theory of diplomacy has long been analyzed in an academic context. But it has been practiced for centuries longer. The authors of the chapters that follow address both the study and practice of the activity. As a former practitioner I think I am typical in not having thought much during my career about ways to reform the system. A practitioner works for one actor in the system whose interests are paramount. Yet the system of diplomacy is essentially a team game where all actors must cooperate and follow the rules and norms if it is to function at all.

The current lack of states' attention to how diplomacy is conducted was not always so. Diplomacy has been addressed as a practical issue by agreeing legally binding conventions and in the rules and legal structure of global and regional institutions of international affairs. Collective diplomacy aims to prevent conflict through a process of dispute settlement. It attempts to create order out of a chaotic world. The chapters here were written in the context of the failings of the global pandemic response which were due to the methods diplomacy applied. The invasion of Ukraine was also a failure of diplomacy because conflict broke out. Some of the pinnacles of modern diplomacy were disparaged. Core articles of the UN Charter, agreed in 1945 and respecting sovereignty of independent states, were breached. Long-standing humanitarian and arms control achievements—such as the Hague Conventions, the creation of the International Committee of Cross, and the Geneva Conventions—have been flouted as war returned to Europe. And major conflicts within states continue to rage in the Middle East and Africa.

The current methods of conducting diplomacy did not happen by accident. They have been built by law and custom. Most are decades old and take no account of the existence of the Internet. The Vienna Conventions on Diplomatic and Consular Relations (VCDR and VCCR), from 1961 and 1963 respectively, remain of critical importance. They continue to be largely respected as was shown during Julian Assange's long sojourn in the embassy of Ecuador in London. But they again were drafted for another era and are obviously antiquated. The era of the 2020s has so far been preoccupied with other global issues than diplomacy such as health and climate. But the way states conduct diplomacy, how they treat other states with which they have diplomatic relations, how they interact to work on issues that no state can solve on its own—this activity is a global issue. Diplomacy is as much a public good as international air traffic control.

As well as arguing that the methods and institutions of diplomacy need more attention this project has sought to suggest some concrete initiatives which are feasible and could make diplomacy more effective. These are discussed further in the conclusions.

The study of the theory of diplomacy enriches how far the world might collectively address reform in the twenty-first century. One clear outcome of decades of academic discussion is that there is no statute-based definition nor a single paradigm through which to interpret the practice. Raymond Cohen (1998) called it "the engine-room" of International Relations but it means different things to different states. The relevance of diplomatic studies to any quest for practical reform is that they may show that certain features of diplomacy evolve without state interventions. They may offer pointers to the way diplomacy will develop if the theories are based on empirical evidence.

For its part, theory may also determine how far diplomacy is likely to reform itself. If norms are fixed for diplomacy then one needs to explain how diplomacy has adapted such norms—for example, by states renouncing some sovereignty through the United Nations and in agreeing to renounce the possession of nuclear weapons. And the diplomatic skills that have evolved should impact how those involved are trained in the future.

A central question for academic study is how far diplomacy establishes methods of behavior in a section of society where diplomats operate. Those who have been termed the constructivist school believe that diplomats have created their own social reality (Bjola and Kornprobst 2018). How far do diplomats establish their own norms which may change over time? The concept perhaps explains how some institutions come to anticipate erosion and loss of effectiveness.

Another issue is the identity of diplomacy. The concept of self-identity, according to John Locke, is based on memory which if forgotten loses its identity. "Our consciousness being interrupted, and we losing sight of our past selves, doubts are raised whether we are the same thinking thing" (Locke 1689). Scholars now discuss how far the very rationale of diplomacy is being forgotten.

Scholars also identify the unique features of diplomats in their role as agents representing their governments. And their capacity to communicate and negotiate on behalf of governments. Their job is to inhabit a world where they represent national interests but also have a stake in creating relationships that are necessary for the promotion of those interests. As Paul Sharp wrote, they "are living separately and wanting to do so while having to conduct relations with others" (Sharp 1999). Equally they are no longer unique as many more actors have entered the field including supranational diplomatic entities like the European Union and African Union and powerful non-state actors such as global charities and businesses. Sharp notes that diplomacy "no longer is the master institution of international society" (ibid.).

Diplomacy is the way states represent themselves to others. Academic study therefore has confronted the issue of hierarchy of states. Is such a hierarchy essential to the functioning of diplomacy? John Searle has analyzed the factors that determine how status of various individuals gives them special status in society (Searle 2010). His research suggests that those who engage in diplomacy have been endowed with such status. But the success of diplomacy depends on how far diplomats recognize each other's functions. Raymond

Cohen (1999) sees differences between cultures as a major factor in how diplomacy is conducted. His analysis impacts how every state will view the prospects of reform of diplomacy. States view the value of diplomatic relations differently and though they recognize reciprocal benefits, they attach different priorities to it. For example some may see it as fundamentally a networking operation where contacts are made as diversely as possible but there is little incentive to build consensus and peaceful solutions. In these cases national interests are in networking for its own sake.

Academic studies have in some instances highlighted the areas where reform might be pursued. These include the erosion of diplomatic norms and the struggles for diplomacy to find a new identity. And diplomats may be losing their unique status as communicators and negotiators. Technology has multiplied the capacity of others to seek to engage in the practice.

Diplomacy Affects Not Only States

Diplomacy is a public good. It benefits all inhabitants of the planet. The Preamble to the United Nations Charter was written in the name of international publics:

> WE THE PEOPLES OF THE UNITED NATIONS DETERMINED to save succeeding generations from the scourge of war, which twice in our lifetime has brought untold sorrow to mankind, and to reaffirm faith in fundamental human rights, in the dignity and worth of the human person, in the equal rights of men and women and of nations large and small, and to establish conditions under which justice and respect for the obligations arising from treaties and other sources of international law can be maintained, and to promote social progress and better standards of life in larger freedom, AND FOR THESE ENDS to practice tolerance and live together in peace with one another as good neighbors, and to unite our strength to maintain international peace and security, and to ensure, by the acceptance of principles and the institution of methods, that armed force shall not be used, save in the common interest, and to employ international machinery for the promotion of the economic and social advancement of all peoples.

After years of the scourge of war diplomacy reorganized itself at the San Francisco conference that established the United Nations in 1945. It had the essential support of the victors of the Second World War. The same conference was observed by over 2000 international press and non-governmental representatives who viewed it as an issue going beyond just the states.

Diplomacy was everybody's business though the states would decide what would be agreed.

Winston Churchill was one of many strong supporters of the Charter though he was not directly involved in its creation. He saw it as essential for the diplomacy of the United States and the big powers to continue to support it. "We must make sure that its work is fruitful, that it is a reality and not a sham, that it is a force for action, and not merely a frothing of words, that it is a true temple of peace in which the shields of many nations can some day be hung up, and not merely a cockpit in a Tower of Babel" (Churchill 1946). From its early years the United Nations survived many challenges including a boycott by the USSR.

Rotary International was one of 42 organizations the U.S. Secretary of State Edward Stettinius invited to serve as consultants to its delegation at the San Francisco conference. Other Rotarians from other continents were members of their own nations' delegations. It is worth noting that Rotary International, alongside many other non-state charitable foundations, remains a major donor to the United Nations World Health Organization. The mood was reflected in the words of the Governor of California, Earl Warren, in welcoming the delegates. He did not use the word diplomacy but the aspiration was clear.

> We recognize that our future is linked with a world future in which the term 'good neighbor' has become a global consideration. We have learned that understanding of one another's problems is the greatest assurance of peace. And that true understanding comes only as a product of free consultation. This conference is proof in itself of the new conception of neighborliness and unity which must be recognized in world affairs. (United Nations 1945)

What was agreed in the United Nations Charter was a set of guidelines and guardrails of state to state diplomacy. And the circumstances in which united action could be agreed in issues of security. It set the principle of one state one vote in the General Assembly. But its terms—including any changes to the text of the Charter—were locked under the veto power of the Permanent Five members. These states—"the Republic of China, France, the Union of Soviet Socialist Republics, the United Kingdom of Great Britain and Northern Ireland, and the United States of America"—remain the only states mentioned in the Charter. The seats of China and the USSR are now the People's Republic of China and the Russian Federation. The Charter was signed on June 26, 1945, by 50 nations—now the membership is 195 which includes the Holy See and Palestine as observers. The vast majority of current UN members took no part in negotiating the articles of the organization. And the world's supreme collective diplomatic institution does not mention the word "diplomacy."

The Vienna Conventions on Diplomatic Relations (1961) and Consular Relations (1963) are more evidence that diplomacy goes beyond an academic study. Precise rules for how diplomatic representations should behave and what immunities and privileges they should receive have been set. Kai Bruns (2014) explained the objectives of these conventions. "International custom had proved too vague and could not keep pace with technological advancements and the increasing number of states within international society."

The VCDR negotiations included discussion not only of codification of existing customary law but also "progressive development of international law." Not every challenging issue of the 1950s and 1960s was included. For example, diplomatic asylum was not mentioned in the Conventions because it was seen as too sensitive in the Cold War era. But in the preamble of the VCDR the aims of the Convention are unequivocal. "Having in mind the purposes and principles of the Charter of the United Nations concerning the sovereign equality of States, the maintenance of international peace and security, and the promotion of friendly relations among nations." They were intended to make diplomacy work better.

Nevertheless the Conventions were never intended to last indefinitely. Bruns notes that "as some delegates pointed out, the Convention was not made for the long term but tailored to immediate Cold War needs" (ibid.). This cornerstone of diplomatic activities has also remained unchanged ever since and the many new states entering the diplomatic arena after 1961 played no part in its drafting.

Why This Era Is Ripe for Reform and Innovation

The authors recognize that there have indeed been many developments since the foundation of the United Nations which have affected diplomatic activity. It is not true that diplomacy has stood still for the last half-century.

Global diplomacy has evolved in key institutional ways. The creation of permanent diplomatic groupings of the major economic powers such as the G7 and G20 and the many regional and state groupings suggests that the post-Second World War structure did not meet diplomatic requirements. The expansion of the United Nations made decision-making too cumbersome. At an early stage some foresaw the likely lack of capacity of the UN for action.

The Vienna Conventions were born in an era of state-centric diplomacy, an era when humanitarian, science, health, and climate diplomacy were largely unknown. Embassies were the focal points of representation and communication. Every state was both a receiving and sending state giving the Convention a basis for reciprocal benefit. The Convention contains a key provision which still underpins the concept of diplomatic relations and the privileges and immunities granted. Article 41 states, "Without prejudice to their privileges and immunities, it is the duty of all persons enjoying such privileges and immunities to respect the laws and regulations of the receiving State. They also have a duty not to interfere in the internal affairs of that State." There is no definition of such interference and in 1961 no one had dreamt of the new possibilities of such interference generated by the Internet.

One question this volume seeks to examine is how far the activity of diplomacy influences the outcomes of its negotiations. How diplomats and those they network with behave in crises is critical to the outcomes. But they seldom address the linkages between, for example, science, climate, and health diplomacy. Or between urban diplomacy and regional diplomacy. Nutrition and access to clean water affect multiple UN agencies and non-state actors. But diplomatically there is little formal coordination. A world of considerable interdependence and interconnectedness generates different types of crises where multiple interests are at stake. Diplomacy seldom pulls together the same institutions, types of resources, forms of communication, or partners to respond to each.

A key issue in determining whether there is an appetite for reform of diplomacy is how contemporary leaders view its effectiveness. Do they recognize its shortcomings and the need for collective action? There is indeed evidence that some contemporary leaders do have a sense of diplomatic malaise.

António Guterres, the UN Secretary General, in his statement to the General Assembly of September 21, 2021, gave a damning indictment of the practice of diplomacy—without ever mentioning the word:

> The pandemic has demonstrated our collective failure to come together and make joint decisions for the common good, even in the face of an immediate, life-threatening global emergency.
>
> This paralysis extends far beyond COVID-19. From the climate crisis to our suicidal war on nature and the collapse of biodiversity, our global response has been too little, too late.
>
> Unchecked inequality is undermining social cohesion, creating fragilities that affect us all. Technology is moving ahead without guard rails to protect us from its unforeseen consequences.

Global decision-making is fixed on immediate gain, ignoring the long-term consequences of decisions—or indecision.

Multilateral institutions have proven too weak and fragmented for today's global challenges and risks.

As a result, we risk a future of serious instability and climate chaos. (Guterres 2021)

It is not only the world's top diplomat who recognizes dysfunction in diplomacy. Xi Jinping, the President of China, has written that China must "uphold the protection of the country's sovereignty, security and development interests, proactively participate in and show the way in reform of the global governance system, creating an even better web of global partnership relationships" (Reuters 2018). Russian President Vladimir Putin in a wide-ranging speech in 2012 gave Russia's views on the inadequacy of global diplomatic mechanisms. "It is important for the United Nations and its Security Council to effectively counter the dictates of some countries and their arbitrary actions in the world arena. Nobody has the right to usurp the prerogatives and powers of the UN, particularly the use of force with regard to sovereign nations" (Putin 2012).

Putin also recognized the new opportunities offered by the Internet to interfere in other countries' affairs. "Regrettably, these methods are being used all too frequently to develop and provoke extremist, separatist and nationalistic attitudes, to manipulate the public and to conduct direct interference in the domestic policy of sovereign countries" (ibid.).

U.S. President Joe Biden has called for "relentless diplomacy" and believes that "we stand… at an inflection point in history. We must work together as never before" (UN News 2021). He concurs that diplomacy must find ways of working more effectively. And the United States must work harder at making diplomacy work: "The world does not organize itself" (ibid.). And the United States should recognize that "the international system that the United States constructed is coming apart at the seams" (Biden 2020).

However, recognizing diplomacy's shortcomings does not mean that national leaders will see it as a priority for their foreign policies.

What Parts of Diplomacy Need Reform?

The issues below are some of those where reform efforts should be directed.

- The need for Diplomacy to be re-addressed as a global issue. The image on this book's cover is the broken chair in front of The United Nations Palais de Nations in Geneva. This recognizes key arms control agreements achieved by diplomacy but the incomplete nature of progress. And that diplomacy has fallen short in its aims. Diplomacy needs to be self-critical again. And open to a reassessment of how better it can achieve its objectives.

* How and with whom states communicate and negotiate. Although the right of free communication between the sending state and its missions abroad has long been established in terms of the inviolability of couriers and the diplomatic dispatches which they carried—so that any interference was covert—in 1961 only those states with advanced technological resources operated transmitters. Today there are no such limits as to how states communicate both to other states and non-state entities. Digital communications have made diplomacy truly borderless. Diplomacy has taken collectively to the social media platforms but public diplomatic communication is often for self-gratification and scoring points to an international audience. This is a not necessarily a new phenomenon for diplomacy but our society's growing penchant for trolling has permeated diplomatic exchanges.
* An interdependent world in trade and investment with the global challenges listed by António Guterres must now coexist with a new world order with multiple power centers and rivalries. As Guterres noted, multilateral diplomacy has proved weak and fragmented. William Burns, former U.S. ambassador to Russia and Deputy Secretary of State, sees the "schizophrenia of an emerging international system with globalization of the world economy alongside the fragmentation of international politics" (Burns 2019).
* The essentials of diplomacy as an alternative to war or animosity between states. The meaning of diplomatic relations and sovereignty requires diplomacy to return to the fundamentals of mutual benefits and respect. States differ in how they view the implications of having diplomatic relations. Diplomacy is valued less and seen more as a simple adjunct of power and an opportunity to damage other. If sovereignty of nations is not respected it gives diplomacy often impossible tasks.
* The responsibility for diplomacy. Should diplomacy be left to successive national leaders to extemporize on how the activity is conducted? Or can diplomacy only be revived by concerted action where states not individual leaders make new pledges to renew the rationale for the benefits that diplomacy brings to all? Any readdressing of the activity will need cooperation and assistance from the leadership of the United Nations and the regional diplomatic organizations. And drawing from the history of diplomacy the

integration more of the non-state sectors, particularly the big technology companies and their platforms.
- The United Nations Charter and its principles. If reform of the Charter was straightforward it would have been done long ago. Any analysis of the prospects for reaffirmation of the principles of the organization needs to start from this assumption. The United Nations itself has been active at looking at collective reform. The problem has been enlisting the attention of states. As part of its 75th anniversary commemoration the United Nations has urged a new look at a "Common Agenda" and has made the case for effective multilateralism to craft "a new global deal to deliver global public goods and address major risks." They say that multilateral action is urgently required in four legally recognized "global commons"—the atmosphere, the high seas, Antarctica, and outer space—each of which is in deep crisis.
- The P5—The permanent members of the UN Security Council. Their role is pivotal in the UN Charter. Global diplomacy has to contend with its history of failures, procedural disputes, vetoes, and theatrics. But it is there and it should not be avoided in any discussion about reform. Many recognize, as does William Burns, the P5 are the "jealous guardians of an outdated system" (Burns 391). Diplomacy needs to accept that imaginative solutions could be devised within the UNSC's existing framework. One idea is suggested in the Conclusions.
- Upgrading of and providing new aspirations for the United Nations to deal with the problem of implementation. The United Nations has urged an expansion of global commitments in new areas. For example, they have proposed a Global Digital Compact covering the risks of internet fragmentation, data protection, and accountability for misleading content. The United Nations will appoint a new Global Envoy for Future Generations—a new Future Labs. And a High-level Advisory Board led by former heads of state and government on improved governance of global public goods. This would complement The United Nations high-level Advisory Board on Economic and Social Affairs established in 2018. It aims to bring new impetus to multilateralism and promote involvement and new commitments of states and non-state actors. Implementation of this reform—not the direction proposed—will be the major challenge.
- The responsibility of states for the behavior of their citizens which affect international relations. This principle is embodied in Article 22 of the VCDR which deals with the protection of diplomatic premises. "The receiving State is under a special duty to take all appropriate steps to protect the premises of the mission against any intrusion or damage and to

prevent any disturbance of the peace of the mission or impairment of its dignity." In other words, any threat from a citizen or other resident of the Receiving State to diplomatic premises is the responsibility of Receiving State which must take action to eliminate the threat. Now the borderless digital world means that the capacity of citizens of one state to harm another state and its citizens has greatly increased. They can cyber-attack for ransom or other motives a key installation such as a power grid or energy pipeline. This is a significantly dangerous development for diplomacy and the cause of peace.

- The practice of disinformation and weaponizing of information. Both activities are seeking to undermine the trust which is central to the practice of diplomacy. It will muddy the waters of any negotiation that diplomatic relations try to promote. And it may be designed to sow seeds of conflict. There is the pernicious problem of difficulty of attribution so states and others can camouflage their identities in this. This is not a new issue for diplomacy but it has been exacerbated by the digital age. Again, this should be a core issue in any attempt to redefine the principles of diplomacy.
- The decline of the western Liberal Democratic Model. This will be seen through different eyes across the world and is being welcomed by some states. But the attractions of populism and authoritarianism mean that accountability for diplomacy to national electorates is diminishing. So is the capacity of leaders to work multilaterally. In a personalization and politicization of diplomacy it matters little to a president unshackled by checks, elections, or a constitution if there are collective objectives or guidelines in diplomatic behavior. The outcome is judged by how it reflects domestically on the personal prestige of political leaders. This is not perhaps as recent a problem for diplomacy as many assume.
- The stovepipe problems of international diplomacy. Major global issues are treated largely separately by core groups. Information and policy approaches do not get properly dispersed. This is also relevant to the regionalism of diplomacy. The various fora where global issues are debated and measures proposed may be better frameworks for action but may conduct their negotiations with little regard for other regional actors. This is a well-discussed issue for reform and the recent pandemic has again brought it to the fore. For example, health issues affect security which affects climate mitigation measures, migration, and sustainable development. Yet the solutions to or progress on common actions in each may well be dependent on others. Diplomacy needs to be the catalyst to connect the implications of these complex issues. Yet the coordinating and central roles of Foreign Ministries are being eroded.

- The historic treaties and conventions of modern diplomacy. Only an irredeemable optimist would think that the widespread revision of these legally binding texts is feasible. But the institution that has played a leading role in revision of such texts—The UN International Law Commission—could do so again and also be an instrument for the key principles of the UN Charter to be reaffirmed.
- The value and status of Foreign Ministries, embassies, and the cadres of diplomatic corps. The Foreign Ministry has a central role in the VCDR. Without it as central coordinating feature diplomatic objectives are increasingly blurred. And the expense and vulnerability of diplomatic missions on their current scale are perhaps not justified. Digital diplomacy offers the possibility of more tele-diplomacy which might make it more effective just as health consultancies and education can be delivered remotely.
- The non-state interested parties. As noted above, many non-state actors were interested when the United Nations was founded. Many now play an integral and indispensable part in diplomacy, whether as implementing state-based decisions, wealth-generators who provide the funding for diplomacy, philanthropy, awareness-raisers, or tech platforms. Climate agreements are just one example of state policies which cannot be implemented without the commitment and cooperation of non-state actors. They are the distinguished non-state diplomatic legacies of the International Committee of the Red Cross and the Nobel Foundation. As Ole Jacob Sending (2011, 528) and his colleagues have argued, "as innovative relationships develop among an increasingly heterogeneous cast of diplomatic actors, the nature and functions of diplomacy also evolves." Their work needs to be more fully integrated into government decisions. The UN-proposed Global Digital Compact offers a major opportunity for significant diplomatic collaboration between the state and non-state sectors.
- Non-state actors interested in global prosperity and stability should coalesce more to assist states promote better diplomacy. The tech companies have as much interest in a peaceful, stable world as the ICRC and Greenpeace. And it would serve everyone's cause if they recognized that consensus-building between states will not happen without their input. They could make their individual contributions to specific causes more effective if they collaborated in efforts to improve diplomatic procedures and to recognize that global consensus-building through diplomacy by states is in all their interests.
- Losers and winners if diplomacy proves increasingly incapable of meeting today's challenges. The losers would be everyone. But if the world increasingly sees diplomacy as a zero-sum game and fragments in its responses to

problems no one country can solve then among the biggest losers would be global businesses. Within the business sector global tech companies would be particularly vulnerable because their businesses depend more on global cooperation than such sectors as manufacturing which must be physically dependent on specific geographical locations.
- Diplomacy's long-term adaptability. There are future challenges where diplomacy is largely stalled. One is the governance of outer space. Diplomacy needs to be made resilient enough to handle what could determine the future of the planet. Disputes and conflict in space and its implications for governance and dominance outside the atmosphere may increasingly undermine all aspects of diplomacy. One day reformers of diplomacy may have to contemplate how the planet might react collectively to an exo-atmospheric common threat from nature or a hostile civilization. How would diplomacy perform in such a challenge to planetary security from another universe?

Innovation

Innovation is a challenge for diplomacy because it represents change. Again the question is whether collective diplomacy will evolve naturally or do innovative methods require direction? Diplomacy's reaction to innovation is not a new issue. But new technologies, as well as advances such as Artificial Intelligence, need to be applied to collective diplomacy and the risks of using new technologies need to be confronted. This book therefore seeks to address both issues of reform and the opportunities and vulnerabilities to diplomacy from innovation.

Themes Covered

It is not possible in one volume to examine all aspects of the reform of diplomacy and innovation. The authors have sought to demonstrate that in many parts of the world the activity is being reexamined and they discuss how its evolution could be influenced. Their essays are grouped under the following themes.

State of Diplomacy

In "The Closing of the Diplomatic Mind" Kenneth Weisbrode examines the historic issues that make diplomacy in the twenty-first-century struggle to adapt to technological and political change. Diplomacy has failed to apply concepts and approaches developed years earlier. Chas Freeman discusses how the taxonomy of diplomacy needs to evolve to help analyze how diplomacy should be practiced. Jane Knight discusses the neglected area of Knowledge Diplomacy where international education and research have developed significant momentum influencing other areas. Kishan Rana explains why the practice of bilateral diplomacy remains central to the craft and needs reinforcing.

Politicization of Diplomacy

Pauline Kerr discusses the ramifications of the impact of populism and politicization on diplomacy and how this is likely to be a long-term phenomenon. Onur Erpul looks at case of Turkey where digitalization has been harnessed to the cause of populism. Qingmin Zhang and Lize Yang discuss related lessons from China. Tony Leon, as a former politically appointed ambassador, examines how far South Africa's diplomacy continues to be infused with political considerations dating from the early post-apartheid era.

Reforming Institutions

Many states have given attention to reforming their own systems of diplomacy. States often borrow examples of new organizational features from others. But central to the concerns is the diminishing effectiveness of the Foreign Ministry. Antônio Carlos Lessa and Rogério de Souza Farias examine the case of Brazil and the implications of the decline of its Ministry of Foreign Affairs. And Sarah Bressan analyzes a key common feature facing Foreign Ministries—how they need to improve their capacity to respond to multiple crises. Tom Barber and Melissa Conley Tyler discuss how in Australia there are efforts to integrate Defense, Development, and Diplomacy and the advantages of taking this further. Anna Mwaba and Emmanuel Balogun examine how the African Union, one of the more recently established regional groupings, has evolved and how ways of operating might be made more effective. HwaJung Kim analyzes the reform process within the South Korean diplomatic system.

Maxime Lefebvre discusses key stages of evolution in modern French diplomacy, how the EU has influenced that evolution and likely avenues for further reform.

Digital Revolution and Diplomatic Reform

The impact on Diplomacy of the Digital Revolution. Corneliu Bjola and Michaela Coplen examine the challenges that COVID-19 posed to Foreign Ministries in adapting their messaging and trying to integrate that responses with their foreign policies. Volker Stanzel looks at how Artificial Intelligence could be applied to help clarify diplomatic options. Tom Fletcher discusses what has been done right and wrong in using digital diplomacy. And now what needs to be done better without forgetting the traditional and appropriate methods of the diplomatic craft. Juan Luis Manfredi-Sánchez and Zhao Alexandre Huang have focused on how disinformation is undermining diplomacy, diverting resources from more productive areas, and producing a response from states. But the practice of disinformation is also developing new variants. Jorge Heine and Daniel Aguirre examine how ministries in Latin America have diverged in their embrace of digitalization and the reasons for it.

Multilateral Diplomacy and Innovation

Bénédicte Frankinet examines a new approach to developing more effective multilateralism in the United Nations. The United Nations agenda has become over-burdened with too many issues which are not priorities any longer. Concentration and better focus will yield better results. Akiko Fukushima looks at multilateralism in the wider context of diplomacy outside the institution of the United Nations. And in his second essay Chas Freeman argues that diplomacy needs to recognize the dangers to diplomacy caused by promoting spheres of influence. Kishan Rana and Rajiv Bhatia address the reasons behind the successes and failures of such regional and other diplomatic groupings. Martin Wählisch gives an insight in the forces driving innovation in diplomacy and the opportunities yet to be taken. José Antonio Zabalgoitia and Antonio Tenorio look at innovation in international cooperation for development written from the perspective of middle-income countries with Mexico as an example. William Guéraiche uses the example of the UAE to show how a state can use innovative diplomacy to develop new foreign policies. Vesko

Garčević looks at how small states can leverage their impact by identifying key common approaches to diplomacy. Juan Luis Manfredi-Sánchez analyzes the key innovations that cities can bring to multilateralism and add to the effectiveness of diplomacy.

The Diplomatic Agenda

The current diplomatic agenda has many active areas in global issues where diplomacy is vital to progress in consensus building. Mark Storella has examined the long history of health diplomacy, what it has learned from past epidemics, and what the failures and successes of the COVID-19 era have taught us about the strength of current diplomatic mechanisms. Gregory Simons and Anna Velikaya discuss how humanitarian diplomacy can explore new avenues for cooperation and seize opportunities offered by innovation. Kim B. Olsen examines how far the diplomacy involved in sanctions policies needs to be formalized and integrated into wider diplomacy. Paul Arthur Berkman discusses how science can bring different perspectives to wider diplomacy and science benefits from international cooperation. Andrew Gilder and Olivia Trumble discuss climate diplomacy from the perspective of a key developing country—South Africa. Sustainable development is addressed by Felicitas Fritzsche and Karin Bäckstrand as a critique of multi-stakeholder diplomacy in one of the most ambitious of current agendas.

Conclusions: Avenues for Reform

The concluding chapter offers possible avenues to break the deadlock on how diplomacy might be more effective. Diplomacy's evolution does not happen by accident. It needs collective attention just as it had in the past. Diplomacy will not seize new opportunities and confront new vulnerabilities by hand-wringing and ignoring the diplomatic capacity of existing institutions and conventions to adapt in order to generate new purpose and relevance for the activity.

References and Further Reading

Biden, J.R., Jr. 2020. "Why America Must Lead Again." *Foreign Affairs* 99 (2): 64–76.
Bjola, C., and M. Kornprobst. 2018. *Understanding International Diplomacy: Theory, Practice and Ethics*. London: Routledge.

Bruns, K. 2014. *A Cornerstone of Modern Diplomacy: Britain and the Negotiation of the 1961 Vienna Convention on Diplomatic Relations.* London: Bloomsbury.

Burns, W. 2019. *The Back Channel. A Memoir of American Diplomacy and the Case for Its Renewal.* New York: Random House.

Churchill, W. 1946. "The Sinews of Peace." https://winstonchurchill.org/resources/speeches/1946-1963-elder-statesman/the-sinews-of-peace/.

Cohen, R. 1998. "Putting Diplomatic Studies on the Map." Diplomatic Studies Newsletter. Leicester University, May 4.

Cohen, R. 1999. *Negotiating Across Cultures. International Communication in an Interdependent World.* Washington, D.C.: United States Institute of Peace.

Guterres, A. 2021. Speech to the UN General Assembly, September 21. https://www.un.org/sg/en/content/sg/speeches/2021-09-21/address-the-76th-session-of-general-assembly.

Locke, J. 1689. *An Essay Concerning Human Understanding.* Book II Chapter 27.

Putin, V. 2012. "Vladimir Putin on Foreign Policy: Russia and the Changing World," February 27. https://valdaiclub.com/a/highlights/vladimir_putin_on_foreign_policy_russia_and_the_changing_world/.

Reuters. 2018. "Xi Says China Must Lead Way in Reform of Global Governance," June 23. https://www.reuters.com/article/us-china-diplomacy-idUSKBN1JJ0GT.

Satow, E. 2009 [1917]. *Satow's Diplomatic Practice.* 6th ed., ed. I. Roberts. Oxford: Oxford University Press.

Searle, J. 2010. *Making the Social World, the Structure of Human Civilization.* Oxford: Oxford University Press.

Sending, O.J., V. Pouiliot, and I.B. Neumann. 2011. "The Future of Diplomacy: Changing Practices, Evolving Relationships." *International Journal* 66 (3): 527–42.

Sharp, P. 1999. "For Diplomacy: Representation and the Study of International Relations." *International Studies Review* 1 (1): 33–57.

UN News. 2021. "At UN, Biden Pledges New Era of 'Relentless Diplomacy' to Tackle Global Challenges," September 21. https://news.un.org/en/story/2021/09/1100502.

United Nations. 1945. Proceedings of the United Nations Conference on International Organization (April 25–June 26).

Part II

State of Diplomacy

2

The Closing of the Diplomatic Mind

Kenneth Weisbrode

The second half of the twentieth century was a creative period in diplomatic history. The years 1947–50, 1969–75, and 1984–89 saw important advances during which multilateral institutions took a place previously occupied by nation-states in governing the international system. That system may fall short of the ideal world government envisioned since the eighteenth century or reimagined at the turn of the twentieth century by the ideological movement known as Wilsonianism after the American president, Woodrow Wilson. Yet, today's system is more peaceful, prosperous, and interdependent than any plausible alternative that Wilson's opponents may have imagined a century ago.

There are numerous multilateral institutions with acronyms, some familiar like the UN, others less so, active in every part of the world. There are non-governmental organizations working in a public or semi-public way which affect the lives of large numbers of human beings, animals, and the environment. These organizations, which include multinational corporations, not foreign ministries operating in secret, or vast armies marching across battlefields, have been the first resort for solving many of the world's problems. The poverty rate in many countries is at one of its lowest points, perhaps the lowest point, in modern history. And despite a good deal of conflict, some of it

K. Weisbrode (✉)
Bilkent University, Ankara, Turkey

armed, there has been no war among the world's major powers in almost a century.

So why does the early twenty-first century look so grim? Or, one should say, why has a grim public perception become so widespread? The answer is not difficult to find. The worst pandemic in a century, the resumption of war on the European continent, the effects of climate change, the uncertainties and inequities of the post-industrial economy, and a decline in representative governance have multiplied to give that impression, largely but not exclusively in what was known for much of the late twentieth century as the West. The following is a brief discussion and interpretation of how and why all that has happened from a diplomatic perspective.

I

The decline and fall of the West is a familiar and recurring trope. If there is a West, it must be in decline, relative to an "East" or to its own imagined past—or, more precisely, to its own imagined future. That today the terms North and "Global South" are more commonly used makes little difference to this point about imagined geographies. These categories stand less for spatial distinctions than they do for temporal ones inasmuch as they set the standard for what was once called civilization, as framed, enacted, and understood by diplomatic norms and practices. Those norms and practices are now contested nearly everywhere. They are contested because they are said to have failed, or are at risk of failure. They are failing not because they are ill suited to a "post-cold war" world or to globalization, or because they have failed to adapt to such a world. They are failing not because they have become known as just another Western encroachment, or imposition of rules, on "the rest." They are failing, rather, because they lost sight in the 1990s of their own purpose, which was not to establish something like a unified global governance regime, but instead to fortify well-integrated yet associated communities of nations and people whose ways of life demanded adaptation, not to any particular universal standard of political behavior, but instead to the technological and socioeconomic changes with which political structures almost always take too long to catch up. The failure of the early twenty-first-century diplomatic mind is a failure of imagination.

Imagination, it has been said, is the script of optimists. But the usual binary image of optimists and pessimists—a glass half full or half empty—may not be the best one to understand what has happened to the diplomatic mind. A better one may be spatial rather than temporal: open versus closed. The reason is that the diplomacy of the twentieth century—also known as the Wilsonian century, the American century, the Atlantic century—based itself on the concept of openness. The first of Wilson's Fourteen Points in 1918 called for open covenants of peace, openly arrived at. To open, in this sense, was to liberate and to rationalize a more just, more ethical, and more effective diplomacy. If diplomats worked in the open, gained the support of public opinion, and debated, discussed, and resolved their nation's differences in institutions open to public scrutiny and participation, there would no longer be the need for war and the other grievances and animosities that secrecy feeds.

So held the theory. In practice, openness has not always brought about happy results. As Harold Nicolson (1939) noted, open covenants are good things but being openly arrived at is something else entirely. Nobody should want to have too much exposure to the inner workings of the sausage factory, be it a diplomatic negotiation or a parliamentary one. Procedural secrecy can be critical to a negotiation's success. The obvious reason is that public opinion, which was not an invention of the progressive early twentieth century or a reinvention of today's digital era, but has been nagging diplomats for a long time, is often fickle and sometimes hysterical rather than mature, sensible, and prudent.

Such commonsensical objections to Wilsonian openness became the basis for the effort shortly after the Second World War to reformulate another new diplomacy, only this time the aim was not to supplant an older form of diplomacy, be it Wilsonian or another, but rather to combine them into what might be called a moral form of power politics. For that purpose, the Cold War was at an advantage. It offered a closed, or at least a semi-closed, world divided into blocs; but within those blocs—at least within the Western bloc, as it advertised itself—openness was the norm. The West, as it became known, liked to call itself the Free World. Its states had parliaments; its parliaments and their leaders were for the most part elected freely and fairly; its governments were responsible to the people; its economies were, on balance, reliant upon the free market; and its diplomacy, whether bilateral or multilateral, adhered as closely as it could to the rhetoric, and sometimes the reality, of Wilsonian principles.

Dwight D. Eisenhower, whose affiliations first to the U.S. Army and then to the Republican Party, would not easily classify him as a Wilsonian, embraced the image of openness as well as any other leader of his generation. He described it as a moving spiral—growing and moving centrifugally as well as centripetally—by which greater portions of the globe were drawn to the Western way of life as that way of life and the power behind it became stronger, more integrated, and, at the same time, more liberating. This image was related to a commonplace of the time, the expanding polity, noted by the philosopher Teilhard de Chardin and, following him, the statesman Jean Monnet. Once again, it is important to qualify the spatial notion of openness in this way with a temporal notion. Eisenhower's spiral image made sense in a world divided into Cold War blocs only because many Americans were told that the Cold War was a temporary, not a permanent, state of affairs. That was another way of formulating the essence of old versus new diplomacy, as it is also of means and ends. Did the old ways of diplomacy—alliances, treaties, embassies, secrecy, and subversion—persist in the service of a new world order? Or did that all happen the other way around?

Here it may be useful to recall another of Eisenhower's abstractions: the domino. His infamous description of the political reality of Communism in Southeast Asia was said to have caused a succession of bloody wars there, fought to keep too many dominoes from falling. The game of dominoes was the spatial and temporal counterpart to the expanding spiral: where the former spread into a zone of peace, the latter fell into a zone of war. Today it is customary to apply yet another map to this distinction: the zone of peace was not the West, but rather the North; the zone of war was the "Global South." They existed almost as parts of a dialectic. Which is to say, the domino theory *was* the spiral when it moved below the equator, after the Korean War, as the global Cold War fed and sometimes causes a series of hot wars in Asia, Africa, and Latin America, all depicted by outsiders with the belief that dominoes had to be indefinitely propped up. The domino theory applied to both sides of the Iron Curtain, in fact. Each side moved to "contain" or limit the influence of the other in faraway places without fully understanding the meaning of influence in those places or the consequences of intervening there by force of arms.

Abstractions, dating back to Wilson's own new world order, have important but limited utility. Many historians of twentieth-century conflicts will say that they had local origins and differences, and that however much they took place within a global Cold War context, they were not pre-programmed by it or even by a Cold War logic. Every conflict was distinct and, to an extent, different. Yet, their place in the chronology of the twentieth century has given them a significance beyond their local causes and effects. That significance relates as much to their role in tipping the scale of Cold War rivalry, often described as "zero sum" between East and West, as it does to the role of what was called the Third World—a realm cast as the decisive tipping agent on the scale however much some parts of it preferred to call that role "non-aligned"—in a global competition for prestige and power.

That global competition, in turn, has come to redefine the second half of the twentieth century and the first part of the twenty-first century less by the Cold War or post-Cold War than by an interaction of longer duration between and among European and non-European societies, in some cases dating back to the early eighteenth century, if not before. For it was this interaction, characterized by conflict as well as competition and cooperation, that has really defined the modern era as one of expanding and retreating empires. The geopolitical and cultural abstractions of East, West, North, and South, all relate to that definition; they serve abstract means to an end—imperial control, sovereign independence, or, to use the language of Wilson's Fourteen Points, "autonomous development"—and not to geopolitical rivalry or even mastery as an end in itself. The second half of the twentieth century therefore saw the acceleration and perhaps the culmination of contending paths to political and socio-cultural, as well as economic and technological, modernization relative to themselves and their imagined place on a world map.

This is the context in which to understand today's closing of the diplomatic mind. Closing is not so much the result of social and cultural coarseness—in other words, a general decline in civility making itself known in public discourse, the loss of authority of elites, the erosion of trust and professionalism, and so on—boiling to the surface of international relations, but rather follows an opposite path, brought about by the combination of enervation, myopia, complacency, and even arrogance at the highest levels of the international system trickling their way down to more local levels where, paradoxically, more imaginative experiments in governance have been underway as people all over the world attain consciousness of other parts of the world beyond their villages, towns, nations, and regions. A similar diagnosis applied to the social and political breakdown leading up to the First World War in Europe and its colonies. The people advising Woodrow Wilson and the other negotiators at Paris in 1919 came to realize that nearly every problem they faced, starting with redrawing the maps of four dissolved empires, related, on the one hand, to the adjustment of political and socio-economic practices to technological and, to some extent, cultural realities; and on the other hand, to the temporal gradation of that adjustment, according to how ready the negotiators and diplomats at Paris determined the people living in various places on the new map were for what was understood to be enlightened self-government. That gradation meant, in practice, an almost century-long postponement of self-government for much of Africa and Asia. Even in some post-imperial parts of Europe—namely the Balkans—at the end of the twentieth century it was understood that some adjustments to the map were needed for the promises of self-government to be realized. Many of those adjustments were made in blood.

Integrating the former imperial and colonial world with Europe and North America on the basis of sovereign autonomy was diplomacy's principal task after 1919. Another world war as well as a Cold War and a post-Cold War advanced it and at the same time set it back by encouraging additional divisions and postponements. Yet, the twentieth century also saw some important advances in diplomatic theory and practice, or, to put it more accurately, in its form and substance, during the three abovementioned moments: 1947–50, 1969–75, and 1984–89.

During each moment creative renewal occurred alongside a refinement of multilateral diplomacy largely in or with regard to Europe: the first with the establishment of the kernel of what would become the EU as well as NATO; the second with the culmination of Cold War détente with the Quadripartite Agreement and the Helsinki Final Act; and the third with the peaceful termination of the Cold War at the Geneva and Reykjavik summits. In between these moments there took place a number of smaller gains. For example, one might add the Bandung Conference of 1955 as another critical moment when the international system became dramatically less Eurocentric; but the innovation represented by Bandung was primarily political (or geopolitical) rather than diplomatic per se. One might also add, as other chapters in this volume mention, the signing of the Vienna Conventions on Diplomatic and Consular Relations in the early 1960s as evidence of a more focused attention on diplomatic practice. The diplomacy of sovereign powers, later nation-states, which had governed relations in Europe—and here one includes major powers such as the Soviet Union and the United States as extra- or quasi-European inasmuch as they were part of the Euro-Atlantic system as the Ottoman and Russian Empires were in previous centuries—as well as globally in a competitive, sometimes rivalrous, fashion gave way to a community of power along lines that Wilson had imagined. Nation-states and even some kingdoms still exist, but they exist as part of a community that regulates itself, and has for the most part resolved its disputes, more or less peacefully. And multilateral institutions—the European Union, the Organization for Cooperation and Security in Europe, and so on—have not supplanted nation-states but instead coexist with and in many instances have sustained and strengthened them.

These institutions moreover have grown stronger and more important in diplomacy. The EU, which began in 1950 as a modest association overseeing the western European coal and steel industries, was already being described as a nascent superstate by the mid-1980s, and, a decade later, had a flag, a currency, a set of capitals, and an anthem, as well as its own diplomatic service.

The OSCE, which began as a diplomatic conference in the early 1970s, was, a couple of decades later, the first regional organization to unite members of the Cold War blocs following a largely peaceful end of that war. The remarkable aspect about both organizations and many smaller ones like them is their varying capacity to marry power and purpose in Wilsonian terms. They go beyond diplomatic alliances in having acquired the capacity for governance within, as well as between, polities. Yet they have done so also largely in accord with political realities, including national political realities, in ways that Wilson and his generation probably did not entirely predict.

This is all to say that the twentieth century, one of the bloodiest in human history, also was one of important diplomatic progress. By the end of the century it was possible to speak of a "Europe, Whole and Free." To Eurocentrics, the continent's achievement was at long last to have become the center of that expanding spiral. It certainly did expand, just not in the way that most people hoped it would. Expansion—or, to use the terms of the U.S. president, Bill Clinton, "enlargement and engagement"—quickly became more contentious than consensual. As the expanding spiral enacted more divisions, it began to turn back in upon itself. Its contraction did not start 20 years later with "populism" but rather began at the outset of the post-Cold War period as the ambiguity and ambivalence of complacent elites, including some diplomats, turned "globalization" into a dirty word in the same way that modernization and Westernization once had been. It may sound too glib to say that the diplomacy of the second half of the twentieth century won the war and lost the peace, but that is close to what happened. The world of the 2020s is less peaceful, less secure, less ordered, and less free than what was imagined in the 1990s, or even what existed then, at least in the Euro-Atlantic region.

II

The decade of the 1990s has been mythologized as an optimistic, almost hedonistic period during which the end of the Cold War coincided with a new springtime of nations—the emergence of a Europe, whole and free—and the profitable explosion of the new dot com economy. Most myths contain a kernel of truth, and this one does, but the 1990s also began, not only with the end of the Cold War and the collapse of the Soviet Union, but also with the advent of a period of brutal persecution in China, several nasty civil wars—including, again for the first time in a generation, in Europe—and with an economic recession, which was especially harsh in the United States. The decade is remembered unhappily, for example, also in Japan, which has called most of it "lost"; and, above all, in the former Soviet Union (and elsewhere in the former Soviet bloc, e.g., in Cuba), where economies brought privations that people had not experienced in half a century.

These years, then, were moments of triumph, exhilaration, and euphoria for some, but not for most, people in the world. Inasmuch as the 1990s heralded an era of globalization, a provisional verdict is also mixed. Globalization, it is said, is not a choice or a preference but a fact. Perhaps. The political and social response to it, however, is all three of those things. The association of globalization with Westernization and modernization was probably unavoidable; however, during the 1990s, globalization itself became more global, as the East Asian tigers, so called, inspired others, notably China, to pursue their own "paths" to prosperity and power, which included a notable assertiveness in their diplomacy. To many people in the West, these paths are familiar, and rhyme not with anything particularly global in design but rather with old-fashioned nationalism, only now with more global effects. Thus the diplomacy of the 1990s, still adhering to the rhetoric of an expanding Western spiral, worked at the same time to throw its movement into reverse.

By the second half of the 1990s, then, a mantra of enlargement and engagement had given way to one dominated by "ethnic cleansing," "financial crisis," and, increasingly, of national chauvinism. The American senator Daniel Patrick Moynihan in fact had warned of that possibility at the outset of the decade in his book, *Pandaemonium* (1993). There, he noted that the Wilsonian promise of the early twentieth century had finally begun to bring results for most of the world's people but that, in so doing, it had begun to fall victim to its own contradictions. Namely, that its main tenet of self-determination was about to become, in the absence of a viable, diplomatic structure of institutions, laws, and norms as adapted to the technologies and social movements of a new century, mere tribalism, and the Hobbesian war of all against all that Wilsonian diplomacy, like other diplomacies before it, was meant to prevent.

Why did this happen? Most explanations are contested by people with distinct preferences. The decline of international order starting in the 1990s may be described, following the American political scientist, Samuel Huntington, as the start of a global clash of civilizations. Or it may be explained less grandly as the result of Western arrogance and the substitution for an existing, emergent, consensual model of international politics—that is, the Wilsonian model—by older geopolitical methods with an aim of augmenting geopolitical supremacy, starting with that of the United States of America, the self-declared "unipolar" state. Or it may be said that decline was the result of Wilsonianism on steroids, as it were, and the abandonment of long-standing standards of international comity, respect—not least for the limits of state power—by the same people, called "liberal internationalists," who were determined in the 1990s to convert the entire world to a particular standard of governance, even if it meant conversion at the end of a barrel of a gun, or, more likely, on the receiving end of a bombing campaign.

The armed interventions by the UN in Kuwait and by NATO in Kosovo, each resulting in the redefinition or the rectification of political borders by force, were and, at the same time, were not, violations of liberal internationalist principles, depending on whether or not one identifies collective security with the once trendy statement that "human rights trump sovereignty," and on whose human rights, including the right to command spiritual adherents across borders, most matter. Human rights trumped sovereignty in Europe; outside Europe, they did not for the most part, at least not to the extent of defending an external, armed intervention. That is another way of saying that the diplomatic spirit of the post-Cold War period was based at once upon relative and objective truths so that the military intervention in Bosnia is still judged differently from the one that subsequently took place in Kosovo, just as the first Gulf War is contrasted normatively with the later Iraq War. Debating the relative measurements of legitimacy is one price that diplomacy has paid for allowing itself to be subordinated to the needs of military interventions conducted in the name of morality.

The result of so much ambiguity and ambivalence—starting with Huntington's parochial, even perverse, understanding of "civilization," which was more akin to the early twentieth-century concept of *Kultur*—infected other concepts and principles, such as the "responsibility to protect," which in turn went beyond ascribing to Wilsonianism a disingenuous, and sometimes hypocritical repudiation of Wilsonian tenets: imposing what the American diplomat George Kennan once called the "red skein" of moralism but without the legalism, and vice versa. Their other main effect was to dismantle a basic norm of multilateral diplomacy less by design than by confusion. That norm, of course, was collective security and the belief in economic, military, and political integration as the main, effective response to geopolitical and functional interdependence in all those areas of human activity. If the tenets of multilateralism could be so easily appropriated and misused by the most powerful nations for what were widely perceived to be their own necessities, they had not merely substituted objective, universal values with relative, parochial ones; they had also suffered the loss of a moral and a practical reputation. By the end of the decade, self-righteous unilateralism, not principled multilateralism, was once again the dominant trend in diplomacy as much of diplomacy in practice came to resemble little more than public relations. Diplomatic society, like many societies across the world, has become more superficial, dysfunctional, and cacophonous.

The philosopher Allan Bloom, whose *Closing of the American Mind* (1987), was a publishing sensation in the late 1980s, equated closing with forgetting. It would be easy to say that is also what happened in the 1990s. Diplomatic practice was struck with a bad case of moral amnesia. Bad as well as remarkable: for how could people forget so quickly that Nazi Germany had defended its intervention in the Sudetenland, which led to the dismemberment of Czechoslovakia, as a humanitarian action to assist a persecuted minority population? It may sound unfair to many people to draw such comparisons, for example, between NATO's armed intervention in Kosovo and Russia's invasion of Ukraine. To the usual charges of hypocrisy came a predictable appeal to virtuous power and enlightened self-interest; in truth, each situation involved complexities that defy easy, principled comparisons. To see that one need only scratch the surface of Chinese diplomacy, which has been more adept and strategic than Russia's toward Europe, and has managed to somehow remain unencumbered by contradictions, such as in refusing to recognize the Russian annexation of Crimea but at the same time pledging to support Russia in security matters. Even the treaties of Westphalia, the purported basis for the modern system of sovereign states, allowed for the possibility of external intervention in order to uphold the international order.

Forgetting the diplomatic lessons of the past therefore was not the only reason why diplomacy's mind has closed. It was not simply that Wilsonianism had been perverted in practice by some of its most loyal defenders. It was also that the perversion, regarded by its victims and their allies as an abandonment of international norms, was not replaced or followed by a new, clear set of accepted rules and institutions, let alone a new, effective, and legitimate international order. The jaded old ones, at once rejecting and preserving by half the diplomatic successes of the middle twentieth century, adjusted and plodded on.

That strange historical condition can be seen in several of the above-cited instances (Kuwait, Kosovo, etc.) and in the more notable negotiations of the period. For example, during the extensive talks over German reunification in 1990, the representatives of the United States insisted to Mikhail Gorbachev that a new, more stable and peaceful security order had emerged in central Europe, and therefore the Soviet Union should allow for a united Germany to join NATO. Gorbachev responded by asking, if such an order really exists, then why must NATO still exist and why must Germany join it? The reply to that obvious question was, again, double-sided and ambivalent: NATO is now a different organization in a different strategic context, Europe, whole and free. That Europe included NATO and, on principle, any nation that wanted to join it. But it did not include the Soviet Union or, later, Russia, whose post-Soviet leadership sought and began to develop alternatives to diplomatic integration with the West, much as Chinese and other ambitious, formerly middle-ranking, revisionist powers have done. Another result of ambivalence and ambiguity at the highest levels of government in the world's major powers was the breakdown of international order, symbolized by a war in Ukraine that several people predicted and, at the same time, denied it was necessary to prevent.

Ukraine and the other cases reaffirm that the "long peace" of the Cold War was made possible not simply by fear of nuclear war but rather by the institutions that fear of nuclear war made possible. Foremost among these were the tacit but very clear spheres of interest that developed in Europe where the USSR was left to deal with eastern Europe and the United States with western Europe. They will have to be reconstructed, probably again through an enlarged NATO. In the fullness of time it may be possible to return to Europe whole and free but there will have to be an intermediate step. That may be the acceptance of China as a world power with an interest in stability in Eurasia, including the Euro-Atlantic system of nations, and with recognized reciprocal interest in Asia by the United States and its allies. Economic order may play a large role in promoting such an international order but so will nuclear weapons.

During geopolitical transitions, borders are usually redrawn. There were probably bound to be new borders in Europe at some point after the Cold War, acknowledging that however much the Cold War was global, it began and ended in the middle of the European continent. However, the value in Wilsonianism as a classic form of progressive politics was to translate geopolitical boundaries into temporal or chronological borderlands. States negotiated, sometimes in perpetuity, over the standards, norms, and stages of inclusion in such multilateral institutions where transnational "issues" were debated, managed, and resolved, rather than trading pieces of territory or placing borders on maps. Without apparently giving much thought to how today's world would look without an effective UN and similar multilateral organizations, the diplomacy of the post-Cold War years resurrected and re-inscribed the latter, geopolitical form of international relations as the primary agent and allocator of progressive movement. Particular territories were told ahead whether or not they were a "candidate" for membership in this or that organization, and then the terms of membership, the costs, and the benefits were imparted to them. Vague promises of membership may also have been made to others left out of consideration, but by the subsequent decade, candidacy itself, as NATO's "Membership Action Plans" and the EU's *acquis*, became matters of direct geopolitical contention.

Meanwhile, the scope and number of transnational problems have continued to outpace the capacity of existing institutions to manage or solve them. Real global governance is a long way off, nationalism remains strong, and regionalism is not a perfect solution because of the likelihood that regional blocs, like leagues and similar, usually unstable, arrangements in early modern Europe, will, however much they overlap, become closed and hostile rather than open and liberal. One reason for that likelihood is the persistent view of diplomats and others of the "region" (and of geography itself) as a setting for action rather than as an actor in its own right. That gap or fixture in the mental map of the diplomatic imagination has, in turn, led to the creation of a number of transregional "functional" offices in several foreign (as well as other) ministries that compete with regional offices more than they augment or complement them. Some of those offices do well in integrating policies across regions and bureaucracies, and of devoting a higher degree of sustained political attention to transnational and transregional problems. But there is always the counter-potential for such offices to neglect or misunderstand local realities, inter-relationships, and the vital expertise of regional specialists. Thus, a truly multipolar international system need not be one that vitiates peaceful multilateralism, but so far that appears to be what has been developing since the 1990s because the members of multilateral institutions have failed to align their structure and operational missions to political, social, and above all, cultural changes taking place in that system.

III

The historian Reinhart Koselleck (2018) has used the image of sediment to describe a particular relationship of space and time by which existing institutional structures and beliefs are supplanted as well as interpenetrated by newer ones, as he has written, reciprocally yet discretely. The structural adaptations and reformulation facilitate progress as well as retrogression. The institution of diplomacy, including everything from embassies and consulates to ambassadors and consuls to treaties, agreements, and communiqués, has adhered to this composite, chronological model. All the above aspects of diplomacy, dating to the outset of the modern era in European history, if not earlier, still exist. But they exist alongside many of the "new" formulations and expressions described elsewhere in this volume, from Twitter to the 24-hour news cycle and its enacting of domestic politics on a global scale. As chapters in this book demonstrate, all that has brought about a renewed politicization of diplomats and their profession. This shows the problem of diplomats seeking to act as professionals in a world where elected officials have the last word. Whereas in the past in some countries, the integration of diplomats and political figures into the same institutions has brought those institutions an occasional vitality, today, increasingly, such politicization has become worse as it has also become synonymous with professional emasculation, starting with foreign ministries. Still, many professional diplomats survive and some even continue to thrive.

It is not surprising therefore that progress in multilateral, institution-building that took place during the second half of the twentieth century has retreated as other older unilateral and bilateral methods of international relations have persevered and advanced. Such coexistence, borrowing, and mutual antagonism of political, including geopolitical, forms is in the nature of politics. Multilateral diplomatic efforts such as those that succeeded briefly in containing the North Korean and Iranian nuclear weapons programs coincided with the decline in power and influence of multilateral organizations, and with the construction of walls and other types of obstructions to long-standing practices of international comity in many areas, from migration to banking, and even to consular representation, all of which became tools of domestic politics and, in some instances, state persecution. The popular media has described this atavistic development as part of a bottom-up reaction to globalization, but, again, from the perspective of contemporary diplomacy, it is rather the result of pre-existing decay in the intellectual and ideological commitment to internationalism which has seen the nation move from a vital component of international, community-based relations to its latent enemy. Thus, it is also not surprising to note the formidable rise in power and prosperity of the non-European world, particularly of China and other powers in Asia, taking place alongside a rise in nationalism and the political mobilization of the newly urbanized middle class in those places, which anyone familiar with European history from the middle of the eighteenth century would recognize. So, too, the expression of what has very loosely been called "terrorism."

The terrorist attacks around the world at the turn of the twenty-first century were not the marks of a new era but rather were the culmination of resentments and inadequacies in the international system that had been accumulating for several decades. They ought to have brought about a reaffirmation of international interdependence and a renewed commitment to multilateral diplomacy. For a brief moment in 2001 and early 2002, they did. But that moment was lost to the Manichean rhetoric the United States, several of its allies, and many of its enemies, chose to utilize in the new "war on terror." The opportunity to recast diplomatic means and ends, if it had existed, was squandered. Diplomacy was understood instrumentally by most people, even the most educated people in the most advanced society, as a "tool in the toolbox" and not as the sum of relationships between polities with intersecting interests, necessities, grievances, and desires.

Such problems of definition reflect a deeper shift from conceptual, even psychological orientation. There has always been a superficial aspect of diplomatic communication—the necessary secrecy of negotiations, for example, is more often shrouded in a pack of bland generalities than in silence—but diplomacy's tone and vocabulary have become rote to the point of vapidity, and thus harmful to the profession's effectiveness and to its central mission of conducting international relations and managing and resolving disputes. The revolution in electronic communications, as several other chapters in this volume demonstrate, has not spared the diplomatic profession, or diplomats. Some have resisted the changes; others have embraced them. But few have come to fully understand how social media and instant, almost omnipresent global communications have altered, perhaps even transformed, the diplomatic mind from one that, on principle, possesses a sophisticated capacity to discern the medium from the message to another that perceives little difference or boundaries between public and other necessary modes of diplomacy.

It is difficult to know whether digital technology enhances or reduces the value of the diplomat's primary social and institutional currencies—empathy and trust—and whether it may in fact go so far as to set diplomatic reform and innovation at cross purposes. Diplomacy by incantation—a vacuous repetition of "talking points"—has moved from providing a veneer for action to the principal rationale for its existence. Slogans, which may sometimes play a significant role in diplomacy through their clarification of difficult problems for public consumption, and therefore support, have moved from a diplomatic auxiliary to a substitute that can appear little different from the traditional tactical use of the megaphone. Some forms of social media, for example, are designed mainly to reaffirm and magnify, and not to challenge, modify, readjust, set beliefs, and judgments. They operate, in other words, not as clubs or networks but as circuits, which serve to admit or reject members and to light up more brightly with the volume, intensity, and purity of featured praise or condemnation. Their global popularity notwithstanding, social media do not by themselves permit to a redefinition of diplomacy or its institutions and purposes that most people around the world can accept. Technological change has become self-justifying as the pace, scope, and nature of reform are measured and promoted with only a secondary regard for what reforms are meant to accomplish on a consensual basis, and not—within and between ministries, governments, and societies—by digital *diktat*.

At the highest levels of many governments, the actual crafting and making of decisions about foreign policy have in fact become more top-heavy, where voices of professional diplomats and foreign ministries have been overtaken by those of appointed advisers to the heads of government or state working above or outside traditional bureaucratic channels. These courtiers, usually known as "national security advisers," have come to reproduce and in some cases to supplant foreign ministers, and amorphous kitchen cabinets to take the place of foreign ministries. The style and manner of diplomacy have become imperial and therefore discretionary or what is now commonly called "transactional," as if to say that diplomacy amounts to little more than dealmaking. And for the foreseeable future, that tool was idle as other tools of compulsion, namely military tools, were preferred, and came to measure the sum of those relationships. The typical embassy of several nations in the early twenty-first century is a walled fortress.

The innovation of diplomacy on mainly operational and tactical grounds in the past few decades has obscured rather than clarified its principal aim, which is to promote the interests of its sovereigns and, sometimes, the cause of peace. The most effective diplomacy, however, has traditionally been that not of tactical compulsion or dissuasion but instead that of strategic reorientation and reconstruction, which ought to include not only the use of tactical and operational means for strategic ends but also the envelopment of strategic elements in diplomatic discussions on the basis of reciprocity. In other words, diplomacy understood as being synonymous with, rather than as elemental to, statecraft is neither new nor anachronistic. In fact, the less strategically minded a state's diplomacy is, the less operationally and tactically successful it also tends to be. Diplomacy's divorce from statecraft has led to operational decline as well. The Iran and North Korea disarmament plans have not been significantly followed up by regional negotiations covering other areas. Most regional organizations have not become viable security communities and exist for the most part as a combination of talking shops and facilitators of technical and other assistance, even though some new arrangements, such as the Trade and Technology Council, a mainly U.S.-EU effort to harmonize digital policy and standards, appear to be promising areas for diplomatic innovation. About the only area of diplomatic activity that has seen real progress in recent years is diplomatic studies, including diplomatic history, which has begun to experience a small renaissance. Generally, renaissances are detected and understood retrospectively, beyond the onset of cultural and political decadence.

Whether the present-day renaissance in diplomatic studies will lead in turn to a reformation and renewal in diplomatic education, including professional education and training, and practice is not yet known, of course, but the hope that it will do so is an inspiration for this volume. It is but one illustration of a diplomatic mind in flux and so, like diplomacy itself, a kind of microcosm of the present-day state of international relations whose "challenges" and other problems may appear predominant but are not universal. Neither, for that matter, is the closing of the diplomatic mind. That mind has been a largely Western or Western-derived mind, whereas diplomatic theory and practice elsewhere—notably in middle or formerly middle, now large, powers—are today assertive as well as creative. From the perspective of the previous century, the Wilsonian, progressive impulse to align international relations, its institutions, and its historical consciousness with technological and political change also remains valid today, just as the central failure to which it responded—in implementing and enforcing an adherence to "autonomous development" within and among states—dates back several more centuries, and also persists. The failure and the corrective impulse are perhaps made even more difficult by the further interdependence enacted by contemporary globalization; but so too should interdependence provide a more vivid guide to diplomacy, which has little choice but to be global and integrative as well as pragmatic if it is to succeed at all.

References and Further Reading

Barraclough, G. 1964. *An Introduction to Contemporary History*. London: C.A. Watts.
Bloom, A. 1987. *The Closing of the American Mind*. New York: Simon and Schuster.
Burns, W. 2019. *The Back Channel*. New York: Random House.
Connelly, M. 2002. *A Diplomatic Revolution*. Oxford: Oxford University Press.
Hall, T. 2015. *Emotional Diplomacy*. Ithaca: Cornell University Press.
Huntington, S. 1996. *The Clash of Civilizations*. New York: Simon and Schuster.
Ikenberry, G.J. 2020. *A World Safe for Democracy*. New Haven: Yale University Press.
Keohane, R., and J. Nye. 1977. *Power and Interdependence*. Boston: Little, Brown.
Koselleck, R. 2018. *Sediments of Time*, trans. S. Franzel and S.-L. Hoffmann. Stanford: Stanford University Press.
Leebaert, D. 2002. *Fifty Year Wound*. Boston: Little, Brown.
Mattingly, G. 1955. *Renaissance Diplomacy*. Boston: Houghton Mifflin.
Moynihan, D.P. 1993. *Pandaemonium*. Oxford: Oxford University Press.
Nicolson, H. 1939. *Diplomacy*. Oxford: Oxford University Press.
Ninkovich, F. 1999. *The Wilsonian Century*. Chicago: University of Chicago Press.
Rice, C., and P. Zelikow. 2019. *To Build a Better World*. New York: Twelve.

Schroeder, P. 1994. *The Transformation of European Politics*. Oxford: Oxford University Press.
Shultz, G., ed. 2016. *Blueprint for America*. Stanford: Hoover Institution.
Sofer, S. 2013. *Courtiers of Civilization*. Albany: SUNY Press.
Van Middelaar, L. 2014. *The Passage to Europe*, trans. L. Waters. New Haven: Yale University Press.

3

A Diplomatic Taxonomy for the New World Disorder

Chas W. Freeman Jr.

Introduction: Diplomacy as the Management of Relationships

Diplomacy is an instrument of statecraft. It is the art of adjusting international political, economic, cultural, military, and other relationships to national advantage with minimal resort to coercive measures or the use of force. Diplomacy is also how the result of the use of coercive measures or force is translated into desired adjustments in relationships. It faces its greatest challenges in eras of complex, shifting balances of power and relationships between states like that of today.

Diplomacy seeks to redirect perceived interests and ties between states and peoples to the benefit of the state or coalition of states whose interests it advocates. It does so by convincing others to see what it advocates as in their best interests. The most common tools of diplomacy are the persuasive words, personal reputations, charisma, and demonstrated empathy of the officials who carry it out. But it can, if necessary, be coercive, making use of both undeclared and overt punitive measures. And it can shape behavior by creating circumstances that make the result it seeks come to be seen by a state or states as a more advantageous alternative to either the status quo or an ineluctable trend. To succeed, diplomacy needs the backing of every capacity of government.

C. W. Freeman Jr. (✉)
Watson Institute for International and Public Affairs, Brown University, Providence, RI, USA

International interactions are inherently transactional. But, over time, they imbue relationships with trust, which is an essential facilitator of positive interactions, or mistrust, which can be an insuperable obstacle to mutually advantageous problem solving or the perception and pursuit of common objectives. The negotiation of a specific issue is always also the negotiation of a relationship.

Diplomacy is a political performing art that demands precision of expression as well as empathetic understanding of other states' perceptions of situations and their likely consequences. It is most effective when conducted with tactful candor[1] that fulfills others' expectations and builds and sustains mutual trust for the next interaction.

The best predictor that commitments will be faithfully executed is, of course, the self-interest of those who will benefit from their fulfillment. But, as every diplomat knows, once lost, trust is almost impossible to restore. Mistrust impedes the peaceable resolution of problems and can make the use of force seem the only way for a state to achieve its objectives. The reputations of a society and its government for trustworthiness are irreplaceable assets in their conduct of relations with others.

Sometimes distrust of another nation is a product of paranoia or unrelated trauma rather than experience, but—whether fairly or unfairly imposed—a reputation for duplicity or unreliability exacts significant opportunity costs and can stymie or paralyze a state's foreign relations. Distrust can rise to such a level that a state fails to perceive and seize opportunities or ignores advantageous offers from another. An ingrained reflex to disbelieve the other and suspect it of artful deceit rather than earnestness can distort or block a state's perceptions of reality.[2]

---

[1] Addressing a class of diplomats in the late fourth century BCE, the Chinese sage Zhuangzi said: "If relations between states are close, they may establish mutual trust through daily interactions, but if relations are distant, mutual confidence can only be established by exchanges of messages. Messages must be conveyed by messengers [diplomats]. Their contents may be either pleasing to both sides or likely to engender anger between them. Faithfully conveying such messages is the most difficult task under the heavens, for if the words are such as to evoke a positive response on both sides, there will be the temptation to exaggerate them with flattery and, if they are unpleasant, there will be a tendency to make them even more biting. In either case, the truth will be lost. If truth is lost, mutual trust will also be lost. If mutual trust is lost, the messenger himself may be imperiled. Therefore, I say to you it is a wise rule: 'always to speak the truth and never to embellish it. In this way, you will avoid much harm to yourselves.'"

[2] Some would argue (e.g., BBC 2016) that this is what prevented the West from responding to the apparent desire of the Russian Federation to integrate itself into the Western-sponsored international order after the Cold War even as China did so. The subsequent rise of Sino-American distrust now menaces the continued successful management of differences over the relationship Taiwan has or should have to the rest of China. See also Lieberthal (2016) and Freeman (2020a, b).

3 A Diplomatic Taxonomy for the New World Disorder

Confidence in the determination of independent nations to stand by their commitments is the bedrock of a predictable international order. The facilitation of cooperation that advances or defends common interests and the avoidance of strategic surprise are the ultimate rationales for PACTA SUNT SERVANDA—the principle that agreements must be kept. Just as empty bluffing can fatally erode the credibility of ultimata and other forms of coercive pressure, non-coercive diplomacy can succeed only with a measure of trust—confidence that what another party has agreed to do or help happen will, in fact, happen.[3]

The formation and maintenance of reliable relationships with other states and peoples are core competencies of diplomacy, which seeks to shape and leverage ties with other states and peoples to the benefit of the state it represents. Relationships embody reciprocal or asymmetrical expectations as well as varying degrees of commitment or reliance by one party on another. They are composed of and express levels of political, economic, and military entanglement or antipathy. Their quality and character foreshadow state responses to international trends and events and empower or preclude international cooperation, collusion, or coalition.

Judgments about the solidity or frailty of relationships help determine states' strategies for reinforcing, weakening, adjusting, or exploiting their relations with others. This makes understanding relationships and their potential to evolve a prerequisite for a state's successful conduct of strategies and tactics in the international arena. To map the geography of relationships and to perceive a shift or the potential for one in the pattern of another state's alignments, a government must be able to discern and distinguish existing relationships and the balances of expectations and obligations toward which they may be evolving. An accurate diagnosis and classification of relationships is therefore an indispensable contributor to statecraft and diplomatic doctrine.[4]

---

[3] Consider the USSR's response to the 1984 American protest of its clandestine establishment of a huge early warning radar system at Krasnoyarsk, which was a clear violation of the 1972–2002 Anti-Ballistic Missile Treaty. In 1989, wishing to improve relations with the United States, Moscow dismantled the radar and resumed careful compliance with the terms of the treaty, thereby validating President Ronald Reagan's policy of "trust but verify."

[4] Diplomatic doctrine is the set of concepts, precepts, measures, and professional tools that a state's foreign policy apparatus applies to analyze the international environment, inform and guide its strategies and tactics, and realize its objectives or defend its interests.

The Cold War Debasement of Diplomatic Terminology and the New World Disorder

The four-decade-long Cold War largely erased the distinctions describing relationships between states that had previously been central to diplomatic analysis and operations. In an historical aberration, it divided the world into two "blocs." Non-alignment could to some extent avoid entanglement in great power rivalries. Both blocs sought to deny this middle ground to "non-aligned countries but, in practice, they tolerated it,[5] and, occasionally, saw merit in it.[6] Still, membership in a bloc defined a state's geopolitical position and relationships. It reliably predicted a state's political, economic, cultural, and military orientations and affiliations and made it a so-called ally of its bloc's overlord.

In time, the word "ally" ceased to describe a participant in a nominally equal relationship of mutual commitment. It was debased to describe any cooperant on any issue with another nation, rather than its original meaning of a participant in a comprehensive partnership with obligations to match its presumed entitlements. In this now ubiquitous usage, so-called allies can be dependencies or subordinate partners of more powerful states, their commitments can be one-way rather than reciprocal and mutual, and cooperation between them can be asymmetrical, transactional, and issue by issue, not mutual, or an agreed recognition of broadly congruent national interests.

But with the end of bipolarity, complexity is back. Statecraft must now discern, describe, manipulate, and react to a multidimensional dynamic between states. The evolving international order has no fixed poles or centers of gravity. Nations are now distinguished not by their allegiance to one or another overlord but by their place in a shifting constellation of greater and lesser powers operating within tenuously connected but discrete political, economic, cultural, and military domains. To be effective, diplomacy must now rediscover the distinctions that the "with-me-or-against-me" Cold War world order obscured or made irrelevant. A taxonomy of international relationships is once again essential.

---

[5] Consider the cases of Switzerland and India. Ironically, non-alignment and the purely transactional conduct of foreign policy represent the default position and the historical norm in international relations between independent states but, in the bipolar order of the Cold War, they stood out as anomalous.

[6] For instance, in 1955, the United States, USSR, UK, and France concluded the Austrian State Treaty, which ended their occupation of Austria and established it as an independent, non-aligned state.

Deconstructing Relationships Between States

The factors that measure the solidity, vitality, and durability of political, economic, cultural, and military relationships between two or more states or parties include:

- Evolving symmetries and asymmetries in their respective sizes, capabilities, and influence.
- The priority each assigns to the interests that unite or divide it from others and the relative level of importance it attaches to pursuing or safeguarding these priorities.
- The extent to which states' interests overlap or coincide at any given moment. (This shifts as objectives are realized, come to be seen as unattainable, and gain or lose political standing.)
- The perceived costs and benefits a state anticipates from sticking with or altering current alignments.
- The quality of cross-cultural communication and the level of trust or mistrust each has established in previous interactions with each other or with others.
- The clarity of the commitments each has made to others and the value it assigns to the faithful execution of these.

There are few if any certainties in human affairs. What an objective analysis of a state's interests suggests it should do is not always what it actually does. But, in combination, the factors outlined above and the bonds they foster between states constitute indicators of how a state is likely to respond to shifts in the political, economic, cultural, and military environments, challenges from third parties, or potential opportunities.

Statecraft rests on judgments about what is possible, plausible, or probable. Assessments of others' intentions, informed by empathy, are essential to inspire a state's development of appropriate strategies and tactics, its decisions about how and when best to put them in play, and its timely formulation and implementation of contingency plans to counter or bolster anticipated knock-on effects. These strategies and tactics may consist of non-violent suasion through diplomacy or of active coercion through the use of force. Diplomacy is the least costly and risky of these choices, which is why the use of force is generally regarded as a last resort.

The Formation and Staying Power of Coalitions

States form coalitions to add others' power to their own for deterrent[7] or proactive purposes,[8] to co-opt rival states and curtail opportunism by them during an operation or initiative,[9] or, less commonly, to inflate foreign or domestic perceptions of other states' support for their actions to counter controversy about them.[10]

Ad hoc Coalitions

The sudden need to respond to a challenge can catalyze temporary cooperation between states that previously treated each other as rivals, adversaries, or enemies. Such ad hoc coalitions usually paper over contradictions rather than resolve them. Notwithstanding their urgency, they lack both the broad, unconditional mutual commitments of true alliances or the contingency-bounded pledges of *ententes*. They should be confused with neither. Ad hoc coalitions last only for the duration of the exigency they were formed to deal with.[11] Those who join them should anticipate and, if appropriate, seek to mitigate or exploit the post-emergency reemergence of rivalry.

---

[7] Case in point: the formation of the North Atlantic Treaty Organization in 1949.

[8] France offered covert, then, in 1778, overt support for the independence of its British enemy's American colonies, despite Louis XVI's abhorrence of *lèse majesté* and republicanism. France turned against the United States in 1794, after the U.S. concluded a treaty of commerce with Britain. The United States and France were soon engaged in the 1798–1800 "Quasi-War" ["Quasi-Guerre"]. Another instance of an ad hoc coalition involving the United States and France was the "coalition of the willing," composed of NATO member states' forces that conducted UN-authorized but tragic 2011 military intervention in Libya.

[9] This appears to have been a significant factor in the composition of the "Eight-Nation Alliance" to put down the 1889–1901 "Boxer" rebellion in China. While slaughtering large numbers of Chinese, the American, Austro-Hungarian, British, French, German, Italian, Japanese, and Russian participants sought to prevent each other from seizing the lead in the ongoing dismemberment of Qing China.

[10] A recent example of such a pseudo-coalition for the sake of appearances was the assembly by the United States of "the coalition of the billing" that joined U.S. forces in their 2003–11 war in Iraq. With few exceptions (e.g., the British), the three dozen participating armies added little or nothing to U.S. combat power and were excluded from a role in the U.S.-led "Coalition Provisional Authority" that conducted the occupation of Iraq. They were there not so much to fight as to provide a veneer of international support to a misadventure opposed by major U.S. allies and the United Nations. Their assembly was a transparent attempt to replicate the coalition that had conducted the 1990–91 war to liberate Kuwait. But, in that previous war, broad coalitions of Western and Islamic forces had volunteered for service in an operation authorized by the United Nations Security Council.

[11] The 1956 Egyptian nationalization of the Suez Canal resulted in the Protocol of Sèvres by which France, Israel, and the United Kingdom agreed to an Israeli attack on Egypt, followed by British and French intervention ostensibly to divide the warring Israeli and Egyptian forces. After the plan was carried out and drew opposition from both the United States and USSR, the tripartite coalition immediately fell apart, but Franco-Israeli cooperation continued.

The response of Britain, the Soviet Union, and the United States to the threat of conquest by the Axis (Germany, Italy, Japan) during World War II is a classic example of an ad hoc coalition. Naïve misinterpretation of it as an "alliance" incorporating more than temporary common purposes (primarily by the United States)[12] led to the planning failures that divided postwar Europe, including Germany and Korea. These divisions became the fault lines of the Cold War.[13]

Ad hoc coalitions are not limited to politico-military matters. Sometimes they include other elements as well.[14] They are also the norm in the parliamentary diplomacy practiced in international organizations and multilateral trade zones, where votes are traded, and postures struck to secure support for responses to events as well as the passage of treaty provisions and resolutions.

Ententes

Ententes are limited partnerships for limited purposes, often for a limited time. Like ad hoc coalitions, they imply neither broadly shared interests nor values. In fact, they often presuppose serious differences that the parties to them find it expedient to set aside to pursue common interests. But unlike ad hoc arrangements, ententes define the responses of the parties to contingencies before these occur and are frequently but not always formalized in negotiated documents.[15] When the purpose of an entente is deterrence, all or part of

---

[12] British Prime Minister Winston Churchill envisioned a rebuilt Britain, France, and Germany allied with the U.S., as a counterbalance to the Soviet Union, but President Roosevelt fantasized about a post-World War II international order that would be led by what he called "the four policemen of world peace." He proposed that Britain direct affairs in Europe, China do the same in East Asia, the Soviet Union exercise hegemony in Eastern Europe, and the United States control the Western Hemisphere.

[13] Many historians have remarked on the consequences of the U.S. failure to consider the long-term implications of the military lines of control established by World War II campaign plans. For the most part, the places where troop advances halted became the borders of a Europe divided between Soviet and Western occupation forces and the Cold War alignments of the occupied nations.

[14] For example, in 1907, in part in exchange for a loan from France, Japan agreed to guarantee France's strategically vulnerable possessions in Indochina and to reach an agreement with Russia on spheres of influence in northeast Asia. Japan subsequently signed a secret treaty in which it agreed to defer to Russian interests in Mongolia and northern Manchuria, while Russia did the same for Japanese interests in southern Manchuria and Korea.

[15] The "Triple Entente" of 1907 between the Russian Empire, Britain, and France formed to counter the pre-World War I "Triple Alliance" was an oral rather than a written understanding.

the documents establishing it are usually publicized.[16] The same is true when an entente is established to co-opt a rival state and preclude hostile cooperation by it with a third party.[17] When its purpose is compellence[18] or conquest, the existence as well as the substance of an entente are more likely to be kept secret.[19]

Ententes limit commitments to cooperate to specific politico-military and economic contingencies, threats, and opportunities. Unlike alliances, they do not imply broad commitments to the security and well-being of the partners to them, nor do they imply automatic mutual aid.[20] The habits of cooperation they engender can evolve into alliances, though this is rare.[21] Generally, ententes dissolve once the interests that caused their formation have been realized or

---

[16] In the 1882 "Triple Alliance" between Germany, Austria-Hungary, and Italy, each member promised mutual support in the event of an attack by any other great power. The treaty they concluded provided that Germany and Austria-Hungary were to assist Italy if it was attacked by France without provocation. In turn, Italy would assist Germany if attacked by France. In the event of a war between Austria-Hungary and Russia, Italy promised to remain neutral. The existence and membership of the treaty were well known, but its provisions were kept secret until 1919.

[17] The openly proclaimed 1902 Japanese treaty of entente with the United Kingdom called the "Anglo-Japanese Alliance" exemplified this sort of diplomatic maneuver. It provided that, for the succeeding five years, each would support the other in the event of a war challenging its interests in China. The resulting threat of war with Britain deterred France from joining its ally Russia in the Russo-Japanese War of 1904.

[18] Compellence is the use of coercive measures (e.g., a threat to impose sanctions or to use force) by a state or group of states to compel another to take an action. It contrasts with deterrence, which is the threat to use coercive measures to convince another party to refrain from taking an action.

[19] The 1939 Molotov-Ribbentrop Pact is a case in point. This was a non-aggression pact between Germany and the USSR that envisioned the partition of Poland. It contained a secret Protocol, dividing Eastern Europe and the Baltic region into German and Soviet spheres of influence. The existence of this protocol was proven only in the 1946 Nuremberg war crimes trials, which followed the German defeat in World War II.

The secret Sykes-Picot Agreement of 1916 is another example of an entente aimed at enabling aggression against other states and peoples. With the assent of the Russian Empire and Italy, Messrs Sykes and Picot defined how they would partition the Ottoman Empire into British and French spheres of influence in the Middle East.

[20] The post-Cold War relationship between Beijing and Moscow is an entente formed in response to Washington's vocal hostility to both and its efforts to contain their influence beyond their borders. The Sino-Russian entente seeks to counter U.S. unilateralism and global hegemony. Characterizing Sino-Russian cooperation as an alliance both exaggerates the degree of mutual commitment it implies and misestimates its potential to expand. On the other hand, presuming that it will collapse due to historical differences ignores the role of American hostility in its creation and sustainment. The withdrawal of hostility to one or the other country would greatly reduce and possibly end the current Sino-Russian entente. It is not clear what else might.

[21] The Anglo-American relationship that was forged in World War II produced an unprecedented degree of integration between parts of the intelligence, scientific and technological, and military establishments of the two countries. The only mutual commitments of the UK and U.S. to each other are the collective security provisions of the North Atlantic Alliance (NATO). But, in practice, since World War II, the bilateral relationship between the U.S and UK has, with rare exceptions, fully deserved the appellation of "special" and has operated at a level above that between the United States and other NATO countries. It is a comprehensive bilateral compact of mutual assistance and so understood in both countries as well as in third parties. Given the disparities in size and capabilities between the two countries, this must be counted as a major achievement of British diplomacy. A similar evolution occurred in the U.S.-Australian relationship, nurtured and sustained by Australia's willingness to participate in every American war after World War II.

ceased to exist.[22] Then they give way to other sorts of relationships, including those of client states, protected states, rivalry, and adversarial antagonism.

Conversely, ad hoc coalition and protected state relationships can, if the interests of the parties are sufficiently challenged, grow into ententes.[23] But these will, as is the case with all coalitions, last only as long as the challenge that generated them before expiring or transforming themselves into something else.[24]

Alliances

The rarest and most durable form of coalition is an alliance.[25] Alliances are formal pledges by members expressing broad mutual strategic commitments to each other. In a multinational alliance, a challenge to one ally presupposes

---

[22] The North Atlantic Treaty's Article 5 commits member states to consider an attack on one as an attack on all. But once the Soviet menace to Turkey dissipated, Ankara began to pursue purely Turkish interests with its Middle Eastern neighbors and Moscow. Some of these Turkish interests are congruent with those of NATO, the EU, and the United States, but others are at odds with them. In practice, Turkey has transformed its relationship with NATO into something less than a collective security alliance, that is, a de facto entente but one in which the contingencies have become ever more poorly defined. Turkey cannot expect its allies to behave as such when it challenges important interests of theirs. Nor can it expect its formal commitment to defend their interests to remain credible in the absence of reciprocity.

[23] The Sino-American relationship underwent radical changes in the 1970s. It began when U.S. President Richard Nixon realized that there was a credible prospect that a Soviet attack on China could remove China from the geopolitical chessboard to the advantage of the USSR in its contest with the United States. In effect, Nixon reacted by returning China to the status as a protected power (see definition in following pages) that it had had in World War II. In December 1979, the USSR directly challenged both American and Chinese interests by invading and occupying Afghanistan. This propelled the two into an entente relationship focused on the frustration of Soviet strategic ambitions beyond the possible subjugation of China itself.

[24] For example, the collapse of the Soviet bloc in 1989, followed by that of the USSR itself in 1991, removed the challenge to common American and Chinese interests that had driven the evolution of the Sino-American relationship from adversarial antagonism, through stages, to that of a protected state and finally to entente. By the end of the second decade of the twenty-first century, China and the United States had reverted first to rivalry and then to adversarial antagonism.

Meanwhile, with the disappearance of the threat from the Soviet Union, NATO lost its *raison d'être*. Its most fervent supporters argued that NATO would have to go "out of area or out of business." Many thought it should disband. Some thought it should transform itself into a cooperative security organization, devoted to sustaining stability in Europe in coordination with Russia. In the event, NATO cured its enemy deprivation syndrome and preserved itself as a collective security organization. It did so, first, by using force in 1999 to detach Kosovo from Serbia and then, in 2001 by committing itself to expeditionary warfare in Afghanistan as an Article 5 response to the "9/11" (September 11, 2001) Islamist attack on the United States. It exploited Russian weakness to expand into Eastern European countries traditionally regarded by Russia as a "cordon sanitaire." Still later, in what appears to have been an instance of self-fulfilling paranoia, NATO found new purpose in the reimagination of a military threat from Russia and American demands that its European members raise defense spending concomitantly.

[25] As previously noted, the terms "ally" and "alliance" lost their precision during the Cold War, since which they have been used to describe any cooperative relationship between states, including those lacking reciprocal commitments. But the distinctions between reciprocal and unequal, formal and informal, broad and narrow, considered and ad hoc, and durable and temporary forms of coalition are indispensable to accurate strategic reasoning and statecraft.

a sympathetic and supportive response by all the others.[26] In a bilateral alliance, each ally is honor-bound to protect the other. In both cases, alliances are expressed in constitutionally approved, written documents that state their purpose and duration. They may be perpetual, terminable after due notice, or set to expire on a certain date unless renewed. Alliance management is a specialized diplomatic skill. To work well, alliances require the development of common operational standards or doctrines.

Alliances are both assets and liabilities[27] of those who form them. They lend the power of allies to the advancement or defense of shared political, economic, and military interests. Allies benefit from the deterrent effects of the expectation that they will not be alone in defending interests they share. But alliances also place the parties to them on call to assist each other in response to situations involving others that do not bear directly on their interests, that they may have had nothing to do with creating, and that they could not foresee or forestall.[28] And, if alliances cease to serve a state's national interests, it will either hedge its commitments or desert them, thereby de facto weakening or dissolving the alliance.[29] At any moment, then, alliances are only as strong as their weakest link. Evaluating their cohesion and acting to reinforce or undermine the bonds that form them are key tasks of diplomacy.

Treaties of alliance formally engage national honor in ways that other forms of coalition do not. They thereby stimulate efforts to validate commitments by perseverance regardless of the prospects of success or the collateral damage being done. In the end, an ally's concerns about its credibility are more often the product of self-doubt than disbelief in its reliability by third parties.[30] Perseverance in counterproductive or self-injuring relationships or policies is

---

[26] Article 5 of the North Atlantic Treaty is the classic expression of such collective security arrangements.

[27] China regards alliances as liabilities. It has none, though it treats North Korea and Pakistan as protected states and has developed a relationship of entente with Russia in opposition to continued U.S. global primacy.

[28] For example, the 1982 Falklands War between Argentina and the United Kingdom posed awkward choices for the United States, which had alliances with both combatants. Washington first supported peace overtures to Argentina and then, having been rebuffed, provided crucial military support to the UK.

[29] As Charles de Gaulle said, "Treaties … are like girls and roses; they last while they last." Consider the example of the 1954 Mutual Defense Treaty between the United States of America and the Republic of China (Taiwan), which the United States terminated in 1979 when this was thought necessary to consolidate the support of the rival People's Republic of China against the USSR and to develop normal relations with it as a potential great power.

[30] The U.S. defense of the Republic of (South) Vietnam against the northern Socialist Republic of Vietnam was fueled by concerns about credibility expressed in the so-called domino theory. In time, it became an argument for continuing to soldier on regardless of the prospects for success. Few doubted the determination of the United States in Vietnam. U.S. persistence in the war enhanced the American reputation for obstinacy but not for wisdom or strategic reasoning. In the end, the American defeat in Vietnam had little lasting effect on the credibility of the United States.

potent evidence of obstinacy but more likely to undercut a state's reputation for wisdom, realism, and effectiveness than to inspire confidence.

Transactional and One-Sided Relationships

The norm in international relations is noncommittal, transactional relationships between states conducted through interactions based on balanced exchanges of goods, services, or favors. States usually deal with each other at arm's length on the assumption that they owe each other nothing and that their interactions are purely self-interested. But the intensity of their engagement with each other can grow into a determination to preserve the ties they have forged. More commonly, a state decides to extend unilateral protection to another state because the latter's autonomy, policies, or prosperity serve its own vital[31] or strategic interests,[32] domestic political purposes, or ideological imperatives.

Client States

A "client state" is one whose transactions with a stronger patron have produced a degree of mutual reliance and dependency that makes preservation of the relationship a matter of interest to the patron. Client state relationships are asymmetric, but client states are not formally subordinate to their patrons. Client state relationships therefore differ from "satrapies"[33] or "satellites,"[34]

---

[31] Vital interests are those that bear directly on a state's security, well-being, and domestic tranquility. They include the defense of national unity behind secure frontiers, the securing of strategic advantage and its denial to potential enemies, access to resources essential to national power and well-being, immunity from intimidation, and freedom from subversion or intervention by other states. See Freeman (1997, 10).

[32] Strategic interests are those that have the potential, whether addressed or left unattended, to affect a state's vital interests or its capacity to advance or defend them. Ibid.

[33] A "satrapy" is a polity whose domestic and foreign policies are under the openly declared control of a viceroy or "satrap" (governor) appointed or legitimated by an imperial or hegemonic poser. In the age of European imperialism, satrapies were manifested in "colonial possessions," "protectorates," and "mandates." Examples include the Raj in British-controlled India, European colonies in Africa, the U.S.-ruled Philippines, and today's Commonwealth of Puerto Rico. The "Palestinian Authority" is a satrapy of Israel.

[34] A "satellite" is a technically independent state whose foreign policies and international relationships are constrained and controlled by a hegemonic power. Examples include Mongolia and the states of Eastern Europe in relation to the Soviet Union and its "Brezhnev Doctrine," Lebanon while under Syrian occupation, and the former state of Sikkim and contemporary Bhutan in relation to India. In pre-modern times such relationships were known as "suzerainty," and manifested in Mughal or British paramountcy over India's princely states and Qing China's veto power over the foreign relations of the Ryukyu Kingdom, Korea, and Vietnam.

which are nominally self-governing but under the open or acknowledged control of a greater power.

Client states seek a wide variety of benefits from their patrons. These include subsidies and subventions; development assistance and project finance; trade preferences, arms transfers, and military training; political, economic, military protection against rival states and adversaries[35]; and support for those in power.[36] In return, client states may offer their patrons preferred access to natural resources,[37] investment and sales opportunities, supportive stances in international organizations, political support by their followers in the patron state or elsewhere abroad,[38] and strategically useful military bases or access to ports and airfields.[39] Such concessions qualify the sovereignty of client states. If they are perceived as domineering or unfair, they can energize nationalist opposition to continued cooperation with the patron.

Despite their transactional nature, client state relationships can still foster unrealistic expectations. To the extent the client state is able to rely on backing from its patron, it may become less risk averse. Client-state adventurism can impose unwelcome and sometimes costly choices on its patrons.[40] The client state has assumed no obligation to add its power to that of the patron when the patron's interests are challenged.[41]

---

[35] The Republic of Djibouti has used its strategic location near the Bab al Mandeb to cultivate client state relationships with multiple patrons. These relationships are central to Djibouti's economic development and national security policies. By 2021, Djibouti had become the principal entrepôt for trade in the Horn of Africa and the site of military bases from China, France (which also hosts German and Spanish forces), Italy, Japan, Saudi Arabia, the United Kingdom, and the United States. It receives development assistance from all of these countries.

[36] For example, U.S. relationships with the Central American "banana republics."

[37] Consider the U.S. relationship that President Franklin D. Roosevelt forged with Saudi Arabia by which, in return for security guarantees, American companies gained preferred access to Saudi hydrocarbons.

[38] For example, wealthy members of Israeli, U.S., and UK lobbies incentivize politicians to defer to Israel on issues of concern to the Zionist state. And Israel leverages the allegiance of American and British politicians to recruit support in third countries.

[39] The ultra-wealthy Persian Gulf Arab state of Qatar, which is located between the regional great powers of Iran and Saudi Arabia, has sought to guarantee its independence by balancing relations with both while catering to the economic and military interests of as many other great power patrons as it can recruit. It has loaned a major airbase to the United States, and welcomed a strong Turkish military presence, while building political and economic ties with China, India, and Russia.

[40] For example, since 1964, when the United States dropped its arms embargo on Israel, the Zionist state has been a U.S. client state. Israel's 1967 surprise attack on Egypt, Jordan, and Syria resulted in its occupation of all of Palestine and parts of Syria and Egypt. Its refusal to withdraw from the Sinai triggered a 1973 surprise attack by Egypt. In both instances, Israel's military actions risked war between the U.S. and USSR. In 1973, they led to a rupture in U.S. relations with almost all Arab countries and an economically catastrophic Arab oil boycott of the United States and other Israeli patron states. Israel's cruelties to its captive Arab populations have earned it widespread international opprobrium, which spills over on its U.S. patron.

[41] Still, it must weigh the fact that failing to support its patron in times of need will reduce its ability to extract benefits from the relationship in future.

Client states are always liabilities; they are seldom active strategic assets.[42] Patron-client relations and expectations require dispassionate judgments by the parties to them about how they will be affected by trends or developments. The willingness to do business with another state is not a pledge of affection, still less loyalty to it.[43]

Protected States

A "protected state" is one whose patron seeks to deny it or its resources to an adversary or to sustain its independent geopolitical position because this serves the patron's strategic interests. Protected states may also be client states despite the absence of tangible benefits to their patrons. Patron states typically demand little, if anything, concrete from those they protect other than policy continuity and continued autonomy.[44] The benefits of the relationship to the patron state are its intangible effects on the strategic judgments and policies of rivals, adversaries, or enemies, rather than active support by the protected state for the patron's policies.[45] Protected state relationships are primarily defined by the patron's strategic interests rather than mutually with the protected state.

---

[42] Consider the example of Serbia as a putative client state of diverse patrons, whose interactions with it catalyzed an unprecedentedly devastating war between them. To bolster Christian opposition to the Ottoman Empire, the Austro-Hungarian Empire sought to incorporate Serbia as a satellite. But the proudly independent Serbs acted in ways that undermined Austrian influence in the Balkans and exacerbated Austrian relations with both the Ottomans and Russians. Serbia soon came under Russian protection, as Russia attempted to form a pan-Orthodox counterweight to the Roman Catholic Austro-Hungarians. Russia regarded its essentially transactional relations with Serbia as an alliance, entente, or protected state relationship. In 1914, when the Austrians attacked Serbia despite repeated Russian warnings, the Tsar felt obliged to mobilize his army, helping to set off a chain of events that led to a devastating war in Europe and to revolutionary upheaval in Russia itself.

[43] "You get what you pay for."

[44] China's relationship with Pakistan fits this pattern. Its primary utility is to offset Indian hegemony in South Asia and thus distract and weaken a potential Chinese adversary. Pakistan has no obligation to come to China's aid even in conflicts with the two countries' common adversary, India.

[45] The relationships between the United States and China during World War II and during the latter phases of the Cold War are examples of such a relationship. In World War II, China was strategically important not for its military capabilities, but because it consumed Japanese military resources and tied down Japanese troops that might otherwise have been deployed elsewhere. There was no expectation or demand from the ad hoc coalition of so-called Allies that China attempt to defeat Japan or actively contribute to their war with Germany, Italy, or other members of the "Axis."

After China broke with the Soviet Union in the Cold War, the United States sought to bolster Chinese independence and defense capabilities because these consumed Soviet military resources and diverted Soviet attention from the more consequential European front. It asked nothing of China other than that it remain ornery and independent.

Relations between patron states and protected states are often misportrayed as "alliances,"[46] but patron states have no reasons, other than self-interest and the cultivation of a reputation for reliability, to come to the aid of a protected state. The occupation of defeated former enemies can underscore the importance of their place in a post-war order and lead to their becoming protected states.[47] The purposes of their patron's protection can include preventing their reemergence as geopolitical actors that might again challenge the patron's interests.[48]

Buffer states are a form of protected state,[49] sometimes with more than one patron.[50] Sometimes, too, events suddenly reveal a previously unrecognized interest in strategic denial of a state and its resources to yet another state, justifying efforts to repel or reverse threats to its independence.[51]

Non-committal, Transactional Relationships

States typically do not form passionate attachments or extend commitments to each other but deal with each other dispassionately based on their judgments of the costs and benefits of specific interactions with each other. It takes the emergence of a common threat or, less often, an opportunity for them to form coalitions, alliances, ententes, or otherwise develop commitments or

---

[46] The U.S. defense treaties with various Asian "allies" (e.g., Japan, South Korea, and the Philippines) are titled "mutual defense treaties" but impose defense obligations only on the United States. In return for undertaking their defense, the United States maintains forces and installations on their territory that are essential to the power projection capabilities that make America a global military power.

[47] After its defeat in 1945, the two parts of Germany initially became protected states of their Western (American, British, and French) and Soviet occupiers and patrons. But they evolved into allies with formal obligations enshrined in the NATO and Warsaw Pacts. Japan underwent no such evolution and remains an American protected state as does the Republic of (South) Korea (ROK). Tokyo has no obligation to come to the aid of its American patron. In recent years, however, it has begun on its own to acquire the option to do so in limited circumstances involving the defense of its own territory and armed forces against neighboring states. In order to confirm and consolidate American protection, the ROK earlier volunteered forces in support of the U.S. in Vietnam and Iraq.

[48] The U.S. relationships with the Federal Republic of (West) Germany and Japan were structured to serve this end.

[49] In relation to China, the Democratic People's Republic of (North) Korea (DPRK) is a buffer against the presence of hostile U.S. forces in the ROK. Ukraine is a potential buffer state between the European Union (EU) and Russia.

[50] For example, Belgium before World War I. Despite the absence of an agreement to do so, China and India treat Nepal as a buffer state, and each seeks to deny paramount influence in it to the other. The relationship of Thailand and Vietnam to Cambodia is similar.

[51] This was the case with Kuwait in 1990. U.S. relations with Kuwait then were troubled and there was no intimation that Americans might intervene to aid it if it were attacked by either Iran or Iraq. But Iraq's invasion and attempt to annex it underscored the importance of denying Iraq monopoly control and the ability to dictate prices for Persian Gulf energy supplies and led to the formation of U.S.- and Saudi-led coalitions to liberate Kuwait and restore a balance of power in the Gulf region.

antagonism to each other. In the absence of such external challenges or revolutionary change at home, they will continue to deal with each other transactionally. As they do, they establish reputations for either probity or duplicity. These reputations enable or constrain cooperation when states find it necessary to support each other. They may also ease or retard a slide into antagonism when states develop opposing interests.

Competitive Relationships

Any power, great or small, seeks to expand its influence and weaken the relative position of its perceived adversaries. Competition between and among states is normal, but it can be benign, malign, or existential in nature.

Rivalry

Rivalry pits parties against each other in a competition to excel. Each seeks to best the other primarily by improving its own capabilities and performance, rather than seeking to impair those of the other. Rivalry is typical of economic[52] and technological[53] competition, but it can also be military[54] or political.[55] It is most dynamic in international systems composed of multiple, relatively small states.[56] It usually involves more posturing than direct confrontation between the parties and seldom includes efforts by one party to inflict injury on another. Rivalry can be a spur to self-improvement and thus an engine of progress for those engaged in it.

---

[52] Competition for markets is a prime example of this. In the age of imperialism, this took the form of efforts by European states to bring underdeveloped areas of the world like sub-Saharan Africa under colonial control and to block the efforts of their rivals to do the same.

[53] The Cold War's space race epitomizes technological rivalry.

[54] Arms races typify military rivalry.

[55] Contests for political influence are the lifeblood of diplomacy. The relationship between a rising United States and weakening Great Britain at the end of the nineteenth and beginning of the twentieth centuries illustrates a broad rivalry for international prestige and influence. (Thanks to a British decision to appease and court, rather than oppose, the United States, the contest remained civil and did not evolve into a situation in which one side's loss was necessarily the other's gain.)

States may also have rival messianic ideologies, for example, the Soviet Union (Marxism-Leninism) and the United States (laissez-faire economics and constitutional democracy) in the Cold War.

[56] For example, the Greek city states, the Spring and Autumn period in China, pre-Mauryan India, the Mayan city states, Arab Spain, and Renaissance Europe.

Adversarial Antagonism

But rivalry can too easily become a zero-sum competition, in which the parties rely as much on crippling each other as on upping their own performance. Economic warfare through trade and financial sanctions is a form of adversarial antagonism. It invites retaliation, not always in kind.[57] In the absence of a potent deterrent,[58] if a party to such an adversarial relationship comes to consider the threat to it to verge on the existential, the contention can escalate into the most extreme form of zero-sum competition—enmity expressed in a war of annihilation.

Enmity

Enmity treats the interests of an adversary as illegitimate and rejects all notions of compromise. It seeks the adversary's incapacitation, conquest following unconditional surrender,[59] annihilation,[60] or genocide.[61] It is a relationship fraught with peril for all concerned.

Conclusion

Relationships among states evolve between categories. Occasionally, they leap across them.[62] But, for the most part, if they are not clearly ad hoc, relationships are more durable than fragile. This is what gives them their predictive value. The sounder the analysis of the character and quality of relationships, the sounder a state's diplomacy.

---

[57] In 1941, Japan's perception that the United States intended to hamstring it, halt its continuing modernization, and oppose its imperial expansion led to a vain attempt to turn the tables with a preemptive attack on the U.S. fleet at Pearl Harbor. Instead of inducing U.S. compromise, as its proponents hoped, this galvanized U.S. enmity.

[58] The Cold War relationship between the United States and the Soviet Union and current U.S. interactions with China are examples of adversarial animosity constrained by nuclear deterrence. Only the fear of a mutually fatal nuclear exchange kept the competition between the U.S. and USSR in check. More recently China, India, and Pakistan have skirmished along their disputed frontiers without escalating their conflicts into full-scale warfare that might risk nuclear exchanges between them.

[59] The United States demanded this of its enemies in the American Civil War, World War I, and World War II.

[60] The classic example is Rome's fear-driven determination in the third and second centuries BCE to destroy Carthage once and for all.

[61] As in the Biblical extermination of the Amalekites or "the only good Indian is a dead Indian."

[62] The 1971–72 opening and visit to China by U.S. President Richard Nixon and the 1977 visit to Israel by Egyptian President Anwar Sadat are examples of such a leap.

3 A Diplomatic Taxonomy for the New World Disorder

Alliances may evolve into ententes[63] or vice versa, but the parties to these relationships are unlikely to revert overnight to the international norm of transactionalism.[64] Protected states may become entente partners[65] or devolve into transactionalism but are unlikely to become allies. The fact that rivalries can become adversarial antagonisms or even enmities underscores the need for prudent handling of competitive relationships.

In the shifting constellations of power of the new world disorder, countries are reexamining inherited relationships and alignments.[66] Smaller and middle-ranking powers are regaining agency.[67] The pace with which relationships evolve is quickening. A more rigorous diplomatic terminology than that of the Cold War is needed to analyze, describe, and manage the increasingly dynamic and multidimensional relationships between states. The lack of such a taxonomy expands the risk that foreign policy decisions will prove counterproductive.[68]

---

[63] "NATO à la carte," for example, the 2011 Libyan intervention, is an example of an entente implemented with the military operational doctrines and infrastructure created by the decaying NATO alliance.

[64] The Trump administration's efforts to transform alliance relationships into transactional relationships damaged transatlantic cooperation but did not succeed.

[65] As noted, this happened in U.S.-China relations after the 1979 Soviet invasion of Afghanistan.

Such a transformation may be in progress in the U.S.-Japan protected state relationship. Japan is reasserting a leadership role in its region and developing its own policies, military capabilities, and ties to neighbors. It can now either support the United States or act independently as it judges appropriate. The emerging Japanese-American entente awaits definition.

[66] The perennial example of this is France. Its reaction to the American usurpation of its preferred strategic partnership with Australia in the September 2021 AUKUS agreement is a case in point.

[67] Consider the maneuvers of the mini-state of Qatar in relation to its Saudi Arabian, Emirati, and Iranian neighbors, and its leveraging of its relationship to the Afghan Taliban to make itself an essential partner in diplomacy toward Afghanistan. In West Asia and North Africa, as the United States steps back, the region's states are stepping forward to deal with each other and solve problems they had earlier delegated to their American patron or regarded as insoluble due to American opposition.

[68] The misperception of Sino-Soviet relations as an alliance rather than an entente caused the consequent failure by the United States to seek at the outset to split the "Sino-Soviet bloc." The British and French wrongly assumed that their alliance with the United States would oblige it to support them in their collusion with Israel in an attack on Egypt and the Suez Canal in 1956. But the alliance was limited to mutual support in European, not Middle Eastern contingencies. London and Paris were surprised when Washington actively condemned and opposed their breach of the peace. Misapprehension of ties between China and the "Democratic People's Republic of (North) Korea" as an "alliance" or client state relationships rather than a protected state relationship with few client state elements inspired an ineffectual American outsourcing of policy to China, which shared some American interests but not all, had different priorities on the Korean Peninsula than the United States, and had much less influence in Pyongyang than the architects of American policy imagined. Conversely, the misperception of twenty-first-century Sino-Russian relations as an alliance rather than an entente has entailed numerous opportunity costs by inhibiting efforts to cooperate with one or the other on matters where their national interests diverge or are not engaged. The persistent American effort to create an "alliance" with India runs afoul of Indian "nonalignment" and precludes the pursuit of entente (limited cooperation for limited purposes), which is acceptable to India as entangling alliances are not.

References and Further Reading

BBC. 2016. "Russia and the West: Where Did It All Go Wrong." https://www.bbc.com/news/world-middle-east-37658286.

Freeman, C.W., Jr. 1997. *Arts of Power: Statecraft and Diplomacy*. Washington, D.C.: United States Institute of Peace.

———. 2009. *The Diplomat's Dictionary*. 2nd ed. Washington, D.C.: United States Institute of Peace.

———. 2011. "The Incapacitation of U.S. Statecraft and Diplomacy." *The Hague Journal of Diplomacy* 6: 413–32.

———. 2018a. "Diplomacy as Strategy." https://chasfreeman.net/diplomacy-as-strategy/.

———. 2018b. "Diplomacy as Tactics." https://chasfreeman.net/diplomacy-as-tactics/.

———. 2018c. "Diplomacy as Risk Management." https://chasfreeman.net/diplomacy-as-risk-management/.

———. 2020a. "On Diplomatic Relationships and Strategies." https://chasfreeman.net/on-diplomatic-relationships-and-strategies/.

———. 2020b. "War with China over Taiwan." https://chasfreeman.net/war-with-china-over-taiwan/.

Lieberthal, K. 2016. *Addressing U.S.-China Strategic Distrust*. Washington, D.C.: The Brookings Institution. https://www.brookings.edu/wp-content/uploads/2016/06/0330_china_lieberthal.pdf.

4

Knowledge Diplomacy: A Conceptual Analysis

Jane Knight

Introduction

Diplomacy is a phenomenon and term which is used and defined in diverse ways. Many diplomacy scholars and experts (Cooper et al. 2013; Leijten 2017; Bjola and Kornprobst 2013) acknowledge that there are multiple terms related to diplomacy such as representation, negotiation, communication, foreign policy, intelligence gathering, and image making; and that the definitions and use of these terms are contested. Each term has its pros and cons, and has been chosen by the scholar, diplomat, or policymaker for specific reasons. It is evident that "one size does not fit all" and the local context of each actor, country, and sector must be respected. However, the plethora of terms is not helping to advance a robust analysis or reform of contemporary diplomacy.

Surprisingly, there is little discourse analyzing why so many interpretations of diplomacy exist (Cooper et al. 2013) or why there is a lack of conceptual research to identify the salient features that differentiate one term from another. It is true that individual disciplines and sectors use their own particular taxonomies to discuss concepts. Nevertheless, further efforts are needed to allow for a more rigorous approach to understanding the meaning and implications of the multiple definitions of diplomacy.

J. Knight (✉)
University of Toronto, Toronto, ON, Canada

At the macro level and in a generic way, diplomacy is described as a lens to understanding international relations (Pouliot and Cornut 2015). But the more specific definitions vary according to whether diplomacy is being articulated in terms of issues, functions, forms, or actors and whether the theory or practice of diplomacy is being examined. Kerr and Wiseman (2013) identify two fundamental aspects regarding the ongoing debates about contemporary diplomacy. The first debate relates to the epistemological underpinnings as they believe that "what we mean by diplomacy" is breaking down. The second is identifying the key differences between contemporary diplomacy and traditional diplomacy (Kerr and Wiseman 2013).

The purpose of this chapter is to explore the need and strategies for further conceptual analysis of the phenomenon of diplomacy. It aims to illustrate how one form of contemporary diplomacy, that being knowledge diplomacy, can be conceptualized through the use of analytical tools such as definitions, descriptions, and conceptual frameworks, and how it can be differentiated from other types of diplomacy as well as soft power.

Why Knowledge Diplomacy

Knowledge diplomacy relates to the role and contributions that international higher education, research, and innovation can play in strengthening relations between and among countries. The phenomenon of knowledge diplomacy has been chosen as an example of conceptual analysis for the following reasons. First, the number of global challenges facing a more turbulent world cannot be solved by one nation alone or by one sector. It requires research, expertise, resources, and political will from a diverse set of state and non-state actors using a multi-lateral approach and finding common ground. Knowledge diplomacy is key to addressing these challenges.

Secondly, a recent review of both the diplomacy and higher education literature (Knight 2022) has revealed that there are about fourteen terms used to describe the role of international, higher education and innovation (IHERI) in international relations (IR) often causing confusion and misunderstandings among the terms. The most common terms used to frame the role of IHERI in IR are cultural, science, education, and public forms of diplomacy as well as soft power. To complicate matters further, the definitions of these individual terms vary significantly across the two fields of study as well as within the same field. This is a current example of terminology chaos. Such a diversity of terms does not lead to a robust understanding of the role of IHERI in IR, it results in more confusion than clarity.

Thirdly, both diplomacy and higher education scholars frame the role of IHERI as a type of diplomacy that can be simultaneously used as an instrument of soft power. This raises the question as to whether this is a contradiction in terms given the different intentions, values, modes, and outcomes of diplomacy versus a soft power approach. Thus, given the importance and relevance of the role of IHERI in contemporary IR and the multiple terms and labels being used to describe it, the concept of knowledge diplomacy has been proposed.

Analyzing Knowledge Diplomacy: A Definition and Description

Given that the conceptualization of knowledge diplomacy is the focus of this chapter, not theories, practices, policies, or geo-political dimensions of diplomacy, it is important to elaborate on the three key analytical tools used—definition, description, and conceptual framework. According to Nordquist (2010), a definition is a concise statement of the meaning of the key concept while a description provides more details and often includes characteristics such as actors, purposes, and instruments. Ravitch and Riggan describe conceptualization as a process of defining and elaborating the meaning of terms and the use of conceptual frameworks help to make conceptual distinctions and organize information, observations, perceptions, and ideas (Ravitch and Riggan 2016).

This explanation suggests that a definition of knowledge diplomacy should be succinct and limited to addressing the fundamental ideas of knowledge diplomacy. Based on this perspective, the definition proposed for knowledge diplomacy is *the process of building and strengthening relations between and among countries through international higher education, research and innovation* (Knight 2021, 161). In this definition, diplomacy is intentionally framed as a process—a means to an end, a series of actions to achieve a result—not a policy or theory per se. This approach to defining knowledge diplomacy is consistent with the understanding that diplomacy is commonly understood as the process of developing relations between and among countries to operationalize foreign policies (Griffiths et al. 2014).

It is important that a generic definition of knowledge diplomacy be used in order to increase its relevance and use in a diversity of settings, cultures, or countries and to emphasize that it is a means to an end. Many of the proposed definitions of diplomacy relate to a specific issue or set of circumstances making it difficult to use the definitions more broadly. To illustrate the difference between a "definition" and a "description," an example of a description of knowledge diplomacy is proposed as follows: knowledge diplomacy involves diverse state and non-state actors involved in collaborative education, research, and innovation initiatives which are based on mutual benefits and reciprocity and designed to build and strengthen relations between and among countries to increase mutual understanding and address global issues. This description includes strategies and intended outcomes and is different from a concise definition. A conceptual framework goes further and explains the fundamental elements of a phenomenon such as intentions, actors, principles, modes of operation, and strategies.

Worth noting is that the proposed definition of knowledge diplomacy does not actually include the term "knowledge." Instead, higher education, research, and innovation are used as the fundamental concepts to represent the transfer, production, and application of knowledge. These three concepts form the backbone of the definition and are defined as follows. *Higher education* is a form of knowledge transfer and refers to the different processes of teaching and learning whether it be in a formal or informal manner. *Research* is aimed at producing new knowledge through the gathering of information on a subject, investigation, or experimentation. *Innovation* refers to the application of research findings and new knowledge to produce change or new ideas.

Not including knowledge in the definition was deliberate and can be both a strength and a weakness. While knowledge is inclusive of higher education, research, and innovation, it can also be used in many different and contradictory ways. Knowledge can be used to empower and also to disenfranchise. Different disciplines and sectors have their own lens to understand and define knowledge and there are countless ways to modify the concept of knowledge such as implicit knowledge, tacit knowledge, indigenous knowledge, technical knowledge, and scientific knowledge (Lehrer 2000).

Furthermore, by including "knowledge" in the definition, the term knowledge diplomacy could be misunderstood as a form of issue diplomacy and become one more hyphenated type of diplomacy such as climate, health, or refugee diplomacy where advocacy plays a key role. It is important to avoid knowledge diplomacy being seen as relating to the nature or type of knowledge such as tacit, indigenous, or technical rather than the use of knowledge, as represented by education, research, and innovation. In this way, the meaning of knowledge diplomacy is similar to the concept of cultural diplomacy and different from climate diplomacy. Cultural diplomacy is not about advocating for or solving issues about culture; it is about using culture to promote relations and understanding between and among countries. This differs from climate diplomacy or food security for example, which is about addressing and solving the issues of climate change and not using climate to strengthen relations between countries. Furthermore, it is important to clarify that knowledge diplomacy is not "knowledge *about* diplomacy" but how knowledge is used in managing and strengthening relations between and among countries.

It is recognized that the working definition of knowledge diplomacy is not neutral, as it infers a positive outcome. While the intention is to strengthen relations between and among countries there can also be unexpected negative outcomes. Unstable and conflicted relations between states can have negative repercussions on IHERI and vice versa. Even though knowledge diplomacy is oriented to positive outcomes, it is not intended to be a normative concept in the sense that it is suggesting what a state ought to do or that it is the preferred approach. Different needs, priorities, rationales, and expected outcomes in the use of IHERI in international relations can necessitate different approaches. The use of IHERI in knowledge diplomacy is one of these approaches which has an intended positive response in strengthening relations between states and societies to address global issues based on collaboration and reciprocity. There are instances where using IHERI in a more competitive and dominant approach would also serve national interests as in soft power.

Knowledge Diplomacy in Relation to Cultural, Science, Public, and Education Diplomacy

The review of scholar and experts perspectives and research from both diplomacy and higher education fields of study revealed that there are at least 14 different terms used to define or describe the role of IHERI in IR. They include (1) cultural, public, citizen, exchange, science, education, innovation, knowledge, science and technology, and academic forms of diplomacy; (2) cultural relations, education relations, and science cooperation; and (3) soft power (Knight 2022). This section examines the most frequently used terms—cultural diplomacy, science diplomacy, education diplomacy, and soft power—and discusses the differences between them and knowledge diplomacy.

Cultural Diplomacy and Knowledge Diplomacy

Cultural diplomacy has been a popular term for decades. While the meaning and activities have evolved it is primarily oriented to international exchanges, exhibitions, and events in all fields of the arts, music, theater, literature, film, media, architecture as well as sports and other cultural expressions (Goff 2013). The goal of cultural diplomacy is primarily to enhance cross-cultural awareness, trust, and relations between and among countries (Gienow-Hecht and Donfried 2010). When higher education is referred to as part of cultural diplomacy the most common activities cited are student/scholar exchanges, language learning, international sport competitions, and cultural events (Pajtinka 2014). While cultural diplomacy can include a wide range of people-to-people education and cultural exchanges, it is not broad enough to include the central elements of IHERI such as research and innovation. Furthermore, the focus is primarily related to people's mobility as in student/scholar exchanges. The recent increase in the scope and scale of universities and other private higher education providers moving across borders to offer foreign education programs and qualifications in the students' home country is not usually accommodated in the notion of cultural diplomacy. Thus, while cultural diplomacy can include some key IHERI activities, and is an appropriate term to discuss student and scholar mobility and exchange, the concept is not broad enough to encompass the wide range of contemporary higher education, research, and innovation activities.

Science Diplomacy and Knowledge Diplomacy

Increased attention is being given to science diplomacy as evidenced by an increase in national government science policies, international meetings on the topic, and the rising number of academic references and projects. A frequently asked question is whether science diplomacy and knowledge diplomacy are not one in the same. This is a question worthy of consideration and depends on how broadly science is being defined and used. If science is broadly interpreted to mean knowledge as in the Latin word *scientia* then there is a close relationship. But traditionally science diplomacy has been seen in terms of natural sciences and more recently it has been placed within the broader framework of science and technology (Rungis 2018). There is no doubt that this reflects the centrality of science and technology in today's knowledge economy (Kim and Lee 2015). However, the focus on science and technology excludes, to a large extent, other sectors and issues related to the social sciences and humanities. For instance, it is unlikely that science diplomacy initiatives or negotiations would include humanitarian or societal issues such as migration, aging, refugees, gender, poverty, or human rights initiatives. Thus, while full acknowledgement is given to the importance and role of science diplomacy it does not exclude the necessity of knowledge diplomacy which is a more inclusive concept in terms of higher education and the production and application of knowledge and is consistent with the holistic concept of knowledge society (Cerroni 2020). It is likely that different countries and actors will continue to use both "science diplomacy" and "science and technology diplomacy" according to their own policy priorities and contexts. However, the difference between these terms and the more comprehensive perspective of knowledge diplomacy needs to be recognized.

Education Diplomacy and Knowledge Diplomacy

Surprisingly, there are very few scholars and experts who used the term education diplomacy. Piros and Koops (2020) examine the terms education, academic, and exchange diplomacy and conclude that "given these multi-faceted and wide-ranging definitions of education and academic diplomacy it is indeed impossible to offer a catch-all definition. Instead, we view 'education diplomacy' as an umbrella term that includes all dimensions" (Piros and Koops 2020, 119). Yet, they state that "there is no unified, single definition of education diplomacy, just as there is not unified single definition of cultural diplomacy" (ibid.). This reflects the reality (and confusion) of how the terms education and cultural diplomacy are used in relation to framing the role of IHERI in IR and how further work on conceptual frameworks might provide some clarity.

In contrast to the diplomacy scholars' use of the term education diplomacy, it is seldom used by higher education scholars as it is usually only applied to basic education. The Association for Childhood Education International (ACEI) asserts that "education diplomacy uses the skills of diplomacy grounded in human rights principles to advance education as a driver for human development" (Hone 2016). This raises the question as to whether the term education diplomacy or knowledge diplomacy is more appropriate for higher education because in addition to education and training, knowledge diplomacy includes the use of research and new knowledge for innovation. These two areas are not usually associated with basic education. Furthermore, the drivers and outcomes differ. Education diplomacy, as interpreted by ACEI, is oriented to human development while knowledge diplomacy has a broader mandate and focuses on strengthening relations between and among countries. It also addresses a diversity of global challenges which face countries in all regions of the world which are not usually part of early childhood education.

Public Diplomacy and Knowledge Diplomacy

The introduction and evolution of the concept of public diplomacy highlight the engagement of a broad range of actors using diverse methods to reach foreign, as well as domestic, publics. Public diplomacy has been described as a "country's efforts to create and maintain relationships with publics in other societies to advance policies and actions" (Melissen and Wang 2019, 2). This involves a wide range of strategies and instruments and can be oriented to an equally broad spectrum of issues. There is no doubt that public diplomacy can include IHERI-related actors, issues, and strategies as evidenced by the substantial number of IR scholars and experts from all regions of the world who framed IHERI's role in IR as public diplomacy. Thus, while public diplomacy clearly can include and be applied to IHERI issues, strategies, and actors (both senders and targets) it is somewhat limited in highlighting or specifying the higher education, research, and innovation activities. While public diplomacy is definitely appropriate, it is a wide umbrella concept and the term knowledge diplomacy is more focused on specific state and non-state actors and activities related to international higher education, research, and innovation.

This discussion on differentiating knowledge diplomacy from related terms acknowledges the need for a more rigorous approach to defining concepts and terms. While an umbrella term acknowledges different actors and activities it is a conceptual challenge to work with a term that is not clearly defined and can be interpreted in multiple ways in different contexts. This underlines the importance of developing conceptual frameworks and classification systems for the large number of diplomacy-related terms in order to understand similarities and differences among them and to use them in a more precise and informative manner.

Toward a Conceptual Framework for Knowledge Diplomacy

As discussed, this chapter uses conceptual frameworks as an analytical tool to explore the meaning and deepen the understanding of a phenomenon and concept such as knowledge diplomacy, it does not use empirical evidence or quantitative data. Table 4.1 presents the foundational elements of the proposed knowledge diplomacy framework structure including intentions, actors,

Table 4.1 Conceptual framework for IHERI in a knowledge diplomacy approach

Intentions Purpose 1	Actors Partners 2	Principles Values 3	Modes Approaches 4	Activities Instruments 5
To build/strengthen relations between and among countries through international higher education, research, and innovation (IHERI)	Government departments and agencies related to education, science, technology, innovation at all levels	Reciprocity Mutuality Cooperation Common ground Partnership Common good Inter-disciplinary Multi-sector Transparency	Negotiation Communication Representation Conflict resolution Compromise Collaboration Exchange Mediation Conciliation Partnerships Building trust Dialogue	*Generic*: Networks Joint projects Conferences Summits Coalitions Track two agreements Working groups Institution-building
To use IHERI to help address global challenges and promote peace and prosperity	Intergovernmental agencies related to IHERI NGOs related to IHERI HEIs Research centers Think tanks Centers of excellence Research networks Foundations Innovation centers Experts Private sector, multi-national corp.			*IHERI specific*: Intl joint universities Student/scholar exchanges Joint research networks Regional universities Education/Knowledge hubs Scholarships ODA projects Twinning and joint degree programs
To strengthen IHERI through enhanced relations between and among countries				

Adapted from Knight (2021)

principles, modes, and activities. The examples noted in the framework are meant to be illustrative not comprehensive. However, the principles and values remain steadfast and are key to understanding the process of knowledge diplomacy.

Each of the five constituent elements of the conceptual framework is discussed in the following subsections.

Intentions, Purpose, Rationales

Because knowledge diplomacy brings together a network of partners from various sectors to address common issues there will be different intentions, self-interests, and implications for the individual countries and actors involved. This means that in spite of common concerns, actors will bring different needs, priorities, and resources to the relationship. These differences will need to be respected and negotiated to ensure that the strengths and opportunities for each partner are optimized. This is done through a horizontal collaborative type of relationship that acknowledges the different rationales, needs, and resources of the group to reach a common understanding and agreement.

Actors and Partners

A multi-actor and stakeholder approach to diplomacy is needed in today's interconnected world and where countries face common challenges (Pigman 2010). While universities and research organizations are key players in knowledge diplomacy there is a broad range of other state and non-state IHERI actors involved. These include national, regional, or international centers of excellence, foundations, think tanks, innovation networks, professional associations, private sector companies, non-governmental organizations, education and knowledge hubs, and different governmental departments/agencies. In many cases the IHERI actors are working with other sectors and/or disciplines depending on the nature of the initiative. Common partners include industry, civil society groups, foundations, and various governmental agencies. Working with a diversity of IHERI and other partners is a key feature of knowledge diplomacy.

Principles and Values

Principles and values are an integral part of diplomacy (Rathbun 2014) and foreign policy (Srinivasan et al. 2019) and thus core to understanding knowledge diplomacy. As identified in Table 4.1 the values of cooperation, reciprocity, and mutuality are fundamental building blocks of knowledge diplomacy. Diverse needs and resources of actors will result in different benefits (and potential risks) for partners. Mutuality of benefits does not mean that all actors/countries will receive the same benefits in a symmetrical fashion. It does mean, however, that the principles of mutuality and reciprocity will guide the process and there will be collective and different benefits accrued for the actors and states involved.

The conceptual framework makes the fundamental principles and values of knowledge diplomacy explicit. Whether these values are interpreted to be inherently good or desirable is in the eye of the beholder. Making values explicit does not necessarily imply that they are normative in nature and indicating a preferred approach. For instance, cooperation and reciprocity can be seen as desirable in some cases where in other circumstances competition and dominance can be seen as more attractive and advantageous.

Modes and Approaches

Knowledge diplomacy is based on horizontal relationships between and among major actors and countries and focuses on collaboration, negotiation, and compromise to ensure that the goals are met and there are benefits for all. There is no doubt that in spite of common concerns, there will be potential conflict given inevitable differences in self-interests and expectations among actors. It is naïve to deny this reality. However, a diplomatic approach in general, and knowledge diplomacy more specifically, relies on negotiation, mediation, and conflict resolution to address these differences and find a common ground. In general, knowledge diplomacy is based on a collaborative win-win approach to addressing common issues as well as meeting individual country self-interests.

Activities and Instruments

The activities/instruments generally associated with international relations and diplomacy include joint meetings, conferences, track two negotiations, summits, coalitions (Cooper et al. 2013). These are central to diplomacy in general and also apply to knowledge diplomacy. However, because knowledge diplomacy has international higher education, research, and innovation at its core, there are additional salient activities which differentiate it from other types of related diplomacies. These include activities such as international and regional joint universities, student/scholar exchanges, thematic research networks, education/knowledge hubs, regional centers of excellence, scholarships, development cooperation projects, international branch campuses, alumni networks, other centers of excellence, and twinning programs to name a few.

Application of the Knowledge Diplomacy Framework

The purpose of this section is to demonstrate a real-life application of the key concepts forming the conceptual framework for knowledge diplomacy. The Pan-African University (PAU) is an example of a contemporary IHERI initiative involving a university with multi-campuses located across the African continent. PAU was initiated in 2013 to establish a regional university system to serve the entire continent in key development areas and to strengthen the regional integration goal of Africa's Agenda 2063.

Pan-African University: A Regional University

The PAU was initiated by the member states of the African Union and is funded jointly by the African Development Bank, host African countries, the World Bank, and international partners. It is made up of five post-graduate, training, and research institutes, hosted at leading universities in the West, North, East, Central, and South regions of the African continent. Each institute focuses on one of the strategic areas for African advancement, as determined by the Conference of Ministers of Education of the African Union. The research institutes are: (1) Kenya: Basic Sciences, Technology, and Innovation located at Jomo Kenyatta University of Agriculture and Technology, (2) Nigeria: Life and Earth Sciences, including Health and Agriculture, located at University of Ibadan, (3) Cameroon: Governance, Humanities, and Social Sciences located at University of Yaounde II, (4) Algeria: Water and Energy Sciences located at the Abou Bakr University of Tlemcen, (5) South Africa (future plan): Space Sciences Institute located at Cape Peninsular University of Technology (Africa Union Commission 2016).

Intentions, Purpose, Rationales

The PAU is considered to be a key player and contributor to the operationalization of the first ten-year phase of the African Union's Agenda 2063. The Agenda 2063 outlines a vision for pan-African unity for the creation of an "integrated, prosperous and peaceful Africa, driven by its own citizens, representing a dynamic force in the international arena." The Agenda 2063 document, ratified in 2015, charts a path for "inclusive and sustainable development, a politically integrated continent, peace and security, fused together by a strong cultural identity, common heritage, shared values and ethics" (African Union 2015).

The five regional networks of universities and research partners are connected and strengthened by a continental framework. A review of the stated objectives reveals how PAU strives to enhance collaboration and integration between and among African countries through IHERI activities. The two primary academic objectives are to (1) stimulate collaborative, internationally competitive, cutting-edge fundamental and development-oriented research, in areas having a direct bearing on the technical, economic, and social development of Africa while recruiting, training, and retaining African talent, and (2) enhance the mobility of students, lecturers, researchers, and administrative staff between African universities to improve teaching, leadership, collaborative research, and create regional/continental integrating networks.[1]

Actors

The African Union, the African Development Bank, and five national African governments are the key state drivers behind the PAU. State and non-state actors include universities, centers of excellence, foundations, and research centers that are members of the five regional networks. International universities and governments are additional partners, and share expertise, participate in joint research projects, and provide some funding opportunities. For instance, Germany cooperates with the research institute in Algeria; Sweden works with the institute in Cameroon; India and Japan are involved in supporting the institute in Nigeria; and China collaborates with the institute in Kenya. The European Union has also been involved by providing initial funding for student scholarships. The African Development Bank was the main funder of the project and the World Bank provided additional start-up funds.

Key Principles/Values

Partnership and collaboration are key principles driving the development and operation of regional networks which are coordinated by a continental wide strategy. Cooperation with African-based public and private organizations for

---

[1] https://pau-au.africa/

internships, joint research, and knowledge exchange is a priority and illustrates the importance of mutual benefits. The theme of each network illustrates the multi-sector and interdisciplinary nature of the entire PAU initiative. In terms of mutual benefits, African researchers and graduate students benefit from the increased collaboration in their region as well as the international support and exchange with their international thematic partners. National governments in the host African countries have benefited from increased research capacity at their institutions and their leadership role in their region to collaborate with industry and non-governmental organization while addressing major societal issues facing the continent. International partners have benefitted from finding common ground, building trust, and deepening relationships with African research institutes and industry. In turn, these activities and benefits contribute to the operationalizing of the Agenda 2063 goal of "inclusive and sustainable development, a politically-integrated continent, peace and security, fused together by a strong cultural identity, common heritage, shared values and ethics" (ibid.).

Modes

A project as large and ambitious as the Pan-African University is not without conflicts and differing priorities among the major players and funders. Negotiation, conflict resolution, mediation, and compromise are necessary to reach common ground and a way forward. The creation of five regional networks consisting of multiple state and non-state actors also requires a consultative and collaborative approach to negotiating priorities, budgets, and strategies. These are fundamental modes used in diplomatic relationships.

Activities

Based on the primary goals and operating principles of PAU, the main IHERI activities focus on graduate level programs including internships, knowledge production, and innovation; academic exchange of students and scholars across Africa; and joint research within the networks and with international partners. Scholarships are available to students from African countries as well as those of the African diaspora. Enrolment quotas are in place to ensure regional representation and gender parity. No more than 20 percent of new students can be from the host country and an equal number of men and women must be accepted. An interesting and important feature of PAU is that graduate programs are designed to intentionally build a unified African identity beyond national differences. Students are required to take two general education courses to further this aim: General History of Africa and Gender and Human Rights. All students are required to collaborate with industrial or governmental partners throughout their program, with internships being mandatory. Finally, students must sign a contract committing to work in Africa after the completion of their program to ensure that the new talent continues to work toward African development priorities.

Two flagship research projects illustrate the emphasis on collaboration, partnerships, and mutuality of benefits as well as the types of global/regional issues being addressed. The West African Science Center on Climate Change and Adapted Land Use project was developed jointly by researchers from the Universities of Cotonou (Benin), Bonn (Germany), and Miami (United States), and their industry and governmental partners. The aim of this project was to create sustainable institutional relationships that develop a community of experts in areas of natural resource management aiming to conduct joint research and offer practical applications. The Institute for Water and Energy Sciences in Algeria offers another example of the PAU's collaborative research projects with its researchers working with German universities to host international research symposia bringing together specialists in water and energy sciences from around the world (Koli et al. 2019). Table 4.2 summarizes and illustrates the application of the five key elements of the knowledge diplomacy conceptual framework as applied to the PAU.

When fully realized, the PAU will be the sum of five thematic regional institutions/networks with 50 related centers of excellence across the African continent working toward and using IHERI as a means to achieve the long-term goal and core aspiration of Agenda 2063 which is to make Africa a strong, united, resilient, and influential global player and partner (African Union Commission 2015).

Differentiating Knowledge Diplomacy and Soft Power

A definition, description, and conceptual framework for the role of IHERI in a knowledge diplomacy approach has been proposed, discussed, and illustrated. This section analyzes the differences and similarities between IHERI in a soft power approach and a knowledge diplomacy approach through the comparison of their conceptual frameworks. This is important because the review of both the diplomacy and higher education literatures revealed that many scholars and experts perceive the contemporary role of IHERI in

Table 4.2 PAU: application of key elements of knowledge diplomacy conceptual framework

Element of conceptual framework	As illustrated in the Pan-African University initiative
Intentions/purpose	PAU is seen as a key player to realize Agenda 2063 which charts a path for "inclusive and sustainable development, a politically-integrated continent, peace and security, fused together by a strong cultural identity, common heritage, shared values and ethics" (African Union Commission 2015).
State and non-state actors and partners	African national governments, universities, research centers, and industry The African Union, the African Development Bank, World Bank International partner governments, universities, foundations, and industry
Guiding principles and values	Partnership Cooperation Mutual benefits Commonality of issues Multi-disciplinary/multi-sector
Modes/approaches of relationship	Negotiation Conflict resolution Mediation Compromise Collaboration Dialogue
IHERI activities	Joint research projects among African universities, research centers, industry, governmental agencies Collaborative academic and research initiatives between African and international universities, foundations, research centers, industry Scholarships for African graduate students, industry internships Student and scholar mobility within Africa Regional, continental, international workshops and seminars hosted in Africa

Adapted from Knight (2021)

international relationships as a form of soft power whether it be labelled explicitly as soft power or as a soft power instrument in the context of cultural, public, and science diplomacy. It is therefore necessary to acknowledge and explore how IHERI can be used for soft power purposes and outcomes and how it is different from the role of IHERI in knowledge diplomacy. For example, scholars such as Nye (2013), Lo (2011), and Wojciuk (2018) were clear that international higher education initiatives can be used to advance self-interests, to gain competitive advantage especially in the fields of science and technology, and for hegemonic reasons. This type of relationship can

Table 4.3 Differences between the role of IHERI in knowledge diplomacy and soft power approaches

	IHERI in a knowledge diplomacy approach	IHERI in a soft power approach
Self-interest	National self-interests leading to mutual benefits	National self-interests dominate
Modes	Negotiation Mediation Communication Conflict resolution Conciliation Collaboration	Attraction Persuasion Competitive advantage Dominance
Values	Reciprocity Mutuality Common ground	Cooption Compliance
Outcomes	Win-win with mutual but different benefits	Win-lose
Nature of relationships	Horizontal Collaborative	Vertical Top down

Adapted from Knight (2021)

occur between developed countries as well as between developed and developing countries where soft power can also be perceived as a means of neo-colonization (Woldegioris 2018).

To illustrate the relationship between diplomacy and soft power, Table 4.3 proposes and summarizes the fundamental elements and differences between the role of IHERI in a knowledge diplomacy framework versus a soft power framework. This analysis is based on the multiple interpretations and definitions for diplomacy and Nye's widely used perspectives on soft power. However, in the real and messy world of international relations, the difference between these two approaches is blurred and complex; but in a conceptualization process the differences must be explored and clearly articulated.

It is clear that in both approaches national interests are at play; but meeting them involves using different modes and values underlying each approach. To analyze and elaborate the role of IHERI in a soft power relationship a conceptual framework is presented in Table 4.4. The same structure used in the development of the knowledge diplomacy conceptual framework (see Table 4.1) is used to elucidate a soft power approach and to facilitate a comparison of the differences and similarities in terms of the foundational elements and core concepts.

It is important to note is that the shaded columns in Table 4.4 are dramatically different than the same three columns in Table 4.1 for knowledge diplomacy. As expected, the IHERI actors in column two are similar for both

Table 4.4 Proposed conceptual framework for IHERI in a soft power approach

Intentions Motivations 1	Actors Partners 2	Principles Values 3	Modes Approaches 4	Activities Instruments 5
National competitive advantage economically, politically, scientifically, culturally, etc. Advancement in technology and innovation To serve self-interests	Intergovernmental agencies—all levels related to IHERI NGOs related to IHERI HEIs research centers Think tanks Centers of excellence Research networks Innovation Centers Experts Knowledge hubs Private sector multi-national corps	Domination Competition Self-interests	Attraction Persuasion Compliance Negotiation Cooption	Networks Joint projects Conferences Summits Track two agreements Working groups Education programs *IHERI specific*: Student/scholar exchanges Research networks Education Knowledge hub ODA projects Twinning and joint degree programs

Adapted from Knight (2021)

approaches as are some of the activities and instruments identified in column five. The fundamental difference between the two frameworks relates to intentions, guiding principles/values, and the modes used to reach desired outcomes. Soft power is focused on meeting self-interests and foreign policy objectives first and foremost. Soft power uses attraction and persuasion to achieve compliance or cooption and is therefore often seen as a top-down and unequal relationship rather than a horizontal collaborative relationship. Interestingly, soft power is based on voluntary actions by the target audience given the use of attraction and persuasion by the sender but, the end result is compliance and competitive advantage for the sender (Nye 2021).

Soft power is not typically based on principles or practices related to promoting cooperation, mutual understanding, and reciprocity. Yet, noting important exceptions, many higher education scholars, and several diplomacy scholars, portray IHERI as a tool of soft power to further mutual understanding and collaboration which is the antithesis of the way soft power is understood by Nye and even by his critics (Bakalov 2019). Perhaps higher education scholars see soft power as more positive and palatable than the hard power of force and coercion, and thus attribute the positive outcomes of mutual understanding and cooperation to it. But this explanation is most likely an oversimplification and requires further research. It is also important to ask whether there is an inherent contradiction in using a soft power approach based on compliance and cooption to further mutual understanding, capacity building, and knowledge sharing based on principles of exchange and reciprocity.

It is anticipated that scholars and experts in diplomacy and international higher education may take exception to the articulated differences between IHERI's role in a knowledge diplomacy approach versus a soft power approach as in the real world these differences are not as sharp as in the process of conceptualization. However, the distinction between the use of IHERI in a knowledge diplomacy approach versus a soft power approach is similar to the way the British Council (2021) report *International Cultural Relations: Soft Power and Cultural Relations Institutions in a Time of Crisis* addresses the issue of soft power and cultural relations. The British Council clearly states that soft power and cultural relations are different concepts and should not be confused. The report articulates the difference by noting that the "the primary purpose of soft power is pursuit of influence in the national interest" while "the primary purpose of cultural relations is to create the conditions for collaboration between like-minded people and countries in pursuit of the common good…" (ibid., 3). The report refers to cultural relations not cultural diplomacy as the term cultural relations is understood as including both state and non-state actors while cultural diplomacy involves state actors only. This is debatable but nevertheless, it is a good example of differentiating soft power from cultural relations based on the stated purpose and intentions. The same rationale can be applied to differentiating soft power from knowledge diplomacy as discussed in the British Council report *on Knowledge Diplomacy in Action* (Knight 2019).

Concluding Remarks

In conclusion, this chapter has addressed the challenges associated with the multiple definitions of diplomacy and has proposed a more rigorous conceptualization of diplomacy through the use of analytical tools such as definitions, descriptions, and conceptual frameworks. The phenomenon of knowledge diplomacy was used to demonstrate the application of these conceptualization tools and the Pan-African University was used as an example of how the knowledge diplomacy framework can be applied to an existing IHERI initiative.

Four commonly used terms to label the role of IHERI in IR were also examined in relation to their similarities and differences with knowledge diplomacy highlighting the importance of clear and concise definitions. Two conceptual frameworks were used to examine the different foundational elements of a knowledge diplomacy approach versus a soft power approach in examining the role of IHERI in IR. The purpose is to highlight the use of conceptual frameworks as an analytical tool not to suggest that one approach is more desirable than the others. However, further work is critical to develop more robust ways to understand, define, and reform the complex but increasingly important role of knowledge diplomacy in today's more turbulent and challenging world.

Note This chapter uses excerpts from Knight, J. 2021. "Towards a Knowledge Diplomacy Framework: The Role of International Higher Education, Research and Innovation in International Relations." Unpublished PhD Dissertation, University of Antwerp, Belgium.

References and Further Reading

African Union. 2015. *Agenda 2063: First Ten Year Implementation Plan 2014–2023*. Addis Ababa: African Union.

———. 2016. *Revised Statute of the Pan Africa University*. Addis Ababa: African Union.

Bakalov, I. 2019. "Whither Soft Power? Divisions, Milestones, and Prospects of a Research Programme in the Making." *Journal of Political Power* 12 (1): 129–51.

Bjola, C., and M. Kornprobst. 2013. *Understanding International Diplomacy: Theory, Practice, and Ethics*. London: Routledge.

British Council. 2021. *International Cultural Relations: Soft Power and Cultural Relations Institutions in a Time of Crisis*. London: British Council.

Cerroni, A. 2020. *Understanding the Knowledge Society: A New Paradigm in the Sociology of Knowledge*. Camberley: Edward Elgar.

Cooper, A., J. Heine, and R. Thakur, eds. 2013. *The Oxford Handbook of Modern Diplomacy*. Oxford: Oxford University Press.

Gienow-Hecht, J., and M. Donfried. 2010. *Searching for a Cultural Diplomacy*. New York: Berghahn.

Goff, P. 2013. "Cultural Diplomacy." In *The Oxford Handbook of Modern Diplomacy*, eds. A. Cooper, J. Heine, and R. Thakur, 419–35. Oxford: Oxford University Press.

Griffiths, M., T. O'Callaghan, and S. Roach. 2014. *International Relations: The Key Concepts*. 3rd ed. London: Routledge.

Hone, K. 2016. "Education Diplomacy: Negotiating and Implementing the Sustainable Development Goals – Looking Back and Looking Ahead." Centre for Education Diplomacy and Leadership, Childhood Education International.

Kerr, P., and G. Wiseman. 2013. *Diplomacy in a Globalizing World: Theories and Practices*. Oxford: Oxford University Press.

Kim, Y.K., and K. Lee. 2015. "Different Impacts of Scientific and Technological Knowledge on Economic Growth: Contrasting Science and Technology Policy in East Asia and Latin America: Impact of Science and Technology Policy." *Asian Economic Policy Review* 10 (1): 43–66.

Knight, J. 2019. *Knowledge Diplomacy in Action*. London: British Council.

———. 2021. "Towards a Knowledge Diplomacy Framework: The Role of International Higher Education, Research and Innovation in International Relations." Unpublished PhD Dissertation, University of Antwerp, Belgium.

———. 2022. *Knowledge Diplomacy in International Relations and Higher Education*. Cham: Springer Nature.

Koli, M., E. Tambo, E. Cheo, B.O. Oduor, and A. Nguedia-Nguedoung. 2019. "Pan-African University and German Government Higher Education Cooperation in Algeria." In *Universities, Entrepreneurship and Enterprise Development in Africa – Conference Proceedings 2018*, eds. J. Bode and C. Freitag, 136–45. Sankt Augustin: Bonn-Rhein-Sieg University of Applied Sciences.

Lehrer, K. 2000. *Theory of Knowledge*. 2nd ed. Boulder: Westview Press.

Leijten, J. 2017. "Exploring the Future of Innovation Diplomacy." *European Journal of Futures Research* 5 (20): 1–13.

Lo, W.Y. 2011. "Soft Power, University Rankings and Knowledge Production: Distinctions between Hegemony and Self-determination in Higher Education." *Comparative Education* 47 (2): 209–22.

Melissen, J., and J. Wang, eds. 2019. *Debating Public Diplomacy: Now and Next*. Leiden: Brill.

Nordquist, R., ed. 2010. *Crossing Boundaries*. New York: Peter Lang.

Nye, J.S. 2013. "Hard, Soft, and Smart Power." In *The Oxford Handbook of Modern Diplomacy*, eds. A. Cooper, J. Heine, and R. Thakur, 559–74. Oxford: Oxford University Press.

———. 2021. "Soft Power: The Evolution of a Concept." *Journal of Political Power* 14 (1): 196–208.

Pajtinka, E. 2014. "Cultural Diplomacy in the Theory and Practice of Contemporary International Relations." *Politicke vedy* 4: 95–198.

Pigman, G. 2010. *Contemporary Diplomacy. Representation and Communication in a Globalized World*. Cambridge: Polity.

Piros, S., and J. Koops. 2020. "Towards a Sustainable Approach to EU Education Diplomacy? The Case of Capacity-building in the Eastern Neighbourhood." In

Cultural Diplomacy in Europe, eds. C. Carta and R. Higgot, 113–38. Cham: Springer.

Pouliot, V., and J. Cornut. 2015. "Practice Theory and the Study of Diplomacy: A Research Agenda." *Cooperation and Conflict* 50 (3): 297–315.

Rathbun, B.C. 2014. *Diplomacy's Value: Creating Security in 1920s Europe and the Contemporary Middle East*. Ithaca: Cornell University Press.

Ravitch, S.M., and M. Riggan. 2016. *Reason & Rigor: How Conceptual Frameworks Guide Research*. London: SAGE.

Rungis, C. 2018. *S4D4C Using Science for/in Diplomacy for Addressing Global Challenges – State of the Art Report*. Brussels: EU Horizon.

Srinivasan, K., J. Mayall, and S. Pulipaka, eds. 2019. *Values in Foreign Policy: Investigating Ideals and Interests*. Lanham: Rowman & Littlefield.

Wojciuk, A. 2018. *Empires of Knowledge in International Relations. Education and Science as Sources of Power for the State*. London: Routledge.

Woldegioris, E. 2018. "Policy Travel in Regionalization of Higher Education: The Case of the Bologna Process in Africa." In *European Higher Education Area: The Impact of Past and Future Policies*, eds. A. Curaj, L. Deca, and R. Procopie, 43–59. Cham: Springer.

5

Why Reforms Are Needed in Bilateral Diplomacy: A Global South Perspective

Kishan S. Rana

State-craft: the only trade in the world that can be learnt but not taught.
—Winston S Churchill (1930, 93)

Diplomats should, therefore, reconsider the ways in which they have dealt with ideas such as nationalism and independence in the course of the twentieth century. Should they still be seen as obstacles or residual facts of international politics, for example, which skillful diplomats should seek to finesse, or is it possible to refer to them again as the building blocks of the only international order we are likely to enjoy?
—Paul Sharp (1998, 112)

Introduction[1]

Diplomacy is a public good. That is true in a literal sense, and also in the deeper meaning of an essential service to which citizens of the country are entitled. The manager of the nation's diplomacy is the Foreign Ministry

---

[1] This essay is based on 35 years of experience of diplomatic practice and research over the next 25 years, including information gathered during 20+ years of teaching diplomats from over 80 different countries, and lectures at over 20 foreign ministries. Academic citations are not offered for some of the information furnished, as this has been gathered in confidential conversations and in the course of teaching activities.

K. S. Rana (✉)
DiploFoundation, Gurugram, India

(MFA). It works in partnership with the ministries and the other agencies of the government, and with non-official entities, delivering to them effective management of the country's external interests. Article 3 of the 1961 Vienna Convention on Diplomatic Relations sums up those external interests in five core words: representation, protection, negotiation, observation, and promotion (Denza 2016).

Countries of the Global South, the majority of them developing states that won independence after WWII, face challenges in dealing with international affairs, especially in mobilizing external relations in pursuit of national economic and social development. They are handicapped by a relative scarcity of resources, amid an excess of priority tasks. To raise the living standard of their people, they must use the international system to secure the basic conditions of peace and security, and also to advance their economic and social interests in a dynamic fashion. In practice, it is the latter set of tasks that is at the core of their existential challenge. For them, effective diplomacy means using external relationships for maximum advantage, prioritizing both neighbors and the states that are their major partners, without ignoring states that are "over the horizon." The constant goal: how to benefit the home country, to spur its economic growth, and help home business, especially small and medium enterprises that are unable to address foreign markets, be it for exports, for attracting FDI (foreign direct investment), technology, and for all manner of partnerships, including the education and skilling of their personnel.

The global environment within which international relations are conducted has been complexified after the end of the Cold War in 1990, and evolves continually. The reasons for rapid transformation are many. One is interdependence among countries, which we call globalization, though after the 2020 COVID-19 pandemic, concepts like de-globalization have entered our lexicon. And the February 2022 Russian assault on Ukraine has further impacted on international affairs, adding new complications in dealings between the great and aspirational powers, and above all, the small states. We return to these fast evolving issues at the end of this essay.

These political challenges are accompanied by a new economic paradigm, that some call Globalization 2.0, replacing the "Golden Era" of globalization. Supply chains are now reframed and shorter; a slew of new FTAs and complexified trading arrangements have moved countries away from the "universal" norms of the WTO process. Adding to these economic issues is the urgency of responding to climate change, which produces new norms and environmental regulations. On top of that, migration, both voluntary, driven by a search for a better life, and involuntary, that is, refugees from war-torn and climate-devastated regions, adds to societal challenges and tensions between states.

Bilateral diplomacy remains the foundation and core of international relations. Countries primarily deal with one another one at a time. Even at international and regional conferences, and other group gatherings, whether at the United Nations or other international organizations, it is the home country's relationship with different partner states that informs the interaction with them. According to one seasoned European practitioner, "all countries still perceive their foreign relations in bilateral terms… (there is) an 'illusion of familiarity' among politicians."[2] Diplomacy marches to an assemblage of bilateral tunes, whether uplifting or monotonous, harmonious or discordant.

The *Problématique*

Why do Global South MFAs find it difficult to learn from one another? Is a regional approach feasible? What other blockages do they face in implementing modern, cost-effective diplomatic practices? Can MFA reform overcome this? These are among the issues addressed in this essay.

International affairs now witnesses the presence of multiple, legitimate actors, official and non-official; the latter are autonomous and active, as never before. The net effect: diplomacy management is severely challenged. The C-19 pandemic has pushed nations into constantly shifting patterns of isolation, quarantines, cooperation, and other fear-driven self-protective actions. It has also crippled economic exchanges, especially trade, travel, foreign education, and flows of tourism, also impacting heavily on income generation. It has reshaped social behavior. Countries face new challenges in protecting their population, in mobilizing resources, and in restoring economic growth to normal levels.

Consider the bilateral diplomacy performance gap between Western and Global South countries. Is the gap real or imaginary? We have no norms for comparing performance between countries. Indeed the very notion of performance measurement in a single country poses questions (Rana 2004b). Since the outcomes of diplomatic actions cannot be quantified (except with a few indicators, such as growth through exports, inflows of investments, and numbers of foreign tourists), we have to rely upon perception-derived, that is,

---

[2] A European ambassador at the Wilton Park Conference, UK, January 2003; from the author's notes. Under the Chatham House Rules that apply, participants are not to attribute comments to named persons.

subjective criteria, not objective or quantified, measurement. Yet, broadly speaking, looking to outcomes of diplomatic actions, one finds that the Global South states lag behind in the results they obtain through their diplomatic systems. One must also ask if the gap is being bridged, or if it has become wider than before? What can Global South states do?

Here is an example. Consider how Western MFAs learn from one another. There exist three MFA groups that regularly exchange information on managing MFAs. One is a cluster of Western foreign ministries that meet annually, on an initiative taken by the Canadians in the 2000s. It now includes over 15 countries, including major Europeans, the UK and the U.S. A second periodically meets at the EU Headquarters, consisting of MFA Human Resource heads. A third is run out of Canada, by a Québec-based think tank, and covers almost 20 countries, including Australia and Mexico.[3] DiploFoundation hosted two conferences to exchange views on MFA operations, in Geneva in 2006 and in Bangkok in 2007, each attended by representatives of over 30 MFAs.[4] An Asian country appeared interested in hosting a follow-up conference, but that did not materialize. Going by published information, there exists no Global South forum, or regional group, that regularly shares information on MFA management, or on evolving diplomacy practices.

Bilateral Priorities

Typically, over 90 percent of diplomatic missions are embassies and consulates that handle bilateral work within any country's overseas diplomatic network. At places such as Addis Ababa, Brussels, Nairobi, Rome, and Vienna diplomatic missions are often "double-hatted," handling the bilateral relationship in that national capital, while also accredited to the multilateral agency headquartered in that city. They are co-designated as a "permanent mission." In addition, at New York, Geneva, plus a few other places we find full time permanent missions.[5] As for the MFA's own work remit as a ministry, bilateral tasks may occupy perhaps around 60 percent of its attention—the other

---

[3] Bilaterally, Austria and Switzerland MFAs regularly meet to share experiences. Possibly the Nordics do something similar.

[4] As DiploFoundation teaching faculty, the author was involved in the organization of both conferences. See Rana and Kurbalija, eds. (2007).

[5] At places such as Brussels, non-EU states establish permanent missions to the EU, which also double, often in a minor role, as an embassy accredited to Belgium. That also happens at a few capitals, when countries that have a special engagement with a particular international or regional entity.

actions are: global (especially UN-related) issues; regional diplomacy; plus thematic issues such as disarmament, the environment, trade, inter-ministry coordination, and many other typical headquarters priorities.

MFAs nearly everywhere find themselves handicapped, owing to inadequacies in their diplomatic structures, processes, and methods, plus financial and personnel shortages.[6] These challenges are acute in the Global South. Typical problems:

- Limited material resources for their diplomatic system. Obtaining sufficient funding is a key challenge for most foreign ministries; this is especially acute in developing countries.[7]
- The human resources available are insufficient in numbers, also needing better training and mentoring. This is not always recognized by the MFA decision-makers, leading to persisting inadequacies, at the MFA, and in embassies.
- Enforcing whole of government external actions is a problem everywhere, when each official agency has its own work remit-driven agenda, with its own foreign network. The MFA's coordination role is challenged as never before. The wider goal of whole of nation consistency is even harder to achieve. Myriad non-official agencies (academia, business, cultural entities, the media, thinktanks, and others), each autonomous, carry a legacy of past indifference from official agencies. Yet, they need to work jointly, to advance national interests.

For these and other reasons, MFA reform, in structure and working, is a priority.

Bilateral Diplomacy, New Practices

How has the practice of bilateral work changed in recent years? Consider first the current work environment from an embassy perspective:

1. Expanded, multitasked: The explosion in the issues crowding the international agenda is reflected in the demands made on the bilateral embassy.

---

[6] This is borne out by the budget cuts that MFAs typically face, as much in Western as in Global South countries. The Scandinavians have cut back drastically on their overseas representation. Among the few exceptions are countries such as Turkey and the UAE, which have significantly expanded their diplomatic footprint in recent times.
[7] See Copeland (2009) for a graphic commentary on the financial shortages facing the Canadian MFA.

More than ever before the diplomat is a connector for a multitude of home agencies, especially official, in loco parentis, as it were, deftly promoting their interests. The best ambassadors may require their team to set out each Monday, connecting with institutions and key actors in their work remit, reporting back at the end of the week on the leads established and the follow-up needed. This work is not capital-centric; often provinces, regions, and cities offer great potential, with much less "competition for access," as exists in busy capitals. Often a task force approach works well on cross-cutting issues, be it economic promotion or the media/culture relations (i.e., public diplomacy), or diaspora outreach. In small embassies multi-tasking is the norm. Informal advisory groups are useful, where feasible, bringing in local personalities and the diaspora.
2. Generalist professionals: It follows from the above that a large embassy staffed by specialists, from different ministries, will be less efficient in handling cross-cutting themes, the daily staple of diplomacy generalists, who gain a spectrum of specialized insights via their normal work remit. But unlike full-time experts, they also relate that specialized knowledge to other work domains, finding connections, providing leverage, and working on a wide front. This is at the heart of modern diplomacy.
3. Embassy structure and leadership: Movies and fiction continue to depict the glamor of diplomatic life, but typically the real life embassy is tiny, with just one or two diplomatic officers besides the ambassador. Home-based officials cost many multiples of the cost of locally engaged staff.[8] One response: Norway's standard embassy model is stripped down to just three: the ambassador, a first secretary, and an administrative officer who also supervises consular work, all ranked as diplomats. Other staff are locally engaged. How one wishes this was emulated as a small embassy template in the Global South. The UK has now eliminated home-based personal assistants/secretaries for all its ambassadors, barring a handful of the senior-most; the rest manage with locally engaged secretaries. India and some others have also cut back such support staff, but more is possible. Across the Global South such cutbacks are worth emulation.

---

[8] This is because airfares, furnished housing, medical and children education cost, and foreign allowances are factored into home staff costs. That has prompted a significant cutback in support staff, now implemented in some Global South countries. Over 15 years ago, the Indian Ministry of External Affairs (MEA) had virtually stopped the recruitment of non-diplomatic support staff. Around 2005, Kenya funded the opening of six of seven new embassies by cutting back on home-based support staff, and now some other African countries are thinning out non-diplomatic support staff.

The ambassador is not a one-man band, but must lead from the front. Professional diplomats, who have climbed up through their career, possess accumulated personal "do-how" insights on what that involves. The politically appointed envoy usually lacks those insights; often embassy management suffers in consequence. The exceptions are non-career envoys with vast experience of public affairs, but even in the U.S., which has a high percentage of such personalities among its non-career ambassadors, these are the exceptions (Jett 2014). The situation is far worse, given a large number of non-career ambassadors from Africa and the Latin American and Caribbean states.[9] This is a major handicap in embassy effectiveness. Asia typically sends out fewer non-career ambassadors. And the practice is largely unknown in most of Europe, and in China, India, and Russia.[10] But in a new development, in the past few years, China has taken to appointing a significant number of party figures and officials from other ministries (and the provinces) as ambassadors. This has contributed to a recent combative style in Chinese diplomacy.[11]

> **Box 5.1 Effective Use of Locally-Engaged Staff**
>
> Hard to believe, but for most countries, rich or poor, the cost difference between home-based diplomatic and non-diplomatic embassy staff is tiny, barely 20 percent. And the cost difference between home-based non-diplomatic staff, and locally engaged staff? Be it in Berlin, Paris, Tokyo, or in Conakry or Dacca an embassy can recruit three to four trained, local language-competent local staff for the cost of a single home-based non-diplomat official—and the latter will face a language handicap.
>
> This is a major differentiator between Western and Global South embassies: ineffective use of trained locally engaged staff. What of the "confidential work" argument? Modern IT empowers the diplomat to dispense with support staff in handling cipher communications; phones and laptops now convert speech to text. Private secretaries are a luxury, though IT tools will not get one's morning coffee!

---

[9] In some African states many ambassadors sent abroad are from outside the professional stream. Except for Brazil, a similar practice is followed in many Latin American and Caribbean states.

[10] Right up to the early 1990s, the most important Indian embassies, say in London, Moscow, and Washington, D.C., went to political appointees from outside the Indian Foreign Service, with few exceptions. Those were among the 8–10 percent headed by political appointees, chosen by the prime minister. Thereafter, the pendulum has swung in favor of professionals. After about 2000, the percentage of such appointments has shrunk to 2 or 3 percent. The Chinese practice has recently swung in the other direction; a new trend is that some ambassadors are appointed from outside their MFA.

[11] A widely used misnomer for this is a "wolf-warrior" style (analogy from a popular Chinese movie). A consequence of this rise in egregious aggressive behavior are, evident especially at Chinese embassies, notably in dealings with Australia and a few other countries since 2019. It might relate to the appointment of a senior Communist Party official as the MFA's Party Secretary; earlier, the Foreign Minister doubled in that role. That is part of a pervasive strengthening of control over state and other entities by the Chinese Communist Party. See the chapter by Zhang and Yang in this volume.

4. Western embassy public outreach: Taking advantage of iconic embassy residences, at many locations Western embassies host concerts, fashion shows, product launches, and other glittering events that showcase their cuisine, culture, products, and visiting artistes. They use local public relations specialists and "event organizers" in innovative ways, using social media for wide impact. They also have no inhibition over getting home companies to underwrite National Day receptions. Among Global South embassies, it is mainly the Latin Americans that join this trend (often partnering local hotels), plus a few others, such as Thailand and South Africa that join hands with their airlines and tourism promotion offices.
5. MFA-Embassy relations: The Embassy is now empowered in new ways (covered in the next section). A small example. In the normal course, embassies assist multiple non-official agencies at home, like commerce chambers, think-tanks, cultural entities, and others. Consequently, embassies establish wide and deep connections at home, typically more extensive and current compared with those available at the foreign ministry. These deep connections are a relatively new development, usable as a foreign ministry asset, provided MFAs are alert to this.

Viewed from the foreign ministry, these changes call for attention:

1. MFA-Embassy: The best MFAs have transferred some work to embassies, so as not duplicate embassy expertise. They use modern intranets, treating the embassy as if it were in an adjoining building, working "jointly" as never before. Example: in preparing country briefs and other documents on individual countries, embassies can be trusted to write the briefs, with the MFA adding its comments, as needed. Intranets permit clusters of embassies to collectively produce well-rounded joint analysis on international events. Consequently, on policy issues, the embassy becomes a quotidian contributor to decision-making. This was anticipated with prescience in the German Foreign Office's Paschke Report (Germany, Foreign Ministry 2000). When this new mutual equation is understood and accepted, it takes MFA-embassy collaboration to a new level. We see signs of this in the Global South, but it is often limited by inadequate intranet systems. Further, the smart MFAs entrust embassies with aid project supervision and other comparable tasks. In Global South small states this is often a bridge too far. Shifting to this mode requires both comprehensive intranets and mindset changes.
2. "Whole" policy enforcement: The foreign ministry is challenged in harmonizing actions with other official agencies for a "whole of nation" foreign

policy. This coordination role can only be enforced through voluntary cooperation, supported by oversight from the Office of the Head of Government, or the Cabinet Office. A similar challenge comes up in broad harmonization with non-state agencies active in international relations; the goal is "whole of nation" actions. Both pose challenges. Example: UK's Fletcher Report of 2016 notes: "…the FCO's value in London was questioned frequently by stakeholders during our consultation… We should re-establish where the FCO can best add value to the rest of Government…The FCO must always retain a leading voice on the biggest thematic international issues of the day, even if the lead lies elsewhere in Cabinet" (UK Foreign and Commonwealth Office 2016, 12). If in the UK, with its strong institutions, its FCO's relevance is now questioned, we may imagine how much harder it is in the Global South, where typically MFAs find it hard to reach the decision table, say on multilateral economic issues, like the WTO.[12]

3. Diplomatic Services: In some Global South countries, especially in small states, MFAs are staffed by civil service pool officials, though most are retained over long periods. An MFA needs its distinct permanent staff, as is the norm in most developed countries. The diplomatic service also needs its legal status, as a specialized entity. We see this best in Brazil that has a law that ensures that only diplomats can be sent out as ambassadors; India treats its Foreign Service as a specialized entity but lacks a law confirming its status.

4. Prioritization and forward planning: Former Thailand Prime Minister Thaksin Shinawatra (2001–6) brought in a slew of new governance ideas; for example ambassadors were designated as heads of country teams in their assignment country, with other agency heads required to submit to the ambassador's decision, also giving the ambassador financial control over these agencies. This was confirmed in a law, repealed after Thaksin's exit as PM even while his tenure was politically controversial. Example: in respect of 25 or 30 priority countries unified 5-year plans were drawn up, jointly with all concerned ministries, identifying bilateral cooperation objectives. This was an effective method.

Other countries select, in rotation, a few states for focused attention to expand mutual cooperation. A more systemic forward planning method

---

[12] In India, WTO issues are the exclusive preserve of the Department of Commerce. The MEA struggles for a place at the decision table.

emerged in the mid-1990s, as part of Prime Minister Margaret Thatcher's public service reform. The British Foreign Office started publishing detailed reports on its performance, against a standard template. That began with setting out main priorities. It was a short step to move to "strategic goals" (detailed in the textbox below). That happened in 2004, when after an ambassadors' conference in January 2003 (a first for the FCO), it published a strategic policy document. All departments and embassies had to show how they contributed to policy goals. With this, focus shifted from *process* to *outcomes*; this meant that it was not enough to say that x number of trade delegations visited a particular country, one had to evaluate the impact of those visits on foreign trade with that country. The key point: good relations with foreign countries were desirable, that was not enough. The framework was the strategic objectives.

> **Box 5.2 MFA "Strategic Objectives"**
>
> While nomenclature differs, published MFA strategic plans typically cover a 3-to-5 year cycle. A typical 3-level format sets out: *A. the strategic goals; B. major targets under each goal; C. specific actions designed to attain each goal.* Australia, Canada, UK, U.S. are among countries that publish the main outlines of such strategic plans, though the third level, that is, the specific actions to be taken, is not revealed. Most Western countries, and some others too, surely have similar documents, but these are not in the public domain. Example: New Zealand is at the forefront of such "performance enhancement," placing outline documents in the public space (New Zealand Ministry of Foreign Affairs and Trade 2021).[13] Under such a format, annual plans for embassies can be produced, cascaded from the MFA goals. In response to pressure from the World Bank and the IMF some Global South countries have shifted to these methods, some through lip service. Such documents are not published.

5. Working with ministries and non-state home entities: In dealing with home-partners, be they official or non-state entities, through its diplomatic network, the MFA can do much to help all these agencies. That works effectively only when handled with sensitivity, respecting the work domains of each partner. Example: the Mexican MFA offers a good example of working harmoniously with NGOs and civil society, and with think tanks. This calls for imagination and flexibility, to assist them as feasible, but not dominate them, or reshape their agendas. In the Global South, these agencies have memories of past over-bearing attitudes by their MFA in earlier days, when it was a "quasi-monopolist" handling external relationships.[14] That legacy casts a shadow in many Global South countries.

---

[13] Most European countries, in contrast, do not publish such documents. Nor is it known if similar strategic planning methods are widely used in the Global South, but indirect information suggests otherwise.
[14] In 2020, the Indian MEA established a mechanism for regular consultation with think tanks.

6. Two-way bilateral partnerships: When a bilateral relationship is stable and expanding, with both countries keen on new mutually beneficial actions, bilateral work, especially economic, becomes "open" and collaborative than in the past. Example: the two MFAs, plus their line ministries, can share information, engaging in open dialogue. This applies especially to cultural, economic, education, S&T, and other functional areas. It also then becomes easier to bring into this process a wider range of nonstate partners, than may have been customary even a decade earlier.

All these are instances of evolution in the work practices in bilateral diplomacy. Of course, this is not a complete listing. It would take a full volume to detail these. Suffice it to say, a huge range of changes have taken place in the working practices in different countries. That sets the stage for addressing the core issue of MFA reforms from the perspective of bilateral diplomacy.

Representation Options

The 1961 Vienna Convention provides only for "concurrent accreditation" as an alternative diplomatic representation method, permitting an ambassador in one capital to represent their country in one or more countries. No published study has examined its effectiveness; perhaps there exist internal MFA studies. A question: given the expanded tasks for the resident embassy, is it really credible for it to effectively bear that additional workload?[15]

We now see some innovative representation methods, and attempts to reduce embassy costs. Malta and Singapore have pioneered the "non-resident" ambassador. This is typically a part-time ambassador based in the home country who visits the accreditation country one or more times in the year, providing off-site representation. Singapore selects public figures from business, academia, and other walks of life, but also gives this add-on task to a few home-based MFA officials. Unlike Malta, it sends an MFA desk-officer for follow-up, and to provide continuity. This device is slowly gaining traction in the Caribbean and among Balkan states. The Organization of East Caribbean States (OECS) is the only regional group that has ventured with appointing a joint ambassador, who represents all seven of the full members, Antigua and

---

[15] In the late-1960s, Apa Pant, Indian Ambassador in Cairo, then accredited also to Libya and Yemen, innovatively designated two language trainees, "probationers" (i.e., new Foreign Service entrants, not confirmed in the Service), both third secretaries, as the leads for handling the two countries. It delivered remarkable results, with motivated young officials reaching out to their charges, Libya and Yemen, with imagination and energy. See: Rana (2016, 339–40).

Barbuda, Dominica, Grenada, Montserrat, St. Kitts and Nevis, Saint Lucia, and St. Vincent, and the Grenadines.[16] OECS has joint ambassadors in Ottawa, Brussels, and Rabat. No other regional group has followed that lead, though a few EU countries have examined possibilities of a joint envoy; Germany had passed enabling legislation over a decade back. The EU's Delegations and embassies run by the European External Action Service (EEAS) are another form of group representation, but there are challenges faced even in calling this entity a diplomatic service.[17]

Other variations include the laptop envoy, who typically works out of a hotel and is usually dispatched for a few months, to prepare for a particular event, such as a major bilateral visit, or some special event. A variation is to embed an envoy who is within the resident embassy of a friendly state, working exclusively on a special assignment.[18]

The method of co-locating resident embassies within the premises of a friendly state is easier. It reduces overheads, and encourages collective actions in the assignment country. This is coming into increasing usage, by innovative groups such as the Pacific Alliance, which speaks of "joint diplomatic missions" as a collective goal and has co-located embassies at about a dozen capitals, besides a joint trade office in Casablanca.[19] This is also favored by other states that traditionally work together, like the Nordics.[20]

Two other methods are used. Small countries use their permanent missions at New York—even the smallest states find it vital to be present at this global hub of multilateral diplomacy—for limited contacts with other states, and for initial work on dispatching delegations to foreign countries, or for specific tasks. The other is honorary consuls, who are used for trade promotion, to assist with foreign visits by delegations, and for specific tasks.[21] For small states, this is by far the most effective, virtually zero-cost option that gives a

---

[16] Besides these seven OECS full members, the Associate Members include the British Virgin Islands, Anguilla, Martinique, and Guadeloupe.

[17] The EU Delegations are virtually treated on par with embassies in a good number of countries, carry out joint representation on most political issues; but on major tasks, and in relation to economic promotion work, most EU states act on their own.

[18] A decade ago, a Scandinavian ambassador was to Addis Ababa for the duration of that country's two-year term as an elected UN Security Council member, working out of a fellow-Scandinavian embassy, for liaison with African Union member-states. Some others have used the same method.

[19] The Pacific Alliance consists of four countries, Chile, Columbia, Mexico, and Peru.

[20] Among those that use this are the Scandinavian states, Czech Republic, Hungary, Poland, and Slovakia (the Visegrad Group), and a Canada-UK partnership.

[21] One small African state has used its honorary consul in another African state to prepare for high-level visits from the home country. Of course, this is possible only when this is permitted by the receiving state.

means of "flying the flag" and securing local assistance around the world.[22] Three barriers arise. The first is the difficulty in finding the right kind of honorary consul, providing genuine assistance, not using that appointment exclusively for self-vanity. A related problem is the existence of agents that market such appointments for money, perhaps with the connivance of some in the appointing countries. The third: to use them effectively the MFA must monitor the performance of its appointees. This is not difficult, but needs sensitization among small MFAs and basic training for wider, effective use of honorary consuls.[23]

Overall, diplomacy clearly retains its conservative work ethos, and we are unlikely to see rapid spread of innovative representation options. This works to the disadvantage of states that have limited resources, which blocks them from opening more diplomatic missions, or using the honorary option in optimal fashion.

The MFA and Foreign Trade

Is it useful to entrust foreign trade to the foreign ministry? Over 30 countries, some big, many small, have done this. As far as known, that experience has not been comprehensively studied. The main advantage is that embassies and consulates are better harnessed for trade promotion; it works even better when investment promotion is added to the mix. It should also reduce contestation over turf issues between the MFA and the economic ministries. Examples:

- Australia and Canada have combined the two, but in practice the diplomatic and the trade service are two parallel entities, with staff that do not swap jobs.[24] But there is a sense of common purpose. Other joint ministries: Hungary, Ireland, Jamaica, Kenya, Malta.
- The Scandinavians often combine these tasks within the MFA, but not Norway. The best integration model is in Denmark, which has one MFA state secretary, supervising a unified system that handles foreign affairs,

---

[22] For a detailed account see DiploFoundation (2013). It cites an article in *The Economist* which reported that there are some 20,000 honorary consuls around the world, including 1200 in the U.S. But the United States and China are among a handful of countries that do not appoint any (that was the Soviet practice in the past, but that has changed in Russia).

[23] Smart countries invite their Hon. Consuls to periodic conferences at home. Mauritius, for example, expects them to pay their travel cost, but gives them generous hospitality, to motivate them.

[24] Australia appoints "trade commissioners" who are often nationals of that country; it has around 20 in the U.S., running offices (with no immunities) in different cities. This is cost-effective.

trade, investments, and foreign aid. The Netherlands has done much the same.
- Argentina, South Korea, and Mauritius have flip-flopped over time, first combining, and then separating the two, sometimes again rejoining them.
- The UK had an excellent method which placed in the FCO a joint entity called Trade & Invest UK staffed by officials from the FCO and the Board of Trade. In 2016, as part of early Brexit actions, a separate Department of Foreign Trade was created, with their own overseas offices. The results are not yet available.
- Two years back, the UK combined its Department of Foreign Aid (DIFD) into the FCO, which has become FCDO. Foreign affairs and outbound aid go well together. In 2013, India created a Development Partnership Administration (DPA), within the Ministry of External Affairs (MEA); this has delivered good results.
- For very small states, combining foreign affairs with foreign trade is an efficient cost reduction. We see this in Santa Lucia, Samoa, Solomon Islands, and St. Vincent and Grenadines.

South Africa attempted to combine the two, but gave up in the face of perceived difficulties. In the absence of close harmony, the major loss is that embassies are not fully harnessed for the vital trade and investment promotion tasks. Ireland, Singapore, and several others entrust economic work to special entities, and that too sometimes works well.[25]

How to Reform

Creating institutional consensus in favor of reform is an essential precondition. Should the MFA go public on its plans, or is it better to work quietly, without fanfare? The hinges on the context and national practices. Incremental reform can always be carried out as a normal program of upgrading services, but elected governments might prefer to showcase new policy actions. The MFA confronts many choices as we see below. One tentative conclusion: it pays to shift out of a business-as-usual mode, trying something innovative.

---

[25] Mexico had a special economic promotional entity, ProMexico, which handled all economic promotion activities. When it was wound up in 2019, all economic promotion work reverted to the country's diplomatic missions. The country's embassies and consulates appear to have risen to the challenge.

1. Choose a reform method or model: Is it worthwhile to go for big reforms, or seek continuous improvement, along the lines of what Japan calls its *kaizen* method? Experience shows that gradual change is more acceptable to organizations, and is easier to digest and implement. It is also more realistic, with easier choices to those that must live with and implement the changes. We come back to this method. There are alternative models:

    (a) Big-bang reform: Often involves special commissions, composed typically of retired MFA officials. UK's 1964 Plowden Report and the 1968 Duncan Report are examples, as is the 1966 Indian Pillai Committee report on the MEA.[26] A more recent case is the three-member Dutch commission that ended its two-year study in 2014; none of the three commissioners had any MFA experience.[27]

    (b) Bench-marking: entails visits to selected foreign ministries to study their experiences; the results are uneven, unless detailed studies are undertaken in advance to understand each system and its institutional ethos. Australia and Uganda are among the countries that have carried this out in the past two decades, with uneven results. It is cheaper to use diplomatic sources, plus desktop research, to gather data.

    (c) Crisis-driven change: In 2003, following some public scandals involving misuse of funds by the Japanese MFA's Protocol Division, urgent reform was recommended. Many of the suggested changes did not stick or were implemented in half-hearted fashion (Rana 2007, 104–6).

    (d) External reports: The U.S. has had an abundance of blue-ribbon commissions that have examined the working of the State Department, across the system and in relation to areas like public diplomacy, foreign aid, and other themes. Their reports frame public discussions but seldom produce implementation. Australia's leading foreign affairs think tank, the Lowy Institute, produced an outstanding study, *Australia's Diplomatic Deficit* (2006), which was widely discussed but paradoxically led to further thinning out of that country's External Affairs Department.[28]

---

[26] See Pillai, et al. (1966).

[27] In early 2014 the author spent almost two hours with two members of this Commission, at the residence of the Dutch Ambassador in New Delhi. For the full Dutch Report, see Docters van Leewen et al. (2013).

[28] See Oliver (2009).

(e) Management consultants: Some MFAs have used consultants (Germany,[29] India,[30] Ireland, the UAE, the UK). Sometimes they are used not because the reforms needed are unknown, but because change is more palatable when recommended from outside.

(f) Internal polling: Another way: solicit ideas from within the system, say by asking ambassadors to send their suggestions on the reforms needed. The Indian MEA did this in 2001, and the results were compiled into a single document by Ambassador Satinder Lambah; many suggestions were implemented gradually. Unfortunately, that report has remained unpublished.[31]

(g) Novel approaches: The British FCO was highly innovative in 2000–1, taking internal polling to a much higher level. Foreign Secretary Jack Straw was persuaded by young officials on his personal staff to entrust the process to staff teams, guided by a small group of senior officials acting as mentors. They used the FCO intranet, carrying out system-wide consultations, and in six months produced a reform plan looking to a 10-year horizon. That unpublished internal document, *Foresight 2010*, was rapidly put into effect. John Dickie wrote a vivid account in *The New Mandarins*, (2004), based on his special access.[32] Germany did something similar in 2001–2, again getting suggestions from junior officials.

(h) Technology driven: The MFA can shift to an intranet (i.e., a virtual private network) linking its MFA and embassies within one seamless system. That inevitably produces a flattening of hierarchies, more rapid communication, and shorter response times, plus other gains mentioned elsewhere. Example: the UK is the only country that mandates interviews, using its intranet, for those short-listed for assignments at any diplomatic level; this deserves emulation.

(i) Incremental change: Carried out by many, among them China, India, Japan, and South Africa with uniformly good results. It is easy to accept for the institution, and permits flexibility, the more so when accompanied by pilot projects, to test how the reform ideas work.[33]

---

[29] The management consultant used by the German Foreign Office recommended use of a "costing" approach, to prioritize actions by embassies. This may suit law firms (and business consultants), but cost of diplomatic or consular action is a poor guide for MFAs; a trial run was rapidly ended.

[30] Senior Indian official N. K. Singh was asked by the External Affairs Minister in early 2002 to recommend improvements to India's economic diplomacy, but just before the report was submitted, that minister swapped jobs with the Finance Minister, Yashwant Sinha, and the project was scrapped.

[31] The Indian MEA has an aversion to publication of foreign policy documents, apart from the mandatory Annual Reports that each ministry is required to table in Parliament before the end of the Financial Year, that is, before the 31st of March. For instance, it has not published any official White Paper for almost 30 years, but there is no dearth of official statements on international events.

[32] This method demands a degree of commitment and mutual trust across the institution; at least one effort in another country to emulate that model failed, mainly owing to systemic differences.

[33] The Chinese Foreign Ministry also sent teams to select countries to examine their systems in depth.

(j) Public communication: Improving public communication should be a priority reform objective for any active MFA. This is done using social media, and a host of other instruments to engage home and external publics on foreign affairs issues. The diaspora is a key target in these efforts, both as an ally in their adopted countries and as a link with domestic publics. The Indian MEA has over 6.9 million social media followers.[34] They serve as a feedback loop, and a source for reviewing the public impact of the MFA's communication policy.

> **Box 5.3 Africa: Educating Home Publics on Foreign Affairs and Reform**
>
> Botswana, Kenya, Namibia, and Tanzania are among the countries that have carried out MFA reforms, some more thoroughgoing than others. In 2004 the Namibia MFA published a document: *Namibia's Foreign Policy & Diplomacy*.[35] Not all countries of the Global South have such a base document that sets out the country's essential goals. In 2016, a five-day Foreign Policy Conference was held in Windhoek, attended by a keen audience of 500 to 600, with four or five panels meeting simultaneously; 26 panels met in all. It is hard to find another comparable example in a small country, especially one that is still developing its foreign affairs infrastructure.
>
> Botswana also worked on a similar foreign policy document in 2012, and organized a two-day traditional town hall meeting, a *pitso*, to discuss foreign policy; foreign ambassadors were also invited.[36] Kenya uses its annual meeting of ambassadors to discuss a range of reform issues and improvements in their practices. Tanzania has added reform to the functions of its training institute. These and other countries have also carried out changes in their diplomatic practices, like introducing a bidding method for MFA staff for foreign assignments. Comparable evolutionary change is also visible in some of the small Caribbean countries, within the limits of their size of population and resources.
>
> The challenge is to build this into regular practice, as part of the working style of the MFA, and not as a special or one-off event.

An overall assessment: Incremental change is easily the simplest, and most palatable way of carrying out reform, looking to experiences of many MFAs across the board. It merits special attention in any MFA reform program, especially when combined with pilot projects to test the result.

---

[34] See Ministry of External Affairs. https://meadashboard.gov.in/

[35] In 2000–1, the author worked for six months as a Commonwealth adviser to this MFA and produced the first draft; it underwent further changes, before publication in March 2004.

[36] In March 2012 the author travelled to Botswana as a short-term Commonwealth adviser and worked on that draft document.

What to Reform?

We should next consider the activities most in need of improvement, constituting priority action areas.
  Human resource management

(a) MFA personnel: The only real resource of the MFA is its personnel, and the knowledge that resides in them, and within the MFA system. Typical good actions: widen the recruitment catchment; use psychological and culture adaptability tests; permit limited intake of experts at mid-career levels, but on the basis of using them as full-scope diplomats, blending their specialized knowledge with newly learnt generalist skills. Base promotions primarily on ability, downgrading the importance given to seniority, with objective tests and other criteria.[37] (India and Japan are two countries that continue to rely on seniority over ability, perhaps distrusting objective assessment of ability.) Introducing a bidding system for assignments, also requiring claimants to justify their suitability for the chosen assignment. Grievance redressal, especially for staff at all levels at embassies, requires special attention. Germany has an outstanding practice that hinges on direct feedback to the Foreign Office from all home-based staff at embassies, including security guards (Rana 2013, 79). Cuba gets great value from its spousal teams by ensuring that both the husband and the wife are employed in the embassy; it works in its tough environment, though hard to emulate.[38]

(b) Diplomacy management: The pillars of diplomacy are political, economic, public, and consular/diaspora affairs. While the first is of self-evident importance, the key differentiators are the remaining three. Challenges: better management of economic and public diplomacy, either through a single ministry (see below), or via "joined-up" arrangements. How to manage high policy—through a national security council, or other top coordination body; improving linkages with stakeholders through formal and informal co-operation; handling public diplomacy.

---

[37] For instance, Peru now requires all those seeking promotion to the rank of ambassador hold a doctorate and master two foreign languages; Brazil bases major promotions on strict academic standard tests, including the writing of dissertations. It is not certain that these are good practices. After a DiploFoundation webinar on this subject in 2015, the author wrote a commentary. See Rana (2015).

[38] Cuba's "health diplomacy," which includes high-quality medical education designed to attract foreign students, and dispatch of over 40,000 doctors and health professionals to Global South countries, especially Africa, practiced for over five decades needs closer study.

This especially involves persuading other official partners to accept the MFA's lead role, not because they are obliged to do so, but because integrated actions help all, that is, through a "whole of government policy." Another major challenge: mastering domestic public outreach, using the internet and other means.

(c) Diplomacy techniques: For the past three decades and more, economic diplomacy has become a priority; developing countries seek new export markets and FDI, as advanced countries want to gain in a highly competitive world market. One aim of reform is thus to improve the engagement with economic diplomacy and in the other areas, including public diplomacy.

(d) Staff distribution: Some countries thinned out overseas staff at different times, shifting them to the headquarters (Australia, New Zealand, Singapore). Some work indeed has moved to back offices, as in the corporate world. Outsourcing visa processing is now the norm for countries that face heavy demand, though visa authorization remains with embassies and consulates.[39] Flexible staffing for temporary demand, rapid-response, and crisis management teams are used as needed. Some old tricks are re-learnt: teams that go to "hot" situations, operating from hotels with backpack communications. Sometimes, physical hazards have to be faced.[40] Other changes: outreach agencies manned by local staff; a larger role for local personnel, including special training for them.[41] These are good methods, but counterproductive when overdone.

Tom Fletcher, author of UK's 2016 *Future FCO* report, summed up his narrative: "Less Office, More Foreign." That produced a thinning of the FCO and staff transfers overseas. There is no ideal ratio of headquarters-to-embassy staff. My 20-year research suggests that when the staff at the MFA is 50 percent or more of the total, it is probably over-large, in relation to its embassies; that may lead to micro-management. Conversely, when the ministry's strength falls below 30–35 percent of the total, staff is insufficient to supervise and absorb the embassies output.

---

[39] Outsourcing visa processing has raised travel costs for the consumer. An Indian company, VFS, has the dominant share in this niche market. Overall, visa revenues have become a major income source for countries that receive millions of visitors.

[40] As part of "transformational diplomacy," which became a buzzword in the mid-2000s, the U.S. spoke of "virtual presence posts," run through the internet. Scandinavians and others experimented with "virtual embassies." These experiments have not endured.

[41] The UK is the trend leader in the use of local staff, with Australia, New Zealand, and Canada not far behind. Some consulates, small ones and a few large ones too, are run almost entirely by local staff; it even designates locals as political officers in a few small embassies. Most others, including Europeans, are unwilling to go that far in use of local staff.

(e) Technology: Effective management of ICT is a prerequisite to obtaining full networking and communications gains. This adds to cost; the systems need support and equipment upgrading. The UK, for instance, even uses its intranet for video-interviews for all diplomat-level staff transfers, in which the official who is to supervise the new appointee is included; that level of scrutiny is not found in other systems. Against this, some countries hesitate over full-scale intranets, due to concerns over security (China, India, and possibly Japan).[42] This carries a high opportunity cost. In contrast, small states are inhibited by a shortage of resources and manpower. That widens the performance gap among MFAs.

> **Box 5.4 Training Diplomats**
>
> A simple lesson from contemporary business management has not fully reached many MFAs: training is a vital organization function that merits top priority. Recent experience:
>
> 1. On the plus side, in the past 20 years many small MFAs have created their own training institutions, often as slim entities that use their own academics and retired ambassadors for short-term courses.
> 2. Armenia and UAE have been especially innovative in offering courses (under a year's duration) that cover international relations and its practice. About half the graduates are accepted into the MFA; the remainder find jobs in companies, banks, and others that look to such experience. This becomes an excellent selection device for the MFA.
> 3. UK's Diplomatic Academy, renamed International Academy after 2020, was established in 2014, as a slim entity outsourcing custom-designed training courses to academia, relying on online learning.
> 4. Given that over half the diplomats in any country are stationed abroad, distance or online learning is especially suited to this profession, though some MFAs have been slow to accept this. The C-19 pandemic of 2020 has helped to reshape thinking in favor of such methods.[43]

Overall, administration of the MFA and personnel management are crucial to professionalization, and to obtaining optimal results. They do not always get the needed attention.

---

[42] This is based on research and conversations with well-informed confidential sources.
[43] See Rana (2022).

> **Box 5.5 A French Method: Ambassador's Instructions**
>
> A reform step that offers multiple advantages is the French method of "Ambassadors Instructions."[44] It is customary for newly appointed envoys to visit a wide range of ministers and official agencies, to understand their agenda for the assignment country. The French take that to the next step, where that list of tasks and expectations is synthesized into a document that becomes the Ambassadors Instructions. This is handed over to the envoy by the Quai d'Orsay Secretary General; the document typically runs from two to five pages. Within six months the ambassador presents his own "plan of action" for executing the instructions, plus a demand for additional resources as needed for the tasks. Thereafter, during the course of the ambassador's term, the implementation is tracked through annual programs, calendars of activities, work-plans for individuals, and timelines. The method is Cartesian, and elegant. Germany and Italy have copied this method, but the former only covers the MFA's work demands, and that reduces its effectiveness. The key strength of this method is that it produces a system-wide annual "Action Plan." It can be done even by an embassy acting on its own.[45] The essential point is to orient the bilateral embassy to forward thinking and an action frame. It joins the list of do-able actions that improve the working of bilateral embassies. Essentials: must be written with a clear vision of the objectives; include the wish-list of each major ministry; make it the platform for consequential actions, including a possible performance contract signed by the envoy.

Reform Pitfalls

Why do MFAs not engage in reform in a more regular, assiduous fashion? For one thing, the pressure of contemporary international affairs is relentless, leaving little time for organizational issues. Nor is there a regular forum for MFAs to exchange experiences, except in the most advanced regional organization, the European Union (EU). It is hard to recognize that managing a diplomatic system is not the same as handling international affairs, and that the lessons drawn from business management are as relevant for MFAs as for

---

[44] Of course, all countries give instructions to their ambassadors, and often, mostly covering specific issues. And some countries give a standard set of instructions to all their envoys, including Japan, Turkey, and the United States. The unique aspect of the French method is that they cover the demands from a wide range of official agencies, and roughly cover the full tenure of that assignment.

[45] On my first ambassadorship in Algeria (1975–79), I produced an Annual Action Plan for myself in 1977, and at the year-end, reviewed it too, besides offering the next year's plan. No one in the Indian MEA paid the slightest attention. When I did the same from Prague in 1980, it caught the eye of a senior official and MEA demanded that all embassies follow that practice. The method gained salience during Rajiv Gandhi's Premiership, but fell by the wayside after that, as one more routine activity, not taken seriously by anyone. See Rana (2016, 325–26).

other branches of government.[46] Moreover, foreign ministries are conservative institutions. Their professional heads may have typically learnt on the job; not all are comfortable with new information technology and its impact on public communication. We saw above how some MFAs long resisted setting up training institutions. Not all reform is successful; institutions steeped in tradition tend to be risk averse. On the flip side, in the past two decades we see new and gathering momentum for reform, especially in Global South MFAs. A small country such as Namibia publicly sets for itself the goal of becoming an exemplar (Namibia Foreign Ministry 2004). Overall, the prospects for MFA reform are favorable.

A. Reform should not be hurried. It takes time for constituencies within the institution to formulate reform demands, and to understand the wider context in which these are going to be handled. The motivation behind reform may not be clear, or may be seen as a camouflage for staff cuts or cutbacks in facilities. Communication within the organization is a key factor. As for the recommendations, the sour needs to be mixed with the sweet, to ensure acceptance.
B. Long waits for reform reports and implementation of recommendations are a frequent problem. A good way out is "early harvest" actions, even while the main report is under preparation. This helps to create a favorable momentum. Inculcation of professionalism is a constant, permanent task. Working with and harnessing domestic civil society, engaging them in dialogue, can help make them reform advocates. Is an open foreign ministry a realistic prospect?[47]
C. A sense that reform proposals will come from those that had their professional experience a long while back, or do not fully connect with current issues. The antidote: enlisting young officials is a great device (as the German and UK experience cited above shows). This is vastly superior to the usual consultation process that brings in different constituencies and hierarchies of the MFA.

---

[46] Example: The British Foreign, Commonwealth and Development Office (FCDO, formerly FCO) has a management board that includes top civil servants from other entities and from business and finance; it handles management issues, not international affairs. Italy has a similar advisory group. This practice is virtually unknown in the Global South.

[47] A simple device is for the MFA to accept interns for short-term work with the ministry. It opens up its working, encouraging graduate international affairs students to sharpen their practical skills. It also serves as a fine device for the MFA's public relations. Again this method is not widely used in Global South countries; India adopted this practice about a decade back.

D. Will radical change work? Is the institution ready for this? Pilot projects and small-scale changes are way to avoid falling into major changes that backfire, or show up unexpected problems.
E. Reform fatigue is a real risk. Canada is sometimes given as an example of an MFA that saw too many changes around the period 2000–15. The way out is to pace changes, and opt for incremental changes.
F. Do we know enough of what others do? There are all too few published studies on the working of MFAs.[48] It helps the MFA to build up a collection of comparative studies of diplomatic systems, and get their own officials to narrate their own stories. This can be done in several ways. One is to compile oral histories. Another is to build one's own collection of innovative actions. These are all elements in "Knowledge Management," which is seldom seen as a priority action in Global South countries.

We see again the virtues of regular, in-depth information exchange among MFAs.

Global South Challenges

As a consequence to financial and human resource shortages, several vital MFA functions suffer neglect that impacts on its delivery capacity. Here are some areas, not mentioned hitherto, that need special attention.

Training: This is too often undervalued in developing countries, partly a legacy issue. Senior MFA officials may say: I never received any training, and learnt well on the job. Such thinking misses the challenge: work demands have grown multi-fold. MFAs are told: do more, with fewer staff and resources. Expectations are also transformed, as are other work opportunities. In Global South MFAs one often hears: "hire specialists"—be it for economic promotion or public diplomacy, or any demanding activity. This runs against several obstacles. Cost, and difficulty in integrating specialists into small generalist systems. The better option is to train one's own staff, and build into the system multiple skills, across hierarchies. This works well in Europe and in the larger Global South countries. It can also be adapted in smaller systems.

---

[48] Asking an academic friend about why few universities study the working of MFAs, the author received the blunt response that this is not of interest to academia. Now that many U.S. and other universities have added diplomatic practice to their courses and to the titles of professorial chairs, this may be changing.

> **Box 5.6 Small and Virtual Training Institutes**
>
> When the number of diplomats in the MFA is 200 to 300 or less, the training facility can be virtual, with skeleton staff that organize courses a few times in the year, ideally in partnership with a local university. It pays to encourage retired ambassadors into the part-time faculty.
>
> Regional joint training centers are a chimera. Switzerland pursued several aid projects of this nature, in Malta, East, and West Africa. The main obstacle was the operational cost, bringing in diplomats from neighboring countries. A second challenge was that such entities, placed within universities, took the academic track, while MFAs needed practical, working skills.[49] Each of those Swiss Aid projects ended up as a faculty in the university, mostly losing connections with the MFA. Recently, a regional diplomatic training institute has been set up in Trinidad, at the St. Augustine Campus of University of the West Indies. It remains an experiment in progress.

Build home constituencies: Foreign ministries typically do not enjoy a home constituency. This leaves them vulnerable when national budgets are allocated, often lacking solid support. Example: do we know of lobby groups in Washington, D.C. that take up the State Department's case at Congress? A significant part of former Canadian diplomat Darryl Copeland's *Guerrilla Diplomacy* (2009) makes the case that the diplomatic service is the country's first line of external defense, and laments how this is so little understood.

The situation is more difficult in most Global South countries, where foreign ministries are typically undervalued. The Indian Parliamentary Committee on External Affairs in its 21st report of 2018 had noted that in 2017–18 the Ministry had been allocated only 62 percent of the funds it had sought from the Finance Ministry; it urged the MEA to engage actively with Finance "to convince them about the significance of allocating substantial budgetary allocations to a Ministry that not only has burgeoning foreign policy goals but also is a builder of India's image abroad" (Parliament Committee on External Affairs 2018, 6, 11). Major change has not taken place since, though funds have been found to expand the embassy network in Africa.

It pays foreign ministries to build up themselves as allies of domestic industry and business lobbies, via its economic diplomacy. Domestic think tanks

---

[49] In the 1990s, Kenya hosted a Swiss project for regional diplomatic training. It ended up absorbed within the University of Nairobi, and around 2009, the Kenya MFA set up its own training center.

are also great allies in building external connections, and for advancing the country's international agenda. More widely, domestic public diplomacy is vital in the foreign ministry's arsenal. Outreach to universities helps with the future catchment for the diplomatic service, and builds an articulate constituency.

Diplomacy as a Public Good

Why do we not easily see diplomacy as a public good? While clean water and a secure societal environment are recognized as essential entitlements for citizens, why should effective management of the home country's international affairs, to the maximum advantage of one's home country, also not be an essential citizen right? Is it that the notion is not self-evident, that is, directly visible to home publics? Or is it a deeper failure of foreign ministries, in not connecting better with their home clients? This issue is simply not discussed in most countries.

The societal gains from improved bilateral and multilateral diplomacy (regional and global) are a very obvious public good. In this fashion, MFA reform connects with public benefit and thus with domestic good governance. We have covered above the vital role of public communications and domestic outreach. Widening the recruitment catchment for the diplomatic system, bringing into the MFA young citizens from all segments of society is an obvious benefit.

An issue seldom explored is the role of the MFA within the country's system of domestic governance. An April 2022 report by the Lowy Institute, Australia's international affairs think tank noted: "Key to developing and implementing an all-elements national security strategy is elevating and reframing DFAT's role. The department should be re-designated as a 'central agency' rather than a 'line agency,' to adopt Canberra bureaucrat-speak, joining the departments of Prime Minister & Cabinet (PMC), Treasury, and Finance… Such a change would serve two important purposes. First, it would afford DFAT a clear leadership role in coordinating policy and capability across all arms of international policy. And second, it would elevate diplomacy as the government's primary foreign policy tool" (Piper 2022). In a globalized world, virtually every official agency has foreign connections and an external agenda. Harmonizing these actions to serve a whole of government policy is both vital and difficult. This is at the heart of the complex foreign policy coordination task that all MFAs face.

The World in Flux

Russia's February 24, 2022, invasion of Ukraine is a major turning point, whose direct outcome, on the ground, remains unclear. Many feel that it has challenged and altered the global order. Are we to witness a tectonic shift in world affairs, new major power alignments, plus cascading consequences to the sanctions that will affect all regions and states? How does this alter diplomatic practice?

Much of the action, including efforts by different countries seeking a solution to the Ukraine crisis, has taken place outside the world's premier multilateral institution, the UN. Regional entities, such as the EU and NATO, are in continual session. Individual states have advanced their efforts to find compromise, looking for a negotiated solution, while the war raged in Ukraine. How does this impact the bilateral diplomacy process? For countries large and small, powerful or otherwise, the world is more contentious, complex, and confusing. Dialogue and negotiation in the widest sense are front and center. Professional craft skills, analysis, advocacy, listening, and the ability to present one's case are acutely needed. That makes additional demands on MFAs. New and emerging power equations affect all countries, calling for skillful, sharper, sustained responses. Actions at bilateral, regional, and global levels are part of a continuous, seamless process. Diplomacy, the advancement of the home country's external interests is a single, seamless, continuous task.

But the diplomacy paradigm and its basics are unchanged. We might ask: will this fluidity, unpredictability, and the unexpected consequences of international developments give greater salience to MFAs, and their role in the affairs of each nation? Bilateral diplomacy remains at the core of international affairs. Global South countries need to redouble their efforts to sharpen their skillsets and enhance their professionalization.

References and Further Reading

Barder, B. 2014. *What Diplomats Do: The Life and Work of Diplomats*. Lanham: Rowman & Littlefield.
Bayne, N., and S. Woolcock. 2012. *The New Economic Diplomacy*. 3rd ed. London: Routledge.
Berridge, G.R. 2022. *Diplomacy: Theory and Practice*. 6th ed. Houndmills: Palgrave Macmillan.
Churchill, W. 1930. *My Early Life*. London: T. Butterworth.

Committee on External Affairs. 2018. 21st Report, Lok Sabha Secretariat, New Delhi, March.
Copeland, D. 2009. *Guerrilla Diplomacy*. Boulder: Lynne Rienner.
Denmark, Foreign Ministry. 2006. *Efficiency Enhancement Strategy of the Denmark Ministry of Foreign Affairs*. Copenhagen, February.
Denza, E. 2016. *Diplomatic Law: A Commentary on the Vienna Convention on Diplomatic Relations*. 4th ed. Oxford: Clarendon Press.
Dickie, J. 2004. *The New Mandarins*. London: I.B. Tauris.
DiploFoundation. 2013. *Honorary Consuls – A Booming Trade*. https://www.diplomacy.edu/blog/honorary-consuls-booming-trade/.
Docters van Leeuwen, A., et al. 2013. *Modernising Dutch Diplomacy*. Amsterdam: Government of the Netherlands. https://www.clingendael.org/sites/default/files/pdfs/Report%20Modernising%20Dutch%20Diplomacy.pdf.
Germany, Foreign Ministry. 2000. Paschke Report. https://www.diplomacy.edu/?s=Paschke+report.
Hocking, B., ed. 1999. *Foreign Ministries: Change and Adaptation*. Houndmills: Macmillan.
Hocking, B., and D. Spence, eds. 2002. *Foreign Ministries in the European Union: Integrating Diplomats*. Houndmills: Palgrave Macmillan.
Indian Parliament Committee on External Affairs. 2018. 21st Report, New Delhi, March.
Jett, D.C. 2014. *American Ambassadors: The Past, Present, and Future of America's Diplomats*. Houndmills: Palgrave Macmillan.
Kurbalija, J., ed. 1998. *Modern Diplomacy*. Malta: DiploPublishing.
Namibia Foreign Ministry. 2004. *Namibia's Foreign Policy & Diplomacy*. Windhoek: Namibia Foreign Ministry.
New Zealand Ministry of Foreign Affairs and Trade. 2021. *Strategic Intentions 2021–25*. https://www.mfat.govt.nz/assets/About-us-Corporate/MFAT-strategies-and-frameworks/MFAT-Strategic-Intentions-2021-2025.pdf.
Olivers, A. 2009. "Australia's Deepening Diplomatic Deficit." Sydney: Lowy Institute. https://www.diplomacy.edu/resource/australias-diplomatic-deficit-reinvesting-in-our-instruments-of-international-policy/.
Pillai, N.S., et al. 1966. Report of the Committee on the Indian Foreign Service. New Delhi: Ministry of External Affairs. https://indianculture.gov.in/report-committee-indian-foreign-service-0.
Piper, H. 2022. "Time to Think Big on the Future of Australian Diplomacy." Sydney: Lowy Institute. https://www.lowyinstitute.org/the-interpreter/time-think-big-future-australian-diplomacy.
Rajan, K.V., ed. 2012. *The Ambassador's Club: The Indian Diplomat at Large*. New Delhi: HarperCollins.
Rana, K.S. 2004a. *The 21st Century Ambassador*. Geneva and Malta: DiploFoundation.
———. 2004b. *Performance Management in Foreign Ministries: Corporate Techniques in the Diplomatic Services*. Paper No. 93. The Hague: Clingendael.

———. 2007. *Asian Diplomacy: The Foreign Ministries of China, India, Japan, Singapore, and Thailand.* Geneva and Malta: DiploFoundation.

———. 2013. *The Contemporary Embassy: Paths to Diplomatic Excellence.* Houndmills: Palgrave.

———. 2015. "Promotion Methods in Foreign Ministries – Time for Reform?" DiploFoundation. https://www.diplomacy.edu/blog/promotion-methods-foreign-ministries-time-reform/.

———. 2016. *Diplomacy at the Cutting Edge.* New Delhi: Manas.

———. 2020. *Bilateral Diplomacy: A Practitioner Perspective.* Diplo Policy Papers and Briefs, No. 15.

———. 2022. "Why Should Diplomatic Academies Shift to Online Learning?" DiploFoundation. https://www.diplomacy.edu/blog/diplomatic-academies-shift-to-online-learning.

Rana, K.S., and J. Kurbalija, eds. 2007. *Foreign Ministries: Managing Diplomatic Networks and Optimizing Value.* Geneva and Malta: DiploFoundation.

Robertson, J., and M.A. East, eds. 2005. *Diplomacy and Developing Nations.* London: Routledge.

Sharp, P. 1998. "Who Needs Diplomats? The Problem with Diplomatic Representation." In *Modern Diplomacy*, ed. J. Kurbalija. Malta: DiploPublishing.

UK Foreign and Commonwealth Office. 2016. *Future FCO, Foreign, Commonwealth and Development Office.* https://www.gov.uk/government/publications/future-fco-report.

Part III

Politicization of Diplomacy

6

Diplomats and Politicization

Pauline Kerr

The objective of this volume is to investigate claims that contemporary diplomacy needs to be reformed in order for it to better perform its role as one of the traditional institutions that effectively manage relations between states and their peoples. The aim of this chapter is to examine the proposition that one of the challenges in managing these relations is that diplomacy and diplomats are increasingly being politicized, and that this development impacts the effectiveness of contemporary diplomacy. Such propositions were particularly prominent during the four years of the Donald Trump administration in the United States. In 2017 the *New Yorker* claimed that then Secretary of State, Rex Tillerson, "has presided over the near-dismantling of America's diplomatic corps, chasing out hundreds of State Department employees and scaling back the country's engagement with the world. Most alarming has been the departure of dozens of the foreign services' most senior officials—men and women who had spent their careers living and working abroad, who speak several languages, and who are experts in their fields" (Filkins 2017).

In 2020, reviewing the Trump administration's record on diplomacy, a Democratic Staff Report, prepared for the U.S. Senate Committee on Foreign Relations, titled *Diplomacy in Crisis*, recommended that "our diplomatic professionals…must be…free from politicization and discrimination"

P. Kerr (✉)
The Australian National University, Canberra, Australia

(Democratic Staff Report 2020, 46). The same report argued the "effectiveness" of U.S. diplomacy was being hampered (3). During the 2020 U.S. presidential election the Biden campaign criticized then Secretary of State Mike Pompeo for his "politicization of diplomacy" (Steinhauser and Shaw 2020). Accusations that diplomacy and diplomats are being politicized go well beyond the United States. India's Minister of External Affairs S. Jaishankar has been criticized for politicizing the Indian Foreign Service (Zeeshan 2021). There are claims that the leaders of Poland, Austria, Italy, and Brazil are undermining diplomacy, ministries of foreign affairs, and diplomats (Destradi et al. 2021). In Australia, public policy scholars have long argued that the Australian Public Service is politicized but offer few insights into the experiences of Australian diplomats and the Department of Foreign Affairs (DFAT) (Mulgan 1998a, b).[1]

Despite such frequent and critical reference to the politicization of diplomacy and diplomats in the print and social media and scholarly literatures—such as Diplomatic Studies and International Relations—the meaning of the term and its impact is under-researched and therefore unclear. Particularly obscure is the response of diplomats in foreign ministries and missions to their perception that politicization is taking place. The questions this chapter therefore grapples with are: How do diplomats respond to their perception that politicization is taking place; to what extent are their responses connected to their understanding of the meaning of politicization; what sources of influence and power can diplomats draw upon when responding; and does politicization impact the effectiveness of their country's diplomacy?

The gap in literatures around diplomats' responses is partly understandable. Researching the practices of diplomats is challenging, notwithstanding the recent insightful literature on international practice theory (IPT), which examines patterns in the everyday work of diplomats (see, e.g., Sending et al. 2015; Pouliot and Cornut 2015). Research can be hampered by the traditional stonewalling around diplomacy: around scholars' access to diplomats and to diplomatic communications, such as cables and online exchanges, most of which are classified. Another explanation for the gap is the view that diplomacy and foreign policy-making, like any public policy, are intrinsically political in nature. One senior Australian public servant, Michael Keating,

[1] Several clarifications and definitional points are in order. The terms public service, public servants and civil service, civil servants are used interchangeably. Politicization in this chapter refers mostly to its presence within the Westminster system of governance rather than presidential systems like that in the United States. Given that the meaning of the terms "profession" and "professionalism" is debated, the stipulative meaning adopted here is that public servants and particularly diplomats belong to a profession insofar as they demonstrate their "expert knowledge, ideals of public service and a code of professional ethics" (Matheson 1998, 16).

endorses the view held by a former Australian Governor General: "Sir Paul Hasluck observed that 'the public service cannot avoid politics any more than fish can avoid the water in which they swim'" (quoted in Keating 1999, 44). Disentangling the boundaries between politics and politicization is problematic and perhaps even fruitless, from this perspective.

Nonetheless, there are push-back analyses and arguments to these positions which justify this chapter's focus. First, despite the challenges, IPT is providing more theoretical and empirical insights into diplomats' behaviors. Second, the public policy literature provides pathways through the politics/politicization nexus: not least through definitions of politicization and supporting empirical case studies. Third, there are ways of accessing diplomats' knowledge about their work. *The Hague Journal of Diplomacy* regularly features works by scholar-diplomats and this very volume has many chapters by retired diplomats and indeed by some serving diplomats.

Further justification for the chapter's focus is that because diplomatic practices are context-dependent and context-making (Kerr 2021) it is important to examine the various contexts in which diplomats work: for example, their professional, international, and domestic contexts. However, examination of diplomats' domestic context, beyond the relatively few studies of foreign ministries (Lequesne 2019 and 2022; Hutchings and Suri 2020), is underexplored. This neglect is problematic given that domestic contexts (and international) are increasingly described in terms of "populism," yet, as the 2021 special issue of *European Comparative Politics* on "Populism and Foreign Policy" points out, "the literature that specifically assesses the consequences of populism for international affairs is scant" (Destradi, et al. 2021, 663). Three of the authors of the special issue suggest that, "Empirical research needs… to identify shifts in who the most relevant actors involved in foreign policy-making are, what role is played by foreign ministries, and to what extent populist governments deviate from traditional diplomatic practice" (Destradi et al. 2021, 676). It is important then to explore the possible connections between populism and politicization, making diplomats' responses to both an important research agenda.

This chapter's aim is to respond to the gap in the literature on diplomats and politicization. It argues that politicization is a multilayered concept: it involves social relationships and relations of power between different policy actors—heads of governments, ministers, ministerial staffers, and public servants including diplomats. Diplomats' responses to politicization vary. They include resistance, receptiveness, retreat, and self-reflective reform, responses that depend partly on diplomats' sources of power and influence and how they understand politicization and its impact on their country. Leaders' sources of power are more explicit. These include their electoral mandate to govern. Staffers' power sources include their proximity to ministers and a mostly unregulated work environment. Diplomats' sources of power are more implicit. These include their reputation for professionalism (e.g., codes of conduct such as impartiality, free and frank advice as well as diplomatic knowledge of the "foreign place") but their professionalism depends on political actors giving it respect. Diplomats' power is now being eroded externally: by formal politicization, or leaders undermining diplomatic codes of conduct; and by administrative politicization, or staffers' side-lining or editing diplomats' professional advice. Diplomats' power is also being eroded internally: by their reluctance to change some outmoded aspects of their own professional identity and organizational-culture which predispose them to avoid active engagement in domestic politics and the domestic-international policy-making nexus and which makes them vulnerable to politicization by the other actors. Diplomats' general lack of self-reflective reform often results in self-defeating outcomes, such as diminished budgets for MFAs, reputational costs, and loss of influence to other actors including the public. Diplomats' vulnerability to politicization is further exacerbated by the action-reaction cycles among the actors. To resist politicization (and the related but also different occurrence of populism) and regain their proper place in robust democracies, diplomats should adopt more reflective reforms and restorative practices. For example, when executing their country's national interests, diplomats may find it useful to re-imagine themselves with a two-sided hybrid professional identity. One side consists of their many positive traditional professional attributes complemented by new ones, which enable them to be domestic public servants of the state serving its often fractured, domestic interests; and another side reinforcing their identity as international public servants serving the fractured global interests of their country and those of the fractured, international community.

The argument offers conceptual and empirical contributions that inform the underexplored relationship between diplomats and politicization in the domestic context. The concept of politicization is substantiated and expanded in a number of ways. The power relations between the actors (ministers, staffers, and public servants) and their power sources are highlighted to show that, among other things, politicization involves these actors engaging in action-reaction cycles which can exacerbate the erosion of diplomats' main power source, their professionalism. Diplomats' professionalism is conceptualized as having some unique features, most of which are positive but a few continue to be outmoded and result in self-defeating behaviors, making diplomats more vulnerable to further politicization. These conceptual contributions help to answer the main research question: how do diplomats respond to politicization? Diplomats' responses vary. They include resistance, receptiveness, retreat, and self-reflective reform responses. The argument is supported by the limited literature on diplomats' responses, including those established in a brief case study of Australian diplomats' experiences. Overall, these conceptual and empirical contributions are hypotheses, which hopefully advance the study of diplomats' responses to politicization.

To make the argument this chapter takes three steps. First, it examines three contexts in democracies that diplomats respond to and shape: their professional milieu, the international context, and the domestic context. The rarely explored domestic context is examined through Australian and New Zealand public policy literatures: referring to scholars' definitions, concepts, theories, case studies, and accounts of public servants' responses to politicization. A critique of the literatures is its under-exploration of the power relations and the power resources of the actors—ministers, staffers, and public servants—as well as its neglect of diplomats' responses to politicization. The second step takes propositions from the above examination of general public servants' responses to politicization to guide a review of the small literature on diplomats' responses to politicization, and also, briefly, their responses to populism, since there are presumed connections between the two factors. A third step takes these findings to interpret a brief case study of Australian diplomats' experiences of politicization and their responses to it. Based on the collective findings, the conclusion suggests how diplomats might meet the challenges that politicization presents to them.

Diplomacy, Contexts, and Diplomats' Responses

Diplomats' responses to their everyday work of conducting diplomacy are unsurprisingly multifaceted. In part their responses derive from the contexts in which they operate. Diplomats' responses can also influence and shape these contexts. One defining feature of diplomacy is that it is context-dependent and context-making (Kerr 2021). Diplomacy has many other defining features (Cooper and Cornut 2019). Among them is that diplomacy is a social practice centered on different social relations, on relationships of amity, enmity, and power between actors, nominally states but more accurately between the people who represent, report, communicate, and negotiate their states' interests and values. In more expansive and now popular definitions, diplomacy also involves relationships between groups of people, often within the international community, involved in representing, communicating, negotiating their own interests and values. The people who historically represented principals—be they tribal heads, princes, kings, and occasionally queens—of political units needed to be skilled in the relational nature of their tasks. Starting in France in the sixteenth century, their expertise became recognized as a profession "with an academy, secretariat, archives and manuals" (Adler-Nissen 2016, 98) and eventually with formal codes of conduct and informal behavioral conventions. Their organizational culture and professional identity endowed them with power and influence and they became known as diplomats, now representing states headed by principals called prime ministers or presidents. Over its *longue durée* diplomacy was and continues to be context-dependent and context-making and strongly focused on relations and relationships.

Diplomats' Professional Milieu

Diplomats' responses to their everyday work are partly derived from their professional milieu. It is a unique milieu. Diplomats belong to what is termed state foreign services, which means they work both at home, in the foreign ministry, and abroad in embassies and consulates (Wiseman 2019, 786). It is also unique in that it comprises international law and rituals, codified and informal conventions, knowledge of the "foreign place," and practical skills.

Diplomats act in accordance with international diplomatic law, much of it set out in two conventions, the *1961 Vienna Convention on Diplomatic Relations* (VCDR 1961) and the *1963 Vienna Convention on Consular Relations* (VCCR 1963). The Conventions are rare near-universal agreements among states which facilitate their relations, including through the proper conduct of diplomats. Another layer of professionalism is foreign ministries' special codes of conduct for diplomats, in addition to those that apply to them as public servants. For example, the Australian Department of Foreign Affairs (DFAT) states that the *DFAT Code of Conduct for Overseas Service* "is a statement of the Department's collective commitment to maintaining the highest ethical standards of behaviour" for diplomats serving in missions and consulates (DFAT 2013). Another aspect of diplomats' professionalism is that, as members of the Foreign Service representing their state, they are involved in internationally recognized formal ceremonies and rituals, many of which, for example accreditation, are hosted by the receiving state. Diplomats' professionalism is also anchored in their membership of the diplomatic corps, a select international body comprising diplomats residing in the capital city of the receiving state and at major international institutions. As Geoffrey Wiseman and Paul

Sharp explain, the corps is a "rare tangible expression of international society" (Wiseman and Sharp 2016, 180). Another important element of diplomats' professionalism is their accumulated diplomatic knowledge, generated by their lived experience of the "foreign place," that is, with the cultures, mores, languages, relationships, and histories of the receiving and neighboring states, as well as their familiarity with the workings of the international system.[2] This knowledge sustains diplomats' practical skill-sets for building relationships which help to influence and persuade others. The final layer of diplomats' professionalism is the informal conventions which help facilitate relations of amity. For Harold Nicolson, the ideal diplomat embodies such qualities as "truth, accuracy, calm, patience, good temper, modesty, loyalty" in addition to what he notes are the taken-as-given diplomatic virtues of "intelligence, knowledge, discernment, prudence, hospitality, charm, industry, courage and even tact" (Nicolson 1963 [1939], 55–67). Added to this is the essential element of emotional restraint which, as Fiona McConnell explains,

> is most apparent in the linguistic styles adopted by diplomats as, in seeking not only to advance the interests of their state but also to safeguard the international diplomatic system more generally. (McConnell 2018, 368)

The multiple unique elements comprising diplomats' milieu are the pillars of their traditionally distinctive professional identity. Diplomats believe they have skills and knowledge derived in part from their particular brand of professionalism, which distinguishes them from most other public servants, politicians, and citizens. According to Lequesne, diplomats have a "professional identity of expert that distinguishes the diplomat from both the politician and the ordinary citizen" (Lequesne 2021, 781).

Diplomats' International Context

Beyond their professional context, diplomats' responses to their everyday work, for example representing their country's national interest, are influenced by the international context, in particular by their perceptions of the nature of the international system. Diplomats usually hold what they call a realist view of the international system. Australia's former ambassador in China from 2007 to 2011, Geoff Raby, is a self-confessed realist who

---

[2] The importance of diplomats having a "deep knowledge of places" is the subject of insightful research by the critical geographer Merje Kuus (Kuus 2016, 549). Her work on diplomatic professions and professionals is equally insightful (Kuus 2021).

recommends Henry Kissinger's 1994 book *Diplomacy*, generally regarded by International Relations (IR) theorists as a "Realist" tome (Raby 2021). Yet, unlike most IR Realist theorists, diplomats believe strongly that diplomacy is a necessary (not always sufficient) process for avoiding the use of force to settle differences between states and for facilitating cordial relations between them. They see diplomacy being especially important in the contemporary context where many divisive global problems, such as geopolitics, pandemics, and climate change, can best be managed through diplomatic methods of negotiation, collective action, coalition building, and multilateralism rather than through states' pursuing individualistic interests. However, ironically diplomats' passion for diplomacy and their traditional professional identity as experts can be problematic in the domestic context.

Diplomats' Domestic Context

Much more is known about the ways diplomats respond to demands arising from the international context than the domestic context. It is fair to say that, beyond the surprisingly few studies of foreign ministries until recently (Lequesne 2019, 2021, 2022; Hutchings and Suri 2020), the impact of domestic politics on diplomats and their responses to it are relatively underresearched. An initial observation is that diplomats at home and abroad are subject to the same legislated public service codes of conduct as their public servant colleagues. In Australia the *1999 Australian Public Service Act* (PSA) (Australian Public Service Act 1999), which is based on the Westminster system of government, stipulates the professional expectations of public servants in the Australian Public Service (APS). Among the most important in this act, appearing in *Section 10 APS Value,* is that public servants are expected to be "impartial" in their conduct. DFAT reinforces diplomats' impartiality in *The Ethics, Integrity, and Professional Standards Policy Manual*, stating that the meaning of "Impartial" is that "The APS is apolitical and provides the Government with advice that is frank, honest, timely and based on the best available evidence" (DFAT 2019). Integral to impartiality is the concept of political neutrality. Australian public policy professor Richard Mulgan, points out that

> Political neutrality, or the need to be "apolitical," does not, of course, imply a literal abstention from politics or policy-making, a requirement which would be impossible… But it does require the avoidance of open, personal commitment to particular policies or values over which different governments and parties

may differ. Such commitments run the risk of compromising the impartiality of public servants and their ability to serve different governments and ministers with equal loyalty. (Mulgan 1998a, n.p.)

Although serving different governments and ministers and upholding codes of conduct such as political neutrality and impartiality applies to diplomats wherever they work, the domestic context puts them, like all public servants, at the coal-face of domestic political relationships where the PSA expectation of impartiality can be challenged, including by different types of politicization.

Politicization: A Multilayered Concept and Practice

Politicization has become a multilayered concept. Originally, it was understood as the relationship between public servants and their political masters. A theoretical framing of this servant-master relationship might suggest that, although both groups have a legitimate role in policy making, it is because political leaders are elected officials with a popular mandate to govern, that their claims are stronger than those of public servants. The logic of this framing would be that politicization has little explanatory substance: the views of elected political leaders are and should be more powerful than those of public servants, full stop. However, such a framing misses the point, among others, that there are obligations, on both sides. Public servants are professionally obliged to uphold their codes of conduct, such as being impartial and offering free and frank advice, which are legislated in Acts authorized by their governments. Governments are obliged, as the instigators of such codes, not to interfere with or deter public servants' obligations. Theoretical propositions aside, the concept of politicization has evolved to have different layers which interact.

Ruth Cole argues that today the public administration literature describes three distinct categories of politicization:

> Formal or partisan politicization, whereby merit-based criteria in recruitment and reward is replaced by political criteria (Christiansen et al. 2016); functional (or behavioural) politicization, whereby some public servants overstep their neutral expertise (Mulgan 1998b, 7), or when public servants become responsive to politicians rather than maintaining neutrality (Almendares 2011, 2065); and administrative politicization, where political advisors intervene in the relationship between the Minister and the public service and obstruct or disrupt the delivery of free and frank advice. (Eichbaum and Shaw 2008, 343; Cole 2020, 499)

These three distinct but interactive layers of politicization provide direction for examining politicization within the domestic context, its impact on public servants, and their responses. However, albeit with the rare exception,[3] an underlying dynamic that is underplayed in the categories above is the relations of power between the key actors, as well as their sources of power and influence.

Politicization as Relations of Power

A relevant concept of power for examining the relations of power between the key actors involved in politicization and their sources of power and influence is Robert A. Dahl's. He states: "Power is here defined in terms of a relation between people." Dahl also states that this relation involves "power comparability, or the relative degree of power held by two or more persons." Dahl's usage of the concepts "power, influence, control, and authority" is interchangeable (Dahl 1957, 202).

Examining the relations between the actors involved in politicization through this power lens is illuminating. Elected political officials—prime ministers, presidents, and other politicians—have a unique and potent source of power and authority: their popular mandate to govern for a set period bestowed upon them by their country's electorate. How governments acquire their mandate depends on their political system: liberal democracies usually have more legitimate processes than dictatorships. Regardless, all types of governments frequently respond to challenges—from any quarter—to their policies by invoking their popular mandate to legitimize their position. It is a powerful response. It connects with democratic principles, held universally at least in name. Former U.S. President Donald Trump's response to losing the 2020 election to Joe Biden continues to divide the U.S. electorate because it is based on the claim (albeit incorrect) that Biden does not have a popular mandate to govern the United States. A popular mandate however is not sacrosanct: it does not prevent governments from policy u-turns especially if it helps their perpetual objective to be reelected. Reelection and partisan imperatives are factors driving formal politicization, "whereby merit-based criteria in recruitment and reward is replaced by political criteria" (Cole 2020, 499). Elected officials' sources of power enable them to engage in this type of politicization.

---

[3] For example, Shaw and Eichbaum point out that in regard to the relationship between minister and political adviser it can concern the "structuring and directionality of power" (Shaw and Eichbaum 2017, 18).

Elected ministers and officials have ministerial staff or staffers—chiefs of staff, policy advisors, press secretaries, and other administrative staff—who over time have acquired their own controversial sources of power and influence. Their close physical and ideological proximity to their ministers empowers them to directly advise ministers on policy as well as on partisan reelection strategies and tactics. Being political appointments, ministerial staff, unlike public servants, are stakeholders in the government's reelection.[4] Staffers have opportunities that public servants do not: for example, gatekeeping the minister's time and agenda, and, for senior staffers, speaking on behalf of the minister to public servants, the press, and the public. Gatekeeping increasingly involves ministerial staff controlling policy advice from public servants. The speed of social media and the need to "control the narrative" put senior ministerial staff at the forefront of managing and communicating the minister's and government's policies. Staffers' sources of influence and power enable them to engage in administrative politicization, "where political advisors intervene in the relationship between the Minister and the public service and obstruct or disrupt the delivery of free and frank advice" (Eichbaum and Shaw 2008, 343; Cole, 2020, 499).

In many instances, administrative politicization is facilitated by flaws in the accountability regime of political advisers. Unlike that of public servants, advisers do not generally have legislated codes of conduct. The prospects of this changing are low usually because the power of advisers is endorsed by prime ministers and other ministers. As John Daley argues, in Australia, the 2019 Thodey Review of the Australian Public Service

> recommended that the code of conduct for advisers should be legislated and enforced; and that at least half of all advisers should have public service experience. The Morrison Government rejected these recommendations on the basis that it saw no problem with the current arrangements. (Daley 2021a, 48)

Likewise, in New Zealand research by Shaw and Eichbaum examining relations between political advisers and public servants found that

> very few (13.3%) of the ministers who participated in a survey we undertook felt that New Zealand should adopt standard practice elsewhere by having a

---

[4] Reelection can serve staffers career prospects, including, for some advisers, later becoming a politician. In Australia "over half of all federal politicians had worked as an adviser at some time before they were elected" (Daley 2021a, 47–48). And furthermore, the number of ministerial staff in Australia is increasing (ibid.).

dedicated code of conduct for advisers, and not one believed such a code should be grounded in legislation. (Shaw and Eichbaum 2017, 18–19)

These flaws support Daley's claim that, in Australia ministerial advisers remain largely unaccountable and that in practice there is often a "black hole of accountability" even though "in theory an adviser is accountable because their minister is responsible for their actions" (Daley 2021a, 48). Advisers' power and influence are enhanced by prime ministerial endorsement of a near-absent legislated code of conduct.

By contrast the sources of public servants' power are fundamentally embedded in their codified professionalism. However, their power is implicit and relies on the respect of ministers and their staffers for their professionalism. As indicated earlier, Australian public servants' professionalism is based on the norms and values stipulated in the *Australian Public Servant Act*, derived from the Westminster system of government.[5] For example, public servants are expected to show impartiality and political neutrality, and offer free and frank advice. However, the sources of public servants' power and influence are changing. In the past, in countries adhering to the Westminster model, public servants tended, on the whole, to respond confidently to political leaders with frank and fearless advice. Elected officials expected and respected public servant's neutrality and impartiality, even if they did not necessarily accept the advice. In this context public servants' professionalism had a greater chance of being a source of power than it has today.

For some time now, public servants' Westminster-based professionalism has been challenged, exogenously and endogenously. As far back as 2005, according to a survey of officials by Rhodes and Weller (2005, 7), "53 per cent of respondents think public servants are less likely to provide ministers with free and frank advice than they once were" (quoted by Shaw and Eichbaum 2020, 847). The exogenous factors include structural shifts, for example, toward prime ministers' offices and bureaucratic departments (in Australia, prime minister and cabinet) being the actors that set the cultural tone for other ministerial offices and departments to follow and which can include politicization by ministers and advisers. The endogenous factors include public servants being overly responsive to politicians rather than maintaining neutrality; that is, being unable or unwilling to sustain Westminster

---

[5] In Australia the formalization of the Westminster system at the federal level began on January 1, 1901, following the *Commonwealth of Australia Constitution Act 1900* passed by the British Parliament. Prior to that, from the late 1800s the colonies followed the Westminster model though with oversight by the British Parliament which could overrule the colonies' laws.

professionalism or to adapt or modify it to create a hybrid or new professional culture that empowers them to better do their job.

These endogenous developments show that public servants' professionalism is not just under attack from the outside by ministers and their staffers, but also from within. That is, public servants are not always the victims of other players' power sources and tactics. In these situations there can be as Cole explains, "functional (or behavioural) politicization, whereby some public servants overstep their neutral expertise… become responsive to politicians rather than maintaining neutrality" (Cole 2020, 499). Functional politicization can in fact range along a continuum: from conscious overstepping (driven for example by such factors as self-serving careerism, personal power-seeking, egoism, and bureaucratic status-seeking) to passive accommodation, paralyzing disillusionment, sub-conscious or conscious self-censoring, concern about the competence of other players in the policy process, and even denial that their professional conduct is flawed. One of the more concerning aspects of functional politicization is self-politicization: not just by individuals, or a department but also across the public service. Research by Eichbaum and Shaw shows a cultural malaise revealed in a widespread willingness to appease the minister that "extends beyond individual departments or agencies to the leadership of the entire sector" (Shaw and Eichbaum 2020, 849). These forms of functional politicization show that some public servants, in being receptive, are giving up what power and influence they have (Shaw and Eichbaum 2020; Niklasson et al. 2020).

A final point to consider about politicization and its underbelly of power relations is whether or not it is connected to populism, a development of increasing concern to many. Populism is a contested concept (Destradi et al. 2021). Among its many definitions is that it is an ideology, a logic, discourse, strategy, performance, political style, or something else. The possible connections between the concepts of populism and politicization however are not conceptually or empirically well researched. Wiseman, one of the few scholars grappling with the possible connections, argues that, "populism is an acute form of politicization" (Wiseman 2022, 128). Furthermore, that "[w]hile populism is an obvious indicator, populism is not necessary for politicization to occur" (ibid., 129). And finally, that "[l]oosely speaking, 'politicization' can be seen as the opposite of 'professionalisation'" (ibid.). For Wiseman there are indeed connections between politicization and populism.

In sum, this section has reviewed some recent research on politicization, predominantly by Australian and New Zealand public policy scholars, which examines the responses of general public servants to politicization, rather than diplomats' responses. Several points are made. First, politicization is a multilayered concept which focuses on the different actors involved: formal politicization focuses on political leaders/politicians; administrative politicization on political staffers; and behavioral/functional politicization on public servants. Second, it is a complex and dynamic concept in that there can be interactions between the layers, and often action-reaction cycles which make causal claims challenging. Something often implied but rarely made explicit in these interactions are the power relations between the actors and their different sources of power. Third, the power relations appear to be changing in favor of political leaders and staffers: that is, public servants' professionalism—their impartiality and frank and fearless advice—is under siege from the outside by these other actors, but also surprisingly from the inside by public servants themselves, many of whom often struggle or fail to maintain high standards of professionalism. Fourth, these points are hypotheses and require more research before generalizations or theories can be proffered. Fifth, this part also finds that there are some connections between politicization and populism indicating that it is a relationship to watch. Finally, given that the above points are mined from the experiences of public servants in general rather than from diplomats, the aim now is to use them as a framework for examining the responses of diplomats to politicization.

Diplomats and Politicization

Guided by some of the propositions from the first section above highlighting general public servants responses to politicization, this section reviews the limited academic literature touching on diplomats' responses. Again, the questions that informed discussion in the previous section are raised: what is the nature of their professionalism; what are the sources of diplomats' power; how do diplomats understand politicization; and how do they respond to it?

The nature of diplomats' power receives little explicit examination in Diplomatic Studies (DS), International Relations, and public policy literatures. In DS, the nearest discussion is framed in terms of diplomatic agency (see Adler-Nissen 2016). It is puzzling that explicit analyses of diplomats' power are often avoided, especially since many definitions of diplomacy explicitly refer to relations and relationships between the people who represent states, and these relations obviously involve influence and power. As Robert Dahl's earlier definition makes clear, relations between people involve power. It is a central tenet in feminist studies, for example. Even the literature on diplomats' agency pulls up short when it comes to discussing diplomats' power and their sources. Again, it is surprising because, in principle to have agency, or the capacity to act,[6] involves drawing on sources of influence and power.

Diplomats' power, and for that matter agency, draws on several sources. Uppermost is their professionalism derived from the factors earlier discussed. Collectively, these sources show that diplomats have a unique professional identity which differentiates them from many of those they work with. As Christian Lequesne argues, "Belonging to the corps of career diplomats means in democratic states serving loyally the state, but also assuming a professional identity of expert that distinguishes the diplomat from both the politician and the ordinary citizen" (Lequesne 2021, 781).

Historically, this type of professionalism, based on diplomats being knowledgeable, practical, and expert, gave them a respected professional identity of expert within governments, bureaucracies, and the public. In these earlier times, the adage that "Knowledge is power, it is based on power, and it produces instruments of power" seemed apt (Therborn 2021, 698). However, although ostensibly a professional identity as experts continues to be a reputational attribute of diplomats' professionalism, one issue, which is not so much an indication of diplomats' lack of professionalism (as is the case with the public policy concept of cultural malaise), is their hesitancy at times to adapt their traditional professionalism and organizational culture to evolving contexts. In the contemporary period diplomats need to better adapt to the closer nexus between the domestic and international contexts driven by globalization and the revolution in communication technologies. George Haynal argues that "diplomats too often [appear] to disdain domestic policy concerns" and that this "has not helped them manage the increasingly difficult intersection of national and foreign policy" (Haynal 2002, 24). Diplomats' hesitancy to robustly engage with the wider public service and to actively integrate domestic policy concerns into their domain of international policy, and international policy into domestic policy, has frustrated governments and created a vacuum which other ministries are stepping into, or at least to a considerable degree. In response to this shift, according to Haynal, MFAs failed to adequately respond, and "sought to prove relevance by finding new priorities, for instance in commercial promotion… [and] increasingly

---

[6] "Agency is a synonym of power. As nouns the difference between agency and power is that agency is the capacity, condition, or state of acting or of exerting power" (https://wikidiff.com/power/agency).

[supporting] ministerial diplomacy" (Haynal 2002, 26; see also Brown 2022[7]). Prime ministerial diplomacy in the form of summit diplomacy is increasing, despite views, including Henry Kissinger's, that leaders are not well equipped to master the finer points of negotiations.[8]

The situation described by Haynal can be explained through the lens of politicization as an action-reaction dynamic involving different layers of politicization. Prime ministers and ministers from other agencies plus their staffers engage in formal and administrative politicization partly because diplomats often continue to practice some aspects of their traditional professionalism and organizational culture which are outmoded. Diplomats often believe that their unique professional expertise and knowledge of the "foreign place" and the international system enable them to be better informed than domestic players. Diplomats and foreign ministries then hesitate to adapt to an evolving and new context, becoming overwhelmed and outplayed by other actors and their sources of power. Others' occupation and often dominance of the domestic-international policy nexus then cause a reactive response from diplomats, namely functional politicization, whereby they become receptive, or retreat.

Becoming more active and improving their influence at the domestic-international nexus is increasingly challenging for diplomats. Domestically, diplomacy, in both liberal democracies and populist governments, "remains contested and stigmatized inside national entities" (Cooper 2019, 800). According to Andrew Cooper, "increasingly, not only central agencies of government along with some 'line departments' go around foreign ministries and traditional diplomats; so, too, do aroused and mobilised citizens" (ibid., 801). This "going around" diplomats is now termed "disintermediation." For Cooper, "the concept of disintermediation [highlights] a separation of diplomats not only from other components of governmental bureaucracy but citizens at large" (ibid., 799). Looking broadly at the reasons for this, Haynal argues, "it was governments, disappointed with the effectiveness and attitude of their diplomatic arms, who led in disintermediating the profession" (Haynal

---

[7] Kerry Brown, a former British first secretary in the Beijing Embassy, argues that during his time there in the early 2000s, "foreign services were poor in engaging with new ideas—and didn't do much in terms of actually trying to generate their own unique thinking. They were the ultimate defenders of the current paradigms and resisted the idea of any new ones emerging to make their lives harder. A lot of the work of colleagues back then was in operating as a highly boutique travel agency for visiting politicians" (Brown 2022, n.p.).

[8] In his book *Diplomacy* Henry Kissinger wrote that: "It is almost always a mistake for heads of state to undertake the details of a negotiation. They are then obliged to master specifics normally handled by their foreign offices and are deflected onto subjects more appropriate to their subordinates, while being kept from issues only heads of state can resolve. Since no one without a well-developed ego reaches the highest office, compromise is difficult and deadlocks are dangerous" (quoted in Varghese 2016a, 595).

2002, 26). But now disintermediation involves publics, particularly in countries led by populist leaders who whip up public sentiment against imagined elites, such as diplomats, and accuse them of underplaying the domestic national interest and overplaying international and global interests. Domestic populism is impacting diplomacy and diplomats in negative ways. And populist leaders and their supporters would say (albeit falsely) that diplomats' traditional professional self-identity as being expert, elite, and internationally rather than domestically focused means they only have themselves to blame (*Guardian* 2017).

The challenges that diplomats are experiencing from politicization and populism raise two more questions. First, how do diplomats themselves understand these dynamics: do their understandings resonate with the conceptualizations in the academic and the literatures (formal politicization, functional politicization, and administrative politicization)? Second, how do they respond to politicization and populism?

Geoffrey Wiseman, former Australian diplomat and now Diplomatic Studies scholar, offers an understanding of politicization that mirrors formal politicization, though he does not use the latter term. He argues that politicization of the bureaucracy happens when there is "the substitution of political criteria for merit-based criteria in the selection, retention, promotion, rewards, and disciplining of members of the public service" (2022, 123)—invoking a well-known definition offered by Guy Peters and Jon Pierre (Peters and Pierre 2004, 2). Wiseman argues that formal politicization is rising in MFAs (2022, 120) and that in liberal-democratic practice politicization occurs

> when political leaders apply direct or indirect pressure on MFA staff to gain partisan advantage—stretching the norms and boundaries—in ways that incentivise or put pressure on officials to ignore the evidence and legal merits of a case or to tailor their advice to favour or satisfy their political masters for less than honourable reasons. (2022, 123)

To substantiate his understanding of politicization he points to

> a discernible shift in the proportion of political appointees, along with public scepticism about diplomacy itself and criticism of the ministry by political leaders, [which] is a clear indication of politicization of an MFA. (ibid., 125)

Wiseman's observation, showing that formal politicization is permeating MFAs in liberal-democratic contexts and compromising diplomats, is even more pronounced in MFAs governed by populist leaders. As Visnovitz and

Jenne argue, "the first hallmark of populist foreign policy is the personalization and politicization of diplomacy" (Visnovitz and Jenne 2021, 689). The connections between politicization and populism are increasingly evident.

The connection between formal politicization and populism is further supported by recent, but still limited, research on diplomats' relations with populist governments. Lequesne, another Diplomatic Studies scholar, examines relations between populist governments and diplomats through some 22 semi-directed interviews with politicians and senior diplomats (both acting and retired) in Poland, Italy, and Austria (Lequesne 2021, 779–95). Taking the example of Poland, many interviewees pointed to several of the PiS (the Law and Justice Party) government's decisions to recall numerous career ambassadors and replace them with political appointees close to the PiS and without diplomatic experience; to demote many diplomats who had trained in Moscow at the MGIMO University of International Relations, claiming that this is part of government's efforts at "decommunization"; and, in January 2021, to introduce "institutional limits to the existence of a career diplomacy composed of career diplomats" (Lequesne 2021, 784). For Lequesne, in all these countries there is "the desire of populist governments to politically capture the corps of career diplomats" (Lequesne 2021, 783). His concept of "political capture" explains "the temptation of populist parties to control career diplomats in order to impose the party's line on the foreign policymaking" (Lequesne 2021, 781). Despite not referring to the concept of formal politicization, his concept of political capture and its supporting evidence resonates strongly with it.

The second question, how do diplomats respond to politicization and populism, also has very few answers in the academic literature.[9] Lequesne's already cited 2021 study of diplomats' relations with populist leaders does however reveal several of their responses. Similar to the account above in the first section, explaining public servants' responses to formal politicization, the diplomats in Lequesne's study, as well as those in other studies, include the following responses: some resisted; some retreated and retired from the diplomatic service; others were receptive, engaging in functional politicization; and a few tried to introduce reforms. The following are examples of these responses. In

---

[9] Lesquesne and Wiseman do raise the general question. Lesquesne asks: "Is it possible to observe forms of resistance from diplomats against growing populist politics in the West, or will diplomats just obey and serve loyally populist leaders like Donald Trump in the United States or Viktor Orban in Hungary?" (2019, 782). Wiseman asks "In an age of populist leaders who thrive on being undiplomatic, how do national diplomats, trained in the art of civility and tact, deal internally with embarrassing leaders, serious policy disagreement, or dissent?" (Wiseman 2019, 792). Wiseman also notes that "Resisting overt politicization is challenging for diplomats, sometimes requiring both moral courage and an unwavering professional persona and reputation" (2022, 131).

Poland, an example of resistance and also reform is the decision by several former Polish diplomats to form a unique association within the EU, called the Conference of Ambassadors. This is in response to the PiS February 2021 law "introducing institutional limits to the existence of a career diplomacy composed of career diplomats' with the aim of denouncing the government's intention to de-professionalize Polish diplomacy" (Lequesne 2021, 785). Presumably, these diplomats were aware that de-professionalizing Polish diplomacy negated their professionalism and that the collective action of the Conference of Ambassadors might help restore their remaining power source. In the United States under former President Trump, many diplomats resisted the president's executive order temporarily banning all refugees and immigrants from seven majority-Muslim countries by engaging the State Department's formal dissent channel, which allows officials to formally express "dissenting or alternative views on substantive foreign policy issues" (Lizza 2017). In response, Sean Spicer, Trump's White House press secretary, dismissed his fellow government officials in State as "career bureaucrats," and told them to resign saying "…they should either get with the program [the executive order] or they can go" (Lizza 2017). An example of U.S. diplomats retreating and accommodating politicization (and a populist-leaning president) was when some went along with Trump's assault on the State Department's budget and increased recruitment of political appointees by excusing his disruptive tweets to international players, suggesting that American foreign policy would not be based just on Trump's tweets (Lequesne 2021, 782). An example of diplomats removing themselves from their country's foreign service during the Trump administration is the resignation of several U.S. ambassadors, including James Melville, John Feely, and Elizabeth Shackelford (BBC 2018). An example of diplomats' receptiveness to formal politicization and adopting functional politicization is the present situation in Poland where serving Polish diplomats are unlikely to be employed unless they follow the PiS line and hand-over their professionalism, their source of influence, and power.

The final question is, do diplomats' understandings of politicization and populism influence their views of whether they see either as detrimental to the effectiveness of their country's diplomacy. Regarding politicization, the varied responses of U.S. diplomats to Trump's undermining of the State Department, its diplomats, and U.S. diplomacy suggest that there were mixed understandings of politicization and its impact and indeed its connections with populism. Some diplomats resigned because they believed that Trump's politicization of the State Department was detrimental to the effectiveness of their country's diplomacy: it weakened U.S. diplomacy and undermined global security, and it undermined their professional status, their source of power, and influence. Those who continued with their careers as diplomats and were receptive to what was clearly Trump's undermining of U.S. diplomacy may have done so for many reasons. One may well have been because they did not understand Trump's politicization as being detrimental to the effectiveness of their country's diplomacy. With regard to populism, diplomats' views of its impact on their country's diplomacy also vary. Italy's populist government's desire to politically capture Italian diplomats was restrained by the structure of Italy's political system, relations between the coalitions, and the still high regard of many Italians for diplomats (Lequesne 2021). Italy's serving diplomats may have a different understanding of populism and its impact compared to that of Poland's former diplomats who clearly see the populist PiS's political capture of career diplomats as having a detrimental effect on Poland's diplomacy. Poland's currently serving diplomats would most likely disagree with their former colleagues (Lequesne 2021).

When reviewing these accounts of diplomats' responses to politicization and populism, it is apparent that, despite some differences, there are connections between politicization and populism. On the one hand, both dynamics are concerned with relations of power and influence and both draw on the power of leaders' mandates to govern. On the other hand, populist leaders' mandates are based on a particular part of electorate, the so-called pure people who like their leaders despise the presence of elite or expert professionals such as diplomats. There is a view that diplomats' professionalism is elitist and that they undervalue their country's national interest, preferring to pursue their country's international and global interests. One important conceptual similarity is that both politicization and populism involve formal politicization: leaders expect diplomats to support their government's partisan objectives. Another similarity is the way that diplomats respond to both politicization and populism: that is through resistance, receptivity, retreat, and reform. In contexts of politicization and populism, diplomats' professionalism is undermined.

In sum, from this discussion of the limited literature on diplomats' responses to politicization, this section makes several points. The multilayered nature of politicization and its underbelly of action-reaction cycles of power relations, established in the first section, also usefully illuminate diplomats' responses. Formal politicization involving political leaders is the most common experienced by most diplomats. But diplomats' functional politicization is also apparent: diplomats self-politicize, one dimension of which is to fail to adapt to a context where their traditional professional identity of "expert" needs to be modified. Less apparent, in this literature, is administrative politicization by ministers' staffers. However, given the experience of other public servants with staffers it is likely that diplomats also experience administrative politicization. How diplomats respond to the various categories of politicization varies: the most common forms being resistance, receptiveness, retreat, and occasionally reform responses. When responding to politicization, diplomats can in principle draw on different sources of influence and power which for the most part are the components that make-up their unique brand of professionalism: for example, the codified and informal codes of conduct, diplomatic knowledge of the international context and the "foreign place," and their relationship building skill-sets. In practice, the sources of power a diplomat draws on depend on how they choose to respond to politicization. A diplomat choosing to resist formal politicization by senior politicians may invoke some elements of their professionalism, whereas a diplomat choosing to be receptive to the same type of politicization may ignore their professional codes of conduct, like impartiality, and engage in functional politicization. Diplomats' understanding of politicization and populism impacts whether or not they see either as detrimental to their country's diplomacy and foreign policies. Many U.S. diplomats (during the Trump presidency) and likewise Polish diplomats believed their leader's formal politicization to be detrimental. Others apparently did not. Some Polish diplomats may have believed that their leaders were less involved in politicization and more in pursuing other objectives, for example, "decommunization" of the diplomatic corps. Understanding diplomats' responses to politicization is complex and at this point, given the limited research, any claims like the ones just uttered are hypotheses for further research.

Australia: A Case Study

This third section of this chapter expands the work-in-progress on diplomats' experiences with politicization by applying the propositions from the first two sections to a summary of the author's findings from a short case study of Australian diplomats (also see the chapter by Melissa Conley Tyler and Tom Barber in this volume). The aim is to fathom the largely unexplored experiences of Australian diplomats with politicization. Although the public policy literature on the Australian Public Service canvasses the politicized relations between public servants, ministers, and staffers, it has little to say about Australian diplomats' experiences, and again there is little other published material which does.

The findings from the case study are as follows:

First, the multilayered nature of politicization (formal, functional, administrative) and the underlying power relations between actors, established in the previous sections, usefully illuminate the experiences of Australian diplomats, despite some differences in the terminology used by diplomats and academics. Former Secretary of DFAT (2012–16) Peter Varghese, argues that he

> [does] not subscribe to the view that our public service has become politicized, if by that we mean that the institution has been subordinated to a partisan political agenda, as opposed to the fundamental requirement to serve the government of the day impartially. (Varghese 2016b, n.p.)

Varghese's understanding of politicization is qualified: the public service as an institution is not being subordinated by a "partisan political agenda." Nonetheless, he notes that "…retaining an apolitical public service is not helped by the disturbing trend for incoming governments to sack some Secretaries" (Varghese 2016b). His point suggests that Cole's definition of formal or partisan politicization, "whereby merit-based criteria in recruitment and reward is replaced by political criteria," is appropriate insofar as the number of highly respected secretaries being sacked is increasing (Varghese 2022), suggesting that one explanation is that political criteria, as well as merit-based criteria, are present.

There are other examples where despite the different terminology used by diplomats and academics the experiences of diplomats can be understood as politicization. Varghese refers to developments within the public service which disturb him: "what is worse than politicization is the 'timidity or timiditisation' of some public servants," resulting in their reticence to stand up to pressure from a minister or staffer (Varghese 2022). As he states, "I have little sympathy for public servants who say they crossed the line because of pressure from a minister or a staffer" (Varghese 2016b). Even though Varghese uses the term "timiditisation," its meaning is analogous to Cole's term of functional politicization: "functional politicization [occurs when] some public servants overstep their neutral expertise… or when public servants become responsive to politicians rather than maintaining neutrality" (Cole 2020, 499).

Likewise, Vargheses' description of the pressure on public servants from staffers can be understood as administrative politicization:

> there is… no room in our system for staffers to ask for a submission to be withdrawn or to insist on a particular recommendation in a departmental submission. Or to ask to see a submission in draft. These should be no-go areas and all public servants should have the confidence of knowing that when they resist

such approaches, they will be fully backed up by their departmental leaders. (Varghese 2016b)

For Cole, administrative politicization occurs when "political advisors intervene in the relationship between the Minister and the public service and obstruct or disrupt the delivery of free and frank advice" (Cole 2020, 490).

Overall, despite the different terms used by diplomats and academics, the experiences of Australian diplomats can be understood as forms of politicization. As for how best to respond to politicization, Varghese's advice to "resist such approaches" (Varghese 2016b) is one of the same responses that other country's diplomats were shown to have taken in the previous sections of the chapter.

Second, the experiences of Australian diplomats with the multilayered nature of politicization and its underlying power relations are evident in political commentator Graeme Dobell's 2021 article (Dobell 2021). Dobell also does not describe his observations of Australian diplomats' experiences in terms of politicization. However, his account can readily be understood as formal, administrative, and functional politicization. For example, Dobell argues that "…curbing the power and prerogatives of ambassadors" by governments is now common in Australia and that ambassadors are responding to it:

> Once, ambassadors on post presided and often ruled…. No more… self-censorship had become an ambassadorial art form; well-understood protocols ensured ministers were not told what they didn't want to hear and professional discipline in the department was reinforced by a "culture of compliance," Being creative and dynamic is tough when ministers and minders demand "no surprises," discipline and compliance. Being answerable saps being active. (Dobell 2021, 376)

Through the politicization conceptual lens, the logic of Dobell's argument above and throughout his article is the following. Ambassadors' professional status and entitlements, a major source of their power, are being weakened in several ways. By prime ministers who adopt presidential styles of governance: for example, by increasing the number of political appointees to ambassadorial positions (Bosworth 2021) (sometimes these include politically sympathetic diplomats, financial donors, and friends). This is a form of formal politicization. Ambassadors' power is also being curbed by staffers (Dobell refers to them as minders) whose proximity to ministers gives them gatekeeping powers over diplomat's policy advice. This is administrative politicization.

Ambassadors are also contributing to their loss of professional power: through self-censorship—that is "[ensuring] ministers were not told what they didn't want to hear"—and by a departmental "culture of compliance." This is functional politicization. Ambassadors are responding to politicization by being receptive. Their receptiveness encourages further politicization by the other actors. An overview of the dynamics shows that politicization involves a complex action-reaction cycle, with implications for diplomats.

Third, Dobell's observations, of how some diplomats (in this case ambassadors) are responding to politicization and the culture of compliance within DFAT, point to the earlier discussion about functional politicization and its element of self-politicization. Australian diplomats are sometimes seen as being complicit, knowingly or unknowingly, in this type of politicization: there is a hesitancy to adapt to new contexts and to modify some aspects of their original professional identity and organizational culture which are outmoded, for example assuming their professional expertise is superior to domestic actors and being distant from participation in domestic politics and the domestic-international policy-making nexus. In Canberra's domestic political battles over budget allocation, for example in the Expenditure Review Committee (ERC), DFAT's voice (particularly the foreign minister's) is often missing or drowned out by the more robust bureaucratic actors. The predictable result is that DFAT's budget continues to decline. As Miletic and Langmore argue:

> Australian diplomacy has had a low priority throughout the last quarter century…by 2023–24, Australian outlays on diplomacy will have been cut by 53 percent during the previous 28 years. (Miletic and Langmore 2020, n.p.)

This trend is confirmed in the 2022–23 Budget (Commonwealth of Australia 2022) which has "funding for 'Foreign Affairs and Trade Operations' from more than $1.27 billion in 2022–23 to closer to $1.15 billion in 2025–26" (DFAT 2022).

Dave Sharma, former Australian ambassador to Israel (2013–17) and until the 2022 federal election a liberal party parliamentarian, points out that DFAT receives much less funding than the Defence Department: Australia spends "roughly $28 billion per year on defence, but only $1 billion per year on diplomacy" (Sharma, 2020). Importantly, Sharma also argues that DFAT's budget decline is partly due to the department's own organizational culture toward domestic politics: DFAT fails to "sell its value to the political class, to cultivate champions within the cabinet, or position itself with solutions to the government's challenges" (Sharma 2020). Sharma's claims point to the earlier proposition that functional politicization can include diplomats' hesitancy to adapt to evolving situations and to rely on some outmoded aspects of their professional identity and organizational culture.

This case further demonstrates how the action-reaction cycle in politicization impacts diplomats. Once DFAT lost its rung on the budget allocation ladder it became more vulnerable to politicization because its sources of power began to fade. It lost missions and consulates, and, in these places, its capacity to report and to represent Australia's national interests. This means its diplomats' diplomatic knowledge has less currency in Canberra with resulting reputational costs: including for the foreign minister who has diminished standing within cabinet. DFAT's hesitancy to robustly engage with the domestic-international nexus is noted in official reviews of DFAT. The Australian Public Service Review 2013, *Capability Review Department of Foreign Affairs and Trade*, states that

> DFAT is not seen by other government agencies, or by some of its own people, as performing as well in Canberra as it does overseas. It is perceived as being distant from policy processes outside traditional national security and trade areas, even on issues like the global economy or energy where it has something to bring to the table. (Australian Public Service Review 2013, 11)

Furthermore, as DFAT's power sources diminished, other departments, for example the Department of the Prime Minister and Cabinet (PM&C), brought their traditional expertise in domestic politics and their now international know-how to the domestic-international policy making nexus, at times overpowering and outplaying the diplomats' professionalism and knowledge, thereby undermining their power base. It was no accident that one of PM&C's deputy secretaries was appointed the Australian Sherpa to lead Australia's presidency of the 2019 G20, and that the Department of Treasury was the supporting bureaucracy. DFAT, including its trade diplomats, came in third. Politicization is a vicious cycle of actions and reactions challenging diplomats.

In sum, this summary of Australian diplomats' experience with politicization makes several points. Australian diplomats, like their domestic public service colleagues and diplomats in many other countries, are increasingly exposed to all three categories of politicization: formal, administrative, and functional politicization. However, as with their overseas colleagues, they may not understand or conceptualize this development in the academic terms of politicization, despite the clear evidence. Australian diplomats' response options are also similar to those of other diplomats. Former Ambassador Varghese's advice is to respond by resisting politicization, that is, to continue to rely on professionalism, and to practice codes of conduct of impartiality and free and frank advice. Dobell's study, however, indicates ambassadors are responding to formal and administrative politicization through functional politicization: receptiveness; self-censoring; and some outmoded forms of professional identity and organizational cultural behaviors. Former Ambassador Sharma's reference to DFATs frequent disengagement from domestic politics, including budget battles, is an example of both. This is often a reaction to earlier cycles of formal and administrative politicization, confirming the action-reaction cycles of politicization in which diplomats can slide into self-defeating reactions and responses of functional politicization and further erode their professionalism, their source of power.

Conclusion: Looking Ahead

The chapter's examination of diplomats' responses to politicization shows that the different layers of politicization undermine diplomats' professional capacity to conduct effective diplomacy. Formal politicization by ministers undermines diplomats' professional codes of conduct, including impartiality, political neutrality, and the provision of free and frank advice. Administrative politicization by staffers has a similar impact plus it can include side-lining and editing diplomats' policy advice. Functional politicization by diplomats also reduces their professionalism. Responding to the other actors' politicization by being receptive, that is, by self-politicization and being reluctant to adapt aspects of their traditional professional identity and organizational culture to the now integrated domestic and international contexts, undercuts diplomats' capacity to sustain effective diplomacy: for example, avoiding domestic politics around budget allocations results in cuts to MFAs budgets making international diplomacy less effective. The layers of politicization interact resulting in action-reaction cycles which makes diplomats more vulnerable to others' politicization, since these actors' sources of power override diplomats' professionalism. Politicization in all its different guises requires reflection and reform by all the actors.

Governments, however, are often reluctant to reform their governance shortcomings. In Australia for example, according to the Grattan Institute's 2021 *Report on Government and Public Integrity*, "policy reform… is gridlocked," and this is partly because

> The growing number and power of ministerial advisers make it harder to pursue reform. The public service has been weakened: often it is not asked to provide policy advice, is not capable of providing it, and is overly pliable in serving the political interests of the government of the day. (Daley 2021a, 3)

Nonetheless, as Daley argues, all is not lost, "Australia could break the gridlock in policy reform by increasing the expertise and independence of the public service, reducing the number of ministerial advisers closely tied to political parties and making them more accountable" (Daley 2021b, 1). Although broad governance reform requires going beyond politicization—formal, administrative, and functional—it is clearly an obstacle to effective governance of the state, domestically and internationally.

Effective diplomacy in the context of increasing politicization requires MFAs and diplomats to do many things. One is to revamp their professionalism through their own reflective reforms and restorative practices. Their self-defeating receptive responses—self-politicization and reluctance to adapt outmoded aspects of their traditional professional identity and organizational culture—require diplomats to consider the following when assembling reforms: to recognize their own part in politicization, in particular those receptive behaviors which contribute to the action-reaction cycles and which increase their vulnerability to other actors' politicization; to adapt some traditional behaviors and attitudes that are outdated by further accepting that diplomacy in the international context cannot be separate from the domestic context (Cooper 2019, 805); to adapt to this change by engaging more robustly with domestic politics (particularly around economic policies) and the domestic-international policy-making nexus; to integrate themselves into the general public service in "order to ensure that [diplomats]… bring the external reality into domestic decision-making, and be better at reflecting domestic realities abroad" (Haynal 25); to ensure that this integration will support effective diplomacy through organizational cultural changes including career incentives that validate engagement in the domestic context, positioning the MFA to acquire proper budget allocations in domestic political competitions, and reducing the reputational costs to diplomats caused by their disengagement and reluctance to adapt their professional identity as expert in international diplomacy to the reality that it is necessary but no longer sufficient.

When executing their country's national interests, diplomats may find it useful to re-imagine themselves with a two-sided hybrid professional identity. One side consists of their many positive traditional professional attributes complemented by new ones which enable them to be domestic public servants of the state serving its often fractured, domestic interests, and another side reinforcing their identity as international public servants serving the fractured global interests of their country and those of the fractured, international community.

Acknowledgment My thanks to my colleague Geoffrey Wiseman whose groundbreaking work on the politician-diplomat nexus inspired me to pursue this topic (Wiseman 2022). He, of course, is not responsible for my interpretations of his work.

References and Further Reading

ABC Radio National. 2021. "John McCarthy on How Diplomacy Should be Used," May 15. https://www.abc.net.au/radionational/programs/saturdayextra/john-mccarthy-on-diplomacy-and-politics/13332790.

Adler-Nissen, R. 2016. "Diplomatic Agency." In *The SAGE Handbook of Diplomacy*, eds. C. Constantinou, P. Kerr, and P. Sharp, 92–103. London: SAGE.

Almendares, N. 2011. "Politicization of Bureaucracy." In *International Encyclopaedia of Political Science*, eds. B. Badie, D. Berg-Schlosser, and L.A. Morlino, 2063–65. Thousand Oaks: SAGE.

Altman, D. 2014. "Reflections on Bob Carr's Diary of a Foreign Minister." *Australian Journal of International Affairs* 68 (4): 397–99.

Ashpole, L. 2012. *Ministerial Advisers: How Ministers Shape Their Conduct. A Study of Ministers and Advisers in the Rudd Government*. University of Sydney. https://ses.library.usyd.edu.au/handle/2123/9047.

Australian Public Service. 1999. *Australian Public Service Act 1999*. http://www7.austlii.edu.au/cgi-bin/viewdb/au/legis/cth/consol_act/psa1999152/.

———. 2019. *Australian Public Service Review 2019*. https://www.apsreview.gov.au/.

———. 2022. *Australian Public Service Commissioner's Directions 2022*. https://www.legislation.gov.au/Details/F2022L00088.

Australian Public Service Review. 2013. *Capability Review Department of Foreign Affairs and Trade*. https://www.apsc.gov.au/sites/default/files/2021-06/DFAT%20Capability%20review.pdf.

BBC. 2018. "U.S. Ambassador to Estonia Resigns over Trump's Comments," June 30. https://www.bbc.com/news/world-us-canada-44665862.

Bosworth, N. 2021. "The Changing Face of Australia's Diplomatic Network." *The Interpreter*, July 9. https://www.lowyinstitute.org/the-interpreter/changing-face-australia-s-diplomatic-network.

Brown, K. 2022. "War Represents Failure of Diplomacy. It Pays to Read Past Page One." *The Interpreter*, March 31. https://www.lowyinstitute.org/the-interpreter/war-represents-failure-diplomacy-it-pays-read-past-page-one.

Byrne, C., M. Conley Tyler, and S. Harris Rimmer. 2016. "Australian Diplomacy Today." *Australian Journal of International Affairs* 70 (6): 581–89.

Christiansen, P.M., B. Niklasson, and P. Öhberg. 2016. "Does Politics Crowd Out Professional Competence? The Organisation of Ministerial Advice in Denmark and Sweden." *West European Politics* 39 (6): 1230–50.

Cole, R. 2020. "Maintaining Neutrality in the Minister's Office." *Australian Journal of Public Administration* 79 (4): 495–513.

Commonwealth of Australia. Department of the Prime Minister and Cabinet. 2019. *Our Public Service, Our Future: Independent Review of the Australian Public Service*, eds. D. Thodey, M. Carnegie, G. Davis, G. de Brouwer, B. Hutchinson, and A. Watkins. https://pmc.gov.au/sites/default/files/publications/independent-review-aps.pdf.

———. 2022. Budget 2022–2023. https://budget.gov.au/2022-23/content/documents.htm.

Conley Tyler, M. 2021. "Diplomacy in a Divided World." Rasina Debates, April 21. https://www.orfonline.org/expert-speak/diplomacy-divided-world/.

Constantinou, C., P. Kerr, and P. Sharp, eds. 2016. *The SAGE Handbook of Diplomacy*. London: SAGE.

Cooper, A.F. 2019. "The Disintermediation Dilemma and Its Impact on Diplomacy: A Research Agenda for Turbulent Times." *Diplomacy & Statecraft* 30 (4): 799–807.

Cooper, A.F., and J. Cornut. 2019. "The Changing Practices of Frontline Diplomacy: New Directions for Inquiry." *Review of International Studies* 45 (2): 300–19.

Dahl, R.A. 1957. "The Concept of Power." Department of Political Science, Yale University. https://fbaum.unc.edu/teaching/articles/Dahl_Power_1957.pdf.

Daley, J. 2021a. *Gridlock. Removing Barriers to Policy Reform*. Grattan Institute. https://grattan.edu.au/wp-content/uploads/2021/07/Gridlock-Grattan-Report.pdf.

———. 2021b. *Gridlock. Removing Barriers to Policy Reform, Summary*. Grattan Institute. https://grattan.edu.au/report/gridlock/.

Democratic Staff Report. 2020. *Diplomacy in Crisis*. A Report Prepared for the Committee on Foreign Relations, United States Senate. 1–43. https://www.foreign.senate.gov/imo/media/doc/Diplomacy%20in%20Crisis%20%2D%2D%20SFRC%20Democratic%20Staff%20Report.pdf.

Department of Foreign Affairs and Trade. 2013. *DFAT Code of Conduct for Overseas Service*. https://www.dfat.gov.au/aboutus/publications/Pages/dfat-code-of-conduct-for-overseas-service.

———. 2019. *Ethics, Integrity and Professional Standards Policy Manual*, October 17. https://www.dfat.gov.au/about-us/publications/corporate/ethics-integrity-and-professional-standards-policy-manual/chapter-3-values-and-codes-of-conduct.

———. 2022. *Portfolio Budget Statements 2022–23*. Budget Related Paper No. 1.6 Foreign Affairs and Trade Portfolio. https://www.dfat.gov.au/sites/default/files/pbs-2022-23-foreign-affairs-and-trade-portfolio-budget-statements-2022-23.pdf.

Destradi, S., D. Cadier, and J. Plagemann. 2021. "Populism and Foreign Policy: A Research Agenda." *Comparative European Politics* 19 (6): 663–82.

Destradi, S., J. Plagemann, and H. Taş. 2022. "Populism and the Politicization of Foreign Policy." *British Journal of Politics and International Relations* 24 (1): 1–18.

Dobell, G. 2021. "Fifty Years of Australia's Department of Foreign Affairs: From External to Internal." *Australian Journal of International Affairs* 75 (4): 367–82.

Edwards, P. 2012. "Dancing with Warriors: A Diplomatic Memoir." *Australian Journal of International Affairs* 66 (3): 397–98.

Eichbaum, C., and R. Shaw. 2008. "Revisiting Politicization: Political Advisers and Public Servants in Westminster Systems." *Governance* 21 (3): 337–63.

Filkins, D. 2017. "How Rex Tillerson Wrecked the State Department." *New Yorker*, November 30. https://www.newyorker.com/news/news-desk/how-rex-tillerson-wrecked-the-state-department.

Guardian. 2017. "Farage Says A Lot More Diplomats Should Follow Rogers and Resign," January 3. https://www.theguardian.com/politics/video/2017/jan/03/nigel-farage-calls-for-more-resignations-after-sir-ivan-rogers-quits-video.

Gyngell, A. 2018. "Australian Foreign Policy: Does the Public Matter? Should the Community Care?" *Australian Journal of International Affairs* 72 (2): 85–91.

Haynal, G. 2002. *Diplomacy on the Ascendant in the Age of Disintermediation*. Weatherhead Center for International Affairs, Harvard University. https://projects.iq.harvard.edu/files/fellows/files/haynal.pdf.

Hutchings, R., and J. Suri, eds. 2020. *Modern Diplomacy in Practice*. Cham: Palgrave Macmillan.

Hutchinson, B. 2019. "Both Parties Want to Pursue Public Service Reform." *The Mandarin*, March 28. https://www.themandarin.com.au/106336-aps-reviewer-belinda-hutchinson-both-major-parties-want-to-pursue-public-service-reform/.

Keating, M. 1999. "The Public Service: Independence, Responsibility and Responsiveness." *Australian Journal of Public Administration* 58 (1): 39–47.

Kerr, P. 2021. "China's Diplomacy: Towards ASEAN Way Norms in the South China Sea." *The Hague Journal of Diplomacy* 16 (2–3): 1–29.

Kuus, M. 2016. "'To Understand the Place': Geographical Knowledge and Diplomatic Practice." *The Professional Geographer* 68 (4): 546–53.

———. 2021. "Professions and their Expertise: Charting the Spaces of 'Elite' Occupations." *Progress in Human Geography* 45 (6): 1338–55.

Lequesne, C. 2019. "Why Studying State Foreign Services Remains a Research Priority." *Diplomacy & Statecraft* 30 (4): 780–85.

———. 2021. "Populist Governments and Career Diplomats in the EU: The Challenge of Political Capture." *Comparative European Politics* 19 (6): 779–95.

———., ed. 2022. *Ministries of Foreign Affairs in the World Actors of State Diplomacy*. Leiden and Boston: Brill/Nijhoff.

Lizza, R. 2017. "White House to Dissenters: Quit." *New Yorker*, January 31. https://www.newyorker.com/news/ryan-lizza/white-house-to-state-department-dissenters-quit.

Matheson, C. 1998. "Is the Higher Public Service a Profession?" *Australian Journal of Public Administration* 57 (3): 15–27.

McConnell, F. 2018. "Performing Diplomatic Decorum: Repertoires of 'Appropriate' Behavior in the Margins of International Diplomacy." *International Political Sociology* 12 (4): 362–81.

Miletic, T., and J. Langmore. 2020. "Australian Threadbare Diplomacy in Conflict." *Australian Outlook*, November 26. https://www.internationalaffairs.org.au/australianoutlook/australian-threadbare-diplomacy-in-conflict/.

Miller, G. 2002. "Current and Emerging Challenges to the Practice of Australian Diplomacy." *Australian Journal of International Affairs* 56 (2): 197–206.

Mulgan, R. 1998a. *Politicising the Australian Public Service?* Parliamentary Library Research Paper 3. https://www.aph.gov.au/About_Parliament/Parliamentary_Departments/Parliamentary_Library/pubs/rp/rp9899/99rp03.

———. 1998b. "Politicisation of Senior Appointments in the Australian Public Service." *Australian Journal of Public Administration* 57 (3): 3–14.

Nicolson, H. 1963 [1939]. *Diplomacy: A Guide to the Conduct of Contemporary Foreign Affairs*. Oxford: Oxford University Press.

Niklasson, B., P. Munk Christiansen, and P. Öhberg. 2020. "Speaking Truth to Power: Political Advisers' and Civil Servants' Responses to Perceived Harmful Policy Proposals." *Journal of Public Policy* 40 (3): 492–512.

Page, M. 2022. "A Silver Lining to DFAT's Budgetary Woes." *The Interpreter*. https://www.lowyinstitute.org/the-interpreter/silver-lining-dfat-s-budgetary-woes.

Peters, G.B., and J. Pierre. 2004. "Politicisation of the Civil Service: Concepts, Causes, Consequences." In *Politicisation of the Civil Service in Comparative Perspective: The Quest for Control*, eds. G.B. Peters and J. Pierre, 1–13. London: Routledge.

Pouliot, V., and J. Cornut. 2015. "Practice Theory and the Study of Diplomacy: A Research Agenda." *Cooperation and Conflict* 50 (3): 297–315.

Raby, G. 2021. Geoff Raby on the Skills Required for Good Diplomats. ABC Radio National, Saturday Extra Podcast, June 12. https://www.abc.net.au/radionational/programs/saturdayextra/geoff-raby-on-the-skills-required-for-good-diplomats/13679922.

Rhodes, R.A.W., and P. Weller. 2005. "Westminster Transplanted and Westminster Implanted: Exploring Political Change." In *Westminster Legacies: Democracy and Responsible Government in Asia and the Pacific*, eds. H. Patapan, J. Wanna, and P. Weller, 1–12. Sydney: UNSW Press.

Sending, O.J., V. Pouliot, and I.B. Neumann, eds. 2015. *Diplomacy and the Making of World Politics*. Cambridge: Cambridge University Press.

Sharma, D. 2020. "A Diplomatic Step-up to Match Our Military Step-up." *The Interpreter*. https://www.lowyinstitute.org/the-interpreter/diplomatic-step-match-our-military-step.

Shaw, R., and C. Eichbaum 2017. "Bargains, Compacts, and Conventions in the Core Executive: The New Zealand Case." Paper presented at the 3rd International Conference on Public Policy, Singapore, June 28–30. https://www.ippapublicpolicy.org/file/paper/593dbbccd2b10.pdf.

———. 2020. "Bubbling Up or Cascading Down? Public Servants, Political Advisers and Politicization." *Public Administration* 98 (4): 840–55.

Sofer, S. 2007. "The Diplomatic Corps as a Symbol of Diplomatic Culture." In *The Diplomatic Corps as an Institution of International Society*, eds. P. Sharp and G. Wiseman, 31–38. Houndmills: Palgrave.

Steinhauser, P., and A. Shaw 2020. "Biden Campaign Slams Pompeo's Speech as 'Politicization of Diplomacy.'" *Fox News*, August 25. https://www.foxnews.com/politics/biden-campaign-pompeo-speech-politicization-of-diplomacy.

Therborn, G. 2021. "Knowledge and Power: Social Science and the Social World." *International Sociology* 36 (5): 697–703.

Varghese, P. 2016a. "Australian Diplomacy Today (Speech, August 28, 2015)." *Australian Journal of International Affairs* 70 (6): 590–96.

———. 2016b. "Parting Reflections." Secretary's speech to IPPA, June 9. https://www.dfat.gov.au/news/speeches/Pages/parting-reflections-secretarys-speech-to-ipaa.

———. 2022. Phone conversation, May 11.

Vienna Convention on Consular Relations [VCCR]. 1963. https://legal.un.org/ilc/texts/instruments/english/conventions/9_2_1963.pdf.

Vienna Convention on Diplomatic Relations [VCDR]. 1961. https://legal.un.org/ilc/texts/instruments/english/conventions/9_1_1961.pdf.

Visnovitz, P., and E.K. Jenne. 2021. "Populist Argumentation in Foreign Policy: The Case of Hungary under Viktor Orbán, 2010–2020." *Comparative European Politics* 19 (6): 683–702.

Wainer, D.F. 2022. "The Populist Way Out: Why Contemporary Populist Leaders Seek Transnational Legitimation." *British Journal of Politics and International Relations* 23 (4): 1–21.

Weller, P., and T. Wood. 1999. "The Departmental Secretaries: A Profile of a Changing Profession." *Australian Journal of Public Administration* 58 (2): 21–32.

Wesley, M. 2002. "Australia's Department of Foreign Affairs and Trade and the Challenges of Globalisation." *Australian Journal of International Affairs* 56 (2): 207–22.

Wiseman, G. 2019. "Contemporary Challenges for Foreign Ministries: At Home and Abroad." *Diplomacy & Statecraft* 30 (4): 786–98.

———. 2022. "Expertise and Politics in Ministries of Foreign Affairs: The Politician-Diplomat Nexus." In *Ministries of Foreign Affairs in the World: Actors of State Diplomacy*, ed. C. Lequesne, 119–49. Leiden and Boston: Brill/Nijhoff.

Wiseman, G., and P. Sharp. 2016. "The Diplomatic Corps." In *The SAGE Handbook of Diplomacy*, eds. C. Constantinou, P. Kerr, and P. Sharp, 171–84. London: SAGE.

Woodard, G. 2000. "Ministers and Mandarins: The Relationships between Ministers and Secretaries of External Affairs 1935–1970." *Australian Journal of International Affairs* 54 (1): 79–95.

Woodard, G., and J. Beaumont. 1998. "Paul Hasluck as Minister for External Affairs: Towards a Reappraisal." *Australian Journal of International Affairs* 52 (1): 63–75.

Woolcott, R. 1997. "Pathways of Modern Diplomacy." *Australian Journal of International Affairs* 51 (1): 103–8.

Zeeshan, M. 2021. "The Indian Foreign Service Must Speak Out Against Growing Politicization. The Indian Diplomatic Corps is Being Increasingly Used for Partisan Purposes." *The Diplomat*, May 3. https://thediplomat.com/2021/05/the-indian-foreign-service-must-speak-out-against-growing-politicization/.

7

Digital Diplomacy and International Society in the Age of Populism

Onur Erpul

Introduction

Digital technologies have affected virtually every domain of human life, and diplomacy, the cornerstone of international society and the sine qua non for international order, is no exception. This impact, what we may call the digitalization of diplomacy, lacks a commonly accepted definition (Manor 2017). The digitalization of diplomacy refers on one hand to strictly institutional and organizational changes by focusing on how Internet and Communications Technologies (ICTs) empower (or hinder) diplomacy by creating new capacities and tools for diplomatic agents to communicate with one another and the global public (Manor 2017). On the other hand, the digitalization of diplomacy also reflects deeper, normative aspects of world politics by calling into question the traditional nature of diplomacy as the interactions of an exclusive club of diplomatic agents tasked with promoting their narrowly defined national and common interests. Instead, the digitalization of diplomacy refers to a shift toward an inclusive networked diplomacy in which non-state and private actors can interact with diplomatic agents and affect change on global issues (Heine 2013). Digital diplomacy allows non-hierarchical communication between states and an increasingly active public (Aguirre and

O. Erpul (✉)
The Center for Foreign Policy and Peace Research,
Bilkent University, Ankara, Turkey

Erlandsen 2022, 4). For our purposes, digitalization of diplomacy facilitates and enhances interactions between the international society of states and world society consisting of non-state actors and individuals.

Digital technologies offer considerable advantages for foreign ministries and diplomats communicating their agenda as part of public diplomacy initiatives, enable greater policy transparency, and enhance a state's offline diplomatic policy goals (Adesin and Summers 2017, 2; Bjola 2018; Aguirre and Erlandsen 2022). Despite these obvious advantages, digital diplomacy also has a dark side since the digital world offers plentiful opportunities for potentially harmful actions ranging from state-directed disinformation campaigns to the mobilization of violent non-state actors (Bjola and Pamment 2019). More commonly, and even in benign contexts, back-end diplomatic ruminations may fail to translate into effective front-end diplomatic communication, which, at best, prevents a state from reaching its intended goals and if managed poorly can result in verbal contestation between representatives of states and public audiences. It is at this nexus that digital diplomacy becomes particularly nebulous because social media blur distinctions between diplomacy and domestic politics (Bjola et al. 2020, 19), which operate with different logics. This dual nature of technological advancements (Evans and Commins 2017) is particularly attractive for populist governments that seek to enhance their domestic standing and purposely manufacture online conflicts to mobilize support (Wajner 2021, 663–64). While unlikely to translate into offline diplomatic conflict, the real danger is that by attempting to incorporate the global public audiences, digital diplomacy can indirectly undermine international society by helping to articulate and disseminate transgressive narratives that can gain traction through public engagement.

Trying to assess the impact of digital technologies, and specifically social media, is daunting given the variations in the diplomatic and digital practices of each state. The goal of this chapter is to contribute to the ongoing discussion on the impact of digitalization on diplomacy by investigating digital diplomacy in the context of a populist government that uses its diplomatic capabilities in a dual role. This question is explored in the context of a country that has, at once, a commanding social media presence and a foreign ministry that has become politicized and undermined by growing populism and personalization (Destradi and Plagemann 2019; Uysal and Schroeder 2019; Kaliber and Kaliber 2019; Selçuk et al. 2019).

Investigating the digital diplomatic interactions of Turkey's top official Twitter accounts in the 2016–20 period offers an ideal case study with which to explore the phenomenon of digital diplomacy and its dual role in reaffirming and undermining the idea of international order. Twiplomacy refers to leaders' and their functionaries' use of social media platforms—Twitter, in this case—to communicate with domestic and international audiences (Twiplomacy 2020). Turkey's digital presence steadily grew during this period (Burson et al. 2020), its government employed social media tools to win public support (Saka 2018; Andı et al. 2020), and the country went through domestic and high-profile diplomatic crises with major powers like the U.S. and Russia, which were reflected in Turkey's Twitter interactions (Arapov et al. 2017; Ovalı 2020).

This chapter endeavors to make three contributions. Firstly, it reinforces the notion that while digital diplomacy is a disruptive innovation, its overall impact on diplomacy is neither inherently positive nor negative. Instead, its overall quality and efficacy are set by its practitioners, suggesting that digital diplomatic statecraft indirectly frames positive and transgressive narratives on diplomacy and foreign policy. Secondly, it contextualizes digital diplomacy in terms of its impact on international relations more broadly. Specifically, it builds on the extant discussion of digital technologies on the relationship between states—international society—and the global public and private actors, or "world society" (Lemke and Habegger 2018). This tension is best captured by the English School approach to International Relations (Bull 1977). This perspective envisages for states the possibility of achieving international order through the promotion of mutually held interests through the development of institutions, norms, and practices, of which diplomacy is a vital component (Bull 1977, 63; Buzan 2004; Stivachtis and McKeil 2018). Crucially, institutions need not always promote order but can reinforce points of contention. Diplomacy more generally, and digital diplomacy in this case, exemplifies how practices can bind or divide (Brown 2017, 165–67) international society by indirectly mobilizing the centrifugal forces of world politics. This is because digital diplomacy can amplify ideas and discourses, and frame narratives about international relations (Brown 2017). Rather than fostering a network of responsible citizens that legitimizes a positive agenda on global issues, digital diplomacy can also serve as a platform of uncivil discourse that undermines interstate relations and relations between non-state and private actors across nations. Finally, this chapter contributes to the burgeoning literature on social media use by top official accounts of Turkey, a country whose government has mobilized its diplomatic resources for domestic ends, illustrating the duality of digital diplomacy.

The next section unpacks the literature on digital diplomacy and its implications for international relations, and Turkey's diplomatic practices to situate the duality argument. This is followed by an exploration and discussion of Turkey's twiplomatic activities, followed by a discussion on ideas for enhancing the efficacy of digital diplomacy.

Theoretical Investigations

Digitalization of Diplomacy

Diplomacy is traditionally associated with a closed and hierarchical structure that relies on controlling and moderating interactions through the participation of few actors for the purpose of negotiation and representation among state officials (e.g., Satow 1979; Berridge 2010). Diplomats could engage in diplomatic activities with limited public engagement, meaning that interstate relations, international conflict and cooperation, and interstate interactions were mediated by similarly socialized professionals who shared institutional and personal connections (Heimann and Kampf 2021). A distinct realm of diplomacy helped to maintain international order, reinforce the common values of the society of states (Sofer 2007, 2013, 53), and engender what Bjola (2015, 4–5) calls "change management." The proliferation of democracy in the twentieth century not only allowed but necessitated public involvement in public and international affairs, leading to the spread of public diplomacy (Melissen 2013, 6–9). Public diplomacy was successful not only in setting agendas (top-down) for the broader global public, but also in activating epistemic communities toward addressing global issues and helping to articulate norms and agendas bottom-up. Public diplomacy ultimately aims to help states brand themselves to build and exercise soft power (Nye 2008). In some cases, however, public diplomacy also creates incentives for populism, particularly in instances when diplomatic strategy has been disconnected from public audiences, which allows populists to interject their agendas (Cooper 2019; Surowiec and Miles 2021).

The promises and pitfalls of digital diplomacy can be understood much in the same way. Accounts range from the possibility of achieving a more inclusive and democratic form of diplomacy with the participation of involved and interested stakeholders and enhancing public diplomatic capabilities by helping states to reach global audiences directly, set agendas, and disseminate norms and values (Duncombe 2017; Sotiriu 2015, 36). It could enable much easier connections and communications between diplomatic agents as well. Despite early challenges of adapting to new technologies, such as developing social media capabilities, many Ministries of Foreign Affairs and diplomatic agents were able to adapt to online niches despite the failure of many to progress beyond using social media in traditional ways like bulletins rather than genuinely dialogic instruments (Danziger and Schreiber 2021).

Against the backdrop of these positive developments came the dark side (Bjola and Pamment 2019) of digital diplomacy, which aggravated the problems of public diplomacy. In other words, digital technologies seem to offer some decision-makers incentives to pursue self-aggrandizing rather than primarily diplomatic goals, focusing instead on engaging the public for domestic political reasons and thereby undermining the logic of diplomacy.

These include disinformation, or the purposeful manipulations of states to coercively achieve offline goals, and the role of social media in aiding the mobilization of violent and extremist actors (Walker et al. 2020, 127). The former is particularly concerning for democratic societies since open and pluralistic political culture can be exploited to influence voter behavior as witnessed by Russian interference in the 2016 U.S. elections using ads on social media (Allcott and Gentzkow 2017; Ott 2017). Social media can also aggravate diplomatic relations by facilitating negative communication and various forms of "cheap talk" (Duncombe 2017) to win arguments and depict a particularly favorable image of their state. One also cannot ignore tools like the use of bots and trolls to overwhelm and inundate social mediascapes with a favorable message (Saka 2018). Digital diplomacy is attractive for key authoritative figures and diplomatic agents to communicate their governments' agenda and interests not only to the global public opinion but also to their constituents (Uysal and Schroeder 2019).

In assessing the overall shape of the literature on the problems of digital diplomacy, it is worth reiterating that most of the issues associated with digital diplomacy seem to originate from misuse of public diplomacy or from the purposeful exercise of a maladaptive policy to affect domestic politics more than coercing other states, as is often the case with populist states. On the flip side, states, even populist governments, are more than capable of using digital diplomacy to reinforce common values and reaffirming diplomatic principles when it is convenient to do so. Digital diplomacy's disruptive impact on diplomacy is therefore of a dual nature and its challenges are contingent on the practitioners' preferences. This is also in the nature of diplomacy as a fundamental institution of international society as is discussed in the next section.

Implications of the Digitalization of Diplomacy on International Relations

Diplomacy's traditional function was to serve as a binding agent of international society that facilitated interstate peace, moderated war, and allowed states to articulate and coordinate their common interests (Bull 1977; Sofer

2013; Bjola 2015, 2–4). The exclusive club model of diplomacy could be considered as an exclusive forum allowing the articulation and harmonization of states' competing national interests in favor of *raison de systéme* (Watson 1990, 99–101; Sofer 2013; Terradas 2020), the common interests of states toward coexistence. Diplomacy, particularly the traditional approach, formed at the nexus of institutional practices and agents socialized into a distinct professional ethos that brought together and bound an otherwise disparate and heterogenous group of states (Bull 1977; Buzan, Little, and Jones 1993).

One can interpret subsequent developments in diplomatic practices, such as the evolution of public diplomacy, as an instance of the members of international society intensifying their interactions with one another not only through less formal channels but also indirectly through the mediation of non-state actors. Public diplomacy could, therefore, be interpreted as a way for states to rationally influence one another, legitimize their policies, and reaffirm their commitment to international order. Additionally, public diplomacy can be considered a venue for states to engage with world society (Neumann 2001; Buzan 2004; Stivachtis and McKeil 2018), which is the collective totality of individuals, non-state groups, and their governments. World society is distinct because it is a repository of norms and values pertaining to the collective interests of humanity, as well as those of parochial groups, apart from those that govern traditional diplomacy. One need only consider the tensions between public opinion and the foreign policies as an illustration. Engaging with elements of world society can help states to enhance and legitimize their position in international society. For example, regarding foreign policy, public opinion can contrast with a government and its allies' preferences. In such cases, states can use public diplomacy as a controlled, contained, and civil *habitus* for states to inform or convince international audiences. Likewise, doing so enables the articulation of the interests of world society since public diplomacy offers venues for norm entrepreneurs to positively shape the global agenda (Finnemore 1996).

The advent of digital technologies and the rise of social media have had the effect of increasing the number and intensity of interactions between public officials and diplomats inter se, as well as global public audiences. This function has become even more important in a period marked by rising heterogeneity accompanying the rise of the non-Western world. Diplomatic practices have also evolved to reflect the rising importance of the "low-politics" of trade, human rights, societal developments, and the environment itself (Falkner and Buzan 2019) since the final days of the Cold War and public diplomacy are no exception. Restating the developments in public and digital diplomacy in this lens, the inclusion of non-state actors such as groups and individuals was supposed to promote global solidarity beyond immediate national allegiances and make individuals and groups stakeholders in the articulation of a more encompassing *raison de systéme*. Instead, digital technologies have had a mixed impact. States initially treated social media to exercise soft power (Nye 2008) and engage with common public diplomatic tasks such as informing audiences, legitimizing policies, engaging in nation branding, and engaging in what essentially amounts to propaganda.

Writing on the impact of digital technologies, Lemke and Habegger (2018) note the blurring lines separating international society and world society. The latter potentially has a much greater impact on world politics now that transnational digital communications networks (TDCNs) allow for widespread articulation of ideas and interests, participation of sub-state actors, and transnational mobilization of groups. What the master institution of diplomacy did to enable an international society of states, TDCNs allow by way of facilitating the same interactive and communicative functions that engender the articulation of identities and interests, and mobilization of people and resources. In all respects, then, the digital world can platform and amplify ever more diverse groups and individuals. On one hand, these technologies can work in favor of instilling broader solidarity and promoting democratic values across the globe, which has been a valid normative goal for proponents of cosmopolitanism. On the other, there is no reason to expect that only benign ideologies will flourish since there is ample evidence that TDCNs can amplify those who are discontent with international society and use digital technologies to mobilize violent actors, as in the case of ISIS, for instance (Lemke and Habegger, 311–12). Of course, states are not powerless either way since it is within the power and purview of states to censor or limit access to cyberspace. What remains underexplored is the subtle role that some states play in actively engaging in transgressive contentions and mobilizing intransigent agendas that contradict the values of international society. This makes the institutional choices of governmental entities and the individual decisions of diplomatic agents much more impactful. Depending on how states utilize it, digital diplomacy can be used as either a binding agent that reaffirms the goals of international society, or a dividing practice that underscores short-sighted state interests. The ideal way to explore this duality is through a case study of digital diplomatic practices of a state that engages in both kinds of behavior.

Digital Diplomacy and Turkey

There are several reasons why the Turkish case is useful for understanding the tension between national interest and the broader principles upon which international order lies. To begin with, Turkey is a state in which the foreign ministry has been politicized to accommodate the needs of an assertive and populist government prior to the proliferation of digital diplomacy. Turkey is, moreover, a populous country that enjoys widespread social media consumption, and the Turkish government devotes considerable attention to the exploitation of social media resources (Saka 2018).

Turkey's foreign ministry was once considered to be a largely elitist and exclusive institution that gradually expanded its sociological base (Süleymanoğlu-Kürüm 2021). In the post-Cold War period, Turkey gradually loosened its hawkish foreign policy and underwent a period of democratization in which Turkey's governmental institutions transformed under the auspices of the AKP government (Aydinli and Erpul 2021) in preparation, it was hoped, for EU membership. In addition to the changing demographic and sociological profile of Turkey's governmental institutions, the AKP government took an active role in reframing and instrumentalizing Turkish foreign policy toward domestic ends. This included the Turkish Foreign Ministry itself as then Prime Minister Recep Tayyip Erdoğan often dismissed Turkish diplomats as being out of touch with the rest of Turkish society (Kuru 2019). Well into the AKP government's second term, the Turkish foreign ministry adopted the interstitial practice of annually convening all ambassadors away on missions to attend meetings held in various Turkish cities. While this may have indeed helped to create ties between Turkey's top diplomats and society, instilling a sense of legitimacy in Turkey's foreign policy ahead of Turkey's aggressive soft power foreign policy (Kuru 2019), a far less charitable interpretation could be that this was merely the first step toward politicizing the foreign ministry by way of changing its mission from a foreign and international vocation into a domestic one.

Turkish diplomacy's specific social media track record took shape in a tense environment in which foreign policy came to be dominated by domestic consumption and the traditional role ascribed to Turkish diplomats likewise shifted toward domestic politics, too. This is to say that the Turkish governments' top diplomatic accounts began repeating the escalatory foreign policy discourses of the government on their social media (Benhaïm and Öktem 2015). Uysal and Schroeder (2019), for example, find that Turkey's social media strategy was markedly different from other states with a strong social media presence in that its official accounts targeted domestic and foreign audiences to convey messages, much like a bulletin board. The dialogic and interactive models of diplomatic engagement on social media observed in other cases seem absent in the Turkish case (Danziger and Schreiber 2021). Moreover, they also found that Turkey's social media strategies have increasingly detracted from simply informing audiences to actively engaging in propaganda and aggrandizement in favor of Turkey's president, Erdoğan (Uysal and Schroeder 2019). There is, therefore, strong reason to believe that social media is incentivizing diplomatic practices deleterious to the spirit of diplomacy.

Studying Turkish Diplomacy on Twitter

It is difficult to measure the tangible offline effects of digital diplomacy. Instead, much of the extant literature measures impact through engagement, wherein efficacy is measured through interactivity (Taylor and Kent 2014). Beyond simply measuring the one-way communications of diplomatic agents on social media, the functions on social media sites avail users with different ways of interaction. Twitter, for example, conveniently offers features such as liking/favoriting, replying, and sharing (retweeting), possibly with comments, any given tweet, which allows for a measurement of two-way communication, and which can allow for an analysis of both the positive aspects of public diplomacy online and the negative. Twitter users can articulate and promote some ideas over others and act upon them in real life, particularly in electoral contexts, with the implicit assumption that the content and nature of social media engagements, therefore, have an indirect bearing on influencing broader societal attitudes and, sometimes, electoral outcomes (Bulovsky 2019) since social media (particularly Twitter users) are more likely to be involved in politics and be more vocal and opinionated overall (Andı et al. 2020).

Consistent with this assumption, and with the goal of understanding the representations of the broader goals and interests of international society and parochial interests, this section analyzes the Twitter activity of top Turkish official accounts. The primary dimension involves a simple qualitative content analysis of tweets based on their sentiment. The tweets were categorized and hand-coded as either transgressive (-1), neutral (0), or (1) conciliatory. It is proposed that (1) politically meaningful content is more likely to receive engagements; (2) transgressive tweets are more likely than positive ones to receive engagements from Twitter users; and (3) and neutral tweets that detail merely inform the public about the activities of diplomatic agents and carry non-controversial messages about diplomatic procedures will garner the least interest and engagements.

Transgressive tweets are politically charged messages that derive from a state's parochial interests, exhibiting anti-diplomatic and uncivil qualities. Since the goal of most forms of public and digital diplomacy is to engage foreign audiences, domestically oriented and parochial tweets can be considered undiplomatic. By the same token, direct and hostile engagement with the domestic political actors of another state violates the spirit of the Vienna Conventions and the principles of non-interference in the domestic politics of another state. For example, an ambassador verbally insulting the officials of a receiving state undermines the principles of international society. Defending and justifying internationally controversial state policies can also be considered a contentious message. Finally, being symbolic acts of violence, tweets that contain insults are also included in this category.

Neutral tweets, in the context of this research, take on multiple forms but exemplify the one-way communication that seems to be a hallmark of much of the social media interactions of diplomatic accounts. The so-called bulletin feature of diplomatic institutions seems to account for a majority of twiplomatic activities. Since informing citizens and foreign publics is a major goal of diplomacy, many accounts post notices, advertisements, and other practical information. Moreover, one can expect commonplace functions like positive nation-branding to be within the scope of regular diplomatic engagements (Burke 2017). Diplomatic accounts also like to detail their activities since doing so not only increases transparency but could be considered as being essential to the performance of diplomacy.

Perhaps one of the most important ways in which diplomacy and the notion of international society are reinforced is through moments of expressing solidarity, sorrow, and commemoration (Kampf 2016). While such comments express positive sentiments, they are also expected and seem to exist as yet another item to be checked off a list (Burke 2017). Unless such statements are expressed in the active voice or specifically addressed to a specific person or audience (which would be coded as 1; see below), expressions of solidarity, sorrow, and commemoration were also coded as neutral (0) due to their procedural nature.

Finally, positive tweets also express a political message but ones that are consistent with the broader interests of international society. These interactions express positive framing about developments in world politics, the relations of the state, and positive statements about projections in a country's foreign relations. Meanwhile, interpersonal communication is also an important component of public diplomacy, and active affirmation to a target person or audience (i.e., "my colleague, the American people, my brothers from x country") so was also coded as positive (1) tweets. While focusing on English-language tweets enables the possibility of performing many detailed content analyses of various dimensions, including a sentiment analysis, the context-sensitive nature of diplomatic tweets necessitated hand-coding by the researcher.

The abovementioned framework is explored in the context of Turkey. With an inclusive view of which agents can engage in digital diplomacy, there is a host of promising accounts that speak on behalf of Turkey in a diplomatic capacity. For the purposes of this research, however, the most important accounts, which also have the greatest number of followers, were selected. Given the size of Turkey's digital diplomatic presence, it is not surprising that President Erdoğan is among the top most-followed Twitter accounts with ~19 million followers as of 2022. Other prominent accounts include Mevlüt Çavuşoğlu, the Turkish Minister of Foreign Affairs, the English account of the Turkish Ministry of Foreign Affairs, and the official accounts of the Turkish Embassy in Washington, D.C., and its ambassador, Serdar Kılıç (2013–20). The foreign ministry, foreign minister, and presidential accounts, for example, showcase an extraordinary social media prominence by their sheer numbers alone. The Turkish Embassy in Washington, D.C. and the Turkish ambassador to the U.S., meanwhile, were selected as this diplomatic mission is Turkey's most important, stemming not only from American preeminence and their commonalities as NATO allies, but controversially because of recent vicissitudes in the bilateral relations of the two countries.

The data was extracted from Twitter and covers all English-language messages tweeted by these accounts in the period from September 2016 to December 2020. This is a broad period, but one that offers notable advantages to illustrate the ideas advanced in this chapter. Firstly, it was a period in which Twitter started to gain traction among officials in Turkey. Secondly, this period also covers a controversial period in Turkish politics that saw a fundamental transformation in the political structure of the country in the aftermath of a failed coup attempt (Esen and Gümüşçü 2018). It is worth noting that the analysis begins in September 2016, more than a full month after the coup attempt, to prevent skew in the data since this traumatic event received significant attention on social media and elsewhere. Finally, every official position under scrutiny in this analysis remained constant for the period. It showcases ample instances of domestic political issues featuring in Twitter communications, as well as many instances of hostile communications and rhetoric.

Turkish Twiplomacy by the Numbers

It is clear from the over-time changes of each account that active social media usage is important as evidenced by the growing number of tweets per year for each account. Of the 9273 total tweets extracted from the Twitter accounts in the 2016–20 period, only 3976 are in English. Table 7.1 (see Appendix) displays the year-by-year breakdown of the tweets. Starting with their common features, the first striking feature is the steady rise in the overall number of tweets for each of these accounts, which suggests a recognition of the importance of digital diplomacy by official actors. For example, the president's number of tweets increased by an average of 110 percent annually between 2016–20; the Foreign Ministry's official English account by an annual average of 68 percent; the foreign minister by 33.44 percent; the Turkish embassy in D.C. by 112 percent; and the Turkish ambassador by 111.5 percent. Looking specifically at their breakdown language-wise, there are no discernible changes in ratios despite the overall rise in numbers of tweets, with the only exceptions being Erdoğan's account, which showcases a steady decline in English to Turkish tweets from a ratio of 0.19 in 2016 to 0.02 in 2020, and the Turkish ambassador's rising ratio of English tweets from 0.23 in 2016 to 0.81 in 2020. These findings are not strange given the importance of communicating with domestic audiences and citizens abroad, although the high and rising incidence of Turkish tweets in bilingual accounts demonstrates a social media primarily concerned with domestic rather than international audiences.

Applying the sentiment framework to the tweets intended for international audiences (i.e., English tweets) reveals interesting trends. The following analysis is conducted by measuring the mean number of likes for each type of tweet posted by accounts. Figures 7.1, 7.2, 7.3, 7.4, and 7.5 and Table 7.2 display the means of engagements each account received from their tweets. Overall, transgressive tweets made up 348 (8.75 percent), positive tweets 406 (10.21 percent), and neutral tweets 3222 (81.03 percent) of the total (n = 3976). In all cases, tweets with politically significant content, be it transgressive or positive, received significantly more attention than neutral tweets.

Figure 7.1 shows that, of the 819 tweets by the minister of foreign affairs, transgressive tweets made up the minority of tweets at n = 48 and positive ones the majority at n=164. The former, however, received a mean number of 2696.19 likes while the latter received a mean average of 1241.817 per positive tweet (neutral tweets only received a mean of 379.01 likes per neutral tweet). Figure 7.2 offers an interesting contrast in terms of the number of overall likes. Despite a significantly higher number of tweets (n = 2144), transgressive (n = 46) and positive (n = 86) tweets are rare. However, when

7 Digital Diplomacy and International Society in the Age of Populism 155

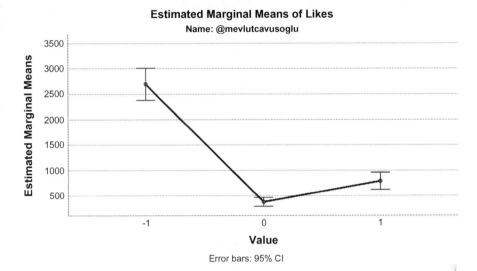

Fig. 7.1 Estimated marginal means of likes (Turkish Minister of Foreign Affairs, 9.2016–12.2020)

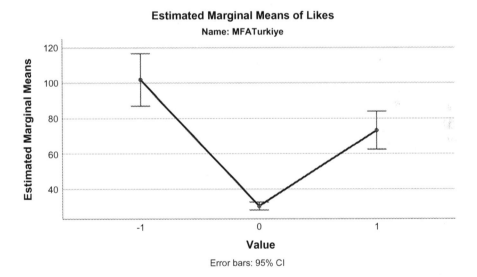

Fig. 7.2 Estimated marginal means of likes (Turkish Ministry of Foreign Affairs, 9.2016–12.2020)

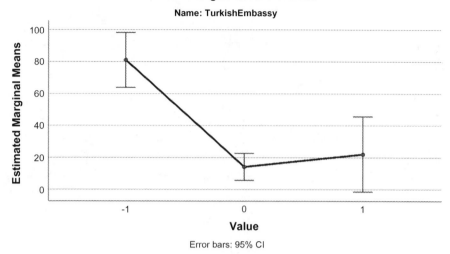

Fig. 7.3 Estimated marginal means of likes (Turkish Embassy, Washington, D.C.), 9.2016–12.2020)

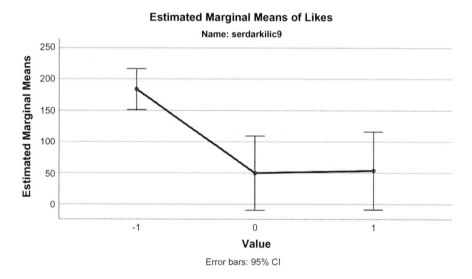

Fig. 7.4 Estimated marginal means of likes (Serdar Kılıç, Turkish Ambassador, Washington, D.C.), 9.2016–12.2020)

Twitter likes are accounted for transgressive tweets receive an average of 101.91 likes, positive tweets 73.19, and neutral ones 30.3.

Turkey's social media strategies via its Embassy in Washington, D.C., and its ambassador's tweets in Figs. 7.3 and 7.4 paint a similar picture. The embassy posted 772 tweets with 138 transgressive tweets, 73 positive tweets, and 561

7 Digital Diplomacy and International Society in the Age of Populism

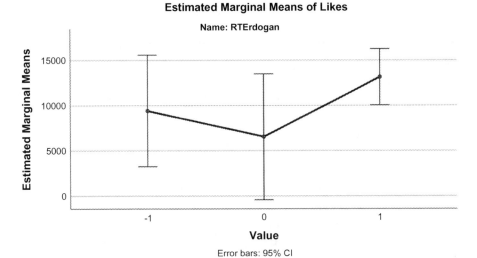

Fig. 7.5 Estimated marginal means of likes (Recep Tayyip Erdoğan)

neutral ones. While neutral tweets make up the bulk of the total, given the practical need for an embassy to engage in traditional one-way communication with expats and host country citizens, transgressive tweets dwarf positive ones in both number and engagements at a mean number of 81.03 likes per transgressive, 52.554 likes per positive, and 20.54 likes per neutral tweets. The Turkish Ambassador's tweets reveal a similar trend, except that most tweets (n = 102) are transgressive with a mean number of 183.85 likes per tweet. By contrast, the 28 positive and 31 neutral tweets have mean likes of 53.61 and 49.77, respectively. The findings on Turkish diplomatic Twitter unambiguously reflect the ongoing bilateral tensions. In fact, some of the most outstanding topics include disagreements over the United States' aid to YPG/PKK, Turkey's military operations in Syria, and engagements with American domestic political actors on the topic of Turkey's domestic and foreign policies. The overall political context seems to have a large impact on the quality and breakdown of the tweets.

On the subject of transgressive tweets, the Turkish president's online presence offers yet another interesting contrast. Erdoğan's Twitter account has far more followers compared to the other accounts in the study (and is among the top most followed accounts on Twitter). Compared to the other accounts, the ratio of English tweets is minuscule (at an annual average of 0.04). Moreover, of the few (n = 80) English tweets, most (n = 55) carry positive messages compared to transgressive (n = 14) and neutral (n = 11) tweets. When combined with the president's larger follower base, the mean average likes for each category of tweets are 9425.43 for transgressive, 6547.91 for neutral, and 13,153.29 for positive tweets. In other words, Turkey's top Twitter account features few tweets targeting international audiences. These are, however, mostly positive in their content and receive comparatively high levels of engagement. Perhaps this can be interpreted as a division of labor among Turkey's top official accounts that also reflects the rising personalism in foreign policy. The presidential account largely focuses on conveying positive sentiments to followers while the task of engaging in transgressive politics falls to other accounts.

These findings corroborate some of the ideas floating around in the literature on the modus operandi of Turkish Twitter accounts and rising personalism in Turkey's social media as a broader reflection on Turkish politics. More importantly, however, is the inescapable fact that politically meaningful engagements, rather than passive and neutral one-way communications, are far more impactful. One could also infer a cultural logic to the behaviors of diplomatic accounts. Proactivity and assertiveness are vaunted qualities, especially in contexts where foreign policy and even the foreign policy institutions of a country are pressured for populist reasons (Kissas 2020). There are strong incentives to politicize public diplomacy and digital technologies, and social media enable both transgressive and positive messages.

What to Do?

One takeaway from the analysis is that neutral and non-political messages seem not to garner as much interest. Perhaps it is a form of public apathy to the perceived proceduralism of most of the neutral diplomatic content that seems to lack emotional heft (Burke 2017). This is not to trivialize this one-way form of communication: it is important and continues to form the bulk of twiplomacy. It does show that digital diplomacy can potentially reach broad audiences, seize public attention, and articulate ideas about international relations to which the public can react and formulate their ideas around. Digital technologies are adding a further layer of complication to institutions already struggling with the task of meaningfully reaching out to and engaging with public audiences. Propaganda, fake news, and extremist mobilization have more tangible offline consequences than the online words of diplomats and politicians. This does not mean, however, that authoritative actors do not indirectly exercise influence over their followers, which is why caution and responsibility are necessary.

The main problem, of course, is that diplomatic concerns are secondary to domestic politics, and the extent to which "cheap talk," "propaganda," or "trolling" behavior are problems for diplomacy depends on the policy priorities of states. This also very likely precludes the possibility of an actionable plan to mitigate the potential pitfalls of digital diplomacy. States and practitioners could theoretically enter into a gentlemen's agreement or codify principles of online conduct to remove undesirable hostility and incivility, but this is neither likely nor desirable since it runs counter to the logic of online engagement, inclusivity, and the free expression of opposing ideas and interests.

There is, however, an obvious solution. Practitioners of digital diplomacy can use their positions to reaffirm positive messages, follow up transgressive or controversial messages with conciliatory ones, and use their platforms to contest the national interest without abandoning civility. The goal would always be to restore dialog premised on civil discourse and conclude on high notes when engaging in personal dialogue with other officials. The need to condense information, particularly for media like Twitter, and the need to react quickly to developments further complicate digital diplomacy. All this is to say that social media literacy and training, combined with a commitment to principled, meaningful, and responsible social media usage, appear to be the most viable ways to moderate transgressive content and benefit from digital diplomacy. As the chapter showed, positive comments that address key issues, offer tangible projections, or even feature active personal communication are better. This is sorely needed given that global politics are becoming less accommodating of liberal, democratic, and cosmopolitan values.

Lessons from Digital Diplomacy for Future Diplomats

The digitalization of diplomacy portends neither failure nor success and its impact is mediated by the preferences of its practitioners. The analysis above suggests an additional nuance. Transgressive content may be detrimental to the spirit of diplomacy, but it is as much a part of international life as it is of social media. Emotionally charged content (Manfredi et al. 2022, 209) serves an important role in communicating disinformation and propaganda. Given the parameters of the medium (Twitter), it is easy to infer an incentive structure favoring officials' abuse of social media to promote parochial and national goals, attract further public interest, and indirectly promote uncivil discourse.

From an institutional perspective, the findings suggest that the kind of impersonal and bulletin-like nature of the Foreign Ministry's social media garners less interest based on Twitter interactions. While unsurprising given the increasing tendency toward personalization, one can infer that a foreign ministry (ministries in general) in such a situation could enhance their online presence by creating unique content designed to repeat and reinforce positive discourses. So long as an institutional account can resonate emotionally and personally, it would enhance the credibility and popularity of the institution, and even appear to the public as a more neutral and authoritative source for information and forum for public engagement.

As for diplomats, one dismaying conclusion could be that there is not much that diplomats can do in this new digital habitus affected by populism. Diplomats tend not to enjoy favorable reputations in many societies and have been targeted by their public and governments as being appeasers or being out of touch with the societies they represent (Kuru 2019; Sofer 2013). Nowhere are these dynamics more visible than in Turkey, and one can speculate that the past dysfunctional relationship between Turkey's diplomatic institutions and populist government will incentivize more online controversy in the future.

These findings, however, are applicable to some of Turkey's major social media accounts in a very specific context. This study is limited due to its scope and conditions, such as focusing on a single country and the strategies of the most highly followed accounts. Extending the analysis to Twitter accounts of missions to other countries, particularly those with proportionally larger numbers of Turkish citizens, or countries with which Turkey enjoys comparatively amicable relations, could have yielded different results. By the same token, the framework could be further tested against the experiences of other countries. Future research can be extended to include other countries and contexts by looking at differences between states based on the regime and the state's qualities, nature of bilateral relations, and other contingent factors. In Turkey's case, exploring additional cases in the form of added diplomatic missions to other prominent states could help to discern more evident general patterns and deviations in Turkey's digital media strategies. Meanwhile, an analysis of the behaviors of foreign missions and mission heads in Turkey under the same premise and framework could yield valuable cross-national data. This could also help to discern differences in the attitudes of social media users who follow diplomatic accounts based on their proclivity to engage with content projecting different kinds of sentiments.

Acknowledgements I would like to thank Hicran Erol and Beyzanur Gençer for their hard work and assistance in helping me gather the data for this research.

7 Digital Diplomacy and International Society in the Age of Populism

Appendix

Table 7.1 Breakdown of tweets by numbers (*n* English tweets = 3976, Turkish tweets = 5089, total *n* = 9056)

Ministry of Foreign Affairs @MFATurkiye					
	Turkish	English	Total	Ratio	Percent change
2016	0	122	122	N/A	N/A
2017	22	394	416	0.06	240.98
2018	19	431	450	0.04	8.17
2019	23	575	598	0.04	32.89
2020	18	621	639	0.03	6.86
Total/Av.	82	2143	2225	0.04	68.44
Minister of Foreign Affairs (Mevlüt Çavuşoğlu) @MevlutCavusoglu					
	Turkish	English	Total	Ratio	Percent change
2016	235	145	380	0.62	N/A
2017	394	191	585	0.48	53.95
2018	461	165	626	0.36	7.01
2019	793	208	1001	0.26	59.90
2020	812	318	1130	0.39	12.89
Total/Av.	2695	1027	3722	0.42	33.44
President (Recep Tayyip Erdoğan) @RTErdogan					
	Turkish	English	Total	Ratio	Percent change
2016	70	13	83	0.19	N/A
2017	358	27	385	0.08	363.86
2018	270	10	280	0.04	−27.27
2019	481	19	500	0.04	78.57
2020	621	11	632	0.02	26.40
Total/Av.	1800	80	1880	0.07	110.39
TR Embassy Washington, D.C. @TurkishEmbassy					
	Turkish	English	Total	Ratio	Percent change
2016	5	33	38	6.6	N/A
2017	56	105	161	1.88	323.68
2018	29	112	141	3.86	−12.42
2019	52	329	381	6.33	170.21
2020	65	194	259	2.98	−32.02
Total/Av.	207	773	980	4.33	112.36
Ambassador, Washington, D.C. @serdarkilic9					
	Turkish	English	Total	Ratio	Percent change
2016	31	7	38	0.23	N/A
2017	66	34	100	0.52	364
2018	64	19	83	0.3	−27
2019	70	41	111	0.59	79
2020	74	60	134	0.81	26
Total/Av.	305	161	466	0.49	111.50

Table 7.2 Estimated marginal means

	"@Cavusoglu"			"@mfa"			"@RTErdogan"			"@serdarkilic9"			"@turkishembassy"			Total	Total percent
Value	Mean	Std. deviation	N	Mean	Std. deviation	N	Mean	Std. deviation	N	Mean	Std. deviation	N	Mean	Std. deviation	N		
−1	2696.19	3516.123	48	101.91	169.970	46	9425.43	11475.242	14	183.85	206.552	102	81.03	236.498	138	348	8.752515
0	379.02	417.381	607	30.43	41.939	2012	6547.91	4913.750	11	49.77	41.542	31	14.16	20.548	561	3222	81.03622
1	789.12	1419.406	164	73.19	96.946	86	13153.29	12457.943	55	53.61	53.062	28	22.03	52.554	73	406	10.21127
Total	596.95	1241.817	819	33.68	52.939	2144	11592.68	11699.713	80	135.39	178.376	161	26.85	105.584	772	3976	

References and Further Reading

Adesin, O.S., and J. Summers (Reviewing Editor). 2017. "Foreign Policy in an Era of Digital Diplomacy." *Cogent Social Sciences* 3 (1).

Aguirre, D.A., and M. Erlandsen. 2022. "Digital Public Diplomacy in Latin America: Challenges and Opportunities." *Revista Mexicana De Política Exterior* (113): 1–17.

Allcott, H., and M. Gentzkow. 2017. "Social Media and Fake News in the 2016 Election." *Journal of Economic Perspectives* 31 (2): 211–36.

Andı, S., S.E. Aytaç, and A. Çarkoğlu. 2020. "Internet and Social Media Use and Political Knowledge: Evidence from Turkey." *Mediterranean Politics* 25 (5): 579–99.

Arapov, S., T. Dadabaev, and C. Laumulin. 2017. "The Use of Digital Diplomacy as a Tool for Symbolic Violence: Framing Analysis of Russian–Turkish Relations on Twitter: Symbolic Violence in the Context of Social Media Diplomacy." *Cambridge Journal of Eurasian Studies* 1 (March): 1–16.

Aydinli, E., and O. Erpul. 2021. "Elite Change and the Inception, Duration, and Demise of the Turkish–Israeli Alliance." *Foreign Policy Analysis* 17 (2).

Benhaïm, Y., and K. Öktem. 2015. "The Rise and Fall of Turkey's Soft Power Discourse: Discourse in Foreign Policy under Davutoğlu and Erdoğan." *European Journal of Turkish Studies* 25.

Berridge, G.R. 2010. "Public Diplomacy." In *Diplomacy: Theory and Practice*, ed. G.R. Berridge, 179–91. Houndmills: Palgrave Macmillan.

Bjola, C. 2015. "Introduction: Making Sense of Digital Diplomacy." In *Digital Diplomacy: Theory and Practice*, eds. C. Bjola and M. Holmes, 1–10. New York: Routledge.

———. 2018. "The 'Dark Side' of Digital Diplomacy: Countering Disinformation and Propaganda." https://www.realinstitutoelcano.org/en/analyses/the-dark-side-of-digital-diplomacy-countering-disinformation-and-propaganda/.

Bjola, C., and J. Pamment, eds. 2019. "Introduction: The Dark Side of Digital Diplomacy." In *Countering Online Propaganda and Extremism: The Dark Side of Digital Diplomacy*. Routledge New Diplomacy Studies, eds. C. Bjola and J. Pamment, 1–10. London: Routledge.

Bjola, C., J.A. Cassidy, and I. Manor. 2020. "Digital Public Diplomacy: Business as Usual or a Paradigm Shift?" In *Routledge Handbook of Public Diplomacy*, eds. C. Bjola and M. Holmes, 2nd ed., 111–26. London and New York: Routledge.

Brown, R. 2017. "Public Diplomacy, Networks, and the Limits of Strategic Narratives." In *Forging the World: Strategic Narratives and International Relations*, eds. A. Miskimmon, B. O'Loughlin, and L. Roselle, 164–89. Ann Arbor: University of Michigan Press.

Bull, H. 1977. *The Anarchical Society: A Study of Order in World Politics*. New York: Columbia University Press.

Bulovsky, A. 2019. "Authoritarian Communication on Social Media: The Relationship between Democracy and Leaders' Digital Communicative Practices." *International Communication Gazette* 81 (1): 20–45.

Burke, R. 2017. "Emotional Diplomacy and Human Rights at the United Nations." *Human Rights Quarterly*, 39 (2), 273–95.

Burson, Cohn, and Wolfe, Ltd. 2020. *Twiplomacy 2020*, November 17. https://tinyurl.com/1tsyzkui

Buzan, B. 2004. *From International to World Society? English School Theory and the Social Structure of Globalization.* Cambridge: Cambridge University Press.

Buzan, B., R. Little, and C. Jones. 1993. "The Logic of Anarchy: Neorealism to Structural Realism." In *The Logic of Anarchy*, eds. B. Buzan, R. Little, and C. Jones, 132–53. New York: Columbia University Press.

Cooper, A.F. 2013. *The Changing Nature of Diplomacy*. Oxford: Oxford University Press.

———. 2019. "Adapting Public Diplomacy to the Populist Challenge." *The Hague Journal of Diplomacy* 14 (1–2): 36–50.

Danziger, R., and M. Schreiber. 2021. "Digital Diplomacy: Face Management in MFA Twitter Accounts." *Policy & Internet* 14 (3): 586–605.

Destradi, S., and J. Plagemann. 2019. "Populism and International Relations: (Un)predictability, Personalisation, and the Reinforcement of Existing Trends in World Politics." *Review of International Studies* 45 (5): 711–30.

Duncombe, C. 2017. "Twitter and Transformative Diplomacy: Social Media and Iran–US Relations." *International Affairs* 93 (3): 545–62.

Esen, B., and S. Gümüşçü. 2018. "The Perils of 'Turkish Presidentialism.'" *Review of Middle East Studies* 52 (1): 43–53.

Evans, N.G., and A. Commins. 2017. "Defining Dual-Use Research: When Scientific Advances Can Both Help and Hurt Humanity." *The Conversation*, February 3. https://theconversation.com/defining-dual-use-research-when-scientific-advances-can-both-help-and-hurt-humanity-70333.

Falkner, R., and B. Buzan. 2019. "The Emergence of Environmental Stewardship as a Primary Institution of Global International Society." *European Journal of International Relations,* 25 (1), 131–55.

Finnemore, M. 1996. "Norms, Culture, and World Politics: Insights from Sociology's Institutionalism." *International Organization* 50 (2): 325–47.

Heimann, G., and Z. Kampf. 2021. "What Makes Them Tick: Challenging the Impersonal Ethos in International Relations." *Cooperation and Conflict* 56 (3): 346–63.

Heine, J. 2013. "From Club to Network Diplomacy." In *The Oxford Handbook of Modern Diplomacy*, eds. A.F. Cooper, J. Heine, and R. Thakur, 54–69. Oxford: Oxford University Press.

Kaliber, A., and E. Kaliber. 2019. "From De-Europeanisation to Anti-Western Populism: Turkish Foreign Policy in Flux." *International Spectator* 54 (4): 1–16.

Kampf, Z. 2016. "All the Best! Performing Solidarity in Political Discourse." *Journal of Pragmatics* 93 (5): 47–60.

Kissas, A. 2020. "Performative and Ideological Populism: The Case of Charismatic Leaders on Twitter." *Discourse & Society* 31 (3): 268–84.

Kuru, D. 2019. "Back at Home: The Ambassadors Conference as an Interstitial Practice." *Global Affairs* 5 (4–5): 295–313.

Lemke, T., and M.W. Habegger. 2018. "A Master Institution of World Society? Digital Communications Networks and the Changing Dynamics of Transnational Contention." *International Relations* 32 (3): 296–320.

Manfredi, J.L., A. Amado, and P. Gómez-Iniesta. 2022. "State Disinformation: Emotions at the Service of the Cause." *Communications Society* 35 (2): 205–21.

Manor, I. 2017. "The Digitalization of Diplomacy: Toward Clarification of a Fractured Terminology." Working Paper. Exploring Digital Diplomacy.

———. 2019. *The Digitalization of Public Diplomacy*. Cham: Springer.

Melissen, J. 2013. "Public Diplomacy." In *The Oxford Handbook of Modern Diplomacy*, eds. A.F. Cooper, J. Heine, and R. Thakur, 436–52. Oxford: Oxford University Press.

Neumann, I.B. 2001. "The English School and the Practices of World Society." *Review of International Studies* 27 (3): 503–7.

Nye, J.S. 2008. "Public Diplomacy and Soft Power." *ANNALS of the American Academy of Political and Social Science* 616 (1): 94–109.

Ott, B.L. 2017. "The Age of Twitter: Donald J. Trump and the Politics of Debasement." *Critical Studies in Media Communication* 34 (1): 59–68.

Ovalı, A.S. 2020. "Turkiye-ABD İlişkilerinde Twitter Diplomasisi." *Uluslararası İliskiler Dergisi* 17 (65): 23–45.

Saka, E. 2018. "Social Media in Turkey as a Space for Political Battles: AKTrolls and Other Politically Motivated Trolling." *Middle East Critique* 27 (2): 161–77.

Satow, E. 1979. *Satow's Guide to Diplomatic Practice*. 5th ed. London and New York: Longman.

Selçuk, O., D. Hekimci, and O. Erpul. 2019. "The Erdoğanization of Turkish Politics and the Role of the Opposition." *Southeast European and Black Sea Studies* 19 (4): 541–64.

Sofer, S. 2007. "The Diplomatic Corps as a Symbol of Diplomatic Culture." In *The Diplomatic Corps as an Institution of International Society*, eds. P. Sharpe and G. Wiseman, 31–38. London: Palgrave Macmillan.

———. 2013. *The Courtiers of Civilization: A Study of Diplomacy*. Albany: SUNY Press.

Sotiriu, S. 2015. "Digital Diplomacy: Between Promises and Reality." In *Digital Diplomacy*, eds. C. Bjola and M. Holmes, 33–51. London and New York: Routledge.

Stivachtis, Y.A., and A. McKeil. 2018. "Conceptualizing World Society." *International Politics* 55 (1): 1–10.

Süleymanoğlu-Kürüm, R. 2021. "The Sociology of Diplomats and Foreign Policy Sector: The Role of Cliques on the Policy-Making Process." *Political Studies Review* 19 (4), 558–73.

Surowiec, P., and C. Miles. 2021. "The Populist Style and Public Diplomacy: Kayfabe as Performative Agonism in Trump's Twitter Posts." *Public Relations Inquiry* 10 (1): 5–30.

Taylor, M., and M.L. Kent. 2014. "Dialogic Engagement: Clarifying Foundational Concepts." *Journal of Public Relations Research* 26 (5), 384–98.

Terradas, N. 2020. "The Quest for Order in Anarchical Societies: Anthropological Investigations." *International Studies Review* 22 (1): 98–121.

Twiplomacy Study. 2020. https://twiplomacy.com/blog/twiplomacy-study-2020/.

Uysal, N., and J. Schroeder. 2019. "Turkey's Twitter Public Diplomacy: Towards a 'New' Cult of Personality." *Public Relations Review* 45 (5): 1018–37.

Wajner, D.F. 2021. "Exploring the Foreign Policies of Populist Governments: (Latin) America First." *Journal of International Relations and Development* 24 (3): 651–80.

Walker, C., S. Kalathil, and J. Ludwig. 2020. "The Cutting Edge of Sharp Power." *Journal of Democracy* 31 (1): 124–37.

Watson, A. 1990. "Systems of States." *Review of International Studies* 16 (2): 99–109.

8

Withering Ministry of Foreign Affairs: Evidence from China

Qingmin Zhang and Lize Yang

The Ministry of Foreign Affairs (MFA) is the core component of modern governance in coordinating domestic and international affairs, and serves as the hub and institutional guarantee for the overall national diplomatic system and processes. Its history exemplifies the evolving features, and its current situation manifests the challenges, of diplomacy. This chapter examines the challenges facing diplomacy through the lens of the Chinese MFA.

China's MFA was chosen as a case study not only to provide a restricted view of the challenges facing diplomacy, but also to address the serious disconnect between international diplomatic scholarship and Chinese diplomatic studies. It has been the tradition of Chinese diplomatic scholars to treat China as so exceptional that they rarely place their research in the larger context of global diplomatic scholarship. It is easy to understand Chinese scholars doing so (Bai 2009; Gong et al. 2009; Zhao 2012). However, the same is true of international scholars who study Chinese diplomacy. For instance, David Lampton, a leading scholar of China's foreign policy and diplomacy, who has keenly observed trends in Chinese diplomacy of "globalization,"

Q. Zhang (✉)
Peking University, Beijing, China

L. Yang
Sun-Yat Sen University, Zhuhai, China

© The Author(s), under exclusive license to Springer Nature Switzerland AG 2023
P. W. Hare et al. (eds.), *The Palgrave Handbook of Diplomatic Reform and Innovation*, Studies in Diplomacy and International Relations, https://doi.org/10.1007/978-3-031-10971-3_8

"professionalism," "pluralization," and "decentralization" (Lampton 1999, 1–33) drew no insight from the international scholarly community on diplomacy in his work. This is bizarre, considering how deeply China has been integrated into the international community.

Scholars in the field of diplomatic theory have not placed China within the scope of their research due to language and cultural barriers. The existing international literature on MFAs rarely addresses the Chinese case (Hocking, eds. 1999; Lequesne, ed. 2022). This is unfortunate considering that China's proactive diplomacy as well as its rising economic clout provide a gold mine for empirical studies. The lack of communication and cross-fertilization between the two groups has drawn the attention of scholars on both sides, who have recently called for attention to the mutual benefits of their interactions.[1] This chapter is such an effort.

As a prominent institution at the heart of state diplomacy, academia has conducted research on the MFA from different perspectives. We intend to conduct a content analysis of the transcripts of the Chinese MFA spokesperson's response to media questions at its regular press conference in order to answer the following questions: What are the challenges facing the Chinese MFA? How does the Chinese government address them? Are these challenges and measures to address them specific to China or are they common features?

MFA and Its Spokesperson System

Compared to the long history of diplomacy, the MFA is comparatively young. According to Harold Nicolson, a pioneer in the study of diplomacy, the MFA was established in 1626 by Cardinal Richelieu to centralize "all responsibilities within the Ministry of External Affairs" (Nicolson 1954, 53). It soon became the hub of liaison and leadership for institutions functioning abroad. As Article 41 of the *Vienna Convention on Diplomatic Relations* stipulates, "All official business with the receiving State entrusted to the mission by the sending State shall be conducted with or through the MFA of the receiving State or such other ministry as may be agreed" (UN 1961).

The international literature on diplomatic studies shows that MFA is the most sensitive part of the diplomatic institution to social changes and has become outspoken in its criticism of diplomacy. After the end of the Cold War, the MFA became more important with the renaissance of diplomacy, but its "credibility" was "questioned" (Hocking 2013). At the turn of the last

---

[1] "Special Issue: China's Global Diplomacy." 2021. *The Hague Journal of Diplomacy* 16, nos. 2–3.

century, the MFA was taunted as the "ministry for foreigners" (Hocking 1998, 171). A decade ago, another study opined that "foreign ministries are at a tipping point between becoming more relevant than ever before and becoming irrelevant as other agencies step into the foreign policy arena" (Netherlands MFA 2011).

The case of China tells a similar story. Criticism of Chinese diplomacy has a long history. Recent criticisms include that China's diplomacy has been too "soft" and "deficient in calcium." A consistent target of criticism of China's diplomacy is the Chinese foreign service profession, which is alleged to be "monopolized and controlled by translators" and whose diplomatic personality is completely distorted by "translation diplomacy" (Hou 2014). More recently, the Chinese MFA has even been referred to domestically as the "sell-out ministry" (Li 1999, 322).

This chapter takes the information department or spokesperson system of MFA as a testing ground, reflecting how MFA has adapted to social development to keep pace with the times. In its early stages, diplomacy was always closely tied to secrecy, conspiracy, and detective work. It became a public interest after the advent of newspapers in the 1830s, when the media was unscrupulous in its efforts to obtain information about diplomacy, regardless of time and occasion. U.S. President Andrew Jackson (in office from 1829–37) was annoyed by the endless media skepticism and is said to have been the first leader to set up a special position of spokesperson as a personal assistant to the president to deal with the relentless interest of the media. After World War I, U.S. President Woodrow Wilson officially set up a presidential spokesperson to promote open diplomacy. After World War II, major countries around the world followed in the U.S.' footsteps and established a press release system with a spokesperson (Zou 2005, 62–63).

The emergence and evolution of China's MFA spokesperson system mirror the changing process of China's diplomatic institution. In the early stages of the establishment of the People's Republic of China (PRC), there was a spokesperson for the Chinese delegation attending international conferences in the 1950s. However, this system did not last long until after China opened up to the outside world in the late 1970s (Qian 2003, 4–6). On March 1, 1983, the Director-General of the Information Department of MFA informed the media that the Chinese MFA has since established a spokesperson system (Zou 2005, 62–63). Its main functions have been expanded and today it is "responsible for releasing information on China's major diplomatic events and clarifying China's foreign policy" and "managing the press coverage of major diplomatic events" (MFA, the Information Department 2022).

One of the major venues for the spokesperson to release information on China's diplomacy is the regular press conference, which has increased from once a week in the 1980s to twice a week in the late 1990s and early part of this century, and to every weekday today. In its initial stages, the spokesperson issued information only on a "no questions, no answers." Gradually, it has not only released information on diplomatic activities and elaborated on China's foreign policy on major issues, but also answered questions on the "unlimited number of questions from the press" today. Since the establishment of the spokesperson system, diplomacy has been placed under public scrutiny.

As stories about Chinese diplomacy increasingly dominate the headlines in China's official media, the MFA spokesperson is quickly garnering attention both at home and abroad. Li Zhaoxing, who served as the MFA spokesperson before he became the Foreign Minister, shared a story in a lecture at Peking University about how the average Chinese person perceives the MFA spokesperson. When he returned to his hometown as Foreign Minister, one of his childhood neighbors, knowing that Li was Foreign Minister, encouraged him to work harder so that he could be promoted to the position of MFA spokesperson in the future. The aggressive foreign propaganda and fighting spirit demonstrated in categorically rejecting any external criticism of China for its management of the COVID-19 virus, the domestic human rights record, and tough policy on Hong Kong have earned Chinese diplomats a nickname, "wolf warrior" (Ye 2020). The current spokesperson, Zhao Lijian, is known worldwide as one of China's top "wolf warrior" diplomats, which has greatly enhanced the spokesperson's international visibility (Martin 2021).

The questions raised by the media at the press conference reflect the public's interest in and concern about China's diplomacy. The answers given by the spokesperson and the news released by the spokesperson at the regular press conference are considered to be the official and authoritative policy and the main sources of media coverage of China's diplomacy. As students of China's diplomacy, we note with interest that in recent years, the MFA spokesperson has always responded to media questions in the following way: "I don't have any information to give you in this aspect," "I am not aware of the situation at the moment," "Please refer to the department in charge," "I have no information about it," and so on. Borrowing from the metaphor of radar and gastroscopy, we regard such questions involving the answers of the MFA spokesperson as information "blind spots." Our interest turned to frustration and triggered this research when the situation of the MFA spokesperson's inability to provide information rose to a kind of "new normal."

Some insiders have suggested that such answers may be an example of "diplomatic language." That is, the spokesperson may not have been authorized to provide the information, or the issue may have been too sensitive, or they may not have been prepared to answer the questions (Zou 2005, 145–47). However, as outsiders, we do not know the exact reasons behind each of these "blind spots." We assume that the distribution and changing patterns should reflect the diverse trends and characteristics of China's diplomatic development. In other words, it should offer clues as to who is undermining or challenging the authority of China's MFA, and whether the Chinese government has taken any measures, or what has been done, to address these issues.

Distribution Patterns of Blind Spots

The Chinese MFA has released a transcript of all regular press conferences since 2002. To study the most recent changes, we selected those from January 10, 2002, to December 31, 2019, as the basic material for our content analysis. Going through a statistical and classification of all answers to media questions by MFA spokespeople during this period, we found a total of 2552 instances in which MFA spokesmen were unable to provide information or referred the media to other relevant departments. Among them, the responses to questions related to Hong Kong, cross-strait relations, Tibet, and domestic social issues appeared a total of 318 times. In view of the domestic nature of these questions, China's diplomacy has always kept domestic issues strictly separate from international issues. Failing to respond to these questions is in itself a political attitude. Therefore, the analysis in this paper excludes these 318 times.

Thus, from the beginning of 2002 to the end of 2019, MFA spokesmen were unable to provide the information requested by the media on 2234 occasions. Longitudinally, there are obvious changing trends in the distribution of information blind spots in the MFA: from 2002 to 2010, information blind spots remained around 100, and exceeded 150 in 2005 and 2008. It dropped sharply to below 50 in 2011–13 with the lowest level in 2013. The lowest information blind spots for the MFA spokesperson were observed in 2012 and 2013, which coincided with the domestic power transition that saw the media focus mainly on China's domestic politics. Since then, the MFA's information blind spots have increased each year since 2013, reaching the highest point in recent years in 2019 with the number exceeding 300 (see Fig. 8.1).

Since there are no restrictions on questions at MFA press conferences, correspondents can ask any questions on topics of interest to them. These questions indicate that these fields are the most active and therefore are areas of public interest for China's diplomacy. As a caveat, we need to clarify that the spokesperson gave clear statements in the vast majority of cases, which is

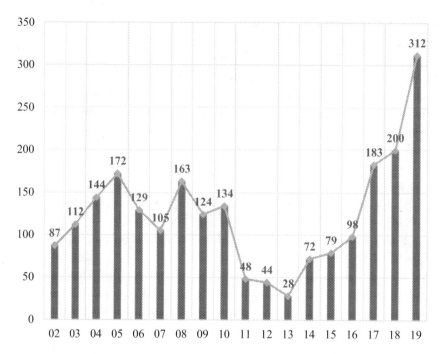

Fig. 8.1 Statistical graph of the quantity of information blind spots by the spokesperson of the MFA (2002–19)

within the expectations of the general public. Blind spots accounted for only a small fraction of the total answers—no more than 10 percent on average, which is the interest and content of our analysis.

From a transversal perspective, the information blind spots are mainly concentrated in nine fields: economic affairs, military affairs, DPRK-related affairs, consular affairs, summit diplomacy, boundary and ocean affairs, high-level diplomacy, cyber security, and terrorism. The blind spots in these nine areas account for almost 85 percent of the total, and the distribution law is obvious (see Fig. 8.2).

Economic Affairs

A total of 625 cases, which exceeds one-fourth of the total number of blind spots, were scattered in the economic field in the areas of China's foreign trade relations, Chinese enterprises' "going out," international financial cooperation, and China's foreign aid to other countries. The blind spots in these areas appeared 306 times, 188 times, 99 times, and 32 times, respectively.

8 Withering Ministry of Foreign Affairs: Evidence from China

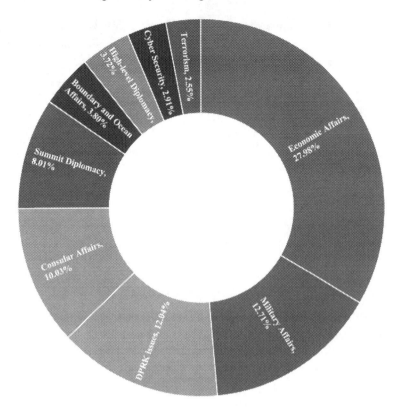

Fig. 8.2 Proportion graph of distribution of information blind spots by the spokesperson of the MFA (2002–19)

First, the blind spots in the economic field concern China's foreign economic and trade relations, which appear 309 times. For example, on September 16, 2010, a reporter asked, "The U.S. has asked the World Trade Organization to investigate China's anti-dumping and anti-subsidy duties on U.S. electrical steel. How do you respond?" On January 22, 2015, a correspondent asked, "The U.S. Department of Commerce will impose high anti-dumping duties on Chinese tires and solar products. The U.S. claims that some Chinese manufacturers have received unfair subsidies from the government. What is your comment on this?" On September 14, 2016, a reporter asked, "The U.S. alleged that China's 'market price support' for rice, wheat, and corn is higher than the level agreed by the WTO, and that the U.S. will file legal actions against China's 'unfair' trade incentives. What is your comment on this?" To these questions, the MFA spokesperson responded, "I'd refer you to the Ministry of Commerce (MOC)" or "Please refer to the Ministry of Commerce."

Second, there is a blind spot in the information on Chinese enterprises' "going out," including the content of Chinese enterprises' overseas investment, Chinese and foreign enterprises' project cooperation, and so on. For example, on December 22, 2016, a reporter asked, "Last night, an Argentine court ruled to suspend the construction of two hydropower stations by Chinese companies due to environmental concerns. Do you have any knowledge about this project? Do you believe that those Chinese companies were treated unfairly by the Argentine side?" An MFA spokesperson said, "I am not aware of the specific situation, but I can give you an answer in principle." In 2012, Iran canceled contracts of hydroelectric dams with Chinese enterprises. When asked twice by this reporter, on May 3 and June 4, 2012, respectively, the MFA spokesperson said, "I am not aware of the situation and suggest you try with the relevant company."

In addition, there are nearly 100 information blind spots in financial fields such as national monetary policy, international financial cooperation, and exchange visits by finance ministers and bank presidents to China. For example, on September 9, 2010, a reporter asked, "The Japanese government recently said that China's purchase of Japanese government bonds has stimulated the appreciation of the Japanese yen. Japan will communicate with China on this issue. Please confirm." A spokesperson for the MFA explicitly stated, "We are not the competent authorities to entertain this question. You can refer to the relevant financial department for specifics."

The Asian Infrastructure Investment Bank (AIIB), an initiative proposed by President Xi Jinping in October 2013, contributes to a large bulk of blind spots in the financial field. As the first multilateral financial institution initiated by China, the AIIB has received a lot of attention from the international community, especially on the occasion of its launching around December 25, 2015. As a result, many questions have been asked by the MFA regarding the progress of the AIIB. However, the MFA spokesperson answered, "I am not aware of that" for a total of six times at the time of its establishment.

Military Affairs

The domain with the second highest number of blind spots is the military domain, which has two categories. One focuses on foreign military relations or so-called military diplomacy, and the other focuses on the military activities of the Chinese People's Liberation Army (PLA). During our study period, the MFA spokesperson responded in a manner such as "I am not aware of the situation" to questions involving the military field a total of 284 times. Of these, the MFA spokesperson was unable to answer or provide information on 135 occasions regarding the content of the Chinese PLA's foreign cooperation. For example, on November 2, 2015, a question was asked about the visit of U.S. Pacific Command Commander Harry Harris to China, to which the MFA spokesperson replied, "I am not aware of the situation. I'd refer you to the military." A day later, a question about the content of Harris' speech at Peking University's Stanford Center was raised again. The MFA spokesperson answered, "I have noticed the relevant reports."

In addition to military cooperation, the MFA spokesman stated 149 times that he was unaware of the situation regarding questions related to the military activities of the Chinese PLA. For example, the movement of the "Liaoning aircraft carrier" (December 27, 2016), China's deployment of surface-to-air missiles in Yongxing Dao (February 17, 2016), the actions of Chinese submarines in the sea area near Japan (November 5, 2015), questions about China's establishment of an Air Defense Identification Zone in the South China Sea (December 22, 2014), China's dispatch of military aircraft to the Air Defense Identification Zone in the East China Sea (November 29, 2013) and patrols carried out by Chinese warships (September 21, 2010). When confronted with these questions, the MFA spokesperson repeatedly answered in the manner of "please ask the military" and "I'd refer you to seek further information from the Chinese Ministry of Defense." A notable case occurred in 2017, when the MFA had the most blind spots regarding military activities, mainly when China's first domestic aircraft carrier was launched that year.

Issues Related to North Korea

The area with the third highest number of blind spots was China-North Korea relations. From 2002 to 2019, the MFA spokesman did not comment on questions related to North Korea for a total of 269 times, accounting for more than 10 percent of the total blind spots. These questions mainly focused on two topics. The greatest number, 187, involved the exchange visits of high-ranking officials between China and North Korea, and 82 blind spots were related to North Korea's development of nuclear weapons or nuclear tests.

In the first kind of situation of being ignorant of it, the MFA spokesperson also pointed out that the International Department of the CPC (IDCPC) Central Committee is the competent department and advised the media to seek concrete information from the IDCPC. Since then, many reporters have repeatedly asked about the visits of high-ranking officials from both countries.

The MFA has said, "I am not aware of it and I have no information to offer," "I have no information to release at present," or "I would refer you to information released by the relevant departments." A telling case was Kim Jong-un's visit to China in May 2018.

PRC and DPRK maintained a high frequency of high-level visits to each other, which were suspended after the death of Kim Jong-il in December 2014. At a time when North Korea and the United States agreed to hold a meeting between U.S. President Donald Trump and North Korean leader Kim Jong-un in Singapore, China welcomed Kim as he visited China between March 25–28, 2018, and May 7–8, 2018. The first visit was kept secret until Kim arrived in Beijing. At the press conference, correspondents inquired about the visit, and MFA spokeswoman Hua Chunying said she was completely unaware of it and could not provide any information. After the press conference, some of the correspondents stayed behind to ask questions about Kim's visit in a very casual manner, and Hua insisted that she really did not know, even though international media were covering Kim's welcome ceremony live at the Beijing railway station.

The second type of information blind spots primarily concerns North Korea's nuclear program. After the end of the Cold War, North Korea bucked the historical trend and stuck to developing nuclear weapons, which was opposed by the international community, including China. From 2006 to 2016, North Korea conducted five nuclear tests, which led to successive UN Security Council resolutions condemning the nuclear tests and imposing sanctions on North Korea. Other than reiterating China's principled position, the spokesperson did not provide any substantive information on the topic.

Consular Affairs

Consular affairs ranked fourth in the number of information blind spots. During the period of our research, spokespersons were unable or unavailable to provide any information in response to questions concerning consular affairs a total of 224 times, including 53 times for consular protection of Chinese overseas nationals and 171 times for management of foreign nationals in China.

On the one hand, consular protection is an important function of the MFA. The Department of Consular Affairs of MFA is charged with the responsibility of "a full range of consular affairs"; "protecting overseas Chinese"; "providing consular protection and assistance, formulating policies and regulations, and issuing early warnings and information on consular protection and assistance; and guiding the consular operations of China's overseas diplomatic missions and foreign affairs offices of local governments" (MFA, the Department of Consular Affairs 2022). With the increasing number of Chinese people going abroad in recent years, the Chinese MFA has done a lot of work in consular protection. However, security incidents of Chinese citizens abroad occur frequently and the need for consular protection has become increasingly prominent. As a result, the MFA is facing an increasing number of information blind spots in the field of security for overseas citizens.

On the other hand, there are more blind spots in the MFA's management of foreign nationals in China. It is reasonable for the MFA to be aware of such information given that the Department of Consular Affairs of the MFA is also charged with the responsibility of "coordinating the handling of criminal and civil cases involving foreign nationals in China and making representations" (MFA, the Department of Consular Affairs 2022). However, many of these cases involve national security and fall under the jurisdiction of the Ministry of State Security or the Ministry of Public Security. The most striking case in recent years involved two Canadian citizens, Michael Spavor and Michael Kovrig, who were arrested in 2018 by the Dandong State Security Bureau and the Beijing State Security Bureau for engaging in espionage activities. The media has repeatedly asked the MFA spokesperson about this matter on several occasions, and the only answer from the spokesperson was that there was no information to provide.

Summit Diplomacy

The area with the fifth number of blind spots is summit diplomacy. Summit diplomacy refers to the direct participation of heads of state or government or other national top foreign policymakers in direct bilateral or multilateral talks. As summit diplomacy has become the main form of China's diplomacy, the MFA has an indispensable role to play, as "handling diplomatic activities between leaders of the CPC and the state with foreign leaders" is one of the top 20 responsibilities of the MFA (MFA). More specifically, the MFA's Protocol Department is "responsible for state protocol matters and ceremonial events. It organizes and coordinates protocol affairs for major state diplomatic functions" (MFA, the Protocol Department 2022). Within the time frame discussed in this chapter, the spokesperson failed to answer questions about summit diplomacy for 179 times.

If this spokesperson was unable to provide information about Kim's visit to China in 2018, it is because the visit was managed by the IDCPC. Its failure to provide information about the summit meeting between China and Japan may indicate something different. The once-active summit diplomacy between China and Japan was suspended in the 2010s due to the disputes over historical issues and the Diaoyu islands (Senkaku islands in Japanese) issues. On April 22, 2015, a question was asked at a regular press conference, "The Japanese side hopes that President Xi Jinping will meet with Japanese Prime Minister Shinzo Abe during the Asian-African Leaders' Meeting in Indonesia. Is China also looking forward to this meeting? What issues will be discussed by both sides?" The spokesperson replied, "I have no information in this regard to provide at present." In fact, that same afternoon, Chinese President Xi was having a meeting with Prime Minister Abe to exchange views on relations between China and Japan. As the department responsible for arranging the diplomacy of the summit, the MFA spokesperson was unaware of anything that caused confusion.

In addition to information blind spots in these five main fields, the MFA also has information of blind spots in four aspects: boundary and ocean affairs, high-level diplomacy, cyber security, and terrorism, which account for nearly 15 percent of the total, appearing 85, 83, 65, and 57 times, respectively. The information blind spots in all four aspects are relatively small, accounting for less than 5 percent each, and we do not analyze them due to the limitation of space.

Types of Challenges Facing the MFA

The blind spots represent two kinds of challenges facing the MFA. The one at the national level, reflected by the large bulk of blind spots in economic, military, and Party affairs, comes from the expansion of diplomatic issues into other fields that were not originally within the scope of the MFA. The other is at the level of the MFA, represented by the blind spots in summit diplomacy and consular affairs. The latter are challenges to the very essence and function of the MFA. These two challenges are common features, rather than characteristics specific to China.

Economic Affairs: Multiple Competitors

It is not surprising that blind spots in the economic field top the list of blind spots, considering that economic elements or economic operations have become increasingly prominent in China's diplomacy since China's reform and opening up. In many foreign economic issues, the Ministry of Commerce is the main protagonist and the MFA is an auxiliary body; in the field of international financial cooperation, the Ministry of Finance is the main protagonist and the MFA plays a subordinate role.

China's active participation in multilateral cooperation mechanisms of an economic nature, such as APEC, the G20, AIIB, the Belt and Road Initiative (BRI), the New Development Bank, and the cooperation mechanism between China and central and eastern Europe, not only increase the prominence of the Ministry of Commerce and the Ministry of Finance, but also bring the National Development and Reform Commission and the People's Bank into these arenas. The MFA, which has little expertise, is not responsible for problems in these fields. Therefore, the spokesperson of the MFA cannot answer the questions asked by reporters in these fields. This is the result of the division of labor among the departments.

The U.S.-China trade war is a case in point. Of the 203 information blind spots in the economic field in 2018 and 2019, 145 were on the progress of the trade war. Bilateral negotiations cover a wide range of subject areas, including intellectual property rights, technology transfer, trade in food and agricultural products, financial services, and so on. This necessitated the participation of different ministries. The MFA officials were certainly involved throughout the negotiations, but the Chinese side was led by the Ministry of Finance (MOF), the National Development and Reform Commission (NDRC), the Ministry of Agriculture and Rural Affairs (MARA), the MOC, and the People's Bank of China (PBC). The MFA was simply a member, and not even a key member of the negotiations (MOC 2020).

Military Affairs: A Thick Wall

The blind spots of military diplomacy are consistent with issues in the economic sphere. However, its rapid growth rate indicates that military diplomacy has become a dynamic aspect of China's diplomacy. As of 2018, China has established 130 military attachés and military representative offices in Chinese diplomatic missions abroad, and 116 countries have established military attaché offices in China. From 2012 to 2018, high-level Chinese military delegations visited over 60 countries, and defense ministers and commanders-in-chief of the three-armed forces of over 100 countries visited China (SCIO 2019). The questions of these military exchanges represent an understandable information blind spot for the MFA spokesperson, who is separate from the PLA bureaucrats.

The second kind of blind spots in military affairs is more recent, more pronounced, and on the rise. Major decisions, especially those of strategic significance, are subject to national security decision-making processes in which the PLA is able to push political decisions to serve its own benefit. However, the PLA enjoys a great deal of autonomy in its own professional and operational details. Moreover, with China's limited international influence, the PLA's involvement in foreign affairs was limited, and its daily normative operating procedures may not need to take international repercussions into account. As the PLA grows in strength, a more confident PLA "no longer shies away from antagonizing its neighbors and the United States through a show of force" (Jakobson and Knox 2010, vii).

Whenever the PLA's activities attract international attention, the media always refer questions to the MFA. However, the PLA is bureaucratically separate from the civil department, including the State Council and its MFA, and has its own "MFA" (the second department of the PLA General Staff), think tanks for strategic and foreign affairs research, and intelligence agencies. As Lampton points out, due to insufficient horizontal coordination between these channels, cases are prevalent in which "there will be instances (sometimes important) where the left hand (the diplomats) do not know what the right hand (the military) is doing" (Lampton 2014, 177). The consequence of the MFA's failure to provide information on these military-related foreign affairs issues has led to global frustration regarding the role of the Chinese military in China's foreign affairs (Swaine 2012; You 2013).

The contest between China's military and diplomacy is a repeat of an old story of hawks versus doves. The military is more willing to flex its muscles as its power increases, putting the MFA under great pressure. Considering that the MFA has been criticized for being too soft and lacking in calcium, they do not want to lose face in defending China's national interests and begin to demonstrate more of a fighting spirit, leading to being referred to as wolf-warriors diplomats or civilian warriors.

North Korea Issues: Special Relationship with a Parallel MFA

The MFA spokesperson's information blind spot concerning relations between China and North Korea reflects a similarity and a peculiarity. The former lies in the fact that it is simply another field similar to economic relations. The peculiarity lies in the rising role of the CPC and its IDCPC in China's overall foreign policy. In the early days of the PRC, most of the countries that established diplomatic relations with China were socialist countries. The Party's foreign relations were intertwined with the state's foreign relations. After the reform and opening up, the 12th Party Congress decided to separate the Party's foreign relations from those of the state. The Party's foreign relations should follow a different principle from the inter-state diplomatic relations.

Relations between China and North Korea are both inter-state diplomatic relations and relations between the two ruling communist parties. Once Sino-North Korean diplomatic relations became plagued by North Korea's insistence on developing nuclear weapons, inter-Party relations became an important link between the two countries. The most recent Chinese ambassadors to the DPRK, Liu Hongcai (2010–15) and Li Jinjun (2015–present), served as deputy ministers of the IDCPC. As such, the IDCPC is responsible for exchanges between senior officials of both parties, and understandably, the MFA spokesperson was unable to provide relevant information in response to media questions.

However, from the perspective of this chapter, the rising role of the IDCPC implies that the role of the CPC in Chinese domestic politics and foreign relations is on the rise. Recently, the IDCPC has become more active in its relations with many foreign political parties. It frequently sends formal "briefing delegations" abroad to explicate CPC policies, promote China's experiences in socialist development, and tell the Chinese story so as to inform, persuade, and inspire foreign political elites. The annual CPC-World Political Party Dialogue was launched in 2014 and upgraded to the CPC-World Political Party High-Level Dialogue in the 2017 Meeting. The CPC-World Political Party Summit was held during the CPC's centennial celebration in 2021 (Shambaugh 2017). Related Party agencies include the Publicity Department and United Front Work Department of the CPC Central Committee, both of which outrank the MFA within the CPC. The former, which controls Chinese media coverage of foreign policy and narratives about the behavior of other countries, dominates Chinese media and public opinion on China's diplomacy. The United Front Work Department has brought overseas Chinese affairs and religious affairs to its portfolio, gaining more attention and prominence on a global scale with its proactive behavior (Joske 2020).

North Korea's nuclear program remains an obstacle between this hermit country and the international community. Many people around the world believe that going through Beijing is the only way to reach Pyongyang; therefore, they are hoping that China will pressure North Korea to abandon its nuclear program. Some even consider North Korea's test of nuclear weapons as a diplomatic "responsibility" or "failure" on China's part (Zhu 2017; Bashir and Laverone 2017). The continuous questions from the media to the Chinese MFA spokesperson on this issue reflect both the desire to see North Korea's nuclear program's development and the expectations that China will live up to its "responsibility." The lack of information from the MFA spokesperson on this issue reflects the fact that "without holding the key to the DPRK's security concerns, China has no leverage to convince this foreign nation to stop its nuclear program" (Fu 2017).

Other domains of blind spots, such as culture, agriculture, and public security, are not discussed because they are relatively insignificant in number. Together, however, they reflect horizontal challenges that share a common feature with the MFAs of most countries, namely diplomatic fragmentation or the horizontal "decentralization" of diplomatic power. China's State Council currently has 25 ministries and commissions in total, including the MFA. With the exception of the Ministry of State Security, whose information is not available, all other ministries and commissions have the International Department or the Department (Bureau) of International Cooperation. These departments are specifically responsible for matters related to foreign contacts and international cooperation in their respective fields of business. With their special expertise, they have become "small foreign ministries" in their respective fields. The international departments within these ministries, rather than the MFA which does not have professional expertise on these issues, are playing an increasingly important role in the implementation of China's policies in these fields.

The MFA has lost its privilege of being the sole or major implementing agency of the country's foreign policy and, like many other MFAs around the world, has been reduced to a "logistics coordinator" at the service of other specialized functional departments and professionals (Rozental and Buenrosto 2013, 237). It is definitely not a pleasant experience for the MFA to be unable to provide information, for which they feel embarrassed, and they complain and have to ask for clarification or information from the relevant agencies. Behind the scenes, there is often competition and bargaining for influence between the MFA and the relevant ministries.

Summit Diplomacy: Eroding the MFA from Above

The failure of the MFA spokesperson to provide information about the Sino-Japanese summit in 2015 and Kim's visit to China in 2018 are not the only cases in this regard. There are many other fragmentary but not insignificant cases of blind spots. A significant case worth mentioning is the "diplomacy of general office" (Hu 2016) between the Director of the General Office of the CPC Central Committee and the Director of the General Office of the President of the Russian Federation, which was acclaimed by the Chinese media as opening up a new channel of cooperation and communication between China and Russia. The existence of close communication and cooperation mechanisms beyond the traditional diplomatic channel has excluded the MFA from the most important part of China's diplomacy.

The rising significance of summit diplomacy is evidence of the centralization of decision-making power and diplomacy (Hocking 2013, 129; Cooper et al. 2013, 16; Greenstock 2013, 107). The blind spots of the Chinese MFA spokesperson in summit diplomacy are evidence of this phenomenon in China. Studies have pointed out that the loss of the halo of the MFA as the "chief diplomat" of their respective countries, with heads of state or government becoming the chief diplomat (Greenstock 2013, 107), signifies the erosion of the MFA's essence from the top.

Consular Affairs: Challenges from Below

The rising blind spots in consular affairs and the activities of state-owned and non-state-owned enterprises abroad represent challenges for the MFA from below. According to the statistics of the National Immigration Administration, the total number of Chinese outbound citizens was only about 17 million in the first three decades after the founding of the PRC in 1949 (Xiong et al. 2019). When China decided to reform and open up in 1978, the number grew rapidly, reaching 100 million in 2014 and nearly 150 million in 2018, the year before the outbreak of COVID-19. By the time COVID-19 curbed the rate of people moving across borders, more than 30,000 overseas Chinese-funded institutions had been established, more than one million exported laborers were working, and 1.37 million overseas Chinese students were studying abroad (Liu and Huang 2018; Xu 2018).

Security incidents involving Chinese citizens and companies have continued to exhibit a trend of multiple and simultaneous outbreaks around the world. The interests of each Chinese citizen are an integral component of

China's overall interests. However, their respective interests, whether individual or corporate, state-owned or private, may not always coincide with the interests of the state. The MFA is not obligated to take responsibility for their behavior beyond providing them with Chinese credentials, and usually does not know about it until they encounter problems or their wrongdoings attract international attention. Such a situation always catches the MFA by surprise. Their illegal behavior may not only undermine China's national interests, but also its international reputation and challenge the capability of the MFA. The MFA spokesperson's response to this issue never asked the media to "refer to the relevant agencies," but said that it would take time to verify the information.

The challenges from above and those from below directly undermine the MFA's traditional function. This chapter does not address other challenges in the MFA, such as its long overseas tenure, underpaid staff, adamant emphasis on political correctness over professional expertise, draconian discipline, and steep climb to top positions (Sun 2017). In the face of all these challenges, expectations of the MFA are not declining, rather they are rising, thanks to the spokesperson. How to cope with these challenges is a common task for major countries around the globe.

Common Features or Chinese Characteristics

In response to these trends, some scholars have suggested the concept of "whole-of-government diplomacy" (Greenstock 2013, 115–16), while others have proposed the establishment of a "national diplomatic institution" to meet the requirements of the times (Hocking 2013, 123) and Chinese leaders have called for a comprehensive or holistic concept of diplomacy. If the challenges facing Chinese MFA share more common features with its counterparts around the globe, then the measures taken by the Chinese government to address the challenges are more "Chinese characteristics," that is, enhancing the CPC's centralized, unified, and absolute leadership over China's diplomacy.

Diplomacy with Chinese characteristics (Zhang 2021, 358–69) was first proposed at the CPC Central Conference on Foreign Affairs in 2014. In his keynote speech, Xi Jinping proposed that "China must have a major power diplomacy with its own characteristics … making China's diplomacy with distinct Chinese characteristics, Chinese style and Chinese manner" (Xi 2017a, b, 443). This has sparked an academic debate about what constitutes Chinese characteristics. The political report of the 19th CPC National Congress explicitly states that "the essential feature of socialism with Chinese characteristics is the leadership of CPC; the greatest strength of the socialist system with Chinese characteristics is the leadership of CPC." The report also requires "the Party to exercise overall leadership in all fields of endeavor in every part of the country," including China's diplomacy (Xi 2017a, b).

Four years later, Xi Jinping's Diplomatic Thoughts were stipulated as the guiding ideology of China's diplomatic work at the 2018 CPC Central Conference on Foreign Affairs. The first of the ten principles of Xi Jinping's Diplomatic Thought is to "uphold the authority of the CPC Central Committee to strengthen the centralized and unified Party leadership over external affairs" (Publicity Department of the CPC Central Committee and MFA 2021, 19). To justify the significance of Party leadership in diplomacy, Foreign Minister Wang Yi wrote: "It has been proven that the Party's leadership is the greatest political advantage of China's diplomacy and the fundamental safeguard for the continuous victory in China's diplomatic endeavor" (Wang 2021a).

With Xi Jinping's Diplomatic Thought guiding all aspects of China's diplomacy, Xi has personally led the practice of China's diplomacy, bringing summit diplomacy to new heights. President Jiang Zemin visited 75 countries during his time in office, while President Hu Jintao visited 83 countries. During his first five-year term, President Xi Jinping visited 56 countries and the headquarters of major international organizations (Wang 2018), visiting more countries annually and staying longer than many of his foreign counterparts. In fact, he became the first Chinese president to outpace his American counterparts in the number, duration, and breadth of presidential trips. Studies show that prior to COVID-19, Xi made an average of 14.3 foreign trips annually and spent about 34 days abroad, notably surpassing his U.S. counterpart Barack Obama's 25-day foreign trips to 13.9 countries annually and Donald Trump's 12.3 countries and 23 days abroad (Thomas 2021).

Xi's personal involvement in summit diplomacy has changed the terminology of summit diplomacy in China. Summit diplomacy (*shounao waijiao*) is referred to as the head-of-government or head-of-state diplomacy. As Xi began to actively engage in diplomacy, the term summit diplomacy was changed to head-of-state diplomacy (*yuanshou waijiao*, presidential diplomacy) only, and the term of head of government diplomacy completely disappeared from the Chinese media. Presidential diplomacy is now extolled in terms of "guiding," "charting a course (*yinling*)," or "setting the direction (*linghang dingxiang*) for China's external relations." More recently, to serve presidential diplomacy has been added to the goal of China's diplomacy, which has been to serve the national interest by creating a peaceful international environment for its domestic economic construction. As Foreign Minister Wang Yi recently wrote, China's diplomacy should "wholeheartedly serve presidential diplomacy to demonstrate the unique appeal of major country diplomacy with Chinese characteristics in the new era" (Wang 2021b). As the defining feature of China's diplomacy is the united and concentrated leadership of the CCP, the very goal of China's diplomacy today is to sever Xi Jinping, the Secretary General of the CCP.

Xi has personally outlined that "diplomacy reflects the will of the state, and therefore its authority must be controlled by the CPC Central Committee" (*People's Daily* 2020). In addition to the theoretical guiding role of Xi's diplomatic thought and his personal engagement in summit diplomacy, diplomatic institutions have been reformed into the leadership of the CPC. Xi heads seven of the 20 or so small leading groups of the CPC Central Committee, in addition to serving as the Secretary-General of the CPC Central Committee, the president as well as the Chairman of the CPC Central Military Commission in his first term. Such a development has led China watchers to refer to him as the "Imperial President" (Economy 2014) or "Chairman of Everything" in China (*The Economist* 2014). However, these do not seem to be enough, and he has taken institutional measures to ensure the Party or his leadership over diplomacy.

With power concentrated in his hand, Xi has basically rewritten the rulebook of China's diplomacy by establishing new diplomatic institutions and reforming old ones. The oldest coordinating institution for diplomacy is the Foreign Affairs Leading Small Group (FASLG), established in 1958 but banned during the Cultural Revolution. It was initially headed by the Minister of Foreign Affairs, but after its re-establishment was headed personally by the State President, the Premier, and now the Secretary-General. The National Security Leadership Small Group (NSLSG) was established in 2000 to coordinate crisis management following the NATO bombing of the Chinese Embassy in Belgrade. As maritime disputes intensified, the Protection of Maritime Rights and Interests LSG (PMRILSG) was established in 2013 to synchronize disparate maritime law enforcement. The FASLG, NSLSG, and PMRILSG shared the same general office at the Central Foreign Affairs Office (CFAO) of the CPC. The Director of the Office was formerly a deputy minister of the MFA and was appointed by the State Councilor at the beginning of this century, and is now served by Yang Jiechi, former Foreign Minister and a member of the Political Bureau. After Xi took over as Secretary-General of the CPC Central Committee, he established the National Security Commission (NSC) in 2013 and upgraded the FALSG to the Central Foreign Affairs Commission (CFAC) in 2018. The boundary between these institutions remains somewhat of a puzzle, but their functions and responsibilities are supposed to enhance the Party's leadership and to strengthen the coordination between bureaucratic agencies involved in foreign affairs. Heading all these organizations provides Xi with the ultimate authority in diplomacy.

Having so many coordinating organizations leads to a problem in which these coordinating institutions also need to be coordinated. However, the important point is that the MFA has not been a crucial component of the process so far. In this government-wide diplomacy with Chinese characteristics, the MFA is not a coordinating institution, but one to be coordinated and can be coordinated by many other coordinating institutions. The third responsibility of the MFA, "to coordinate with relevant government departments in accordance with overall diplomatic planning," is reduced to an empty phrase (MFA 2022). This is because the MFA has neither the legally based power nor the political prestige to coordinate issues in different domains.

In the face of horizontal challenges from its peers and vertical challenges from above and below, the MFA has taken the following measures for its survival. First, in response to the call of the Party Central Committee, the MFA reiterated and took measures to ensure the Party's overall leadership of the MFA. In 2019, to ensure the Party's leadership, Qi Yu, Vice Minister of the Organization Department of the CPC Central Committee, was designated as the MFA's Secretary of the Party Group. In accordance with the unified plan of the CPC Central Committee, the fifth Central Inspection Team regularly inspected the work of the MFA from September to November 2019. The first problem pointed out in the team's final report is that the MFA "has not done enough to thoroughly study and implement Xi Jinping's Diplomatic Thought and the Party's guidelines, principles and policies, and consciously employ the stands, perspectives and methods of Xi Jinping's Diplomatic Thought to analyze the international situation and solve difficult problems …." The report proposes six requirements for the MFA, one of which is that the MFA should "deeply study and implement Xi Jinping's Diplomatic Thought on Socialism with Chinese Characteristics for a New Era" (MFA 2020).

In response to the criticism from the CPC's disciplinary inspection team, MFA Party Secretary Qi Yu said, "The MFA Party Committee accepts them sincerely, treats them seriously, and is determined to reform and correct them." Wang Yi said that the MFA "must study and implement Xi Jinping's Thought on Socialism with Chinese Characteristics for a New Era and Xi Jinping's Diplomatic Thought, and must be brave enough to reform itself and solve existing problems in theory, institution and capability" (MFA 2020). Every year, Yang Jichi and Wang Yi publish articles in authoritative media outlets and journals of the Party, such as *People's Daily* and *Qiushi (Seeking Truth)*, to elaborate on the greatness of Xi Jinping's Diplomatic Thought, pledge the

MFA's loyalty to the Party, and outline plans to implement Xi's Thought in their daily diplomatic work.

The second effort is to upgrade its professional expertise and increase its capabilities within a limited sphere, and to do its best to fulfill its responsibility and live up to a high expectation. The efforts include the following aspects. MFA has made adjustments to its personnel recruitment, promotion system, knowledge reserve, and other aspects, and has prepared them in a targeted manner. As the MFA 2022 recruitment plan for 170 members indicates, applicants are required to have degrees in a variety of fields, including philosophy, law, education, literature, history, administration and the arts, as well as diplomacy and international relations, besides mastering a foreign language (MFA 2021). Recently, the MFA has also intensified exchanges with high-level officials in domestic government branches to enrich their experience and expertise.

The third effort is to do its best to justify its role and function as indispensable. Consular protection is one of the main sources of criticism from the MFA that provides such an opportunity. The assistance received from the diplomatic institutions is the major, if not the only, personal experience of the average Chinese person who influences the perception of China's diplomacy. More resources and personnel are devoted to consular work. As a result, China has more than 240 foreign-service institutions abroad, of which 70 or so are specialized in consular affairs whose main task is to protect the interests of Chinese citizens abroad. Following the principle of "giving priority to prevention and placing equal importance to prevention and emergency management," the MFA uses modern technology to carry out early warnings on consular protection. New columns of "Consular News" and "Notes on Traveling to Certain Countries and Cities" have been added to the official website of the Ministry of Foreign Affairs to report on recent cases.

The fourth effort to shore up the MFA's reputation is to respond to public criticism of China's diplomacy by demonstrating more of a fighting spirit. With the responsibility of disseminating information about China's diplomacy, the spokesperson is more concerned with the views of the general Chinese public than that of the international media. In response to criticism that China's diplomacy is too weak, Foreign Minister Wang Yi promised that "we will continue to uphold the Party's leadership of diplomatic work, fully implement Xi Jinping Thought on Diplomacy, *steel the spine of China's diplomacy* [emphasis added by authors] with the Party's fine traditions" (Wang 2021a, b). Although the fighting spirit demonstrated by the spokesperson has earned them the title of "wolf warriors," which they changed from liking to resenting as the term turned negative globally, it is the safest way for them to be protected, praised, and even promoted.

As China further integrates into the international community and pledges to become a responsible stakeholder, its diplomacy is beginning to have more things in common with other countries, as the challenges facing the MFA indicate. However, the measures taken by the Chinese government to address these challenges valorize the special characteristics of China's diplomacy and reflect a strong sense of political insecurity in the context of globalization. The survival of China's MFA may lie in its global function, but its role lies in its position within the Chinese political hierarchy of the CPC. Evidence from the Chinese case suggests that the future of the MFA depends on international trends, but that its function and role will be determined by domestic politics.

References and Further Reading

Bai, Y. 2009. "Evolution and Innovation of New China's Diplomacy Institution." *World Economics and Politics* 31 (9): 45–56.

Bashir, O.S., and L.T. Laverone. 2017. "The Wrong Way to Coerce China, Trump's Misunderstanding of Sanctions." *Foreign Affairs*, September 13. https://www.foreignaffairs.com/articles/china/2017-09-13/wrong-way-coerce-china.

Cooper, A.F., J. Heine, and R. Thakur. 2013. "Introduction: The Challenges of 21st-Century Diplomacy." In *The Oxford Handbook of Modern Diplomacy*, eds. A.F. Cooper, J. Heine, and R. Thakur, 1–31. Oxford: Oxford University Press.

The Economist. 2014. "Chairman of Everything Xi Jinping Consolidates His Power, and Officials Are Quaking in Their Boots." July 4. http://www.economist.com/news/china/21606318-xi-jinping-consolidates-his-power-and-officials-are-quaking-their-boots-chairman-everything.

Economy, E. 2014. "China's Imperial President, Xi Jinping Tightens His Grip." *Foreign Affairs* 93 (6): 80–91.

Fu, Y. 2017. "The Korean Nuclear Issue: Past, Present, and Future: A Chinese Perspective." John L. Thornton China Center at the Brookings Institution, May. https://www.brookings.edu/research/the-korean-nuclear-issue-past-present-and-future/.

Greenstock, J. 2013. "The Bureaucracy: MFA, Foreign Service, and Other Government Departments." In *The Oxford Handbook of Modern Diplomacy*, eds. A.F. Cooper, J. Heine, and R. Thakur, 106–21. Oxford: Oxford University Press.

Gong, L., H. Men, and D. Sun. 2009. "China's Diplomatic Decision-making Mechanism: Change and Evolution since 1949." *World Economics and Politics* 31 (11): 44–54.

Hocking, B. 1998. "The End(s) of Diplomacy." *International Journal* 53 (1): 169–72.

———., ed. 1999. *Foreign Ministries: Change and Adaptation*. Houndmills: Palgrave Macmillan.

———. 2013. "The Ministry of Foreign Affairs and the National Diplomatic System." In *Diplomacy in a Globalizing World: Theory and Practice*, eds. P. Kerr and G. Wiseman, 123–40. Oxford: Oxford University Press.

Hou, F. 2014. "The Root of Poor Performance of the MFA in Recent Years," May 14. http://www.dacankao.com/thread-27236-1-1.html.

Hu, X. 2016. "Sino-Russian 'Diplomacy Between Two General Offices' Reveal High Level of Mutual Trust [zhong e 'ban gong ting waijiao' tixian gaodu huxin]." *International Herald Leader*, April 5. http://ihl.cankaoxiaoxi.com/2016/0405/1119017.shtml.

Jakobson, L., and D. Knox. 2010. *New Foreign Policy Actors in China*. Stockholm International Peace Research Institute (SIPRI). https://www.sipri.org/publications/2010/sipri-policy-papers/new-foreign-policy-actors-china.

Joske, A. 2020. *The Party Speaks for You: Foreign Interference and the Chinese Communist Party's United Front System*. Canberra: Australian Strategic Policy Institute.

Lampton, D. 1999. *The Making of Chinese Foreign and Security Policy in the Era of Reform, 1978–2000*. Stanford: Stanford University Press.

———. 2014. *Following the Leader: Ruling China, from Deng Xiaoping to Xi Jinping*. Berkeley: University of California Press.

Lequesne, C. 2022. *Ministries of Foreign Affairs in the World: Actors of State Diplomacy*. Leiden: Boston: Brill/Nijhoff.

Li, N. 1999. "Organizational Changes of the PLA, 1985–1997." *China Quarterly* 158 (1): 314–49.

Liu, B., and J. Huang. 2018. "Behind the Rising 'Golden Content' of Chinese Passport." *People's Liberation Army Daily*, February 4. http://www.81.cn/jfjbmap/content/2018-02/04/content_198710.htm.

Martin, P. 2021. *China's Civilian Army: The Making of Wolf Warrior Diplomacy*. New York: Oxford University Press.

Ministry of Foreign Affairs (MFA) of the People's Republic of China. 2021. Answers to Frequently Asked Questions on the MFA Civil Service Recruitment in 2022, October 14. https://www.fmprc.gov.cn/web/wjb_673085/gbclc_603848/bkzn_660695/202110/t20211014_9552884.shtml.

———. 2022. Main Responsibilities. https://www.fmprc.gov.cn/mfa_eng/wjb_663304/zyzz_663306/.

———. 2020. The Central Committee's Fifth Inspection Team's Feedback to the Party Committee of MFA on the Result of the Inspection, January 10. https://www.mfa.gov.cn/web/wjb_673085/zygy_673101/qy/xgxw_673105/202001/t20200110_10418108.shtml.

Ministry of Foreign Affairs (MFA) of the People's Republic of China, the Department of Consular Affairs (Centre for Consular Assistance and Protection). 2022. Main Functions. https://www.fmprc.gov.cn/mfa_eng/wjb_663304/zzjg_663340/lss_665290/.

Ministry of Foreign Affairs (MFA) of the People's Republic of China, the Information Department. 2022. Main Functions. https://www.fmprc.gov.cn/mfa_eng/wjb_663304/zzjg_663340/xws_665282/.
Ministry of Foreign Affairs (MFA) of the People's Republic of China, the Protocol Department. 2022. Main Functions. https://www.fmprc.gov.cn/mfa_eng/wjb_663304/zzjg_663340/lbs_665286/.
Ministry of Commerce (MOC) of the People's Republic of China. 2020. Announcement on Releasing the Phase One China-U.S. Economic and Trade Agreement, January 16. http://english.mofcom.gov.cn/article/newsrelease/significantnews/202001/20200102930958.shtml.
Netherlands Ministry of Foreign Affairs (MFA). 2011. *The Foreign Ministry at a Tipping Point*, a Report of the Ministry of Foreign Affairs of the Netherlands, October.
Nicolson, H. 1954. *The Evolution of Diplomatic Method*. London: Constable.
Publicity Department of the CPC Central Committee and the Ministry of Foreign Affairs (MFA) of the People's Republic of China. 2021. *Outline on the Study of Xi Jinping Foreign Policy Thoughts*. Beijing: People's Press and Study Press.
Qian, Q. 2003. *Ten Episodes of Diplomacy*. Beijing: World Affairs Press.
Rozental, A., and A. Buenrosto. 2013. "Bilateral Diplomacy." In *The Oxford Handbook of Modern Diplomacy*, eds. A.F. Cooper, J. Heine, and R. Thakur, 229–47. Oxford: Oxford University Press.
Shambaugh, D. 2017. "China's Quiet Diplomacy: The International Department of the Chinese Communist Party." *China, an International Journal* 5 (1): 26–54.
State Council Information Office (SCIO) of the People's Republic of China. 2019. "China's National Defense in the New Era," July. http://www.scio.gov.cn/zfbps/ndhf/39911/Document/1660528/1660528.htm.
Sun, J. 2017. "Growing Diplomacy, Retreating Diplomats, How the Chinese Foreign Ministry Has Been Marginalized in Foreign Policymaking." *Journal of Contemporary China* 26 (105): 419–33.
Swaine, M.D. 2012. "China's Assertive Behavior – Part Three: The Role of the Military in Foreign Policy." Hoover Institution, Stanford University, *China Leadership Monitor* 36: 1–17.
Thomas, N. 2021. "China Overtakes America in Presidential Diplomacy." *The Interpreter*. June 9. https://www.nziia.org.nz/articles/china-overtakes-america-in-presidential-diplomacy/.
United Nations, Office of Legal Affairs (OLA). 1961. *Vienna Convention on Diplomatic Relations*. https://legal.un.org/ilc/texts/instruments/english/conventions/9_1_1961.pdf.
Wang, Y. 2018. "Wang Yi Answers Questions on China's Foreign Policy and Foreign Relations at the First Session of the 13th National People's Congress." *People's Daily*, March 9. http://cpc.people.com.cn/n1/2018/0309/c64102-29857110.html.

———. 2021a. Answers to Questions from Correspondents from Chinese and Foreign Media about China's Foreign Policy and External Relations, March 8. https://www.fmprc.gov.cn/mfa_eng/wjb_663304/wjbz_663308/2461_663310/202103/t20210308_9889342.html.

———. 2021b. "Rise to the Challenges, Serve the Nation and Embark on a New Journey for Major-Country Diplomacy with Chinese Characteristics." *Qiu Shi*. http://www.qstheory.cn/dukan/qs/2021-01/16/c_1126985877.htm.

Wen, Y. 2020. "In-depth Study of Xi Jinping's Diplomatic Thought and Strive to Create a New Situation of Major-country Diplomacy with Chinese Characteristics." *People's Daily*, January 6. http://theory.people.com.cn/n1/2020/0106/c40531-31535409.html.

Xi, J. 2017a. *The Governance of China*. Vol. 2. Beijing: Foreign Language Press.

———. 2017b. "Secure a Decisive Victory in Building a Moderately Prosperous Society in All Respects and Strive for the Great Success of Socialism with Chinese Characteristics for a New Era." Speech Delivered at the 19th National Congress of the Communist Party of China, October 18. http://www.gov.cn/zhuanti/2017-10/27/content_5234876.htm.

Xiong, F., Y. Bai, and B. Zhao. 2019. "The 'Golden Content' of Passport Greatly Increased, Going Abroad Getting Easier: Interview with National Immigration Administration Official." *Xinhuanet*, September 25. http://www.xinhuanet.com/2019-09/25/c_1125039799.htm.

Xu, K. 2018. "Motherland is Along with Us: Review of China's Consular Protection Works in 2017." *Xinhuanet*, January 10. http://www.xinhuanet.com/politics/2018-01/10/c_1122240751.htm.

Ye, M. 2020. "Wolf Warriors Blow Hot Before Cooling Down." https://www.globalasia.org/v15no3/focus/wolf-warriors-blow-hot-before-cooling-down_ye-min.

You, J. 2013. "The PLA and Diplomacy: Unraveling Myths about the Military Role in Foreign Policy Making." *Journal of Contemporary China* 23 (86): 236–54.

Zhang, Q. 2021. "Diplomacy with Chinese Characteristics." *The Hague Journal of Diplomacy* 16 (2–3): 358–69.

Zhao, K. 2012. *The Transformation and Position of China's Diplomatic Institutions*. Beijing: Current Affairs Press.

Zhu, F. 2017. "China's Liability on the DPRK: How Washington Can Get Beijing to Rein in Pyongyang," *Foreign Affairs*, July 11.

Zou, J. 2005. *Uncover Secrets by the Spokesperson of MFA*. Beijing: World Affairs Press.

9

South Africa and Its Foreign Alignment and Practice: From Hope to Dashed Expectations

Anthony James Leon

Overtaken by Events

Warren Buffett, the famed U.S. investor, is reputed to have said: "Only when the tide goes out do we see who has been swimming naked." Many of the institutions which we built to maintain our countries and the world and improve their condition do just fine when growth is up and conflict is down. But they sometimes fail and falter when they are stress-tested by adverse currents and rough tides.

The paralysis of the United Nations Security Council over Russia's invasion of Ukraine for example, and its wider impact on globalization; the efficacy of such international bodies as the G20; and the stress-testing of the world's rule-based system of international relations are further highlights of current dark times.

The above snapshot of the world around us is a necessary caution before interrogating certain elements, design faults and implementation challenges which confront South Africa, a middle-ranking world country, as it finds its place and prominence in the world nearly three decades after we became again an admired member of the comity of nations after half century of international isolation and pariah status, under apartheid. The entire notion of political appointees as ambassadors is not confined to South Africa. In the United States, for example, it is commonplace for U.S. presidents to appoint political

A. J. Leon (✉)
Cape Town, South Africa

funders and other partisan eminences to major ambassadorial postings in the world.

In South Africa there are a disproportionately large number of former politicians and ministers who receive diplomatic postings. This is exacerbated by two factors.

Firstly, in 1994 at the end of minority rule, the outgoing administration had a fairly professional diplomatic corps with most ambassadorial postings filled by career diplomats. However, given that the appointees were overwhelmingly white, it would have been impossible for the new democratic majoritarian government to simply leave the status quo in place. Furthermore, since the ANC had never served in government there were no corps of ambassadors-in-waiting ready to be appointed.

For the early years of democratic rule in South Africa the new diplomatic corps represented an amalgam of the professional group of foreign affairs appointees and a new crop drawn primarily from the ranks of the majority party, the ANC, including its own diplomats who had served as representatives in exile during the struggle to liberate South Africa.

The second factor was far more nefarious: the concept of so-called cadre deployment which explicitly was adopted as policy by the ANC in late 1997. The central purpose of the policy was defined at the party conference for "the national liberation movement [i.e., the ANC] to [extend] its power … over all levers of power" (African National Congress 1998). This policy was applied to the deployment of diplomats abroad and the number of political appointees quickly exceeded the professional cadre of diplomats at ambassadorial level at least in all major capitals.

During the current judicial hearings of the judicial commission of enquiry into so-called state capture in South Africa, some career diplomats deposed that the ruling party had used its "deployment committee" to "illegally and unconstitutionally nominate ambassadors, heads of mission and senior diplomats and then shove them down the throats of the [Department of International Relations and Co-operation and the] presidency for ratification" (News24 2022).

It is noteworthy that in South Africa, in contrast to the situation pertaining in the United States for example, there is no ratification by any external body or legislature on the choice of ambassadors.

This writer himself was in a sense a politically appointed ambassador. On standing down from the leadership of the parliamentary opposition, the then president of South Africa, Jacob Zuma, indicated to the writer that it "was important for the face of South Africa abroad be not just ANC faces." At that time there were approximately six or seven high-level diplomats whom had been drawn from the ranks of the opposition parties. Today there are none.

When I served for three years as South African Ambassador to Argentina and surrounding countries, my diplomatic friend, U.S. Ambassador Vilma Martinez, amused her guests one evening around her dinner table at her palatial Buenos Aires residence by telling us that, in State Department-speak, "OBE" meant "overtaken by events."

Although much of the foreign policy bureaucracy in South Africa and the rest of the world has been captured, and remains enthralled, by management consultants, with their emphasis on "business plans," "mission statements," "visions," and the entire gamut of measurable deliverables and other excrescences embedded in the "culture of performance," it is often real-time events, especially those which mushroom into crisis proportions, which test the relevance and limits of any nation's external projection.

Like Andy Warhol's promise that everyone should enjoy fifteen minutes of fame, South Africa in 1994, under the inspiring presidency of Nelson Mandela, debuted in the global spotlight after decades in its shadows.

South Africa's status in the world in the 1990s was achieved as a consequence of the immense strength (a classic example of what Harvard professor Joseph Nye terms soft power) of the example which we provided to the world. This was during the period of our political and constitutional transition from apartheid to democracy during that period. Our power of example, rather than the example of our power back then, created a following wind of high expectation and international goodwill, which we have seldom matched in the more prosaic and difficult three decades since then.

White Paper on Foreign Policy: Box Ticking, Lack of Priority Focus

Midway during my ambassadorship in 2011, and fully 17 years after the election of the post-apartheid government of the African National Congress (ANC), the Department of International Relations and Co-Operation (DIRCO), the rebranded foreign affairs ministry, published its White Paper on Foreign Policy entitled "Building a Better World: The Diplomacy of Ubuntu" (DIRCO 2011).

The title was a nod to an indigenous concept (Ubuntu) of interactive humanity, but it was fairly apparent that the document itself provided neither a definitive nor resolutive priority listing of international objectives, nor indeed a handbook for practitioners to execute and advance policy in a coherent manner.

In the event, the White Paper neither acknowledged some of the core dilemmas and shortcomings of previous iterations of foreign policy. It specifically repeated a lengthy list of national interests, without stating in which order they would be executed and how they would be realized abroad. It contained proposals for further bureaucratic building blocks (e.g., the creation of a single agency to channel development aid—the South African Development Partnership Agency (SADPA) and a South African Council on International Relations (SACOIR)—without defining criteria for its grant allocations, in the case of the former, or for its constitution and powers in the case of the latter).

In the opinion of Ambassador Tom Wheeler (2013), a former South African diplomat and Research Associate at the South African Institute of International Affairs (SAIIA),

> The key focuses of South African foreign policy, its African Agenda, South-South Cooperation, North-South Dialogue, Multilateral and Economic Diplomacy, and bilateral relations with individual countries, have been listed on the DIRCO website for years. Nothing new (in the White Paper) here. Nor is there any attempt to identify the countries which are of special importance to South Africa in promoting its interests. South Africa's current foreign policy has been described as "care and maintenance" of what was created during the Mbeki presidency.[1] The White Paper does little to disabuse that characterisation.

Other analysts were equally unmoved by the White Paper, or thought it added anything of new significance for future use. For example, Mzukisi Qobo, senior lecturer in political sciences at the University of Pretoria, described the exercise and its outcome as "old wine in new bottles ... it includes almost everything under the sun" (Qobo 2011). Policy analyst Greg Mills was crisper and harsher: he described our foreign policy as "a bit of this and a bit of that" (Mills 2011). In the same article he also dismissed our diplomatic techniques as "largely analogue for the digital world, and leadership anodyne, rather than dynamic." This rather painfully chimed with my lived experience as an ambassador.

---

[1] This refers to the presidency of Thabo Mbeki (1999–2008).

Dimming the Light on Human Rights

However, to the extent that a common thread linked the earliest pronouncement on the country's international posture with later iterations of policy it was in the arena of promoting human rights as a cornerstone of foreign policy. This perhaps was unsurprising: the entire system of apartheid was based on the denial of both basic rights for the African majority of the population and oppressive incursions of civil liberties by the state. In 1994 the arrival of full-blown democracy, undergirded by a progressive constitution, strengthened the idea that South Africa would in the international arena give its voice and vote in support of a rights- and rule-based international order.

Twenty-eight years in power had seen the ANC government energetically, and across the world, extinguish Nelson Mandela's promise in 1993 that human rights would be the "light that guides our foreign affairs" (Mandela 1993).

In my own diplomatic hinterland of South America, Venezuela provided a similar case. While President Hugo Chávez was lionized for his staunch anti-Americanism and his populist giveaways, there was at least some measure of basic governance and a vestige of democracy. But after his death in 2013, his successor Nicolás Maduro attempted to recreate his legacy (once dismissed by *The Economist* as a "gaseous concoction of authoritarianism, socialism and populism"), with dismal and bloody results.

A great deal of state-sponsored violence and impoverishment forced the migration of an estimated four million starving Venezuelans to neighboring countries, since the collapsing oil price and runaway inflation had seen, according to economists, the largest economic collapse of any country outside of war in at least 45 years. In its heyday, Venezuela had been the richest country in the region; by 2018, it was reduced to beggary. Maduro closed down the opposition and ruled through violent military oppression, propped up by Moscow and Beijing. There was not the slightest hint of basic rights for its citizens, only their denial and impoverishment.

Into this mix, in July 2018, arrived Ambassador Joseph Nkosi, South Africa's man in Caracas. Ironically, at a commemorative function for Nelson Mandela, he expressed solidarity with the Maduro regime under economic blockade by the U.S., adding, "If it is necessary that we bring our soldiers to fight against the Americans we will do it, we cannot allow ourselves to be dominated by the American administration … The days of the U.S. dominating the world are numbered" (Fabricius 2018). Nkosi was rebuked by Pretoria and recanted. Tellingly, however, Nkosi was neither recalled nor relieved of his duties—and remains in post as of this writing.

A few months later, then ANC secretary general Ace Magashule led a top-heavy ANC delegation to Caracas in support of the beleaguered and ever more tyrannical Maduro regime. On the weekend of the ANC's arrival, regime troops killed and injured dozens of people who were attempting to deliver a convoy of food into the starving country.

By contrast, there was little controversy in the bilateral relationship between South Africa and Argentina during the period of my ambassadorship. It was precisely this absence of any contentious issues which influenced my acceptance of this posting since, as events proved, there would be no conflict between my political principles and any demands of the South African government. However, the one controversy which arose toward the end of my tenure as ambassador to Argentina concerned the stance of the South African government on the evolving situation in Libya in August 2011. I was approached by a group of North African Ambassadors when the SA government had called, ridiculously, for "a negotiated settlement" between Muammar Qadaffi and the armed rebels. And at the point of Qadaffi's ouster, the South African government refused for quite some time to recognize Libya's transitional national council as the government of that country, in contrast to the position adopted by most Arab and Western States.

This posture was informed by the very significant funding Qadaffi had provided both the ANC and several of its leaders over decades. When I protested the inaptness of this stance to the director general of DIRCO in Pretoria, his response was, "from time to time you need to advance positions with which you personally disagree." I left my post twelve months early, this communication being a factor which weighed on the decision (Leon 2013, 238–40).

This visceral anti-Americanism and placing South Africa as "an instinctive supporter of tyrannical leaders hated by their own populations"—as *Business Day* (2019) in Johannesburg editorialized—obtained the imprimatur later from Ramaphosa himself. In April 2020, while hungry residents of Caracas were eating their own pets to stay alive, he posted a warm tweet on his phone call with "my brother President Nicolas Maduro of Venezuela yesterday," noting "Our two countries share a close and historical bond based on friendship, solidarity and cooperation" (Ramaphosa 2020).

There was a grim consistency to all this, in a long roll call across the globe of the South African government violating its own constitutional promises of human decency and democracy and temporizing with tyranny. In 2015 the minister of international relations, Maite Mashabane-Nkoana, bundled out of the country Sudan's tyrant-president Omar al Bashir in defiance of a court order to arrest him. The state had also granted spurious—arguably illegal—diplomatic immunity to Grace Mugabe, wife of President Robert Mugabe of Zimbabwe, after she assaulted a local citizen. It propped up for more than two decades the continuing authoritarianism in neighboring Zimbabwe, and had greenlighted stolen elections across the continent. And it had, infamously, denied a visa to South Africa for Nobel Peace laureate, the Dalai Lama.

There was no difference, and every meeting of the UN Security Council and its Human Rights Council confirmed it, between Russia and China and South Africa on a slew of foreign issues and interventions. And should the assertive cold war between the United States and China go hot, there was no doubt with which side South Africa would align. This would become very apparent in 2022, during Russia's invasion of Ukraine (see below).

The Core of Beliefs

Strangely enough, it was not South Africa's betrayal abroad of its human-rights commitments and the tossing aside of its moral compass that provided the best one-paragraph explanation for the animating impulse behind the country's foreign policy. It was in describing the worldview of former British Labour Party leader, the far-left Jeremy Corbyn, that *The Economist* (2019) summarized matters with pinpoint precision and cynicism:

> The core of his beliefs is not opposition to war but opposition to "Western imperialism." His hostility to "imperial powers" (most notably America and Israel) is so fierce that he is willing to make excuses for "anti-imperial powers" such as Russia and Syria, as well as terrorist organisations like Hezbollah and Hamas. His support for national liberation movements stops short of support for the people of Crimea, Georgia and Ukraine. His sympathy for victims of oppression turns cold when the countries doing the oppressing are Vladimir Putin's Russia or Nicola Maduro's Venezuela.

That was a perfect facsimile, with the addition of Cuba and Zimbabwe, of the past 28 years of ANC foreign policy. It rested, beyond prejudice and hypocrisy, on the faulty and mediocre pillar of a warped and outdated worldview: America and the West are very bad; their opponents always and everywhere are very good. The results of the last cold war, between the West and the U.S.SR, are well known—the U.S.SR disappeared behind the rubble of the Berlin War. But for the ANC it was—childishly, simplistically—never over.

South Africa practices its own version of Corbynista foreign policy from a position of regional pre-eminence, but precisely because of its declining economic significance and less elevated position in the world, post-Mandela, of declining significance.

South Africa's now predictable and consistent re-litigating the struggles of the past and dressing them up in garbs not fit for purpose in the hyper-competitive and often ruthlessly self-interested world in which it operates might not count for much in the forums that matter internationally. Joining the overcrowded balcony of third-world countries is a comfortable zone for an also-ran nation. The price of admission might be cheap, along with the rhetoric; but the problem is that it is a far view from the front-rank places reserved for more serious and engaged players in the world—the place South Africa seemed destined to occupy after 1994, but from which it has slid in succeeding years.

Biting the Hand

Some years back, I had an engaging evening with Gideon Rachman, the influential chief foreign affairs commentator of the *Financial Times*, when he was on a visit to Cape Town. During our dinner I discovered that his parents were South African, and that he had spent some of his childhood years in the country. So behind his polemics there was a background of personal identification.

In February 2018, the day before Ramaphosa was elected president, Rachman wrote a major op-ed for his newspaper entitled "Why South Africa Matters to the World." Rachman (2018) noted that the continent of Africa could either tip into atrophy and induce mass migration into Europe, on the one hand, or, on the other, "if things go really well," could "become a new pole of growth for the world economy." In his view, South Africa's trajectory would "matter hugely in this story." Our country had, rightly or otherwise, become "an informal spokesman for the continent … a standard bearer for Africa." And its new president's responsibilities would "extend beyond the borders of his own country."

Two years later, in 2020, Ramaphosa held another high office, as chair of the African Union, formalizing his spokesmanship for the continent. He did not, however, indicate that he had any intention of moving beyond the familiar terrain of engaging in international posturing based on a pastiche of anti-colonial rhetoric and demands for a seat of influence at the tables of world decision-making. The world, preoccupied with its own concerns, especially the cratered COVID-19 economies, took little notice.

In South Africa, though, there were blowbacks from the gesture politics that animated our foreign policy and positioning, illustrating that these weren't cost-free exercises, and that conspicuous acts of national self-harm resulted. It was perhaps understandable, given the alliances forged in the heat of struggle against apartheid, that there would be a Manichean view of the world by the ANC after it assumed power: "our allies" (Russia, Cuba, et al.) were with us; "the West" was against us.

Of course, this was not strictly true. The armed struggle did far less to topple, or even dent, white-ruled South Africa than the sanctions imposed by the United States, the UK, and Germany. Moreover, beyond an imagined past, there were the more pressing needs of the much-promised (by every president from Mandela onward) attraction of foreign investment and interest to the country. And in this scenario, the United States and the Western world had a big potential role and an influential hand to play, provided South Africa didn't rebuff it. But there was every indication that is precisely what the play was.

Of all the under-remarked achievements for Africa of the presidency of George W. Bush, two are of huge and continuing significance. His multibillion-dollar funding of the President's Emergency Plan For Aids Relief (PEPFAR), which saved millions of lives on the continent; and his championing of the African Growth and Opportunity Act (AGOA), the stated aim of which was to assist the economies of sub-Saharan Africa. Even under protectionist and instinctive Africa-skeptic Donald Trump, the unilateral trade agreement that allowed South Africa and the continent to export, sans restrictions, goods to the United States continued.

The United States is the third-largest export market (after China and Germany) of South African products, but AGOA allows 36 percent of such exports to arrive in the United States on preferential terms (Theobald 2018). Significantly, AGOA is the principal reason why this country even has an automotive industry and car manufacturing at all. Principally because of AGOA, South African vehicle exports to the U.S. soared from $298 million in 2001 (the first year of AGOA) to $1.4 billion in 2015, the year AGOA was renewed.

By contrast, while China had become a large export market for South Africa, the terms of trade for this were dire for South Africa: China was actively assisting the de-industrialization of South Africa, contrary to the ANC mantra seeking the opposite, by dumping its state-subsidized ultra-cheap steel exports into the local market, having the decade before helped, in similar fashion, to destroy the local textile industry. So, 2015 might, in the ordinary world, be the year in which the South African government tipped its hat to such a conspicuous overseas benefactor. However, as the SA Tourist adverts described it, "South Africa is Exceptional."

In October 2015 the ANC gathered for its national general council meeting. Reams of documents were published in preparation, but the section dealing with international relations went beyond the day-before-yesterday ideas in the rest of the policy offers. It was actively hostile to the United State, at one point opining that across the world the United States was "toppling progressive democratically elected governments." Untoppled and undemocratic countries—notably China and Russia (then annexing, illegally and violently, swathes of Ukraine)—received, by contrast, warm approbation as resurging "two emerging world powers."

Amid these shrill denunciations, South Africa was hapless about its economic imperatives and interests. At the same ANC policy conference, then-party secretary general Gwede Mantashe denounced an American demand that that government reconsider a bill mandating that 51 percent of local security companies be locally owned (and thus forcing foreign owners to sell to the ANC-aligned interests looking for a quick-fire sale asset). Actually, the demand was consistent with the AGOA requirement that benefiting countries establish market-based economies "that protect private property rights."

Beyond telling the United States that South Africa "would not be taking instructions" from it, Mantashe refused to invite any U.S. or Western diplomats to the conference—an unprecedented snub. Since the ban was extended to include representatives from the European Union (EU), which was South Africa's largest trading-bloc partner in the world (ka'Nkosi 2015), this was not just childish but damaging.

The best that could be said for the deep vein of anti-American sentiment mined by South Africa was its consistency, from Mandela through to Ramaphosa. And it mattered little to the mandarins in Pretoria whether Barack Obama or Donald Trump or even Joe Biden was in the White House. One telling vignette in this regard was buried deep in the pages of Hillary Clinton's otherwise anodyne account of her years as Obama's Secretary of State.

She relates in *Hard Choices* a telling incident occurred on her last official visit to South Africa in 2012. This was some nine months before the Gupta wedding saga unfolded on the apron of the Waterkloof Air Force Base, and the difference between their reception (whisked in and cleared for landing even though it was for a private party) and the treatment meted out to the U.S.'s most important official was very telling.

Clinton, who was leading a delegation of American business leaders from Fedex, Boeing, General Electric, and other major companies from a country which by then was one of South Africa's largest export destinations, relates:

> In August 2012, the South Africans refused at the last minute … to allow my diplomatic security team to bring weapons and the vehicles they needed into the country. My plane sat on the tarmac in Malawi, waiting to hear how the negotiations unfolded. In the end the matter was resolved, and we were finally able to take off. (Clinton 2014)

No doubt the officials in Pretoria delighted in delaying the arrival of a delegation from the world's hyper-power, heedless of the reputational damage this caused. Little wonder Clinton concluded,

> In some instances, South Africa could be a frustrating partner … Presidents Mbeki and Zuma wanted to be taken seriously on the world stage. That's what we wanted too … But respect comes from taking responsibility and sometimes it was difficult to interpret the reasons behind government actions. (ibid.)

By 2019, in the second year of the promise of Ramaphosa's "investment friendly" administration, the ANC had moved on—it was now also shooting the country in the foot.

Clown-Car Diplomacy

In early 2019 an evening with a Western diplomat from a leading investor nation in South Africa revealed deep levels of frustration with his host nation. "Imagine," he said to me, as we surveyed the sweeping view of Table Mountain from the terrace of a Bishopscourt embassy residence, "if we had said during the struggle for democracy here, 'It's not our business'? And if we had added that the future of South Africa could not be determined by outsiders, least of all by those from the west. And that there may be terrible violations of human rights in the country, but that was for the government and the people of South Africa to sort out?"

My ambassadorial interlocutor hardly needed to remind me that the ANC in exile had taken a radically different view—it had applied, with great success, enormous pressure on Western governments to put the administrations of P. W. Botha (with little success) and F. W. de Klerk (with much better results) under the economic and diplomatic cosh. Now, the ANC in government—in stark contrast to its position in exile, was dusting off the mantra of the NP foreign-affairs playbook, "no external interference in the internal affairs of other countries." (Israel was the singular exception to this new-old rule.)

What had really annoyed my otherwise mild-mannered—and now highly frustrated—host that evening was an almost cartoonish and foolish attack by my old department, DIRCO, on five Western countries, including his. In February 2019 the diplomatic representatives of the United States, the UK, Germany, Switzerland, and the Netherlands—which between them accounted for 75 percent of all foreign investment in South Africa—were summoned to the DIRCO head office in Pretoria, to receive a demarche (a political line of action) registering its displeasure of the conduct of foreign countries.

Some eight months earlier, this ambassadorial quintet had addressed a memorandum (not a diplomatic dispatch) in anticipation of the investment summit hosted by Ramaphosa. The ambassadors had met with his "investment envoys" and at their behest had codified concerns on corruption and other obstacles in the path of foreign investor nations. Notably, the diplomats had flagged concerns at the lack of action on the legal front against state capturers. They had also noted disquiet with government hobby horses, from stringent Black Economic Empowerment codes to moves to weaken intellectual property rights.

Nothing was heard back until the summons to the DIRCO dressing-down. No doubt the briefly serving foreign minister, Lindiwe Sisulu—who was dropped from this post shortly afterwards—wanted to burnish her anti-Western credentials. But my diplomatic friend was both appalled by the clumsy and dilatory action of her department and nonplussed by the response to a request for suggestions from Ramaphosa's so-called listening government. And it was not so much the diplomatic gaffe by South Africa that stunned even the most sympathetic European envoy stationed here. It was the ruling party, the locus of real power, which gave an unvarnished view of how the ANC viewed things. In one of several bile-filled paragraphs it read, in part:

> The ANC has noted with deep concern the interference by the Western imperialistic forces, like condemns this dramatic holier-than-thou stance of these former colonisers and we would not like to relate to them on the history of master-slave relations …. (Umraw 2019)

However jejune such statements appear, they are worth quoting since despite South Africa's democratic institutions, it is the conclaves and councils of the governing party, more than other institutions of state, which more accurately locate the real source of country policy.

Holier Than Thou in the Holy Land

Israel was the one safe space where South African foreign policy felt comfortable to intrude and to suspend the non-interference in domestic politics it offered elsewhere in the world.

In 2014, when Israel invaded Gaza for the second time in five years, the deputy secretary general of the ANC Jessie Duarte found some outsize language to attack Israel as "barbaric," suggesting, additionally, that the Israeli occupation of the Palestinian territories was equivalent to the Nazi "death camps" (Polity 2014).

In truth, more than residual anti-Semitism or solidarity with the Palestinians (though both were features of the anti-Israel policy), the enduring reason for the stance of the South African government was a consequence of its anti-Western approach. This was given voice in 2015 by Obed Bapela, then head of ANC international relations, who advised a radio station that a proposal to deny South African dual citizenship with Israel—allegedly to prevent local Jews taking up arms in the Holy Land then being mooted—was because the "ANC is opposed to the imperialistic agenda of the U.S. and its allies" (Modise 2015).

In that giveaway phrase lay the nub of the issue and the real basis for the anti-Israel prejudice. The Jews are outside "colonisers" and the state of Israel is both a proxy for its U.S. ally and must—as per Duarte—be Nazified to complete the picture. The hypocrisy and historical elisions necessary to arrive at this illogical endpoint are beside the point.

Ukraine War Exposes Limits of South Africa's Approach

On the one hand, the DIRCO (2011) White Paper on South Africa's Foreign Policy explicitly commits the policy to "continue to recognize the importance of multilateralism and a rules-based international system that is governed by international law" (DIRCO 2011).

On the other hand, hard cases make bad law. And this country's response to Russia's invasion of Ukraine on February 24, 2022, proved this adage anew and cast serious doubt on South Africa's international commitments and reinforced the impulses and gestures highlighted above in other contexts. More pertinently for a country ravaged by high unemployment, low growth, and poor rates on internal savings, the elusive quest for direct foreign investment would be a hard sell for a country out of kilter with international sentiments of the major industrialized countries in the world (bar China which also adopted a posture of between support for Russia and neutrality in taking steps to interdict its aggression). In this regard a brief synopsis of South Africa's stance on the Ukraine conflict is both instructive and confirmatory of its anti-Western bias, highlighted above.

Shortly after the commencement of Russia's invasion, international relations minister Naledi Pandor stated "South Africa encourages dialogue in a spirit of compromise" drawing no distinction between aggressor and victim (quoted in Leon 2022). However, stung by searing criticism of this stance, not least the stance against irredentism and expansionism taken by other African countries such as Kenya, Pandor called for the withdrawal of Russian forces to withdraw from Ukraine. This appeared to be a straightforward commitment to the country's normative constitutional dictates and founding moral principles, which as a former South African ambassador expressed it concerned "respect for human rights, sovereignty, democracy and territorial integrity" (Olivier and Olivier 2022).

However, the ink had barely dried on the minister's statement when the president, Cyril Ramaphosa, contradicted her. He advised Parliament that "the war could have been avoided if NATO had heeded the warnings from among its own leaders and officials over the years that its eastward expansion would lead to greater, not less, instability in the region" (Mills and Hartley 2022).

When a motion was presented to the UN General Assembly condemning Russia's aggression in Ukraine, South Africa was among 35 countries that abstained, while 141 countries voted in favor of the resolution and just five voted against. Several weeks later, Ramaphosa did speak to Zelensky, but thereafter repeated his call for a "negotiated settlement" and insisted on referencing both Russia, the clear aggressor in the war, and Ukraine, victim of such aggression, as "co-belligerents." This simply cemented the wide-held view that South Africa, by inference, supported Russia in the conflict. Ramaphosa meanwhile telephoned Vladimir Putin although in the first 45 days of the conflict made no attempt to reach Ukraine president Volodomyr Zelensky. (Belatedly he attempted an outreach which was shunned by Ukraine given that country's perception of South Africa's pro-Russian bias.)

Perhaps tellingly it was the ruling party utterances rather than government statements which expressed sentiments most clearly. Thus, for example, ANC international relations and cooperation committee chair, Lindiwe Zulu, told the *New York Times*, "Russia is our friend through and through" (du Plessis 2022).

South Africa followed through on its studied neutrality on the conflict when further votes at both the UN General Assembly, including the resolution to terminate Russia's membership of the UN Human Rights Council; in all cases the country found itself in the minority. At the time when the focus on Ukraine highlighted South Africa's ambivalence—at best—on core issues of rights and international law, an interview with the author of a study on South Africa's voting pattern at the UN was of interest.

Suzanne Graham authored *Democratic SA's Foreign Policy: Voting Behaviour in the UN*. She advised the *Financial Mail* that while South Africa voted most consistently on issues such as UN reform (the country has long called for the expansion of the UN Security Council and the inclusion of permanent representatives from Africa) and the general advancement of African interests, on rights issues the country "is the least consistent" (du Plessis 2022).

She noted that while South Africa had voted consistently in favor of "thematic human rights resolutions—protecting civil, political, economic and cultural rights un general—and for the right to development and democracy, there's been a less clear line on country-specific votes where other interests are at play" (ibid.). With few exceptions, there has been a rather grim consistency in the roll call of votes: generally, to align against the West and always against Israel specifically, and vote alongside China and Russia.

Early Hopes Dashed by Subsequent Events at Home

Alongside its international positioning, inside South Africa there has been something of an unravelling of the hope and expectation which greeted the country's arrival nearly three decades back into the front rank of emerging democracies.

The national infrastructure has blighted and incapacitated South Africa. A faltering electricity system, shuttered ports and rail network, and the decimation of many state institutions have become a depressing reality in a country, which still by far is home to the most developed and diversified economy in the continent of Africa.

A great deal of the blame for the decimation of the state is, correctly, placed at the door of the immediate past president of South Africa, Jacob Zuma, whose presidency (2009–18) eroded trust in government and saw the plunder of state assets and the embedding of corruption on a truly industrial scale: it is estimated some $90bn was pilfered from the state—and many of its institutions crippled—during his presidency. That is the figure which the judicial commission investigating "state capture," chaired by Justice Ray Zondo, revealed in its first of three reports—published in early 2022—citing "a scarcely believable picture of rampant corruption" (*The Times* 2022).

While Zuma himself is on trial for an unrelated and earlier corruption case and was briefly imprisoned last year for contempt of the Zondo Commission, he still remains ever present in the life and fate of the country. His successor, President Cyril Ramaphosa, is still besieged by Zuma-acolytes in his own party, the African National Congress (ANC), putting at risk his own modest reform menu intended to kick start economic progress in a country once expected to emerge in the front rank of developing economies.

Indeed, one of the greatest blights in recent South African history occurred in July 2021, when mobs of looters rampaged through the Zuma heartland of Kwa Zulu Natal, killing over 300 people, and causing an estimated $628 m of damage to property and businesses. The proximate cause for the rampage was the court decision to imprison Zuma (he was soon released for a "medical parole") and instigated by social media groupings aligned to him. The fact that not a single person who led the rioting has been either arrested or convicted is another indicator of the incapacitation of the state and its security and policing arms, all in varying stages of decline.

Ramaphosa, whose narrow election as party and then state president in early 2018, entered office with the wind of hope and expectation on his back. Yet while incontestably a vast improvement on Zuma, he has not managed to shake off the decline of the previous lost decade as he described the Zuma era. Last year, for example, unemployment (on the back of a very low growth economy aggravated by the COVID-19 pandemic) hit a record high of 47.1 percent on its expanded definition (including those who have given up the search for work). And the reason why the July 2021 insurrection has not likely spread across the country is the provision by the state of social grants which reach 17 m households, an extraordinary total in a country which only has 11 million people in formal work.

But the provision of such an expansive social security network is very expensive: the national debt stands at R4 trillion (approx. $274bn) and the costs of the welfare programs annually amount to R1 trillion ($68bn). Little wonder that the International Monetary Fund (IMF) warned in its December 2021 country report that South Africa "needs to fix its debt problems, public finances and pursue growth friendly fiscal consolidation" (fin24 2022).

The year 2022 is unlikely to see any items on the IMF menu being pursued: Ramaphosa faces a party congress at year end when he is up for re-election and in his four years in office, despite the huge expectations that his election heralded "a new dawn," he has not undone a single policy from the Zuma era or before: these include the controversial "cadre deployment" agenda of placing party comrades, often unqualified, into key posts of state, and rigid implementation of affirmative action prescripts which has seen a skills flight and a decapitation of much expertise from national and local institutions.

In 1994, South Africa's improbable settlement of centuries old conflict and racial division ignited hope that the country could be a beacon of reconciliation and economic progress to the wider world. The decades since suggest this expectation has sadly faded.

References and Further Reading

African National Congress. 1998. "The State, Property Relations and Social Transformation." *Umrabulo* 5 (3).
Business Day. 2019. "SA Diplomats Fluff It Again in Venezuelan Crisis," February 15. https://www.businesslive.co.za/bd/opinion/editorials/2019-02-15-editorial-sa-diplomats-fluff-it-again-in-venezuelan-crisis/.
Clinton, H. 2014. *Hard Choices*. New York: Simon and Schuster.
DIRCO 2011. *Building a Better World – The Diplomacy of Ubuntu – White Paper on South Africa's Foreign Policy*.
du Plessis, C. 2022. "Behind SA's UN Vote." *Financial Mail*, March 10–16.
The Economist. 2019. "Security Questions for Jeremy Corbyn," November 9.
Fabricius, P. 2018. "Washington Sleeps Easy: SA Envoy to Venezuela Calls Off 'Plans' for Military Action against U.S." *Daily Maverick*, August 17. https://www.dailymaverick.co.za/article/2018-08-17-washington-can-sleep-easy-again-sa-envoy-calls-off-plans-for-military-action-against-us/.
fin24. 2022. "Interest Rates, Inflation, and Debt – SA is Facing the Worst of All Worlds, MF Warns," February 21.
ka'Nkosi, S. 2015. "Mantashe: We Won't be Dictated to by U.S." *IOL*, October 9. https://www.iol.co.za/business-report/economy/mantashe-we-wont-be-dictated-to-by-us-1927254.
Leon, T. 2013. *The Accidental Ambassador – From Parliament to Patagonia*. Johannesburg: Pan Macmillan.
———. 2022. "Kenyan Response to Ukraine Crisis Puts SA to Shame." *Sunday Times*, February 27.
Mandela, N. 1993. "South Africa's Future Foreign Policy." *Foreign Affairs* 72 (5).
Mills, G. 2011. "SA's Bit of This, Bit of that Foreign Policy." *Sunday Times*, November 29.
Mills, G., and R. Hartley. 2022. "On Russia and Ukraine, the Opposition, not the ANC, Speaks for SA." *Politicsweb*, March 24.

Modise, T. 2015. "Obed Bapela on Dual Citizenship, 'Imperialism' and Why the ANC's Not Naïve." News24, September 11. https://www.news24.com/fin24/biznews/obed-bapela-on-dual-citizenship-imperialism-why-the-ancs-not-naive-20150911.

News24. 2022. "Jobs for Pals at DIRCO?" May 4.

Olivier, G., and M. Olivier. 2022. "SA Has No Idea of the Consequences of Siding with an Autocratic War Criminal." busineslive.co.za, March 31.

Polity. 2014. ANC: Statement by Jessie Duarte, ANC Deputy Secretary General, on the Situation in the Gaza Strip, July 10. https://www.polity.org.za/article/anc-statement-by-jessie-duarte-anc-deputy-secretary-general-on-the-situation-in-the-gaza-strip-10072014-2014-07-10.

Qobo, M. 2011. "South Africa's Foreign Policy Stuck in the Doldrums." *Mail and Guardian*, September 1.

Rachman, G. 2018. "Why South Africa Matters to the World." *Financial Times*, February 12.

Ramaphosa, C. 2020. Twitter, April 28.

Theobald, S. 2018. "Expropriation without Compensation Puts Preferential Access to U.S. Markets at Risk." *Business Day*, August 13. https://www.businesslive.co.za/bd/opinion/columnists/2018-08-13-stuart-theobald-expropriation-without-compensation-puts-preferential-access-to-us-markets-at-risk/.

The Times. 2022. "Corruption in South Africa under Jacob Zuma Scarcely Believable." thetimes.co.uk, January 5.

Umraw, A. 2019. "ANC Slams 'Interference by Imperialist Forces' over Corruption Warning." TimesLive, February 4. https://www.timeslive.co.za/politics/2019-02-04-anc-slams-interference-by-imperialist-forces-over-corruption-warning/.

Wheeler, T. 2013. "South Africa's Foreign Policy Objectives," January 2. http://www.saiia.org.za/feature/south-africa-s-foreign-policy-objectives-reviewing-the… 2013/02/01.

Part IV

Reforming Institutions

10

From Great Expectations to Dwindling Status: Brazilian Diplomacy's Response to Post-Cold War Upheavals

Rogério de Souza Farias and Antônio Carlos Lessa

Introduction

Brazilian diplomats working in the Ministry of Foreign Affairs (Itamaraty[1]) constitute the main engine behind the implementation of Brazilian foreign policy. This chapter will discuss how political and economic changes since the end of the Cold War affected the institution. Underpinning this narrative is the argument that, despite severe structural changes in global politics, Itamaraty has been slow to update its working methods, governance structure, and mission.

The chapter begins with a broad overview of Brazilian diplomacy from the nineteenth century to the Cold War. We show the unique nature of the diplomatic corps within the Brazilian state and how it managed to increase its role in the foreign policy decision-making process. This was achieved by convincing public opinion that it was an institution above political partisanship and by its efficiency due to top-down organizational centralization. In terms of what diplomats did, we will argue that for a long time they strove to increase Brazilian status abroad by a strategy also followed by other rising powers:

---

[1] A reference to the historic palace that housed the diplomatic bureaucracy in Rio de Janeiro, which at the time was still the capital of Brazil. It moved to Brasília in 1970.

R. de Souza Farias • A. C. Lessa (✉)
University of Brasília, Brasilia, Brazil

"emulation of more advanced powers to be admitted to elite clubs" (Larson and Shevchenko 2019, x).

The second part of this chapter appraises how the demise of the Cold War and the return to democracy in the 1980s challenged Itamaraty. Our analysis in this part will focus on how these structural shifts played out in the context of the rise of the internet. Despite all pressure, the institution in general remained committed to excessive centralization, to a self-important belief in its status in defining Brazilian national interests, and to an effort to "depoliticize" foreign policy to increase its organizational legitimacy.

The Legacy of the Past

Brazil is an outlier among developing countries in the theme of diplomatic capacity. Between 1808 and 1821 Rio de Janeiro hosted the Portuguese bureaucratic apparatus, including the Royal court and the Ministry of Foreign Affairs. Fleeing the Napoleonic wars in Europe, they created a "Tropical Versailles," which hosted diplomats from foreign powers and controlled Portuguese foreign relations and colonial administration (Light 2007; Schultz 2001). When Brazil became independent in 1822, it inherited a full-fledged Ministry of Foreign Affairs, with experienced employees and established diplomatic routines.[2] The fact that it was the only monarchy in a hemisphere of republics created an aristocratic *esprit de corps* and a unique foreign policy orientation in the region. The diplomatic profession became a route for ambitious law graduates to rise in a slave-based economy with few economic opportunities. Forty-four heads of legations and special missions were ennobled during the monarchical period (1822–89), almost all of them serving in Europe and Washington, D.C.[3]

In this period, Brazil aspired to be recognized as a "civilized" country abiding to the rules of a European-led international order. This had racial, cultural, and diplomatic consequences. Despite the conspicuous role of slavery, which was abolished only in 1888, and the fact that much of the population was Black, Brazilian elite promoted foreign and domestic policies designed to empower whiteness. This can be seen both in the intensive quest to bring European immigrants and the active effort to downplay Black and Indigenous

---

[2] Brazil became the seat of a kingdom of its own in 1815. The Portuguese Royal Court returned to Portugal in 1821, but left part of its archives and personnel in Rio de Janeiro.

[3] On the particularity of Brazilian diplomats in South America, see Seckinger (1984). Campos (1913) has the list of all chiefs of missions from 1808 to 1912. Fundação Alexandre de Gusmão (2021) presents an updated and corrected list, but only of chiefs and *chargés d'affaires* of legations and embassies.

culture in how foreign policy promoted the country abroad. Depicting an image of a European monarchy in the tropics shaped both how Brazilian diplomats saw themselves in the region and what modernization projects they embraced.

Brazil withstood several diplomatic and military challenges in South America during the nineteenth century, and fear of a united group of American republics encircling its territory led to a permanent aversion to integration plans for the region. Brazil turned its back on the Americas and envisaged its future as emulating European enlightening modernization strategies and technologies, such as railroads, steamboats, agriculture technologies, and telegraphic communications. Diplomats abroad had to keep an eye on all developments and bring knowledge to Brazil (CHDD 2008, 145; Cribelli 2016, 4, 13–14, 29–30, 163; Loureiro 1825, 4).

The rise of the Republican campaign in the 1870s, the demise of the monarchy in 1889, and increasing trade ties with the United States led to a significant foreign policy reorientation, despite the ambivalence of continuing to crave the recognition as a major power in the Americas (Bueno 1995; Smith 1991; Topik 1996). Baron of Rio Branco, head of Itamaraty from 1902 to 1912 and considered the father of modern Brazilian diplomacy, was the most important symbol of this period. Despite living in Europe for most of his adulthood, he reinforced Brazilian relations to the United States. He considered Brazil a unique rising power, but in the 1907 Hague Conference became convinced about the importance of Brazil to improve relations with other countries from the periphery. Most importantly, he strove to keep a safe distance from domestic politics.[4]

This last aspect began a long-term tendency to consider Brazilian foreign policy as a technocratic field, in which only a professional diplomatic corps could have the legitimacy to act upon. The first victory of this quest for bureaucratic autonomy came with the increasing use of rigorous exams to hire employees. In 1912, the year Rio Branco died while still heading the institution, 92 percent of its 175 employees had entered the institution through political connections. In 1945, the creation of *Instituto Rio Branco*, the diplomatic academy closed the door for political meddling in hiring new employees. In 1965, 90 percent of all active diplomats had entered the institution through exams—an atypical case among other Brazilian bureaucracies (Farias and Carmo 2021).

---

[4] He offered this proposition in the famous speech at the Naval Club in 1902 (Rio Branco 2012, 105–8). See also Santos (2018).

During the Cold War, Itamaraty's quest for a preeminent role in foreign policy continued. After the 1964 military coup, the professional diplomacy managed to curtail rivals, particularly in the economic arena. The institution also absorbed the Brazilian Treasury Office in New York responsible for financing government payments abroad. The biggest victory, however, was reinforcing the idea that foreign policy was a domain best left to professional diplomats. Precisely, 93.5 percent of all 214 heads of embassies during the military regime (1964–85) were career diplomats, and from December 1967 to March 1985 all foreign ministers were also career diplomats (Fundação Alexandre de Gusmão 2021).

There was, however, a dark side in the way the institution amassed technocratic power. First, it had to promote several purges within its ranks, derailing the career or firing diplomats accused of being communist, gay, lesbian, or having specific habits (like drinking too much). Second, it had to spy on Brazilian exiles abroad and perform intelligence gathering activities, something that led occasionally to human rights violations. Third, it had to support the military rule, defend controversial domestic policies, and project a benign image abroad to shore up the regime's international legitimacy (Comissão Nacional de Verdade 2014).

Several diplomats admired the authoritarian regime, others displayed unconcealed opportunism to get promotions and nomination to prestigious posts abroad, but the majority regarded foreign policy as a technocratic and unpolitical domain, framing their actions as contributing to permanent national goals. Much like Rio Branco, they believed foreign policy was above domestic politics. The analysis of series of diplomatic documentation, notably reports and letters exchanged between the most prominent ambassadors and the Ministry, allows us to conclude that they truly believed that foreign policy hovered above domestic policy issues and that Itamaraty had little to do with the ugly face of the military regime. The same can be seen in the memoirs of some of these diplomats, published when they retired. In order to rally behind this image, the institution centralized the decision-making process (Farias, 2021, 7).

As outlined above, in the nineteenth century the tools to help overcome Brazilian relative backwardness were mostly domestic. In this context, diplomats had a significant role as intermediaries in shaping the flow of capital, people, information, and technology. This conception would change, particularly after the 1950s. A group of intellectuals, policymakers, politicians, and diplomats embraced the idea that Brazilian underdevelopment resulted from a rigged international system, in which more prosperous countries set rules to benefit themselves at the expense of the weak (Ioris 2014, 49–82).

This had three consequences for Brazilian diplomats. First, it reinforced a nationalist belief in terms of identity. Instead of taking Europe and North America as role models, a new generation became proud of being a multiracial society with a unique comprehension of world problems and willing to put forward innovative solutions to them. Brazilian diplomats could now say they understood the plight of decolonization and could bridge the dialogue between the First and Third World.[5] This official rhetoric, however, was far from convincing. Foreign observers never failed to note that Brazil supported Portuguese colonialism in Africa until the bitter end in 1974. Also, despite praising the myth of racial integration, Brazilian military, political, economic, and diplomatic elites were overwhelmingly white (Dávila 2010).

The second consequence was the portfolio of activities diplomats performed. With the expansion of American (U.S.) hegemony and multilateral rules after the Second World War, Brazilian foreign policy became particularly active in trying to shield domestic policies from international pressure. This quest for autonomy was particularly acute in the economic domain. As the country progressively embraced an import substitution model to accelerate industrialization, diplomats worked to preserve the Brazilian economy from international competition. They were successful in performing those tasks during the Cold War, one of the reasons Itamaraty preserved and expanded its power in several bureaucratic skirmishes. Itamaraty prepared itself to act dynamically on commercial issues—the opening of new consumer markets for the traditional sectors of the economy, and, especially for the industrial sector, seeking to expand its operations in Africa and Latin America. The economic sectors of Brazilian embassies were expanded, and diplomats began to act more intensively on prosaic issues of the trade agenda, such as market prospecting, and the organization of participation in international fairs.

The third dimension is related to the former two. While authorities assessed that abiding to international rules devised by developed countries would perpetuate Brazilian backwardness, it was clear that the country had few resources to reshape the international order by itself. It was in this context that Brazil reviewed its place in Latin America and framed its strategic role in a group of like-minded reformists developing countries (Hurrell 2013, 96 –97). In this context, Brazil could count on its bilateral ties to offset multilateral limitations. From 1945 to 1990 the number of embassies abroad rose from 45 to 98. The presence in Asia and Africa was particularly relevant, growing from 6 to 48 embassies. This occurred concomitantly with an expansion of Brazilian foreign trade. Diplomats used an increasing number of state companies and

---

[5] The first case is the 1953 Brazilian plan to demilitarize Jerusalem. See Uziel (2019).

government institutions to imprint a global presence, exporting arms to South American neighbors, selling industrial products to West Africa, providing services to build roads in the Middle East, and framing a technological partnership with China.

This activism would be severely curtailed by 1981, when a profound recession hit the Brazilian economy, followed by 13 years of failed economic reforms, massive inflation, and a diminishing international profile. The ensuing economic chaos hindered Brazilian diplomats' ability to implement foreign policy. Even the maintenance of embassies, missions, and consulates would suffer, with smaller budgets and fewer diplomats posted abroad.

After the Cold War

The demise of the Cold War coincided in Brazil with the enactment of a new constitution and the first free presidential elections in Brazilian history since 1960. In 1994, a successful economic plan curbed inflation, liberalized foreign trade, privatized state companies, and improved Brazilian capital markets. This new domestic framework gradually aligned Brazilian foreign policy with the basic tenets of global regimes on subjects such as nuclear nonproliferation, human rights, and environment. This allowed diplomats to frame a less defensive stance abroad, increasing the country's profile with international partners in international negotiations (Fonseca Jr. 1998; Cepaluni and Vigevani 2009).

The 1988 Constitution had one article on foreign policy principles (the previous six constitutions did not have it), and deputies and senators in the following years would increasingly show interest in international themes. Today this involves setting up fact-finding missions, discussing foreign policy issues in specialized commissions, building ties with legislators from other countries, creating bilateral caucus to support specific countries in the Brazilian Congress, appreciating legislative bills with foreign policy impact, and leading embassies and Itamaraty itself—three senators became foreign ministers in the last three decades.[6]

Itamaraty's effort to keep foreign policy out of domestic politics has been far from successful, and professional diplomats occasionally became entangled in wider political controversies. The most recent case was during the COVID crisis. The government relied on its diplomatic network to procure vaccines and guarantee export licenses from foreign governments. As in other

---

[6] Fernando Henrique Cardoso (1992–93), José Serra (2016–17), and Aloysio Nunes (2017–18).

countries, this entire process was followed closely by the press and by opposition parties in the Congress. Diplomats were invited to hearings and their activities in Brasília and in strategic posts abroad closely monitored. An overlooked aspect of this process was how the Brazilian Congress used its constitutional power to gather classified diplomatic documents to oversee the Executive. Confidential assessments about the global politics of fighting the pandemic and procuring vaccines were actively discussed in Congressional hearings and in the press.

This oversight was almost nonexistent during the Dictatorship period (1964–85), when diplomats worked without fearing their communications would be publicized. The 1988 Constitution and two laws—one from 1991 and other from 2011—created stringent limitations on Itamaraty's ability to work in the shadows. Gradually, the institution was overwhelmed with information requests. Nevertheless, users are far from satisfied. According to the Brazilian federal comptroller, Itamaraty is the 30th in demands for information of 306 federal institutions, but the 241st in response time and the 179th in satisfaction (Government of Brazil 2022).

Requests can be summarized in two broad categories. The first originates from historians and political scientists interested in Brazilian foreign relations. They have been helped by the work done by the *Comissão Nacional da Verdade* (National Truth Commission), a working group which conducted investigations on human rights violations perpetrated in Brazil from 1946 to 1988. An ongoing surge of articles and books have not been kind to Itamaraty as an institution and professional diplomats as a career (Simon 2021; Gomes 2019).

The second category, comprising most of the requests, is associated with current themes, from how Pentecostal pastors got diplomatic passports to the expenditure of presidential trips abroad. Journalists are particularly fond of digging for information, and their work fuels conflicts between opposition and government parties in the Congress. This exponential rise in transparency had an unintended consequence for the decision-making process, as diplomats gradually reduced the use of official channels of communication to record ongoing negotiations and activities. The number of electronic telegrams sent or received peaked in 2012 (335,566), one year after the 2011 freedom of information law, and decreased 24.72 percent to 252,592 in 2017.[7] It is a fact that the public exposure caused by the Law forcing the opening of information did not seriously affect the organizational culture of Itamaraty. But it is a fact too that, for the first time in its history, the Ministry had to respond quickly, and with great care to requests for information on

---

[7] Data was shared by a Brazilian diplomat on condition of anonymity.

topics that were sometimes sensitive or uncomfortable, which arrived through requests for access to information.

Fear of using official diplomatic channels cannot explain by itself the drastic reduction in official communications. Diplomats continue to interact actively, but they have been doing it through other channels. The technological revolution in communications in the last decades, therefore, had great weight in diverting information flows. The first transformation came with the reduction in the cost of international calls and the introduction of fax machines in Itamaraty during the late 1980s. The use of phones was hardly new, but it transitioned from being an emergency tool for high-level decision makers to become a daily equipment available to nearly all diplomats, even junior secretaries. The use of fax machines also played a role in diverting information from official and more secure channels. The portability and speed became key factors in transmitting sizable print material that was usually sent by air mail.[8]

This first revolution was supplemented by a second: the rise of workstation computers. Their use was also not a novelty. Since the 1970s, Itamaraty has used Burroughs computers to perform specific activities, such as calculate salaries (Cardoso 1980).

The spread of personal computers, however, was slow. In 1985 computer terminals were still considered specialized machines outside the daily routine of most diplomats, who continued to use electric typing machines. In 1991, for example, the Brazilian Embassy in Caracas had only four computers (all of them to support management systems) and diplomats had to rely on their private units to use word processing software to type telegrams.[9] Change came only in the second half of the 1990s, with the bulk procurement of more user-friendly computers. They became a pervasive fixture in offices in Brasília and in posts abroad, substituting typing machines and streamlining the process of drafting documents and transmitting information using floppy disks.

The third round of transformations came with the internet. The first step was the creation in August 1992 of a Bulletin Board System (BBS) to share data on MERCOSUR decisions, events, and press releases (Almeida 1993). It was not a success, as Brazilian state monopoly in communications and protectionist trade policies reduced the number of potential users. The progressive deregulation of the domestic market changed the landscape and in 1997

---

[8] The first thermo-fax machine was acquired in the early 1960s, but it was used for copying documents. It was only in the early 1980s that the system became a permanent channel for communication. See Guimarães (1981).

[9] In 1985 the challenge was to use computer terminals to reduce expenditure in copying machines. See Duarte (1991); Rodrigues (1985).

Itamaraty already had a website. It resembled a yellow page book and content was seldom updated, but two years later it started to become a valuable tool. Three areas were outliers in this process: consular assistance, economic diplomacy, and press relations. In the first case the Ministry provided contacts, guides, and the manual of consular assistance. In the second, the focus was on export promotion, particularly the calendar for trade fairs and in connecting Brazilian producers with foreign clients—in April 1998, the institution created BrazilTradeNet, the first effort in using the internet in trade promotion activities.[10] The press relations area of the website was updated routinely, and rapidly became a reference to journalists and foreign diplomats. The launch of websites was such an important theme in this period that the Brazilian president attended the Brazilian Embassy in London's webpage inauguration in a live event in 1995 and a similar event at the Brazilian mission to UNESCO in Paris in the following year.[11]

The most important transformation in this juncture was the use of e-mail. The first private Brazilian e-mail server was created in 1996 and in the same year we can find diplomats using Itamaraty's e-mail server. In 1999, 91 embassies, 47 consulates, and 7 missions to international organizations already used them. While Brasília had influence in instructing all posts to set up accounts, its use depended in the early years much more on the profile of chiefs of posts than on standard procedures mandated from home. While the Paris embassy had 15 e-mail accounts, the embassy in Rome had only 2.[12] The use of personal e-mails disrupted official communications and proved a more consequential innovation than the use of word processing software. Diplomats now had a cheap, fast, intuitive, and reliable channel to interact outside the formal and bureaucratic telegraphic system.[13] The institution faced a strenuous battle in recording the decision-making process, as officials became adept in exchanging e-mails before using the official telegraphic channel.

The latest disruptive change was the rise of social digital networks and instant messaging apps (IMA).[14] They became essential tools in the diplomatic work, both in signaling international partners and in internal work routines. Like other Ministries of Foreign Affairs, Itamaraty and its units

---

[10] BrazilTradeNet was launched in 1999.

[11] Information about the event is available at CPDOC's archive, particularly in folder LFL mre1 1995.01.01 (1).

[12] Itamaraty's 1999 webpage is archived at https://web.archive.org/web/19990429084457/http://www.mre.gov.br/.

[13] The fax machine, progressively abandoned and in the 2000s, would be used mostly to have certificated copies of official documents.

[14] We refer to institutional use by embassies and other divisions of the Ministry's structure. Diplomats can have their own personal accounts—but posting on current foreign policy topics is not allowed.

created accounts on Facebook, Twitter, Spotify, Instagram, YouTube, Soundcloud, and Flickr; and today diplomats must draft both traditional and new contents—such as tweets and Facebook posts. This new digital environment changed the relationship between Brazilian diplomacy and society, as anyone can now directly interact with information provided by the institution, offering feedback and reactions—a situation different from before, when traditional media companies performed the role of intermediaries. This new reality has brought challenges in how to face criticism. Itamaraty has repeatedly closed the comment sections of its accounts.

A separate issue is the use of IMA. Brazil is the second largest country in WhatsApp accounts and its use brought significant impact to the economy and the formal political process (Gualtieri 2021, 150). While social digital networks usually work as a new venue for public diplomacy, IMA became a crucial tool for daily operations in Brazilian diplomacy in three specific dimensions. First, it connects Brazilian diplomats to their counterparts in foreign governments. Both during preparatory talks and actual negotiations it helps to set the agenda and exchange draft documents. It is interesting to note that representatives from countries in which WhatsApp is not popular are using it when interacting with Brazilian authorities. A second dimension is how WhatsApp is being used within the government. Brazilian diplomats are widely recognized as excelling in coordinating the decision-making process and this app became the cornerstone in interacting with other government agencies to collect information and recommendations. Today there are no clear rules on the use of IMA and detailed directives on what kind of information can be shared. The example from the top is far from reassuring, as instructions to ambassadors abroad are occasionally sent by WhatsApp (Amado 2021).

As we noted above, Brazilian diplomacy confronted dictatorship at home and complexity abroad during the Cold War by increasing decision-making centralization at the top. It might be surprising to note that the forces of globalization, democratization, and revolution in communications did not significantly change this institutional feature. The minister's and the secretary general's cabinet still have a firm grip on minor administrative tasks. Even the allocation of low-level diplomats to obscure posts is within their purview.

Centralization is also a feature of substantive work. Documents with scant policy relevance are cleared sometimes by four hierarchical levels, including the minister's cabinet before dispatched, and there is significant effort in controlling the interaction with outside organizations and the press. Even undersecretaries and heads of departments discuss with both cabinets the wording of trivial telegrams, e-mails, and, more recently, WhatsApp messages and tweets—many of them of dubious relevance to major policy issues. This situation partially results from the initiative of diplomats themselves, who want an opportunity to have face time with both cabinets and are usually anxious about being disapproved by superiors—something that might jeopardize future promotions and work assignments.

Apart from mere fear, there are several reasons explaining the persistence of this situation. First, a centralized framework offers a better guarantee that decisions will provide unambiguous messages to international partners and that they will be consistent with diplomatic precedents. Second, it is an inducement to motivate hard work and prevent divergent behavior—becoming an essential instrument to guarantee a cohesive cadre of officials. Third, it is a performative ritual that reinforces a traditional ethos of professionalization—as we pointed out in the last part, Itamaraty for decades strived to define foreign policy as a technocratic field outside other public policies.

Brazilian diplomats usually argue that Itamaraty has a tradition of reformism, referring to the number of administrative reforms to which the Ministry was submitted, which did not necessarily lead to a change in administration practices.[15] There are worrying signs that excessive centralization in a highly hierarchical structure might jeopardize modernization initiatives. First, there is excessive demand on high-level decision makers, reducing the response time for non-critical issues. Second, much of daily routine is influenced by the subjective proclivities of leaders at the top, creating long-term uncertainty in managing the institution. Third, morale is sapped by excessive delays and a constant fear of innovating.

Some justify reliance on traditional hierarchy by defending that diplomacy is a unique activity, seldom compared with other professions in terms of disruption by technological innovation.[16] This belief, however, is questionable. The disintegration of the Soviet Union, the rise of globalization, and the upheaval caused by modern communications are associated with a decreased reliance on hierarchical systems and the rise of networked structures—a trend highlighted in popular academic literature from Thomas Friedman's *The Lexus and the Olive Tree* (1999) to Niall Ferguson's *The Square and the Tower* (2017). Even military organizations—a source of comparisons cherished by some Brazilian diplomats—are rapidly adjusting. Several armies have been

---

[15] In addition to the institutionalization of recruitment through public tender and the procedural changes introduced by Paranhos, to which we referred above, Itamaraty underwent two major institutional reforms, in 1931 and 1938, which unified the services of the Secretary of State and the consular services. Finally, this process concludes with the creation of the Rio Branco Institute. Another major change was introduced in 1971 with the creation of the Department of Trade Promotion.

[16] This is usually the case with speeches diplomats give in the Day of the Diplomat, commemorated on April 20. They are published in the journal *Resenha de Política Exterior do Brasil*.

changing traditional command and control structures to more decentralized systems, particularly in the backdrop of hybrid battlefield coalitions, technology-driven systems, and the rise of special operations forces. While this is far from rejecting the role of hierarchy, there is now a rising preference for allowing operational units more freedom in detecting opportunities, maneuvering, and using force—displaying a start-up mentality under flexible tactical guidelines.[17]

Itamaraty's quest for centralization is increasingly challenged by an environment of political polarization, making it hard to portray diplomats as a career aloof to the grubby reality of domestic politics. During the Dictatorship, Brazilian diplomats were encouraged to keep themselves from controversies and those who deviated could be dismissed; even unauthorized interviews to newspapers could cause serious troubles. The transition to democracy became more challenging to prevent dissent (Lopes 2011).

One symbolic case to illustrate this transition occurred in 2001. The negotiation of a Free Trade Area of the Americas (FTAA) was the most important foreign policy issue in Brazil and became a contention issue domestically, dividing political parties, trade unions, non-government organizations, business associations, and even the church. Diplomat Samuel Pinheiro Guimarães, the head of a research institute linked to Itamaraty, criticized the official government stance.

His public remarks were used by the biggest opposition party (Workers Party or *Partido dos Trabalhadores*—PT) to attack Brazilian foreign policy. As a result, Guimarães would soon be ousted from his position. Inspired by the case, foreign minister Celso Lafer approved a new rule prescribing that all diplomats had to get authorization before publicly manifesting an opinion on foreign policy issues. Lafer argued that despite diplomats having the right to free speech, expressing public opinion contrary to the official policy line discredited Brazil to international partners, something that could not be tolerated (Ministério Das Relações Exteriores 2001; Lafer 2001).

The decision was an unsuccessful attempt to put the genie back into the lamp, as punishing dissent had unintended and contrary effects—Guimarães, for instance, would rise to become Itamaraty's secretary general as soon as PT gained the presidential office in 2003. The task of reviewing beforehand a

---

[17] This is not exactly the case of the Brazilian army, which, although recognizing the elements that shape the conflicts of the future and considers them in its strategic planning and military transformation project, shows difficulty in effectively incorporating them. Examples: Capabilities-Based Planning has been studied and gradually introduced for nearly 15 years after being incorporated into the National Defense Strategy in its original 2008 edition. Force interoperability is still a very distant goal. Integrated projects, even more. Finally, in the case of Brazilian Army, there are many qualifications regarding the preparation for a new operational scenario. It is tuned in to changes but reacts very slowly.

diplomat's posting in the age of Facebook, Instagram, and Twitter is impossible to implement. Besides better training and post-facto reviews of these activities, the only remaining tool to coax diplomats behind the official policy line is the use of career promotions and the nomination to leadership positions in the institution. But even with the use of these instruments dissent has been rife. Also, participation in the digital arena is an important task for public diplomacy.[18] Excessive constraints on it might jeopardize the attainment of long-term foreign policy goals.

Diplomats have been highly active in public debates, from the 2015–16 impeachment process of President Dilma Rousseff to more recent controversies of the Bolsonaro government. The most significant episode was an open letter supported by 300 diplomats in March 2021 criticizing Ernesto Araújo, the first head of Itamaraty during the Bolsonaro administration. Araújo rose from obscurity in 2018. During the national elections he published a laudatory article on Donald Trump's foreign policy and created a blog promoting his ideas and Jair Bolsonaro's presidential candidacy. This caught the attention of an influential group of right-wing politicians and intellectuals, securing for him the much-coveted position of foreign minister after Bolsonaro was elected. He would soon set himself apart from his predecessors in three crucial dimensions. First, instead of following the tradition of discreetly offering expert advice for politicians, he brazenly criticized specific political parties and contentious themes of the domestic agenda, from abortion to corruption. He caused more uproar for continuing to write on his blog and use his private Twitter account to criticize journalists, politicians, and academics—he even attacked the Chinese Ambassador in Brasília and accused a senator of being coopted by the Chinese government, something that would eventually lead to his dismissal. The brash rhetoric of social media suddenly spread to diplomatic discourse (Farias et al. 2022, 9–10).

Second, he jettisoned the argument that diplomacy was a technocratic dimension that had to be preserved from the turbulence of domestic politics and guided by aloof professionals. By countering the belief of foreign policy as a secluded policy arena, he attacked the source of legitimacy Itamaraty nurtured for decades. For him, diplomats were not above governments and had to actively engage domestic politics as the shock of global values played out at this level (Araújo 2021, 22). It is no surprise that Araújo would take part in

---

[18] Although not the object of this study, it is important to note that over the last three decades, a peculiar concept of public diplomacy has been consolidated at Itamaraty, by which actions to promote Brazil's image abroad are understood (such as cultural diplomacy, sports diplomacy, technological innovation, etc.), and a sense of approximation or opening up of the Ministry and of the foreign policy to public debate and to the scrutiny of civil society. It would be a belated reaction to the process of democratization of the political process in Brazil and the growing pluralization of Brazilian society.

political rallies with the president and engage actively with niche YouTube channels, blogs, and internet right-wing celebrities—bypassing the traditional media to directly reach out groups who supported Bolsonaro.

Third, while most of his predecessors regarded the international global order as reflecting the interests of great powers, Araújo considered that recent changes in the international system resulted from a coalition of powerful individuals scattered at the top of companies, media outlets, state bureaucracies, and multilateral organizations. According to him, they shaped economic globalization to promote communism, quash Christianity, and create a world without borders and identities. He defined the ideology guiding these actors as globalism—a set of ideas on political correctness, climate change, "gender ideology," "racialism," scientism, and antinationalism (Araújo 2021, 26, 55, 85; Casarões and Farias 2021).[19]

Araújo was atypically critical of many Itamaraty's traditions and managed to conduct a limited administrative reform allowing some lower-level positions in Brasília to be filled by junior officers. This was an important signal, as the institution usually links tasks, responsibilities, and leadership positions to career seniority. In this framework, bright and dedicated diplomats must subordinate themselves to older and sometimes less competent colleagues. Reforms in the last decades have been slow to tackle this issue and this is increasingly a problem. Older employees are usually frustrated to perform activities associated with lower career ranks when they lose leadership positions. Having a less senior colleague as a boss, in the few cases in which this is possible, is also particularly disliked. Motivating this unhappy group has been a challenge. Some of them stay months or even years in what is informally known as *Department of Stairs and Corridors*—wandering aimlessly through Itamaraty's offices without any work assignment.

While Araújo was certainly a rupture, he shared a crucial characteristic with his predecessors: the belief that Itamaraty's foreign policy mirrored Brazilian society identity and aspirations. As we overviewed above, during the Cold War the Brazilian diplomacy's quest to shape alliances in the developing world was partially justified by the belief the country had succeeded in integrating all races in a harmonic society.[20] He also believed that foreign policy had to reflect what he considered core Brazilian values—Christianity and attachment

---

[19] Araújo's conception of globalism is different from the definition in the academic literature. See Rosenboim (2017) and Slobodian (2018).

[20] This is usually denominated as the "racial democracy" thesis and it was embraced by Brazilian diplomats for decades, becoming the cornerstone of Brazilian foreign policy. Today it is completely debunked in academia, but still influences conservative groups. On why it remains in the public discourse see France Twine's study on race relations in the city of Vasalia in Twine (1998).

to the West. This justified how he prioritized ties to the United States and Israel instead of relations with China and other developing countries (particularly those headed by left-wing governments).

While in both cases professional diplomats have portrayed themselves as privileged interpreters of Brazilian national interests, the diplomatic career is still highly perceived as elitist, being demographically divorced from the rest of the population—85.42 percent of the 3012 diplomats hired from 1889 to 2018 were males and 81 percent were born in the southeast and south of Brazil, 35 percent of which were from Rio de Janeiro. Despite being 54 percent of the country's population, only in 1979 the first Black candidate was approved by competitive exams to the career and until 2009 none of the 110 Brazilian first-class ministers (usually referred as ambassadors) were Black (Lima and Oliveira 2018, 808).[21] Gender disparity also stays a problem. The proportion of Brazilian female diplomats hovers around 25 percent of new entrants—a proportion close to their current participation in the career. They face more difficulties to be promoted and are rewarded with fewer opportunities for leadership positions (Balbino 2011; Friaça 2012). The Rio Branco Institute established in 2002 a Diversity, Equity, and Inclusion policy, but only aimed at the inclusion of Black people. The program grants a scholarship so that Black candidates have some means to pay for preparatory courses, and purchase books and other resources necessary for their preparation for the career admission contest. There are no policies or actions specifically designed to compensate for the deficit in female participation in the admission or throughout female diplomats careers.

The mismatch between identity and aspirations also plagues the broader sense of what is the mission of Brazilian diplomacy. This results to a certain extent from the country's declining international status after 2014, which marked a reversal from recent history. During Lula's and most of Dilma Rousseff's administrations (2003–16) Brazil became a rising star in the Global South. High GDP growth fueled an ambitious foreign policy symbolized by a preeminent role in multilateral negotiations and substantive improvements in bilateral ties with the developing world. The country transitioned from being a recipient of foreign aid to sustain sophisticated cooperation initiatives abroad. The demand to have a seat in a reformed United Nations Security Council became the crowning jewel of this period (Spektor 2022; Gardini, 2016; Dauvergne and Farias 2012).

---

[21] In 1961 Raymundo Souza Dantas, a Black journalist and not a career diplomat, became the first Black person to head an embassy. About his short stint ahead of the Brazilian embassy in Ghana, see Koifman (2021). The Brazilian government has been trying to change this situation. In 2002 the institution created an affirmative action program.

Celso Amorim, the longest-serving foreign minister in Brazilian history (1993–95 and 2003–10), epitomized a renewed focus on prestige. Both he and President Lula believed the country had a unique contribution to the management of the international system, even in fields and geographical areas in which Brazil historically had scant interest or influence, like the Middle East.[22] It is important to note that, differently from earlier periods, Brazil not only refrained from emulating developed countries' modernization projects but created a singular mix of public policies that inspired other developing countries. This policy mix included conditional cash transfer to alleviate extreme poverty, high-tech agricultural support by state companies, subsidies to emerging industrial conglomerates, reliance on ethanol as a less polluted source of energy, and affirmative action programs to support historically disadvantaged groups. In terms of foreign policy strategies, Brazil became particularly active in promoting coalitions of emerging countries—such as the BRICS and other regional agreements like UNASUR—in addition to demanding the reform of multilateral institutions in which it was believed that Brazil could play a more prominent role, such as the UN and more specifically, the UN Security Council. Finally, Itamaraty worked intensely for the resumption of policy for Africa, which lost relevance throughout the 1990s, among other action fronts, many of which were the subject of much controversy in domestic debates.

The whirl of foreign policy ambitions, however, had the unintended effect of crystalizing beliefs, routines, and rules that precluded Itamaraty from reforming itself. Amorim was an energetic leader in substantive themes but refrained from challenging the status quo. Apart from few changes, there was no rethinking of the professional role of Brazilian diplomats in the early twenty-first century. He also expanded the oversight of his cabinet over substantive and trivial matters. Even with these challenges, soaring aspirations motivated an enthusiastic and hard-working career, which absorbed the biggest increase of personnel in Brazilian history—the total number of diplomats rose from 1091 in 2002 to 1593 in 2010.[23]

---

[22] He even tried to mediate with Turkey a nuclear agreement with Iran to reduce international tensions. On this topic, see Amorim (2018).

[23] A two-year stint in *Instituto Rio Branco* was (and still is) mandatory for all newcomers. The literature and Itamaraty's official tradition emphasize this period as a critical factor in imparting a body of knowledge in newcomers and shaping a unified institutional ethos. A curriculum analysis from dozens of classes since 1946 shows, however, that most disciplines are just superficial overviews of themes already studied for the admission exams. The conception that the *Institute* promotes a strong socialization process akin to what is called "total institution" is also an exaggeration—any newcomer to the Presidency, both from the left and the right, can recruit diplomats with convergent worldviews. See Cheibub (1985, 1989); Ministério Das Relações Exteriores (1955, 2010); Moura (2007).

The economic boom which supported Lula's ambitious foreign policy did not last. From 2014 onward the crisis sent Brazilian diplomacy into a tailspin. Funds for cooperation project dwindled, several embassies and employees abroad failed to settle expenses, and Brazilian payments to international organizations collapsed. The situation gave visibility to internal structural problems in Itamaraty, such as the lack of cost-benefit analysis in opening and keeping embassies, questionable operational choices in export promotion, serious bottlenecks in the career advancement of diplomats, lack of training in foreign languages, and absence of transparency in operational activities (Comissão de Relações Exteriores 2016).

The crisis started a much-needed overview of Brazilian foreign policy. Itamaraty contacted NGOs, academics, other government agencies, and businesspeople to take part in discussions on a white book encompassing concrete information on principles, priorities, and policy actions (Nascimento and Coelho 2017). It was an excellent opportunity to define what diplomats had to focus on, but the institution soon retrenched itself to defensive procrastination. The white book project was forsaken, shelving the last systematic attempt by the government to rethink diplomacy, foreign policy, and the role of professional diplomacy.

The self-centered nature of an institution characterized by being system-oriented and not goal-oriented led to losses in bureaucratic battles. In 2008 the agrobusiness sector and the Ministry of Agriculture managed to overcome Itamaraty's resistance to create the position of agriculture attaché in Brazilian posts abroad. In the same year, the Brazilian Intelligence Agency created the position of intelligence attachés abroad. In 2022, the Ministry of Economy also prevailed over diplomats' resistance to create a representation office in Washington. Despite being a regular feature in other countries, the permanent posting of other civil services personnel abroad was rare until very recently. The spurt of encroachment from outsiders is another signal that the diplomatic profession in Brazil is being pressured to review its mission and values.[24]

---

[24] The posting of military personnel in Brazilian embassies and permanent multilateral missions, however, is common at least since the first decades of the twentieth century.

Conclusion

Brazilian diplomats might be an atypical case. They created an image of technical expertise and reached great dominance in the foreign policy arena—since the Cold War, the overwhelming majority of chief of posts and foreign ministers have been professional diplomats. Their excellence results from outstanding employees hired through competitive entrance exams, a continuous effort to detach themselves from domestic politics, policy-making centralization at the top, and an institutional culture based on the idea that foreign policy should be left to a technocratic class.

This chapter argued that after Cold War the communication revolution pressured Brazilian diplomats to rethink their working methods. The internet changed the portfolio of activities they performed, but also created an unfiltered channel through which Itamaraty can be criticized—even by its employees. Notwithstanding the underlying shift, the institution muddled through with its highly centralized decision-making structure.

The communication revolution, particularly the rise of the internet, also changed the long-held belief Brazilian diplomacy had about serving a national interest that was disconnected from domestic politics. Foreign policy problems became increasingly engulfed by the polarized domestic environment, affecting how Itamaraty's top diplomats curtailed internal dissent. The politicization of Brazilian diplomacy developed in the context of the enactment of transparency laws. They obligated the Ministry to disclose internal communications, but Brazilian diplomats managed to use the internet to reroute internal communications to maintain a degree of confidentiality.

Celebrating the image of a multiracial democracy and setting themselves in the position of privileged interpreters of the national interest became difficult in the context of the predominance of white males from the southeast (particularly from Rio de Janeiro). How could this group question the legacies of colonial hierarchies of the international system if domestically they represent an institution displaying similar inequalities? Current debates on Brazilian foreign policy point out this mismatch, and pressure is mounting particularly on increasing the role of women in the diplomatic career.

One of the primary concerns of Brazilian diplomacy was and is to help reduce the country's economic backwardness. Until the Cold War this usually meant emulating Europe's development strategies, particularly in the use of specific technologies. This conception changed and, instead of taking developed countries as role models, Brazilian diplomacy embraced an original worldview associating underdevelopment to a rigged international system.

During Lula's and Rousseff's administrations (2003–16), diplomats championed the belief that Brazil had an indigenous model that could help other developing countries rise from poverty. The economic crisis that began in 2014 wrecked this framework. Brazil's dwindling status since then has pressured Itamaraty to adapt itself to withstand stringent budget conditions, a more complex domestic environment, and the challenge of modern tools of communication. So far, the institution has been erratic in finding a new framework.

References and Further Reading

Almeida, P.R. De. 1993. "Informative Note to Rubens Barbosa. 9 March." Rba mpc i 1991.05.16. Rio de Janeiro: CPDOC.
Amado, G. 2021. "Itamaraty usou WhatsApp para enviar orientações polêmicas a embaixadas sobre pandemia." *O Globo*, May 15.
Amorim, C. 2018. *Teerã, Ramalá e Doha: Memórias da política externa ativa e altiva*. São Paulo: Benvirá.
Araújo, E. 2021. *Política externa: soberania, democracia e liberdade. Coletânea de discursos, artigos e entrevistas do ministro das Relações Exteriores*. Brasília: FUNAG.
Balbino, V.R. 2011. *Diplomata: substantivo comum de dois gêneros. Um estudo sobre a presença das mulheres na diplomacia brasileira*. Brasília: FUNAG.
Bueno, C. 1995. *A República e sua política exterior (1889 a 1902)*. São Paulo e Brasília: Editora da Universidade Estadual Paulista e Fundação Alexandre de Gusmão.
Cardoso, A.J.S. 1980. *Memo to DCD. 12 March. Confidential*. Brasília: Ministério das Relações Exteriores.
Casarões, G.S.P., and D.B.L. Farias. 2021. "Brazilian Foreign Policy under Jair Bolsonaro: Far-right Populism and the Rejection of the Liberal International Order." *Cambridge Review of International Affairs*.
Cepaluni, G., and T. Vigevani. 2009. *Brazilian Foreign Policy in Changing Times: The Quest for Autonomy from Sarney to Lula*. Lanham: Lexington Books.
CHDD. 2008. "Instruções 1822–1840." *Cadernos do CHDD* 7 (12): 9–252.
Cheibub, Z.B. 1985. "Diplomacia e construção institucional: o Itamaraty em uma perspectiva histórica." *Dados* 28 (1): 113–31.
———. 1989. "A carreira diplomática no Brasil: o processo de burocratização do Itamarati." *Revista de Administração Pública* 23 (2): 97–128.
Comissão de Relações Exteriores. 2016. *Relatório sobre o requerimento n° 4 sobre o MRE. Rapporteur: T. Jereissati*. Brasília: Senado Federal.
Comissão Nacional de Verdade. 2014. "A participação do Estado brasileiro em graves violações no exterior." In *Relatório da Comissão Nacional da Verdade. Parte II. As estruturas do Estado e as graves violações de direitos humanos*, 175–217. Brasília: CNV.

Cribelli, T. 2016. *Industrial Forests and Mechanical Marvels: Modernization in Nineteenth-century Brazil*. New York: Cambridge University Press.

Dauvergne, P., and D.B.L. Farias. 2012. "The Rise of Brazil as a Global Development Power." *Third World Quarterly* 33 (5): 903–17.

Dávila, J. 2010. *Hotel Trópico: Brazil and the Challenge of African Decolonization, 1950–1980*. Durham: Duke University Press.

de Campos, R.A. 1913. "Relações diplomáticas do Brasil: contendo os nomes dos representantes diplomáticos do Brasil no estrangeiro e os dos representantes dos diversos países no Rio de Janeiro de 1808 a 1912." Rio de Janeiro: *Jornal do Commercio*.

de Moura, C.P. 2007. *O Instituto Rio Branco e a diplomacia brasileira: um estudo de carreira e socialização*. Rio de Janeiro: Editora FGV.

Duarte, S. de Q. 1991. "Embassy in Caracas (Inspection Visit)." In *Confidential*. Brasília: Ministério das Relações Exteriores.

Farias, R. de S. 2021. "The Rise, Fall and Rebirth of Foreign Policy Planning in Brazil (1949–2018)." *The Hague Journal of Diplomacy* 16 (4): 547–64.

Farias, R. de S., and G. Carmo. 2021. "Base de dados de diplomatas brasileiros do período republicano (1889–2017)." Unpublished paper.

Farias, D.B.L., G. Casarões, et al. 2022. "Radical Right Populism and the Politics of Cruelty: The Case of COVID-19 in Brazil under President Bolsonaro." *Global Studies Quarterly* 2 (2): 1–13.

Ferguson, N. 2017. *The Square and the Tower: Networks, Hierarchies, and the Struggle for Global Power*. London: Allen Lane.

Fonseca, G., Jr. 1998. *A legitimidade e outras questões internacionais*. São Paulo: Paz e Terra.

Friaça, G. 2012. "Mulheres diplomatas no Itamaraty (1918–2011): uma análise de trajetórias, vitórias e desafios." In *Thesis, Curso de Altos Estados*. Brasília: Instituto Rio Branco.

Friedman, T. 1999. *The Lexus and the Olive Tree*. New York: Farrar, Straus and Giroux.

Fundação Alexandre de Gusmão. 2021. *Legações e embaixadas do Brasil*. Brasília: FUNAG.

Gardini, G.L. 2016. Brazil: "What Rise of What Power?" *Bulletin of Latin American Research* 35 (1): 5–19.

Gomes, P.C. 2019. *Liberdade vigiada. As relações entre a ditadura militar brasileira e o governo francês: do golpe à anistia*. Rio de Janeiro: Record.

Government of Brazil. 2022. Statistical panel of the Law of Information Access. http://paineis.cgu.gov.br/lai/index.htm.

Gualtieri, A. 2021. "The Brazilian Case: The Effect of Social Media on a Democratic Regime of Today." In *Democracy and Globalization: Legal and Political Analysis on the Eve of the 4th Industrial Revolution*, eds. C. Sieber-Gasser and A. Ghibellini, 149–70. Cham: Springer.

Guimarães, L.F. de M.S. 1981. *UNIDAS, Divisão das Nações. Comunicações. Uso do sistema fac-simile. Memo DNU/70. 21 de maio.* Brasília: Ministério das Relações Exteriores.

Hurrell, A.J. 2013. *The Quest for Autonomy: the Evolution of Brazil's Role in the International System, 1964–1985.* Brasília: FUNAG.

Ioris, R.R. 2014. *Transforming Brazil: A History of National Development in the Postwar Era.* New York: Routledge.

Koifman, F. 2021. *Raymundo Souza Dantas: o primeiro embaixador brasileiro negro.* Salvador: Saga Editora.

Lafer, C. 2001. "O alegado expurgo do Itamaraty." *Folha de São Paulo*, April 19.

Larson, D.W., and A.D. Shevchenko. 2019. *Quest for Status: Chinese and Russian Foreign Policy.* New Haven: Yale University Press.

Light, K., ed. 2007. *A viagem marítima da família real: a transferência da corte portuguesa para o Brasil.* Rio de Janeiro: Jorge Zahar Ed.

Lima, R. de C., and A.J. Oliveira. 2018. "Manutenção e mudanças no Ministério das Relações Exteriores: perfis do corpo diplomático e padrões na carreira." *Revista de Administração Pública* 52 (5): 797–821.

Lopes, D.B. 2011. "A política externa brasileira e a 'circunstância democrática': do silêncio respeitoso à politização ruidosa." *Revista Brasileira de Política Internacional* 54 (1): 67–86.

Loureiro, A.J. da S. 1825. *Código mercantil da França, traduzido do francês e oferecido ao muito alto e muito poderoso senhor D. Pedro I.* Typografia Nacional: Rio de Janeiro.

Ministério das Relações Exteriores. 1955. *Anuário do Instituto Rio Branco 1953/1954/1955.* Rio de Janeiro: Ministério das Relações Exteriores.

———. 2001. "Circular aos postos sobre a manifestação pública de diplomatas. 20 de fevereiro." *Resenha de Política Exterior do Brasil* 88 (1): 242–44.

———. 2010. *Anuário do Instituto Rio Branco.* Brasília: Ministério das Relações Exteriores.

Nascimento, A.L., and R.M.G. Coelho. 2017. "Relações exteriores e modernização administrativa do MRE." *Cadernos de Política Exterior* 3 (6): 63–96.

Rio Branco, B. do. 2012. *Obras do barão do Rio Branco IX: discursos.* Brasília: Funag.

Rodrigues, C.C. 1985. Circular Memo SG/12. Redução de gasto com cópias Xerox. Comunicações, January 31. Brasília: Ministério das Relações Exteriores.

Rosenboim, O. 2017. *The Emergence of Globalism: Visions of World Order in Britain and the United States 1939–1950.* Princeton: Princeton University Press.

Santos, L.C.V.G. 2018. *Juca Paranhos, o barão do Rio Branco.* São Paulo: Companhia das Letras.

Schultz, K. 2001. *Tropical Versailles: Empire, Monarchy, and the Portuguese Royal Court in Rio de Janeiro, 1808–1821.* New York: Routledge.

Seckinger, R. 1984. *The Brazilian Monarchy and the South American Republics, 1822–1931. Diplomacy and State Building.* Baton Rouge: Louisiana State University Press.

Simon, R. 2021. *O Brasil contra a democracia: a ditadura, o golpe no Chile e a Guerra Fria na América do Sul*. São Paulo: Companhia das Letras.

Slobodian, Q. 2018. *Globalists: The End of Empire and the Birth of Neoliberalism*. Cambridge, MA: Harvard University Press.

Smith, J. 1991. *Unequal Giants: Diplomatic Relations between the United States and Brazil, 1889–1930*. Pittsburgh: University of Pittsburgh Press.

Spektor, M. 2022. "Strategies of Rising Brazil: Postmortem Review, Looking Forward." *Contemporary Politics* 28 (1): 20–37.

Topik, S. 1996. *Trade and Gunboats: The United States and Brazil in the Age of Empire*. Stanford: Stanford University Press.

Twine, F.W. 1998. *Racism in a Racial Democracy: The Maintenance of White Supremacy in Brazil*. New Brunswick: Rutgers University Press.

Uziel, E. 2019. "A Diamond of Intense Brilliance in the Diadem of Brazilian Diplomacy: The 1953 Plan for Peace in Jerusalem." *Diplomacy & Statecraft* 30 (1): 1–25.

11

Crisis Prevention and Stabilization Made in Germany: Meeting the Demands of Modern Diplomacy?

Sarah Bressan

Introduction: Diplomatic Reform and Crisis Diplomacy

A main goal of contemporary European diplomacy—the diplomacy of the European Union and its member states—is to prevent another war on the scale of what the European continent saw in the twentieth century. With this goal in mind, European diplomacy not only aims to show the world by example that peace, reconciliation, and prosperity among neighbors are possible even after horrific atrocities, but in recent years also by offering their diplomatic services to mediate between parties to conflict worldwide and to foster crisis prevention. This includes traditional forms of diplomacy like mediation to avert crises, a field in which both the EU and member states like Germany leverage their reputation as trustworthy mediators, as in the example of negotiating the Joint Comprehensive Plan of Action, named commonly as the Iran nuclear deal (see Herrberg 2021). Current challenges to peace and security in a more interconnected world, however, require new additional approaches to avert and mitigate crises. Those include, for example, digitally assisted methods to assess information about impeding crisis given an ever greater availability of real-time data, as well as funding and steering projects for conflict

S. Bressan (✉)
Global Public Policy Institute, Berlin, Germany

prevention and stabilization—tools with which European foreign policy aims to enhance its role as a constructive actor in countries at risk of conflict (see Bressan and Bergmaier 2021).

In 2013, Jorge Heine described how the paradoxical decrease in budgets for foreign services in the face of increasing globalized challenges was the consequence of a failure to adapt and fill the gap in global governance (Heine 2013). With the return of great power competition, optimism about globalization and interconnectedness has waned, and the emphasis on classical modes of (bilateral) diplomacy and statecraft returned (e.g. Mattelaer 2019). At the same time, the world's largest challenges—such as climate change, regulating digital technologies, and fighting pandemics—have illustrated that the scope of global problems that require global solutions goes well beyond inclusive economic growth and peace.

How to manage a succession of multiple crises has become a common topic of discussion in global and academic discourse (Freeden 2017; Ikani 2020). This is particularly true for Germany as a country that has benefitted from a postwar "peace dividend" for decades and is in the process of waking up to a reality with plenty of challenges, such as 2021 Russian invasion of Ukraine and subsequent significant policy shift, labeled a *Zeitenwende* or historical turning point (see Mair 2022; Risse 2022). To what extent this will lead to a permanent shift in Germany's approach to political crises beyond the extra-budgetary 100 billion euros for the German military remains to be seen. Given the importance of Russia policy and German relations with Russia for German and EU foreign policy, the coming years will likely see further significant shifts.

While globalization and political crises on a global scale have meant that domestic government portfolios from health to energy are becoming increasingly international, responding to crises that challenge control over territory, as well as sovereignty, remains the core business of diplomacy, and therefore of diplomatic reform. Yet, due to a persistent status quo bias—because it is almost always easier not to change established structures and habits—bureaucratic reform and innovation are counterintuitive developments that represent the exception rather than the norm and therefore need explanation. Seen from the perspective of historical institutionalism, "once a country or region has started down a track, the costs of reversal are very high. There will be other choice points, but the entrenchments of certain institutional arrangements obstruct an easy reversal of the initial choice" (Levi 1997, 28). The timeframe since Heine's (2013) observations is particularly fitting to study the case of the German Federal Foreign Office, which has undergone since 2014 the most substantive foreign office reforms since the postwar period. It was in that year that it launched a year-long consultative process on the role and priorities of German foreign policy, published as "Review 2014—A Fresh Look at Germany's Foreign Policy" (Auswärtiges Amt 2015).

This chapter discusses innovation and institutional reform in the German Federal Foreign Office since 2014 and particularly the establishment of directorates of stabilization and international order. First, it explains the reforms and discusses some of the enabling conditions. Then, it applies a lens of diplomacy as relational practice of governance (see Sending et al. 2015; Adler-Nissen 2015) to show how those reforms and the emerging practices exemplify a new type of engagement and skillset needed for modern diplomacy; and then it analyzes remaining obstacles. In doing so, it draws from original research on how methods for crisis anticipation are used and integrated into diplomatic bureaucracy. This chapter concludes with an outlook on the conditions for and limitations of innovation and reform in both Germany and elsewhere.

Germany's Review 2014: Crisis, Order, Europe

Germany's "Review 2014" debate process on foreign policy titled "Crisis, Order, Europe" clearly reflects the then-prevalent view that a number of global crises—from the climate crisis and global health emergencies, to arms control, justice, and conflict resolution—suffered from a lack of functioning global governance mechanisms. The year-long Review process served to debate what needs to change in German foreign policy through interactive discussion formats with civil servants, politicians, and civil society experts, and to recommend reforms. The final report explains the view—obviously rooted in the country's privileged peaceful and prosperous postwar history—that global crises and the absence of global governance and resolution mechanisms challenge Germany's reluctance to lead, after a coordinated call by leading politicians to take on more international responsibility (Auswärtiges Amt 2015).

The Review report ended with seven areas in which German foreign policy should "do better," which can really be grouped into three areas. First, it restates the desire for a peaceful and just global order and a stronger connection to the EU, emphasizing the central role multilateralism and European identity play in postwar Germany's identity and foreign policy. Second, the report calls for better communication, more openness for civil and broader society, and a better mobilization of expertise within. Finally—and first on the original list—it states the need to "better anticipate crises and expand the diplomatic toolbox," including strengthening instruments for prevention, early warning and crisis management with a mix of classic and modern instruments of foreign policy (Auswärtiges Amt 2015). This was to be realized in the form of a new directorate general, in order to allow "more room for strategic reflection," including the use of joint scenarios, strategic foresight exercises, and more systematic evaluations to inform strategy (Auswärtiges Amt 2015). As a consequence, the foreign office set up two new directorates, *OR* for international order, and *S* for stabilization, conflict prevention, humanitarian aid, and post-conflict reconstruction, adding cross-cutting thematic centers of expertise to a structure that was traditionally dominated by geographic working units for different regions of the world.[1]

Conditions for Reform

As mentioned, the establishment of the two directorates was a clear case of an institutional reform resulting from the perception of crisis and lack of global governance mechanisms, which require the redefinition of the role of a country and the tasks of its diplomatic service. This is true even though according to an insider's account, "the administrative questions were superseded by the political discussions" and "briefly before the results of Review 2014 were presented to the public, the outline of a strategic reform was hastily cobbled together" (Bartonek 2020, 198–99).

In addition, reform took place in a moment of leadership change when foreign minister Frank-Walter Steinmeier took office for the second time, already knowing the organization from his first term as minister, and after the office had been led by another party and government coalition for the past four years (see Bendiek 2015; Bartonek 2020). Establishing a broad consultation process as the foundation for serious reform was designed to avoid what former minister Joschka Fischer had run into in the late 1990s when he rather unsuccessfully and unsustainably tried to reform the ministry with the help of ad-hoc working groups (Bartonek 2020, 197). However, a comparison of the two reform efforts in the 1990s and 2014 has not been studied systematically. Steinmeier's experience in the civil service and his reputation in the diplomatic service are seen to have played an important role, as did the increased pressure on Germany to assume more international responsibility. Minister

---

[1] Full original title: Directorate for International Order, United Nations and Arms Control, International Cyber Policy, Combating Terrorism and Drug Trade, International Development and Social Affairs, UN Global Compact, which—in addition to Directorate S—was added to the existing General Directorates for Political, Economic, Legal, Cultural Affairs, and Protocol and Management.

Fischer, who infamously wore tennis shoes to his inauguration, did not enjoy those benefits to the same extent.

The reforms themselves were dependent on and enabled by Germany's budgetary and economic conditions. Since the Review 2014 and subsequent reforms, the budget allocated to the Federal Foreign Office has grown steadily, from 3.32 billion euros in 2012 to 7.10 billion euros in 2022, which amount to 1.08 percent and 1.63 percent of the overall government budget respectively (Bundesministerium der Finanzen 2022; Auswärtiges Amt 2022). In 2021, 3.49 billion euro or over half of the Foreign Office's budget was allocated to "safeguard peace and stability," including support to the United Nations and other multilateral organizations (221 million euro); 2.11 billion euro in humanitarian aid channeled through directorate S, as well as 434 million euro for crisis prevention and stabilization (Auswärtiges Amt 2020). So while innovation and reform are difficult, and bureaucratic competition continues, reforms are arguably easier in a time of greater budgets and responsibility. In the German case, the availability of resources for the new directorates was indisputably one of the biggest enabling factors of reform. This becomes especially evident in contrast with other cases, such as the diplomatic services of France or Italy, which have not invested into new tools and methods for crisis anticipation and prevention at a comparable scale, not least due to budgetary constraints (see Bressan and Bergmaier 2021; Barguès-Pedreny et al. 2019).

The establishment of the German directorate S with its approach to stabilization and conflict prevention was also inspired by international approaches and the institutional design of multilateral organizations such as the World Bank and the EU, and of other nations such as the United Kingdom (see Bernstein 2017; World Bank and UNDP 2018). As outlined above, a perception of multiple and evolving crises that were not adequately addressed paved the way for a return to prevention as a priority for Germany. That was facilitated by the fact that Germany's foreign policy, by definition, sees itself as only ever acting within the framework and in the interest of the postwar multilateral global and European order, and by the fact that Germany was, as one of the world's largest economies, figuring out how to increase its contribution to international stability (see Brockmeier and Rotmann 2019, 11–12; Eberle and Miskimmon 2021).

On stabilization, a first set of "Interministerial Guidelines for a Coherent German Policy towards Fragile States" was issued already in 2012 (Auswärtiges Amt et al. 2012; see Rotmann 2016, 2). At a time when "'stabilisation' has become the new mainstream catch phrase for what to do when high levels of political volatility and violence lead to humanitarian and political crises"

(Rotmann 2016, 1), the Federal Foreign Office's policy planning department commissioned a study to compare institutional and conceptual approaches to stabilization in different countries and their ministries for the purpose of informing its own approaches (Rotmann and Steinacker 2014). The establishment of directorate S and subsequent interministerial guidelines and strategies reinforced Germany's policy focus on stabilization, clearly inspired by those of partner countries (see Rotmann and Steinacker 2014). Similarly, the need to better anticipating crises with the help of data and foresight as a precondition for prevention featured in this work at directorate S. This was in part inspired by government investments into conflict forecasting and foresight elsewhere, as in the United States, and at the European External Action Service with its EU Early Warning System. Capacities at the EU and the domestic level were, however, not developed in a coordinated or complementary manner, and there is little evidence to suggest that Europeanization in the sense of Germany adopting EU politics has played a significant role (see Bressan and Bergmaier 2021).

A Relational Perspective on Diplomatic Evolution

An anonymous author from within the institution described the German foreign office's reforms since 2014 in an academic journal article as a process of "socialization" (German: *Vergesellschaftung*), in which a former elite and aristocratic bureaucracy became increasingly egalitarian and representative of broader society (Bartonek 2020). While this is an observable trend in many democratic governments, it neither explains the reasons for nor the particular direction of reforms in the areas of international order, crisis prevention, and stabilization. Rather, a relational approach to the analysis of diplomacy can help to explain some of the substantive decisions the German foreign office took in 2014, as well as the remaining challenges it faces in order to realize the ambition it has formulated in its 2014 Review.

Scholars focusing on diplomacy as a relational practice have problematized and questioned the definition of diplomatic practice as a special "third culture" that stands above and beyond the other cultures between which it mediates (see Adler-Nissen 2015; Sending et al. 2015; Avant et al. 2010). They argue that international relations have tended to ignore what is "going on in the engine room of global politics" (Sending et al., 1), as "IR scholars have ignored that diplomacy helps constitute world politics" (ibid., 285). More research on diplomacy as practice, for example using ethnographic methods (e.g., Lequesne 2015, 2022), is emerging. But scholarship about German diplomacy still suffers from the problem of secrecy and difficulty of access that is so common in the study of diplomacy (see Lequesne 2020), and thus contains surprisingly little research on the "how" of foreign policy that very much defines the substantive "what" of a modern democracy.

Because "diplomacy is constitutive of international society and that diplomats produce, through the practice of diplomacy, an international system that would otherwise be different … it is important to pinpoint and account for how diplomatic practice may change" (Sharp 2009, 105–7; see Sending et al. 2015, 19). To add precisely to the understanding of how diplomatic practice affects international politics, a relational lens sees "diplomacy as an infrastructure for the making of world politics," in which international structures are created through the interaction of diplomats (Sending et al. 2015, 7f.; see Adler-Nissen 2015). The relational lens helps show, for example, that diplomacy has moved from mere representation of national interests to the creation and maintenance of a system of global governance through the practice of maintaining diplomatic relations, and finally into the active governance of that global system (Adler-Nissen 2015, 302–3; see Sending et al. 2015).

Applying this definition to Germany's reforms, the establishment of directorate OR for international order in 2014 can be seen as an answer to the challenge of not just representing interests toward other countries and regions, but also coordinating a diplomatic institution's contribution to creating and shaping a multilateral system with thematic units for the challenges of global governance. Meanwhile, directorate S for stabilization fills a gap that is concerned with questions of governance in areas where state authority is either contested or needs to be supported. The stabilization directorate is responsible for spending a large share of the ministry's additional budget in aid of what the German foreign office calls *Außenpolitik mit Mitteln* (literally translated to foreign policy with means/funds), including humanitarian aid and project-based stabilization and prevention measures with which the department essentially funds projects proposed by external actors who implement them (Auswärtiges Amt 2018). This mode of engagement is similar to the direct funding of projects in foreign aid for humanitarian operations, which has become increasingly professionalized (see Koddenbrock and Hoffmann 2017; see also the chapter by Simons and Velikaya in this volume), and represents a non-traditional way of doing foreign policy and diplomacy inasmuch as it devises strategies for managing projects with contractors on the ground in crisis contexts alongside traditional diplomatic methods of representation and negotiation undertaken by diplomats. Stabilization as an area of practice borrows from development and humanitarian policy with its contracting and management approaches, but applies such projects to core diplomatic domains under or on behalf of state authority.

While scholarship on these reforms is still rare, the establishment of directorate S has attracted greater interest than other reorganizations of government ministries. The relational view helps clarify why that it is the case: because it exemplifies a shift in diplomatic practice that comes with a different mode of doing diplomacy which has potential consequences for the nature of international politics and global governance, and which—according to the relational view—are nevertheless created through the actions of diplomats.

New Job Descriptions and New Methods?

Because reform involves long-term processes of change and adaptation, it is difficult to identify a clear point in time for a final evaluation. In addition, the study of institutional reform suffers from a biased sample. Many reform proposals and ideas that are discarded within bureaucracies and so never see the light of day. Failed bureaucratic and structural reforms in diplomacy hardly ever get publicly scrutinized (see Bartonek 2020, 197). Nevertheless, observable challenges to implementing reforms can help identify what is needed for diplomacy to succeed in the future. In the German case, two adaptations relating to staff expertise and integrating structures are illustrative of such challenges.

Foreign offices engage in stabilization of state authority elsewhere because their unique selling point as opposed to other parts of government is representing and negotiating state authority and negotiating the terms of international relations in the space where representatives of state authority interact. The German case shows that realizing project-based stabilization and conflict prevention creates the need for a different skillset: the daily work in those areas does not mainly consist of formulating national interests and negotiating them with foreign diplomats, but instead of funding projects through contractors abroad. Seabrooke (2015, 204) explains that "diplomatic-tacit knowledge has affinities with the legal profession, economic-systematic knowledge with the economics profession, and programming-managerial with the quasi profession of management consultancy." Rather than the traditional diplomatic art of "holding secrets," representing and negotiating national interests through tacit knowledge, the "economic-systematic knowledge" that is required to manage projects that are to make possible and improve governance in fragile contexts "is concerned with locating incentive structures for action and pricing them via a 'good science' understanding of the relevant and applicable theories" (see Seabrooke 2015, 204).

This framework helps understand the need for skills outside the traditional diplomatic job description. Arguably, changes in the complexity of conducting international politics and diplomacy in an era of global governance alone create a need for these skills. So the reforms were not the ultimate cause, but rather a shift in setting demanded them. The result was the need for staff working on cross-cutting topics such as conflict analysis, governance, rule of law in fragile contexts, as well as a number of staff to administer the projects in directorate S (Rotmann 2016; Bartonek 2020). Staff were relocated from other directorates and embassies to the new directorates and the service was opened to temporary expert staff in a "slow and painful adjustment" (Rotmann 2016, 5). A lack of staff and difficulties to fill all posts, creating career pathways beyond the traditional regular rotation model for generalists, and an appreciation for much-needed experience in crisis contexts, are issues the German foreign office is grappling ever since (Brockmeier 2020; Kurtz and Meyer 2018, 9). At the same time, cooperation with researchers through projects with universities and think tanks, in which external experts inform the work of the directorate S, grew—for example by setting up an academic advisory board for conflict forecasting (see Bressan and Bergmaier 2021; Bartonek 2020).

For crisis prevention, Kurtz and Meyer (2018) suggest—among others informed by research on the German case since 2014—that there has been an excessive focus on a technocratic understanding of conflict prevention that privileges data-based analysis and toolbox approaches and neglects the need for diplomacy as an "art" for conflict prevention. Our own findings (Bressan and Bergmaier 2021; Bressan 2021; Bressan et al. 2019; Rotmann et al. 2021a; Baykal et al. 2021) show that this may be true but overstated: for while there are investments into technocratic analysis, there is a significant gap between data-driven analytical methods, for which the Foreign Office has hired external experts and advisors, and the traditional skillset and self-conception of diplomats as negotiators of the national interest. This is an obstacle to connecting more structured analysis based on quantitative data and other systematic analytical methods to decision-making and diplomatic practice. Temporary expert staff describes the problem as a double-blind: while data analysts ask diplomats what they need to make better decisions, diplomatic core staff asks analysts what better information they can provide. Both sides lack an understanding of how the other side operates. At the same time, producing valuable analytical products is hindered by the fact that analysts have to participate in the daily exercise of bureaucracy that consists of drafting memos, participating in update rounds, and responding to requests, instead of working on analytical products.

Regarding the structural changes needed to integrate new working modes into a traditional bureaucracy, Germany has lagged behind in the development of functioning interagency planning processes that improve coordination between foreign, development, defense, and related portfolios compared with other governments (Rotmann 2016, 8). This includes more systematic use of foresight methods for joint planning and strategizing, in which individual German ministries including the foreign office have recently increased the investments and started sharing assessments in interagency working groups. The ambitions of the 2014 Review to allow "more room for strategic reflection" (Auswärtiges Amt 2015, 45) with joint scenarios and deep analysis at times clash with the day to day operations of a hierarchical bureaucracy. As we found out in a three year research project on the use of structured foresight methods to inform conflict prevention policy making in European foreign services, including the German foreign office, "foresight exercises continue to be employed as one-off events that might help get a different perspective on an intractable policy problem, rather than as part of continuous threat-scanning and a systematic machinery of early warning for more effective prevention," which would be needed to realize any added value (Rotmann et al. 2021a, 26). Among countries, including Germany, time constraints and a lack of incentives to reflect on the fundamental strategic direction and devise alternatives were the most frequently mentioned reasons by diplomats for not using structured foresight methods more regularly, and for the results not having greater impact on policy. What's more, "even those institutions with several years of experience with different kinds of foresight exercises remain untouched in their core institutional cultures" (Bressan et al. 2019, 71).

When traditional bureaucratic structures and new project-related tasks meet, developing and carrying through strategic policy proposals is difficult. While bureaucrats are, on the one hand, often stuck in the daily operations of administering conferences, country visits, and—on the other hand—administering project funding, "the combination of insufficient resources, outdated processes, and increased political expectations makes it impossible for bureaucratic institutions to deliver policy options that meet the needs of political leaders and the public. Overstretched institutions are stuck in a perpetual state of reactive short-termism. … A main chunk of policymakers' time goes into coordinating responses between different stakeholders, resembling more a management than a policymaking role" (Rotmann et al. 2021a, 48). This becomes clear when looking at the concrete outcomes, for example in the way that crisis prevention funding is spent by Germany as the largest international donor in this policy area, which ends up being spent in a way that is not strategic, not informed by existing risk assessment and early warning analyses, and not focused enough to make a considerable difference in countries at risk of violent conflict and crisis (Rotmann et al. 2021b).

Outlook: Reform Requires Different Practices

Many have argued that globalization changes diplomacy, as it becomes more networked, transparent, and open, while other government portfolios such as environment, health, and energy become more globalized. Theories that define diplomacy by the particular way it is conducted get into trouble when foreign policy and other policy fields converge. Relational and practice theory approaches to analyzing diplomacy are helpful to de-mystify diplomacy and explain that what sets diplomacy apart from other professions is its claim to represent state authority and negotiate the terms of interaction between states. At the same time, diplomacy has moved from mere representation to the construction of a global governance system through diplomatic relations and, increasingly, questions of global governance. So the absence of governance mechanisms at the global level and the local level in areas at risk of conflict rightly concerns diplomats. Dealing with crises that call into question state authority and the rules of international relations thus remains the core business of diplomacy, but the ways of doing so have changed in recent years.

Institutional reforms in the German Federal Foreign Office since 2014 provide a glimpse of how diplomatic institutions adapt to the challenge of governing a global system and managing or hoping to prevent crises. This chapter has offered a reading of those reforms through a relational lens of diplomacy in practice. It finds that a cross-cutting working unit on international order took up the challenge directly; the German directorate for crisis prevention, stabilization, and related topics borrowed methods of managerial bureaucracy, professional development, and humanitarian aid to fill the gap of state authority and governance elsewhere, and in the absence of global governance mechanisms that can substitute for legitimate state authority in "fragile" areas. The discussion of Germany's context at the time of reform shows that a perception of multiple global crises in the context of challenged global governance, availability of funds, and the ambition to take responsibility created the conditions for institutional changes. An inclusive debate process taking place both internally and externally, the leadership of a minister with civil service experience, and the ability to build on exemplary reforms of partner governments and the

EU, which have developed similar working units and policy fields in recent years, were all additional enabling factors.

While institutional structures were successfully reformed to adapt to new challenges, emerging research shows that the process of transformation to a new practice of diplomacy that was also discussed in the German context (e.g., Bagger and Heynitz 2012) is far from complete. Some remaining obstacles like the difficulty of establishing intergovernmental decision-making structures in a coalition government are specific to the German context. Others, like the difficulty in adapting diplomatic career pathways to meet contemporary needs and creating structures in which different types of doing diplomacy—from representation to structured analysis and strategic steering of project funding—may be similar for other countries and they may be more successful in meeting them. Comparative research of the conditions that enable and shape the outcomes of reforms, as well as the diffusion of approaches between different levels of international governance and national bureaucracies, can help better understand how diplomacy can adapt. For this, it is essential that diplomacy as a research object is further de-mystified from a "third culture" to a bureaucratic practice that focuses on the core business of state sovereignty—a process that in principle may become easier as the diplomatic profession itself evolves.

Finally, a large set of challenges will continue to be present across countries: the need to match the increasing need for and supply of managerial, scientific, data-based, and structured analysis and policy development skills with the traditional ways of doing diplomacy. Arguably, both will be needed, but the challenge of integrating them is a significant challenge that diplomatic services need to accomplish. After all, the ability to anticipate, prevent, and manage crises as its core aim will always be the criteria on which successful diplomacy turns.

Acknowledgments For research referenced in this chapter, the author has received funding from the European Union's Horizon 2020 research and innovation program under grant agreement no. 769886 (EU-LISTCO project, 2018–21).

Special thanks to Sarah Brockmeier at Peace Research Institute Frankfurt for graciously sharing her expertise on diplomatic reform in Germany. The chapter reflects only the author's views.

References and Further Reading

Adler-Nissen, R. 2015. "Conclusion: Relationalism or Why Diplomats Find International Relations Theory Strange." In *Diplomacy and the Making of World Politics*, eds. O.J. Sending, V. Pouliot, and I.B. Neumann, 284–308. Cambridge: Cambridge University Press.

Auswärtiges Amt. 2015. "Review 2014 – Außenpolitik weiter denken" *Abschlussbericht*. https://www.bundesregierung.de/breg-de/service/publikationen/review-2014-aussenpolitik-weiter-denken-735224.

———. 2018. "Drei Jahre, Außenpolitik mit Mitteln." https://www.auswaertiges-amt.de/de/aussenpolitik/themen/humanitaere-hilfe/-/1697156.

———. 2020. Germany's Foreign Policy Budget. https://wien-io.diplo.de/iow-de/karriere/haushalt/229742.

———. 2022. "Ohne Geld geht Außenpolitik nicht: Der Haushalt des Auswärtigen Amtes." https://www.auswaertiges-amt.de/de/aamt/auswdienst/haushalt/2283092.

Auswärtiges Amt, BMVg, and BMZ. 2012. "Interministerial Guidelines – For a Coherent German Government Policy towards Fragile States."

Avant, D.D., M. Finnemore, and S.K. Sell, eds. 2010. *Who Governs the Globe?* Cambridge: Cambridge University Press.

Bagger, T., and W. von Heynitz. 2012. "'Der vernetzte Diplomat': Von Vernetzter Sicherheit zu einer netzwerkorientierten Außenpolitik." *Zeitschrift für Außen-und Sicherheitspolitik* 5 (1): 49–61.

Bargués-Pedreny, P., A. Bergmaier, F. Bicchi, A. Buchwald, K. Eickhoff, P. Morillas, G. Sanchez, and A. Schmauder. 2019. *Does Resilience Permeate Foreign Policy?* EU-LISTCO Working Paper No. 4.

Bartonek, E. 2020. "Journeying into the Diplomatic Unknown: The Vergesellschaftung of the German Auswärtiges Amt." *The Hague Journal of Diplomacy* 15 (1–2): 196–205.

Baykal, A., S. Bressan, J. Gabriel, and P. Rotmann. 2021. *Report on Four Strategic Policy Design Exercises*. EU-LISTCO Project.

Bendiek, A. 2015. "The '2014 Review': Understanding the Pillars of German Foreign Policy and the Expectations of the Rest of the World." Note du Cerfa (123). French Institute of International Relations. https://www.ifri.org/en/publications/notes-de-lifri/notes-cerfa/2014-review-understanding-pillars-german-foreign-policy-and.

Bernstein, T. 2017. "United Nations Secretary-General António Guterres: The First 100 Days." ZIF Policy Briefing.

Bressan, S. 2021. "Crisis Early Warning: The Path From Foresight to Prevention." https://peacelab.blog/2021/06/crisis-early-warning-berlins-path-from-foresight-to-prevention.

Bressan, S., and A. Bergmaier. 2021. "From Conflict Early Warning to Fostering Resilience? Chasing Convergence in EU Foreign Policy." *Democratization* 28 (7): 1357–74.

Bressan, S., J. Gabriel, P. Rotmann, and D. Seefeldt. 2019. *Report on Four Threat-Scanning Workshops*. EU-LISTCO Project.

Brockmeier, S. 2020. "The German Foreign Office at 150: Time to Shake Things Up." https://www.gppi.net/2020/04/08/the-german-foreign-office-at-150-time-to-shake-things-up.

Brockmeier, S., and P. Rotmann. 2019. *Krieg vor der Haustür: Die Gewalt in Europas Nachbarschaft und was wir dagegen tun können*. Bonn: Dietz.

Bundesministerium der Finanzen. 2022. Bundeshaushalt Datenportal. https://www.bundeshaushalt.de/DE/Datenportal/datenportal.html.

Eberle, J., and A. Miskimmon. 2021. "International Theory and German Foreign Policy: Introduction to a Special Issue." *German Politics* 30 (1): 1–13.

Freeden, M. 2017. "Crisis? How Is That a Crisis?! Reflections on an Overburdened Word." *Contributions to the History of Concepts* 12 (2): 12–28.

Heine, J. 2013. "From Club to Network Diplomacy." In *The Oxford Handbook of Modern Diplomacy*, eds. A.F. Cooper, J. Heine, and R. Thakur, 54–69. Oxford: Oxford University Press.

Herrberg, A. 2021. "Translating the Peace Ambition into Practice: The Role of the European External Action Service in EU Peace Mediation." *European Foreign Affairs Review* 26 (1): 133–48.

Ikani, N. 2020. "European Foreign Policy in Times of Crisis: A Political Development Lens." *Journal of European Integration* 42 (5): 767–82.

Koddenbrock, K., and S. Hoffmann. 2017. "There is No Alternative." *Zeitschrift für Friedens-und Konfliktforschung* 6 (1): 73–106.

Kurtz, G., and C.O. Meyer. 2018. "Is Conflict Prevention a Science, Craft, or Art? Moving Beyond Technocracy and Wishful Thinking." *Global Affairs* 5 (1): 23–39.

Lequesne, C. 2015. "EU Foreign Policy through the Lens of Practice Theory: A Different Approach to the European External Action Service." *Cooperation and Conflict* 50 (3): 351–67.

———. 2020. "Ministries of Foreign Affairs: A Crucial Institution Revisited." *The Hague Journal of Diplomacy* 15 (1/2): 1–12.

———. 2022. *Ministries of Foreign Affairs in the World: Actors of State Diplomacy*. Boston: Brill.

Levi, M. 1997. "A Model, a Method, and a Map: Rational Choice in Comparative and Historical Analysis." In *Comparative Politics: Rationality, Culture, and Structure*, eds. M.I. Lichbach and A.S. Zuckerman, 19–41. Cambridge: Cambridge University Press.

Mair, S. 2022. "The National Security Strategy and the Zeitenwende in German Foreign Policy." *Verfassungsblog*. https://verfassungsblog.de/the-national-security-strategy-and-the-zeitenwende-in-german-foreign-policy/.

Mattelaer, A. 2019. *The Resurgence of Bilateral Diplomacy in Europe*. Egmont Paper 104, January. http://www.egmontinstitute.be/the-resurgence-of-bilateral-diplomacy-in-europe/.

Risse, T. 2022. "Zeitenwende?" *Internationale Politik*, June 10. https://internationalepolitik.de/de/zeitenwende-2.

Rotmann, P. 2016. "Toward a Realistic and Responsible Idea of Stabilisation." *Stability: International Journal of Security and Development* 5 (1): 1–14.

Rotmann, P., and L. Steinacker. 2014. *Stabilisierung: Begriffe, Strukturen und Praxis im Vergleich*. Global Public Policy Institute. https://www.gppi.net/media/rotmann-steinacker_2014_stabilisierung-gppi-studie_DE.pdf.

Rotmann, P., A. Baykal, S. Bressan, J. Gabriel, A.F. Tollefsen, and S.A. Rustad. 2021a. *Analysis of Cross-Cutting Findings and Lessons on Forecasting and Foresight*. EU-LISTCO project.

Rotmann, P., M. Li, and S. Stoffel. 2021b. *Die 9-Milliarden-Euro-Frage: Was und wie investiert Deutschland in Krisenprävention?* Global Public Policy Institute. https://gppi.net/2021/12/20/die-9-milliarden-euro-frage.

Seabrooke, L. 2015. "Diplomacy as Economic Consultancy." In *Diplomacy and the Making of World Politics*, eds. O.J. Sending, V. Pouliot, and I.B. Neumann, 195–219. Cambridge: Cambridge University Press.

Sending, O.J., V. Pouliot, and I.B. Neumann, eds. 2015. *Diplomacy and the Making of World Politics*. Cambridge: Cambridge University Press.

Sharp, P. 2009. *Diplomatic Theory of International Relations*. Cambridge: Cambridge University Press.

World Bank and United Nations Development Programme. 2018. *Pathways for Peace: Inclusive Approaches to Preventing Violent Conflict*. Washington, D.C.: The World Bank.

12

Integrated Statecraft and Australia's Diplomacy

Tom Barber and Melissa Conley Tyler

Introduction

In Australia, as in many countries, the practice of diplomacy has lost prestige. This has spurred an interesting example of diplomatic innovation bringing together diplomacy, development, and defense. This chapter will look at what has changed in Australia's circumstances and the impact this has had on diplomacy. It will then look at a modest innovation trying to push against this tide.

So if diplomacy has lost its privileged position, when was the high-water mark of Australian diplomacy? There are a few eras that merit consideration: the immediate post-war period where Australia played an important role in the formation of the United Nations; the late 1980s and early 1990s when Canberra played a leading role in the formation of the Asia-Pacific Economic Cooperation forum and the signing of the Paris Peace accords ending the conflict in Cambodia; and the "creative middle power diplomacy" of the late-2000s in which Australia was central to the formation of the G20 and East Asia Summit. Each of these periods are important and collectively they help demonstrate how the prestige of Australian diplomacy has fallen in recent years.

To be sure, this is not a phenomenon unique to Australia. Across the globe, diplomacy is under strain on several fronts. Populism's derision of elites

---

T. Barber • M. Conley Tyler (✉)
Asia-Pacific Development, Diplomacy & Defence Dialogue,
Canberra, Australia

© The Author(s), under exclusive license to Springer Nature Switzerland AG 2023
P. W. Hare et al. (eds.), *The Palgrave Handbook of Diplomatic Reform and Innovation*, Studies in Diplomacy and International Relations, https://doi.org/10.1007/978-3-031-10971-3_12

downplays and undermines the important function that diplomacy serves, while the polemical and maximalist positions being staked out by partisans in democracies are antithetical to the compromise and negotiation that diplomacy entails. Rising nationalism likewise prioritizes the domestic over the international, and the dawning of a new, more contested era has seen defense budgets balloon at the expense of diplomatic investment, building on the groundwork of the prioritization of national security in the post-9/11 world. Since 2001, for example, Australian military spending has increased by 122 percent in real terms, while funding for the Department of Foreign Affairs and Trade has shrunk by 9 percent (Australian Strategic Policy Institute 2021; Wise 2022). More subtly, there are reports of the Department of Foreign Affairs losing its "heft" in decision-making, with diplomats not consulted on important foreign policy decisions (Dziedzic 2018; Gyngell and McCarthy 2021; Seo 2019). In addition, trends like technological change continue to redefine the practice of diplomacy in the twenty-first century. Taken together, it is perhaps no surprise that diplomacy has lost some of its luster.

But the decline of diplomacy is not a *fait accompli*. Newton's third law—that for every action, there is an equal and opposite reaction—can apply to politics as much as physics. The steady erosion of Australia's diplomatic capacity is being contested by a resolute constituency that includes prominent academics, experts, and former practitioners, including former Secretaries of the Department of Foreign Affairs and Trade (Broadbent et al. 2009; Conley Tyler 2019; Costello 2021; Langmore et al. 2020; Oliver and Shearer 2011; Wise 2022). Whereas previously the consequences of diplomatic underinvestment were only apparent to the informed who knew where to look, it is now beginning to be visible in public debate in a way not seen before (Conley Tyler 2021b; Galloway 2021).

At a surface level, remedying the problem would appear quite simple: increase the diplomatic budget. But it is more complex than that. Prestige is not something that can be immediately reacquired; investment needs to be long term, systematic, and comprehensive. There is a need to treat the underlying causes and not just dress the symptoms. Because the decline of diplomacy cannot be pinned down to one particular factor—it is the result of many that are dynamic and interacting—any attempt to rectify the problem must take this into account.

In that context, an interesting, if modest, experiment is taking place in Australia that seeks to arrest the decline by bringing together the development, defense, and diplomacy communities to advocate for Australia to use all the arms of its statecraft in a difficult and contested world (Asia-Pacific Development, Diplomacy & Defence Dialogue 2021a). In doing so, it is taking inspiration from similar initiatives in other countries promoting a "3D" approach that integrates development, diplomacy, and defense including the United States, United Kingdom, Canada, and the Netherlands (Conley Tyler 2021a).

According to Allan Gyngell (2016, 2), Australian statecraft "embraces all the attributes of state power, domestic as well as international, military as well as diplomatic." Foreign policy is a central method by which statecraft is pursued, with diplomacy best conceptualized as its operating system. The 2017 Foreign Policy White Paper (Department of Foreign Affairs and Trade 2017, 17) said that Australia's "diplomacy promotes regional stability, security and prosperity, through our work with bilateral partners and in multilateral forums. We cannot impose our views or our will overseas. Our ability to protect and advance our interests rests on the quality of our engagement with the world."

But statecraft as a whole also encompasses defense and development programs as distinct pillars that have established roles and outlooks. Over time, Australian departments and specialized communities have coalesced across these constituent components of Australian statecraft, leading to siloed approaches taking hold. The wording in the 2017 Foreign Policy White Paper makes this division clear: "In the decade ahead, strong diplomatic, defence and national security capabilities will be essential to shape events to our advantage. Our development assistance will support efforts to build a stable and prosperous world, with a focus on the Indo–Pacific" (Department of Foreign Affairs and Trade 2017, 2).

By encouraging more interchange between the different elements of statecraft, and implementing an overarching strategic coherence that guides them toward complementary and shared goals, a 3D approach that leads to more integrated statecraft is beneficial for each of its constituent elements. This chapter will look at what has changed in Australia's circumstances in recent decades and the impact this has had on diplomacy. It will then look at this new initiative that has been established to reinvigorate Australian diplomacy. Challenges to diplomacy have provided the impetus for this innovation.

Australia's Foreign Policy

Australia's foreign policy technically only came into being in 1942 with the adoption by parliament of the Statute of Westminster, which formally gave Australia full sovereignty over its foreign policy. The context in which this decision was made—immediately following the fall of British Singapore to the forces of Imperial Japan—reveals a deep, underlying fear of abandonment that has permeated thinking on Australia's place in the world since European settlement (Gyngell 2017). With the British defeated in Asia and focused on the war in Europe, Prime Minister John Curtin looked to the United States to fill the void, "free of any pangs as to our traditional links or kinship with the United Kingdom … we shall exert all our energies towards the shaping of a plan, with the United States as its keystone, which will give our country some confidence of being able to hold out until the tide of battle swings against the enemy" (National Museum of Australia 2021).

This decision exemplifies how the fear of abandonment underpins a central pillar of Australian foreign policy: the cultivation and maintenance of a relationship with a great and powerful friend. The Australian desire to ally itself with a strong external power—the UK by history and the U.S. by choice—spoke to a deep unease about its geography. Upon federating, one of the first acts of Australian parliament was to pass the Immigration Restriction Bill, otherwise known as the White Australia policy, which essentially blocked non-European immigrants from entering the country. The threat that Imperial Japan posed during the Second World War was the manifestation of a long-held fear of invasion from the North.

In the years following the end of the Pacific War, however, with the United States emerging as the clear dominant power in Asia, these anxieties were somewhat alleviated, or at least became repressed. Cold War episodes—such as the conflict in Vietnam and the subsequent concerns about the implications of the Nixon Doctrine—demonstrated that the fear of abandonment was still very much alive in the Australian imagination. But for the most part, U.S. primacy precipitated a remarkable period of stability in Asia that allowed other pillars of Australian foreign policy to emerge, solidify, and flourish.

Decolonization meant that Australia's neighborhood was now filled with independent, sovereign states rather than outposts of European empires. The formation of the Association of Southeast Asian Nations (ASEAN) in 1967 and subsequent emergence of Asian regionalism, as well as the rapid industrialization of the "Tiger economies," presented Australia with a dilemma; not so much a fear of being invaded, but a risk of being left out. Whereas Australia had previously seen the region through a prism of threat, Asian economic opportunities were now becoming clear. Merchandise exports to Europe began a steady decline from around 70 percent of Australia's total immediately prior to World War II to less than 5 percent by 2015—a mirror image of exports to Asia over the same period (Department of Foreign Affairs and Trade 2015, 8).

Increasing economic enmeshment in the region, as well as the desire to maintain peace and stability, provided impetus for more Australian diplomatic engagement in Asia. Australia established formal relations with ASEAN in 1974—the first non-member state to do so—and followed up with the creation of the annual ASEAN-Australia Forum in 1977 (Gyngell 2017). It instituted the Colombo Plan in the 1950s in order to forge stronger links with the region through education. It recast its relationship with Japan as one of mutual trading benefit. The central role that Canberra played in the formation of the Asia-Pacific Economic Cooperation forum is likewise testament to the diplomatic capital spent on ensuring that Australia sought security "in" and not "from" Asia.

Australia's approach to the region was reflective of its growing multilateral inclinations more broadly. As a middle power, Australia saw benefit in the UN ecosystem of multilateral institutions born out of the San Francisco Conference, as well as the obligations outlined in the Bretton Woods agreement (both of which it helped draft). Australia was likewise instrumental in the formation of the Asia-Pacific Economic Cooperation forum and the Cairns Group agricultural trading bloc—the former as a result of the compelling logic for the creation of "formal intergovernmental vehicle of regional cooperation" in response to global trade liberalization; the latter to ensure such trade liberalization took place on an even playing field (Gyngell 2017). The advantages of a system of rules that govern international behavior were and remain highly appealing to a country that depends on maritime trade and who would be at the mercy of great powers in a "might is right" order. The emphasis in recent years on support for a "rules-based order" is not a new phenomenon—it is merely a more vocal manifestation of a longstanding view.

The need for such vocalizations, however, reveals how the longstanding underpinnings of Australian foreign policy have come under challenge of late. Rod Lyon argues: "Much like individuals, states can be thought to have strategic personalities, a set of ingrained habits which reflect their relationship with the world," and which "is the product of its history and culture, the 'ingrained habits' of its long-term interactions with the world." Because of this: "In the strategic personality stakes, states change only slowly" (Lyon 2019).

The United States' Cold War triumph and resulting addition of a liberal prefix to "international order" heralded a time of optimism and confidence, at least among those in the West, that liberal democracy and free markets would prevail. Australia found itself in a remarkably benign environment—benefiting from an international order that reflected its own values and interests and allied to an unrivaled unipolar hegemon that shared them too. From this privileged position, Canberra was able to pursue an agenda of middle power activism that belied its size and built a reputation as a respected diplomatic operator and international citizen that "punched above its weight." The "active middle power diplomacy" of the Rudd government in response to the Global Financial Crisis—leading to the elevation of the G20 as "principal manager of the global economic system" (Cotton and Ravenhill 2011, 6)—as well as less successful attempts to promote international cooperation on climate change and to establish an Asia-Pacific Community, typified the diplomatic ambition of Australian governments throughout the first decades of the post-Cold War world. But this all began to change soon after the new century dawned.

A range of factors including the continued rise of China as a peer competitor to the United States and its authoritarian turn under Xi Jinping, along with the impact of rising populism in democracies across the world and the knock-on effect that it has had on international institutions and multilateralism, have disrupted and threatened to break down the rules-based international order from which Australia has so benefitted. In a March 2022 speech, Australian Prime Minister Scott Morrison said that "A new arc of autocracy is instinctively aligning to challenge and reset the world order in their own image" (Morrison 2022). Indeed, some have argued that "the order we have known for the past seventy years has ended. It's not being challenged. It's not changing. It's over" (Gyngell in Lowy Institute 2018). COVID-19 has acted as an accelerant for many of these negative trends.

For Australian policymakers, this is unwelcome news. Four years of erratic Trump administration policies, pronouncements, and Twitter pontification have raised doubts over whether the United States can be relied upon as a responsible and dependable ally in the future (Wyeth 2021). China, Australia's largest trading partner, continues to wage a campaign of economic coercion via tariffs and sanctions on Australian exports (Hanson et al. 2020). And the steady erosion of the international rules-based order more broadly threatens the foundations upon which modern Australian security and prosperity are built. This is an era in which the stability of the Indo-Pacific region cannot be assumed and the rules and institutions that help maintain peace and security are under strain.

The speed at which events are proceeding and change is occurring means that the demands being placed on Australia's diplomatic corps are increasing in intensity, complexity, and urgency at every level of analysis. Australian diplomacy is in a state of flux, with the need to continually respond and adapt inhibiting the ability to proactively shape and influence. This can be attributed to three overarching challenges facing Australian diplomacy today: a lack of coherence with respect to what the core purposes of Australian diplomacy are; a paucity of public debate and understanding of Australia's national interests and diplomatic priorities; and the systematic under-resourcing of the Department of Foreign Affairs and Trade (Byrne et al. 2016).

Australia's Declining Diplomacy

Security has always held a privileged status in the realm of international relations. In an anarchic society, the most basic responsibility of a sovereign state is to ensure its citizens' physical safety and survival. Human security and state security are complementary, and it is from this base that all other functions of the state are built on. Over the centuries a latticework of mechanisms, institutions, and norms have been established and refined that guide countries' interactions with each other to try and prevent misunderstanding and conflict and smoothen the anarchic edges of the international order. If we think of this structure as the hardware of international relations, then diplomacy is its operating system.

In times of relative global order, diplomacy is easier to pursue. For Australia, the late 1980s and 1990s were such a time: the "end of history" had been declared and Australia's privileged position as outlined above afforded it the latitude to attempt and pull off some adroit diplomatic successes, such as the coalition-building efforts that led to the formation of the Cairns Group of agricultural exporters in 1986, the establishment of the Asia-Pacific Economic Cooperation forum—"the first trans-Pacific governmental organization" (Gyngell 2017, 145)—in 1989, and the 1995 Australia-Indonesia Agreement on Maintaining Security (Fathana 2018). That is not to underplay the agency of talented diplomats and ambitious leaders, but to highlight how structural and environmental factors can open up the space for diplomacy.

Following the 2001 terrorist attacks in New York, however, the factors favorable to Australian diplomacy began to change. If the world's most powerful nation could not prevent an attack on its own soil, then how should less powerful nations like Australia prepare? In response to the risk of terrorism, Australia began to invest more heavily in national security and defense capacity. Subsequent wars in Afghanistan and Iraq, as well as further Islamist terrorist attacks around the world—including those that killed Australians in Indonesia—gave further prominence to defense and national security perspectives. This period can be thought of as one in which Australian foreign policy was securitized, insofar as it marked the beginning of an era in which the security domain was given prominence over other elements of statecraft such as diplomacy (Behm 2020).

Following the emergence of a new, more assertive China under the stewardship of General Secretary Xi Jinping, Australia's relationship with its biggest trading partner has also been largely securitized, with the domestic China debate increasingly being framed around national security issues—both in a bilateral sense following China's sanctions on Australian exports, but also in terms of the regional and global implications of U.S.-China geostrategic competition (Chubb 2022). This is reflected in public perceptions, with Lowy Institute polling recording a 22-point increase (41 percent to 63 percent) in Australians viewing China as "more of a security threat to Australia" from 2020 to 2021; while those viewing China as "more of an economic partner to Australia" decreased from 55 percent to 34 percent over the same period (Lowy Institute 2021a).

Australia's 2020 Defence Strategic Update reflected such concerns and revealed how key foreign policy issues are being increasingly framed in national security terms. This tendency is most visibly evident in the first of three strategic objectives outlined in the update: to shape Australia's strategic environment (Department of Defence 2020). The other two objectives—to deter actions against Australia's interests and to respond with credible military force, when required—are traditional defense responsibilities. This stands in contrast to the first, which has historically been a whole of nation endeavor that is built on influence deriving from diplomacy, development, and trade.

At the current time, Australia's international engagement more broadly is often refracted through the dominant prism of national security. It is a highwater mark for bringing all aspects of life within a security view when activities like study abroad, artistic exchange, export bureaus, and trade delegations are scrutinized as issues of national security, as occurred with Australia's new *Foreign Relations Act* in 2020 (Conley Tyler 2021c).

The decline of diplomacy and increase in prominence of defense can be detrimental to Australia's international engagement in peacetime. Security thinking tends to paint in black and white, as enemies or friends. The focus is on denying the enemy its interests and every concession can be painted as a loss of sovereignty rather than a trade-off. This is appropriate when in conflict. But in peacetime, problems arise if this approach subordinates a less adversarial civilian perspective and creates a self-fulfilling prophecy. Along with the securitization of Australia's international relations "comes the attendant risk that Australia will not just be dragged into unnecessary conflict, but also that an unbalanced posture might help precipitate it" (Moore 2020).

Nevertheless, the trend toward a hard power-centric view of international affairs endures and has been strengthened by Russia's 2022 invasion of Ukraine. Australia's prime minister has spoken of the need to defend against an "arc of autocracy" in the context of Australia facing its "most difficult and dangerous security environment in 80 years" (Morrison 2022). In conjunction with declining diplomatic budgets and increasing defense spending, such rhetoric serves to further entrench the dominance of national security perspectives within Australian foreign policy-making, insofar as it implies that diplomacy has been ineffective or is somehow unsuited to the task. What results is a feedback loop wherein resource allocation gets more skewed, which in turn places additional strain on an already stretched diplomatic capacity, thus further solidifying perceptions that diplomacy is ill-equipped to deal with security challenges, and that defense spending must be increased as a result.

While Australia has its own distinct idiosyncrasies, its experience should nonetheless be understood as part of a broader global phenomenon around the decline of diplomacy. The impact of domestic factors like populism and nationalism that can devalue diplomacy (as discussed below) as well as international trends like the breaking down of the rules-based order and deterioration of the strategic environment—which can be portrayed and perceived as failures of preventive diplomacy—have elicited similar declines in the esteem in which diplomacy is held across the world, however unfair these criticisms might be.

In recent decades, diplomacy has had to evolve quickly in response to fundamental changes, especially in transport and communications technology, meaning that diplomats no longer have the exclusive gatekeeper role they once held in international affairs. During what is often depicted as a golden age of diplomacy before the end of the twentieth century, diplomats belonged to an exclusive club that managed international engagement. Today, real-time communication technologies and ease of travel give the (false) impression that anyone can communicate seamlessly across borders. While the information revolution might well contribute to the democratization of diplomacy, it can also contribute to a decreased appreciation of the tradecraft and skillset that diplomats have. With "traditional distinctions between domestic and foreign audiences, elite and general publics, producers and consumers" becoming "less relevant than ever before," it is understandable that diplomacy might no longer be widely regarded as a special skill (Byrne 2020).

Moreover, such perceptions can lead not only to the erosion of diplomats' power and dismissal of their craft as politicized, overvalued, or exaggerated (see Pauline Kerr's chapter on politicization and diplomats in this volume), but to depreciation of the important work that they do and denigration of their profession. Populist leaders are often associated with centralizing foreign policy decision-making within the leader's close inner circle of family and loyal advisors (Conley Tyler 2021d). They tend to express suspicion of professional diplomats who are, definitionally, elites, and instead prefer to conduct leader-on-leader diplomacy through summits (or loudspeaker diplomacy via Twitter). Populism offers simplistic answers to complex problems. If difficult multifaceted questions become party political, it tends toward lowest common denominator debate. Worse, if issues become totemic of political identity, it stymies productive thinking, with decision-making becoming a matter of identity, rather than policy (Conley Tyler 2020).

Diplomacy means living with compromises, stopgaps, and partial solutions (Conley Tyler 2021d). It accepts that friction is unavoidable; the task of diplomacy is to manage, contain, and ease the effects of friction. Diplomacy deals with nuance (which can sound like being an apologist) and engagement (which can sound like appeasement). Diplomats have to understand how issues look from other countries' points of view (which can sound like agreeing with the other side). Being an intrinsically subtle and incrementalist enterprise, diplomacy is rarely revolutionary. Such qualities are conspicuously incongruous within a milieu of rapid change where immediate solutions to problems are in high demand. In "a post-truth, hyperemotional world," the "pragmatic nature of traditional diplomacy prevents it from employing a similarly emotional response. In the eyes of socially engaged publics, this delegitimizes traditional diplomacy" (Emrich and Schulze 2017, 5).

Another major challenge for diplomacy is domestic politics: specifically, domestic nationalism and the desire to be seen as tough on foreigners. An example of this has been China's wolf warrior diplomats—named after a patriotic movie franchise—who have conducted foreign policy with an eye to domestic audiences wanting to see an assertive China pursuing its national greatness. This phenomenon is considered a direct response to President Xi Jinping issuing diplomats a memo in 2019 to show more "fighting spirit" (Zhai and Tian). But demanding that one's diplomats be demonstratively patriotic means it is difficult for them to do their job in terms of connecting with their host society. Diplomats operate in a curious liminal space between domestic constituencies and foreign audiences where an air of duplicity and slipperiness is hard to shake (Byrne 2020). They must constantly maintain their legitimacy, managing "the suspicion of their host state and that of their own state, demonstrating to both their honesty, reliability and capacity" (Hall 2010, 249).

If there is a common theme among these challenges—be it securitization, populism, or domestic politics—it is that simplistic explanations of international trends and events have been to the detriment of diplomacy. But that is not to say such negative trends have gone unnoticed or unopposed. In

Australia there has been a concerted advocacy effort over a number of years to attempt to arrest the decline in diplomatic prestige and capability. The Lowy Institute has for over a decade charted the decline in resourcing allocated to the Department of Foreign Affairs and Trade; not only in reports dedicated to the issue—such as Diplomatic Deficit (2009) and Diplomatic Disrepair (2011)—but in other products that shine a light on it, such as the Asia Power Index which shows Australia's diplomatic influence "trending down" in key metrics over time compared to other regional countries (Lowy Institute 2021b). Alex Oliver (2020) has been at the forefront of this debate, pointing out how Australia's "diplomacy has been sapped by increasingly strained budgets, relentless 'efficiency dividends' and workforce cuts," making it particularly challenging to pursue a "strenuous diplomatic agenda" given that this "requires a diplomatic corps operating at peak ability" (Oliver 2020).

As well as analysts and academics, several high-profile former practitioners have lamented the decline of Australian diplomacy and securitization of Australian foreign policy. Former Ambassador to Thailand James Wise (2022) has been critical of Australia's undervaluing and under-resourcing of diplomacy, advocating for a new capability statement and funding to match. According to former Department of Foreign Affairs and Trade (DFAT) secretary Michael Costello (2021): "diplomacy seems to have been forgotten in the febrile alarmism that has taken hold in Australia's security establishment and now dominates our national discourse on external relations. The relative decline in DFAT's resourcing and influence is a critical related factor." Former Director-General of the Australian Office of National Assessments, Allan Gyngell, and former ambassador John McCarthy have similarly tried to draw attention to the dire state of Australian diplomacy, underlining the disparity between diplomatic and defense investment and criticizing the number of political appointments to diplomatic postings (Gyngell and McCarthy 2021).

Yet despite these interventions, there has been no discernible effect in terms of reversing the decline of Australian diplomacy as underpinned by decades of systematic bipartisan neglect. Australia's combined budget for diplomacy and overseas development assistance has contracted from $8.3 billion for the 2013–14 financial year (adjusted for inflation) to $7.26 billion for 2020–21 (Conley Tyler 2019; Treasury 2021, 67–69). The foreign aid component has been held at a baseline of $4 billion (supplemented by temporary and targeted measures), a reduction of $1 billion since 2013, meaning it is at its lowest point ever as a percentage of gross national income at 0.2 percent (Conley Tyler 2019; Department of Foreign Affairs and Trade 2021).

In 2019, Australia was ranked twentieth of twenty-nine among developed nations in the Organization for Economic Co-operation and Development

(OECD) for its diplomatic resources. With 118 diplomatic missions abroad, Australia is below the OECD average of 132, and nowhere near the G20 average of 196. It is outranked by countries such as Portugal, Greece, and Chile, which have smaller populations and less than 20 percent of Australia's GDP (Lowy Institute 2019).

And even these figures overstate Australia's reach: many of its diplomatic posts are micro-missions, with as few as two or three staff posted from Canberra, meaning they have limited outreach and spend much of their time on administration (Wise 2022). The ever-growing number of Australians traveling abroad has meant an increase in the proportion of funding allocated for passport applications and consular assistance (now 23 percent of DFAT's budget) at the cost of its broader diplomatic mission. Given the complexity and scale of issues it faces in the fast-moving international environment, DFAT's funding is beyond lean, which also has implications for recruitment and retention of talented staff.

A Diplomatic Innovation

Considering the challenges outlined above, and given the limited impact of advocacy to date in reinvigorating Australian diplomacy, it is worth exploring and encouraging new approaches that might prove more successful in reversing the decline of diplomacy. In this context, a current effort is underway in Australia that adopts an innovative approach based on bringing together the development, diplomacy, and defense communities. The Asia-Pacific Development, Diplomacy & Defence Dialogue (AP4D) (2021a) is based on what has been termed a 3D approach that appears to have had an effect in other countries (Conley Tyler 2021a). This seeks to bring together each of the constituent parts of statecraft—broadly defined as development, diplomacy, and defense—and institutionalize mechanisms so that each element of statecraft is complementary, mutually reinforcing, and guided by the same overarching strategic vision.

A 3D approach argues that in an era of rolling change, crises, and disruption that are increasingly blurring the lines between previously more distinct facets of international interaction—such as the emergence of geoeconomics and the rise of political interference—maintaining a traditional siloed approach to foreign policy risks impeding its overall effectiveness. It promotes the case for a more integrated approach to foreign policy that incorporates each of the elements of statecraft in complementary ways. As the 2010 U.S. Quadrennial Defense Review made clear: many "authorities and structures assume a neat divide between defense, diplomacy, and development that simply does not exist" (U.S. Department of Defense 2010, 74).

In the United States, a 3D approach to international engagement was actively promoted during the Obama Administration by Secretary of State Hillary Clinton (2019) and Secretary of Defense Robert Gates (Silberman 2014). More recently, President Biden appointed Samantha Power as U.S. AID administrator and elevated the role to the National Security Council "to ensure our development agenda is a core pillar of our foreign policy" (Biden 2021). In his first foreign policy speech at the State Department, Biden told his nation's diplomats "the message I want the world to hear today: America is back. Diplomacy is back at the center of our foreign policy." He described "leading with diplomacy" as including "standing shoulder-to-shoulder with our allies and key partners once again" but also "engaging our adversaries and our competitors diplomatically, where it's in our interest, and advance the security of the American people." Biden also announced a Global Posture Review so that "our military footprint is appropriately aligned with our foreign policy and national security priorities" (White House 2021), and his administration's 2021 budget request responded to what it described as "years of neglect" by making critical investments in diplomacy and development (Garver 2021). These requests were largely approved by Congress. Subtracting the amounts designated as emergency funds, funding for the Department of State's total foreign operations increased from U.S.$34.88 billion in the 2021 financial year to U.S.$40.95 billion in the 2022 enacted budget, while the spend on bilateral development assistance increased from U.S.$22.9 billion in the 2021 financial year to U.S.$27.4 billion in the 2022 enacted budget (Congressional Research Service 2022, 28–34). The Biden administration's 2023 budget request included "[U.S.]$67.6 billion for the State Department, the United States Agency for International Development and other international programs for the 2023 fiscal year, an increase of 18 percent from the amount enacted in 2021" (Wong 2022).

In the United Kingdom the 3D approach has progressed to the point that the government produces an Integrated Review of Security, Defence, Development and Foreign Policy rather than separate white papers. The integrated review promises "an approach that puts diplomacy first" (UK Government 2021, 14) and defines effective diplomacy as "a critical tool in the UK's ability to deliver for British citizens in the world" (ibid, 45). As in the United States, this prioritization in the United Kingdom is not at the expense of other arms of statecraft. The review makes the case for deeper integration across government, "bringing together defence, diplomacy, development, intelligence and security, trade and aspects of domestic policy in pursuit of cross-government, national objectives" (ibid, 19). Britain's indicators of diplomacy are strong. The resourcing gap is smaller than in the United States, with defense funding only four times greater than foreign/development (although the current trend is increasing the gap). The fact that strategic planning is now integrated across defense, diplomacy, and development itself is an indicator of giving diplomacy weight.

The 3D approach has also been applied by the governments of Canada and the Netherlands. The Dutch applied a 3D framework as part of their International Security Assistance Force (ISAF) responsibilities in Uruzgan province in Afghanistan. As in Australia, development and diplomacy are already integrated within a single Ministry of Foreign Affairs in the Netherlands, and coherence is sought with the Ministry of Defence. The Afghanistan mission further developed this integration by involving non-government organizations and business partners, although it has been criticized for being too vague and broad and thus not necessarily a 3D approach to be emulated (van der Lijn 2011, 24–25).

Canada's 3D experiment also began with its mission in Afghanistan. As its ISAF responsibility switched from Kabul to Kandahar province, the Martin Liberal government released "an International Policy Statement (IPS) detailing how Canada would take a leading role in the world by leveraging the combined efforts of the Department of Foreign Affairs and International Trade (DFAIT), the Department of National Defence (DND), and the Canadian International Development Agency (CIDA)" (Boisvert-Novak 2019, 1–2). The 3D approach was subsequently kept and rebranded as "WoG" (Whole-of-Government) by the Conservative Harper Government when it won office in 2006, and continues to shape Canada's international engagements, as well as some domestic armed forces operations. Despite criticisms that WoG has become "a catch-all term without any formal grounding in policy, procedures or practices" (ibid., 2), the longevity of the concept—whether articulated in 3D, whole-of-government, or comprehensive approach terms—demonstrates that it has purchase.

These examples suggest that, while taking an integrated approach to international strategy is not a panacea, the process by which one is instituted can allow policymakers to step out of constraints, re-evaluate risks and opportunities, and chart a new course. It cannot miraculously create a whole-of-government, whole-of-nation culture where it is lacking, but it can help to build one where it is sought.

Australia has arguably been an outlier in its reluctance to embrace more holistic policy-making (Sussex 2021). It has not yet commissioned a process similar to the UK's integrated review, outlined commitments to critical investment in diplomacy akin to those of President Biden, or formally adopted a 3D foreign policy framework.

However there does seem to be an appetite among Australian policymakers for a more integrated approach to foreign policy. There has been increased use of 3D language across both sides of politics. Prime Minister Scott Morrison (2020) has spoken about the need to use all elements of statecraft to shape the world he wants to see. Minister for International Development and the Pacific Zed Seselja (2021) have committed to use "all the tools of statecraft." Minister for Foreign Affairs Marise Payne has described Australia's response to COVID-19 in the region as a "whole-of- government framework" that draws on "the full suite of our development, diplomatic, and defence capabilities" (Minister for Foreign Affairs 2020).

This is mirrored across the political divide with Shadow Minister for International Development and the Pacific Pat Conroy MP calling for "greater coordination between development, diplomacy and defence policy" (Conroy 2021) and "more strategic and joined-up thinking between the domains of diplomacy, defence and development" (Conroy 2022). In the words of Shadow Minister for Foreign Affairs Penny Wong:

> Maximising our influence means we need to use all the tools we have. Military capability matters ... But we need more than that. We need to deploy all aspects of state power—strategic, diplomatic, social, economic ... Foreign policy must work with other elements of state power to succeed—in this the whole is greater than the sum of the parts. (Wong 2021)

It is in this context that a new initiative is seeking to implement and broaden the 3D approach in Australia. Given that in Australia an integrated approach is still in its nascency, this gives the chance to go beyond what has been done to date and add a further element to the existing 3D approach. The Asia-Pacific Development, Diplomacy and Defence Dialogue (AP4D) creates a new dimension in Australia's international policy-making by bringing together the development, diplomacy, and defense communities, and by consciously including dialogue as the fourth D. Its inaugural program—"Shaping a shared future—deepening Australia's influence in Southeast Asia and the Pacific"—aims to generate more effective approaches to advancing Australia's influence in Southeast Asia and the Pacific through the integrated application of development, diplomacy, and defense perspectives.

AP4D brings together experts from these 3D communities, with the overarching objective of cultivating a 3D constituency over time that can precipitate a cultural shift in the way Australia foreign policy is formulated and operationalized. The specific aims of the inaugural program are pursued through a sequenced methodology, and involve bringing together perspectives from all three communities at all stages.

The first step in the process are online diagnostic forums. For the Southeast Asian component of the inaugural program, five such events were held with a total of 29 experts in order to surface problems and raise questions about Australia's approach to Southeast Asia. Key issues identified included the shift in Australian foreign policy fundamentals—such as the fraying of the rules-based order, increased geostrategic contestation and the fast-changing Southeast Asian strategic landscape—a lack of Australian foreign policy coherence, and questioning of Australian foreign policy assumptions, and an overly responsive approach. One of the main suggested strategies to come out of the diagnostics was that Australia values the region in its own right, instead of only seeing it through the prism of great power competition. In conjunction with this step, a compendium of research was produced that included key extracts of literature covering Australia's (and the region's) policy foundations, notable policy speeches and documents, expert commentary, and analysis (Asia-Pacific Development, Diplomacy & Defence Dialogue 2021b, 2022c).

Along with the feedback from the diagnostics, the compendia serve as a baseline for the second step—a series of dialogue events. Three Southeast Asia Dialogues were held with a total of 124 development, diplomacy, and defense experts, with the aim of including more voices (including those from the region), exploring more in-depth the issues flagged in the diagnostics, and identifying and triaging the most pressing. During the interactive sessions, participants offered their thoughts on what they thought were the issues in most need of attention, which were then collated in real time, and voted on to establish a consensus.

Those results then formed the basis for five topics of focus which, in the third step, cross-sector working groups of development, diplomacy, and defense experts formed around and collaborated on for a period of two months (2022b). The objective of each working group was to produce an options paper that outlined a vision for what an integrated approach to foreign policy would look like in practice for Australia in Southeast Asia. A feedback opportunity was also built into the process in the form of a Chatham House roundtable with senior officials from the Departments of Defence and Foreign Affairs and Trade, and the options papers are very deliberately framed in a future-facing, propositional, and problem-solving way, so as to present policymakers with practical options moving forward, rather than rehash critical analyses of past decisions and failures.

The options papers follow the same structure: they outline why the subject matter is important and why current approaches need revision or enhancement; appraise Australian and regional views on it, and consider whether there exist opportunities for alignment; flag any potential obstacles and evaluate the realistic prospects for success; articulate a positive, future-facing vision of what a shared future could look like; and offer pathways and strategies by which such a future could come to fruition (whether immediate, medium-term, or ambitious).

The options papers were titled to reflect the future-facing, propositional, and constructive tone of AP4D: Namely, what does it look like for Australia to be a:

- Partner for Southeast Asian Recovery and Growth (Asia-Pacific Development, Diplomacy & Defence Dialogue 2022d). This paper focused on areas where Australia can have outsized effect, including in systems, regulation, and technology and as a pivotal education partner contributing to skills development across the region.
- Partner in Climate Leadership in Southeast Asia (Asia-Pacific Development, Diplomacy & Defence Dialogue 2022e). This paper looked at how Australia can help build the region's ability to manage the impacts of climate change, such as through regional risk assessments and disaster preparedness, in addition to outlining ways Australia can be part of the region's green economy transition.
- Effective Security Partner in Southeast Asia (Asia-Pacific Development, Diplomacy & Defence Dialogue 2022f). This paper looked at how Australia can find common ground with Southeast Asian leaders across a broad spectrum of cooperation, in particular with respect to shared interests in human security and effective governance. It outlined why Australia's national security and international engagement strategy should see investing in human security and state security as complementary and mutually reinforcing endeavors, not competing paradigms.
- Catalyst for Southeast Asian Civil-Military Cooperation (Asia-Pacific Development, Diplomacy & Defence Dialogue 2022g). This paper looked at how Australia's strong civil-military collaboration and governance framework represent an avenue through which it can enhance and expand its engagement in Southeast Asia, and leverage community-level connections with civil society in the region to more effectively engage in the region.
- Strategically Coherent Actor in Southeast Asia (Asia-Pacific Development, Diplomacy & Defence Dialogue 2022h). This paper looked at how Australia could ensure alignment and coordination of each arm of state-

craft to maximize impact. For example, defense cooperation that supports stability, resilience, and sovereignty in the region contributes to economic growth and development, meaning that defense has a place at the table when it comes to recovery and growth in the region.

The results of the Southeast Asia component were launched at a symposium event in February 2022 (Asia-Pacific Development, Diplomacy & Defence Dialogue 2022a, b) along with private briefings to senior bureaucrats, parliamentarians, and advisors (see below).

Given the initiative is a relatively new at less than year old (with the inaugural program still underway), and considering the limitations in determining policy impact in the short-term of what is intended to be a long-term and somewhat unquantifiable objective (improving Australian statecraft), there are limits to how the impact of AP4D can be measured. Nevertheless, the metrics and indicators collected so far[1] suggest that AP4D is garnering genuine and substantive engagement on its core theory of change—that an integrated approach to foreign policy will result in greater recognition of the distinct and complementary role of diplomacy, development, and defense, in turn resulting in better statecraft to maximize Australia's influence in a difficult, dangerous and complex world.

The program has attracted substantial political support with relevant portfolio ministers, shadow ministers, and parliamentarians from across the political spectrum providing strong public and private statements of support for the initiative and participating in tailored briefings. Australia's Minister for Foreign Affairs, Marise Payne, delivered a message to the AP4D Southeast Asia Symposium in which she described AP4D as "a valuable contribution at a time of rapid change" (Payne 2022). Shadow Minister for International Development and the Pacific Pat Conroy also delivered a message at the Symposium, stating that

> AP4D is an important initiative because now, more than ever, Australia needs innovative thinking on foreign policy. We need more strategic and joined-up thinking across the domains of diplomacy, defence and development and we

---

[1] The AP4D website had 837 unique page visits in the three weeks following the launch of the Southeast Asia options papers, with 346 publications being downloaded by users. In the same period, social media impressions increased by 338.5 percent, including retweets, shares, and likes from Australia's Ambassador to ASEAN, Will Nankervis, and Australia's High Commissioner to Brunei Darussalam, Luke Lazarus Arnold. In April 2022, AP4D gave a briefing to the Shadow Minister for Foreign Affairs, Senator the Hon Penny Wong, during the federal election campaign. AP4D and AP4D's work has been featured on multiple mainstream media platforms, such as the *Sydney Morning Herald*, *Australian Broadcasting Corporation*, *Jakarta Post*, *Solomon Times*, and *Philippine Inquirer*.

need more collaboration and better partnerships between government, academia, civil society and the private sector. That's why for me the formation of AP4D was a lightbulb moment, a powerful idea whose time has come. (Conroy 2022)

For the Southeast Asia component, sixteen private briefings were held with more than 67 people across six departments and agencies, seven ministerial and shadow ministerial offices, and the Joint Standing Committee on Foreign Affairs, Defence, and Trade. The purpose of these briefings was to go through the findings from AP4D's Southeast Asia and summarize the key takeaways, tailored to the specific audience receiving the briefing. A key message for defense and security audiences, for example, was the need to model effective civil-military engagement and support strong civil society, as well as integrate a climate perspective into bilateral defense cooperation and defense diplomacy. Whereas for a development audience, the message was that Australia should focus development cooperation on three priority areas that underpin sustainable growth and development: health, education, and economic cooperation.

The feedback received from the senior public servants, parliamentarians, and advisors receiving these briefings was overwhelmingly positive. Some verbatim responses include:

* "We're huge believers in the scheme of work and approach. It looks entirely palatable for government."
* "The type of work you're doing is really valuable for us."
* "Really excellent work and ideas and a valuable contribution to discussion."
* "A brilliant package of research and ideas."
* "Thanks for sharing a copy of the report. Integration of the elements of national power is an increasingly pressing challenge. I look forward to reading the report and discussing with colleagues."
* "Well-aligned with what we're thinking of."

This demonstrates that AP4D's work has been well-received by policymakers as a valuable, timely, and constructive contribution in promoting the benefits of integrated statecraft—and outlining practical pathways to achieve it—within the broader Australian foreign policy debate. While it is too early to expect any changes to investments in diplomacy to result from it, these early indicators show that the program is delivering on the first steps in its theory of change.

In wider debates, foreign policy and statecraft are increasingly being articulated by politicians, senior officials, and commentators in 3D terms, a trend that precedes the establishment of the program but for which it can reasonably claim some credit. For example, pitching to voters prior to the 2022 federal election, Leader of the Opposition Anthony Albanese has spoken of the need for Australia "to step up in terms of our diplomatic efforts," lamenting the "short sighted" budget cuts that had undermined the capacity of the Department of Foreign Affairs and Trade to "engage in soft diplomacy" and "build relations over a period of time." He said there would be "a much bigger effort, both in terms of quantity but also in terms of quality" to reverse "the marginalisation that has occurred" if his party won government (Albanese 2022).

Conclusion

Despite the challenges it faces, it is unlikely that diplomacy will become obsolete or redundant any time soon. That leaves two options: either let the decline continue or try to reverse the trend to bring diplomacy back to the forefront of foreign policy. The scale of international problems suggests that the former isn't an option. As former Department of Foreign Affairs and Trade Secretary Peter Varghese argues diplomacy can contribute to the really big issues, including forging a new strategic equilibrium in the Indo-Pacific, making a case for an open economy and refashioning the institutions of a revamped international order: "To get out of the difficulties that we're currently in, diplomacy has to come to the fore again: to make sense of a period of some considerable uncertainty and to lead the institutional rebuilding we need" (Conley Tyler 2021d).

With traditional forms of advocacy not showing great dividends, it is worth considering innovative approaches, including promoting greater integration of the arms of statecraft through a 3D approach. By bringing together the three communities, a coalition can be built to promote a more central role for diplomacy in achieving international goals. This sort of process creates a new dynamic. It builds a constituency that is appreciative of the unique benefits that diplomacy offers and creates new coalitions. Such coalitions can make the argument that shaping Australia's strategic environment is a job for all three elements of statecraft. Each has a distinct and complementary role to play, applying the right resources in the right combination to be most effective. At a time that new ways of thinking are needed, it is worth supporting such initiatives.

References and Further Reading

Albanese, A. 2022. An Address by Opposition Leader – Anthony Albanese. Lowy Institute, March 10. https://www.youtube.com/watch?v=Z1Jhl-7bZnI&t=2700s.

Asia-Pacific Development, Diplomacy & Defence Dialogue 2021a. https://www.asiapacific4d.com/.

———. 2021b. Southeast Asia Pre-Dialogue Compendium, September. https://uploads-ssl.webflow.com/60c387a5a55520deb6151bbc/61b82c1591a8ec1f7ec9c5ae_Shaping%20a%20Shared%20Future%20-%20Southeast%20Asia%20Compendia.pdf.

———. 2022a. Asia-Pacific Development, Diplomacy & Defence Dialogue – Southeast Asia Symposium, February 10. https://www.youtube.com/watch?v=VFWJCyQqryQ.

———. 2022b. *Australia and Southeast Asia: Shaping a Shared Future*. https://uploads-ssl.webflow.com/60b8844010f77f30cd04bf93/622a17db4f1c4b676ab712c8_Synthesis%20Report.pdf.

———. 2022c. Pacific Islands Pre-Dialogue Compendium, February. https://uploads-ssl.webflow.com/60c387a5a55520deb6151bbc/62281fff28cb1403a546dced_AP4D%20-%20Shaping%20a%20Shared%20Future%20Pacific%20Islands%20Compendium.pdf.

———. 2022d. *What Does It Look Like for Australia to be a Partner for Southeast Asian Recovery & Growth*. https://www.asiapacific4d.com/shared-future/recovery-and-growth.

———. 2022e. *What Does It Look Like for Australia to be a Partner in Climate Leadership in Southeast Asia*. https://www.asiapacific4d.com/shared-future/climate-leadership.

———. 2022f. *What Does It Look Like for Australia to be an Effective Security Partner in Southeast Asia*. https://www.asiapacific4d.com/shared-future/effective-security-partner.

———. 2022g. *What Does It Look Like for Australia to be a Catalyst for Southeast Asian Civil-Military Cooperation*. https://www.asiapacific4d.com/shared-future/civil-military-cooperation.

———. 2022h. *What Does It Look Like for Australia to be a Strategically Coherent Actor in Southeast Asia*. https://www.asiapacific4d.com/shared-future/strategically-coherent-actor.

Australian Strategic Policy Institute. 2021. Australian Department of Defence Funding Database. https://drive.google.com/file/d/1jX70EGfSD42TknqyBpZ-il47YauIPOYX/view.

Behm, A. 2020. *Securitisation – Turning Problems into Threats*. Australia Institute, June. https://australiainstitute.org.au/wp-content/uploads/2020/12/200604-Securitisation-WEB.pdf.

Biden, J. 2021. President-elect Biden Announces Ambassador Samantha Power as His Nominee for USAID Administrator. Biden-Harris Presidential Transition YouTube channel, January 14. https://www.youtube.com/watch?v=0Ud_sfC4lTE&list=UUzDolbZ-zDzZ-DxapEQPALQ.

Boisvert-Novak, A. 2019. *Different Yet Similar: Comparing Canada's Whole-of-Government Approach Abroad and at Home*. Canadian Forces College. https://www.cfc.forces.gc.ca/259/290/308/286/novak-boisvert.pdf.

Broadbent, J., W. Maley, B. Orgill, P. Shergold, R. Smith, and A. Gyngell. 2009. *Australia's Diplomatic Deficit: Reinvesting in Our Instruments of International Policy*. Lowy Institute, March. http://archive.lowyinstitute.org/sites/default/files/pubfiles/BlueRibbonPanelReport_WEB_1.pdf.

Byrne, C. 2020. "Truth, Lies and Diplomacy: Fostering Co-operation in a Fractured World." *Griffith Review* 67. https://www.griffithreview.com/articles/truth-lies-and-diplomacy/.

Byrne, C., M. Conley Tyler, and S. Harris Rimmer. 2016. "Australian Diplomacy Today." *Australian Journal of International Affairs* 70 (6): 581–89.

Chubb, A. 2022. "The Securitization of 'Chinese Influence' in Australia." *Journal of Contemporary China*, n.p.

Clinton, H. 2019. "Hillary Clinton: Reflections on Foreign Policy: Defense, Diplomacy, and Development." Gerald R. Ford School of Public Policy, October 10. https://fordschool.umich.edu/video/2019/hillary-clinton-reflections-foreign-policy-defense-diplomacy-and-development.

Congressional Research Service. 2022. *Department of State, Foreign Operations, and Related Programs: FY2022 Budget and Appropriations*, April 1. https://sgp.fas.org/crs/row/R46935.pdf.

Conley Tyler, M. 2019. "Solving Australia's Foreign Affairs Challenges." *Australian Foreign Affairs* 7. https://www.australianforeignaffairs.com/articles/the-fix/2019/11/the-fix/melissa-conley-tyler.

———. 2020. "Foreign Policy Identity Politics is a Dangerous Path." *The Interpreter*, August 18. https://www.lowyinstitute.org/the-interpreter/foreign-policy-identity-politics-dangerous-path.

———. 2021a. "How Does an Integrated Approach Help Defence?" *Australian Naval Review* 2 (December): 57–61.

———. 2021b. "Australia Has Not Just Had a 'Diplomacy Fail' – It Has Been Devaluing the Profession for Decades." *The Conversation*, November 15. https://theconversation.com/australia-has-not-just-had-a-diplomacy-fail-it-has-been-devaluing-the-profession-for-decades-171498.

———. 2021c. "Foreign Policy Is More Than Defence." *Evatt Foundation Journal* 20 (1). https://www.evatt.org.au/post/foreign-policy-more-than-defence.

———. 2021d. "Diplomacy in a Divided World." *Raisina Debates 2021*. https://www.orfonline.org/expert-speak/diplomacy-divided-world/.

Conroy, P. 2021. Address to the Australian Council for International Development National Conference, September 30. https://youtu.be/9g2tKATTHAI?t=112.

———. 2022. Message Delivered at the Asia-Pacific Development, Diplomacy and Defence Dialogue Southeast Asia Symposium, February 10. https://www.youtube.com/watch?v=vtXnERMRpls.
Costello, M. 2021. "When Ineptitude Goes Nuclear." *The Saturday Paper*, October 9. https://www.thesaturdaypaper.com.au/2021/10/09/when-ineptitude-goes-nuclear/163369800012635#hrd.
Cotton, J., and J. Ravenhill. 2011. *Middle Power Dreaming: Australia in World Affairs 2006–2010*. Melbourne: Oxford University Press.
Department of Defence. 2020. *2020 Defence Strategic Update*. https://www.defence.gov.au/about/publications/2020-defence-strategic-update.
Department of Foreign Affairs and Trade. 2015. *Australia's Trade since Federation*. https://www.dfat.gov.au/sites/default/files/australias-trade-since-federation.pdf.
———. 2017. *2017 Foreign Policy White Paper*. https://www.dfat.gov.au/sites/default/files/2017-foreign-policy-white-paper.pdf.
———. 2021. *Partnerships for Recovery: Australian Official Development Assistance*. https://www.dfat.gov.au/sites/default/files/pbs-2021-22-aid-budget-summary.pdf.
Dziedzic, S. 2018. "Senior Diplomats Not Consulted about Prime Minister's Decision to Review Location of Australian Embassy in Israel." ABC News, October 25. https://www.abc.net.au/news/2018-10-25/dfat-told-of-jerusalem-consideration-day-before-announcement/10427396.
Emrich, R., and D. Schulze. 2017. "Diplomacy in the 21st Century – What Needs To Change?" *German Institute for International and Security Affairs*, December, Working Paper 22. https://www.swp-berlin.org/publications/products/arbeitspapiere/WP_Diplomacy21_No23_Final_Presentation.pdf.
Fathana, H. 2018. "Cabinet Papers 1994–95: How a Security Agreement Allayed Australian Anxiety over Indonesia." *The Conversation*, January 1. https://theconversation.com/cabinet-papers-1994-95-how-a-security-agreement-allayed-australian-anxiety-over-indonesia-89143.
Galloway, A. 2021. "Australia's Foreign Policy is Getting Clumsy and Arrogant." *Sydney Morning Herald*, September 18. https://www.smh.com.au/politics/federal/australia-s-foreign-policy-is-getting-clumsy-and-arrogant-20210918-p58ssr.html.
Garver, R. 2021. "Biden Budget Substantially Boosts Foreign Aid, Diplomacy, but Raises Defense by 1.7 Percent." *Voice of America*, May 28. https://www.voanews.com/a/usa_us-politics_biden-budget-substantially-boosts-foreign-aid-diplomacy-raises-defense-17/6206352.html.
Gyngell, A. 2016. "Statecraft, Strategy and Foreign Policy." Address to Australian Institute of International Affairs National Conference Canberra, November 21. https://www.internationalaffairs.org.au/wp-content/uploads/2016/12/Allan-Gyngell-Speech.pdf.
———. 2017. *Fear of Abandonment: Australia in the World Since 1942*. Melbourne: La Trobe University Press.

———. 2021. "The Year Ahead." *Australian Outlook*, February 19. https://www.internationalaffairs.org.au/australianoutlook/the-year-ahead.

Gyngell, A., and J. McCarthy. 2021. "Australia Lacks the Diplomacy to Win Friends and Influence." *Australian Financial Review*, October 26. https://www.afr.com/policy/foreign-affairs/australia-lacks-the-diplomacy-to-win-friends-and-influence-20211025-p5930t.

Hall, I. 2010. "The Transformation of Diplomacy: Mysteries, Insurgencies and Public Relations." *International Affairs* 86 (1): 247–56.

Hanson, F., E. Currey, and T. Beattie. 2020. "The Chinese Communist Party's Coercive Diplomacy." *ASPI International Cyber Policy Centre*, Policy Brief Report No. 36/2020, August. https://s3-ap-southeast-2.amazonaws.com/ad-aspi/2020-08/The%20CCPs%20coercive%20diplomacy_0.pdf?4M_JTUAd05Bjek_hvHt1NKKdCLts4kbY.

Langmore, J., T. Miletic, A. Martin, and B. Breen. 2020. *Security Through Sustainable Peace: Australian International Conflict Prevention and Peacebuilding*. University of Melbourne, July. https://arts.unimelb.edu.au/__data/assets/pdf_file/0004/3495721/Security-Through-Sustainable-Peace-Report.pdf.

Lowy Institute. 2018. *Australia's Security and the Rules-Based Order: Tracking a Decade of Policy Evolution*. https://interactives.lowyinstitute.org/features/rules-based-order/.

———. 2019. *Global Diplomacy Index*. https://globaldiplomacyindex.lowyinstitute.org/country_comparison.html.

———. 2021a. Lowy Institute Poll 2021 – "China: Economic Partner or Security Threat." https://poll.lowyinstitute.org/charts/china-economic-partner-or-security-threat/.

———. 2021b. *Asia Power Index 2021 Edition*. https://power.lowyinstitute.org/data/diplomatic-influence/.

Lyon, R. 2019. "Strategic Personalities and a Changing World." *The Strategist*, May 16. https://www.aspistrategist.org.au/strategic-personalities-and-a-changing-world/.

Minister for Foreign Affairs. 2020. "Standing with Our Region in Response to COVID-19," October 23. https://www.foreignminister.gov.au/minister/marise-payne/media-release/standing-our-region-response-covid-19.

Moore, R. 2020. "Into the Dragon's Mouth: The Dangers of Defence-led Foreign Policy." *Australian Outlook*, July 10. https://www.internationalaffairs.org.au/australianoutlook/into-the-dragons-mouth-the-dangers-of-defence-led-foreign-policy/.

Morrison, S. 2020. Address, Aspen Security Forum – "Tomorrow in The Indo-Pacific," August 5. https://www.pm.gov.au/media/address-aspen-security-forum-tomorrow-indo-pacific.

———. 2022. An Address by Prime Minister Scott Morrison. Lowy Institute, March 7. https://www.lowyinstitute.org/publications/address-prime-minister-scott-morrison.

National Museum of Australia. 2021. Fall of Singapore. https://www.nma.gov.au/defining-moments/resources/fall-of-singapore.

Oliver, A. 2020. *Revaluing Australia's Diplomacy.* Lowy Institute, June. https://interactives.lowyinstitute.org/features/covid-recovery/issues/diplomacy/.

Oliver, A., and A. Shearer. 2011. *Diplomatic Disrepair Rebuilding Australia's International Policy Infrastructure.* Lowy Institute, August. https://archive.lowyinstitute.org/sites/default/files/pubfiles/Oliver_and_Shearer%2C_Diplomatic_disrepair_Web_1.pdf.

Payne, M. 2022. AP4D Southeast Asia Symposium – A Message from Australian Foreign Minister Marise Payne. *Asia-Pacific Development, Diplomacy & Defence Dialogue*, February 10. https://www.youtube.com/watch?v=5rjWHGAntWk.

Seo, B. 2019. "Dave Sharma Warns DFAT is Being Sidelined." *Australian Financial Review*, April 22. https://www.afr.com/policy/foreign-affairs/dave-sharma-warns-dfat-is-being-sidelined-20190422-p51g2c.

Seselja, Z. 2021. Address to the Australian Council for International Development National Conference, September 30. https://youtu.be/9g2tKATTHAI?t=92.

Silberman, Z. 2014. "The Defense Secretary Who Fought for the State Department's Budget." U.S. Global Leadership Coalition, January 16. https://www.usglc.org/blog/the-defense-secretary-who-fought-for-the-state-departments-budget/.

Sussex, M. 2021. "Why Australia Needs an Integrated Review." *Australian Journal of Defence and Strategic Studies* 3 (1): 75–82.

Treasury. 2021. *Agency Resourcing Budget Paper No. 4 2021–22.* https://budget.gov.au/2021-22/content/bp4/download/bp4_2021-22.pdf.

U.S. Department of Defense. 2010. *Quadrennial Defense Review*, February.

United Kingdom Government. 2021. "Global Britain in a Competitive Age: The Integrated Review of Security, Defence, Development and Foreign Policy," March. https://assets.publishing.service.gov.uk/government/uploads/system/uploads/attachment_data/file/975077/Global_Britain_in_a_Competitive_Age-_the_Integrated_Review_of_Security__Defence__Development_and_Foreign_Policy.pdf.

van der Lijn, J. 2011. *3D 'The Next Generation" Lessons Learned from Uruzgan for Future Operations.* Netherlands Institute of International Relations 'Clingendael.' https://www.clingendael.org/sites/default/files/pdfs/20111130_cscp_rapport_lijn.pdf.

White House. 2021. Remarks by President Biden on America's Place in the World, February 4. https://www.whitehouse.gov/briefing-room/speeches-remarks/2021/02/04/remarks-by-president-biden-on-americas-place-in-the-world/.

Wise, J. 2022. *The Costs of Discounted Diplomacy.* Australian Strategic Policy Institute. https://www.aspi.org.au/report/costs-discounted-diplomacy.

Wong, P. 2021. "Expanding Australia's Power and Influence": Speech to the National Security College – Australian National University, November 23. https://www.pennywong.com.au/media-hub/speeches/expanding-australia-s-power-and-influence-speech-to-the-national-security-college-australian-national-university-canberra-23-11-2021/.

Wong, E. 2022. "Biden Requests an 18 Percent Increase in Spending to Address Global Diplomacy, Crises and Threats." *New York Times*, March 28. https://www.nytimes.com/live/2022/03/28/us/biden-budget-proposal/biden-requests-an-18-percent-increase-in-spending-to-address-global-diplomacy-crises-and-threats?smid=url-copy.

Wyeth, G. 2021. "After Trump, Can Australia Trust the United States?" *The Diplomat*, January 12. https://thediplomat.com/2021/01/after-trump-can-australia-trust-the-united-states/.

Zhai, K., and Y.L. Tian. 2020. "In China, a Young Diplomat Rises as Aggressive Foreign Policy Takes Root." *Reuters*, March 31. https://www.reuters.com/article/us-china-diplomacy-insight/in-china-a-young-diplomat-rises-as-aggressive-foreign-policy-takes-root-idU.S.KBN21I0F8.

13

African Union Reform: Challenges and Opportunities

Emmanuel Balogun and Anna Kapambwe Mwaba

Introduction

The African Union's (AU) official transition from the Organization of African Unity in 2001 marked the major shift in African international relations. The OAU was no longer equipped to address the challenges it was established to address in 1963 marking a need for reform: "the decision to re-launch Africa's pan-African organization was the outcome of a consensus by African leaders that in order to realize Africa's potential, there was a need to refocus attention from the fight for decolonization and ridding the continent of apartheid, which had been the focus of the OAU, towards increased cooperation and integration of African states to drive Africa's growth and economic development" (AU 2022a). As the organization continues to face challenges in a dynamic global environment, the need to reform persists.

During the AU's 28th Ordinary Summit of Heads of State and Government, AU member states committed to implementing a series of reforms that support a shared understanding of ownership, financing, accountability, monitoring, and evaluation of AU institutions. Under the direction of Rwandan

E. Balogun (✉)
Skidmore College, Saratoga Springs, NY, USA

A. K. Mwaba
Smith College, Northampton, MA, USA

President Paul Kagame, the AU pan-African advisory team found several key findings that necessitated institutional reform. Among them were a failed perception of relevance to African citizens, a chronic failure to implement AU decisions, and an overreliance on external partner funding, and an unclear division of labor between the AU Commission and the regional economic communities (RECs) (Kagame 2017). Despite Kagame's recommendations, there still appears to be a disconnection between the desires for AU reform and AU reform in practice (Nantulya 2022).

The AU's reform process began in September 2017 following the Reform Troika's report with the AU's Commission (AUC) appointing Professor Pierre Moukoko Mbonjou and Ms. Ciru Mwaura as Head and Deputy Head of the Institutional Reforms Unit. To date, reforms include progress on the sustainable financing of the Union and the Peace Fund as well as the adoption of Continental Free Trade Area. As of June 2020, 17 of the 55 member states were at various stages of implementing the 0.2 percent levy to assist in financing the Union; contributions to the Peace Fund were at approximately $176 mission (68 percent of the expected $400 million); and new financial management "Golden Rules" were implemented (AU 2020). The New Partnership for Africa's Development (NEPAD) has become the African Union Development Agency (AUDA-NEPAD),[1] and the African Peer Review Mechanism (APRM) has been integrated into the AU budget with an extended mandate covering conflict prevention. The countries that have yet to join the APRM were encouraged to do so by 2023 (APRM 2019).

However, despite the progress on reforming the African Union, there has been little progress on the reform of key organs such as the African Court of Justice, the Pan-African Parliament, and others within the African Union Commission. Compounding the slow pace of reform is the lack of coordination between the principal organs of the AU and the regional economic communities (RECs).

In this chapter, three causes that limit the progress of institutional reform in the AU are considered. First, that there are internal political factors that impact leader's ability to manage their positions in the region (clout); inconsistency in how AU leaders prioritize certain issues (commitment); and inconsistency in the application of AU rules and norms (credibility). Considering these "3Cs," how much the AU commits to institutional reform may account

---

[1] See https://www.nepad.org

for shifting political contexts both on the African continent and in the international system. The AU partners with other states and international organizations; however, practicality is one of the stumbling blocks to the AU's partnerships with other international actors, along with the pressures of a challenging economic, social, and political environment.

There are two pathways in order for the AU to overcome challenges of clout, commitment, and credibility toward diplomatic reform. First, the AU needs to consider how to bridge the institutional divides between the AU Assembly and the AU Commission (AUC) as well as the AU Commission and the Regional Economic Communities (RECs). While the Assembly serves as the "AU's supreme policy and decision-making organ," the AU Commission and the practitioners therein also play a primary role in determining policies, establishing organizational priorities, and implementing AU policies and decisions (AU 2022b; Tieku 2017).

Second, this chapter argues that the AU needs to strengthen its diplomatic relationships with domestic institutions, civil society, and non-governmental organizations. The driving mechanism in both of these pathways is an empowered and autonomous practitioner class within the AU, which is able to leverage their ability to coordinate in a centralized manner through the AU Commission and formal interactions with AU organs and instruments, while also building decentralized networks with domestic institutions, regional civil society organizations, and other stakeholders.

Diplomatic reform in the AU may be contextualized as a change in the political relationships between the AU and other critical stakeholders—national and international along with its interaction with the AU Commission. Put differently, diplomatic reform considers structural and functional changes to the organization, but also reform in the practice of reform. The implications of diplomatic reform are two-fold. First, embracing diplomatic reform will change how the AU assembly engages with AU practitioners at the commission, and with other, non-African Heads of States. Second, diplomatic reform can also identify institutional mechanisms to facilitate engagement across scales of governance. The AU as an institution needs to reform for the sake of functional and efficient governing, but it also needs diplomatic reform to empower practitioners to build relationships beyond the institution to fill in capacity gaps across multiple scales of governance.

An exploration of the prospect of AU reform follows using the conceptual frameworks of informal international politics, international practices, and regionalism, to highlight the multitude of ways AU practitioners can bridge the gap between legal mandate and action.

Clout, Credibility, Commitment, and the AU's Performance

Why is the African Union seeking reform? The impetus for reform for most international organizations often relates to organizational performance (Lall 2017). Institutional design is often a predictor of organizational performance. Institutional design choices can lock in organizational characteristics that delimit the prospect of reform, particularly at the organization's founding moments (Balogun 2022). Institutional design choices can also offer flexibility to organizations that allow them to adapt their structures according to changes in the political context.

For example, critics of AU performance often refer to its reliance on external donors. At its creation, the AU did not require a community levy from its member states, but later adopted a 0.2 percent levy on imports. Sixty-seven percent of assessed member state contributions come from this community level and have caused the AU to frequently seek out external funding. This has caused the AU to work on creating a consensus among member states toward financial autonomy. AU leaders and practitioners mentioned that the need for predictable and sustainable funding is part of the AU's normative foundation, yet also acknowledge that the road to consensus is mired in competing interests between member states, and that institutionally, RECs and Regional Mechanisms (RMs) have a political will and comparative advantage over existing AU mechanisms to create sustainable financing. These challenges are an example of the hurdles underlying AU governance performance and why the AU seeks reforms.

Another issue of AU performance and institutional design is how negotiations operate and decisions are made (Krause 2002). Specifically in the AU, the importance of debates and norms of engagement are crucial in moving forward political agendas. While AU practitioners and leaders follow formal legal processes, there is a high degree of informality that undergirds the policy cycle and decision-making in the AU. As such, informal international rules (IIRs) and how they are used to move the AU's agenda forward and in certain cases, serve as pre-laws, gap-fillers, enablers, and spoilers in the policy cycle (Tieku 2019). However, this informal nature of diplomacy can limit the ability of international organizations to address their goals. Politics undermines independent processes where "processes that ought to be less political in nature take on a more direct political role and are often subverted by it" (Sarkin 2018) which can be viewed as regional politicking.

The AU has institutions to manage regional governance, yet matters of clout, commitment, and credibility (the 3Cs) highlight the diplomatic challenges of implementation. The following cases illustrate how diplomacy has undermined the AU's ability to fulfill its mandate and move forward on critical areas for reform.

Clout

Issues of clout manifest as leaders struggle to manage their positions in the region due to challenges in collaboration within the AU itself and with other international institutions and RECs. A case of agency toward the world versus contestation within. Tensions between Nigeria and South Africa within the AU are well documented—ranging from early disputes as to what direction to take the organization, to the violation of the norm that neither country would head the AUC, to diplomatic rows that led to the deportation of nationals from each country, to how to further integrate the continent's two largest economies on their terms. Uganda and Rwanda's political issues—Rwanda accusing Uganda of harassing its nationals and supporting dissidents and Uganda accusing Rwanda of illegal espionage—led to their Gatuna border being closed for three years, which negatively impacted trade between the two countries (Reuters 2022). These internal diplomatic disputes where the "law of the strong" (Bew 2015, 33) has prevailed not only have economic, political, and social implications, but have also stalled action on urgent matters.

Along with these high-level diplomatic disputes, the AU also deals with internal disagreements, such as the one that directly places its political arm, the Assembly, against its technical/operational one, the AUC. While the AUC has the authority to operationalize the AU's mandate and programs as an implementing actor (Tieku 2021), the Assembly as the Heads of State and Government is the decision-making body. The realpolitik of the leaders matters in terms of advancing debates and equitably apply decisions across continental issues. Leaders can use their political clout to challenge established rules and norms. One example of this is The Gambia's former president, Yahya Jammeh in January 2017, who initially agreed to step down if he lost to then-candidate Adama Barrow. Jammeh reversed course and refused to step down, despite calls by the AU and the Economic Community of West African States (ECOWAS) to do so. His refusal led the AU Peace and Security Council

(AUPSC) announcing that it would no longer recognize Jammeh as president after January 19, 2017, and ECOWAS deploying air and navy troops around Gambia to facilitate the transfer of power (Bappah 2018).

Similarly, the Democratic Republic of Congo resisted the AUC's call for the recount of election votes following the election in December 2018 where it was apparent that the opposition leader Felix Tshekedi won the majority of the votes. Yet another example is Somalia's rejection of the AUPSC's proposal (AU Peace and Security Council 2021) to turn its peacekeeping force, the African Union Mission to Somalia (AMISOM), in Mogadishu into a hybrid mission. The Somali Ministry of Foreign Affairs and International Cooperation (MOFA) publicly stated its opposition, arguing that the AU PSC did not consider the views of the Somali government and the Somali defense minister argued that the AU PSC "continued to disregard Somalia's sovereignty, territorial integrity, and political independence" and that a hybrid mission "violates the basic rights of a member state" (MFA, Somalia 2021). Following further discussions, on March 8, 2022, the African Union Transition Mission in Somalia (ATMIS) was authorized by United Nations Security Council Resolution 2628 to replace AMISOM with effect from April 1, 2022. This plan includes the handing over of security operations to the Somali security forces and state institutions by December 2024 (AU Peace and Security Council 2022).

Another diplomatic row involving Somalia involves tensions with Kenya. In 2019, the Somalia's MFA issued a statement that called a tweet by Kenya's government referring to Somaliland as a country to be "an affront to Somalia's sovereignty, unity and territorial integrity" (Africanews 2019; Hiiraan Online 2019). These tensions came to a head when Somalia summoned its ambassador to Kenya and requested that the Kenyan ambassador to Somalia be recalled on November 29, 2020—effectively severing all diplomatic ties—following accusations that it was meddling in its electoral process (Dahir 2020). The Ministry of Foreign Affairs and International Cooperation of Somalia argued that Kenya was infringing on its sovereignty and political independence. Soon after, President Kenyatta hosted Somaliland's President Muse Bihi Adbi (Obala 2020).

Despite warming relations, with the resumption of the import of Somali *khat* (a natural stimulant) following a two-year ban, Somalia's government requested an apology after the Somaliland flag was displayed and an envoy was present at a diplomatic event in Nairobi. This request, prompted by the Ambassador Mohamoud Ahmed Nur walking out of the event, led to the Kenyan Ministry of Foreign Affairs issuing an apology statement affirming the sovereignty of the Somali government (Africanews 2022). But this statement resulted in the Somaliland government issuing its own response expressing its disappointment at the situation saying that this reaction on the part of the Somali government demonstrated "the hatred and long-term enmity of Somalia towards the Republic of Somaliland and its people" (Agence France Press 2022).

As shown, the use of clout is often associated with the claims of sovereignty and political independence, which can limit the AU's implementing ability. Claims that AU activities or policies violate member state rights also highlight the functional limitations of the AUC and its disconnect from the AU Assembly Heads of States. Leaders who can leverage their clout are often able to obtain favorable outcomes, such as maintaining the governing status quo in their countries or not having to comply with AU rules. However, we do see variation in the effectiveness of clout. For example, former president of The Gambia, Yahya Jammeh, attempted to use his clout to reject election results, which led to a principled stance by the AU and ECOWAS in facilitating the election of Adama Barrow.

However, sometimes clout can be used to move forward policies that are in line with influential countries within the AU. In these cases, the AUC is allowed to act without restrictions. Regarding regional stability, the AU sought to strengthen its ability to support member states during electoral processes by mandating that all elections were to be observed by the AU in direct response to the violence in Kenya following its 2007 elections (African Union 2013, 23).

Clout is also a factor in how the AU positions itself with other international institutions. For example, the relationship between the AU and the International Criminal Court (ICC) has been strained for some time because of accusations by the AU that the ICC unfairly targets African countries leading to threats that these countries would leave the institution. Similarly, the A3 (Ghana, Gabon, and Senegal) in the UN Security Council, in conjunction with the AU Assembly and AUC, has taken a firm stance of non-alignment in the 2022 Russian-Ukraine crisis, even though Russia, the EU, and the United States, among other Western allies, have tried direct appeals to the AU. These dynamics encourage international bodies to hold annual leadership summits to court the AU to build upon existing partnerships and facilitate new areas of cooperation. The common African position on the ICC and the Russia-Ukraine crisis are illustrative of how member states choose to use their diplomatic weight to insulate themselves from control from other international institutions and is a recognition by AU member states and the AUC of their clout.

However, despite these instances where AU member states and the AUC can demonstrate clout, the motivations can lead to challenges in coordinating between AU organs. The challenges of collaboration and division of labor noted between the AU and RECs continue despite the existence of the 2008 Protocol on AU and REC relations (AU 2008a) and as highlighted in the 2017 Reform Report leading to the first coordination meeting between the AU and RECs in Niamey, Niger, on July 8, 2019. This meeting led to a proposal to amend the existing protocol to address these coordination challenges. This proposal expands the scope of relations to include the environment, marine resources, migration, and the African Governance Architecture (AGA), in addition to economic, social, political, and cultural fields including gender, peace, and security. It also proposed the establishment of three new organs for coordinating policies, measures, programs, and activities of RECs, and ensuring the implementation of the protocol. These organs are the Mid-Year Coordination Meeting, the Committee on Coordination, and the Coordination Secretariat. Each institution presents a means for moving coordination and policy implementation forward.

Composed of the Bureau of the Assembly and the Chairpersons of the RECs, the Mid-Year Coordination is tasked with assessing the status of continental integration and coordinating efforts to accelerate the integration process. The Committee on Coordination, consisting of the chairperson, the chief executives, and the chief executives of the financial institutions of the Union and AUDA-NEPAD, is responsible for providing policy orientation pertaining to the implementation of this Protocol. Finally, the Coordination Secretariat, made up of the representatives of the chairperson responsible for coordination of the activities of the RECs, the representatives of the chief executives of the RECs responsible for the coordination of integration with the Union, the representatives of the AUDA-NEPAD, and the representatives of the chief executives of the financial institutions of the Union, is in charge of preparing and submitting reports to the Committee on Coordination on a number of issues (AU 2008b). These proposed changes highlight the need for a framework on the working relationship between the AU and RECs.

While these advances indicate a willingness to increase the capacity for collaboration, the reforms improve the working capacity for the functional and technical side of the institution. These functional reforms do little to bridge the governance divide between the AUC and the Assembly Heads of State. However, they offer incremental progress toward collaboration between the AUC and the RECs. AUC/REC collaboration would be a significant step forward as an institutional reform; however, the functional changes should also account for issues of clout playing out at the subsidiarity level. Improved collaboration between the AU and RECs would need to consider existing governance instruments at the REC level and envision what AU support and autonomy would look like. Given the informal dynamics at the political level, the technical organs would need to be reformed to ensure member states fulfill their obligations, or these functional reforms would need to be strengthened to empower practitioners in the RECs and the AU with the authority to overcome the leverage from political and economic clout of dominant member states.

Commitments

The AU governance profile extends over dozens of different policy areas, such as health, peace and security, development, finance, youth engagement, gender, and many others. The breadth of issues areas limits a depth of coverage in each area. The AU, being an international organization with a general scope, has a problem with over-commitment and consistency in how it prioritizes its commitment. While the AU may try to do too much, there are ways in which the AU works to ameliorate this concern through its partner engagements. Two issues condition the AU's commitment problem: funding challenges and variations in institutional autonomy. Given a lack of predictable and sustainable funding, the AU becomes reliant on partner engagements for institutional support. A consequence of relying on partner engagements is a limited or varied ability to build autonomy through the partner relationship. The second issue is the variation in institutional autonomy among AU organs.

Funding Challenges

The AU's increasing governance space has meant a significant increase in the budget to run the AU. As a result, the AU identified that on assessed contributions alone, it cannot fulfill the mandate of many of its commitments. In 2016, the AU adopted the Kigali Decision, a funding mechanism that would require AU members to pay 0.2 percent import levy as assessed contributions to the union. So far, only 17 countries have indicated that they were at various stages of domesticating the Kigali Decision.

The Kigali Decision was a welcome step by most AU member states, specifically because it offers flexibility for states to domesticate the Kigali Decision in line with their national and international policies, so long as they express the predictability of their contributions. Any excess contributions would be used to finance other issues of importance to the member state.

Despite the advantages, many countries have not committed to the Kigali Decision and are not able to be held accountable for being in arrears to the AU, given the lack of enforcement mechanism to collect the levy. The Kigali Decision also presents challenges for some AU members, as the levy conflicts with their obligations to the World Trade Organization's Most Favored Nations principle as well as other tariff commitments that would yield less than they are required to pay the AU in assessed contributions.

The Kigali Decision is the kind of reform that could lead to financial autonomy for the AU, however, it also highlights constraints and uneven economic development among AU member states. One way the AU works within to amend these constraints is through partner engagements. The AU relies on formal external partnerships that lay the foundation for collaboration but are also avenues for financial assistance. For instance, the AUC-United States High-Level Dialogue, started through a Memorandum of Understanding in 2013, has facilitated political and economic partnerships, while also tying the African Growth and Opportunity Act to the relationship, as a means to help generate revenue to African countries through trade. FOCAC or the China-Africa Cooperation Forum has also been a key external partnership for the AU, as China has used the forum to indicate its strategic priorities and points of cooperation with Africa, strengthen partnerships, exchanges, and investments on the continent. President Xi of China recently indicated in his 2035 Vision for China-Africa cooperation an investment of over 60 billion USD in Africa and a significant increase in trade flows between the two countries. The AU has similar partnerships with the EU, South Korea, South America, India, Turkey, and Japan.

These partnerships are both signals of the larger diplomatic engagement with Africa globally, but also signals of a necessity for the AU to use its partnerships as a means of generating revenue for its operations. These external partnerships, while commonplace among international organizations, lend the AU toward a dependence on maintaining the partnerships out of necessity and limit their ability to be fully autonomous in their engagements. These existing partnerships also create conditions of forum shopping, meaning the AU chose whichever arrangement/partnership that it views will offer them the best chance of fulfilling its operational and political objectives, however, at the expense of alienating or diminishing partnerships in other domains. Forum shopping may be fruitful in the short term, but there are long-term implications that could lead to fits and starts with external partnerships that are neglected or create imbalances in the partnerships. One area where this dynamic is emerging is the growing trade imbalance between China and Africa. China now holds about a 41.5 billion USD trade surplus with Africa, an increase of 243 percent from 2019 (People's Republic of China, Ministry of Commerce 2021). Taken together, the reliance on external partnerships can be seen as an institutional pathway around funding constraints, however, they also pose significant challenges in getting the AU to uphold its commitments.

Variations in Institutional Autonomy

Another key commitment challenge is the functional differentiation between AU institutions. The functional differences between the AUC and the AU Assembly have been highlighted; however, within the commission, AU organs are given different degrees of autonomy. Two organs highlight the variation in autonomy: the AU PSC and the African Centres for Disease Control (Africa CDC).

The AU PSC is the main decision-making body that works with the chairperson of the AUC to interpret violations of AU rules and norms regarding internal and external conflicts and disputes on the continent. The AU PSC is also the arbiter of sanctions, election security, and implementer of conventions relating to democracy and good governance. The mandate of the AU PSC is tethered to the constitutive act, the mandate of the AUC, and the unit composition comes from the AU Assembly Heads of State. The AU PSC is functionally a deciding and implementing body in the AU, meaning the body is responsible for interpreting and handing down decisions, but also making sure it adequately aligns its decisions with existing protocols and mandates. This creates an institutional disconnect, in that it was established to predict and manage existing crises but is also charged with interpreting member state violations and challenges to existing rules. Further, the AU PSC is meant to create partnerships with RECs and the UN, to ensure that relevant stakeholders are also involved with the mandate. Member state interest and clout condition the AU PSC's ability to commit to uniformity across all institutional contexts. This is an institutional design issue—the scope of responsibilities held by the AU PSC makes it difficult for members of the body to act independently and through its own discretion, as there are many factors the body has to consider beyond its technical/implementing mandates.

By contrast, the Africa CDC has emerged as an AU institution with significant autonomy. Following the declaration of COVID-19 as a Public Health Emergency of International Concern (PHEIC), the AU scaled up the development of the Africa Centres of Disease Control, despite the global attention to China, Italy, and the United States during the first few months of the pandemic. The AU Assembly decided early on that it would empower the Director General of the Africa CDC to seek out partnerships and work collaboratively to facilitate a response to the pandemic. The Africa CDC and by extension, the AU, was one of the first and only regional bodies to opt for a multilateral approach to respond to the pandemic (Patterson and Balogun 2021). Africa CDC worked directly with the World Health Organization to facilitate the dissemination of personal protective equipment across Africa, and Africa CDC was a key partner in fast-tracking vaccine trials in Africa. Guided by a "new spirit of pan-Africanism" the African Union's initial response to the pandemic was highly collaborative, which addressed a threat that many thought would impact the continent more severely than it did (Patterson and Balogun 2021; Tieku 2021). Africa CDC also facilitated many "community of practice" dialogues with health practitioners across throughout the pandemic, to encourage best practices on the continent. Because of these actions, Africa CDC was elevated to the status of a Continental Public Health Agency, an autonomous entity, rather than a technical arm of the AU.

The differences in the trajectories of the AU PSC and Africa CDC can be explained by the amount of institutional space given to each organ to stick to its commitments. While the AU PSC has to consider the political will of member states and function as a coordinating body for all regional stakeholders (this is also conditioned by the breadth of non-AU security arrangements that exist on the continent), AU leaders delegated authority to the Africa CDC and created the institutional space for its practitioners to address issues related to the pandemic without the bureaucratic hurdles that other AU institutions have to face (Balogun 2021).

Credibility

Finally, credibility refers to organization's struggle to follow through with plans. One example is the inconsistent application of the anti-coup norm and the different ways the AU and RECs approach sanctioning an unconstitutional transfer of power. Since 2020, there have been several recent coups or coup attempts in African countries—Mali (2020, 2021), Niger (2021), Chad (2021), Guinea (2021), Sudan (2021), Burkina Faso (2022), and Guinea-Bissau (2022). While the AU has often articulated its rejection of unconstitutional transitions of power and showed this with its suspension of Burkina Faso, Guinea, Mali, and Sudan following their coups, the AU PSC did not do the same for Chad. This move called attention to the fact that current AUC chairperson Moussa Faki Mahamat is a Chadian national raising concern surrounding the organization's credibility. The inability in a consistent manner really undermines the organization and overshadows all that the organization has achieved since its treaty was ratified in 2001. Similarly, issues of subsidiarity and paternalism create challenges to the AU's credibility.

Issues of credibility challenge the AU's authority as an appropriate diplomatic actor. The AU has several instruments that are meant to increase the credibility of the rules and norms established in the constitutive act. For example, the AU's Panel of the Wise, embedded in the AU PSC, calls for the inclusion of "highly respected African personalities" that have made outstanding contributions to peace and security, as a means to enhance the credibility and objectivity of institutional decision-making. The Panel of the Wise is also one of the few areas of the AU that explicitly incorporates RECs into its formal structure. Similarly, the African Peer Review Mechanism serves as another formal institution that relies on member states submitting information about their progress toward democracy, good governance, economic and sustainable development. Countries that are members of the APRM are reviewed once they become members and every four years after. Countries can also request review by APRM members as a mechanism of early warning. Critics of the AU often ignore these institutions designed to increase member state accountability, however, these organs show that the African Union has innovative existing institutions that can help solve issues on the continent, if they were empowered. Further, these institutions lack credibility because they require buy-in from key African actors as well as a more concentrated connection between the outcomes generated from the institutions and the impact on the lives of citizens in member states.

Looking Ahead

This chapter has outlined three areas in which the AU would benefit from diplomatic reform—clout, commitment, and credibility. Its challenges in these areas undermine its ability to fully undertake its institutional mandate. Looking ahead, we offer a few solutions to addressing these issues.

One pathway to reform is to empower and build capacity in its existing institutions. This would involve amending the goals and outcomes of existing institutions to connect with locally led civil society organizations and a democratization of AU governance to focus less on the self-interest of member state governments, toward a more inclusive governance space. Functionally, that would require AU Heads of States empowering AUC practitioners with more delegated authority to structure partnerships with civil society organizations, activist groups, and political parties, for example, that could change the governance landscape across the continent. There are a number of ways in which civil society organizations (CSOs) can serve as pivotal partners. The most apparent is the role that CSOs play in popularizing the organization. In Afrobarometer's most recent Round 8, 25.1 percent of the population surveyed answered "don't know" to the question "In general, do you think that the economic and political influence of each of the following organizations on [country] is mostly positive, mostly negative, or haven't you heard enough to say? African Union," and 52.7 percent answering "somewhat" or "very positive" (Afrobarometer 2022). These numbers indicate that AU needs to prioritize informing citizens of its member states of what its role is. The AU can take the example of ECOWAS, who partners with the West African Network for Peacebuilding (WANEP) to assist with early warning and peacebuilding capacity in West Africa.

Another way the AU can functionally prioritize the citizen perspective would be to empower and elevate the relevance of its Civil Society, Citizens, and Diaspora Directorate (CIDO). CIDO is a coordinating division under the AU tasked with supporting intercontinental consultations between the AU and its external partners, and facilitating CSO input in the AU's external partnerships. CIDO already tasks itself with building capacity to improve information gaps between civil society and AU governance. A way forward would be for there to be higher-level diplomatic engagement with CIDO or a more institutionalized role for CIDO in more prominent governance areas. Where this has some policy congruence is in the AUs urging of CSOs' support and promote the implementation of the AU's Free Movement Protocol (FMP) and Migration Policy Framework for Africa (MPFA). Building the capacity of existing institutions by incorporating civilian input provides a direct link to member state populations, democratizes the governance process, and can make diplomatic reform more durable by generating popular consent for national and continental initiatives.

Second, given the challenges that diplomatic disputes and political rivalry pose, the AU has an opportunity to improve its institutional conditions for diplomatic engagement and clarify instances of subsidiarity. As noted in Kagame's report, there is a lack of clarity in the relationship with RECs, which provides an opportunity for the AU to clarify the working relationship with the RECs and also facilitate REC autonomy in response to continental issues. This would require a more robust engagement that goes beyond the current Mid-Year Coordination meetings between the AUC and RECs and considers how RECs maintain their autonomy and subsidiarity, while also aligning their action plans with the AU 10-year implementation plan and Agenda 2063. Addressing the division of labor issue between the AUC and RECs could create an opening for RECs to have more ownership in their domain, while allowing the AU to act as an overarching body and liaison at the continental level (as a bridge between the various regional bodies). This can be done by using Memorandums of Understanding (MOUs) more strategically. Better coordination will facilitate compliance with existing and future efforts.

Third, there is a need to reimagine how reform and innovation can be applied. There are key areas where institutional reform has been successful and where regional consensus has worked, such as global health and the environment. Despite this, there is an opportunity for the AU to cease on its penchant for collaboration and solidifying a collective posture on the global stage, to advocate for technological innovation in medicine, climate change, and food security. Positive diplomatic engagement would lend itself to member states addressing the international community from a common position and move quickly in addressing these critical matters.

Finally, an obvious path forward would be for the AU to figure out how to create financial self-reliance. While there is a shared understanding and political will to create financial independence, the capacity is lacking. The AU could serve as a forum for the African Continental Free Trade Area (AfCFTA) tariff negotiations, focused on creating conditions for Small Island States and other African countries with low capacity for trade to begin working groups to eliminate trade barriers to make AfCFTA work. Member states with the largest share of continental trade can also use the AfCFTA to build on the Kigali Decision as a means of facilitating the community levy. Using the AfCFTA to facilitate AU financing would also provide a functional bridge for AU-REC collaboration, specifically through sub-regional trade and custom regulations. Finally, the AfCFTA could be used to engage private, Africa-based financial firms in providing capital to support AU priority areas. Partnerships like this exist currently, evidence by the African Development Bank (AfDB) providing a 5 million USD grant to scale-up the Tony Elumelu Entrepreneurship Programme. AfDB provides an example of the kind of mutual investment that is possible through public private partnerships and the African Union has already prioritized private sector reform as part of its COVID-19 response (African Union 2021).

Taken together, the prospect for AU reform is not insurmountable, but will require a shift in priorities and a deliberate engagement with underutilized stakeholders in the region.

References and Further Reading

African Peer Review Mechanism. 2019. *2018 APRM Secretariat Report v.11.01.2019*. https://www.aprm-au.org/wp-content/uploads/2019/08/APRMANNUAL REPORT2018.pdf.

African Union. 2008a. Protocol on Relations between the African Union (AU) and the Regional Economic Communities (RECs). https://archives.au.int/handle/123456789/1621.

———. 2008b. Draft Protocol Amending the 2008 Protocol on Relations between the African Union and the Regional Economic Communities (RECs). https://archives.au.int/handle/123456789/8441.

———. 2013. *African Union Election Observation Manual*. https://www.eisa.org/pdf/au2014EOMmanual.pdf.

———. 2020. *Financing the Union: Towards the Financial Autonomy of the African Union*. https://au.int/sites/default/files/documents/38739-doc-report_on_financing_of_the_union_jun_2020_002.pdf.

———. 2021. African Private Sector Forum. https://au.int/en/pressreleases/20211115/public-private-partnership-viable-path-africas-economic-recovery-african.

———. 2022a. Overview. https://au.int/en/overview.

———. 2022b. Assembly. https://au.int/en/assembly.

Africanews. 2019, July 2. "Somaliland Steps Up Diplomatic Efforts to Secure International Recognition." https://www.africanews.com/2019/07/02/somaliland-steps-up-diplomatic-efforts-to-secure-international-recognition/.

———. 2022, June 6. "Kenya, Somalia in Fresh Diplomatic Row." https://www.africanews.com/2022/06/15/kenya-somalia-in-fresh-diplomatic-row//.

Afrobarometer. 2022. Round 8 Survey Data. http://www.afrobarometer.org.

Agence France Presse. 2022. "Somalia Protests to Kenya over Somaliland Presence at Briefing." Reprinted in *Barron's*. https://www.barrons.com/news/somalia-protests-to-kenya-over-somaliland-presence-at-briefing-01655233507.

AU Peace and Security Council. 2021. Communiqué 1037th Meeting on Somalia AMISOM. https://www.peaceau.org/uploads/eng-psc-communique-1037th-meeting-on-somalia-amisom.pdf.

———. 2022. Communique of the 1068th Meeting of the AU Peace and Security Council on ATMIS Mandate. https://amisom-au.org/2022/03/communique-of-the-1068th-meeting-of-the-au-peace-and-security-council-on-somalia/.

Balogun, E. 2021. "African Agency in Practice: Acquiring Agency and Institutional Change in the West African Health Organisation." *Africa Spectrum* 56 (3): 293–313.

———. 2022. *Region-building in West Africa: Convergence and Agency in ECOWAS*. London: Routledge.

Bappah, H.Y. 2018. "ECOWAS Protagonists for Peace: An Internal Perspective on Policy and Community Actors in Peacemaking Interventions." *South African Journal of International Affairs* 25 (1): 83–98.

Bew, J. 2015. *Realpolitik: A History.* Oxford and New York: Oxford University Press.

Dahir, A.L. 2020. "Somalia Severs Diplomatic Ties with Kenya." *New York Times*, December 15. https://www.nytimes.com/2020/12/15/world/africa/somalia-kenya.html.

Hiiraan Online. 2019. "Somalia Summons Kenyan Ambassador over PS's 'Offensive' Tweet," July 1. https://www.hiiraan.com/news4/2019/July/164541/somalia_summons_kenyan_ambassador_over_ps_s_offensive_tweet.aspx.

Kagame, P. 2017. *The Imperative to Strengthen Our Union: Report on the Proposed Recommendations for the Institutional Reform of the African Union*, January 29. https://au.int/sites/.../32777-file-report-20institutional20reform20of20the 20au-2.pdf.

Krause, K. 2002. "Multilateral Diplomacy, Norm Building, and UN Conferences: The Case of Small Arms and Light Weapons." *Global Governance* 8 (2): 247–63.

Lall, R. 2017. "Beyond Institutional Design: Explaining the Performance of International Organizations." *International Organization* 71 (2): 245–80.

Ministry of Foreign Affairs and International Cooperation, Federal Republic of Somalia. 2021. Press Statement (For Immediate Release). https://www.mfa.gov.so/wp-content/uploads/2021/10/AMISOM.pdf.

Nantulya, P. 2022. *The African Union at 20: Much Accomplished, More Challenges Ahead*. Africa Center for Strategic Studies. https://africacenter.org/spotlight/african-union-20-much-accomplished-more-challenges-ahead/.

Obala, R. 2020. "Uhuru Hosts Somaliland Leader Amidst Tension." *The Standard*. https://www.standardmedia.co.ke/nairobi/article/2001397220/uhuru-hosts-somalilandleader-amidst-tension.

Patterson, A.S., and E. Balogun. 2021. "African Responses to COVID-19: The Reckoning of Agency?" *African Studies Review* 64 (1): 144–67.

People's Republic of China, Ministry of Commerce. 2021. *China-Africa Trade and Cooperation*, April 12. http://xyf.mofcom.gov.cn/article/tj/zh/202104/20210403051448.shtml.

Reuters. 2022. "Rwanda Re-opens Border with Uganda But Says Grievances Remain," January 31. https://www.reuters.com/world/africa/rwanda-re-opens-border-with-uganda-says-grievances-remain-2022-01-31/.

Sarkin, J. 2018. "The Need to Reform the Political Role of the African Union in Promoting Democracy and Human Rights in Domestic States: Making States More Accountable and Less Able to Avoid Scrutiny at the United Nations and at the African Union, Using Switzerland to Spotlight the Issues." *African Journal of International and Comparative Law* 26 (1): 84–107.

Tieku, T.K. 2017. *Governing Africa: 3D Analysis of the African Union's Performance*. Lanham: Rowman & Littlefield.

———. 2019. "Ruling from the Shadows: The Nature and Functions of Informal International Rules in World Politics." *International Studies Review* 21 (1): 1–19.

———. 2021. "The African Union Makes Its Mark in the Pandemic." *Current History* 120 (826): 127–77.

14

What Motivates South Korea's Diplomatic Reform and Innovation?

HwaJung Kim

Introduction

South Korea's policies, including its national or diplomatic security strategy, have been heavily affected by exogenous factors. During the Cold War, South Korea lacked autonomy and subjectivity (Milani et al. 2019), which is considered an example of the second image reversed (Gourevitch 1978). This means that South Korea aligned its international and regional strategies with U.S. global strategy and its East Asia strategy to prevent the spread of communism, protect liberalism, and develop a democratic market economy. In the absence of regional and Korean Peninsula-specific strategies, efforts to improve inter-Korean relations were limited and often politicized for domestic politics.

After the establishment of the South Korean government in 1948, South Korea's foreign policy spearheaded by the president was largely focused on two issues: security and the economy. Specifically, South Korea sought to develop favorable relationships with the United States from the 1950s to 1960s by forming a security alliance with the United States and Asian countries and by promoting economic alliances and seeking military aid from

H. J. Kim (✉)
Ewha Womans University, Seoul, South Korea

European countries. From the 1970s to 1980s, the country aimed to facilitate economic development and resource diplomacy (Ministry of Culture, Sports, and Tourism [MCST] 2010). Under the Chun Doo-hwan presidency (1980–88), a transition period from an authoritarian dictatorship to a democratic government occurred, but still, the government was dominated by the military. There were also attempts to diversify diplomatic relationships with Southeast Asia and Africa to secure natural resources and to maintain the political and economic stability of the Northeast Asia region by strengthening economic and security alliances among the United States, Japan, and South Korea. Hosting mega sporting events, such as the 10th Asian Games (1986), the 24th Seoul Olympic Games, and the 8th Seoul Paralympic Games (1988), raised the country's global reputation (Kim 2022).

Meanwhile, South Korea's June 1987 nationwide pro-democracy movement and the end of the Cold War enabled the country to set independent external strategies beyond the Korea–U.S. alliance. In particular, democratic reforms taking place in the same year had a significant impact on conceptions of the country's national role, constructed by both policymakers and citizens, since it became possible to apply democratic control (Kim 2020) to foreign affairs and security regarding international and regional strategies, as well as inter-Korean relations. The tendency to follow the U.S. strategy was put into question. Since then, South Korea's policies, national, and diplomatic security strategies have been extensively affected by government-led reform and innovation to meet international expectations and domestic demands. Thus, the country's diplomacy has continued to evolve over time.

This chapter aims to discover what motivated South Korea's reform and innovation after the pro-democracy movement in the late 1980s by analyzing the country's diplomatic practices. The next section introduces the background of South Korea's contemporary diplomacy practice. The subsequent section examines six administrations, starting with the first civilian president Kim Young-sam (1993–97) followed by Kim Dae-jung (1998–2002), Roh Moo-hyun (2003–7), Lee Myung-bak (2008–12), Park Geun-hye (2013–16), and Moon Jae-in (2017–22), to reveal driving forces affecting diplomatic reform and innovation. The last section summarizes the key findings and considers their implications.

Background to South Korea's Contemporary Diplomatic Practice

The year 1987, when the pro-democracy movement occurred, was a turning point for South Korea because the Ministry of Foreign Affairs had overhauled the organization and focused efforts on ensuring the manpower necessary to strengthen the country's international status, to take an appropriate role in world politics, and to cope with protectionism trends and the rapidly changing international economic environment (Ministry of Foreign Affairs and Trade [MOFAT] 2009). Major reforms were made in three areas: economic diplomacy, public relations and cultural affairs, and the computerization of foreign administrations.

Since the 1990s, various forms of diplomacy, including "eastern" and United Nations (UN) regional economic cooperation diplomacy, have been pursued. By capitalizing on the atmosphere resulting from the successful hosting of the 1988 Seoul Olympics, the country's economic development, the dismantling of the Eastern Bloc, and the "northern" foreign policy were actively promoted. The two Koreas signed up to be UN member states simultaneously during President Roh Tae-woo's administration (1988–93). Subsequently, the Framework Agreement between South and North Korea went into effect. This transitional period saw South Korea convert from an industrial era to a democratization era and expand its diplomatic relations with the Soviet Union, China, and Eastern European countries, the so-called *Nordpolitik*, to expand the scope of the country's diplomacy (MCST 2010). Notably, the government expanded the horizons of cultural diplomacy, establishing the Cultural Agreement and Cultural Joint Committee, cultural exchange, academic exchange, sports exchange and promotion, tourism promotion activities, local government and private diplomacy support activities, and other activities.

In 1991, a foreign policy planning office was established to efficiently design and promote comprehensive mid-term foreign policy. Furthermore, three policy deliberators, the policy general department, and the security policy department were established (MOFAT 2009). To efficiently support overseas diplomatic missions and manage state-owned property, two deliberators and a state-owned property officer were newly established as part of the Planning and Management Office. Although the Roh administration sought contemporary diplomatic practices, meaningful innovation based on democratic governance came with the next president, as Roh's government was still an authoritarian regime (Kim 2022).

Case Study: South Korea's Diplomatic Reform and Innovation

The Kim Young-sam Administration (1993–97)

The "*Munmin* [civilian]" government, a catchphrase coined by President Kim Young-sam, represented the first general citizen government with the first civilian president elected, putting an end to 32 years of military governments. The *Munmin* government laid the groundwork for government reforms and innovations for adaptation and adjustment to a rapidly changing environment. The primary slogan of the *Munmin* government was made of three parts: establishing a "New Korea," internationalization, and globalization to align with a liberally democratic world. The first half of Kim Young-sam's presidency mainly focused on the system reform of public administrations to distinguish the *Munmin* government from previous authoritarian governments, which affected diplomatic goals, objectives, and tasks. In the second half of his term, President Kim Young-sam engaged in more diplomatic efforts and economic development to pursue internationalization and globalization (Korea Institute of Public Administration [KIPA] 2008).

Reforms in public administration during the period made it possible for South Korea to establish a democratic government through a bottom-up process (Oh 2019). According to President Kim Young-sam's speech in 1993, the reforms, regarded as successful democratic experiments and signaling the construction of a democratic government, were welcomed by the United States and other Western countries. Public administration reforms, including the real-name financial system, were implemented to eliminate political corruption and economic and social injustice (*Kukjung Shinmun* 1993). Additionally, the newly established Ministry of Information and Communication constructed high-speed information and communication infrastructure that raised the global competitiveness of the entire country (Chung et al. 2022). This effort made it possible to implement a small and efficient government.

As a result of these government reforms, the Ministry of Foreign Affairs raised its effectiveness by upgrading its system, organizations, departments, and personnel. For example, six headquartered departments were reduced to one new department in 1994; in the following year, the administrative and legal officers of the Planning and Management Office were merged into the Public Administration Legal Affairs Office to improve the organization, quota management, and personnel system. In 1997, the International Economic Bureau established an economic organization dedicated to the Organization for Economic Cooperation and Development (OECD)-related affairs (MOFAT 2009).

President Kim Young-sam laid out so-called new foreign policy upholding normative values, such as democracy, freedom, social policy, and security, at a time of radical transition in the world to create a new framework for peace, co-existence, and co-prosperity heading into the twenty-first century (*Kukjung Shinmun* 1993). To achieve the goal of the internationalization of South Korea in the context of globalization, the *Munmin* government developed coping strategies to expand and deepen economic cooperation in the Pacific region and to further develop security alliances by actively participating in international, functional organizations (World Trade Organization [WTO], OECD, Asia-Pacific Economic Cooperation [APEC], and Asia-Europe Meeting [ASEM]); hosting international competitions, such as the Daejoen Expo (1993) and the Muju-Jeonju Winter Universiade (1997); and winning the bids for co-hosting the 2002 Korea-Japan World Cup and the 2002 Busan Asian Games (MCST 2010). South Korea became seen as an economic powerhouse by the international community and was ranked 11th in economic power in the world, particularly when the country joined the OECD with a per capita income of more than $10,000.

While the Korea-U.S. alliance was strengthened, continuing diplomatic and security ties, Korea's relationship with Japan deteriorated due to historical debate between heads of states in spite of the *Munmin* government's reforms for internationalization. The North Korean nuclear threat and its leader Kim Il-sung's death further strained inter-Korean relations, raising concerns from neighboring countries. In addition, the 1997 financial crisis came as a result of the failure to manage foreign debt, which made it difficult to properly evaluate the economic achievements of the Kim Young-sam administration.

Nonetheless, the achievements of democratic reforms in the *Munmin* government led South Korea to adjust its diplomatic affairs in accordance with the liberal world and realize the administration's vision of a New Korea. By doing this, the Ministry's organizational changes helped the country become more open to the rest of the world. Therefore, it can be said that national aspirations for the democratic transformation of the country have improved the fundamentals of the country's overall public administration system as well as the Ministry of Foreign Affairs' organizational system.

The Kim Dae-jung Administration (1998–2002)

President Kim Dae-jung, representing the "*Kukmin* [people]" government, the first progressive government since democratization, began his term by tackling the East Asian economic crisis, as he made every effort to overcome the financial difficulties. The administration concentrated on restructuring initiatives, such as through public, corporate, financial, and labor reforms. The adaptation of the Washington Consensus caused the country to make changes and improvements throughout the entire government system under neoliberal economic prescriptions (Lee et al. 2005; KIPA 2008, 541). As a result, the Republic of Korea overcame the foreign exchange crisis in the shortest time compared to other countries in the world (MCST 2010). In the latter half of his term, President Kim Dae-jung's administration employed information technology to reinvent administrative work, laying the foundation for an e-government (Chung et al. 2022).

Under the *Kukmin* administration, the Ministry of Foreign Affairs experienced significant organizational reform, institutionalizing the MOFAT, human resource restructuring, and the improvement of public servants. Following the governmental organizational reforms, the Ministry of Foreign Affairs embraced economic affairs, becoming the MOFAT in 1998, newly instituting the Minister for Trade (Presidential Decree No. 15710). The Trade Negotiations Headquarters, a ministerial body under the MOFAT, was also established to serve in the model of the U.S. Trade Representative. Since 1998, the MOFAT has comprehensively established foreign policy related to trade, negotiations, and foreign investment to strengthen the country's economic and trade functions in a globalized market. The Kim Dae-jung administration also engaged in organizational and human resource innovations in the Ministry by enacting the Foreign Service Officials Act in 2000. This Act created open positions for public servants, abolishing the classification of public officials and implementing qualification assessment criteria (MOFAT 2009).

There were also changes in foreign policy directions following the Kim Dae-jung administration's policies, which sought comprehensive partnership relationships with neighboring countries based on mutual trust (MOFAT 2001). The *Kukmin* government pursued the country's independent position in power struggles among four strong nations (the United States, China, Japan, and Russia) over issues on the Korean Peninsula and implemented a policy of reconciliation and cooperation with North Korea through the so-called Sunshine Policy. President Kim Dae-jung won the Nobel Peace Prize for his contributions to the establishment of a peace regime in Northeast Asia by holding the first inter-Korean summit since the establishment of the democratic government and drawing up the Six-Party Talks involving the four nations alongside the two Koreas (MCST 2010).

In addition, the MOFAT created a comprehensive foreign strategy in the areas of commerce, negotiations, and foreign investment. The Ministry enhanced the country's multilateral diplomacy in international organizations, including Association of Southeast Asian Nations (ASEAN) and the European Union (EU), deepened trilateral relations with Japan and China by utilizing the newly instituted mechanism of ASEAN Plus Three, and expanded its scope of cultural diplomacy to enhance the national image (MOFAT 2001). The successful co-hosting of the 2002 World Cup with Japan also paved the way for reconciliatory sentiments between the two countries. The National Image Committee was established by the Kim Dae-jung administration to maintain the country's global reputation.

However, even though this administration overcame the financial crisis, promoted economic growth and political democratization, and established peaceful sentiments on the Korean Peninsula by way of the Sunshine Policy, there were still issues related to North Korea's provocations, which threatened the fragile peace between the two Koreas and their respective allies. These remained unfinished tasks at the end of President Kim Dae-jung's administration. Furthermore, the 9/11 attacks in 2001 raised concerns about world security.

Overall, there were two driving factors that led to reform and innovation. The capacity building of the country in accordance with a globalized market based on the neoliberal world order was one main factor in actualizing the *Kukmin* government's diplomacy reform. Another determinant factor lies in the advancement of information and technology, which has reinvented administrative work in the Ministry.

The Roh Moo-hyun Administration (2003–7)

President Roh Moo-hyun created a progressive and reformative policy by representing the "*Chamyeo* [participatory]" government in consolidating the development of democratic efforts in the face of the influence of globalization and the information age (KIPA 2008, 156). The Roh administration had to deal with the rapid changes in the international environment, North Korea's provocations, and related growing demands from South Korean society, and anti-Americanism when two Korean girls were killed by American military vehicles (Kim 2022). Given this backdrop, President Roh aimed to establish a democracy with the people, the balanced development of society, and peace and prosperity in Northeast Asia.

The administrative reforms of the *Chamyeo* government were carried out with a clear roadmap featuring information policy and e-government initiatives, ushering the country into an era of digital governance (Chung et al. 2022). This digital transformation, along with the Roh administration's policy of realizing a participatory democracy, heavily affected diplomatic reforms and innovation in the MOFAT, which pivoted toward a new people-oriented paradigm. In addition, the increasing number of traveling and overseas Koreans required more protection assistance since incidents such as the London bombings, Hurricane Katrina, and the Bali bombings put Korean nationals in danger. The MOFAT developed high-quality consular services and organizational and human resource innovations, such as providing short messaging service (SMS) alerts in cases of emergency, as well as establishing a Consular Call Center to respond to accidents and share information, a Rapid Response Team, and an Overseas Emergency Alert System, making Korea the first nation in the world to provide alert messages via mobile phones (MOFAT 2006, 199). After the legal and institutional groundwork was completed for the establishment of the Innovation Committee, the completion of organizational restructuring to enhance diplomatic capacities was carried out in the latter half of 2006.

As such, the paradigm shift to people-centered foreign policy enabled the MOFAT to implement public diplomacy initiatives, making 2005 the starting year of diplomacy with the people. These efforts expanded dialogue with the public and built overseas information networks. Furthermore, the MOFAT established foreign policy lecture circuits in major cities, the Visit MOFAT Programs, and visits to middle and high schools. The existing MOFAT homepage was revamped with user-friendly features, and the Ministry's portal site "e-World" and Overseas Information Network were established to provide real-time communication (MOFAT 2006, 207–9). Public diplomacy efforts mainly focused on cultural and public relations for the promotion of a "Dynamic Korea," the catchphrase of the Roh administration, and the *Hallyu* (Korean Wave).

The Roh administration sought advanced diplomacy with the rise of the country's economic power, actively participated in major international organizations, reflected its position in UN reforms, spread universal values, dedicated itself to solving problems, and enhanced soft power through cultural diplomacy. The MOFAT diversified diplomatic practices via the systematic promotion of omnidirectional summit diplomacy, active participation in economic diplomacy through the Free Trade Agreement (FTA), and regional diplomacy by deepening substantive cooperation with the EU, Latin America, and the Middle East. Additionally, the 2011 IAAF World Championships in Athletics in Daegu, the 2012 International Exposition in Yeosu, and the 2014 Asian Games in Incheon were successfully hosted by South Korea. In doing so, the Roh administration promoted balanced pragmatic diplomacy for peace and prosperity in Northeast Asia, the development of comprehensive partnerships, and multilateral diplomacy in Northeast Asia.

Through balanced practical diplomacy with the United States, Japan, China, and Russia, the Roh administration sought an integrated order for peace in Northeast Asia and produced the first Korean UN Secretary-General in history (MCST 2010). In contrast to the policies for the Cold War during the Kim Dae-jung presidency, the resolution of problems on the Korean Peninsula was the core of the Roh administration's strategy, and regional strategies around the country were implemented. However, the principle of bilateralism regarding the Korea-U.S. alliance remained the same (Kim 2020). Regardless of the peace policy efforts extended toward North Korea, nuclear threats and tensions on the Korean Peninsula have yet to be resolved.

Essentially, the same forces continued to drive change and innovation. Beginning from the previous government, the advancement of information and technology is a major determinant factor of the *Chamyeo* administration that has opened a new era of digital governance. In addition, the rise of people-centric sensing in foreign policy has motivated the Ministry's openness and diversified diplomatic practices.

The Lee Myung-bak Administration (2008–12)

The Lee Myung-bak administration marked the return of the conservative government after a decade of progressive regimes, as it was born at the behest of the people's desire to cope with the economic downturn. Critical public opinion on sluggish economic performance during progressive administrations heightened concerns about the global financial crisis in 2007 (Kim 2020). President Lee pledged to enact MB-nomics, a pragmatic economic policy that promised 7 percent growth, a per capita income of $40,000, and the making of Korea as the seventh-largest economy within his term (Chang 2008). The Lee administration pursued *creative pragmatism* with a vision of a "Global Korea" through a harmonious balance between continuity and change in the face of challenges in the early years of his term. His administration faced challenges such as the North Korean nuclear threat, the global economic crisis caused by the bankruptcy of Lehman Brothers, the Eurozone crisis, issues related to the FTA, the candlelight vigils to protest the imported beef scandal, the abduction of Korean nationals in Afghanistan, and the rise of China (Chung et al. 2022; MOFAT 2008a; MOFA 2013).

The Lee administration's vision was to make South Korea an advanced nation. The vision of a Global Korea pursued national interests on the world stage with confidence based on economic development, relied on the strong Korea-U.S. alliance to ensure security (Park 2008), and allowed Korea to be regarded as a secure country that could be an exemplary model for developing countries (Kim 2020). Additionally, the Lee administration focused on the systematization and institutionalization of a national task system by providing strategies and tasks for national affairs according to indicators through the online national task management system (Kim 2020). The National Informatization Strategy Committee constructed an integrated national knowledge infrastructure, accelerating the motto of "Low Carbon, Green Growth," which nurtured new sectors, enhanced services through information technology (Chung et al. 2022), and launched the new era of "Government 2.0," where two-way communication between the government and people was made possible (Bloter 2010; Lee n.d.).

At the beginning of his term, the Lee administration led organizational reform. The Multilateral Diplomatic Treaty Office was formed by merging the Multilateral Diplomatic Office with the Treaty Bureau (MOFAT 2008b). The Ministry's direct energy resource ambassador and climate change ambassador were appointed to promote energy resource diplomacy and increase the capacity to negotiate international climate change terms. The Trade Negotiations Headquarters was reformed rather than removing the interim Free Trade Agreement Promotion Group for efficient FTA activity to simplify the organizational system, boost working-level manpower, and secure accountability for organizational operations (MCST 2010).

Additionally, the MOFAT continued its efforts to improve consular services. To meet the growing demand to ensure the safety of Koreans living overseas, the MOFAT established travel safety and travel alerts information dissemination methods, carried out visa waiver agreements with various countries, and extended the Working Holiday Program in 2009 (MOFAT 2010). There were significant reforms in human resources management in the second half of the Lee administration. In 2011, the Korea National Diplomatic Academy Act was created with the goal of identifying and educating excellent diplomats to help develop a twenty-first-century diplomatic system. The Foreign Service Officer Act was changed to establish an institutional foundation for workforce planning based on the values of fairness, transparency, and competitiveness (MOFAT 2012).

At the diplomatic practice level, the MOFAT tackled the difficulties of an ever-changing worldwide environment, as symbolized by globalization and the digital revolution, under the slogan "With the People, Towards the World." To promote the vision of a Global Korea effectively, the Lee administration established the Presidential Committee on National Branding in 2009 using a whole-of-government approach to public diplomacy. In May 2010, the first year of public diplomacy was declared, and Ma Young-sam was appointed as the first public diplomacy ambassador under the circumstances that next year's organization would not be reorganized. Since 2013, when Korea's first official public diplomacy project took place, the public diplomacy capacity-building project has been secured and increased every year (Choi 2018, 255). South Korea's standing in world politics became eminent through the successful hosting of a series of international events, such as the G20 Seoul Summit in 2010, Yeosu Expo 2012, the 2012 Seoul Nuclear Security Summit, and the Busan High Level Forum on Aid Effective in 2012. Furthermore, it won the bid to host the 2018 Winter Olympics Games in PyeongChang in the same year.

South Korea's foreign policy behavior prominently contributed to global governance throughout Lee's presidency. For example, Korea became a member of the G20 steering group, and the OECD Development Assistance Committee (DAC) developed a sophisticated Official Development Assistance (ODA) system and implemented the UN Peacekeeping Operations (PKO) Participation Act. At the regional level, the MOFAT promoted the "New Asia Initiative," which facilitated friendly ties with Asian countries, including ASEAN, while also expanding cooperation with Central Asia, Africa, the Middle East, and Latin America, clearing the way for cooperation with the EU through "Comprehensive Partnership." South Korea actively engaged in international conversations regarding global concerns like climate change, the global financial crisis, and rising oil prices. To deal with the issues surrounding North Korea, the Lee administration established a Secretariat for Trilateral Cooperation for Korea, Japan, and China while maintaining a strategic partnership with the United States (Um 2010, 54–55).

While the Lee administration achieved diplomatic gains through innovative pragmatism (Lee 2008, 49) and successfully built an image of a Global Korea, the North Korean nuclear threat, North Korea's regime change due to the death of Kim Jung-il, the sinking of South Korea's navy vessel Cheonan, and the artillery strike on Yeonpyeong Island intensified military tensions on the Korean Peninsula (MOFA 2013; Kang 2013, 87).

The Lee administration demonstrated South Korea's contribution to global governance in several notable ways. It strengthened the global competitiveness of the country, including not only the Ministry and its public servants, but also its people based on informational technology and knowledge infrastructure. In a similar vein, the systematization and institutionalization of national affairs, once considered less important, also contributed to the capacity building of public sector and the people.

The Park Geun-hye Administration (2013–17)

The Park Geun-hye administration was inaugurated in 2013 against the backdrop of a more critical diplomatic scenario, North Korea's provocations, and a sentiment of mistrust among Asian countries that was greater than ever before. The first female president in Korea's and Northeast Asia's history moved the national paradigm even further away from governments and toward individuals, presenting a vision of happiness for the people of the Korean Peninsula, Northeast Asia, and eventually the global village. President Park sought a balanced regional strategy as the president of a middle power to correct the excessively global-based diplomacy of the previous administration.

The Park administration engaged in organizational changes. For the first time in 15 years, the government's industry and trade activities were reunited to raise the effectiveness of internal talks at the domestic level. That is, the MOFA separated its trade affairs and reduced the size of the organization and the number of personnel. Furthermore, the Ministry of Trade, Industry, and Energy, newly created by combining the Ministry of Knowledge Economy and trade-related tasks, transferred the positions of overseas representative to the MOFA (Lee and Lee 2013). The Korean government created a new diplomatic recruiting system based on the previous government's initiatives regarding the Korea National Diplomatic Academy, with the goal of boosting Korea's diplomatic skills. To promote digital government, the Park administration adopted "Government 3.0" policies, regulations, and governance, altering the previous administration's information policy framework with the slogan "for *people-centered* focusing on suppliers" (Chung et al. 2022).

The MOFA promoted *trustpolitik*, or the trust process, the Northeast Asia Peace Cooperation Initiative, and the Eurasian Initiative in collaboration with the people and in line with new government goals, such as economic restoration, citizen happiness, and cultural enrichment. Furthermore, the MOFA established the groundwork for peaceful unification by taking a critical role in creating long-term peace on the Korean Peninsula and in Northeast Asia (MOFA 2013). By emphasizing the significance of public support in making diplomacy successful (Mo and Hahn 2005), the MOFA also focused on the institutionalization of public diplomacy by way of establishing a legal basis and infrastructure and enacting the Public Diplomacy Act (MOFA 2017).

During the first half of Park's administration, the MOFA practiced middle-power diplomacy by contributing to the following global concerns: humanitarian diplomacy by taking leadership roles in major UN groups; unification diplomacy by persuading the international community that Korean unification would be a "bonanza"; network diplomacy by supporting the *trustpolitik*, establishing the Northeast Asia Peace and Cooperation Initiative, and participating in regional multilateral organizations; Eurasia Initiatives to engage Russia and Central Asia; Mexico, Indonesia, Korea, Turkey, Australia (MIKTA), a cross-regional consultative organization comprising five middle powers; and regional cooperative diplomacy by forming cooperative networks with various international organizations.

In 2014, the world faced both traditional and non-traditional challenges, such as North Korea's provocations, rising tensions between China and Japan over the East and South China Seas, the Ukrainian crisis, foreign terrorist fighters, the unprecedented spread of trans-boundary epidemics, and cybersecurity issues. The MOFA reinforced the crisis management capabilities of embassies, along with providing risk alert social services and emergency interpretation services in six languages—English, Chinese, Japanese, French, Spanish, and Russian—as part of its efforts to prepare for potential terrorist attacks and violent extremism.

In response to North Korea's escalating nuclear threat in 2015, the Park administration exerted multi-faceted diplomatic efforts (MOFA 2015). President Park's participation in China's Military Parade (September 3, 2015) was a pivotal point in the ROK-China relationship. As a result, for the first time in three and a half years, the China-Japan-Korea Trilateral Summit was held, followed by the Korea-Japan Summit Meeting. The long-standing issue of reparations for comfort women was ultimately settled with a historic accord reached during the Korea-Japan Summit. However, diplomacy in China raised criticisms at the ROK-U.S. summit (October 16, 2015). In addition, the Ukraine crisis led the Eurasia Initiative to a different mode of cooperation.

In 2016, North Korea conducted its fourth nuclear test, and the Park administration's unification diplomacy reverted to a traditional conservative model, strengthening sanctions against North Korea and the Cold War-style quasi-aligned ROK-U.S.-Japan alliance (Lee 2020). This resulted in the closure of the Kaesong Industrial Complex, the deployment of Terminal High

Altitude Area Defense (THAAD), and the signing of the General Security of Military Information Agreement (GSOMIA). In early 2017, President Park was impeached due to a political scandal at the domestic level, and she was also blamed for the unsatisfactory negotiation results with Japan regarding the comfort women. Nonetheless, some of the Park administration's structural reforms continued. Even though the Park administration's efforts at reform and innovation were discontinued, their effects did not entirely disappear; that was because structural reform has aligned with national aspirations for upgrading the country's diplomatic practice in a way that preserves the residual impact of previous administrations' institutional reforms, that is, by way of so-called path-dependence.

The Moon Jae-in Administration (2017–22)

The year 2017 was turbulent for South Korea due to its first historic incident of the impeachment of a president through a democratic protest, which resulted in candlelight vigils. Additionally, there was growing uncertainty at the international level stemming from North Korea's advancement of nuclear and missile capabilities, anti-globalization sentiments since Brexit, the rise of nationalism and populism, and challenges to the U.S.-led liberal rule-based order triggered by the launch of the Trump administration and China's pursuit of the "Chinese Dream" under President Xi's renewed leadership. From the progressive party, President Moon Jae-in was elected through hopes for change and intercommunication with the people.

Under the new national vision of the Moon administration, which aimed to achieve a "Nation of the People, a Just Republic of Korea," the MOFA exerted efforts to meet people's expectations, to diversify diplomacy by expanding diplomatic horizons, and to further realize *diplomacy for the people* that reflects people's will through communication via strengthening public diplomacy practice and creating a new mechanism of participatory diplomacy (MOFA 2018). The MOFA's Innovation Roadmap entailed three themes: people-themed tasks, the theme of national interest, and tasks for capacity building that brought about innovation and reforms during Moon's presidency.

A structural reform of the MOFA improved working conditions, promoted work-life balance, and carried out innovative pilot projects, such as Town Hall Meetings, mentoring programs, and the launch of the Online Innovation Platform and the Advisory Committee (MOFA 2018). In addition, there has been domestic-wide innovation since the MOFA declared the year 2018 to be the first year of "Participatory Diplomacy" while establishing a Participatory

14 What Motivates South Korea's Diplomatic Reform and Innovation?

Diplomacy Center under the Public Diplomacy and Cultural Affairs Bureau. These efforts were part of the people-themed task specified in detail through the 2018 Comprehensive Plan for Government Innovation. Specifically, these innovative diplomatic practices and styles aimed to raise awareness of citizen participation in diplomacy from decision-making processes to the implementation and execution of foreign policy. Accordingly, *diplomacy with the people* was realized (MOFA 2019). The MOFA enacted the Act on Consular Assistance to protect overseas Koreans, launched the Protection of Overseas Korean Nationals and Crisis Management Division, and assisted Korean enterprises in job creation and promoting the well-being of the people (MOFA 2019).

During the first half of the Moon administration, the MOFA focused on restoring summit diplomacy, particularly with its neighboring countries, and pursuing peace and stability on the Korean Peninsula, although a higher level of nuclear threats from North Korea exacerbated security dilemmas (Kim 2020). The MOFA also implemented the New Southern Policy and New Northern Policy, engaged in diplomacy with Europe, Latin America, the Caribbean, Africa, and the Middle East, and strengthened economic diplomacy (MOFA 2018).

The year 2018 started a new era of peaceful sentiments on the Korean Peninsula due to North Korea's participation in the PyeongChang Winter Olympic Games, which led three inter-Korean summits and the first North Korea-U.S. summit in history (MOFA 2019). In 2019, the world witnessed rapid changes in inter-Korean relations and U.S.-North Korea relations, which enabled South Korea to take a leading role in the peace negotiation process (Kim 2020). The Moon administration made it possible for North Korea to alter its nuclear diplomacy through close coordination with the Trump administration. However, North Korea revived its military plans later in mid-2020, bombing a joint liaison office in Kaesong as nothing materialized (Bicker 2020).

In 2020, the COVID-19 pandemic swept through the entire world, forcing borders to close and governments to focus on domestic quarantine measures against the pandemic. The fourth year of the Moon administration was greatly challenged, as it had to find ways to protect the interests of the country and safeguard its people in the midst of the global pandemic. Accordingly, the MOFA fully mobilized its capabilities, allowing 50,000 Koreans to return home safely, activated special entry permission agreements with other countries to help 23,000 Korean business people continue their activities, and contributed to joint responses to the pandemic at the international level (through the UN and WHO) as well as at the regional level by launching the Northeast Asia Cooperation for Health Security (MOFA 2021).

The MOFA announced a self-innovation plan called the MOFA Innovation Roadmap and Second Innovation Plan, which highlighted the necessity of continued efforts to promote innovation during the pandemic. Specifically, the plan proposed to reorganize the Crisis Management Division, open the second Center for Participatory Diplomacy, upgrade online and offline training systems, secure gender equality in the workplace, improve digital and online infrastructure, and introduce digital systems such as Cyber Cabinet and a mobile-based work system. The plan also proposed improvements to a system for advanced diplomacy, the establishment of Africa II and Eurasia I, the creation of the Korea-ASEAN Financial Cooperation Center under the Korean mission in Jakarta, Indonesia, and the enhancement of diplomatic capacity through the installment of efficient management methods for human resources.

The Moon administration's willingness to take risks in times of difficulty, such as the impeachment of the previous president and an unprecedented global pandemic affecting countries all over the world, was seen in its efforts at diplomatic reform and innovation. It also continued to advance civic capacity in the field of diplomacy.

Key Findings and Implications

This chapter has traced various factors that determined South Korea's diplomatic reform and innovation over a period spanning three decades from the early 1990s to the early 2020s by comparing six administrations in terms of globalization, democratization, information and technology advancement, national aspirations, capacity building and global competitiveness, risk taking, and the rise of people's power.

The major factor during the Kim Young-sam administration involved the nation's aspirations for democratic transformation, which led to the improvement of its overall public administration system and that of the Ministry of Foreign Affairs. That continued under the Kim Dae-jung administration with its reforms in the areas of capacity building to cope with globalization and the preparedness for the information and technology that shape public administration at all levels. The advancement of information and technology also motivated the Roh Moo-hyun administration's reforms, which came along with the rise of people-centric sensing in foreign policy. As globalization accelerated, the notion of the global competitiveness of the country became the main driver for the Lee Myung-bak administration's reforms, bringing about the systematization and institutionalization of national affairs. National aspirations and residual impacts of the previous government were identified as the Park Geun-hye administration's determinant factors for upgrading the country's diplomatic practice. Taking risks and the power of domestic opinion were the major factors in the Moon Jae-in administration's reforms and innovation in diplomacy. Despite significant continuities, such determinant factors also differed by administration. Why is this so?

South Korea's diplomatic reform and innovation go beyond the organizational level toward the political philosophy of a new administration whose effectiveness in policy engineering must be better than that of the previous administration at all levels. This is because the 1987 Constitution builds a system of a five-year single-term president, which makes the president the most powerful element of government and, at the same time, affects administration changes on whether or not to continue the ruling party's authority. The prerequisites for the implementation of reform and innovation are diverse, and implementation itself is a complex and challenging process, facing institutional constraints. Therefore, it is important to find a strong driving factor that makes innovative governance in diplomacy possible.

The tendency of each administration to seek greater effectiveness generates contrasting phenomena. On the one hand, this tendency has made institutional (re)arrangements move faster according to the goals and objectives of a new administration, and has enhanced the responsiveness and resilience of ministries, particularly the Ministry of Foreign Affairs. These features have facilitated a better functioning system at the level of the UN and regional groupings, such as APEC, ASEM, ASEAN Plus Three, or MIKTA. That is, the country's five-year single-term president system, in turn, strengthens the leadership of the president in diplomacy and brings about adaptability of the MOFA to the constantly changing diplomatic environment.

On the other hand, it lacks a long-term approach to foreign policy planning and consistency in diplomatic practice, as shown in the different modes of governance in diplomacy of each administration. Success or failure of reform and innovation largely depends on the president's leadership rather than the willingness and autonomy of the ministry; thus, it challenges the organizational-decision-making structure in the implementation of the national agenda of foreign affairs. Different administrations' geopolitical calculations about North Korea add to the uncertainty in inter-Korean relations and make it harder for diplomats to work with neighboring countries in a consistent way.

Therefore, in this regard, it is important to think about the president's leadership as well as administration changes when looking at South Korea's diplomatic reforms and innovation in addition to the abovementioned determinant factors. The new president, Yoon Suk-yeol (2022 onwards), from the conservative party, has just begun with visions and strategies driven by a variety of roadmaps and action plans, but the biggest problem in diplomacy still lies in two Koreas. In order to accomplish the goals and objectives of the Yoon administration, the government requires enormous changes across all areas of the MOFA.

Acknowledgments This work was supported by the Ministry of Education of the Republic of Korea and the National Research Foundation of Korea (NRF-2021S1A5B5A16078325).

References and Further Reading

Bicker, L. 2020. "North Korea Blows Up Joint Liaison Office with South in Kaesong." BBC News. https://www.bbc.com/news/world-asia-53060620.

Bloter. 2010. Beyond Government 2.0. Bloter & Media. https://www.bloter.net/newsView/blt201008100005.

Chang, J.C. 2008, *MB-nomics Mixture will Brew 7% Growth*. SERIWorld, January 25. http://www.seriworld.org/05/wldColumnV.html?mncd=0105&p_page=6&key=200804150001&mncd=0105.

Choi, K.J. 2018. *People Diplomacy, Public Diplomacy in the Era of the Fourth Industrial Revolution*. Seoul: Gwangjin Munwha Publication.

Chung, C., H. Choi, and Y. Cho. 2022. "Analysis of Digital Governance Transition in South Korea: Focusing on the Leadership of the President for Government Innovation." *Journal of Open Innovation: Technology, Market, and Complexity* 8 (2): 1–28.

Gourevitch, P. 1978. "The Second Image Reversed: The International Sources of Domestic Politics." *International Organization* 32 (4): 881–912.

Kang, J.H. 2013. "Rho Moo-hyun, Lee Myung-bak Regimes' Inter-Korean Relations and Public Opinion Analysis." *21st Century Political Science Review* 23 (3): 83–109.

Kim, S.H. 2020. "Study on South Korea's Policy Advocacy vis-à-vis the United States: Rho Moo-hyun Administration and Lee Myung-bak Administration." In *South Korea's Knowledge Public Diplomacy and Policy Advocacy Towards the United States*, ed. W.H. Lim. Daejeon: KDI Publication.

Kim, H.J. 2022. "What Affected South Korea's Behaviors in Hosting the Olympic Games?" In *Exploring Cities and Countries of the World*. New York: Nova Publication.

Korea Institute of Public Administration. 2008. *Korean Public Administration, 1948–2008*. Paju: Bobmun Publication.

Kukjung Shinmun. 1993. *The Kim Young-sam and New Diplomacy*. Korea Policy Briefing, November 18. https://www.korea.kr/archive/governmentView.do?newsId=148749450&pageIndex=1.

Lee, S.H. 2008. "New Government's Direction of Security and Diplomacy and Its Assignments." *Strategic Studies* 15 (1): 42–72.

Lee, J.C. 2020. "Study on South Korea's Policy Advocacy vis-à-vis the United States: Park Geun-hye Administration and Moon Jae-in Administration." In *South Korea's Knowledge Public Diplomacy and Policy Advocacy Towards the United States*, ed. W.H. Lim. Daejeon: KDI Publication.

Lee, J.Y. n.d. "Government 3.0-Public Information and New Values," *Naver*. https://terms.naver.com/entry.naver?docId=3576731&cid=59088&categoryId=59096.

Lee, J.U., and S.H. Lee. 2013. "Park Geun-hye Administration's Reform." *Dong-A Ilbo*, January 16. https://www.donga.com/news/Politics/article/all/20130116/52349874/1.

Lee, K., B.K. Kim, C.H. Lee, and J. Yee. 2005. *Visible Success and Invisible Failure in Post-crisis Reform in the Republic of Korea: Interplay of the Global Standards, Agents, and Local Specificity*. World Bank Policy Research Working Paper 3651, June.

Milani, M., M. Dian, and A. Fiori. 2019. "Interpreting South Korea's Foreign and Security Policy under the 'Asian Paradox.'" In *The Korean Paradox: Domestic Political Divide and Foreign Policy in South Korea*, eds. M. Milani, A. Fiori, and M. Dian. New York: Routledge.

Ministry of Culture Sports Tourism. 2010. *Policy Briefing about South Korea*. Seoul: Daehanminkuk Policy Briefing.

Ministry of Foreign Affairs. 2013. *Diplomatic White Paper 2013*. Seoul: Ministry of Foreign Affairs.

———. 2015. *Diplomatic White Paper 2015*. Seoul: Ministry of Foreign Affairs.

———. 2017. *Diplomatic White Paper 2017*. Seoul: Ministry of Foreign Affairs.

———. 2018. *Diplomatic White Paper 2018*. Seoul: Ministry of Foreign Affairs.

———. 2019. *Diplomatic White Paper 2018*. Seoul: Ministry of Foreign Affairs.

———. 2021. *Diplomatic White Paper 2021*. Seoul: Ministry of Foreign Affairs.

Ministry of Foreign Affairs and Trade. 2001. *Diplomatic White Paper 2001*. Seoul: Ministry of Foreign Affairs and Trade.

———. 2006. *Diplomatic White Paper 2006*. Seoul: Ministry of Foreign Affairs and Trade.

———. 2008a. *Diplomatic White Paper 2008*. Seoul: Ministry of Foreign Affairs and Trade.

———. 2008b. *South Korea's Diplomacy for Sixty Years: 1948–2008*. Seoul: Ministry of Foreign Affairs and Trade.

———. 2009. *Diplomatic White Paper 2009*. Seoul: Ministry of Foreign Affairs and Trade.

———. 2010. *Diplomatic White Paper 2010*. Seoul: Ministry of Foreign Affairs and Trade.

———. 2012. *Diplomatic White Paper 2012*. Seoul: Ministry of Foreign Affairs and Trade.

Oh, C.H. 2019. *Government Innovation, Looking Back Last Two Years and Preparing for the Future*. Seoul: Daehanminkuk Policy Briefing.

Park, B.C. 2008. "The Lee Myung-bak Administration and the U.S. Diplomacy Strategy." *Unification Strategy* 8 (2): 57–100.

Um, T.A. 2010. "Korean War and the Future of the U.S.-ROK Alliance." *Quarterly Journal of Defense Policy Studies* 26 (1): 35–72.

15

The Transformations of French Diplomacy

Maxime Lefebvre

The tradition of French Diplomacy is very much associated with the prestigious legacy of the past: the striving for "grandeur" and "rank" carried by Louis XIV, Napoleon, Charles de Gaulle, and others; the aristocratic figure of Talleyrand, who served the French Republic as well as the French Empire and the French Monarchy; the magnificent palace of the "Quai d'Orsay" inaugurated for the Congress of Paris under Napoleon III, and where Robert Schuman made a famous declaration launching the process of European integration.

But things have changed with time. The French diplomatic service has little to do with the small aristocratic system which prevailed at the time of the Congress of Vienna. It has become a strong institution. Today several transformations are at work, and this chapter discusses four of them in particular.

The first one is *professionalization*. Admission into the diplomatic service not being a privilege restricted to a small social elite is hardly new, and is today based on fair and competitive exams (*concours*) open to all. The principal of equal access to civil service positions was established under the French Revolution, and the French Republic has consistently imposed the principles

---

The views of the author do not reflect the official position of the French Ministry of Foreign Affairs.

M. Lefebvre (✉)
ESCP Business School, Paris, France

of recruitment by *concours*, of a neutral civil service loyal to the political power, of competence and experience-based careers.

In the recent period, the ministry has strengthened the internal mechanisms ensuring the professionalization of diplomacy. Diplomats undergo a systematic and ongoing evaluation throughout their careers not only by their superiors but also by their subordinates when they are in charge of running a team. This means that diplomats are not only judged on the basis of their original diplomas or their intellectual qualities, but also on their behavior and their sense of service. This is quite new compared to the past, when some ambassadors (by far not the majority) could sometimes behave as all-powerful despots. Also the inspection service of the French MFA attaches more and more importance to issues of management, exemplarity, and public service; and it is not uncommon that ambassadors or other managers are recalled or dismissed following some problems.

This all relates to the reform of the public service designed by President Emmanuel Macron's government. The reform has been caricatured as the suppression of ENA (the National School of Administration, created in 1945 as part of the republican re-foundation following the "Liberation" from German occupation and Vichy authorities) and of the corps of prefects and diplomats which could appear as *Etats dans l'Etat*. In reality the reform does not mean an evolution toward a U.S.-inspired "spoils system." Diplomats will still exist with another name (*Administrateurs de l'Etat*, maybe nicknamed *Administrateurs du Quai*); they will still be recruited both by specific exams and by the successor institution of ENA (INSP: *Institut national du service public*); and they will continue to run a diplomatic career managed by the Ministry of Foreign Affairs. The objective of the reform is to increase the level of inter-ministerial mobility but not to decrease the level of professionalization which specific diplomatic competences and jobs require. The arbitrary appointment of political figures as ambassadors or directors has always been possible (this is a principle of the French Constitution that such appointments are made at the discretion of the French government) but it is a reality that under the previous mandate of President Macron the practice of appointing qualified and experienced persons has been maintained: only a very limited number of non-diplomats hold positions of ambassadors, consuls, or directors in the French MFA. Thus it may be assumed that the professionalization of French diplomacy will continue also under the new system.

The second important evolution is *Europeanization*. It has to do with the creation of the European External Action Service (EEAS) in 2010, which has to recruit (on a rotating basis) one third of its agents from national diplomatic services. The objective of this fixed "quota" was to facilitate mobility between national and European diplomatic services and to help create a common European diplomatic culture. Some top French diplomats have served in the EEAS, for example Ambassador Pierre Vimont as the Secretary General (2010–15) and Charles Fries as Deputy Secretary General (since 2020). Many French ambassadors have been appointed as heads of EU delegations abroad. Many French diplomats have occupied temporarily some positions in the EEAS or its delegations before serving again in the French system.

Undoubtedly such examples of mobility contribute to the Europeanization of Foreign Policy. French diplomats bring into the European service their specific French knowledge and expertise, for example when they serve in African countries or as political-military experts. When they return to the French service, they can better integrate the knowledge of the European system.

This fully supports the European ambition of France at a time when President Macron has drawn a vision of "European sovereignty" in his Sorbonne speech of 2017, including on foreign and security policy issues. While taking a strong stance on the Brexit negotiations, the French president has reinvigorated the Franco-German partnership (see the new Franco-German Treaty of Aachen in January 2019). He was repaid by a Franco-German agreement for the nominations at the top of the EU institutions in 2019 (with Christine Lagarde being appointed as head of the European Central Bank and Thierry Breton as EU Commissioner for the internal market), and by the Franco-German proposal for an ambitious recovery plan financed by EU public debt in the context of the COVID pandemic in 2020.

All diplomats who come back from the EEAS are not so enthusiastic about their experience. The EEAS is sometimes described as a cumbersome bureaucracy which tries to assert itself as a 28th Ministry of Foreign Affairs. Its real power against the European Commission remains limited. Member states and especially the bigger ones retain their power and their means of action in foreign and security policy. Maybe things will change in the future; maybe the European countries will become more united in their foreign policy, which can be seen in the context of the war in Ukraine; maybe qualified majority will be used some day in foreign policy as it is used in other policy issues. However, despite the President Macron's efforts both to reform the EU (through citizens' dialogues in 2018 and a conference on the future of Europe in 2021–22) and to boost European sovereignty and European defense, it seems that the appetite among member states for a revolution in the EU system is quite limited. Significantly, one of the biggest successes of the French EU Presidency in 2022 was the adoption of the "strategic compass": but if this document strengthens the EU's role in security and defense, it does not really challenge the role of NATO in Europe's collective defense, which remains pivotal and has moved away from the "cerebral death" which Macron claimed for it at the end of 2021.

Most probably, the EU will in the future still need to rely on strong member states to play an international role. France as a permanent member of the UN Security Council, as a nuclear weapon state, as a strong military power, as a top-ranking diplomatic actor in Europe, Africa, and the Middle East as well as in the multilateral system, will still need a strong national diplomatic service integrated with European institutions. It has been revealing that Macron's France does not consider leaving its permanent seat in the UN Security Council for the benefit of the EU (as it is sometimes proposed in the German debate) and has insisted on having a clause in the Aachen Treaty that it is a joint French and German objective to have a second seat for Germany.

The third major evolution is *Feminization*. Woman empowerment is a very strong tendency in all parts of the society and nothing can stop it. The first woman admitted to the French diplomatic service was Suzanne Borel in 1930 (she later married the French Foreign Minister Georges Bidault). The first French woman to be appointed ambassador was in 1972. The first woman appointed as foreign minister was Michèle Alliot-Marie (for a short time period, 2010–11), and Catherine Colonna, a career diplomat who already served as European Affairs Minister in 2005, was designated as foreign minister in May 2022 at the beginning of Emmanuel Macron's second mandate.

The Sauvadet law of 2012 forced the ministry to appoint 40 percent of women as first appointed ambassadors (*primo-ambassadeurs*) or directors. Through this voluntarist policy women today represent 35 percent of ambassadors in the French diplomatic network. A woman like Sylvie Bermann was the first woman appointed to major countries abroad (Peking, London, Moscow): today she is retired and has been rewarded by the title *Ambassadeur de France*. Before becoming foreign minister, Catherine Colonna was also Ambassador to UNESCO, Italy, the OECD, and the United Kingdom, and was also rewarded with the title *Ambassadeur de France*. Another woman, Anne-Marie Descôtes, previously Ambassador to Germany and also *Ambassadeur de France*, has become Secretary General of the Ministry. Until now no woman has been appointed to the top positions of Director of the Minister's Private Office, or Political Director, but that time will definitely come.

For men this makes things more complicated. The diplomatic corps is made up of a large majority of men. Given the rapid promotion in women's careers, it means a real deterioration of the ratio between candidates and available posts for men. Many men in particular in their advanced career remain unoccupied, or receive positions which do not match their qualifications and grades. Some of them try to leave the ministry and start a new professional career, for example in business or in other professional environments.

The last notable evolution is the *reduction of means and resources* under strong budget constraints. The cost of diplomacy amounts only one percent of the state budget, but the necessity to reduce public debt and the deficit does not spare the Ministry of Foreign Affairs, which has lost one third of its job positions in the past 20 years (reaching today a bit more than 13,000 agents). France still has the ambition to maintain a universal diplomatic network throughout the world, and is the third largest after the United States and China with 160 bilateral embassies and 16 permanent representations. But it had to close down many consulates and cultural institutes. It also had to sell or reduce many real properties in order to decrease the cost of its diplomatic expenditure and reimburse the public debt. Digitalization offers an opportunity to lower the number of permanent jobs and the payroll, and to increase the proportion of precarious contracted positions. This, alongside fears about the reform of the public service, fuels a social malaise which explains that French diplomats were partially on strike in June 2022, for only the third time in their history.

This orientation is there to stay. French public debt has reached 115 percent of the GDP. It will be necessary to continue budgetary efforts. Some diplomats try to find in the EEAS or in new professional positions outside the ministry a possibility to escape these gloomy perspectives. However, the Quai d'Orsay continues to attract younger people. The appeal of diplomacy to new generations in a world more and more subject to geopolitical tensions and crises remains very strong.

All these transformations are not always perceived as positive but they are also necessary adaptations to the modern world. All in all, there is no doubt that the French Ministry of Foreign Affairs has not only a prestigious past but also a brilliant future.

Further Reading

Charillon, F., ed. 2021. *La France dans le monde*. Paris: CNRS Editions.
Lefebvre, M. 2021. "Europe as a Power, European Sovereignty, Strategic Autonomy: A Debate that is Moving Towards an Assertive Europe." *European Issue* 582, February 2.
———. 2022. *La politique étrangère de la France*. Paris: Que sais-je?
Lequesne, C. 2020. *Ethnographie du Quai d'Orsay. Les pratiques des diplomates français*. Paris: CNRS/Biblis.
Vaïsse, M. 2018. *Diplomatie française. Outils et acteurs depuis 1980*. Paris: Odile Jacob.

Part V

Digital Revolution and Diplomatic Reform

16

Digital Diplomacy in the Time of the Coronavirus Pandemic: Lessons and Recommendations

Corneliu Bjola and Michaela Coplen

Introduction

In *The Republic*, Plato famously remarked that the "real creator, as it appears, will be our needs" (Book II, Section 369)—a phrase that has been construed in the contemporary context to mean that necessity is the mother of invention. Echoing Plato, many diplomats would likely agree that the COVID-19 pandemic has indeed been the necessity that has pushed them to reinvent how to communicate and negotiate in a post-physical, virtual space (Bramsen and Hagemann 2021; Bjola and Manor 2020a). Impacted by the rise of digital technologies, especially social media, diplomacy has already reinvented itself in recent decades by learning how to adapt many of its activities to the online medium, such as crisis communication, diaspora engagement, and public diplomacy. Diplomats have also had to draw on their previous "analogue" experience of handling propaganda and learn how to cope with the "dark side" of new technologies, that is, digital disinformation (Bjola and Pamment 2018), which unfortunately has become rampant during the pandemic. The COVID-19 pandemic has not only accelerated these trends, but it has also created new pressure points for diplomatic adaptation (Bjola and Manor 2022). The goal of this chapter is to unpack how ministries of foreign affairs

C. Bjola (✉) • M. Coplen
University of Oxford, Oxford, UK

(MFAs) have digitally coped with the pandemic and to trace the implications of these adaptations for the conduct of diplomacy—generating critical lessons learned and recommendations for further diplomatic reform.

To that end, this chapter analyzes the digital interventions of various MFAs in five broad areas which MFAs have prioritized during the pandemic: crisis management; international collaboration; foreign policy continuity; countering disinformation; and digital innovation. The pandemic has posed new questions for diplomats in each of these areas. How can digital tools best be used to manage crisis communications, and how might these digital interventions be received by an online public? What forms of digital collaboration might emerge in a pandemic context, and how could these approaches enhance existing forms of collaboration? How can MFAs continue to advance their policy agendas through virtual engagement? How has disinformation changed throughout the pandemic, and what new approaches are most effective in countering its spread? What digital innovations have MFAs adopted during the pandemic, and how might these changes affect the nature of their work moving forward? Taken together, how will the adaptations of the COVID-19 era affect digital diplomacy in a post-pandemic world?

This chapter draws on three main sources to articulate and address these questions. First, key emerging scholarship on pandemic diplomacy and its constituent adaptations is reviewed in each area, elaborating on key concepts and their relevance. Second, examples of notable MFA digital interventions are drawn from social media posts and other media produced from March 1 to September 1, 2020, during the first wave of the pandemic. The diplomatic strategies illustrated in these texts and images are analyzed according to their instrumentalization as tools of crisis management, international collaboration, foreign policy continuity, countering disinformation, and digital innovation. Third and finally, recommendations in these areas are drawn from direct observations of the digital diplomacy efforts undertaken by various MFAs during the pandemic. These observations were conducted in a series of webinars convened by the Lithuanian, Israeli, and Japanese MFAs, which one of the authors attended and contributed to as a member of the University of Oxford's Digital Diplomacy Research group, between May and September 2020.[1] These sources are triangulated to present findings that are not exhaustive, but illustrative of key challenges to digital diplomacy throughout

---

[1] The Digital Diplomacy Research group is an academic collaborative that engages members of the diplomatic community in London and Europe through workshops, trainings, and public events. For more details, see https://www.qeh.ox.ac.uk/content/oxford-digital-diplomacy-research-group.

COVID-19, offering lessons learned for the future of digital diplomatic practice.

After outlining broader themes of research in global trends of diplomatic adaptation during COVID-19, each of the areas above will be discussed in turn, drawing on illustrative examples and summarizing key lessons. This chapter will conclude with recommendations for the collective reform of diplomacy in the post-pandemic period.

A Shifting Diplomatic Landscape

At the outset of the COVID-19 pandemic, the unfolding health crisis rapidly generated travel bans, border closures, and social distancing measures, while the global economy faltered and international cooperation on issues such as climate change stalled. While diplomacy has always had to adapt to shifting realities in international relations, emerging technologies, and new challenges and opportunities therein, the COVID-19 pandemic presented a significant and immediate rupture with the old order. MFAs around the world moved to rapidly adapt their diplomatic activities to a digital footing. As the dust settles, diplomats and academics alike are taking note of how COVID-19 has altered the focus, priorities, and practice of diplomacy—and specifically, are learning how to navigate the digital challenges of conducting diplomacy in the post-pandemic period. What states expect of their diplomats and what publics expect of their states—the very actors and audience of digital diplomacy, respectively—has clearly shifted in the (post-) pandemic landscape in ways that have not been fully anticipated, especially with regard to the role of virtual platforms in supporting and facilitating diplomatic activities.

On the one hand, it is evident that pandemic considerations have in many cases accelerated or generated nationalist impulses within state governments—a phenomena reflected in their digital diplomatic presences. As Pipa and Bouchet write, "the immediate response by countries to COVID-19 was primarily unilateral rather than multilateral," focusing on internally protective policies such as border closures and supply stockpiling; these responses generally reflected concern for national reputation over interests in international coordination (Pipa and Bouchet 2020, 600). Similarly, Manor and Pamment argue that COVID-19 measures have provided an opportunity structure for countries to "reassert sovereignty," using their public diplomacy and digital communications to "demonstrate their ability to provide good governance" for their own citizens in times of crisis (Manor and Pamment 2022a, 1). This sometimes has entailed MFAs promoting their own national image at the expense of others. The blame game relating to COVID-19 outbreak and spread, as well as subsequent vaccine nationalism messaging, offers further evidence that COVID-19 has led some states to adopt a more explicitly nationalist form of digital diplomacy.

On the other hand, the pandemic has also shifted the public opinion toward a renewed internationalism. As Zaharna writes, in some country contexts the pandemic has been a "wake-up call," as publics demand more coordinated international solutions to mutual, global problems. In this way, COVID-19 has constituted a "new global mandate for collaborative problem solving for the global good" (Zaharna 2021, 4). As pointed out by Cull, "the transnational pandemic emphasized the need for transnational collaboration and provided opportunities for countries to associate themselves with collective solutions" (Cull 2021, 19). Therein, reputational security has become more contingent on a country's diplomatic participation within global problem-solving forums. This trend is evident in pandemic-era digital diplomacy, as MFAs have sought to promote their engagement in international collaboration through their digital messaging. Whether or not the pandemic marks a genuine turn toward humanity-centered public diplomacy, this research suggests that publics increasingly expect their diplomats to represent and promote the ideal of international collaboration, and not just the pursuit of narrowly defined national interests.

Another area of the diplomatic landscape that the pandemic has drawn into focus is the importance of sub-national and transnational networks for managing global crises. As Manfredi-Sánchez writes, networks of civil society organizations, cities, private sector firms, and non-governmental organizations "can provide distinctive value in building an environment of trust and efficiently carrying out campaigns for the prevention, surveillance and monitoring of COVID-19" (Manfredi-Sánchez 2020, 518). In the same vein, Vera and De la Casa note that the COVID-19 pandemic made it necessary for international non-governmental organizations (INGOs) to actively respond to the situation of health and economic vulnerability of a large segment of the global population. They have done so by using the digital sphere to demand the suspension of the external debt of poor countries, or by campaigning for COVID-19 vaccines to be offered as a free universal public benefit, and even by promoting forms of food assistance and minimum income provision to curb world hunger (Vera and De la Casa 2020, 630–631). By stepping into quasi-governmental roles in managing the pandemic response through innovative means, networks of actors that have not always or traditionally been engaged in diplomacy thus proved their value for facilitating governance and international collaboration—cementing their status as an important feature of the digital diplomatic landscape.

While each of the phenomena outlined above—namely the pull between nationalist and internationalist digital messaging, and the growth of non-state actor networks as partners in global governance and digital diplomacy—is by no means new, the COVID-19 pandemic accentuated the need for the collective reform of diplomacy, and particularly digital diplomacy, to navigate and accommodate these shifts. This chapter proceeds by articulating how this has played out across five priority areas for MFAs, articulating some examples of best practice and lessons learned for each.

Crisis Management

Emerging research in public diplomacy suggests that a country's reputation in a state of emergency is largely contingent on public perceptions of their government's competence in crisis communications (Lee and Kim 2020). This entails not only countries' ability to keep stakeholders (both domestic citizens and diaspora) abreast of accurate and reliable information (Vériter et al. 2020), but also their ability to manage crisis logistics such as consular assistance and repatriation efforts (Udovič 2020). How can digital tools best be used to facilitate these crisis communications, and how are such digital interventions received by the online public? Examining MFA digital strategies for communicating repatriation information in the first wave of the pandemic shows that MFAs generally pursued one of three models in their early crisis communications: adapt, improvise, or ignore (see Fig. 16.1).

When Italy announced a national lockdown on March 9, 2020, most countries were initially slow to recognize the scope of the threat and respond accordingly. Countries that had established digital crisis communications systems were at an advantage, as they were able to adapt these systems more quickly to the COVID-19 context. The U.S. State Department, for example, established the Smart Traveler Enrolment Program (STEP) in the post-9/11 context; this program was designed to register expatriates travelling abroad, disseminate information regarding potential security threats, and share consular resources. In March 2020, the STEP program was rapidly adapted to share information regarding COVID-19 and repatriation opportunities. Tweets promoting STEP enrolment were among the most widely shared communications by the U.S. State Department in this period. Similarly, the UK FCDO adapted its established travel advice resources and communications,

Fig. 16.1 Crisis communication approaches: adapt, improvise, and ignore

successfully sharing checklists for essential travel that were tailored to COVID-19 developments.

While the EU was not poised to adapt existing crisis communications systems and were initially slow to develop their own, they soon improvised new means of digital crisis management. The case of German MFA digital diplomacy is particularly illustrative. While in the first weeks of March 2020, most digital communications stressed Germany's engagement in collaborative sense-making exercises with the broader international community, these messages were later adjusted to focus on communicating details of the response. These response communications entailed sharing information on the improvised regional crisis management strategy and promoting solidarity with the rest of the EU (Bjola 2021). As Fig. 16.1 illustrates, by the end of March, the European Commission had established an "EU Emergency Response Coordination Centre" to handle repatriation logistics. Their digital communications effectively raised awareness and celebrated the successes of this (among other) improvised emergency systems.

The "adapt" and "improvise" strategies are in stark contrast to the "ignore" approach that some countries initially attempted as COVID-19 pandemic unfolded. Turkey, for example, did not tweet any information regarding COVID-19 throughout March 2020. Their MFA's most-shared tweet in this period was an image of the Lycian ruins at Patara. Similarly, Russia's MFA did not offer travel advice or information. The highlight of their March 2020 digital communications was a tweet regarding foreign minister Sergey Lavrov's 70th birthday. While these MFAs' attempts to ignore COVID-19 and project an image of "business as usual" could have been viewed at the time as a message of reassurance, this digital strategy ultimately backfired. MFAs that fail to provide crucial information to their nationals in a time of crisis face higher reputational costs. It is also important to note that the "ignore" approach was more enthusiastically embraced by countries with an authoritarian profile (Salecl 2020, 151). This suggests that political concerns involving possible acts of public contestation of the regime's leadership and legitimacy might have taken precedence over considerations of public health, hence the attempt to ignore or mask the effects of the pandemic.

While the "ignore" approach employed by some countries is therefore not advisable, "adapt" and "improvise" can both be beneficial models of digital crisis communication when implemented promptly and effectively. Three important lessons emerge in this regard. First, it is easier to adapt than to improvise; MFAs should therefore upgrade their crisis response systems now and test them regularly. Second, if the situation requires improvisation, it is best to act quickly without panicking. This requires MFAs to examine their internal systems and pinpoint possible barriers between "sense-making" and "response," so that they can adapt and improvise more rapidly in the future. Third, care should be taken to manage public expectations, both domestically and with expatriate and diaspora audiences. Proactive crisis communication will likely reduce the costs of managing the crisis and allow the MFAs to more effectively use their diplomatic network and capacity to steer the crisis on a less hazardous path.

International Collaboration

As mentioned above, COVID-19 provided an opportunity structure for many countries' leaders to employ increasingly nationalist rhetoric. In the United States, President Donald Trump was a particularly egregious offender, as he and his staff members insisted on labelling COVID-19 the "Wuhan virus" (Hudson and Mekhennet 2020), and repeatedly maligned China's containment efforts. Trump did not limit his blame-game politics to China, however, but also later responded to domestic criticism by publicly comparing U.S. case rates to higher per capita death tolls in other countries, such as Belgium (Schultz 2020). In the face of potentially divisive crisis events, what can digital diplomacy do to increase international collaboration? What forms of collaboration emerged during the pandemic, and how might these new approaches complement diplomatic practice moving forward? Throughout the pandemic, MFAs have generally sought to promote collaborative problem-solving through either unilateral or multilateral messaging.

Publicized aid and gift-giving often fell under the first category. These included donations of money, supplies, and volunteer medical workers to countries that were more affected and/or poorly equipped to manage climbing case rates. As Cull reminds us, this "public diplomacy of deeds" carried additional rhetorical symbols (Cull 2021, 19). Toward the end of March 2020, for example, China's MFA released digital messaging promoting its government's pledge of aid to 82 countries, the World Health Organization (WHO), and the African Union (as seen in Fig. 16.2). Reframing China's early experience with COVID-19 as a positive, this messaging positioned China as a leader in treatment and containment strategies with valuable knowledge and resources to share. While mentioning international collaboration, the thrust of the digital messaging was on what China has to give. However, when read in the context of the country's internal political dynamic and its strategies for geopolitical and regional influence, these messages may have caused target audiences to suspect a mixed motive (Kowalski 2021).

Other countries also sought to leverage domestic policies to international effect. Israel, for example, published digital messaging on "World Health Day" reminding Twitter followers that "it's up to us all to break the chain of infection"—linking to a video that promoted mitigation measures such as basic hygiene and social distancing. The video was well received online and served as a source of digital inspiration for public health initiatives in other

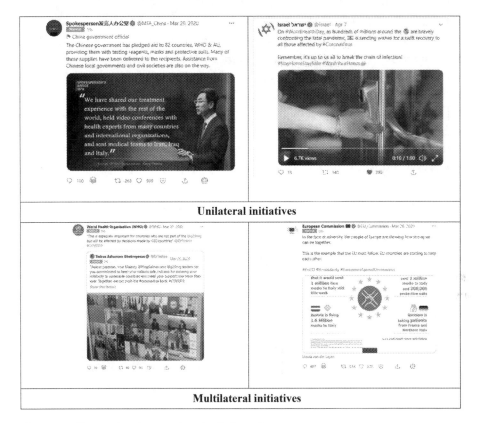

Fig. 16.2 Showcasing international collaboration

countries, such as in Ukraine.[2] In this way, situating domestic public health policies in light of an international struggle against COVID-19 served to bolster the country's reputation while creating opportunities for strengthening relations with countries similarly affected.

More multilateral approaches to promoting international collaboration can again be found in the EU communications throughout this period. In addition to their institutional commitments to funding the WHO and the COVID-19 global response pledging conference, the EU signaled regional solidarity by highlighting multiple countries' aid and gift-giving simultaneously. By the end of March 2020, the EU tweeted an infographic listing the forms of aid that several EU countries had dispatched to Italy, complete with the caption: "In the face of adversity, the people of Europe are showing how strong we can be together" (with tags such as #EUsolidarity and

---

[2] Personal communication with the Head of Digital Diplomacy, Israel Ministry of Foreign Affairs, June 2020.

#EuropeansAgainst Coronavirus). In a post-Brexit EU, the EU moved quickly to ensure that messaging around the COVID-19 response was genuinely multilateral, stressing European strength in solidarity. Emphasizing this collaborative approach therefore did not only bolster national reputations, but also served to reinforce public buy-in and inspire meaningful support, building regional solutions for a transregional problem. Even broader multilateral messaging was published by international organizations such as the WHO. In publicizing the G20 meeting at the end of March, for example, the WHO Twitter account not only stressed the collaboration between the G20 countries, but it also emphasized that "this is especially important for countries that are not part of the [G20] but will be affected by decisions made by G20 countries."

Throughout the COVID-19 pandemic diplomacy, countries faced particular challenges to promoting their international collaboration, not least when members of their own governments were involved in a damaging blame game. Digital signaling stressing the importance of international collaboration was crucial in getting the diplomatic train back on track. Three lessons learned emerged in this area. First, MFAs need to avoid rhetorical jabs that articulate or exacerbate false or gratuitous accusations of blame as the spiral of inevitable controversy could severely hinder collective efforts necessary to address the crisis. Second, they need to demonstrate solidarity through digital messaging. While unilateral support for international partners is always good, sharing messages about multilateral solidarity and support could work even better. And third, MFAs' digital efforts would benefit from contextualizing domestic experiences of managing the crisis in light of international challenges in order to generate opportunities for bilateral or multilateral partnerships.

Foreign Policy Continuity

As the early days of the COVID-19 outbreak passed and governments began to settle into the so-called new normal, MFAs turned from crisis management and messages of collaboration to another key challenge: foreign policy continuity. In the ongoing pandemic, a key challenge for MFAs has been the issue of maintaining and enhancing their diplomatic visibility: how could they simultaneously manage crises and advance their policy agendas? Strategies for foreign policy continuity can roughly be categorized as either building policy linkages or expanding virtual presences (see Fig. 16.3).

MFAs began to adapt existing and long-term communications strategies to the COVID-19 context by building policy linkages. One such example is the

16 Digital Diplomacy in the Time of the Coronavirus Pandemic...   333

Fig. 16.3 Showcasing international collaboration

Swedish MFA's emphasis on gender equality, a key component of their national and foreign policy agenda (Aggestam and Bergman-Rosamond 2016). By April 2020, the Swedish MFA Twitter account began sharing articles under the tag #FeministFriday that explicated COVID-19's impact on women and girls specifically. This digital strategy served to reiterate Sweden's support for mainstreaming gender considerations in domestic policy, as well as to reinforce their global image as leaders in gender equality. Another example of policy linkage, but in more negative colors, was evident in the Russian approach to their vaccine promotion. As examined by Manor and Pamment, the Russian MFA synthesized vaccine rollout communications with their long-term communications strategy of fostering Russian nationalism and anti-Western sentiment (Manor and Pamment 2022b). Their digital messaging clearly invoked Soviet nostalgia—going so far as to set up a Twitter account to promote Sputnik, the Russian vaccine.

As MFAs developed digital messaging that linked COVID-19 to existing policies, they also developed new modes for maintaining diplomatic continuity via virtual presence. For some, this entailed adapting international conferences to virtual platforms or selecting virtual venues for ongoing negotiations. As the incoming chair of G20 meetings in 2020, the Saudi MFA moved quickly to convene all preparatory events and the Leaders' Summit in a virtual format. The task proved challenging, as virtual venues offered limited opportunities for ceremonial and informal talks (Naylor 2020), but it was accomplished professionally. Some MFAs went beyond simple videoconferencing, establishing hybrid setups that allowed for some in-person interaction while upholding social distancing precautions (Bjola and Manor 2022). Still others invented new modes of virtual presence, such as promoting diplomatic visibility by setting themselves up as hubs for knowledge-sharing. As shown in Fig. 16.3, Israel's MFA was notably ahead of the curve in this regard. By the end of March 2020, they had developed a series of online courses for "Coping in the Midst of the Corona Crisis," with modules on managing cybersecurity and child education while working from home.

These examples provide several lessons learned for foreign policy continuity in the digital space. First, diplomatic goals do not need to be put on pause indefinitely. MFAs should develop policy linkages as soon as appropriate to reintroduce key foreign policy goals in the crisis context. Second, developing modes of virtual and hybrid presence are key in showcasing MFAs' ability to adapt and collaborate as partners in the virtual space. Third, as will be discussed in the fifth section on innovation, expanding virtual presence does not just mean engaging in virtual substitutes for in-person meetings. It also involves developing new virtual programming and establishing the MFA as a center of learning and engagement, which requires, in turn, original thinking.

Countering Disinformation

As most scholars agree, "the pandemic has revealed the shortcomings of the international information disorder," especially the fact that disinformation "circulates at great speed from screen to screen" (Manfredi-Sánchez 2020, 518). While disinformation is by no means a new phenomenon, digital media have increased the speed and economy of spreading it (Bennett and Livingston 2018). The spike in digital activities during the COVID-19 pandemic has only accelerated these trends. In a dynamic information ecosystem, publics sought reliable sources of information—and often, were met by propaganda and conspiracist narratives (Stephens 2020). While conspiracy thinking is in some ways a natural phenomenon of crisis coping (as an anxious public struggle to make sense of rapid and significant changes to their way of life), unchecked, these narratives not only diminish adherence to public health guidelines, but promote distrust in public institutions and authorities and thus generate instability (Veriter et al. 2020). This is particularly dangerous in a global pandemic, where misdirection regarding public health measures threatens public, economic, and human security. In light of these developments, how have MFAs coped with the challenge of digital disinformation?

MFAs and international organizations have increasingly countered disinformation by asserting themselves as reliable sources of information validation and knowledge-sharing. As Fig. 16.4 shows, this task has been accomplished

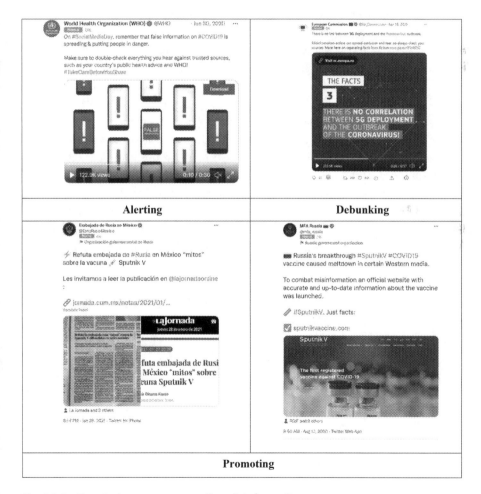

Fig. 16.4 Countering versus promoting disinformation

with varying levels of responsibility. Some of these institutions have taken their role seriously and tried to educate their online audiences about the dangers of disinformation, including alerting publics to disinformation threats as well as debunking specific narratives in their digital communications. By the end of April 2020, for example, the European Commission was producing digital messaging explicitly countering conspiracy theories such as the "5G" narrative. The EU was also actively denouncing disinformation from Russian and Chinese outlets, as well as those from unattributable sources (Beaumont et al. 2020). In June, the EU released a Joint Communication on countering COVID-19 disinformation, calling for coordinated action to increase digital platforms' responsibility through regulation and boost awareness and media literacy (European Commission 2020).

Others, such as the Russian MFA and its network of embassies, have seen the pandemic as an opportunity to weaken their geopolitical rivals (namely the EU, UK, and U.S.), including by actively promoting disinformation on their digital platforms. Russian media outlets repeatedly stoked vaccine disinformation and portrayed COVID-19 as a bio-weapon deployed by the United States (Woodruff Swan 2020). Some Kremlin-supported media even repeated conspiracy theories such as claiming the virus was intentionally spread by Bill Gates (Barnes et al. 2020). Beyond allowing these narratives to go unchecked, Russian diplomats actively promoted disinformation through their official communications channels. As shown in Fig. 16.4, the Russian Embassy in Mexico City used its Twitter account to share Spanish-language stories that falsely claimed U.S. media had "remained silent" on deaths caused by the Pfizer vaccine (Barnes et al. 2021). In this and similar digital communications across Latin America, Russian diplomats leveraged disinformation to not only promote sales of the Russian-made Sputnik vaccine, but to diminish U.S. credibility and influence in the region.

Examining the different approaches adopted by MFAs and international organizations (IOs) to countering COVID-19 disinformation offers four lessons for future digital diplomats. First, MFAs need to proactively monitor the online space for emerging disinformation narratives. This requires establishing systems to analyze media output and track networks, including competing MFAs, which are known to be sources or propagators of disinformation. Second, not all disinformation narratives spread easily and with the same level of intensity. Protocols are required to set thresholds for debunking interventions in order to avoid unnecessarily raising the profile of narratives that might dissolve independently. Third, when a disinformation threat does cross this threshold, MFAs and their institutional partners must act rapidly to face it down. Fourth and finally, MFAs need to work together with other governmental institutions and international organizations, in non-crisis times, to build greater societal resilience to disinformation and conspiracy thinking.

Innovation

As mentioned at the outset of this chapter, the COVID-19 pandemic has also seen a range of diplomatic innovations borne out of necessity. Two simple, yet by no means mutually exclusive, categories of innovation are particularly relevant and they both promise to affect working procedures moving forward: programmatic innovation and technological innovation.

The first concerns the content, producers, and partners of the cultural programs that often constitute public diplomacy. The volume of digital cultural production and its global consumption have drastically increased during the COVID-19 pandemic. As Grincheva writes, this increased cultural output is largely due to non-state actors like museums, libraries, and public institutions taking up the mantle of not only public service delivery—offering social and educational programs to their own citizens—but also engaging in various forms of cultural diplomacy with global audiences. Livestreaming educational events or curators' lectures, for example, augmented the scope and reach of museum diplomacy (Grincheva 2022, 9). Sub-national and local governments have similarly innovated their digital engagement as city-to-city networks like the "C40 Cities Climate Leadership" group continued to meet and develop joint programing (Pipa and Bouchet 2020). Local and regional government networks such as the United Cities and Local Governments (UCLG), Metropolis and UN-Habitat launched, for instance, in March 2020, a live learning experience, #BeyondTheOutbreak, to discuss the challenges they confronted and the actions they needed to take to raise public awareness and implement emergency mechanisms that could help maintain the orderly functioning of services (UCLG 2020).

Beyond these programmatic innovations, more traditional diplomatic actors also had to adopt technological innovations to keep up with public demands in the fluid COVID-19 context. The novelty of the situation and the lack of human resources forced MFAs and IOs to develop and deploy chatbots for providing health info and real-time updates about the evolution of the pandemic. As shown in Fig. 16.5, the WHO was among the first institutions to develop a WhatsApp-based chatbot to guide individuals through information regarding COVID symptoms and local case rates, complete with "myth-busting" and "travel advice" features. MFAs did the same. The

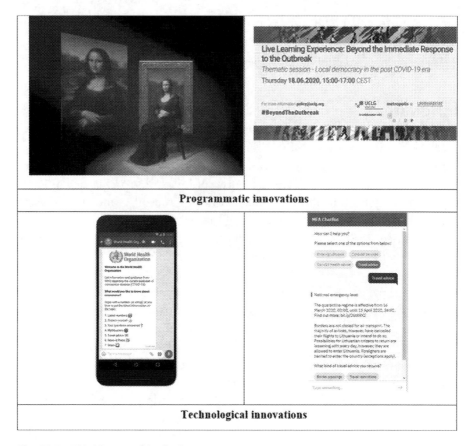

Fig. 16.5 Thinking outside the box

Lithuanian Ministry of Foreign Affairs deployed an AI-assisted chatbot that provided COVID-19-related health advice as well as information on travel restrictions, consular services, and conditions for entering and leaving the country during the quarantine (Bjola and Manor 2020b). Drawing on their previous experience of developing and using travel apps, some other countries, such as Canada, created new apps for citizen services such as registering passenger locator forms for travel. In keeping with its regional approach, the EU launched a "Re-Open EU" app, allowing users to quickly select and compare information on COVID-19 rates, restrictions, and travel requirements across EU countries to support "#EUtourism."

In terms of integrating new programmatic innovations, two lessons are apparent. First, MFAs should continue to develop relationships with cultural institutions and sub-national government leaders outside of crises in order to strengthen trust and potentially advise their programmatic development for integration in diplomatic activities. Second, MFAs need to establish communications and coordination networks during crises to promote unity of effort and linkages between MFA policy agendas and digital programming. Effectively working with cultural, sub-national, and transnational partners will serve to amplify MFAs' digital diplomacy strategies in the future. Experiences of integrating technological innovation into digital diplomacy have offered two additional lessons. First, similar to developing crisis communications systems, consular chatbots should be upgraded and regularly tested by the public to streamline information and service delivery. User experience should be a priority consideration in development and design. Second, MFAs also need to think ahead and develop systems to trial and integrate emerging tech (e.g., AI-based decision-making assistants) into their crisis tool repertoires, but in a manner that observes privacy concerns and data-protection standards in the development of apps.

Conclusion

Having reviewed key instances of MFA digital diplomacy in the five priority areas of crisis management, international collaboration, foreign policy continuity, countering disinformation, and digital innovation, one overarching question remains: How will the adaptations of the COVID-19 era affect digital diplomatic practice in a post-pandemic world? While COVID-19 represented a significant, perhaps even unprecedented, global challenge in recent decades, diplomats must now capitalize on the resulting opportunities—consolidating diplomatic gains, learning from mistakes, and incorporating new techniques in post-pandemic diplomacy. To that end, the recommendations below are divided into immediate, medium-term, and long-term priorities.

Several lessons learned can be immediately implemented to great effect by diplomats and their MFAs. Foremost, MFAs should work to upgrade their crisis response and crisis communications systems now, and to test them regularly. Further, diplomatic leaders and their staff should work to avoid blame game messaging in crisis situations, instead framing digital diplomacy around themes of international collaboration and solidarity. Relatedly, diplomats should work to develop linkages between policy objectives and unfolding crises—building creative messaging that speaks to public concerns, without sacrificing the continuity of digital campaigns. MFAs should also proactively monitor the online space for emerging disinformation narratives, acknowledging that this may require not only analyzing media output, but also the digital communications of other MFAs that may be involved in promoting disinformation for strategic reasons. Finally, diplomats should work in the immediate future to develop and share connections between MFA activities and non-traditional diplomatic partners such as cultural institutions and sub/trans-national networks.

Implementing these recommendations in the immediate term will increase MFAs' capacity to cope with ongoing and future crisis situations. Implementing more medium-term recommendations will enable even greater readiness. Medium-term recommendations include conducting internal systems analyses, such as after action reviews, of MFA crisis functions with a specific focus on identifying institutional bottlenecks or barriers between sense-making and crisis response. Similar systems analysis and development is necessary in expanding modes of virtual and hybrid engagement, including increasing research and training in digital diplomatic practices such as negotiation in virtual venues (Bjola and Coplen 2022). Another area for medium-term diplomatic reform includes building more robust systems for managing disinformation—from using AI research tools to identify emerging narratives, to developing internal protocols for rapid and effective counter-messaging.

Ultimately, long-term reforms are necessary to ensure that digital diplomacy, and diplomatic practice more generally, is not only resilient during future crises, but capable of effectively navigating in the shifting (post-)pandemic landscape. In the area of disinformation, long-term efforts may include establishing education and awareness campaigns to increase public capacity to identify disinformation narratives. Further investment in technological innovation in crisis communication management, including AI-assisted apps, can aid continuity of service delivery and digital MFA presence through crises. Additional innovations in programmatic landscape and scope will also be necessary—requiring diplomats to think beyond digital diplomacy as a substitute for in-person engagement, and instead capitalize on the strengths of hybrid and digital means of engagement as diplomatic tools in their own right. Adopting these long-term recommendations, and fostering cultures of innovation within MFAs, will ensure that invention is not only borne after necessity, as Plato suggested centuries ago, but that diplomats are also empowered to anticipate and enhance MFA preparedness to meet future needs.

References and Further Reading

Aggestam, K., and A. Bergman-Rosamond. 2016. "Swedish Feminist Foreign Policy in the Making: Ethics, Politics, and Gender." *Ethics & International Affairs* 30 (3): 323–34.

Barnes, J.E., M. Rosenberg, and E. Wong. 2020. "As Virus Spreads, China and Russia See Openings for Disinformation." *New York Times*, March 28.

Barnes, J.E., S. Frenkel. and M. Abi-Habib. 2021. "Russian Campaign Promotes Homegrown Vaccine and Undercuts Rivals." *New York Times*, February 6.

Beaumont, P., J. Borger, and D. Boffey. 2020. "Coronavirus Sparks Perfect Storm of State-led Disinformation." *Guardian*, April 24. https://www.theguardian.com/world/2020/apr/24/coronavirus-sparks-perfect-storm-of-state-led-disinformation.

Bennett, W.L., and S. Livingston. 2018. "The Disinformation Order: Disruptive Communication and the Decline of Democratic Institutions." *European Journal of Communication* 33 (2): 122–39.

Bjola, C. 2021. "Digital Diplomacy as World Disclosure: The Case of the COVID-19 Pandemic." *Place Branding and Public Diplomacy* 18 (1): 22–25.

Bjola, C., and M. Coplen. 2022. "Virtual Venues and International Negotiations: Lessons from the COVID-19 Pandemic." *International Negotiation*.

Bjola, C., and M. Holmes. 2015. *Digital Diplomacy: Theory and Practice*. Abingdon: Routledge.

Bjola, C., and I. Manor. 2020a. "NATO's Digital Public Diplomacy during the Covid-19 Pandemic." *Turkish Policy Quarterly* 19 (2): 77–87.

———. 2020b. *Digital Diplomacy in the Time of the Coronavirus Pandemic*. U.S.C. Center on Public Diplomacy. https://uscpublicdiplomacy.org/blog/digital-diplomacy-time-coronavirus-pandemic.

———. 2022. "The Rise of Hybrid Diplomacy: From Digital Adaptation to Digital Adoption." *International Affairs* 98 (2): 471–91.

Bjola, C., and J. Pamment. 2018. *Countering Online Propaganda and Extremism: The Dark Side of Digital Diplomacy*. Abingdon and New York: Routledge.

Bramsen, I., and A. Hagemann. 2021. "The Missing Sense of Peace: Diplomatic Approachment and Virtualization during the COVID-19 Lockdown." *International Affairs* 97 (2): 539–60.

Cull, N.J. 2021. "From Soft Power to Reputational Security: Rethinking Public Diplomacy and Cultural Diplomacy for a Dangerous Age." *Place Branding and Public Diplomacy* 18 (1): 18–21.

Duncombe, C. 2017. "Twitter and Transformative Diplomacy: Social Media and Iran–U.S. Relations." *International Affairs* 93 (3): 545–62.

European Commission. 2020. *Tackling COVID-19 Disinformation – Getting the Facts Right*, June 6. https://eur-lex.europa.eu/legal-content/EN/TXT/?uri=CELEX%3A52020JC0008.

Grincheva, N. 2022. "Cultural Diplomacy under the 'Digital Lockdown': Pandemic Challenges and Opportunities in Museum Diplomacy." *Place Branding and Public Diplomacy* 18 (1): 8–11.

Hudson, J., and S. Mekhennet. 2020. "G-7 Failed to Agree on Statement after U.S. Insisted on Calling Coronavirus Outbreak 'Wuhan Virus.'" *Washington Post*, March 25. https://www.washingtonpost.com/national-security/g-7-failed-to-agree-on-statement-after-us-insisted-on-calling-coronavirus-outbreak-wuhan-virus/2020/03/25/f2bc7a02-6ed3-11ea-96a0-df4c5d9284af_story.html.

Kowalski, B. 2021. "China's Mask Diplomacy in Europe: Seeking Foreign Gratitude and Domestic Stability." *Journal of Current Chinese Affairs* 50 (2): 209–26.

Lee, S.T., and H.S. Kim. 2020. "Nation Branding in the COVID-19 Era: South Korea's Pandemic Public Diplomacy." *Place Branding and Public Diplomacy* 17 (4): 382–96.

Manfredi-Sánchez, J.L. 2020. "Introduction to the Forum on Covid-19." *The Hague Journal of Diplomacy* 15 (4): 517–19.

Manor, I. 2019. *The Digitalization of Public Diplomacy*. Cham: Palgrave Macmillan.

Manor, I., and J. Pamment. 2022a. "At a Crossroads: Examining Covid-19's Impact on Public and Digital Diplomacy." *Place Branding and Public Diplomacy* 18 (1): 1–3.

———. 2022b. "From Gagarin to Sputnik: The Role of Nostalgia in Russian Public Diplomacy." *Place Branding and Public Diplomacy* 18 (1): 44–48.

Naylor, T. 2020. "All That's Lost: The Hollowing of Summit Diplomacy in a Socially Distanced World." *The Hague Journal of Diplomacy* 15 (4): 583–98.

Pipa, A.F., and M. Bouchet. 2020. "Multilateralism Restored? City Diplomacy in the Covid-19 Era." *The Hague Journal of Diplomacy* 15 (4): 599–610.

Plato. *The Republic* (Book II, Section 369). http://www.perseus.tufts.edu/hopper/text?doc=urn:cts:greekLit:tlg0059.tlg030.perseus-eng1:369.

Salecl, R. 2020. *A Passion for Ignorance: What We Choose Not to Know and Why*. Princeton: Princeton University Press.

Schultz, T. 2020. "Why Belgium's Death Rate Is So High." National Public Radio, April 22. https://www.npr.org/sections/coronavirus-live-updates/2020/04/22/841005901/why-belgiums-death-rate-is-so-high-it-counts-lots-of-suspected-covid-19-cases.

Stephens, M. 2020. "A Geospatial Infodemic: Mapping Twitter Conspiracy Theories of COVID-19." *Dialogues in Human Geography* 10 (2): 276–81.

UCLG. 2020. *Live Learning Experience #BeyondTheOutbreak*. https://www.uclg.org/en/issues/live-learning-experience-beyondtheoutbreak.

Udovič, B. 2020. "Consular Protection in Slovenia During the First Wave of Covid-19." *Teorija in Praksa* 57 (4): 1147–66.

Vera, J.M., and J.M. Herranz de la Casa. 2020. "How Influential Are International NGOs in the Public Arena?" *The Hague Journal of Diplomacy* 15 (4): 624–35.

Vériter, S.L., C. Bjola, and J.A. Koops. 2020. "Tackling Covid-19 Disinformation: Internal and External Challenges for the European Union." *The Hague Journal of Diplomacy* 15 (4): 569–82.

Woodruff Swan, B. 2020. "State Report: Russian, Chinese and Iranian Disinformation Narratives Echo One Another." *Politico*, April 21. https://www.politico.com/news/2020/04/21/russia-china-iran-disinformation-coronavirus-state-department-193107.

Zaharna, R.S. 2021. "The Pandemic's Wake-up Call for Humanity-centered Public Diplomacy." *Place Branding and Public Diplomacy* 18 (1): 4–7.

17

Exploring the Usefulness of Artificial Intelligence for Diplomatic Negotiations: Two Case Studies

Volker Stanzel

On February 24, 2022, the Russian army invaded Ukraine. The invasion had been preceded by years of attempts to negotiate between Russia and its Western partners in order to find a modus vivendi for a peaceful partnership serving the interests of both sides. These negotiations have failed with tragic consequences. This failure raises the question, as always in wars, of how the negotiations could have been conducted to arrive at a satisfying result that would have avoided war. Among the various options to be examined, this essay deals with the possibility of the future use of artificial intelligence (AI) and presents two case studies that may indicate where in diplomatic negotiations AI might be of use.[1]

---

[1] This chapter is based on the study "Diplomacy and Artificial Intelligence: Reflections and Practical Assistance for Diplomatic Negotiations," written in 2021 by my colleague Daniel Voelsen and myself at the German Institute for International and Security Affairs in Berlin (SWP). I express my gratitude to Daniel Voelsen, to the German Foreign Office for its support, and to the company Aleph-Alpha for their cooperation on the first of our two case studies.

V. Stanzel (✉)
German Institute for International and Security Affairs, Berlin, Germany

The Nature of Diplomatic Communication and Interaction

Christer Jönsson, in perhaps the broadest definition, describes diplomacy as a "timeless phenomenon" of human existence, meaning the effort of human communities to balance their interests with each other, before or after the attempt to employ armed force (Jönsson 2012, 3; also Voss 2016, 17). Conflicting interests have to be defused and balanced in order to create a modus vivendi that is as durable as possible in the long term. Since the emergence of at least partially sovereign territorial states, diplomacy has almost exclusively represented the interests of such states.

Diplomatic communication begins when decisions have to be made in at least one state that affect the interests of at least one other state. Unless it is merely a matter of clarifying easily resolved issues, communication takes the form of interaction—negotiations that usually lead to an outcome: a new or confirmed status in relations between the states involved, joint or unilateral concerted action, the failure of negotiations or their transfer to a different temporal, geographic, or institutional framework. The consequence of failure may be the use of military or non-military means of coercion. Even if the problem remains unsolved, a solution may be sought by other means, such as with the help of other states or by redefining priorities. In negotiations of any kind, therefore, there is always, with varying clarity but unmistakably, what has been the normal case throughout history, interrupted only by pauses in which negotiations took place: the use of coercive means; hence the statement of King Frederick II: "Diplomacy without weapons is like music without instruments." Today, the term "weapons" has a broader meaning, since in times of global interdependence of trade chains, non-military sanctions are often used—markets as "one of the most important battlefields" (Lohmann 2019, 25).

Once the negotiations end—one way or another—the work of diplomacy is done for the time being. Negotiations are thus the core of what diplomacy is all about (Jönsson and Hall 2005, 82; Meerts 2015, 20).

Elements Determining the Process and Outcome of Diplomatic Negotiations

Despite the general prohibition of the use of force codified in Article 2 of the UN Charter, a state's power ultimately means its ability to assert itself in varying forms. This ability is the function of material resources, technical know-how, strategic savvy, the self-image of the population, and the international environment. Negotiations and the possibility of using coercive measures in diplomatic dealings thus go hand in hand as the result of a cost-benefit analysis to be carried out continuously by governments. Consequently, regarding the negotiating parties, a comparison of the power of the involved parties and the means to use that power becomes the first criterion for assessing the process of a negotiation and for deciding on the next steps to be taken. However, just as the outcome of armed conflicts cannot be predicted by comparing the number of troops and tanks, the outcome of a negotiation process cannot be reliably predicted on the basis of a state's total resources for the use of coercive measures. Beyond the criterion of the means of power available to the negotiating partners, therefore, other elements must be considered that can provide information about the expected process of negotiations.

One such element is the strategy pursued by the negotiating parties. If the strength of one side means that no progress can be expected, attempts must be made to change the parameters of the negotiations. This can be done by introducing new factors that previously did not seem relevant. Such factors can take various forms, such as:

- changing context, such as new coalitions;
- changing conditions for the implementation of intended agreements—such as differing economic, financial, or technological circumstances;
- different points of departure—such as the mood of the public and its platforms, the media—a new government or special attention from important international as well as national actors;
- changes within a negotiating party, that is, possibly fragile cohesion, if interests of groups within a coalition shift.

Another element is the personality of the negotiating individuals—that is, their characteristics as well as their professional competence. This means that peculiarities of interpersonal communication such as joy, anger, embarrassment, surprise, lies, and openness can play an often-unexpected essential role. This can happen through purely emotionally based mutual or one-sided suspicion or mistrust among the negotiators. Knowledge of the negotiators and their character should therefore be able to help assess the direction and results of negotiations in advance. Differences between the negotiating partners also play a role here, which cannot be traced back to character traits of individual persons, but to traditional—"cultural"—patterns.

Another essential factor is the intermittent process of the negotiations themselves. This is only a targeted, straight line when it is a matter of minor individual issues that need to be resolved quickly. In most cases, it runs over several stages, at each of which the course of events to date is evaluated and decisions are made about the next steps; and this often includes the content. Changes in one's own interests can be a reason for a different process. But new knowledge about the other side also may lead to modified or new strategies, perhaps the suspension or abandonment of negotiations, the use of coercive means, or the search for coalition partners. And external "shocks," ranging from changes in the global economic situation to natural disasters, can even lead to the unwanted breakdown of negotiations.

Power, strategy, personality, and process may therefore be essential criteria for assessing negotiations and their chances of success. However, diplomatic negotiations take place in their own social sphere with its own rules, starting with the norms of international law. At the same time, their outer edges are permeable to a variety of external influences. Often, and thanks to increasing real and virtual mobility and globally facilitated communication more and more often, these are "uninvited negotiators" such as the electronic and traditional media with their range of easily accessible platforms and the temptation to use them to intervene in negotiation processes. There are also other actors, such as NGOs or popular movements (like Fridays for Future), who try to intervene publicly or non-publicly in the negotiations. On the other hand, they, like the media, offer themselves to the official negotiators as mouthpieces and as instruments for manipulating the other side through the various publics (Iklè 1964, 52–55; Starkey et al. 2015, 108–10). In this way, however, the negotiation process moves into areas that can hardly be calculated in advance. Thus, the question that arises here is, which part of the complex mosaic that negotiations present is predictable and to what extent, possibly by employing AI means.

Artificial Intelligence

The attention "artificial intelligence" (AI) has gained in recent years is due to technological advances: the performance of computer processors has been increasing every year for decades, and advances in memory technology have been added to this. In sum, it is now possible to process more data faster than ever before. In parallel to these developments in computer hardware, the recent rise of AI has been made possible by advances in software, that is, in research on AI algorithms. In this context, we understand AI as a collective term for a variety of data processing methods. Underlying our reflections is an understanding of AI that sees it as a cipher for machine learning (ML) methods. These methods are characterized by the fact that the corresponding algorithms—that is, the rules according to which a program processes a problem—are designed in such a way that they can evolve independently within certain parameters. In this limited technical sense, they are learning machines.

Basically, in ML we can distinguish between a deductive and an inductive approach. The deductive approach starts with abstract concepts that are used to tap into the diversity of empirics. The inductive approach takes its starting point in empiricism and condenses it into concepts in the course of machine learning. For some years now, the second strand has been predominant—made possible by the mass of data available today and the advances in memory and processor technology. Here again, the method of "deep learning" is currently being used: based on the structures of neuronal networks in the human brain, an algorithmic structure is created that allows complex and nested statistical calculations to be carried out. The method of "deep learning" relies on very large amounts of data in order to be able to balance the neural network with sufficient precision.

Once a system is set up with a training data set, it can be used to analyze further data. Usually, an evaluation takes place here as an intermediate step: ML methods are particularly suitable for recognizing patterns in large amounts of data. The complexity of neural networks allows large data sets to be broken down into a large number of individual data points, which can then be processed using statistical methods. For example, an AI system divides an image into different components and searches them for clues that allow the identification of what is being depicted.

In this way, a wide variety of data inputs can be analyzed: for example, text, image/video, sound, weather data, event data, metadata. The advantage of AI systems is that, like any computer, they are generally better than humans at sifting through large amounts of data without getting tired, sloppy, or simply terribly bored. Still, current forms of ML are not capable of uncovering causal relationships. Neural networks work with probabilities to detect patterns; but they cannot test these patterns for causality; or at least not yet (Dickson 2021).

One of the most prominent examples of AI-based analysis is the analysis of attitudes toward people, institutions, and products ("sentiment analysis"). What AI can do is an independently performed identification of central themes in a text, or even in a mass of texts. AI systems can also capture the emotional content of texts. This is used, for example, by agencies that offer companies the service of monitoring coverage of a company or individual products. In most cases, newspaper reports and presentations in publicly accessible social media profiles (especially Twitter and Instagram) are evaluated. One problem here is that, despite all the advances, AI systems are still not very good at grasping overarching contexts of meaning. While systems are getting better at correctly recognizing the content of individual sentences or even entire texts, they have so far failed to contextualize them appropriately: who is writing about what topic in what place and why? What is the social and historical context of a text?

Recommendation or predictive systems are probably the best-known example of this kind of ML. For example, based on the analysis of customers' past behavior, predictions are made about their future preferences. Such recommendation systems are also used by many "social media" providers to select from the multitude of possible information for display those that are likely to be of most interest to users. The most prominent example of this is Facebook's "News Feed," which aims to show Facebook users precisely the information from their network that interests them most—and which subsequently leads them to use Facebook longer.

A particularly politically controversial example is forecasting in the context of police work ("predictive policing"). Another form of forecasting involves developing recommendations for action. In games such as chess and Go, AI systems are now superior to human players. They can draw on enormous amounts of data and process it faster than their human counterparts can. Interestingly, some AI systems have discovered strategies that humans had never thought of before (Deepmind 2019).

Two Case Studies

What questions would AI systems now face in specific cases of diplomatic practice? We have brought together the considerations made so far by looking at two concrete diplomatic negotiation contexts. In a first step, the two case studies are used as concrete examples to sound out what information was available to German diplomats regarding the power resources and goals of the other states involved in the negotiations. The second step is to consider what additional information would have been available to the diplomats had they been able to draw on AI-based analyses.

The two cases were chosen to cover two different aspects of negotiations. The first case study on the German-Austrian negotiations in 1930/31 on a customs union is in many respects typical of bilateral negotiations. A counterfactual verification, so to speak, is not possible here. However, we come close to this in the second case. The second case study takes the United Nations as an example of multilateral negotiations. Here, we are concerned with the negotiations in 2018/19 on a resolution introduced by Russia to pave the way for a new convention on cybercrime.

Case Study 1: The German-Austrian Customs Union

In the first case study, we examine a concrete example of where problems arose in the negotiation process that led the negotiations to an impasse, caused them to encounter problems that were difficult or impossible to overcome, and/or led them down wrong paths that led to worse than hoped-for results or to no results at all: Success or failure does not arise of its own accord, but is always the result of the negotiations. In each case, this then raises the question of whether AI could have brought about a better situation here, if not a solution to the problem that caused the negotiations. For the sake of simplicity, we have initially chosen a case in which the emphasis of the negotiations was on bilateral issues, even when this bilateralism could no longer be maintained.

This case study deals with a moment in the history of German-Austrian relations when both sides intended to establish a bilateral customs union. Negotiations with this goal in 1930 and 1931 took place primarily between the two countries until third parties intervened, one of them by means of such a purposefully coercive approach that the consequence was the abandonment of the customs union project. This outcome was a possible one—feared—that the two main parties had had in mind from the beginning, but ultimately could not prevent.

The essential features of the entire negotiation process are documented in the *Akten zur Deutschen Auswärtigen Politik* (for the sake of simplicity, the analysis is limited to the German files). In this negotiation process, four essential stages can be distinguished, in each of which questions arose whose answers determined the direction of the following negotiation steps. These questions were:

1. Early in 1930: How could general opposition by other states to the tariff union project be neutralized?
2. Mid-1930-early 1931: How could concrete distrust by other states of Germany's true intentions be avoided?
3. March 1931: How could increasing French opposition to the project be overcome?

4. Spring/Summer 1931: How could Austria's fiscal problems be managed so that they could not be used against the project, especially by France and Czechoslovakia?

The Background

The Treaty of Versailles, which also legally ended World War I in 1919, cut Germany's and Austria's territories considerably, by far the most in the case of Austria: From what used to be the largest state in Europe after Russia, the Habsburg Empire, only a state of about the area of today's Austria remained. The Geneva Protocol of 1922 prohibited a German-Austrian merger. The League of Nations supervised compliance with all post war agreements, with economic matters to be overseen by the "Study Commission for European Union" established by the Briand Plan of 1929/30.

The position of the most influential players in the negotiation process differed considerably on the issues affecting the problem:

1. Germany: With initially rapid economic recovery from the war, the foreign policy of the Weimar Republic had strong revisionist features. In 1925, the cabinet decided on the goal of creating a country with borders that would encompass all ethnic groups wishing to join. Here, trade with Austria was seen as an instrument to bring the two countries closer together and eventually to achieve political unification.
2. Austria: With the disappearance of most of the former Habsburg Empire, the economic situation deteriorated increasingly from 1925 onward. Large parts of the Austrian economy subsequently cooperated more closely with the German economy. In 1930, Chancellor Schober came to the conclusion that Austria would only be able to survive economically and financially if it merged with a larger economic area.
3. France: An important element of French foreign policy was the goal of preventing any development that might have strengthened Germany. France had therefore concluded an alliance with Czechoslovakia in 1924.
4. Czechoslovakia: The country—created as a sovereign state only after the World War—depended economically on its relations with Germany and Austria. Unification of these two would have meant a considerable weakening of Czechoslovakia's political position. Against this background, Foreign Minister Edvard Benes declared in 1924 that a German-Austrian union would mean war.

The Negotiations

A. German-Austrian Agreement on the Customs Union Project
Problems:
It seemed to both sides that there would be opposition to the project among some of the victorious powers. After the establishment of the customs union, problems would arise for parts of the Austrian economy.

Solution:
June 4, 1930: Instruction from the Foreign Office to the German embassies in Berne, Brussels, Budapest, Bucharest, London, Paris, Prague, and Rome, referring to the German-Austrian consultations of February 23–24 at the Chancellor level:

> Austria's internal situation demands joint efforts for the country's economic recovery. We will try to achieve a convergence of economic conditions. On the other hand, a weakening Austrian economy may make the country more dependent on France and Italy. We must therefore strive for Austria's economic recovery. (*Akten zur Deutschen Auswärtigen Politik* 1982)

B. Start of Negotiations
Problems:
Germany is now developing—apparently with Austria's approval—differentiated considerations for dealing with feared opposition from the Allied Powers (and other states). Guidelines: For the time being, the project is to be stripped of its broader political objectives. It should appear as a purely economically oriented project and be submitted only to the international body responsible for economic matters in Geneva.

Solution:
The German approach seems prudent, especially in its intention to deceive its international partners and even the public. In retrospect, however, it is obvious that the problem of resistance on the part of France and Czechoslovakia was not sufficiently recognized and evaluated in relation to the behavior of other states. From today's perspective, there was no matrix for a differentiated approach to the various parties (only the attitude of the United States seems to have been given special consideration) and no correspondingly applied diplomatic measures.

C. Dealing with the French Problem

Problem:

The task for both sides is now no longer to avoid the emergence of resistance to a suspected German plan for unification with Austria. The task became to neutralize particularly the French resistance, only now expected with vigilance and concern.

Solution:

March 18, 1931: Instruction of the German foreign minister to the German ambassadors in London, Paris, and Rome: You and your Austrian colleague are to inform your host government of the negotiations of the German and Austrian foreign ministers. They have reached agreement to begin negotiations on the conclusion of a customs union which will be open to the accession of other states.

D. The End of the Customs Union Project

Problems:

While in March France was apparently still looking for ways, with the help of international institutions and other states, to simply put obstacles in the way of the customs union project, in the aftermath of the outbreak of the world economic crisis with the difficulties for the Austrian banking system, from April France was given a considerably more effective hand to prevent the project completely. Germany could have prevented French intervention in favor of Austrian banks only by transferring money to Austria itself. That proved impossible.

Solution:

September 3, 1931: The German and Austrian foreign ministers issue a declaration at the European Committee in Geneva that their countries will not pursue the project of a customs union.

Evaluation of the Determining Elements of Diplomatic Negotiations

Power: On the one hand, differences in the strength of Germany and Austria do not play a recognizable role in the negotiations between the two sides at the level of the present documentation. There is, however, a clear imbalance of power between Germany/Austria on the one hand and the Allied powers (which had still occupied territories on the left and right of the Rhine until June 30, 1930) which could count on the support of other states and international institutions. Even Czechoslovakia, militarily weak, possessed considerable structural power through its alliance with France and France's interests. It seems to have become clear to the German side only gradually that the customs union would be difficult to implement against France's various means of power.

Strategy: After agreeing on the customs union, Germany and Austria proceeded aggressively, insisting on the right to establish such a purely economically oriented union (with, of course, long-term political aspirations) even against France.

Personalities: Little can be discerned in this regard, but there seems to be a high degree of mutual trust; with a clear German leadership role.

Process: The moves in the international context are well-devised and implemented, taking into account the findings on the attitude of France in particular.

Conclusion: Taking on the solution of the simpler problems first seems rational. In hindsight, it is evident that the problem of resistance from other parties would have required earlier action. The strategic decision to continue negotiations on the customs union must have been based on the assumption that the resistance of the European states would ultimately be low and that Germany and Austria would be able to prevail against the remaining resistance. In retrospect, this assumption proved to be wrong. The will and the ability of the other sides to oppose the project were underestimated, especially of course once an event such as the world economic crisis struck. Could this have been recognized and tackled with AI help?

No matter how elaborate the data analysis, it is unlikely to be an effective antidote to hubris. For the purposes of this analysis, however, we will first assume that governments generally have an interest in being able to realistically assess their negotiating situation. The question, then, is whether it would have been possible to assess the political stance of European states more accurately—and whether, if so, AI-based analysis could have helped.

Had the German government had today's possibilities for using AI analyses at its disposal at that time, would that have translated into a strategic advantage? It would be conceivable to have AI systems automatically analyze all public statements made by representatives of the government as well as socially influential groups (in this case, e.g., industry associations and trade unions) in the relevant states in order to obtain a picture of the political mood toward the customs union project. However, it seems unlikely that such an analysis would have yielded superior insights. The circle of relevant actors was clearly limited, and Germany had sufficient diplomatic capabilities and resources at that time to conduct the necessary analyses based on information from the embassies.

Had there been interest in doing so, it would not have required AI-based analysis.

However, AI systems exist that deductively harness comprehensive amounts of human knowledge ("the knowledge of the world"), such as OpenAI's Generative Pretrained Transformer. Here, the device searches for semantic patterns and "learns" to discover associations in order to derive "comments" (OpenAI 2019). Such systems can also design "scenarios" for future developments. We therefore asked the German company Aleph-Alpha to use such a system to design scenarios for the final question of our case study. Aleph-Alpha produced five brief machine-generated scenarios. Some of them were useless, such as the proposals to exclude Austria from the Customs Union, or to include the United States. One, however, suggested admitting Czechoslovakia. In reality, it would now have been up to the diplomats to evaluate the usefulness of the AI-generated "proposals."

It is now interesting to note that a document dated February 21, 1931, contains a reference to the fact that the major "cause of resistance" to the Customs Union in fact lay in Czechoslovakia. The conclusion: the Czechoslovak and thus French distrust might perhaps be minimized if Germany declared "beyond doubt" its willingness "to admit France and Czechoslovakia into the economic bloc as equal partners and thereby… to finally secure the peace of Central Europe." These considerations are also conclusive from today's point of view and, against the background of the actual course of the negotiations, were perhaps more promising than those actually pursued in that they showed a path to possibly overcome Czech and French opposition to the project. From the perspective of the time, they were sufficiently persuasive to be submitted to the minister by the Political Department of the Foreign Office—albeit, for reasons our files do not tell us, unsuccessfully.

A single example of this kind is not sufficient to make a definitive statement about the utility of AI in complex cases such as this one. Nevertheless, that such a result can be reached without further contextual knowledge of the computer indicates that this avenue deserves further exploration.

Case Study 2: The UN General Assembly Cybercrime Resolution

For the 74th session of the UN General Assembly in 2019, a resolution entitled "Countering the use of information and communications technologies for criminal purposes" was introduced by a group of states led by Russia. This built on a resolution with the same title from the previous session but went a decisive step further. The goal of the new edition of the resolution was to begin a process to develop a new convention to deal with "cybercrime." To this end, the draft resolution provided for the establishment of an "open-ended ad hoc intergovernmental committee of experts."

It was clear to the stakeholders that such a new convention would be in competition with the so-called Budapest Convention of the Council of Europe, which entered into force in 2004 and is also intended to regulate the handling of "cybercrime." The Budapest Convention has so far been ratified by 65 countries, including the United States. Russia is the only member of the Council of Europe that has neither signed nor ratified the resolution.[2] In statements made during the discussion of the draft resolution in the Third Committee of the United Nations, however, the signatories of the Budapest Convention—first and foremost the United States—expressed their concern that the new convention called for by Russia could undermine the mechanisms provided for in the Budapest Convention for the protection of fundamental or human rights. Although the resolution was initially intended to establish "only" a process, the discussion was thus understood as a confrontation of liberal and more authoritarian ideas about the normative order of the digital space.

In December 2019, the resolution was adopted by the UN General Assembly (UNGA). However, judging by the practice of the UNGA, the result was close: the resolution was adopted with 79 votes in favor to 60 against. Thus, only 40 percent of the 193 member states voted in favor of the resolution; 28 percent of the states abstained or did not participate in the vote. Looking at these figures, it becomes clear that a change in the voting behavior of only a few states could have brought about a different—for Europe and its allies desirable—result. Whether it would have been possible cannot be conclusively answered on the basis of the information publicly available today. However, it is possible to ask whether, on the basis of the information available to the opponents of the resolution at the time, it would have been possible with the help of AI to gain new insights into the likely behavior of the states in this vote—in order to be able to identify those states that would have been most willing to change their position and thus bring about a rejection of the resolution.

---

[2] https://www.coe.int/en/web/conventions/full-list/-/conventions/treaty/185/signatures?P_auth=HchL3alQ.

Unlike the previous case study, it is not (yet) possible in this case to gain insight into the strategic considerations of the actors involved. The focus here is therefore on what signals the states send out during votes and other formal procedures within the UN framework. In this respect, it is a view "from the outside" of the negotiations, focusing on the moments in which intermediate states of the negotiations become publicly visible.

UN General Assembly Session 73

On November 2, 2018, the draft resolution "Countering the use of information and communications technologies for criminal purposes" was made public. In practical terms, the draft formulates a mandate for the UN Secretary-General to prepare a report on the topic to capture states' perspectives on cybercrime. At the meeting of the Third Committee on November 9, the draft resolution was introduced by Russia. In the vote that followed, the draft resolution was adopted in the Third Committee by 88 votes in favor, with 55 votes against.

An analysis of voting patterns in the Third Committee reveals some interesting patterns:

* A large proportion of the authors and "sponsors" of the resolution are classified as "authoritarian" in various indices. However, the group of supporters also includes Brazil, India, and South Africa, three states that are considered predominantly democratic and are in close political exchange with Europe.
* A similar picture emerges when looking at the 88 states that voted for the resolution in the Third Committee. Most of these are widely classified as non-democratic.
* All 28 member states of the EU at that time voted against the resolution in the Third Committee.

On December 17, 2018, the resolution was then put to a vote in the General Assembly. Essentially, the result here was the same as the vote in the Third Committee: 94 states voted in favor of the resolution, 59 voted against, 33 abstained, and 7 did not participate.

In view of the above criteria for the course of diplomatic negotiations, two points are of particular importance for these first votes on the cybercrime resolution in session 73: With regard to power relations, a certain ambivalence is apparent. As can be seen from the voting results, Russia was able to organize the necessary majorities. At the same time, even these first votes were highly controversial by UN standards; in the General Assembly, the resolution did not even achieve the approval of half of the 193 member states, with 94 votes in favor.

Without insight into the considerations of the actors involved, conclusions about the underlying strategic calculus are possible only to a limited extent. Some observations can be made, however:

- Russia seems to have deliberately chosen the forum of the UN General Assembly and to have targeted authoritarian states in particular. It is also possible that Russia deliberately counted on the fact that the other side would offer little resistance to a resolution with limited practical consequences.
- To the extent that the dispute over the resolution has become a conflict between the major powers, a comparatively large number of states appear to have attempted to avoid the conflict by abstaining or not participating in the vote.

UN General Assembly Session 74

A new draft resolution on the topic was published on November 5, 2019, and was quickly introduced by Russia in the Third Committee on November 7. The new draft went beyond the previous year's resolution in key respects. Paragraph 2 mandated the process to develop a new convention on cybercrime. In addition to Russia, another 26 states were among the authors of the draft resolution. Of the total 27 authors, 19 were also authors of the previous year's resolution. Another 28 states declared themselves "sponsors" of the draft resolution before the vote in the Third Committee.

At the Third Committee meeting on November 18, 2019, the draft resolution was adopted. Eighty-eight states voted in favor, 58 against, and 34 abstained (which also indicates that 13 states did not participate in the vote). On December 27, 2019, the resolution was then adopted in the General Assembly (A/RES/74/247). Here, 79 states voted in favor of the resolution, 60 voted against, 33 abstained, and 21 did not participate in the vote. Some aspects of this voting result are worth highlighting:

- Ten states that had voted in favor of the resolution in the Third Committee abstained or did not participate in the vote in the General Assembly.
- The 28 EU member states voted unanimously against the resolution.

From the perspective of Germany and its Western allies, the result is a defeat. Unlike the previous year, this resolution clearly was to have concrete consequences by establishing a process for a new cybercrime convention. Thus, it would have been important to ensure that the resolution would not be adopted. And based on the experience of the previous year, it was to be expected that this year's decision would again be a close one. It is true that Russia and its allies were able to push through the resolution against the largely united opposition of the Western states. On the other hand, approval in the General Assembly was even lower than in the previous session: with 79 states, only 41 percent of member states voted in favor of the resolution.

With regard to the strategy, as in the previous year, the comparatively high number of states that neither clearly supported nor opposed the resolution is noteworthy. It can be assumed that supporters as well as critics of the resolution tried to lobby states for their position. In fact, the proponents of the resolution lost 15 votes, but the opponents gained only one vote at the same time. Accordingly, there again was a large number of states that avoided a clear position by abstaining. Although the specific circumstances for non-participation in a vote in the General Assembly cannot be clearly determined, it can be assumed that among the 21 non-participating states there were also some that wanted to evade a decision.

The Problem

After the "test balloon" of the first cybercrime resolution in 2018, it had become apparent that there would be a sharpened confrontation between two political camps on this topic: The supporters of the resolution were led by Russia. The opponents of the resolution were led by the U.S. and had the EU on their side. The challenge for the opponents of the resolution was therefore to achieve a majority by the time the new version was voted on in the Third Committee and possibly then in the General Assembly.

As a first approximation, it can be seen which states can be clearly assigned to one of the two sides:

* Twenty-three states appeared in session 73 as authors of the draft resolution, another six declared themselves "sponsors" of the resolution in the corresponding session of the Third Committee. These public signals from a total of 29 states are to be understood as a strong "commitment," so that it could be assumed that these states would also support a corresponding

resolution in session 74. In fact, of these states, 26 voted in favor of the resolution at the vote in session 74, 2 abstained, and 1 did not participate.
* As can be seen from the minutes of the Third Committee meeting, Australia, the U.S., and Japan were already clearly opposed to the resolution at that time. In addition, Austria expressed the EU's opposition. At this point, 31 states had clearly declared their opposition to the resolution. In fact, of these states, all 31 voted against the resolution at the vote in session 74.

Against these 60 clearly positioned states thus stood 133 states whose future voting behavior was still open to a certain extent. It is true that the voting behavior of these states in session 73 provided indications of their probable behavior in the future. As with Case Study 1, the question arises as to whether it would have been possible to use AI to obtain clues as to which states were potentially to be won over to the side of the opponents of the resolution.

AI as an Answer?

The difference to the first case study is that it concerns a comparatively large number of states, but at the same time more information is available about the preferences of the states. This raises questions of data collection as well as data analysis.

Data Collection

Data on the voting behavior of UN member states on resolutions in the General Assembly are available for all votes since the founding of the UN. In addition, it is common practice in the UN General Assembly to introduce resolutions on the same subject matter in slightly different forms every year or every two years. These "recurring resolutions" provide an opportunity to study the voting behavior of states over many years.

In April 2021, the SWP released a new dataset on voting behavior in the UN General Assembly. The dataset reprocesses information on voting behavior in the General Assembly as provided by the UN through the Digital Library. The dataset starts with session 49 (1995/1996) and currently extends to session 74 (2019/2020). For the dataset, the content keywords assigned by the UN were used to assign the resolutions to topic areas.[3]

---

[3] The dataset itself and further information can be accessed via the SWP website: http://www.swp-berlin.org/unga-dataset.

In addition, it is in principle possible to obtain further information on the preferences of states with regard to a specific resolution in the sense of the "media monitoring" already discussed. Many UN ambassadors, for example, are represented on various platforms today, which could be automatically evaluated to determine whether statements on a topic or even a specific resolution can be found there. Another source would be to use automated text analysis tools ("natural language processing") to evaluate the statements made by member states in the relevant UN committees.

In the specific case of the cybercrime resolution, a further source of this kind is the report of the Secretary-General of July 2019 in which 61 states comment on the topic of the resolution. Here, comments on the subject can be found from 29 of the states that are still unclear. Instructive are, for example, positive references of a number of states to the "Council of Europe"—which can be understood at least as a distance to Russia's initiative. Even a cursory search shows that "Council of Europe" appears 115 times in this document. With the help of tools for "sentiment analysis," it should be possible to automatically detect whether the reference here is positive or negative. While this is relevant for large data sets, in this specific case it would probably be even easier to analyze the 61 statements manually to use them as input for further data analysis.

Data Analysis

Once all of the above information has been compiled, a fairly comprehensive data set emerges—even for just one resolution. If similar information is collected for all resolutions in the context of the UN, the amount of data reaches a considerable scale. In the first step, such a data collection allows targeted queries on past events. This refers to the kind of information used in the presentation and discussion of this case study, such as detailed analyses of voting results. The U.S. State Department, for example, has been producing annual reports to Congress since the 1980s that quantitatively evaluate the voting behavior of states in the UN. The focus is on which states voted with or against the U.S. and how often.

However, in view of the volumes of data generated in this way, it is also promising to examine them with the machine-learning algorithms common today. This holds out the prospect of finding patterns in the data that have so far escaped the human gaze but which might provide indications as to where voting behavior of at least some states might be influenced. These patterns, in turn, can be sharpened into the form of predictions, in principle very similar to other AI applications. In the concrete case, then, the idea would be to forecast the behavior of the 133 states that had not previously been clearly assigned to one of the two camps. This would make it possible to specifically identify those states that are in all likelihood still largely undecided, that is, can still be won over.

The ultimate test of such AI-based analyses is whether they offer added value compared to analysis by experts or purely descriptive processing. Last but not least, it is important to determine what characterizes such added value in this specific case. The forecasts would have to be at least as good as forecasts made "manually" by diplomats. Added value would arise if the forecasts were better than human forecasts and/or could be produced more quickly or with fewer resources. A conclusive evaluation is not yet possible here without more extensive practical experience. However, experience with AI analysis in other areas suggests that this path can be pursued by applying findings to negotiations with states that might reconsider their decisions on how they will vote. It is also likely that the systems will become more powerful as more extensive and systematic data on states' preferences are collected and available for analysis in the future.

A few pieces of information on the U.S. State Department's website indicate that it is already considering this. As part of the work on an "Instability Monitoring & Analysis Platform (IMAP)," there also seem to be attempts to forecast the behavior of states in negotiating situations.

To assess the potential of AI for predicting the voting behavior of states in the UN General Assembly, we conducted a pilot project on the concrete applicability of machine learning in this context. The data basis for this was the new dataset on voting behavior in the UN General Assembly created by SWP. We selected a subset of resolutions from this dataset: These are recurring controversial resolutions in the area of human rights. We combined the voting data for this subset with additional information on the states (e.g., regime type, membership in organizations). From the resulting constructed dataset, we used UN sessions 49 to 72 as training data to predict, using a random forest algorithm, which states are likely to change their voting behavior on recurrent resolutions in subsequent sessions 73 and 74. Since we had the real voting results from these two sessions, we were able to measure the accuracy of the prediction against actual voting behavior.[4]

---

[4] More information on the pilot project can also be found on the SWP website: http://www.swp-berlin.org/unga-dataset.

AI as a Tool for Diplomatic Negotiations

The potential of AI as a tool for diplomatic negotiations can be measured by how large the intersection between two groups of information problems is: on the one hand, those information problems that regularly occur in diplomatic negotiations from the perspective of (potential) negotiation participants and have high practical relevance; on the other hand, those information problems that can be profitably solved with machine learning methods.

The four determining elements for the course of diplomatic negotiations identified above correspond to "information problems" which the actors are regularly confronted with in diplomatic negotiations:

1. What power resources do the actors have, and what is the power structure between the actors?
2. What strategic signals do the actors send? How consistent and credible are these signals? What options for action are available to the actors? What formulations in the agreed text increase the prospects of reaching an agreement?
3. On the personality of the negotiators: Are there pre-existing relationships or cultural peculiarities?
4. The process: What internal and external events or what contextual factors (e.g., institutional ties) might influence the course and outcome of the negotiations?

The questions about the framework of a negotiation (1) seem unsuitable for processing with machine learning tools. Here, it is not about searching large amounts of data for patterns, but about qualitatively assessing what the parameters of a specific negotiation situation consist of. Even the strategic questions (2) and the individual qualities (3) of the actors involved can only be answered qualitatively. Here, however, there is perhaps the greatest potential for the use of ML of the kind offered by Aleph-Alpha. A second starting point is AI-based text analysis of diplomatic documents ("natural language processing"). A conceivable extension of this approach would be to not only analyze diplomatic documents in an automated way, but also to have text proposals for negotiations developed automatically. In the best case, such systems could come up with new solutions and thus break down established thought patterns; in the worst case, however, the results would be little more useful than mediocre automatized translations.

The situation is again more difficult when it comes to questions about the actors' options for action in the process of negotiations (4). It is logically conceivable to describe the totality of all possible external influences and all possible options for action of the participants. Combining this information with all other information relevant for the respective negotiation would then make it possible to search for patterns in this total quantity and thus, on the one hand, to "calculate" the probable outcome and, on the other hand, to give the actors involved strategic recommendations on how they can influence the outcome in the light of their interests.

If all the necessary information is available, this does not require any prior theoretical assumptions about the expected interactions. All that is required is "parsimonious" modeling that provides information about the relevant actors and the courses of action available to them. On this basis, at least in principle, all conceivable combinations of actions can be run through in order to arrive at the desired analysis results. This is, in simplified terms, the procedure with which ML is used today to master games such as chess or Go. However, as complex as negotiations are in themselves, an important complication is that diplomatic negotiations are often linked to other negotiations (layered negotiations). Also, unlike in a chess game, it is often possible for the actors to disregard the rules, to set new rules themselves or simply to leave the playing field of a concrete negotiation situation. These complications create a kind of gray area that makes it difficult to name a set of possible options for preparing or conducting negotiations conclusively and completely. It seems, therefore, that we as human beings are able to usefully process great amounts of information—directed by what we like to call "gut feeling," which in effect means an intuitive "computing power of our brain" (Daniel Voelsen) without conscious data crunching lying behind it.

Relieved as we as human beings might feel about this advantage we still seem to have over artificial intelligence, there still is a profound and grave problem. Returning to Russia's invasion of Ukraine of February 24, clearly all the "computing power" of our brains employed in the negotiations with Russia preceding the invasion has not sufficed to prevent what happens the very moment this is being written. The question thus may well be justified whether crossing the "creepy line" beyond which AI outperforms human intelligence is not something we in fact should wish and work for. Such an ambition would need to assume that a future AI's "political power of judgment" (Hannah Arendt) would be guided by ethical standards more than humans are able to achieve. That is, it would develop solely scenarios or recommendations (as Aleph-Alpha in our first case study did) that would prevent the employment of armed force. The question then is whether in order to prevent a war such as the one we see on the ground in Ukraine presently, we are able to devise machines that with their computing power also possess an "ethical" power of judgment. And that then would need to reach a degree that helps avoid the tragic traps we as humans throughout our history set up for ourselves, and all too obviously cannot avoid stepping into.

References and Further Reading

Akten zur Deutschen Auswärtigen Politik. 1982. Series B: 1925–1933. K 59/K 006 781–90. Göttingen: Vandenhoeck & Ruprecht.

Berridge, G.R. 2005. *Diplomacy: Theory and Practice*. Houndmills: Palgrave Macmillan.

Citron, K. 1989. "Experiences of a Negotiator at the Stockholm Conference." In *Processes of International Negotiation*, ed. F. Mautner-Markhof, 79–84. Boulder: Westview.

Deepmind. 2019. *AlphaStar: Mastering the Real-Time Strategy Game StarCraft II – DeepMind*. https://deepmind.com/blog/alphastar-mastering-the-real-time-strategy-game-starcraft-ii.

Dickson, B. 2021. *Techtalks Newsletter*. https://bdtechtalks.com2021/03/15/machine-learning-causality.

Faizullaev, A. 2014. "Diplomatic Interactions and Negotiations." *Negotiation Journal* 30 (3): 275–99.

Gilboa, E. 2000. "Mass Communication and Diplomacy: A Theoretical Framework." *Communication Theory* (August): 275–309.

Iklé, F.C. 1964. *How Nations Negotiate*. London: Harper & Row.

Jönsson, C. 2012. "Psychological Causes for Incomplete Negotiations." In *Unfinished Business: Why International Negotiations Fail*, eds. G.O. Faure and F. Cede, 167–84. Athens: University of Georgia Press.

Jönsson, C., and M. Hall. 2005. *Essence of Diplomacy*. Houndmills: Palgrave Macmillan.

Lohmann, S. 2019. "Diplomaten und der Einsatz von Wirtschaftssanktionen." In *Die neue Wirklichkeit der Außenpolitik: Diplomatie im 20. Jahrhundert*, ed. V. Stanzel, 23–33. Baden-Baden: Nomos.

Mautner-Markhof, F. 1989. "International Negotiations: Mechanisms for the Management of Complex Systems." In *Processes of International Negotiation*, ed. F. Mautner-Markhof, 65–78. Boulder: Westview.

Meerts, P. 2015. *Diplomatic Negotiation: Essence and Evolution*. The Hague: Clingendael.

OpenAI. 2019. *Better Language Models and Their Implications*, February 14. https://openai.com/blog/better-language-models/.

Stanzel, V., ed. 2019. *The New Reality of Foreign Policy: Diplomacy in the 21st Century*. Baden-Baden: Nomos.

Stanzel, V., and D. Voelsen. 2022. *Diplomacy and Artificial Intelligence: Reflections and Practical Assistance for Diplomatic Negotiations.* SWP Research Paper 1. Berlin: German Institute for International and Security Affairs (SWP).

Starkey, B., M.A. Beyer, and J. Wilkenfeld. 2015. *International Negotiation in a Complex World.* Lanham: Rowman & Littlefield.

Voss, C. 2016. *Never Split the Difference: Negotiating as If Your Life Depended On It.* London: Random House Business.

Zartmann, I.W., and J.Z. Rubin, eds. 2000. *Power and Negotiation.* Ann Arbor: University of Michigan Press.

18

Beyond Meeting and Tweeting: The Next Challenges for Innovation in Diplomacy

Tom Fletcher

Like every industry or craft, diplomacy—a world once dominated by protocol and platitudes, maps, and chaps—has already been hugely disrupted by digital technology.

Also like many professions, the most visible impact has been on the tools: better equipment, better communications (internal and external), faster pace. Again like many, the real impact has been less visible, and is about culture: the humility that comes from understanding how power has shifted, the agility that the new tools allow, the effectiveness that comes from being more inclusive, and the transparency that comes from increased public understanding of what was once a closed world.

In 2011, I was posted as Her Majesty's envoy to Lebanon. At 36, I was young for the role. The Arab Spring was firing up young people across the region and I wondered if technological change could transform the way statecraft engaged with people. I began experimenting with what we started to call (after a few clunky options like "Twiplomacy") "digital diplomacy." A decade on, digital diplomacy has already moved through several phases—three in fact—and stands on the threshold of a fourth. Much has been achieved. But if it is to succeed in putting more streetcraft into statecraft, we must take into account what we did right and wrong.

T. Fletcher (✉)
Hertford College, Oxford, UK

The First Phase Was "Brave New World"

The first email between heads of government was sent on February 4, 1994, from the Swedish Prime Minister Carl Bildt to the U.S. President Bill Clinton. Bildt congratulated Clinton on the lifting of the Vietnam embargo and added that "Sweden is one of the leading countries in technology, and it is only appropriate that we should be among the first to use the Internet for political contacts and communications around the globe." Clinton replied the following day, in hindsight perhaps with less panache than the moment required: "I appreciate your enthusiasm for the potential of emerging technologies. This demonstration of electronic communication is an important step toward building the global information highway." The language was as clunky as the software, but e-diplomacy was under way.

With its twenty-first-century statecraft program under Secretary of State Hillary Clinton, the U.S. State Department led a period of excitement and optimism about the way that diplomats could use the new tools of communication and connection. For the ambassadors of that era who genuinely adopted and adapted, these were heady times. The rules from capitals were loose: one minister told me that he did not care what I tried so long as it stayed out of the UK media. Many of us were able to proceed until apprehended. There were plenty of mistakes. And risks: the smartphone I tweeted relentlessly from was also the device that terrorists used to track my movements.

But this was a period when we could surprise people with a desire to connect, engage, and show some humility. It seemed possible to imagine that social media would open up societies and promote real agency and freedom. One British ambassador even suggested that the most powerful weapon in the Middle East was the smartphone. I was wrong about that, so far.

Several foreign ministries adjusted to social media far more quickly than to any previous technology. Having been one of only four UK ambassadors on Twitter in 2011, within a few years all but four were, with some like John Casson in Egypt amassing over one million followers. For a profession without many ways to assess impact, there was real willingness to experiment with social media. I spoke at over twenty conferences of ambassadors, urging colleagues to give it a try, show the human behind the handle, and engage (rather than transmit). I used to tell them it was like the largest diplomatic reception they could imagine: don't stand at the margins, say nothing, or bellow across the room. Yes, there were risks. But the biggest risks were not to be in the conversation.

The second phase was the institutionalization of digital diplomacy. As more adopted the approach, foreign ministries faced new trade-offs over agility versus confidentiality of their communication. My 2016 review (FCO 2016) of the Foreign Office recommended a pivot toward the former: perhaps Sir Kim Darroch, the outstanding UK Ambassador driven out by President Trump over his leaked cables—might subsequently have disagreed. But we became more reliant on that ability to communicate at speed.

Traditionally, diplomats have always tried to minimize and manage the amount of direct contact between leaders. We encased their exchanges in protocol, prepared lines and statements. I worked for one minister in Tony Blair's government, Chris Mullin, who admirably made a point of not being connected by phone or pager, despite the strenuous efforts of his party's whips and managers. As I used to tell him, this is a civil servant's fantasy. But his technological detachment did not seem to stop the world from turning.

New ways of communicating broke down the restrictions that officials put up. Leaders started to text, email, and tweet each other directly. During negotiations, the text or WhatsApp messages between them (and between their advisers) became more substantive and critical to the outcome than the conversation at the table. Neither Bildt nor Clinton could have anticipated the speed at which the "global information highway" was being built around them. In terms of diplomacy, it was Twitter and Facebook that built it. @jack (aka Jack Dorsey, Twitter's founder) sent the first tweet at teatime on March 21, 2006. Within three years, a billion tweets had been sent.

Bildt was the first minister to make it compulsory for ambassadors to have social media accounts. Leaders began to wrestle control of their own social media accounts from their staff. They recognized that if you were not tweeting yourself, you were not really on Twitter. In early 2014, John Kerry tweeted "It only took a year but @StateDept finally let me have my own @Twitter account," and used the hashtag #JKTweetsAgain. Increasingly, such accounts replaced carefully scripted formal and less engaging statements.

Diplomats need to pick arguments. Twitter and other social media tools allowed them to do that in new ways. One of the pioneering digital diplomats, the former U.S. ambassador to Russia Michael McFaul, had online fights with the Russian ministry of foreign affairs over freedom of assembly and speech. He saw it as a way to avoid having his views censored or filtered through traditional Russian media. UN Security Council arguments between permanent representatives were played out in real time on Twitter. The brilliant French ambassador to the U.S., Gérard Araud, regularly took on U.S. presidential candidates and others in public. This would all have appeared unseemly just a few years previously.

Diplomats put these tools to increasingly creative and effective use. In Iran, both the U.S. and UK had virtual embassies—allowing them online engagement without the physical risks of locating diplomats. I remember how dangerous it felt to be organizing a joint town hall meeting between the UK and Chinese premiers in 2009, the first of its kind in China. There were now virtual town halls everywhere online.

Some of the most innovative digital diplomats were from smaller countries. Perhaps they found it easier to embrace a more fleet-footed, start-up approach. Estonia led the diplomatic market in the use of blockchain technology (a way of distributing digital data globally across thousands of computers), and online citizenship. Since its independence in 2008, Kosovo had been recognized by only half the world. So its deputy foreign minister, Petrit Selimi, persuaded Facebook to allow users to place their location in Kosovo, and not in neighboring Serbia. The success of this effort meant that Kosovo's existence is more widely recognized online than offline. Digital media were also increasingly important resources for those responding to humanitarian crises. Humanitarian agencies got social media channels and devices to those hit by disasters, and used Google Earth to locate survivors. In Lebanon, we used smart cards to deliver cash to the neediest refugees, and sophisticated social media mapping tools to locate them.

Of course, all of this digital diplomacy brought risks. In September 2012, while under direct attack as the result of unrest caused by the rapid spread of a video critical of Islam, the U.S. embassy in Cairo condemned the efforts of some to "hurt the religious feelings of Muslims." The backlash in the United States, where some felt that the tweet attacked the very principles of free speech that U.S. institutions ought to be upholding, led to the White House disowning it. Separately, the U.S. ambassador in Egypt had to apologize to his sensitive hosts when the embassy Twitter feed retweeted a clip from *The Daily Show* with Jon Stewart that criticized the Egyptian government.

So digital diplomacy was not without its critics. The former British ambassador Oliver Miles wrote in 2010 (when William Hague was Foreign Secretary) that we need to "Stop the blogging ambassadors. The immediacy of social media does not lend itself to the measured nature of international diplomacy…. The issues with which ambassadors have to deal are better dealt with *penseroso* rather than *allegro*. Blogs by ambassadors were bound to end in tears. Let's hope William Hague will blow the whistle." "Il Penseroso" is Milton's poem about sober contemplation, as opposed to the frenetic world of "L'Allegro." Personally, I think Milton would have tweeted. If the whistle was blown, it was too *piano* to hear. Of course there will always be a need for considered diplomacy, but diplomats will also have to be part of the conversations that everyone in the real world is having.

Sir Leslie Fielding, another former UK ambassador, has also lambasted the "trivial chirpiness and dumbing down" of social media, saying that it "cuts no mustard when applied to the sheer complexity of many world issues. The global waters are often opaque, even muddy." He was right, of course, about the fiendish complexities of foreign policy, and indeed the inane nature of much social media. But that is not an argument against trying to communicate in new ways, and to use the new tools to make the global waters a little less murky. The examples of diplomatic digital disasters—inadvertent insults to former opponents, misguided attempts at humor in serious situations, disgruntled hosts—will not seem so dramatic in a few years. There is no other way to pursue digital diplomacy effectively except through loosening the reins of control.

In the second phase we also started to create structures around the wider dialogue between the old emperors and the new. Worried by the implications for geopolitics of the pace of technological change, I left the UK government to try to make the case for the urgency of this effort. After a report (UN 2017) I had written for the United Nations in 2017, the UN launched an effort for Big Tech and government to talk *to* rather than *past* each other. Both the UN's High Level Panel and the Global Tech Panel were genuine and effective attempts to translate between those disrupting global politics, economics, and society and those nominally still in charge, an alternative to trying to summon the [Mark] Zuckerbergs before parliamentary or congressional committees. In *The Naked Diplomat* (Fletcher 2016), I had proposed that countries should appoint "tech ambassadors." The Danes went for it, with success, challenging the tech companies to engage with states in a veritable dialogue. But fewer others followed than we anticipated. Many stuck to the traditional model, upgrading Consuls General in San Francisco. Others looked instead to recruit more tech savvy diplomats.

The third phase of digital diplomacy overlapped with the second: the empire struck back. Authoritarian governments found new ways to use digital technology to suppress freedom. Trump exploited Twitter to exploit and augment xenophobia, prejudice, and insurrection. More creatively he also used it—as at home—to court potential diplomatic allies and to pressure diplomatic opponents. Meanwhile, Russia's Vladimir Putin weaponized the internet against democracy and built troll factories. Twitter mobs made it harder to share the nuance of complex diplomatic positions, let alone use social media to reach compromise and common ground. Polarization was clickbait, and the center did not hold. Governments realized that cyber was the new battleground, and started to think in terms of defense.

Meanwhile, Big Tech grew, morphing in some cases into entities more powerful and sometimes more reactionary than governments. Mischievously I had wondered aloud in 2013 whether we should ask Google to be on the UN Security Council. Google might now ask why it should bother. While Big Tech grew and flexed its muscles, it quietly recruited the talent, depriving governments of human capital as well as taxes. Symbolically, and perhaps inevitably, the (excellent) first Danish Tech Ambassador was poached by Microsoft and Britain's Liberal Democrat leader poached by Facebook. As the legal arms race intensified, the EU's titanic clashes with Big Tech over data or incitement were a long way from the idealism of the Brave New World phase, when we genuinely believed that we could solve more problems together.

Where does this leave us today? I am now more of a realist about technology and diplomacy, but I remain an optimistic one. We can still crack challenges together, including the Sustainable Development Goals. But to do so, governments must be more honest about what they cannot do alone. Tech needs more patience to stick with slower moving and often clumsy states, and more honesty about where it has become part of the problem.

Meanwhile, diplomats can continue to use technology to make them more effective: my research group at New York University worked on wearable technology to help a diplomat read a room; a Diplopedia to do a better job of conserving diplomatic records; and intelligent and transparent use of sentiment mining to better understand public opinion. I stand by the hypothesis that the more oversight the public has of issues of war, the more peaceful government policy will be. Perhaps one of the most exciting areas for diplomacy will be the potential to combine it with the latest advances in collective psychology (such as the Larger Us campaign) and social media to make peace between societies rather than between states, and between nations and their histories.

The next phase of digital diplomacy should also see work on the next great peace processes: with the planet, with Big Tech, between young and old, between hosts and migrant communities, and ultimately maybe with technology itself. I think digital diplomacy can help us get and deliver better outcomes on each of those. It can provide the tools to connect discussions in a more effective way, and it could contribute to shifting the social media environment in a more collaborative, consensus building direction. New forms of meeting and interaction can make it easier for government and technology companies to establish a more trusting and action focused dialogue. And social media can continue to diversify and distribute power in fairer ways, creating a sense of power and agency among groups that are currently disadvantaged.

Finally, the next phase of digital diplomacy—like James Bond putting the gadgets aside in Skyfall—will see diplomats returning to the basics of the craft. We will need a more focused effort to develop citizen diplomats, equipped with vital diplomatic skills like empathy and emotional intelligence: education is therefore upstream diplomacy. We will need an old school pen and paper effort to rewrite the global rules for protection of our freedoms in an online world. We will need embassies to escape from the confines of buildings and return to their original mission as groups of people sent to connect. And we will need diplomats who can still do what Edward Murrow called the "last three feet," that crucial human connection that will be the last diplomatic skill to be automated.

For a trade that relies on communication, diplomacy has obviously had to adapt to successive waves of dramatic technological disruption. The most important innovations to shape statecraft throughout history were language, writing, ships, rules, the printing press, trains, the telegraph, telephones, and now the internet. So the tools of diplomacy are constantly evolving. Diplomats now compete over who has the most Twitter followers rather than where they are placed at a diplomatic dinner. Many of Talleyrand's contemporaries, if not the adaptable character himself, would have been out of his depth in a twentieth-century summit, just as John Kerry would be in a twenty-second-century summit. Diplomacy had surrounded itself by the late twentieth century with immense paraphernalia—titles, conferences, summits, rules, and codes. But strip these away, and we can identify the diplomatic skills that made our ancestors more likely to survive the hostile 200,000 years of hunter-gathering, the eight millennia of the Agricultural Age, and the two centuries of the Industrial Age. Maybe these can get us through the new uncertainties of the Digital Age.

Diplomats have always been most effective when they have understood, channeled, and represented real power. When states became the dominant power brokers, diplomats started ministries and tried to get as close as possible to their elected (or unelected) leaders. As democracy took hold in the West, diplomats reinvented themselves as its most ardent supporters, while trying to ensure that their trade stayed out of its sight. We need to consider what this means for diplomacy in an age when power is once again shifting and diffusing. If diplomats are not where the power is, they are simply slow journalists with smaller audiences.

The history of diplomacy also shows us that, at key points in our collective story, and normally following shocks such as war, shifts in power required diplomats and politicians to work together strenuously to recalibrate systems and establish new rules of coexistence. Modern diplomats are standing on the shoulders of the curious, canny, and sometimes courageous individuals behind the Peace of Westphalia, the Congress of Vienna, the creation of the League of Nations and the Bretton Woods Conference. Two centuries after the Congress of Vienna, are we again at such a moment of flux and uncertainty, and do diplomats have the legitimacy and credibility to help manage the next global reset?

Diplomacy over the last two years would have been unimaginable without Zoom and WhatsApp. For a profession that used to do everything to minimize direct contacts between leaders, diplomats were quick to embrace video-conferencing once the tech made it a serious option. The pandemic drove summits and conferences online, saving enormous amounts of carbon with little obvious negative impact on the outcomes. Perhaps we may even look back on an era of social and national distancing and discern ways in which the pandemic *improved* diplomacy. It has reminded the world—and diplomats—why the craft matters. It has given a much-needed technological jolt to diplomacy. And it has exposed the fundamental dividing lines between nationalism and internationalism. The inadequacy of the global infrastructure was not created by COVID, the retreat from Kabul, and the invasion of Ukraine: it was exposed by those moments. If in passing the pandemic marks the end of the unnecessary summit, of diplomacy measured in air miles rather than outcomes, and a resistance to automating the parts of diplomacy that are better done by technology, that will be a bonus.

That is an exciting and urgent agenda. If diplomacy did not exist we would need to invent it. But now we need to *reinvent* it. And that is too important to leave to diplomats.

References and Further Reading

Fletcher, T. 2016. *The Naked Diplomat*. London: HarperCollins.
Foreign and Commonwealth Office (FCO). 2016. *Future FCO Report*. https://www.gov.uk/government/publications/future-fco-report.
United Nations (UN). 2017. *United Networks: The UN Needs You*. https://www.unitednetworks.ae/.

19

Disinformation and Diplomacy

Juan Luis Manfredi-Sánchez and Zhao Alexandre Huang

The field of communication has a neutral definition regarding the term "information," and it is an act of communication in which the actor notifies other individuals, organizations, groups, or civil society to brief about an event. However, in military and strategic competition areas, information is seen as a tool that can be effectively designed and constructed to frame and legitimate the authority of a specific interest group. In fact, discourse, as the critical carrier of information, is regarded as the center of social construction (Schneider 2015); moreover, the process of discourse formation is also interpreted as pre-formulating and pre-integrating diverse language and rhetorical elements to forge the target audience's positive perception and acceptance of information more subtly (Huang 2020). For this reason, it is usually regarded as a strategic carrier of communication actions to help its initiators gain and maintain a decisive persuasive advantage in the communication process.

The discussion on the importance of information in diplomacy does not only lie in (re)formulating strategies that allow actors to adapt to change in the geopolitical environment while achieving (pre-)fixed objectives better (Krieg-Planque 2009). Further, this importance is also reflected in content

J. L. Manfredi-Sánchez (✉)
School of Foreign Service, Georgetown University, Washington, D.C., USA

Z. A. Huang
Université Paris Nanterre, Paris, France

production to radiate state influence abroad. Thus, information, the narrative, and the rhetoric based on it have been seen as an essential persuasive instrument implemented by a government to deploy its soft power (Roselle 2010). Diffusing information depends on communication channels. The development of information and communication technologies (ICTs) has expanded the traditional mediation techniques of diplomatic propagation, especially the popularization of digital media, which has also created new dilemmas in diplomacy related to information disorder.

What Is Information Disorder?

Information disorder is one of the most relevant topics in diplomacy and international relations (Wardle and Derakhshan 2017). Diplomats, journalists, militaries, and policymakers are interested in the way the messages are created, distributed, shared, and understood. The phenomenon has several dimensions. Social networks and platforms have reduced the private space, so that information flows without filters. The multiplication of sources has augmented the noise and the inability of citizens to articulate and discern the quality of the information they receive. Information systems do not take responsibility for the content they release, separating technology from content. Journalistic companies are weakened and compete for social attention with clickbait techniques and free content, thus increasing the noise and not the quality of public information. These problems, although more widespread, are not that new. Information disorder has long opened new avenues for anti-diplomacy practices. As Der Derian (1987, 135) wrote, "diplomacy is negotiation between states, while anti-diplomacy is propaganda among peoples."

Disinformation impacts three elements of diplomacy. On the political level, it weakens trust between parties and resurrects propaganda practices as a vehicle for interfering in international affairs. On the multilateral level, disinformation is also one of a number of joint concerns. The meaning and method of conflict resolution are disputed, as there is no consensus on the scope of disinformation, freedom of expression, or the normative power of states. Ultimately, it causes the diplomatic corps to abandon traditional discretion to discuss aspects of foreign policy in public and on social networks. This shift from the private to the public makes diplomatic culture uncomfortable. Disinformation in the diplomatic field can be defined as false or forged information and politically motivated to gain influence in the local and global audience. It fosters a culture of suspicion, because to succeed it does not require construction of a plausible, alternative reality. To corrupt reality, it is enough to distribute incomplete and inaccurate data, not necessarily false, to generate doubt. Out-of-context information is confusing and does not require a complete, homogeneous, or meaningful narrative.

Disinformation is a dynamic policy, sustained over time and endowed with resources. It is connected to foreign policy as a visionary and strategic part of external action and is allied with intelligence services, economic affairs, or cultural relations. It is not an isolated action, but the systematization of hostility through all the communication tools and strategies. Unlike traditional propaganda, it does not pursue a specific political objective, but rather the discrediting of institutions, social polarization, or the propagation of inaccurate data that contaminate public opinion. It is an active and strategic policy because its mission entails exploiting the vulnerability of the adversary and affecting the quality of public opinion, the credibility of the political system, or the capacity to build consensus in terms of external action. Disinformation is successful, then, not because of the achievement of defined political objectives (electoral interference, economic promotion, cultural diversity), but because of its capacity to condition the reality in which international activity operates. In the academic literature, disinformation fits in with hybrid strategies, the gray zone, and other literary references that link political action, diplomatic routines, military deployment, and economic relations with a global project of external action. Under this terminological umbrella, the study of disinformation in the diplomatic field includes the use of fake news (Yablokov 2015), the rise of fact checking (Powers and Kounalakis 2017), the disqualification of opponents, the populist management of social networks (Manfredi-Sánchez et al. 2021), and other psychological operations (Nisbet and Kamenchuk 2019).

Disinformation includes "fabricated or deliberately manipulated audio/visual content. Intentionally created conspiracy theories or rumours" (Wardle and Derakhshan 2017); misinformation comes from unintentional mistakes and inaccuracy; and mal-information means leaking and spreading private information to harm others, for instance, during election campaigns to discredit candidates. Bennet and Livingston underline disinformation's purpose as disseminating "intentional falsehoods… as news stories or simulated documentary formats to advance political goals" (2018, 124). The preferred technique, as noted, is the propagation of doubts. It is a matter of taking advantage of contemporary reality to introduce informative elements that manipulate, and are false or biased. Factual truth competes with other hypotheses, not as a source of healthy skepticism toward institutional communication or the scientific method, but as a space for cynicism and generalized distrust.

The disorder is relevant when truth is contested by emotions, opinions, and interpretations (Arendt, 1967). Disinformation builds an order called to compete with factual reality, a sort of epistemology where facts and emotions are combined to create a forged narrative. In the mix, emotions (myths, nostalgia, conspiracies, rage, historical humiliations, antiscientific discourse) are more relevant than facts and arguments. Disinformation is a key part of this disorder.

Truth and lies compete on the same dimension and, therefore, disorder appears. There is no clear separation between conventional propaganda, journalistic activity, fiction, or satire. Technological and digital development has blurred the boundaries between media, content, and information producers, so that the public sphere receives a continuum of digital content. The risk represents a serious threat to open societies: facts compete with emotions and reality is confused with desires and opinions. This all corrodes public trust and represents a conflict for other political basic goods, namely freedom of expression and freedom of information. In addition, from the perspective of social psychology, information disorder can also make people deviate from or reverse facts and truth. Because as the recipient of information, the audience cannot filter a large amount of ambiguous, complex, and changeable information in a short period (Rathbun 2007). Insecurity results when the audience makes decisions, which will further generate a "generalized and unspecified sense of disequilibrium" regarding communicated information at the cognitive level (Turner 1988, 61). This insecurity breaks the cognitive balance between the sender and the receiver in information communication, making people more willing to accept false information wrapped in emotions (Huang 2021).

Disinformation may be understood with a twofold analysis. First, it is a political motivated activity. Actors disseminate disinformation to advance a political agenda. There is no specific objective (to win an election, to approve a trade agreement), but rather to promote a broad political agenda. Mistrust, institutional discredit, and the culture of suspicion are not measured by performance indicators, unlike traditional propaganda. This political orientation makes countermeasures difficult. Disinformative actions are not consistent with each other; they produce dissonant messages and target very different audiences. Thus, public health disinformation or electoral interference calls for specific measures, adapted to each sociodemographic segment and institutional moment (Jeangène Vilmer 2021). Four challenges are identified for the prevention and fight against disinformation: a) the promoters of the messages are not clear: they are not states, but assimilated actors: news agencies, NGOs, and so on; b) censorship does not proceed in an open society: expelling journalists creates dangerous precedents and is often repeated by third countries;

c) freedom of expression is menaced: artists and satirists need a certain dose of creativity and subversion; and d) securitization of speech produces norms against dissidents and alternative voices to official discourse.

Second, disinformation is a relevant economic activity. Disinformation is produced in technological factories that turn a profit from the global syndication of content, which poses a threat to the news industry governed by professional and ethical standards (Carlson 2017). In the U.S. market, technological companies define themselves as non-media firms to avoid any responsibility over content management, moderation, or hate speech distribution. In the European market, technological companies are reactive, and are not involved in preventing disinformation. Investments in fact checking and editorial verification are not enough as the audience is not willing to do it by themselves (Eurostat News 2021). Under these conditions, disinformation is a growing industry where often amateurs championing a cause and motivated by the profits can be reaped from programmatic advertising and the invention of hoaxes. Benkler et al. (2018, 9) have classified these actors as "'Fake News' Entrepreneurs/Political Clickbait Fabricators." On-demand disinformation mixes the agenda of verifiable events (election calls, social movements, corporate behavior, sports results, etc.) with the mood of readers, the recommendations of their inner circles, and the most popular content, even though it does not match their own profile (Bakshy et al. 2015). Meanwhile, the systematic effort to counteract disinformation generates a high economic cost for democracies (Cavazos 2019). It has been approached as a security problem, as a social issue that requires its own discipline (media and digital literacy), or as a structural weakness of the journalistic system (fake news, fact checkers).

Disinformation has generated its own theoretical noise. The impact of communication campaigns on electoral results, social behaviors, or political decisions has been overestimated. Such a functionalist approach reduces international communication to a process of information injection that modifies the course of decisions. There is no such cause-effect relationship, nor is there a zero-sum game. Disinformation works because it exploits pre-existing weaknesses in social life, the need for audiences to accept an explanation for their bias. Disinformation has grown in a political and social environment where polarization exists for different reasons. Internally, countries are facing increased inequality, problems of legitimacy of the political system, economic crises, or unemployment. Externally, the collapse of the global governance system (Eurozone crisis, Trumpism, COVID, Russian aggression) leads political actors to want to produce their own new legitimacy narratives. International actors use such discontent to interfere in domestic affairs. It affects public opinion, institutions, electoral processes, media ownership, or social media campaigns. The dissemination of inaccurate ideas and facts aims to affect judgment (value judgment about a decision) and perceptions (stereotypes) but will hardly affect voting behavior automatically. Meanwhile, Russian and other state interference (e.g., in the U.S. presidential elections and the Brexit vote) cannot be singled out as the only factor causing social unrest. The problems of liberal democracies are not the sole result of disinformation. One point should be clarified: the producers of disinformation take advantage of the diversity of problems and audiences to produce and distribute personalized pieces. In their disinformation strategy, the stories do not have to be consistent with one another, and the inconsistency allows them to reduce the public space for coexistence in order to reinforce prejudices and falsehoods. There lies the gain for authoritarian states which can exploit the degree of openness and transparency of democratic countries (Lanoszka 2019).

Why Now?

Communication is at the heart of any diplomatic strategy. The rise of public diplomacy, and alongside it, the management of memory and nostalgia, the multiplication of international television channels financed by governments, the use of social networks for deterrence and negotiation, the growth of transnational social movements, the application of marketing to cities and territories, and the interference of private actors and capital in electoral processes all affect diplomatic practice and challenge it to develop new methodologies, contents, and perspectives.

Three sets of changes are at the root of this process of diplomatic mediatization: a) technology, b) political time, and c) international journalism.

Technological development has fragmented audiences. There is no room for a single narrative of war, peace, or negotiation because audiences find more and more channels for information and propaganda. It is no longer possible to study a "CNN effect" when there are at least ten major global television operators, as well as other platforms, social networks, and individuals armed with a cell phone. There is not one diplomatic audience, but many. In fact, domestically, citizens do not feel concerned about their own information or the need to "rally around the flag" in case of conflict. In many countries, citizens consume information from the sources they choose, not from official or the government's own sources. The fragmentation of audiences overlaps with polarization, which affects exposure to sources. International information and foreign policy have abandoned the incorporation of national consensus into the general policy debate. In the 2016 and 2020 elections, the mere idea of Russian interference in the U.S. presidential election did not serve to unite the electorate, but to divide it. In Latin America, the label "Chavista candidate" is used to signal possible Venezuelan interference in domestic affairs. Part of society welcomes such interference, whether real or figurative, because it coincides with its domestic political objectives.

Yet, the state still maintains a preponderant role in strategic narratives in some countries, as evidenced by Russia or China investing in global televisions, advertising insertions, digital campaigns, and social networks (Xu and Wang 2022). Similarly, populism and illiberal leaders create their own communicative space to validate themselves (TeleSur, TRT World, Press TV). Technology accelerates the distribution of content, facilitates the construction of alternative spaces (Entman 2008), drives new editorial projects (Elswah and Howard 2020), and breaks English-language hegemonies over diplomatic discourse (Mattelart and Koch 2016).

In relation to political time, mediatization has reduced discrete and confidential spaces. Discretion no longer has much value (Amado, 2016). Technology accelerates the feeling of real time and of live broadcasting. Real time does not allow for negotiation or conversation but summarizes actions into a binary code of response. Traditional diplomacy succumbs to the digital rhythms of conspiracy theories, antagonisms with reference journalism, or mere messianism (citations, examples needed). Digital logic clashes with diplomatic corporate culture and affects the institutionalization of diplomacy, as well as the recognition of actors and legitimacy. By its nature, diplomatic communication is secretive and prefers activity on the margins of public opinion. However, today, diplomacy is mainly exercised in the media with declarations and audiovisual scenography.

Political representatives exchange tweets, diplomats respond or provoke controversy, militaries reveal images of deployments. Secrecy has vanished, because there is always someone in the audience who records, shares, and leaks. Without secrets, the culture of suspicion is cultivated; trust between the parties is undermined; and the space for confidentiality is reduced. Moreover, diplomats are called upon to participate on an equal footing with journalists, citizens, lobbyists, or politicians to distribute their story on different platforms and according to the corresponding visual or semiotic codes. Diplomats, international politics, multilateral organizations, or chancelleries have been incorporated into the hybrid logic that involves participation in 24/7 communicative flows, the direct relationship with citizens, the creation of their own strategic narrative that is not mediated through the journalistic industry, the use of "memes" and "emojis," the management of a digital audience, or the interaction with trolls and serial disinformers. It is novel precisely because of its performative quality: to the extent that they act, their behavior has political and diplomatic consequences. A Donald Trump tweet about recognizing the status of Western Sahara affects Spanish-Moroccan relations. Ukraine's MFA memes to address the crisis introduce humor to attract others to join its side in the crisis. Videos of U.S. influencers visiting China offer an attractive and open image of the country. Tik-tokers narrating their experience of fleeing a besieged Ukraine employ digital semiotics and open a new stage in war communication.

The rise of diplomatic communication coincides with the decline in the number and strength of correspondents. The journalistic perspective competes with other actors, companies, influencers, or governments. The structural crisis of the newspaper industry prevents the maintenance of a capillary network of journalists, editors, and photographers on a global scale. In the absence of journalistic professionals, interest groups act as information providers with their own cognitive biases and conceptual frameworks. Moreover, the credibility crisis in the media makes it difficult to impose a single agenda, framework, or linguistic definition (e.g., "illegal annexation," "invasion," "terrorist group"). Journalism does not set itself up as an interlocutor to convey messages, but rather individuals organize themselves into reading communities through social networks, instant messaging, or YouTube channels. Technology has widened the gaps among them. In February 2022, the distribution of photographs of Russian military movements on the Ukrainian border came from satellites, not from journalists on the ground. The agencies themselves warned of their own inability to assess the quality of audiovisual information, then devalue their own information product. The erosion of professional journalism facilitates the expansion of the post-truth political culture, since no one can question the political and diplomatic power for decisions, show inconsistencies, or reveal scandals.

On the content level, the audience embraces new values of participation and subjectivity. Objective and impartial information and the status of professional reporters are no longer dominant values in international news. The latter has fallen into the game of "emotional contagion": emotions, feelings, traumas, and humor set the value of international communication to the detriment of analysis or the provision of information. Contagion opens the door to ignorance, popular beliefs, and anti-scientific discourse. Ignorance, anti-scientific discourse, conspiracy is cool (Ecker et al. 2022).

Diplomatic activities are no longer the monopoly of ministries of foreign affairs or of diplomats but is exercised and responded to from a multitude of channels. This phenomenon of deinstitutionalization poses risks to the unity of external action and opens the door to other actors contesting the authority of the federal government. Diplomacy ceases to be a specialized space reserved for professionals to make room for more actors—with and without legitimacy—to participate in diplomatic affairs. Diplomatic communication is not reduced to the relationship between public administration, the diplomatic corps, and the specialized press, but allows for the advancement of other actors. Consequently, cities, corporations, NGOs, terrorist groups, insurgents, social movements, and stateless nations can engage with journalists and publics with the aim of influencing their perception of international events. It may be liked or disliked, be in accordance with international law, or arouse misgivings, but the exponential growth of non-traditional participants, sources of law, and non-normative actions is undeniable. These actors have seized the opportunity to leverage their capacities through public communication, either to increase transparency and accountability or to increase noise and misinformation.

Second, the communication exercise redefines diplomacy. Public diplomacy ceases to be an after-the-fact communication tool for foreign policy objectives and becomes a major part of state strategy. Diplomacy is public, it develops in real time in a hybrid ecosystem (Chadwick 2017). The publicity of agreements, messages, epistolary exchanges, or negotiations affects the nature of the profession. There is no longer a public diplomacy complementary to the political activity of leaders and the diplomatic activity of chancelleries. Diplomacy is public and happens in campaigns, persuasion, audience engagement, production of audiovisual fiction, database management, access to networks, promotion of hate messages, and creation of cognitive frameworks and platforms. The new diplomatic environment must demonstrate an awareness of the dynamics and scope of the changes to navigate the uncertainty of an information system different from the one inherited from the twentieth century. Thus, diplomatic success is strongly linked to understanding new media structures (Pamment 2014; Manor and Crilley 2020). Chancelleries learn in real time how to navigate the new media ecosystem. What is new is the volume (total quantity), variety (diversity of sources), and speed (real time) of information distribution. MFAs are overwhelmed and require new institutional capacities to receive, manage, and understand public information. The diplomatic challenge is not, therefore, to deal with public conversations, the multiplication of actors, or the profusion of disinformation, but to be able to interpret information (veracity) and have criteria (create public value). Once again, it is a matter of distinguishing between the noise and the signal in order to be able to create knowledge that serves the achievement of foreign policy objectives.

Diplomatic Goals

Disinformation serves diplomatic interests as a tool to advance political and economic objectives. This configuration is based on acts of communication and governance, and it manifests the process of power creation. Price (2015, 8) describes this phenomenon as "the organized advocacy of 'narratives of legitimacy' as a way to provide moral and consensual bases for modes of governance."

The first instrument is the framing. Framing remains relevant as it is a basic mechanism for defining problems, identifying causes and actors, constructing a moral and belief response, and offering solutions. Framing fixes the vision, values, and agency of both international audiences and local voters. Russian activity provides three recent examples. In information activity, neighboring countries are associated with poor political status and dependent on Russian input. Crimea needs protection and order (Szostek 2014). Ukraine's borders contested. Kazakhstan, Georgia, and Belarus need external intervention to maintain internal stability. The emotional framing is central to the disregard for verifiable facts, as it contributes to the extension of biases. McIntyre explains that, in the absence of factual reality, "politicians can defy facts and pay no political price for it" (2018, 43). The epistemic communities (really, networks) of disinformation do not aspire to widen the range of arguments or to find contradictory arguments but pursue ideas and facts that serve a certain way of believing and behaving. Ideology and moral principles take precedence over evidence. The cognitive process is ordered on a criterion, an attitude toward the observed facts. Framing is fundamental in the construction of disinformation because it hierarchizes facts and associates them with moral values. Disinformation anticipates the validation or legitimization of political decisions, so that emotions (which are true) serve for the fabrication of collective truths. The effectiveness of disinformation lies not in its capacity to manipulate and change beliefs but in its ability to appeal to prior beliefs.

China's public diplomacy to Africa, for example, is based on framing positive emotions carried out by information and diverse mediatization techniques and infrastructures. The starting point of China's public diplomacy toward Africa is rooted in the ideological conflict between the two camps during the Cold War (Huang and Hardy 2019). The Mao Zedong government decided to use foreign economic and technical assistance to participate in African countries' anti-colonial wars, gain the support and endorsement of newly established African countries on the international stage, and promote the Chinese government's legitimacy. This history is packaged as a historic brotherhood by Beijing in the current narrative of the China-Africa community, and it is repeatedly referenced in the media it controls. For example, in the Beijing-led coverage of the 2018 Forum on China-Africa Cooperation (FOCAC), we found a series of articles in *People's Daily*—the organ newspaper of the Communist Party of China (CPC). Their titles showed the importance of positive emotions in China-Africa themed narratives: "singing the main melody of win-win cooperation and common development between China and the (01/09/2018)"; "China and Africa are writing new chapters in cooperation (05/09/2018)"; "the Sino-African friendship has been and will be transmitted from generation to generation (09/09/2018)." These titles are formulated to concretize Beijing's conception of China-Africa cooperation's golden age while echoing President Xi's advocacy for the "China-Africa Community with a shared future." In addition, Beijing has also actively strengthened the construction of information dissemination infrastructure in Africa. This initiative can be traced back to 2011, when China launched its media "going out" policy of expanding its influence with a $7 billion media infrastructure investment plan. It aims to enhance China's state-owned media's framing capacity on the global stage, especially in the African community (Zhang et al. 2016). Thus, China Central Television (CCTV) has been operating an African channel in Nairobi since 2012, and CCTV-Africa (today: CGTN-Africa) is a relay critical to Chinese public diplomacy. Besides, the Chinese government uses *Star Times*, a Chinese operator of digital terrestrial television (DTT) in Africa, to enhance Chinese cultural attractiveness. *Star Times*, labeled as the "key enterprise for cultural export" by the Chinese Ministry of Culture (Ministry of Commerce, People's Republic of China 2021), is a private company supported by Chinese investment. In 2014, it created the center for producing and distributing cultural products in Nairobi. Its objective is to import Chinese films or television programs and dub them into African languages. Chinese cultural products could be widely disseminated on the African continent (Rønning 2016). Finally, Confucius Institutes are also regarded as a medium for China to build its influence and have been laid on the African continent to subtly influence the target audience's perception of China's development and rise through grassroots daily communication (Huang 2021).

This series of actions contribute to the deployment of China's foreign policy and the implementation of the communication strategy with Chinese characteristics to African audiences. From creating mass media channels to providing digital TV and internet access for residents to cultural and academic communication of Confucius Institutes, Beijing aims to holistically embed African civil society in its communication channels for long-term, lasting, daily communication and communication to frame China as a friendly, peaceful, attractive, cooperative, and responsible great power. Such message productions subtly express themes not of politics but cultural and social life in most contexts. However, Chinese communicators carry out these activities by abiding by the CPC's public opinion censorship principles. It aims to circulate exclusively positive information on African countries or information with selective truths vis-à-vis specific political/public affairs. Indeed, it is a question of carefully avoiding demeaning subjects on Africa in general, allowing China to ensure local political leaders' support (Thussu 2016).

Like such propaganda, disinformation serves political leadership with charisma. The charismatic leader is placed at the center of the narrative and above institutions, and confers stability to the aforementioned society by giving meaning to three questions: who we are as a nation, why we are important to the world, and where is our future going (Wivel and Grøn 2021). Disinformation diplomacy is emotional and therefore allows a) history to explain contemporary problems and draw lessons from the past, even if not in an imprecise or legendary way; b) causal analyses based on perception, values, and morals, so that affronts are not objectifiable; and c) symbolic and performative solutions rather than sustainable agreements or alliances. Populist leaders foster the atavistic tendency to tribalism by highlighting the morality that polarizes one group with another on the basis of a value system (Waisbord 2018). To promote leadership, disinformation generates emotions (admiration, respect, but also hatred or fear). Given the approach, disinformation contributes to symbolic violence or rhetorical coercion (Krebs and Jackson 2007). This leap toward argumentative or verbal pressure conflates actual and representational sociopolitical forces (Mattern 2005). Coercion generates fear and impacts the ideas and beliefs of an audience which is predisposed to support or resist foreign policy decisions (Graham 2014). Disinformation, then, does not achieve specific policy objectives, but rather prepares audiences for a series of decisions.

Cull (2019) has coined the term "reputational security," which advocates a defensive interpretation of international communication. In the current context, reputational security represents a change in the ethos of diplomacy. The priority for most states is security, legitimacy, and defense of territorial integrity. Disinformation is used to blur international communication and place in the global imaginary a catalog of political demands, which include the defense of certain values and the capacity to lead alternative multilateral projects. China gives another good example. China has expanded its actions to "tell the story well" and position itself as a dominant alternative to the dominant United States. It aims to build a reputation based on positive values and long-term stable relationships to accompany investments, especially in Africa and Latin America. Media acquisition pursues integration into the local culture and attention to the Chinese diaspora. Russia operates in another political dimension. It is not interested in reputation management vis-à-vis Western countries or institutions, but in reinforcing an internal message of pride and belonging. Thus the idea of "Russkiy Mir" and "compatriot" is understood as an emotional response, not as a journalistic discourse. The nostalgic narrative seeks to discredit the EU or NATO in order to set itself up as the only authority in the ex-Soviet space, a spatial logic based on geopolitics and security. Chaos is the message in the face of the strengths of Vladimir Putin's presidentialism. Both countries have deployed their strategy in networks and digital media with a customized message for different audiences. They share the adaptation to digital culture with campaigns designed for rapid expansion in different formats and platforms. Both have weakened the independent journalistic ecosystem with the erosion of freedoms with the argument of security.

Challenges

Disinformation poses four challenges. The first is the naturalization of antidiplomatic behavior, the breakdown of the ethical framework of relations between actors. The erosion of credibility (expertise, trust, goodwill) affects institutions, which operate in a scenario of growing distrust. This approach hinders the exercise of diplomatic functions under the Vienna Convention (1961), as disinformation professionals are accredited with diplomatic protection (see the cross-accusations between the Russian and German governments regarding the real role of the RT and DW television stations (Bahgat 2022)). International and national laws (data protection, privacy, electoral interference) have been violated; propaganda and the discrediting of interlocutors and their requests have hindered negotiations; hate speech and other aggressive statements have hindered friendly relations and have discredited traditional mediators (journalists, artists, creative professionals). The ethical circulation of information affects the exercise of diplomatic and consular functions, which have become more subordinated to other foreign policy objectives. The consequences on the ground affect the diplomatic profession, which operates in two scenarios, one of factual facts (government instructions, *notes verbales*, accountability, relations with the accrediting country) and the other of communication management (production of messages for local and international audiences). Disinformation separates the two functions with dire consequences for professional diplomacy.

The second element is the struggle with misinformation. The use of emotional arguments represents a substantial shift in argumentation. Persuasion is not based on arguments, facts, and data, but on the ability to generate a discourse that interests the audience. Thus, disinformation based on stories that polarize the audience, nostalgic arguments based on traumas of history and other mechanisms alien to rational use multiply. The emotional approach promotes polarization (for or against vaccines, Russian aggression, or negotiation in Venezuela) without nuance.

In the fight against both misinformation and disinformation, the production of sound and objective counter-information is not enough. An active role of societies is necessary: "these values—including polarization—are there before disinformation arrives" (Gerrits 2018). Disinformation acts as a social parasite that radicalizes pre-existing problems. The success of disinformation lies in the fact that it provides each social group with a solution to their concerns, so it focuses its communication strategies on confirming cognitive bias. Disinformation hardly changes the opinion of those affected. On the contrary, it seeks to reaffirm one's own beliefs and generate doubts about the dissemination of reliable information. Thus, the inaccuracy or the "drop of poison" contaminates the information source and the population becomes infected because it is shared on social networks, self-convinced of the informative value of the tweet or message. It is not necessary to intervene in the entire information chain; it is enough to introduce some messages into the public conversation.

An analysis of disinformation serves to define the pattern. The growing sense of inequality and partisan polarization facilitate the entry of divisive messages with concrete effects on institutional or political credibility. News distributed by RT and Sputnik on European affairs, for example, accentuates political divisions and lack of unity in institutions. The tangle of bots creates a divisive narrative on social media and the media itself echoes the controversy. Sponsored tweets and content contribute to the speculation, as well as their distribution in newspaper chains in countries with deficiencies in the media industry. The process legitimizes the origin of the information before the audience ("foreign media") contributes to the echo chamber with the same arguments against European policies. The digital dimension makes it difficult to monitor and evaluate Russian disinformation.

On this information front, the European Union has taken several decisions and implemented joint action plans. In 2015, the East StratCom Task Force was created to systematically respond to the attacks following the invasion of Crimea. The reference service, available in digital format, is *Disinformation Review*, which lists Russian actions on EU territory. In 2018, the EU recognized disinformation as the "biggest challenge" and Russia as the "biggest threat" (European Commission 2018a). The EU has accused Russia of waging disinformation campaigns that are "systematic, well-resourced, and with different scales of impact" (European Commission 2018b). The European Parliament has also pointed out the need to push for a legal doctrine at the international level to prevent disinformation and cyber weapons from becoming tools of destabilization in the service of the Russian Federation (2016). In February 2022, the European Commission took a further step in this fight. It banned the distribution of RT and Sputnik signals because it considers these TV channels to be part of the Russian propaganda strategy and, in times of war, to be linked to defense operations.

The Russian challenge connects with the third diplomatic element. The securitization of freedom of expression has led to a zero-sum calculus that hinders the exercise of journalism, particularly as regards government criticism. This too is part of a decline of digital freedom (Freedom House 2017). Legislative action allows the control of content and the restriction of freedoms under different political and legal standards. China and Russia are entrepreneurs of anti-digital freedom norms that flout those standards by alternative security framing (Finnemore and Hollis 2016; Flonk 2021). Both countries see security as a performative act. The mere classification of an event as affecting "national security" anticipates an agenda of political performances and behaviors (Buzan et al. 1997). The performance obliges the identification of the authorities responsible for subduing the threat, the singling out of enemies, the restrictive measures against the conventional order, the extension of the policy of exceptionality, the constitution of emergency powers (state of alarm, siege, war, emergency), and the limitation of individual liberties. In short, all that is a transformational act. The threat value works to articulate a successful discourse that prioritizes security over the rights and freedoms of the individual, including in cybersecurity and data protection. A review of current measures points to a push for this approach without proper institutional and journalistic counterweights. In the international scene, securitization signals an enemy, or more precisely, a "friend/enemy" dichotomy. In the internal politics, the phenomenon allows the identification of a common public good of an abstract nature (security, homeland, culture, identity) from which emanate principles and behaviors to adhere to. COVID-19 too has provided insight into how public health issues are constructed as security threats and subsequent extraordinary measures with less political control (Kirk and McDonald 2021).

In the context of falsehood, diplomats have the opportunity to regain spheres of influence and exercise their power of mediation. In global affairs, one works with a sensitive capital that is trust, which is damaged by fake news and the flood of propaganda in the form of bots and trolls. International trust is earned through the defense of a specific position, the veracity of the technical information and facts being promoted, as well as consistency between word and action. Trust is not earned through advertising campaigns or isolated tweets, but through recurrent participation in the international digital arena. In an environment of uncertainty and specific or recurring problems, the international relations professional is a reliable articulator of messages, a connector of public and private interests, a creator of narratives and arguments. On the audience side, on the other hand, the international relations professional can contribute to education and media literacy. Global issues are complex, so it is important to identify sound sources, provide technical specificities, and use an informative language, neither expert nor ambiguous. Against the profusion of alternative facts and the pernicious use of artificial intelligence, this task will be multilevel, public and private, with governments, technology multinationals, users, and academics.

Conclusion

Disinformation is a transformative phenomenon in diplomacy. There is no consensus on the definition of disinformation. Without a joint definition, diplomatic actors cannot move forward in the search for solutions. The United Nations General Assembly resolution 76/227 on "Countering disinformation for the promotion and protection of human rights and fundamental freedoms" is ambiguous and lacks the necessary force to address the problem. The Human Rights Council (A/HRC/49/L.31/Rev.1) links disinformation with the devaluation of human rights. Within UNESCO, a basic response is agreed upon, consisting of training journalists, supporting community journalism, media literacy, and the provision of public information (UNESCO 2022). Thus, diplomatic solutions reflect a growing division of the world into geopolitical blocs. Of particular note are the EU's East StratCom Task Force, NATO's StratCom Center of Excellence, and the Helsinki Hybrid Center of Excellence. In the G7, cyberthreats and disinformation point to Russia as the main adversary. In contrast, the G20 has failed to put the issue on the agenda on a regular basis. The United States has strengthened its capabilities through the Global Engagement Center and the U.S. Agency for Global Media. Sweden has launched the Swedish Psychological Defense Agency, which brings together military, media, and academic actors to promote media literacy, detect fake news, and help citizens. This model is in line with the growth in the number of civil society actors contributing to the fight against disinformation. Among the most relevant are Bellingcat, the Alliance for Security Democracy's Hamilton 68 (German Marshall Foundation), and EU DisinfoLab. In short, the tension between freedom of expression and censorship has jeopardized international action while divisions caused by Russia's invasion of Ukraine make global diplomatic efforts to discuss disinformation unlikely. Multilateralism is penalized and individual actions reflect largely unilateral action and defense, but not the protection of the global public good that is information.

Public theoretical construction fades in the face of a changing political and information system in which ministries and diplomats compete for audience attention, narrative construction, and news dissemination (Golan et al. 2019). There is increasing pressure on statements and negotiations, already public in nature, and operating in real time in the new media ecology (Manor and Crilley 2020). The offensive use of disinformation is sanctioned in the management of political warfare and has opened a new stage in the study of international communication, public diplomacy, and propaganda where emotions predominate (Solomon 2014; Nisbet and Kamenchuk 2019). Since the legal system in most countries protects freedom of expression, censorship is a path contrary to democratic political principles, yet the attitude of audiences varies depending on who distributes, produces, or pays for the information. Lying does not build one's own side's credibility, but it does weaken that of the opponent and therefore enhances the vulnerability of audiences in general through representational force (Entman 2008; Mattelart and Koch 2016).

Mediated diplomacy also deinstitutionalizes official channels (heads of state and government, chancelleries) and increases the number of actors who claim official legitimacy. The more actors that participate in the conversation about diplomatic policy, the more complex it becomes. In this space, misinformation finds gaps in the public conversation. The gaps are in tune with the non-material demands of de-globalization (identity, homeland, nation, religion) and with the breakdown of the local/global divide in international communication. Disinformation therefore increases the noise in the political environment. The assignment of political and diplomatic responsibilities to non-government actors, such as journalistic companies, think tanks, or virtual communities, makes for a broader field of action than conventional propaganda (Cull 2019).

The narratives of variable international legitimacy project values and defend foreign policies. Populist practice has consolidated such legitimacy with the cult of personality (Cooper 2019). As opposed to propaganda, the disinformative narrative projects proposals and ideas into the future on non-factual epistemological grounds. This narrative is not explanatory or argumentative, but visionary about the future, which allows the inclusion of an important moral variable.

As a consequence, disinformation is structured as a polysemic phenomenon in which stories, campaigns, and operations converge (la Cour 2020). Isolated stories contribute to the spread of hoaxes and the weakness of official sources in order to construct an alternative and polarizing narrative. In short, disinformation affects the foundations of diplomatic relations and calls out for a strategic review. Both foreign ministries and multilateral institutions should devote more time and resources to thinking about and responding to the challenge with measures, normative actions, and training, as well as active communication strategies aimed at engagement with digital society. This shift will affect diplomatic practice.

It is important to be well versed in the management of disinformation to protect national and international interests, as well as general ethics. The desire to mislead, profit, or deceive through the production and dissemination of manipulated or false information makes it difficult for political actors to talk to each other. Without mutual trust, diplomacy cannot move forward. This is not to indulge in wishy-washy idealism: diplomats defend the interest of one party, not all. However, if they engage in lying, it is difficult to establish avenues for collaboration. The last element to consider is the measurement of results. In democratic societies, the fight against disinformation generates fatigue in the political system, because it touches on freedom of expression and other ethical goods. Therefore, measures must be cautious in order to rebuild public trust.

References and Further Reading

Amado, A. 2016. *Política pop: de líderes populistas a telepresidentes*. Buenos Aires: Ariel.

Arendt, H. 1967. "Truth and Politics." *New Yorker*, February 17. https://www.newyorker.com/magazine/1967/02/25/truth-and-politics.

Bahgat, F. 2022. "DW's Moscow Bureau Closes after Russian Ban." *Deutsche Welle*, February 4. https://www.dw.com/en/dws-moscow-bureau-closes-after-russian-ban/a-60657233.

Bakshy, E., S. Messing, and L.A. Adamic. 2015. "Exposure to Ideologically Diverse News and Opinion on Facebook," *Science* 348 (6239): 1130–32.

Benkler, Y., R. Faris, and H. Roberts. 2018. *Network Propaganda: Manipulation, Disinformation, and Radicalization in American Politics*. New York: Oxford University Press.

Bennett, W.L., and S. Livingston. 2018. "The Disinformation Order: Disruptive Communication and the Decline of Democratic Institutions." *European Journal of Communication* 33 (2): 122–39.

Buzan, B., O. Waever, and J. de Wilde. 1997. *Security: A New Framework for Analysis*. Boulder: Lynne Rienner.

Carlson, M. 2017. "Facebook in the News: Social Media, Journalism, and Public Responsibility Following the 2016 Trending Topics Controversy." *Digital Journalism* 6 (1): 4–20.

Cavazos, A. 2019. *The Economic Cost of Bad Actors on the Internet*. Baltimore: CHEQ/University of Baltimore.

Chadwick, A. 2017. *The Hybrid Media System: Politics and Power*. Oxford: Oxford University Press.

Cooper, A.F. 2019. "Adapting Public Diplomacy to the Populist Challenge." *The Hague Journal of Diplomacy* 14 (1–2): 36–50.

Cull, N.J. 2019. *Public Diplomacy: Foundations for Global Engagement in the Digital Age*. Cambridge: Polity.

Der Derian, J. 1987. *On Diplomacy: A Genealogy of Western Estrangement*. Oxford: Blackwell.

Ecker, U.K.H., S. Lewandowsky, J. Cook, P. Schmid, L.K. Fazio, N. Brashier, and M.A. Amazeen. 2022. "The Psychological Drivers of Misinformation Belief and Its Resistance to Correction." *Nature Reviews Psychology* 1 (1): 13–29.

Elswah, M., and P.N. Howard. 2020. "Anything that Causes Chaos: The Organizational Behavior of *Russia Today (RT)*." *Journal of Communication* 70 (5): 623–45.

Entman, R.M. 2008. "Theorizing Mediated Public Diplomacy: The U.S. Case." *International Journal of Press/Politics* 13 (2): 87–102.

European Commission. 2018a. Joint Communication to the European Parliament, the European Council, the Council, the European Economic and Social Committee and the Committee of the Regions. "Tackling Online Disinformation: A European Approach." Brussels, April 26. https://eur-lex.europa.eu/legal-content/EN/TXT/PDF/?uri=CELEX: 52018DC0236&from=EN.

———. 2018b. Joint Communication to the European Parliament, the European Council, the Council, The European Economic and Social Committee and the Committee of the Regions. "Action Plan Against Disinformation." Brussels, December 5. https://eeas.europa.eu/sites/eeas/files/action_plan_against_disinformation.pdf.

Eurostat News. 2021. "How Many People Verified Online Information in 2021?" December 16. https://ec.europa.eu/eurostat/web/products-eurostat-news/-/ddn-20211216-3.

Finnemore, M., and D.B. Hollis. 2016. "Constructing Norms for Global Cybersecurity." *American Journal of International Law* 110 (3): 425–79.

Flonk, D. 2021. "Emerging Illiberal Norms: Russia and China as Promoters of Internet Content Control." *International Affairs* 97 (6): 1925–44.

Freedom House. 2017. "Freedom on the Net 2017. Manipulating Social Media to Undermine Democracy." https://freedomhouse.org/report/freedom-net/freedom-net-2017.

Gerrits, A.W.M. 2018. "Disinformation in International Relations: How Important Is It?" *Security and Human Rights* 29: 3–23.

Golan, G.J., I. Manor, and P. Arceneaux. 2019. "Mediated Public Diplomacy Redefined: Foreign Stakeholder Engagement via Paid, Earned, Shared, and Owned Media." *American Behavioral Scientist* 63 (12): 1665–83.

Graham, S.E. 2014. "Emotion and Public Diplomacy: Dispositions in International Communications, Dialogue, and Persuasion." *International Studies Review* 16 (4): 522–39.

Huang, Z.A. 2020. "Servir le soft power et la diplomatie publique à la chinoise: Analyse communicationnelle de l'Institut Confucius de l'Université de Nairobi" (These de doctorat, Paris Est). Paris Est, Marne-la-Vallée, France. http://www.theses.fr/2020PESC2022.

———. 2021. "The Confucius Institute and Relationship Management: Uncertainty Management of Chinese Public Diplomacy in Africa." In *Public Diplomacy and the Politics of Uncertainty*, eds. P. Surowiec and I. Manor, 197–223. Cham: Springer International Publishing.

Huang, Z.A., and M. Hardy. 2019. "#Guanxi @ChineAfrique: La mobilisation des relations interpersonnelles dans la diplomatie publique chinoise à l'heure de numérique." *MEI.Médiation et Information* 48: 75–86.

Jeangène Vilmer, J.B. 2021. *Effective State Practices against Disinformation: Four Country Case Studies*. Hybrid CoE Research Report 2. Helsinki: The European Centre of Excellence for Countering Hybrid Threats.

Kirk, J., and M. McDonald. 2021. "The Politics of Exceptionalism: Securitization and COVID-19." *Global Studies Quarterly* 1 (3): 1–12.

Krebs, R.R., and P.T. Jackson. 2007. "Twisting Tongues and Twisting Arms: The Power of Political Rhetoric." *European Journal of International Relations* 13 (1): 35–66.

Krieg-Planque, A. 2009. *La notion de formule en analyse du discours: Cadre théorique et méthodologique*. Besançon: Presses Universitaires de Franche-Comté.

La Cour, C. 2020. "Theorising Digital Disinformation in International Relations." *International Politics* 57: 704–23.

Lanoszka, A. 2019. "Disinformation in International Politics." *European Journal of International Security* 4: 227–48.

Manfredi-Sánchez, J.-L., A. Amado-Suárez, and S. Waisbord. 2021. "Presidential Twitter in the Face of COVID-19: Between Populism and Pop Politics." *Comunicar* 29 (66): 83–94.

Manor, I., and R. Crilley. 2020. "The Mediatisation of MFAS: Diplomacy in the New Media Ecology." *The Hague Journal of Diplomacy* 15 (1/2): 66–92.

Mattelart, T., and O. Koch, eds. 2016. *Géopolitique des télévisions transnationales d'information*. Paris: Mare et Martin Editions.

Mattern, J.B. 2005. "Why 'Soft Power' Isn't So Soft: Representational Force and the Sociolinguistic Construction of Attraction in World Politics." *Millennium* 33 (3): 583–612.

McIntyre, L. 2018. *Post-truth*. Cambridge, MA: MIT Press.

Ministry of Commerce, People's Republic of China. 2021. Notice on Publicizing the List of National Cultural Export Key Enterprises and Key Projects in 2021–22, July 27. http://www.mofcom.gov.cn/article/gztz/tzbjg/202107/20210703180727.shtml.

Nisbet, E.C., and O. Kamenchuk. 2019. "The Psychology of State-sponsored Disinformation Campaigns and Implications for Public Diplomacy." *The Hague Journal of Diplomacy* 14: 65–82.

Pamment, J. 2014. "The Mediatization of Diplomacy." *The Hague Journal of Diplomacy* 9 (3): 253–80.

Powers, S., and M. Kounalakis. 2017. *Can Public Diplomacy Survive the Internet?: Bots, Echo Chambers, and Disinformation*. Washington, D.C.: U.S. Advisory Commission on Public Diplomacy.

Price, M. 2015. *Free Expression, Globalism and the New Strategic Communication*. New York: Cambridge University Press.

Rathbun, B.C. 2007. "Uncertain about Uncertainty: Understanding the Multiple Meanings of a Crucial Concept in International Relations Theory." *International Studies Quarterly* 51 (3): 533–57.

Rønning, H. 2016. "How Much Soft Power Does China Have in Africa?" In *China's Media and Soft Power in Africa*, eds. X. Zhang, H. Wasserman, and W. Mano, 65–78. London: Palgrave Macmillan.

Roselle, L. 2010. "Strategic Narratives of War: Fear of Entrapment and Abandonment during Protracted Conflict" (SSRN Scholarly Paper No. ID 1643331). Rochester: Social Science Research Network. https://papers.ssrn.com/abstract=1643331.

Schneider, M. 2015. "Mobilising the Masses: A Grass-roots Communication Strategy for TTIP." *European View* 14 (2): 201–7.

Solomon, T. 2014. "The Affective Underpinnings of Soft Power." *European Journal of International Relations* 20 (3): 720–41.

Szostek, J. 2014. "Russia and the News Media in Ukraine: A Case of 'Soft Power'?" *East European Politics and Societies* 28 (3): 463–86.

Thussu, D. 2016. "The Scramble for Asian Soft Power in Africa." *Les Enjeux de l'information et de La Communication* 2 (17): 225–37.

Turner, J.H. 1988. *A Theory of Social Interaction*. Stanford: Stanford University Press.

UNESCO. 2022. *Journalism Is a Public Good: World Trends in Freedom of Expression and Media Development*. Global Report 2021/2022. Paris: UNESCO.

Waisbord, S. 2018. "The Elective Affinity between Post-truth Communication and Populist Politics." *Communication Research and Practice* 4 (1): 17–34.

Wardle, C., and H. Derakhshan. 2017. *Information Disorder: Toward an Interdisciplinary Framework for Research and Policy Making*. Informe al Consejo de Europa. https://shorensteincenter.org/information-disorder-framework-for-research-and-policymaking.

Wivel, A., and C.H. Grøn. 2021. "Charismatic Leadership in Foreign Policy." *International Affairs* 92 (2): 365–83.

Xu, W.W., and R. Wang. 2022. "Nationalizing Truth: Digital Practices and Influences of State-affiliated Media in a Time of Global Pandemic and Geopolitical Decoupling." *International Journal of Communication* 16: 356–84.

Yablokov, I. 2015. "Conspiracy Theories as a Russian Public Diplomacy Tool: The Case of *Russia Today (RT)*." *Politics* 35 (3–4): 301–15.

Zhang, X., H. Wasserman, and W. Mano, eds. 2016. *China's Media and Soft Power in Africa: Promotion and Perceptions*. London: Palgrave Macmillan.

20

Digitalizing South American MFAs: Reform and Resistance

Jorge Heine and Daniel Aguirre

Latin America's international self-image has traditionally been that of the "middle-class of nations" (Orrego 1975). This would place it somewhere between the developed, mostly North Atlantic countries, on the one hand, and those of Africa and Asia, on the other. This comfortable role, modest enough not to threaten anyone, yet sufficiently rewarding to allow for a certain degree of smugness and self-satisfaction, is now contested, as the region slides downhill in its international standing. From representing 12 percent of world exports in 1955, Latin America represents less than half of that in 2021, 5.6 percent. With the rise of China and India, and the growing international role of ASEAN, the notion that in any hierarchical ordering of continents, Asia would rank below Latin America would strike most observers as wrong—after all, there is a reason why it is said that this will be the "Asian century." In turn, according to several indicators that measure degree of internationalization, Africa is also starting to leave Latin America behind (González et al. 2021). If anything, the COVID-19 pandemic, of which Latin America, with 8 percent of the world's population and 30 percent of the world's deaths from it, became effectively Ground Zero, and would seem to confirm this diagnosis

J. Heine (✉)
Boston University, Boston, MA, USA

D. Aguirre
Arizona State University, Tempe, AZ, USA

of downward mobility among the world's regions, as Latin America is displaced from the periphery to the margins of the international system (Malacalza 2021).

This was not always so. The early national experiences of Argentina and Brazil offer evidence of considerable influence within fledgling international systems. In the late nineteenth century, the United States was at one point concerned about the rise of Chile as a Pacific power that could threaten Washington's own role in the Asia-Pacific region (Burr 1974). The first Pan-American institutions at the turn of the twentieth century showed an active Latin American diplomacy in which the region's states dealt with the United States as equals (Hart 2013; Cull 2018; Schindler 2018). In effect, both world wars and the post-World War II emergence of U.S. power in world affairs point to an engagement with the region predicated on the notion of seeking mutual support with the region's leading powers, including Mexico, and some South American nations. Latin American participation in the establishment of a multilateral order, via the League of Nations first and the United Nations later (at which point, Latin American countries made up 40 percent of the United Nations founding members), reflected the response of a Latin American elite that found partnership with the great powers in that endeavor, as well as the creation of a rules-based order, very much to their advantage.

In turn, the emergence, in the 1960s, of dependency theory, arguably Latin America's single most important contribution to the social sciences, reflected the degree to which the region felt the imprint of its condition of underdevelopment, yet one still torn between the First and the Third Worlds. Once the United States consolidated its unrivaled global role, Latin America's pivot to the developing world shifted from the intellectual sphere (Fajardo 2022) to that of direct action (e.g., Cuba in Africa). Strategies to engage the world included regional integration schemes, a search for autonomy, and partnership with emerging actors and reemerging global powers such as China.

This "intersectionality" of Latin America, firmly part of the Global South according to most indicators, yet still longing for the days when it considered itself a sort of European bastion in the New World, offers some insights into the conduct of its diplomacy. Special attention deserves the sparks of diplomatic resourcefulness to be found within claustrophobic, self-contained institutions with a strong corporativist and bureaucratic bent. In the past decade, MFAs in the region, while still constrained by traditions and established modus operandi, did experience a wave of moderate modernization in matters of digital diplomacy via loose, and in rare cases, formalized processes of reform. This chapter draws on interviews done by one of the authors with diplomats from Argentina, Brazil, Chile, and Peru in 2016–18. Despite a strong aversion to change, some progress took place.

We frame these changes within the broader shift from club to network diplomacy (Heine 2008, 2013). This means the switch from the practice of statecraft within a small circle of diplomats, policymakers, and selected members of the local elite, to a much broader group of people, including civil society, political parties, trade unions, and NGOs. This reflects the changing realities and expectations of democratic societies, and the demand for transparency and accountability that permeates today's world. Far from being limited to his or her office and elegant salons, contemporary diplomats are supposed to reach out deep into the host societies to regions, provinces, and towns to convey and project his or her country's message. In the digital age, this entails the deployment of digital tools: most prominently, but not exclusively, social media.

The rise of digital diplomacy has gone hand in hand with the resurgence of public diplomacy (PD) that has taken place after 9/11 (Melissen 2005). Yet, although PD has come into its own in many countries around the world, especially in North Atlantic nations, and in a few rising powers, it has not really taken off in Latin America. Seen as propaganda by some traditional diplomats, and thus alien to the practice of statecraft, the last thing resource-starved MFAs want to do is to engage in expensive PD campaigns that would divert budgetary allocations from the bread-and-butter of diplomacy. It is in this context that the emergence of digital diplomacy posed a special challenge. In an increasingly competitive media environment, in which traditional media was being partly displaced by the new digital tools, the *blasé* attitude toward communicating the country's key foreign policy objectives became unsustainable. In a competitive international environment, digital can no longer be ignored.

What are some of South America's leading nations doing to bring their MFAs up to speed in the digital age? Are they embracing digital diplomacy to deal more effectively with an inhospitable environment, or is this very upgrading exercise itself falling victim to some of the same forces that have been pulling the region down, including inertia, bureaucratic sclerosis, and resistance to innovation?

To answer these questions this chapter is organized as follows: the first section examines the rationale behind the initial digitalization impetus; the second surveys the state of play after the proliferation of a number of digital tools and resources in order to ascertain the degree to which the global transition to network diplomacy identified by Heine has expressed itself in the modernization efforts of South American MFAs, and particularly in the shift toward digital diplomacy, in Argentina, Brazil, Chile, and Peru; the third section looks at organizational and cultural variables, and the disruption digitalization has brought to club diplomacy and established MFA mores. The fourth section deals with the by now formalized ways in which digital diplomacy is currently present within the MFAs in question. This chapter concludes with a summary of the findings and observations from Twitter data, interviews conducted in the various MFAs, and Jorge Heine's own perceptions as a participant-observer, while head of mission from 2014 to 2017, at a time when the Chilean MFA made its first forays into digital diplomacy.

Digitalizing Diplomatic Practices

In Everett Rogers' (1962) seminal work on the diffusion of innovations, a typology of "entities" explains how new practices and tools are incorporated over time in organizations. Rogers distinguishes between Innovators, Early Adopters, Early Majority, Late Majority, and Laggards. The adoption of digital diplomacy in these South American MFAs provides us with a revealing case study of how a key innovation such as digital diplomacy has expanded (or not) in them. Digital diplomacy, by which we mean the use of social media platforms as well as other digital tools in the conduct of statecraft, is especially relevant in this regard. This is not simply another, albeit more efficient communication tool in the diplomatic kit. Far from being just another instrument (as, one might say, the telephone was in its day), digital diplomacy has in some ways arguably altered the fundamental manner by which business is conducted in diplomacy. The WhatsApp groups with which many diplomatic entities instantly communicate with each other are but one example of this transformation.

In some ways, though, it is Twitter that epitomizes the tension between traditional and digital diplomacy. The social media platform, launched in 2006, originally limited to 140 characters (now 280), asks a simple question: "What's Happening?" allowing users to vent on all matters under the sun. Given that the whole idea is to reach more people rather than fewer, a premium is placed on being as funny, provocative, and unpredictable as possible. The greater the provocation, the bigger the response. This mixes uneasily with diplomacy as we have known it. Humor in statecraft seldom works. Provocation is considered unfriendly. And predictability is considered the ultimate diplomatic virtue. All of this is added to the compressed and immediate nature of tweets, so different from the long-form and reflective character of that long-established genre, the diplomatic cable (Heine and Turcotte 2012). Not surprisingly, many diplomats were reluctant to join Twitter. Yet today, Twitter, though by no means as widely used as other social media platforms, remains in many ways the platform of choice of many diplomats.

In terms of the rise of digital tools, one could arguably identify three key moments: 1) the emergence of the internet in the mid-1990s, and the associated widespread use of e-mail as the leading communications tool; 2) the advent of social media—especially Twitter in 2006 (Heine and Turcotte 2012); and 3) the COVID-19 pandemic in 2020, with its widespread disruption of travel, in-person meetings, and the analog world in general (Riordan 2020). What until then had been a slow trickle of digitalization in diplomacy, suddenly became a flood, as virtual meetings became the rule. Many of the trusted verities of traditional diplomacy ("look your counterpart in the eye"; "check how firm his/her handshake is"; "invite him/her to a few drinks") were evidently thrown out the window, and there was no alternative but to adapt to this brave new world.

As argued elsewhere (Aguirre et al. 2018a, 2018b; Aguirre 2020), the digitalization of politics with the rise of social media soon spread globally as campaigning and fundraising via online platforms became the norm. Experimentation with online voting albeit with mixed outcomes was part of this "digital boom" that enthralled candidates for office and political consultants alike. Taking cues from President Obama's use of digital tools in his campaigns (Hayden 2011) and the U.S. State Department's digital diplomacy offensive (Cull 2013; Brown and Hensman 2014), Latin American politicians followed suit. Thus, Latin American presidential candidates and presidents themselves embraced Twitter in the late-2000s. MFAs did not take long to catch up, but institutional followership remained modest in relation to presidential accounts. Hampered by institutional rigidities, ministerial accounts had trouble in gaining traction. Digital diplomacy made headway mostly via individual ambassadors, with more personalized approaches. The result was the creation of "influencers" within the foreign policy sphere but aiming at both domestic and international publics. MFAs' social media accounts themselves at times had most of their interactions with its own nationals, breaking the mold of conventional public diplomacy exercises.

In short, the second decade of the new century ushered in the use of a variety of social media platforms by Latin American MFAs and diplomats. Still, Twitter remains the "indispensable" one in the region. As shown in Table 20.1, in Argentina, Brazil, Chile, and Peru, 60 percent or more of content posted in social media by their MFAs was via Twitter. Among the four, Peru is the one that has diversified the most, adding Facebook and Instagram to its regular use. In the case of the three other countries, MFAs prefer Twitter seven to eight

Table 20.1 Platform use for digital diplomacy 2021

Country MFA	Posts Twitter	Posts Facebook	Instagram	Total social media footprint	Percent Twitter	Percent Facebook	Percent Instagram
Brazil	1994	302	258	2554	78	12	10
Peru	1459	553	402	2414	60	23	17
Argentina	1117	218	117	1452	77	15	8
Chile	981	339	41	1361	72	25	3

Source: The authors

times out of ten of their total social media postings. That said, even to get to this level of relatively low digital diplomacy development has been a struggle.

Resisting Change

In some ways, the structure of MFAs is akin to that of military organizations. Their vertical nature entails written and unwritten rules. The former mostly follow and make explicit certain expectations about functions within globally established diplomatic conventions. They have been implemented over decades, are guided by the Vienna Conventions, and are reflected in routinized practices woven into the fabric of these organizations. In this context, some MFAs stand out as reference points. Itamaraty, the colloquial name (after the palace of its original headquarters in Rio de Janeiro) by which the Brazilian MFA is referred to, is considered the epitome of what a foreign ministry should be.[1] Its sheer size (with some 4000 officers), generous budget (which allowed it to have at one point in the second term of President Lula, 2007–11, 35 embassies in Africa, more than the UK), and high degree of institutional autonomy make it the envy of its counterparts in the rest of the region.

Itamaraty's rigorous selection process and high-quality training have cemented its prestige, attracting the country's best and brightest. The corporate spirit of the Brazilian foreign service is such that the expectation is that, not only will *all* ambassadors be recruited from its ranks (leaving almost no room for political appointees—the latter being an established practice in most other MFAs in the region), but that even the foreign minister himself will be a career diplomat. This has been the case during much of the past 35 years, that is, ever since Brazil's transition to democracy in 1985 (Gobo and Santos

---

[1] See the chapter by Farias and Lessa in this volume.

2022). Taking this one step further, Brazilian presidents will sometimes pick career diplomats and appoint them as cabinet ministers in other portfolios, a telling indicator of their standing. The corporate spirit of the Brazilian Foreign Service, in turn, translates into an insular diplomatic culture. Arguably, Brazil's very size and global aspirations fully justify such a grand undertaking, although recent crises and the international *capitis diminutio* Brazil experienced under Jair Bolsonaro mean whatever weight and leadership in the region and in the Global South Brazil would like to bank on in the present are based more on its past than on its current standing (Peron and Perreira 2018; Pestana 2020).

At a smaller scale, yet similarly structured, the Peruvian MFA, known as Torre Tagle, after the name of the palace it is headquartered in Lima, shares some of the features of Brazilian diplomatic institutions and organizational culture. A carefully guarded institutional autonomy, a quasi-monopoly on head-of-mission appointments, and a strong preference for foreign ministers from the foreign service itself, can all be found in Torre Tagle. Vertically organized and command-driven, its directors and high-ranking officials supervise large staffs, with the latter expected to seek clearance on almost every single action, however minute. Peruvian diplomacy, similarly to Brazil's, enjoys a high standing in the region, due to its effectiveness, organizational outputs, and an active agenda that make it punch above its weight in regional and global affairs. In the case of both Brazil and of Peru, distinctive cultural identities provide them with a level of differentiation they have been able to translate into considerable soft power resources. Few other Latin American countries have been able to deploy such soft power, with the partial exceptions of Mexico and, to a lesser degree, of Colombia. Peru has been especially adept at mobilizing "gastrodiplomacy" (the use of a country's cuisine to promote its image abroad; see Wilson 2013), building on its strong and highly sophisticated culinary traditions, and making the most of this fast-growing specialty in diplomatic studies (Rockower 2012; Mendelson Forman 2016).

A very different picture is the one provided by the Chilean MFA. On the one hand, over the past thirty years, Chile has built up quite a record of foreign policy accomplishments, both on matters like international trade (with the highest number of foreign trade agreements signed by any country) and in multilateral fora. In this, presidential leadership and competent foreign ministers, many of them professional IR scholars, have played a key role. A remarkable foreign policy continuity, especially in the 1990–2018 period, across governments from different ruling coalitions, also helped. On the other hand, severe budgetary constraints, and self-imposed administrative limitations (like the absence of a mandatory retirement age and a fixed number of ambassadors), as well as a rigid and highly centralized structure in which many decisions can only be taken by the minister, have meant bureaucratic bottlenecks and an increasingly unwieldy apparatus. A modest reform approved in 2018 did little to change this. In this context, individual initiatives to circumvent formal channels to engage in newer practices, such as digital diplomacy, until the rest of the organization catches up, have emerged as an alternative to following anachronistic rules and conventions. Lone wolves and complementary issue-specific agencies arose to deal with and to anticipate new agendas. Thus, a number of ambassadors were given free rein to embark on their own use of various digital platforms, which was especially the case with Twitter. The Press Division, under the office of the Minister, was also empowered to strengthen the Ministry's digital toolkit and outreach.

In some ways, the case of Argentina is the mirror opposite of that of Chile. Over the past thirty years, the foreign policy pendulum has swung from one extreme to the other, from radical Third Worldism on the one hand, to sending warships to support the United States in the first Iraq war, on the other. In this setting, a competent and highly professional body of diplomats has been left to deal with such unpredictable behavior. In the more recent past, this became especially apparent when dealing with the change that took place from President Cristina Fernández (2007–15) to Mauricio Macri (2015–19). As Amorim Neto and Malamud (2020) have shown, this entailed a shift from presidential diplomacy to one that relied more on the MFA. That in turn facilitated change by allowing diplomats to play a larger role in the conduct of foreign policy. While not fleshed out in formal legislation, the Argentine MFA undertook internal restructuring aimed at formally incorporating and promoting the use of digital tools. This led to the creation of an ambassador-led unit to oversee digital and subnational diplomacy initiatives. A larger press unit, to deal with the bigger digital footprint required by hosting the G20 summit in December 2018, was also established. All of this was a major change from a digital diplomacy model driven largely from the Casa Rosada, the Argentine presidential palace, under President Fernández, during her two administrations (Erlandsen and Hernández 2018 in Aguirre et al. 2018a, 2018b; Centurión and López 2019).

Shifting toward the Digital Now

How did digital diplomacy spread in these MFAs? Though more research needs to be done on this question, a key first step was the development or borrowing of manuals on how to manage digital tools. A second one was the enlistment of consultants to provide training on the subject to cadets at diplomatic academies. The expectation was that a newer breed of young diplomats from the junior ranks would bring about organizational change. This stands in stark contrast with, say, the approach of the British FCO, which as early as 2013 had made the use of Twitter mandatory for all heads of mission. Annual meetings of the Latin American diplomatic academies and student exchanges among them also furthered the use of digital tools. These cautious steps reflected the widespread resistance to what were seen as largely frivolous, if not downright alien practices that had little to contribute to the ancient craft of diplomacy. "Why do you spend your time uploading pictures, instead of writing cables, Ambassador?" was the way one old-school diplomat put it to one of the authors of this chapter one morning in Beijing.

Conventions arise from institutionalized practices derived from years of experience in the field. Conventions will often buttress what in foreign policy analysis is referred to as standard operating procedures (SOPs) (Allison and Zelikow 1999). They also interact with organizational culture in a variety of ways. A key role in hindering change and protecting established practices, however idiosyncratic, is played by institutional gatekeepers. Within MFAs, gatekeepers are those that protect the established ways of practicing the ancient craft. They tend to be career FSOs, and their associations of various kinds will often be especially protective of the status quo.

In highly centralized organizations such as the MFAs we are discussing, the role of the minister is critical, and one could think that a change-oriented foreign affairs minister wishing to modernize the foreign policy machinery might bring about major changes by sheer force of will. In practice, it does not work that way. In the case of Chile, for almost thirty years repeated efforts to reform a ministry with an anachronistic structure and a budget dating back to the days of military rule failed. This was not because ministers were not fully aware of the need for reform, but because ministers had no interest in picking a fight with the diplomats' union, ADICA. As mentioned above, the 2018 reform was largely pro forma, elevating the position of the Director General for international economic relations to that of deputy minister, and dealing with several administrative loose ends, but otherwise doing little to solve the underlying organizational and bureaucratic problems of an entity whose design, career structure, and incentive system are steeped in the world of the 1950s. The one thing it did, though, was call for a shift from the existing press division to a strategic communications one designed to deploy digital diplomacy.

In short, the practice of digital diplomacy, in many ways so antithetical to the established ways of statecraft, could not but rub many the wrong way, and the diplomatic establishment in these South American countries has been reluctant to embrace it. This is not surprising. Reservations about adopting digital diplomacy mirror those about adopting network diplomacy (Heine 2008), as it entails leaving the cozy comfort zone of club diplomacy. Again, this shift has meant a supplantation of the traditional club model of diplomacy—wherein diplomats are largely confined to their own peers and fellow government officials—to a network model, which sees diplomats increasingly creating and maintaining relationships with actors outside the immediate diplomatic community.

Assumedly the use of digital tools comes more easily to younger generations more familiar with the second model. In the case of diplomatic cadets and junior diplomats, there was no steep learning curve to master the mechanics of social media platforms like Twitter (let alone TikTok) as was often the case for their less adaptable colleagues. The downside of this was that it raised thorny issues of hierarchy within such vertical entities as MFAs. In addition to this generational push, though, a significant role was played by a few select heads of mission, often political appointees, who made their mark by taking up digital diplomacy *pace* institutional constraints. The bottom-up approach of digitally empowering junior diplomats was complemented by "trickle-down digitalization," with leading ambassadors acting as institutional influencers, legitimizing digital practices at the senior level. This dispensed with the flippant notion of Twiplomacy as a frivolous exercise unsuited to heads of mission.

The networked nature of the Internet allows diplomats to pepper messages with links to longer pieces of writing, video, and audio. The brevity of the medium also means that diplomats can interact with the public without dedicating copious amounts of time to it. In contrast to traditional media, Twitter is also dynamic and interactive. It has the benefit of broadcasting media and of interpersonal communication. Twitter is short, crisp, and informal—precisely the sort of medium favored by the young, although other platforms like TikTok are intruding on its terrain. It also allows diplomats to reach directly to the public of the host country, skipping gatekeepers and intermediaries, like the editors of traditional media.

Continuity within MFAs is provided by the country's declared foreign policy principles and objectives. A certain set of issues is defined and pursued across different administrations, making it possible to support and enhance diplomatic action and interaction with their counterparts. This provides a set of behaviors that can be anticipated by others, with predictability being a prized diplomatic virtue. That said, you can have too much of a good thing, and an excessive emphasis on continuity stifles innovation. In the case of

Chile, this is epitomized by the term *política de Estado*, the notion that "politics stops at the water's edge," and that the give-and-take of domestic politics does not apply to the realm of foreign policy. Yet, while there is much to be said for foreign policy continuity, an associated danger is that of a "package deal," in which both substance and form go together, producing a traditional approach to the conduct of foreign policy, with procedures that do not reflect current realities and are not responsive to a rapidly changing environment. This has been one of the obstacles to the deployment of digital diplomacy. The latter requires a nimbleness and flexibility that is not just alien to traditional statecraft but seen by some as the exact opposite of it. To a certain degree, all four countries defined for a time certain issues as untouchable (such as *política de Estado* and how to pursue it). This, in turn, is associated with a set of do's and don'ts as interpreted by diplomats and MFA staff (with a strong emphasis on the "don'ts"). In a sense "don't veer off" our conventions and established practices.

In this context, it is high-ranking officials within the MFA that have the most significant political capital to spend on digital diplomacy. Thus, well-established ambassadors, and a few mid-to-high level FSOs, were active on various social media platforms, tweeting or posting on topics related to their country or on international affairs more generally. This made them into de facto enterprising diplomatic agents. In addition, a group of lower-level diplomats argued in favor of digital practices and championed them in various ways, including from the Diplomatic Academy. These "early adopters," borrowing Rogers' terminology, were relatively few, and some ended up engaging in more exchanges with fellow diplomats from other countries, rather than with everyday citizens—in other words, in a sort of networked club diplomacy.

A hitherto understudied aspect is that of the digital interaction of diplomats with citizens of their home countries—not on, say consular matters, an area in which there has been quite a boom (Romero et al. 2021)—but more generally on bilateral relations. In countries such as those we are concerned with in this chapter, the interaction of MFAs with citizens and the public, especially the public outside the capital city, is quite limited. An active digital diplomacy agenda is thus not only significant when it comes to engage the public in the host country, but also when it comes to "selling" bilateral issues and foreign policy objectives at home.

The practice of presidential digital diplomacy is often even more selective, as heads of state and government engage mostly with other leaders on Twitter and other platforms, and do not necessarily establish two-way communication with citizens. As can be seen from Table 20.2, much more than enterprising diplomatic agents, presidents tend to follow a broadcast model of

Table 20.2 Presidents during two waves of digital diplomacy

Presidents in 2015	Followers	Tweets	Retweets	Replies
@CFKArgentina (Cristina Fernández—Argentina)	3,650,743	7268	884,581	1
@dilmabr (Dilma Rousseff—Brazil)	3,334,741	4530	599,658	38
@Ollanta_HumalaT (Ollanta Humala—Peru)	1,190,823	708	32,363	29
Presidents 2020	**Followers**	**Tweets**	**Retweets**	**Replies**
@Alferdez (Alberto Fernández—Argentina)	1,564,138	26,016	1286	859
@Jairbolsonaro (Jair Bolsonaro—Brazil)	6,558,312	9224	265	979
@Sebastianpinera (Sebastian Piñera—Chile)	2,473,049	4222	220	290
@MartinVizcarraC (Martín Vizcarra—Peru)	966,325	1729	530	65

Source: Elaborated by the authors from official data

messaging that remains closed to user interaction. There is a key difference here: in the case of a regular press conference, presidents are confined to whatever segments of it the media are willing to broadcast. By using social media, presidents and other government officials reach the public directly, skipping the intermediaries. The concern about open-platform criticism (let alone trolling) plays a role, but also calculated risk-taking regarding issue treatment means balancing what might be understood as a two-level game (Putnam 1988; Bjola and Manor 2018). In effect, the messaging on international affairs from presidential accounts tends to be on what are considered to be safe issues. In turn, the global rise of populism has brought to the fore increased suspicion of the various ways in which the internet is deployed to promote "fake news" (Cooper 2019). Populism, with earlier manifestations in Latin America in the first half of the twentieth century, is opening the doors to the darker side of digital diplomacy, namely mis/disinformation (Pamment and Bjola 2018; Aguirre and Avila 2020).

A Reluctant Digitalization

Certain critical events accelerated the adoption of digital diplomacy in Itamaraty and in Torre Tagle. In Brazil, hosting the FIFA World Cup in 2014 and the Olympic Games in 2016 offered a unique opportunity to project Brazil's image (*o pais mais grande do mundo*, "the world's biggest country" in popular parlance) on the world stage. In Peru, a border dispute with Chile that reached the International Court of Justice (ICJ) triggered a digital media offensive that stood the country in good stead. Lacking any such "push" factors, both Argentina and Chile were slower in reacting to the digital challenge.

The Argentine case is one of restricted digitalization. The government of President Fernández centralized the use of digital tools in *La Casa Rosada*, and when competition (like that of foreign minister Héctor Timerman, such a frequent tweeter that he became known as "Twitterman") arose, the order came down from above both to the minister and embassies abroad to stop using social media (Erlandsen and Hernández 2018 in Aguirre et al. 2018a, 2018b). The Twitter accounts of both Fernández and Timmerman are pioneering for Argentine diplomatic standards. Yet, President Fernández's tweets on foreign policy crowded out other voices, making it difficult to institutionalize digital diplomacy within the Argentine MFA. Mauricio Macri's coming to power in December 2015 changed this.

Macri's foreign minister, Susana Malcorra, an old UN hand, encouraged younger staff to embrace social media platforms, both at headquarters and at embassies and consulates. This started with broad user guidelines and manuals but acquired momentum with the establishment of a public diplomacy and inter-institutional affairs department within the ministry, thus formalizing the deployment of digital tools. Information officers were tasked with performing their duties more and more in the digital sphere.

Interestingly, the case of Chile, often described as a pioneer on a variety of foreign policy initiatives (Stallings 2009), is one of late adoption. Arguably, the highly vertical chain of command in the Chilean MFA, in which even the smallest initiative needs approval from the minister, who in turn is unwilling to take on established mores and conventions, conspired against reform. Yet, the minister himself, Heraldo Muñoz, and individual ambassadors like Juan Gabriel Valdés and Jorge Heine were early adopters and even advanced users of digital tools. As per several interviews, this would respond to a certain political strategy, in which, from 2014 onward, in the second administration of President Michelle Bachelet, foreign minister Heraldo Muñoz and a select group of heads of mission worked in lockstep, in an intermediate stage of network diplomacy. Also in 2014, the MFA press division began the shift toward social media platforms. Eventually, even President Bachelet rejoined Twitter in 2016, giving an additional impetus to Chilean digital diplomacy, which was able to capitalize on her strong international reputation. The Chilean MFA's latecomer condition in this matter, in a country widely considered to be a forerunner and "conceptual leader" in foreign policy, as well as, paradoxically, the most digitalized in Latin America, would seem to confirm the risk-aversion strategy followed by the ministerial leadership, as well as the power of inertia, established mores, and traditional club diplomacy within the organization.

The Peruvian experience, in turn, is mixed. On the one hand, it was one of the earliest MFAs in the region to open institutional accounts and to deploy its message on a variety of social media platforms. It is also in many ways the most successful digital adopter in South America. On the other hand, the evaluations of the practitioners themselves are a bit more nuanced. Cases of audacious or exemplary work are described as being the result of fortuitous outcomes and individual skill in the context of reputational and bilateral crises, rather than of institutional design or conscious policies (Neyra and Rubio 2018). An ostensible reluctance to engage with foreign publics, and an inordinate emphasis on consular information to the exclusion of much else, would seem to reflect a skeptical view of the MFA leadership about the utility of digital diplomacy. This would be based on the alleged fickleness of public opinion, as well as on the dangerous terrain represented by the polarization of views within social media. The spontaneity of digital engagements is seen a risk to be managed, rather than an opportunity to be leveraged, risk that Peruvian diplomats and supporting staff were able to navigate, given the organizational "jack of all trades" resilience forged in what was characterized by several interviewees as an underfunded MFA.

In Brazil's Itamaraty, the impetus for digital diplomacy was driven by two factors. As mentioned above, the hosting of two major world sports tournaments, the FIFA World Cup in 2014 and the Olympic Games in 2016, was seen as an opportunity to make a mark on international public opinion at a moment when the country was still riding high and President Dilma Rousseff quite popular. In turn, this happened at a time when a push for greater transparency in government was taking hold. The net result was that the digitalization of Brazilian diplomacy was framed more along the lines of domestic public accountability, than along the ones of impacting international public opinion. The pushback and criticism of what was considered excessive government spending on stadiums and other infrastructure needed for these sports events, in a country where poverty is still rampant, became an object lesson in the "boomerang effect" of projects designed to be matters of national pride, but that end up exploding in the face of government leaders at a time when the transparency of public budgets is the norm. This was, in many ways, a cautionary tale about the perils of unfettered digital enthusiasm.

Despite the varying uses of Twitter over the years by all four MFAs, follower growth as evidenced by comparison from years 2020 and 2015 in Figure 20.1 increased exponentially of institutional accounts. In Figure 20.2, the growing follower count of each institutional MFA handle measured in

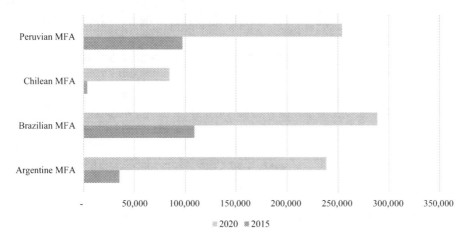

Fig. 20.1 Institutional Twitter followers in 2020 versus 2015. Source: The authors

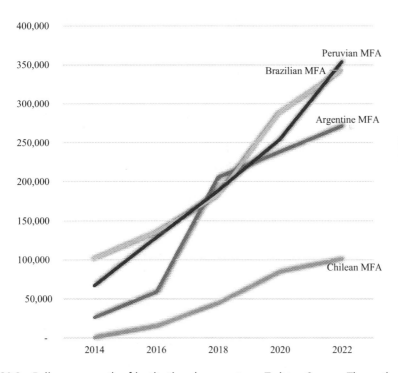

Fig. 20.2 Follower growth of institutional accounts on Twitter. Source: The authors

two-year intervals[2] points to interest and recognition by users of digital diplomacy as a sought-after means of interaction on foreign policy issues with official actors. Notably, Peru surpasses Brazil in the number of followers and Argentina's follower growth is also quite high, as compared to a much slower increase in Chile. A charitable interpretation would be that in the latter case, follower growth may have been affected by the 2019 social uprising. Follower growth in the other three countries may be attributed to the consular effect upon the accounts in a moment of desperate search for information and assistance for Peruvians, Brazilians, and Argentines during the pandemic.

Embracing Innovation and Reform: Organic and Formal Change

Institutional changes are hard to come by. Bureaucracies are resistant to mend their ways. This is especially true of MFAs, home to the practitioners of what is sometimes described as "the world's second oldest profession." These features are even more pronounced in the case of Latin American MFAs. The latter are marked by the Iberian centralist tradition, on the one hand, and their existence in a region of "coups and earthquakes," meaning extreme political oscillations, on the other. In a part of the world where the MFA is often the only government department having a proper civil service, aiming for continuity is an overriding goal. Diplomatic conventions, institutional predictability, sacrosanct standard operating procedures, and supposedly unalterable foreign policy principles all help to cope with an uncertain *milieux*.

In a setting in which risk-aversion is the norm, adopting new tools such as those of digital diplomacy, that change not just the mechanics of communication but its very dynamic and tempo, cannot but be seen as a dubious, even dangerous, proposition. Thus, unless strict orders come down from the highest levels, or a demonstration effect takes place through the example of senior officials, not much progress will take place on the digital frontier. Ministers, in turn, have little interest in antagonizing the diplomats' union or spending much time in projects designed to reform established procedures, from which they believe to have little to gain, as compared to the time they could spend interacting with their counterparts abroad on much more reputedly glamorous international issues. Yet, the digital age is with us, and even such a relatively highly cloistered profession as diplomacy cannot ignore it. Thus, despite the resistance to it, digital diplomacy has made strides and has established a

---

[2] The data utilized is publicly provided by Twiplomacy and missing data corresponds to 2019 and 2021.

regular albeit limited presence in these four South American countries. Yes, there is the danger of diplomatic backsliding (Aguirre et al. 2018b; Manor 2019), but most observers would agree with the proposition that, if anything, the COVID-19 pandemic has shown the increasing centrality of digital diplomacy in a world in which travel is no longer what it was, and virtual conferences and Zoom calls are routine.

Nonetheless, in a world in which one-third of humanity is on Facebook, the notion that explicit legislation, formal authorization, and special incentives are needed for foreign policy professionals to use social media platforms will strike many people as odd. Yet, such has been the pattern in Latin America so far. Chile and Mexico have approved legislation modernizing their MFAs that includes references to various aspects of digital diplomacy but remain the exception. The irony is that the use of advanced digital diplomacy need not be monopolized by the big powers. In fact, some of the smallest countries in Europe, like the Baltic nations, have been particularly successful in it and in e-government more generally. The difficulty of the South American MFAs discussed in this chapter to adapt to the digital age reflects a broader problem of attitudes—from reluctant to resistant—toward embracing change during the last decade.

References and Further Reading

Aguirre, D. 2020. "Public Diplomacy in Latin America: An Emerging Field of Practice?" In *The Routledge Handbook of Public Diplomacy*, eds. N. Snow and N.J. Cull, 368–78. London: Routledge.

Aguirre, D., and C. Avila. 2020. "Propaganda and Populist Communication in Bolivia, Ecuador and Venezuela." In *The SAGE Handbook of Propaganda*, eds. P. Baines, N. O'Shaughnessy, and N. Snow, 476–91. London: SAGE.

Aguirre, D., M. Erlandsen, and M.A. López. 2018a. *Diplomacia pública digital: el contexto iberoamericano*. San José: Editorial Escuela de Relaciones Internacionales Universidad Nacional de Costa Rica.

Aguirre, D., I. Manor, and A. Ramos. 2018b. "The Digitalization of Public Diplomacy: Towards a New Conceptual Framework." *Revista Mexicana de Política Exterior* 113: 7–13.

Allison, G., and P. Zelikow. 1999. *Essence of Decision: The Cuban Missile Crisis*. New York: Longman.

Amorim Neto, O., and A. Malamud. 2020. "Presidential Delegation to Foreign Ministries: A Study of Argentina, Brazil, and Mexico (1946–2015)." *Journal of Politics in Latin America* 12 (2): 123–54.

Bjola, C., and I. Manor. 2018. "Revisiting Putnam's Two-level Game Theory in the Digital Age: Domestic Digital Diplomacy and the Iran Nuclear Deal." *Cambridge Review of International Affairs* 31 (1): 3–32.

Brown, K., and C. Hensman. 2014. *Data-driven Public Diplomacy: Progress Towards Measuring the Impact of Public Diplomacy and International Broadcasting Activities*. Washington, D.C.: United States Advisory Commission on Public Diplomacy.

Burr, R.N. 1974. *By Reason or Force: Chile and the Balancing of Power in South America, 1830–1905*. Berkeley: University of California Press.

Centurión, E.L., and F.A. Trinadori López. 2019. "Diplomacia digital: los cambios y las continuidades en el uso de Twitter de las administraciones de Cristina Fernández y Mauricio Macri (2011–2018)." Unpublished thesis. Buenos Aires: Pontificia Universidad Católica Argentina.

Cooper, A. 2019. "The Disintermediation Dilemma and Its Impact on Diplomacy: A Research Agenda for Turbulent Times." *Diplomacy & Statecraft* 30 (4): 799–807.

Cull, N.J. 2013. "The Long Road to Public Diplomacy 2.0: The Internet in U.S. Public Diplomacy." *International Studies Review* 15 (1): 123–39.

———. 2018. "Prólogo." In *Diplomacia pública digital: el contexto iberoamericano*, eds. D. Aguirre, M. Erlandsen, and M. López, 11–20. San José: Editorial Escuela de Relaciones Internacionales Universidad Nacional de Costa Rica.

Erlandsen, M., and M.F. Hernández. 2018. "Argentina en manos de@ cfkargentina. Diplomacia pública digital: el contexto iberoamericano." In *Diplomacia pública digital: el contexto iberoamericano*, eds. D. Aguirre, M. Erlandsen, and M. López, 155–91. San José: Editorial Escuela de Relaciones Internacionales Universidad Nacional de Costa Rica.

Fajardo, M. 2022. *The World that Latin America Created: The United Nations Economic Commission for Latin America in the Development Era*. Cambridge, MA: Harvard University Press.

Gobo, K., and C. Santos. 2022. "The Social Origin of Career Diplomats in Brazil's Ministry of Foreign Affairs: Still an Upper-class Elite?" In *Ministries of Foreign Affairs in the World*, ed. C. Lequesne, 15–38. Leiden: Brill Nijhoff.

González, G., et al. 2021. "Coyuntura crítica, transición de poder y vaciamiento latinoamericano." *Nueva Sociedad* 191: 49–65.

Hart, J. 2013. *Empire of Ideas: The Origins of Public Diplomacy and the Transformation of U.S. Foreign Policy*. Oxford: Oxford University Press.

Hayden, C. 2011. "Beyond the 'Obama Effect': Refining the Instruments of Engagement through U.S. Public Diplomacy." *American Behavioral Scientist* 55 (6): 784–802.

Heine, J. 2008. "On the Manner of Practising the New Diplomacy." In *Global Governance and Diplomacy*, eds. A. Cooper, B. Hocking, and W. Malley, 271–87. London: Palgrave Macmillan.

———. 2013. "From Club to Network Diplomacy." In *The Oxford Handbook of Modern Diplomacy*, eds. A. Cooper, J. Heine, and R. Thakur. Oxford: Oxford University Press.

Heine, J., and J. Turcotte. 2012. "Tweeting as Statecraft: How, against All Odds, Twitter Is Changing the World's Second Oldest Profession." *Crossroads* 3 (2): 59–72.

Malacalza, B. 2021. "Sudamérica, una periferia convulsionada." *Nueva Sociedad* 295: 29–41.

Manor, I. 2019. *The Digitalization of Public Diplomacy*. New York: Springer International.

Melissen, J., ed. 2005. *The New Public Diplomacy: Soft Power in International Relations*. Basingstoke: Palgrave Macmillan.

Mendelson Forman, J. 2016. "Foreign Policy in the Kitchen." *Global Policy*, October 10. https://www.globalpolicyjournal.com/blog/10/10/2016/foreign-policy-kitchen.

Neyra, A., and R. Rubio. 2018. "Cancillería peruana: de la digitalización a la modernización." *Revista Mexicana de Política Exterior* 113: 141–61.

Orrego, F., ed. 1975. *América Latina, clase media de las naciones*. Santiago: Institute of International Studies, University of Chile.

Pamment, J., and C. Bjola. 2018. *Countering Online Propaganda and Violent Extremism: The Dark Side of Digital Diplomacy*. Abingdon: Routledge.

Peron, V., and S. Perreira. 2018. "Medios sociales y la diplomacia pública digital brasileña: Un análisis sobre el uso de Twitter por Itamaraty durante el proceso de juicio político del Gobierno de Dilma Rousseff." In *Diplomacia pública digital: el contexto iberoamericano*, eds. D. Aguirre, M. Erlandsen, and M. López, 195–241. San José: Editorial Escuela de Relaciones Internacionales Universidad Nacional de Costa Rica.

Pestana, A. 2020. "The Brazilian Approach to Public Diplomacy." In *Routledge Handbook of Public Diplomacy*, 342–49. London: Routledge.

Putnam, R.D. 1988. "Diplomacy and Domestic Politics: The Logic of Two-level Games." *International Organization* 42 (3): 427–60.

Riordan, S. 2020. "Covid-19 and the Digitalization of Diplomacy." *Journal of Diplomacy* 24: 124–31.

Rockower, P.S. 2012. "Recipes for Gastrodiplomacy." *Place Branding and Public Diplomacy* 8 (3): 235–46.

Rogers, E. 1962. *Diffusion of Innovations*. New York: The Free Press.

Romero, L., A. Alfaro, E. Hudson, and D. Aguirre. 2021. "Digital Diplomacy and Covid-19: An Exploratory Approximation towards Interaction and Consular Assistance on Twitter." *Comunicación y Sociedad* 18: 1.

Schindler, C.E. 2018. *The Origins of Public Diplomacy in U.S. Statecraft*. Cham: Palgrave Macmillan.

Stallings, B. 2009. "Chile: Pioneer in Trade Policy." In *Competitive Regionalism: FTA Diffusion in the Pacific Rim*, eds. M. Solís, B. Stallings, and S. Katada, 118–38. Houndmills: Palgrave Macmillan.

Wilson, R. 2013. "'Cocina Peruana para el Mundo': Gastrodiplomacy, the Culinary Nation Brand and the Context of National Culture in Peru." *Exchange: The Journal of Public Diplomacy* 2 (1): 1–8.

Part VI

Multilateral Diplomacy and Innovation

21

Toward a More Credible Multilateralism at the United Nations: A Few Practical Steps

Bénédicte Frankinet

In many respects, UN multilateralism has become dysfunctional. There are many reasons for this unsatisfactory state of affairs.

The most obvious is the selective use, or indeed the complete disregard, by Permanent Members of the Security Council, of the responsibilities entrusted to them by the UN Charter: preventing war and maintaining peace and, consequently, acting together in good faith for the common good. Without this basic understanding, the UN cannot function, as illustrated most recently by the escalation and dramatic events leading to the invasion of Ukraine, in February 2022. As Secretary General António Guterres reminded us, "the principles of the UN Charter are not an à la carte menu."

This chapter, however, is not about global geopolitics, nor about the dynamics of the Security Council. It does not deal with the need to modernize the composition of the Council, nor with revisiting the right of veto. These have already received ample attention, both in academic research and diplomatic conversations, and they will most probably continue to do so.

The relevance of the United Nations extends far beyond the functioning of the Security Council. This chapter seeks, in a pragmatic way, to address the apparent shallowness and inefficiency that characterize much of today's multilateral diplomacy, in particular at the UN and across the organization's multiple mandates and areas of work.

B. Frankinet (✉)
Brussels, Belgium

Multilateral declarations and commitments, solemnly made by Member States at the UN or about the UN, do not match with the deficit of urgency, creativity, or political will when it comes to implementing these pledges and turning words into action.

Moreover, in the 75 years of the United Nations' existence, path dependence in diplomatic practice and bureaucratic habits have turned the organization into an almost unmanageable instrument in terms of achieving the objectives of the Charter. Routine and aloofness have progressively contributed to shrinking the potential of the UN as an efficient instrument of global governance. Worse, this situation easily passes nowadays for normal, or even for the only way to handle multilateral issues.

If carried forward, this trend can only further undermine the credibility and the reactive capacity of the United Nations and of the global multilateral system as a whole. This contribution is about the need to change our ways, and to make the best possible use of all the resources, experience, and expertise of the UN and maximize the potential of the organization, in its various incarnations, for global cooperation.

The suggested improvements are of a practical order. They are inspired by the conviction that it is high time to break with outdated, repetitive, and unimaginative habits in multilateral diplomacy, and to re-energize UN multilateral diplomacy with a sense of vision, of priority, and of common purpose.

This contribution is based on a practitioner's experience. For the sake of clarity, it deliberately considers the United Nations system as a whole, without distinguishing between its various fora and mandates. This might strike UN connoisseurs as an oversimplification.

The United Nations in History

In 1945, after two catastrophic world wars, preventing the resurgence of deadly conflicts and nurturing a lasting peace was the ultimate goal of the international community. Such were the role and responsibility entrusted to the United Nations and, in particular, to the Security Council. Although the UN force that was originally planned never materialized, the Council had at its disposal a set of instruments for discharging this essential function: mediation, negotiation, good offices, judicial settlement, and the right to authorize the use of force. The protection of human rights and international cooperation also played a role in reducing tensions and in promoting mutual understanding. They became an integral part of the global prevention and peace architecture. International peace and security were the most sought after public good, and universal cooperation under the Charter would help secure it. The implementation, in good faith, by all Member States, of the decisions they made jointly at the UN became a prerequisite for successful multilateralism.

With time, however, the unity of vision and purpose that formed the basis of the Charter faded. Evidently, the international context had evolved. Not all the Charter's promises had materialized. Member States did not always avail themselves of the peaceful options it contained. UN instruments did not always deliver the expected results for the maintenance of international peace and security. More importantly, the international mood in favor of peace and cooperation through multilateralism waned. The mutual understanding that had briefly prevailed among the founding members unraveled, firstly in the face of the Cold War and later of the renewed competition among the superpowers in a multipolar world. Meanwhile, numerous newly independent states joined, changing the majority in the General Assembly and pressing for a prioritization of development issues. The North-South divide in the membership became more entrenched. Furthermore, new global challenges emerged, such as the environment and climate change. As with many international organizations, the work of the UN and its specialized agencies, funds and programs grew rapidly and became increasingly specialized and fragmented.

Global threats and challenges have, indeed, shifted and morphed. Besides wars between states, threats to international peace and security now include terrorism, transnational crime, domestic conflicts, and impunity, among others. More importantly, new realities and new concepts have emerged about what now constitute existential threats to humankind, such as climate change or the loss of biodiversity, opening new lines of priority for the UN and the multilateral system.

The changing global environment, the multiplication and increasing complexity of the tasks entrusted to the UN, and the subsequent growth of the organization have progressively distracted decision-makers and diplomats from the core business of multilateral diplomacy. They may also have disenfranchised some of the weaker Member States. Yet, for all the lapses and missed opportunities, the United Nations, its civil servants, its various organs and governing bodies, and its Member States have together produced major evolutions and achievements in global governance and international cooperation. The reasons and circumstances that have enabled the success of these processes and outcomes need a more detailed analysis, should we later want to draw on the lessons learned to improve the overall relevance of the UN.

The dynamics initiated under the 1994 United Nations Framework Convention on Climate Change and its successive protocols and agreements may appear to be too slow and to lack ambition in view of the magnitude of the challenges. The implementation of the commitments made in the successive Conferences of the Parties (COP), once again, lags behind. Nonetheless, the Convention can rightly be hailed as the launch of a legitimate and ongoing multilateral process to address a new global threat. This inclusive process allows for the meaningful participation of the smaller—and often most affected—countries. The adoption, in 2015, of Agenda 2030 and the Sustainable Development Goals, by the UN General Assembly, is another example of a participative and successful negotiation producing a consensual and global vision. In spite of its imperfections, the Agenda is a common roadmap for balancing progress for "people, prosperity, and planet" and for responding to universally recognized challenges, such as poverty, inequality, and environmental threats. More recently, the World Health Assembly, with the help of WHO staff, professionals, and researchers, has managed to issue much-needed guidance to the entire world and provide the elements of a global response to face the COVID-19 pandemic. Given the necessary political will and the right focus, the United Nations can make a difference.

The perception of our mutual interdependence in the face of global threats has become sharper. We also understand better how, where, and why these new threats develop and how they can become mutually reinforcing. The need to devise, negotiate, and agree swift, coherent, global responses is obvious and palpable. Nevertheless, responding adequately, agreeing on common approaches and solutions, and, above all, implementing them steadfastly and in good faith remain an arduous path.

The role of the United Nations is, indeed, irreplaceable, and its added value is beyond question when it comes to reacting to complex problems affecting the entire international community and requiring common responses at the global level, like climate change, pervasive poverty, global health, migration, conflict, loss of biodiversity, and the overexploitation of natural resources, to name but a few. In this evolving context, the original commitment under the Charter to act together as a community of states and of peoples when faced with common threats remains a useful compass, especially when moving forward demands balancing short-term, national, or narrow interests with a long-term vision and win-win solutions for the common good.

It is essential that all Member States participate in the decision-making, and from a level-playing field. UN multilateralism should not be a disguise for promoting the priorities of a few or, even worse, an excuse for inaction. Without true ownership and commitment by Member States, many UN decisions remain inoperable, nor will they deliver credible results. Without the reaffirmation of a common political will to act, the credibility of the United Nations and the sustainability of its actions will always remain fragile.

In an ideal world, a keen and deep sense of political purpose and priorities, a cooperative spirit, and the will to work hard to reach meaningful solutions would infuse multilateral policy and the diplomatic practice of Member States. This overall vision and perspective is unfortunately often absent from the daily practice of officials and diplomats representing their countries at the UN, of their counterparts in their respective capitals, and of international civil servants, too. There are many exceptions of course, but their present working methods, routines, and reflexes are not conducive to the reinforcement of the credibility, the efficiency, and the authority of UN decision-making or of the public image of the organization.

What follows are a few practical suggestions relating to the day-to-day work at and for the United Nations. They might sound trivial, or even bureaucratic. Their overall aim, however, is also to reinject significance and a sense of purpose into the activities of UN bodies, into the work of UN diplomats, and into multilateral diplomacy in general.

Move beyond Declarative Multilateralism

For many of its Member States, the United Nations has a highly symbolic value. Consequently, symbolic gestures and ritual expressions of support for multilateralism have too often become substitutes for active engagement and efficient solutions to issues of global concern through the work of multilateral organizations. There is a pervasive disconnect between the support for the United Nations rhetorically professed by Member States and their actual willingness or capacity to act decisively. This support should extend beyond words and symbols. It should materialize into dynamic and constructive participation in the work of the UN. The central aim remains to improve global cooperation and governance in order to prevent or to respond to shared threats and challenges. In short, to bring forward useful initiatives, to follow them through and to work out compromise solutions for their adoption and implementation.

Many government representatives, including at the highest level, seem actually to be content with a combination of high visibility opportunities and public statements at the UN, which are presumed to vouch for their commitment to multilateralism. The unfolding of the annual opening of the General Assembly, with a competition for photo ops, speeches destined mostly for national audiences, delivered in a half-empty hall, and hundreds of competing side events, is a case in point. We need to reflect on the added value of these limelight moments, on the honesty of the promises made from the podium, and on their role in the chain of steps leading to concrete global action. How could they better serve the substantial work at and of the UN? It is worth questioning long-established practices, re-examining priorities, and switching mindsets to more result-based approaches. Lofty exchanges must not be an end in themselves; their role as possible launching pads for policy and action needs to be revisited.

Think through Multilateral Initiatives Thoroughly

The world changes and the UN has to adapt its priorities accordingly, especially if it is to remain a dynamic and proactive organization. Decisions adopted by the international community in the past are not sacred. In an evolving global context, they may progressively outlive their relevance. As a result, they may become inadequate to respond to new types of challenges. Some will remain, as useful historic references or as stepping-stones for the future, but many should objectively no longer qualify as recurrent items on the agenda of the UN, as was mentioned above.

Not all new processes engaged in by Member States at the United Nations are equally important in terms of global governance. Some are vanity projects. Others, while well-intended, lack depth or support from the start. Thankfully, many new proposals also emerge from the various parts of the UN Secretariat, which is often better equipped to provide the necessary guidance and coherence.

Member States could play a useful part in selecting relevant topics and means for action. They could, for instance, conduct thorough and honest reviews of the motivations, the efficiency, the successes and failures, and the relevance of their past initiatives at the UN; or they might look at the reasons behind their support or opposition to other members' proposals. These internal exercises would allow them to reflect on the significance and the added value of their own multilateral policy, beyond self-promotion or visibility, as meaningful contributions to global governance, before launching new processes.

When tabling or supporting proposals for new directions, new priorities, or new areas of work at the United Nations, Member States need to tread carefully and selectively. Relevance and efficiency should be paramount. Not every worthy cause, no matter how popular with domestic audiences, is fit for automatic transposition into a multilateral initiative. National concerns are not necessarily shared by the majority of other Member States. Proposals conceived mainly as a response to the preoccupations of national opinions, no matter how legitimate, do not always meet the basic criteria for support at the UN. As stated above, symbolic actions are neither appropriate nor very credible.

Before launching or supporting a new initiative at the UN, Member States could also submit it to a tight screening process at the national level, to objectively assess its relevance and chances of success. What is its intended objective? Its possible complementarity or competition with existing initiatives, possibly from other Member States? Its chances of achievability? What realistic contribution will it make to resolve a distinct issue of common concern in global governance, for instance climate warming, human trafficking, migrations, or plastic pollution? Is the UN the most appropriate forum and why? What degree of support can be expected from the UN membership?

Such a relevance-based review process of a planned multilateral initiative, involving all the domestic stakeholders concerned, would help clarify its intended impact on the UN global agenda. It would inform the international community as a whole, but also relevant national actors, of its purpose and its benefits. It would identify possible hurdles ahead. It would provide negotiators and other parties involved with useful references and arguments to promote, at the national and international levels, new concepts and approaches.

During negotiations, all national stakeholders need to be regularly informed and consulted, in particular those whose tasks will include the domestic implementation of the final UN product. Bringing them in at an early stage would help pave the way for devising suitable and fine-tuned implementation mechanisms should the new multilateral instrument or decision under consideration be adopted.

Modernize and Accelerate National Implementation Procedures

For all its work overload and cumbersome working methods, the UN offers a unique framework for developing groundbreaking and innovative global policies and instruments. The Arms Trade Treaty, the UN Conventions on Climate Change and on Biodiversity, the Convention on the Law of the Sea, Agenda 2030, and the Sustainable Development Goals all represent major achievements in global governance.

However, if they are not followed by swift implementation, by Member States, of the commitments and obligations they entail, many of these instruments remain ineffective and incomplete. The consequent adoption of relevant national or regional policies, legislation, plans and programs, enforcement and financing mechanisms is key. Yet translating multilateral commitment into action at the national level is often a very slow and disjointed process, as if the successful conclusion of negotiations at the UN was the ultimate step. This lack of systematic implementation by Member States undermines the very purpose of multilateral cooperation.

This state of affairs is another manifestation of the discrepancy, mentioned already, between the Member States' public expressions of support for the UN and multilateralism, on the one hand, and their apparent unwillingness or lack of capacity to operationalize their UN obligations, on the other. Whether these are legally binding or not is, in practice, of little relevance. The amount of ambition, time, expertise, and credibility invested in vital UN negotiations would otherwise make little sense.

The minimum requirements for completing the circle of multilateral engagement are: systematically translating UN decisions into national instruments, paying national contributions to the UN budget on time, respecting the letter and the spirit of UN Conventions, monitoring implementation and, if necessary, adopting corrective measures. The UN multilateral system will remain lame and impotent if Member States do not follow up and rigorously apply the decisions they have jointly agreed.

Mainstream Multilateral Diplomacy

Many nations' Departments of Foreign Affairs often consider multilateralists as belonging to a separate branch, specializing in somewhat abstract issues, operating in a different universe, and relying on distinct networks and codes. To reach its full potential, multilateral diplomacy needs mainstreaming. Breaking traditional silos, and bringing in new ways and new actors, both at home and at the UN, is indispensable.

The contribution of bilateral diplomats, in their capitals or in the field, can bring new dynamics to multilateral diplomacy. Through their deeper knowledge of local contexts and sensitivities, they can enrich the understanding of third countries' positions. They can relay useful information on the perception of the role of the UN in specific countries. They can help develop or fine-tune targeted and convincing arguments for respective partners. They can bring a degree of realism into analyses and expectations. In order to fulfill these tasks, however, bilateral diplomats need to be properly informed about these responsibilities, as well as about the evolution of the relevant multilateral dossiers.

A well-oiled triangular exchange of information between capital cities, representations to the UN, and bilateral posts is also a precious tool. It helps to build a more complex picture of the decision-making processes and the motivations behind the positions of third countries on UN issues than can be gathered from their public statements at the UN. In particular, in the case of a vote or of a protracted obstruction, knowing who has the right to the final cut is most useful. Is it the Head of State, the Minister of Foreign Affairs, or the Permanent Representative to the UN? The information provided by these triangular exchanges is essential to appropriately direct the arguments and demarches and to maximize their efficiency.

Multilateral commitments and policy certainly do have direct implications for bilateral relations and policy. As said, the functioning of the UN system is predicated on the participation, in good faith and on an equal footing, of its members in its decisions and in their implementation. In practice, though, not all countries have the human resources or the capacities to invest in all the intricacies of the UN agenda; even less, to evaluate and factor in the consequences of UN negotiations and decisions on their national policies. Consequently, the implementation of UN resolutions ranks low in their priorities.

In order to keep members on board, the concern for effective implementation of multilateral decisions—including the financial commitments of richer countries—should be factored into bilateral relations and policies in all relevant areas: political, development, but also sectoral, such as climate, oceans, or agriculture.

Today, maybe with the exception of climate change, migration, and some acute geopolitical crises, the opportunities for in-depth discussions on UN issues in bilateral meetings remain minimal. This sends the wrong signals about the importance of multilateral policy and may, again, convey the message that multilateralism relies more on words than on deeds. The role of the UN in general and the relevance of specific multilateral dossiers need to find their place on bilateral agendas.

Bilateral contacts, at all levels, represent an excellent opportunity to convey the importance of improved multilateral dynamics, to spell out in more detail national positions, motivations, and proposals at the UN, to elicit support, to build alliances, or to frankly broach the concrete and efficient implementation of UN decisions. These conversations should not only take place in the margins of UN meetings or during negotiations in New York, Geneva,

Vienna, Rome, or Nairobi; they should also become standard practice in bilateral diplomacy.

Diplomats accredited to or responsible for multilateral organizations other than the UN, in particular regional organizations, can play a role too, if mobilized and kept in the information loop. They are better informed of the positions and decisions already adopted in the respective organizations, on which initiatives can be built at the global level. They can also identify the inclinations of individual members of these organizations relating to specific subjects and, consequently, the potential for cooperation or disagreements at the UN on similar matters.

Thematic diplomacy (on climate, on human rights, or on migration) is a welcome addition to the toolbox. It brings together bilateral concerns and multilateral solutions and allows for more focused exchanges. The content and the results of these specialized conversations should also become part of broader bilateral agendas, including at a high level.

Build Long-Term, Flexible, and Actionable Alliances

In global governance and in multilateral diplomacy, alliances are key; building long-term trust and a common understanding of issues is equally important. As hinted above, bilateral networks can play a useful role in this regard.

The hurdles should not be underestimated though; reaching the intended level of commonality of purpose for joint action at the UN can at times remain out of reach. Limited means disenfranchise many ministries of foreign affairs and governments. Few decision-makers feel at ease discussing intricate multilateral issues.

The general inertia of multilateral settings is also partly to blame. The regional and thematic group system at the UN (the African group, the Group of 77, the Non-Aligned movement, the Least Developed Countries, but also the EU) is still a reflection of the traditional North-South divide and therefore limits the possibility to influence and convince individual Member States. The different groups provide support and information to their respective members. Their most influential members are often in charge of carrying out negotiations. Once adopted, each group's negotiating positions and tactics leave little space for bilateral considerations and understandings, no matter how relevant. As a result, bilaterally agreed positions might in the end not carry much weight in UN deliberations.

Diplomats at the United Nations should be encouraged to leave the comfort zone of the group(s) to which their own country belongs and to reach out regularly to other colleagues, to develop and nurture a broad network of actionable contacts. Building cross-regional alliances on a specific multilateral issue at the UN is a long-term investment. Once launched, their chances of success also depend on a vigorous and dynamic follow-up, involving relevant bilateral and multilateral administrations and diplomatic posts.

Fortunately, group dynamics evolve: new groups are emerging and new alliances are built, as demonstrated, for instance, by the cooperation between the very vocal group of Small Island States and the European Union on climate issues. Hopefully, rolling back COVID and providing vaccines to all will benefit from joint approaches between developed and developing countries, across the usual dividing lines.

Streamline and Update UN Agendas and Priorities

Over the decades, a growing number of meetings, mandates, requests, and tasks, on a very wide range of topics, have accumulated at the UN. Little guidance is provided as to their actual relevance, their degree of urgency or their level of priority. Many issues have run their course. Overtaken by new events and by new approaches, they have lost a great deal of their significance for the international community. Nonetheless, for the Member States who initiated them, they often acquire a symbolic and sentimental value, as testimonies of their achievements and successes. Ritually submitting identical proposals (or paragraphs) for discussion and decision also offers countries a safe and comfortable area for action and visibility, and strengthens their historic profile at the UN. The benefit of these processes for global governance or the functioning of the organization is apparently of little consideration for their sponsors. This routine and the exponential consequences of this seemingly benign activity have resulted in an immense, and partly unmanageable, workload, both for the UN Secretariat and for Member States' delegations. Agendas are repetitive, overloaded, and mostly unfathomable.

This repetitive work has also created a bubble of comfort, both for UN delegates and for members of the Secretariat, whose talents and experience could be put to much better use. As a result, for delegations battling with a large number of non-priority issues, little time remains to invest in the production of new ideas, in substantial reflection, or in meaningful discussions and negotiations. Year after year, the UN Secretariat sees itself tasked with producing "updated reports," which are barely read. This entire process results in constant lack of focus and consumes a large amount of precious time, energy, financial and human resources. It distracts from real priorities, dilutes the real significance of the role of the United Nations, and negatively affects its image.

With this in mind, successive presidents of the General Assembly, or of other UN organs, have made several attempts at rationalizing agendas. Their efforts have so far been met with either indifference or with resistance from many Member States, who consider these exercises as merely bureaucratic and of little significance.

Agendas and programs of work need to be trimmed, reframed, and refocused on a regular basis, to take into account the changes in the context in which the organization operates. They need to be turned into proactive and dynamic policy and priority-setting instruments. Such a change might contribute to redefining the way the UN works. Leaving the routine behind, eliminating deadwood, and refocusing on the crucial issues might help turn around the common perception that the UN is, at best, a blunt instrument of soft power. Once again, this will require foresight, determination, goodwill, and cooperation from all Member States, as well as some delicate trade-offs. Posturing should make place for the will to deal in-depth with issues where the added value of the multilateral approach of the UN is both indisputable and necessary. This rationalization would allow the UN to breathe. It would help Member States with limited human and financial resources to take a more active part in decision-making processes. It would help the Organization, as well as its Member States, to concentrate their efforts and means on issues of global relevance that require urgent multilateral solutions.

Instill New Values in Multilateral Diplomacy

UN delegates' daily practice consists of meetings, consultations, discussions, and negotiations, both formal and informal. This permanent exposure to different viewpoints and exchanges with colleagues from a number of different countries is, without a doubt, one of the most enriching experiences, both at the personal and at the professional level. However, the UN context has also produced, over the years, a particular brand of "experts," who specialize, each in his or her area of work, in the drafting of texts and the elaboration of compromise formulations. This is, of course, a welcome and necessary skill at the United Nations.

Given the specialized, technical, and formatted nature of these negotiations, Permanent Representatives and capitals rely on their experts and on their knowledge of the intricacies and dynamics of a specific negotiation. Experts often enjoy a broad degree of freedom within the framework of their instructions. Others are under such strict supervision, from their hierarchy or their capital, that their natural instinct is to seek refuge in the repetition of the status quo. Consequently, the products of negotiations are highly coded—or ambiguously formulated—texts, barely understandable for non-specialists. Compromises are reached based on recycled "agreed language" or copy-paste paragraphs from previous resolutions. Year after year, lengthy negotiations stall on the same issues. They succeed or break down over a few symbolic words or expressions, no matter how important the challenge at stake. It is often tempting to settle for half-baked decisions or to ritually block progress, rather than help moving real issues forward.

Understandably, many UN delegates have become very adept and also very proud of their skill in these "drafting games." The same is true for their counterparts in capitals, and even for representatives of civil society organizations, who follow the work of the United Nations closely. Fighting eternally contentious issues and winning the day with a few words, with little concern for the broader picture or for the meaning of these repetitive and fruitless efforts, is objectively of little use or interest.

Of course, an ambiguously formulated agreement is sometimes the only achievable result in view of the gaps between the respective positions of Member States. Nonetheless, the way delegates and experts approach their work at the United Nations needs redefining and reframing.

During their training and throughout their briefings, diplomats at the United Nations should be reminded of the broader significance of their work and the importance of multilateral diplomacy. They need to learn to develop a sense of priority and purpose, and to put their negotiating and drafting skills at the service of an overall vision, extending beyond the narrow range of their specific dossiers.

Improve Communication about the UN and Multilateralism

It should come as no surprise that the perception of the UN remains blurry to say the least, even for generally well-informed audiences. Few political leaders undertake to thoroughly inform their own government or indeed their citizens, not only about the significance of the UN decisions they have agreed to, but also on the need to implement them at home without delay.

Dynamic communication about the UN is not easy, except in times of crises. The understanding by the general public of the importance of the UN is, at best, patchy. The same is true for their grasp of the reasons for working through a multilateral organization to address global issues. Only a few items reach the headlines, but the patient—if sometimes protracted—work necessary to curb arms proliferation, to tackle climate change, or to reduce world poverty is not well understood.

The complexity of the agenda, the lack of prioritization, the formulation of UN decisions are all partly responsible. There are notorious exceptions: communication on climate change and successive Conferences of Parties is now reaching a broader audience. It might inspire efforts to better inform on other UN issues. The work of the UN, its urgencies and priorities, its contribution to global governance, peace and well-being deserve more finely tuned presentations and explanations for domestic audiences, parliaments, academia, civil society, and the general press, in a language accessible to all. They should highlight the benefits and the necessity of the multilateral approach, and concrete achievements, while highlighting the complexity of the process and the difficulties encountered, as well as the expected results.

Promote Academic Research on UN Achievements

The United Nations, its functioning, its successes, and failures have been the subject of a vast quantity of research papers and academic production. Yet, after 75 years, we sometimes remain at a loss to comprehend the basic dynamics of the organization. These, of course, have also fluctuated over time.

How can we deepen and refine our understanding of the life of concepts and approaches that have made the UN—in certain cases—both efficient and irreplaceable? Where were they born? What path do new ideas and proposals for better governance lead? Who are, in each case, the relevant actors: initiators, supporters, propagators, opponents? What circumstances and environment have contributed in the end to success or rapid failure? Why have some innovative proposals been embraced by the international community, while other valuable contributions have remained forever on the back burner?

Even if the answers to these questions will probably remain complex, a better understanding of the dynamics of success at the UN would offer useful guidance to the United Nations and to its Member States.

Concluding Remarks

Over the years, the United Nations has, in a way, been overtaken by its own success, as the common house of its Member States. In the process, many stakeholders have lost track of the importance, for the Organization, of being able to discharge its fundamental duties and responsibilities fluently and efficiently. The suggestions offered in this chapter are just a few practical examples of possible remedies for the present state of affairs. It is clear, however, that without the political will of governments to abide by their obligations under the Charter, no amount of reforms will be able to restore the authority and the legitimacy of the United Nations as a unique instrument for peace, global cooperation, and common solutions.

Further Reading

Biscop, S. 2020. "For Multilateralism to Work, There Must be Consensus on What It Is Supposed to Do and Can Realistically Achieve." In *The Multilateral Order Post-COVID: Expert Voices*, 6–7. Dublin: Institute of International and European Affairs.

Gordenker, L. 2018. "The UN System." In *International Organizations and Global Governance*, ed. T.G. Weiss. London: Routledge.

Kamau, M., P. Chasek, and D. O'Connor. 2018. "Pulling It All Together: The SDG's and the Post-2015 Development Agenda." In *Transforming Multilateral Diplomacy*, eds. M. Kamau, P. Chasek, and D. O'Connor. London: Routledge.

Morris, J. 2000. "UN Security Council Reform: A Counsel for the 21st Century." *Security Dialogue* (September): 265–77.

Müller, J. 2020. *Reforming the United Nations: Fit for Purpose at 75?* Leiden and Boston: Brill.

Peterson, M.J. 2005. *The UN General Assembly*. London: Routledge.

Weiss, T.G. 2009. "What Happened to the Idea of World Government?" *International Studies Quarterly* 53 (2): 253–71.

22

A New Logic of Multilateralism on Demand

Akiko Fukushima

Introduction

In recent decades, it has been asserted that "multilateralism matters." Many articles and books have been written with this title such as John Gerard Ruggie's book *Multilateralism Matters* (1993) and Margaret P. Karns' article, "Multilateralism Matters even More" (1988). The very fact that such an assertion has been made reflects that multilateralism is a weak form of diplomacy. Yet, despite its ups and downs, multilateralism has not disappeared from diplomatic history since the Concert of Europe.

In the twenty-first century, against the background of changing geopolitics, multilateralism has been emphasized even during the U.S. Donald Trump administration, which asserted "America first" and turned his back on alliances and partnerships. Denial of multilateralism by some has been rescued by other willing powers. As an illustration, while the United States left the Trans-Pacific Partnership Agreement (TPP) that it once led, Japan, Canada, and others rescued the agreement by concluding the Comprehensive and Progressive Agreement for the Trans-Pacific Partnership (CPTPP) with 11 remaining member countries. The UK, China, Taiwan, and the Republic of Korea (ROK) have subsequently applied for membership.

A. Fukushima (✉)
The Tokyo Foundation for Policy Research, Tokyo, Japan

Yet, the United Kingdom decided to leave the European Union (EU). Nevertheless, the EU has maintained its institutional multilateralism. The North Atlantic Treaty Organization (NATO) has expanded its membership to the east after the end of the Cold War and has been strengthening its ties among members and partners. Its key member, the United States, under President Joe Biden decided to revive the alliance beyond his predecessor's negative attitude. Solidarity has further strengthened after Russian aggression against Ukraine in February 2022.

While existing multilateral institutions have been shaken, the global community has generated a new variety of multilateralism different from those created immediately after the end of the Second World War. Facing new global and regional challenges, ad hoc minilateralism or multilateralism not based on an institutional framework has emerged, such as the Alliance for Multilateralism, the Quadrilateral Security Dialogue (QUAD), and the Free and Open Indo-Pacific vision/strategy/outlook.[1]

With the spread of the pandemic by the COVID-19 virus since the end of 2019, despite initial retreat, states are reinforcing multilateral cooperation to emerge from the pandemic and its aftermath. Yet, the pandemic has revealed the shortcomings of existing international institutions in responding to the global spread of virus, causing victims comparable to wars around the globe.

The Russian aggression against Ukraine in February 2022 has arguably shattered the liberal international order maintained since the end of the Second World War. Such order has been discussed as weakening, as needing refitting since the turn of the century, but the war has revealed that it faces tectonic change. The war has threatened the collective security mechanism at the United Nations and confidence-building measures taken since the end of the Cold War in Europe and in Asia-Pacific. The legal framework to prohibit the use of force built in the twentieth century has also been challenged by aggression. The crisis has tested multilateralism hard and has shattered the liberal international order visibly. Multilateralism now demands a new logic.

This chapter reflects on a logic of multilateralism developed over the years, examines what multilateralism can cater to, and analyzes new trends. Beyond the immediate crisis, this chapter also examines a new logic of multilateralism on demand that will be effective for peace, stability, and prosperity in the twenty-first century, responding to the demands of today.

---

[1] The nouns used for the Free and Open Indo-Pacific concept varies by countries and regions. For example, the United States and France use "strategy," while Japan uses "vision." ASEAN uses "outlook."

What Is Multilateralism?

What is multilateralism? Robert Keohane (1990, 731–33) defined multilateralism as "the practice of coordinating national policies in groups of three or more states, through ad hoc arrangements or by means of institutions." This definition holds true even today with a wide variety of multilateral institutions, participants, and modus operandi. According to this definition, multilateralism includes those institutions with global membership such as the United Nations (UN), the World Bank, those at regional level with institutions such as the European Union (EU), and the North Atlantic Treaty Organization (NATO). Multilateralism also includes forum types such as the East Asia Summit (EAS), ad hoc arrangements on a specific functional agenda such as the Proliferation Security Initiative (PSI), or conference centered architectures such as ASEAN plus three (Japan, China, and ROK) and the ASEAN Regional Forum (ARF). There are also those with a fewer number of participants which is sometimes called plurilateralism or minilateralism, such as the Quadrilateral Security Dialogue (QUAD). While all these variants fit the definition of multilateralism by Keohane, a whole variety of adjectives have been used. William Diebold (1988) used "formal and substantive," and "nominal" or "qualitative." Meanwhile John Gerard Ruggie defined multilateralism to "refe[r] to coordinating relations among three or more states in accordance with certain principles." Like Keohane, he regarded the number of participants as not mattering so long as it is more than three. However, Ruggie emphasized shared principles as being important to sustain multilateralism. Willing powers now emphasize values such as democracy, freedom, and rule of law—principles which are gaining importance in multilateralism.

On the other hand, in launching multilateralism membership is always a difficult entry point for debating who is in and who is not. In some instances, exclusive frameworks have been dubbed a containment strategy. Luis Simon distinguishes "inclusive" and "exclusive" multilateralism explicitly. Simon (2021) argues that Europe prefers a more inclusive format of multilateralism so long as the members share standards and norms. Simon names the Organization for Security and Co-operation in Europe (OSCE) as an example of inclusive multilateralism.

Yet, there is another type of multilateralism different from existing frameworks illustrated by the "Free and Open Indo-Pacific (FOIP)" vision initially proposed by Japan in 2016. The Free and Open Indo-Pacific did not start as a multilateral framework but was launched as Japan's strategy. Subsequently the United States, Australia, India, Germany, France, and the Netherlands individually, and ASEAN and the EU as regional institutions, launched respective Indo-Pacific visions/strategies/outlook for cooperation. The choice of the noun shows the comprehensive, visionary nature of respective policy initiatives. The Indo-Pacific conception has subsequently led to bilateral and multilateral cooperation for enhancing quality infrastructure, both physical and digital, and for enhancing connectivity, or for fortifying maritime security in the Indo-Pacific. The Free and Open Indo-Pacific, in other words, has become a platform for bilateral, minilateral, and multilateral cooperation.

Multilateralism has been consistent in its definition but has evolved in its form and modus operandi responding to the changing geopolitics and the nature of transnational challenges. To consider the future of multilateralism, the next section reflects briefly upon its past.

Multilateralism in History

Today's multilateralism dates to the Congress of Vienna in 1814–15 after the Napoleonic wars when nations agreed to launch a multilateral arrangement to prevent national revolution and wars. This was called the Concert of Europe. Charles and Clifford Kupchan (1986, 120) argued that the arrangement was characterized by the dominance of great powers within a concert. It was not based on a pre-arranged mechanism but was made by informal negotiations and consensus. The Concert was based on the understanding of the participants that their peace was indivisible, which prompted members to act together to prevent aggression. However, the arrangement eroded and crumbled, perhaps because some war memories faded but also because competing alliances emerged (Jervis 1982, 368).

In the twentieth century multilateralism became more institutionalized. The post-World War I Paris Peace Conference led to the creation of the League of Nations and its Covenant, which were meant to prevent another world war. Moreover, the Kellogg-Briand Pact (Pact of Paris) was signed in 1928, which banned the use of war to resolve disputes or conflicts. Nevertheless, neither the League of Nations nor the Pact of Paris prevented the Second World War. That was in part because the Covenant did not include provisions to penalize members who did not observe the provisions. Although the League of Nations was more institutionalized than the Concert of Europe, the institution was not robust enough to prevent the Second World War. Moreover, the United States, which was instrumental in launching the League of Nations, did not participate in the institution due to domestic opposition.

In 1945 after the Second World War the UN was created with its Charter to prevent another world war. The organization has so far been successful in preventing a third world war but also failed to prevent the Korean War, the Vietnam War, conflicts in former Yugoslavia, Middle East, Africa, and most recently, in Ukraine.

John Gerard Ruggie (1993, 32) has argued that multilateral institutions exhibit durability and adaptability once launched. The key to successful multilateralism is whether such institutions exhibit diffuse reciprocity—benefits from multilateral cooperation over the long haul and over multiple dimensions—among participants. Multilateralism most often cannot show specific reciprocity—equal immediate benefit at each round of cooperation—which stands in for bilateralism. When participants to multilateral arrangements do not insist on specific reciprocity but look for diffuse reciprocity, such institutions can be sustained. Dissatisfaction over existing multilateralism as time lapses has been expressed at the UN and other international institutions insofar as they do not reflect changes in the balance of power. When left unattended, dissatisfaction can also weaken existing multilateralism by members not observing rules.

Scholars have examined the nature of the crisis of multilateralism in the twenty-first century. Edward Newman (2006, 161, 173) observed that crises "generally result from environmental variables" such as changing power relations, international threats, and security. The deepening of confrontation between the United States and China in the recent decade has produced geopolitical tensions, urging other powers to take sides. As a result, competing visions of the international order have made multilateralism less and less effective. Having witnessed less than expected functioning of the UN, the World Trade Organization (WTO), the World Health Organization (WHO), and other international institutions, participants have lamented their weakening and have complained that "multilateralism matters" out of a sense of crisis.

Multilateralism Matters

Multilateralism has its advocates and detractors. The Koerber Foundation in Germany observed that in one camp people observe that "multilateral cooperation has caused them more harm than good." In the other camp, "we see the hashtag #MultilateralismMatters reassuringly pop up across multiple social networks. Leading politicians and technocrats repeat variations of the mantra, 'global problems need global solutions.'" The Koerber Foundation further observed that the division of the two camps on multilateralism has been deepened by the COVID-19 crisis due to the failures of the international institutions in securing medical equipment, drugs, and vaccines. These failings have "not only reinforced the sceptics' view, but [have] also sown doubt even among avid multilateralists, since global cooperation is failing when it is most needed" (Koerber Foundation 2021, 1–2).

As the preceding section reflected, multilateralism has evolved in response to changing circumstances, most notably wars. The international institutions created after the Second World War have supported the liberal international order over seven decades led by the United States. However, after the turn of the century, other rising powers expressed their dissatisfaction with the existing institutions and sought to alter the existing international liberal order to their liking. They have taken measures such as an aggressive seizure of top positions of institutions to change rules and standards, or the creation of possible international orders more reflective of their wishes. Should that happen, the world will fall into instability if not chaos. Willing powers should aim at maintaining and refitting the rules-based order.

Hans W. Maull in 2019 observed the consistency as well as the evolution of the liberal international order. The constant factor he observed is the principle of sovereignty and non-interference which has been maintained from the Concert of Europe to today (Maull 2019, 7). The evolution, Maull wrote, is based on the fact that the Concert of Europe was built on equality among sovereign states. That led to the second-generation liberal international order following the Atlantic Charter, the United Nations, and the Bretton Woods institutions. The principles of the order were national self-determination and decolonization, individual human rights, and democratic governance. Although this order suffered from the Cold War confrontation, it reasserted itself by the collapse of the Soviet Union, as reflected in the Charter of Paris.

After the end of the Cold War, the second generation of the liberal international order has been strained by Iraqi invasion of Kuwait, civil conflicts in the former Yugoslavia, and the Rwandan genocide. Then came such institutional reforms as the establishment of the World Trade Organization (WTO) succeeding from GATT and the indefinite extension of the Non-Proliferation Treaty. But then came 9/11 and the American war on terror which Maull observed as a trigger for another transformation. The liberal order was further weakened by crises such as the failure of the Doha round of the international trade regime leading to conclusion of numerous bilateral free trade agreements (FTAs); nuclear tests by India, Pakistan, and the DPRK; and developments in the Middle East, namely conflicts in Libya and Syria, leading to massive migration of refugees. These symptoms led Maull and others to call the liberal international order a "myth" and to state that "liberal institutionalism needs recalibration" (Fukushima 2017, 157–58).

On the other hand, concerns have been mounting about how to manage the transformation of the existing international order without a war this time around. Philip Zelikow (2017), for example, argued that "the world is today suffering from a 'grave systemic crisis." That is, until 2022 and the onset of Russian aggression against Ukraine. Maull cautioned that "the contemporary liberal order may itself have entered a period of accelerated transformation – and perhaps dissolution" (Maull 2019, 7).

Moreover, dissatisfied powers have taken their own path. China has built its Belt and Road Initiative (BRI) as well as founded its own international bank, the Asian Infrastructure Investment Bank (AIIB). Russia has mounted its dissatisfaction with its fate after the collapse of the Soviet Union, witnessing its former allies and partners joining NATO and/or EU. This led Russia to opt for their war in Georgia and in Crimea as well as in Ukraine.

Multilateralism Challenged

The world is faced with serious transnational challenges that demand responses by multilateral institutions, most notably the UN and its specialized agencies as well as regional institutions such as NATO and EU, and global forums such as G7. Their failures have deepened the division between those for and against multilateralism. The latter has gained more steam. Among versatile challenges that strain multilateralism, this section examines two challenges, namely the COVID-19 pandemic and the war in Ukraine.

COVID-19: Revealing the Failings of Multilateralism

The COVID-19 pandemic has affected lives of people around the globe. In two years since its outbreak, the world by March 2022 lost more than 6 million people according to the COVID-19 Dashboard of Johns Hopkins University (2022). The total deaths are comparable or even more than war deaths relative to the time duration: 8.5 million during the First World War, and 9.1 million during the Second World War.

The pandemic exposed shortcomings, if not failures, of the existing institutions, most notably the World Health Organization (WHO). At the time of the outbreak of the COVID-19 in Wuhan, China, the WHO was slow to recognize the disease as a pandemic and was slow to investigate the disease spreading in China. The virus quickly spread to Europe, North America, elsewhere in Asia, and subsequently to the whole world. Different from other infectious diseases such as HIV/AIDS or Ebola which affected mostly developing countries, COVID-19 spread almost simultaneously around the globe. Since the world lacked medical and pharmaceutical prevention and a cure, countries initially turned inward to take domestic measures of lock down or restriction on the public contacts to avoid the further spread of the pandemic. After one year, the vaccines for COVID-19 by private pharmaceutical companies such as Pfizer and Moderna were introduced. As wealthier countries in Europe and the Americas secured vaccines, poorer nations had to wait for a long time to get supplies. Meanwhile, the WHO and other multilateral institutions were unable to respond to the needs of vaccines, leaving the world to suffer from inequality and allowing some to take advantage to expand their sphere of influence in return for supplies.

Many people called for the reform of the WHO to be more independent and not to be influenced by big powers. The United States decided to halt its funding to the WHO, criticizing it for being too close to China. Experts demanded that the WHO improve equitable access to vaccines to prevent COVID-19 (Kelland and Mason 2021).

While the WHO has been the target of criticisms, the United Nations itself was slow in acting. The UN General Assembly belatedly adopted two resolutions: one on April 2, 2020, four months after the outbreak, which called "for intensified international cooperation to contain, mitigate and defeat the pandemic." The second resolution adopted on April 20, 2020, urged global action to rapidly scale up development, manufacturing, and access to medicine, vaccines, and medical equipment. On the other hand, the UN Security Council had a hard time in agreeing on its resolution on the COVID-19 due to the dispute between its permanent members, the United States and China, over what to call the coronavirus. Although the Secretary-General António Guterres on March 23, 2020, called for global ceasefires to better tackle the pandemic, it took 90 days for the Security Council to adopt a resolution demanding a general and immediate cessation of hostilities in all situations.[2]

These episodes demonstrated the limits of the UN Security Council in taking necessary actions to deter the spread of COVID-19 and to assist those member states affected by the pandemic. As a matter of fact, in the past the Security Council adopted resolutions related to public health three times

---

[2] UN Security Council Resolution S/RES/2532 (2020).

which were effective. The first was in 2000 which was over the spread of HIV/AIDS and its devastating impact on stability and security.[3] This was followed up by another resolution on HIV/AIDS in 2011. The occurrence of HIV/AIDS has been curbed. In 2014, the Security Council determined that the unprecedented extent of the Ebola outbreak in Africa constituted a threat to international peace and security, and took measures to control the spread.[4] These precedents show that the organization was fully aware of the health threat to international peace and security. In the case of COVID-19, however, different positions of the permanent members, namely the United States and China, prevented a swift move on the pandemic, costing millions of lives.

Since WHO reform will take time, numerous multilateral bodies have engaged in cooperation such as the EU, ASEAN, the Quadrilateral Security Dialogue (QUAD), and G7. As an illustration, the QUAD has included their cooperation on the COVID-19 explicitly. When the QUAD leaders from the United States, Japan, Australia, and India met in Washington, D.C., on September 24, 2021, they agreed to donate more than 1.2 billion vaccine doses globally, in addition to the doses QUAD countries finance through COVAX (White House 2021). Other multilateral institutions such as the EU have returned to multilateral cooperation over COVID-19 after their initial emphasis on domestic measures.

Multilateralism Facing Russian Aggression against Ukraine

In 2022, the world was faced with yet another serious challenge to multilateralism, this time in a form of war, that is, the Russian aggression against Ukraine. Witnessing the horror on the ground and the huge number of evacuees fled from Ukraine, multilateral institutions and forums such as the NATO, the EU, and the G7 swiftly caucused and discussed measures to halt the Russian aggression to Ukraine such as placing economic sanctions on Russia, granting assistance to Ukraine and its neighboring countries, as well as providing humanitarian assistance to evacuees.

The UN whose main mission is to maintain international peace and stability certainly responded but revealed its limits. On February 24, 2022, Secretary-General Guterres (2022) made it clear that "such unilateral measures conflict directly with the United Nations Charter." The UN Charter clearly stipulates that "All members shall refrain in their international

---

[3] UN Security Council Resolution 1308, S/RES/1308 (2000).
[4] UN Security Council Resolution S/RES/2177 (2014).

relations from the threat or use of force against the territorial integrity or political independence of any state, or in any other manner inconsistent with the purposes of the United Nations." He stated that "the use of force by one country against another is the repudiation of the principles that every country has committed to uphold." He immediately called the Russian Federation to stop its military offensive, as well as to establish a ceasefire and to return to the path of dialogue and negotiations which Russia ignored.

The UN Security Council swiftly met but failed to adopt a resolution to condemn Russia and to urge Russia to withdraw from Ukraine, due to the veto by Russia. Nevertheless, the UN Security Council adopted the decision to convene an Emergency Special Session of the General Assembly based on the resolution adopted in 1950 entitled "Uniting for Peace." On March 1, 2022, the General Assembly adopted the resolution deploring Russian aggression of Ukraine and calling for the immediate withdrawal of its forces with 141 member states out of 193 voted for the resolution while five voted no and 35 abstained. The five countries voting no were Belarus, North Korea, Eritrea, and Syria in addition to Russia. The resolution is officially entitled "Aggression against Ukraine," and stated that the UN "deplores in the strongest terms the aggression by the Russian Federation against Ukraine" (UN 2022). The resolution is not legally binding for Russia but demonstrated a majority view of the international community. Furthermore, as Russia continued its aggression, the General Assembly resumed its emergency special session and adopted another resolution entitled "Humanitarian consequences of the aggression against Ukraine" (A/RES/ES-11/2) on March 24. The resolution stated that the UN "deplores humanitarian consequences of the hostilities by the Russian Federation against Ukraine" and "demands an immediate cessation of the hostilities by the Russian Federation against Ukraine" to protect the lives of civilians. The second resolution was again adopted by 140 member states in favor, the same five member states voted no while 38 member states including China and India abstained.

An Emergency Session of the General Assembly based on the Uniting for Peace resolution was called 11 times in the past. Particularly the one called in October 1956 when France and the United Kingdom protested the nationalization of the Suez Canal by Egypt has relevance to the war in Ukraine in 2022. The Security Council met to discuss British and French troops in the Suez Canal Zone after the Israeli attack on Egypt but failed to reach a conclusion because of French and British vetoes. From November 1 to 10, 1956, the General Assembly was called to discuss a ceasefire and the withdrawal of all foreign forces from occupied territories. It was significant, however, that the General Assembly resolved to dispatch the first United Nations Emergency Force (UNEF) to secure and supervise the cessation of hostilities to the area. This subsequently led to the creation of UN peacekeeping operations (PKO). In 2022, the General Assembly was unable to push their draft resolution to the extent of use of force or a possible dispatch of peace operation mission nor political mission in March 2022. It was inevitable because the situations on the ground in Ukraine did not allow any UN members to dispatch their military troops avoiding a direct clash against Russia and the possible use of weapons of mass destruction.

Nevertheless, though limited, the United Nations has further responded to the war. First, as the veto prevented actions by the Security Council again in facing Russian aggression, the General Assembly took another action. Since the rules on the veto of the permanent members of the Security Council entail the amendment of the UN Charter which requires adoption by a vote of at least two-third of the members of the General Assembly and ratification by at least two-third of the members including all Security Council permanent members, the General Assembly took another route. On April 27, 2022, the General Assembly adopted a resolution that aimed at holding the five permanent members accountable for their use of the veto. The resolution A/77/L.52 entitled "Standing mandate for a General Assembly debate when a veto is cast in the Security Council" decided that the General Assembly President "shall convene a formal meeting of the 193-member organ within 10 working days of the casting of a veto by one or more permanent members of the Security Council and hold a debate on the situation as to which the veto was cast, provided that the Assembly does not meet in an emergency special session on the same situation." Lichtenstein drafted the resolution, and it was co-sponsored by 83 member states, including three permanent members—France, the United Kingdom, and the United States.

Soon after the Russian aggression began, the International Court of Justice (ICJ) and the International Criminal Court (ICC) started their investigations. The ICJ held hearings in March following application from Ukraine to denounce claims by Russia that it was merely acting to prevent the genocide of Russian-speaking minorities in Ukraine. On February 28, the chief prosecutor of the ICC announced that he would open an investigation on possible war crimes in Ukraine. This would be the ICC's second such investigation, after one that ran from 2014 to 2020 on Russian aggression in Crimea and which concluded in a statement that evidence of war crimes had been found and that formal investigation would proceed.

In late April 2022, UN Secretary-General Guterres visited Russia and Ukraine. On April 26 in his meeting with President Vladimir Putin in Moscow, he did not use his good-offices mechanism to negotiate a ceasefire. However, he agreed with President Putin in principle to cooperate with the evacuation of citizens from Mariupol involving the UN and Red Cross. On April 28, Guterres also visited the Kyiv suburbs of Borodianka, Bucha, and Irpin, which are reportedly sites of suspected war crimes. He also met with President Vlodomyr Zelensky of Ukraine and promised further humanitarian aid (UN News 2022a).

On May 6, 2022, the Security Council President for the month of May, Ambassador Linda Thomas-Greenfield of the United States, on behalf of the ambassadors issued the presidential statement on Ukraine. The statement expressed deep concern on peace and stability of Ukraine and expressed strong support for the Secretary-General to find a peaceful solution (UN News 2022b). It was significant that the Security Council could issue the presidential statement, but it could not contain condemnation to Russia nor request immediate cessation of the aggression by Russia. The wording was carefully chosen so that Russia would not bloc the statement.

The Russian aggression in Ukraine and the war are different from most conflicts the UN has dealt with since its foundation. It is not a case of a weak state or a failing state suffering from intra-state conflicts but a case of a functioning sovereign state attacked by another member of the UN. This made the functioning of the UN tougher. Yet, the UN has demonstrated its role, representing voices of member states which can be found in statements by Ukraine. The remarks by the Permanent Representative of Ukraine to the UN, Ambassador Segiy Kyslytsya, at the UN Security Council meeting on May 5, 2022, after the Secretary-General's visit to Russia and Ukraine alluded to a role the UN plays on peace and security. He on behalf of the President of Ukraine thanked the Secretary-General for making progress on the possible evacuation of civilians from Mariupol and said that "the whole world has learned about the role of the UN and the International Committee of the Red Cross (ICRC) in this. This has shown that international organizations can be effective," rescuing civilians from Azovstal and the city blocked by the Russian Army (Permanent Mission of Ukraine to the United Nations. 2022). He also told the Japanese journalist that "it is wrong to say that the UN as a whole has failed. If the UN does not exist, the evil can win easily. It is important to make it clear who is responsible for this atrocity" (*Asahi Shimbun* 2022).

A New Path to Effective Multilateralism

Beyond asserting that "multilateralism matters," numerous attempts and calls are underway to turn the strained situation around. New initiatives for multilateralism which are an extension of, or different from, their historical precedents, are unfolding.

Reforming Existing Institutions Anew Beyond Rhetoric

A familiar course in the history of multilateralism when strained is to reform the existing institutions to refit to the demands of the time. It is rare that institutions are disbanded except a case of major war, be it cold or hot as illustrated by the League of Nations with the outbreak of the Second World War, SEATO with the Vietnam War, and the Warsaw Treaty Organization with the collapse of the Soviet Union and the end of the Cold War.

After facing a crisis, UN created mechanisms such as peacekeeping operations to respond to conflicts. Member states of the United Nations have often been disappointed with the dysfunctional Security Council as illustrated in the two cases examined. For too long, member states have included the reform of the Security Council in the annual agenda of the General Assembly. Secretary-Generals submitted their reform recommendations as well as established numerous advisory panels to recommend them. Nevertheless, the Security Council has not been reformed substantively. The UN member states have nearly quadrupled to 193 since its foundation, but the size and the composition of the Security Council, the UN's highest decision-making body, has remained unchanged since its foundation, except a slight enlargement in 1965 of adding four non-permanent seats. The veto of permanent members which is a source of the problem has been maintained for over seven decades. The General Assembly resolution to hold permanent members accountable once they exercise their veto is the only development so far.

Security Council reform is hard to realize. Yet we should recall why vetoes were given to the five permanent members of the Council. It was to avoid war between great powers and to avoid proxy war. Instead of denying vetoes, conditional use of veto should be considered unless members opt for another war in the future.

The wave for demanding reform is hitting other international organizations, such as the WHO and the World Trade Organization (WTO). After succeeding GATT, the WTO despite high hopes has failed in its round negotiations and has demonstrated that it is not functioning as an effective organization for trade. The failures have resulted in numerous bilateral and regional Economic Partnership Agreements (EPAs) and Free Trade Agreements (FTAs) resulting in fragmented trade rules. Moreover, the WTO rules were written more than a quarter of a century ago and need refitting. The organization has to reform its rules to reduce discrepancies between developed and developing members. It also needs to introduce new rules on e-commerce, climate change, and other areas. The COVID-19 pandemic has exposed its problems. Director-General Ngozi Okonjo-Iweala after taking office on March 1, 2021, called on members to "do things differently" to achieve reforms to keep the WTO relevant (WTO 2021). The WTO's highly valued Dispute Settlement System also needs reform, and its Appellate Body must be restored. Carlos María Correa, Executive Director of the South Centre, pointed out that "the COVID-19 crisis has shown the world the profound asymmetries that exist in many economic, social and health aspects. The post-pandemic reality should be an opportunity to create a new system based on equality and solidarity which is truly effective" (WTO Public Forum 2021).

The logic of multilateralism must be considered in reform efforts. The logic of sovereignty, non-interference, and equality must stay. However, many of the existing multilateral institutions were created by the allied nations that won the Second World War. It is based on the logic of agreed rules laid down in old treaties or charters. The institutions are membership driven, most often based on consensus. Special privileges were given to the allies who won the war, such as the veto. Since geopolitics and geoeconomics have evolved over the past seven decades, such privileges should be revisited to fit the current distribution of world power. The agenda of institutions should expand or prioritize transnational challenges of the day such as climate change. Multilateral institutions need genuine reform beyond rhetoric, or they will face dissolution.

Forums as Leverage for Innovation

Sharing a sense of crisis, there emerged a new logic of multilateralism, not to start from institution building but from caucusing on cooperation. This line of efforts is illustrated by "Alliance for Multilateralism" led by German Foreign Minister Heiko Maas and French Foreign Minister Jean-Yves Le Drian in September 2019. They observed rising nationalism and isolationism and launched this initiative to support multilateralism. They have chosen the venue of the annual General Assembly of the United Nations as the place to convene their forum.

This initiative has been developed further as an informal forum with more than 70 countries, international organizations, and representatives of civil society participating in 2021. The Alliance for Multilateralism is a new type of multilateral forum. It does not have a formal structure or institutions. The Alliance has taken up two causes, a humanitarian call for action and the joint fight against the COVID-19 pandemic. In the meeting held in September 2021, the Alliance discussed how to close gaps in the international health, how to promote cooperation to achieve equality for women and girls on a global scale, and how to stop climate change. Rather than choosing from a predetermined agenda, the Alliance has identified those commonly shared by participants in the forum. The Alliance did not start from an explicit membership but is open to those who share its interests. Thus, this is truly inclusive multilateralism.

As a matter of fact, there were precedents for such a forum. When the notion of human security was debated by two camps over a narrow and a broad definition, the UN World Summit Outcome Document stipulated in paragraph 143 that "we stress the right of people to live in freedom and dignity, free from poverty and despair. We recognize that all individuals, in particular vulnerable people, are entitled to freedom from fear and freedom from want, with an equal opportunity to enjoy all their rights and fully develop their human potential. To this end, we commit ourselves to discussing and defining the notion of human security in the General Assembly."[5] Japan followed up this paragraph and led the discussion on the concept of human security by the Group of Friends of Human Security in 2006. This group is open to any member state or international organization that is interested in the concept of human security. This group held several meetings until 2009, which led to the General Assembly Resolution on a common understanding of human security (A/RES/66/290) adopted in 2012. This helped to end the debate on the definition of the concept of human security and has opened the avenue for the operationalization of human security. On June 9, 2021, Japan, Costa Rica, and Senegal co-chaired another round of discussions of this group on human security.

Forum diplomacy may develop a different avenue from the existing modus operandi of multilateralism and can be an innovative avenue to promote collective diplomacy fitted for the need of generating a new model of

---

[5] The UN World Summit Outcome Document, (A/RES/60/1), 2005, para.143. https://www.un.org/en/development/desa/population/migration/generalassembly/docs/globalcompact/A_RES_60_1.pdf.

multilateralism when there is no hegemon to lead multilateral cooperation. A logic here is to gather those states who share an agenda—so-called like-minded countries—in an open-ended manner and to discuss topics of interest. Whether this logic can lead to sustainable and robust multilateralism depends on whether they can gather a critical mass or not.

Individual Policy Initiatives Leading to Multilateral Cooperation

Yet another path to multilateral cooperation is for an individual state to launch a vision, subsequently shared by others, still individually, and form bilateral or multilateral cooperation on elements they commonly share. Individual initiatives have led to bilateralism, minilateralism, as well as multilateralism. This can be illustrated by the Free and Open Indo-Pacific (FOIP) cooperation that Japan has led.[6]

The origin of Japan's vision on the Free and Open Indo-Pacific (FOIP) dates to the former Prime Minister Shinzo Abe's speech at the Indian Parliament on "the Confluence of the Two Seas, the Indian and the Pacific Oceans" in August 2007 and his subsequent article to *Project Syndicate*, entitled "Asia's Democratic Security Diamond" in December 2012. Combining these two ideas, Japan officially launched its Free and Open Indo-Pacific (FOIP) strategy in August 2016 at the Sixth Tokyo International Conference on African Development (TICAD VI) held in Kenya. Prime Minister Abe said that "Japan bears the responsibility of fostering the confluence of the Pacific and Indian Oceans and of Asia and Africa into a place that values freedom, the rule of law and the market economy, free from force or coercion, and making it prosperous." This value-backed initiative is a feature of the FOIP vision which lent itself for wider resonance in the region and beyond. Since Japan wishes to share the Indo-Pacific concept with like-minded countries, Japan has softened the edges of the strategy. Japan has made it clear that the FOIP is not an exclusive but inclusive concept as was described in the *Diplomatic Bluebook* 2020 (MOFA 2020).

U.S. President Donald Trump launched his own FOIP when he spoke in Vietnam in November 2017, which was followed by the U.S. National

---

[6] Although there is a debate over who was the first in launching the Indo-Pacific, Japan was, at the least, one of the first countries to launch the broader regional framework. In fact, Australia was an early mover on the Indo-Pacific as reflected in the 2013 Australian Defense White Paper.

Security Strategy at the end of 2017. President Joe Biden did so anew in February 2022 (White House 2022). Indian Prime Minister Narendra Modi explained India's share of the vision of an open, stable, and prosperous Indo-Pacific when he spoke at the Shangri-La Asia Security Conference in June 2018. India tries to balance its quest for strategic autonomy and for necessary partnerships in the region. ASEAN which was initially dubious of FOIP with a possible impact on ASEAN centrality in regionalism, announced its ASEAN Outlook on the Indo-Pacific (AOIP) in 2019 (ASEAN 2019).

Beyond the geographical scope of the region, France issued its Indo-Pacific strategy in 2018 which was updated in 2019. France identifies itself as an Indo-Pacific resident power since it has its own territories in the region. In September 2020, Germany published its Policy Guidelines for the Indo-Pacific. The Guidelines expressed a broader interest from trade, order, peace, and security, to digital. It also emphasized its relations with ASEAN. The Netherlands also published its Guidelines in the fall of 2020. These initiatives culminated in the EU strategy for Cooperation in the Indo-Pacific released on September 16, 2021 (EU 2021), which included several references to Japan's FOIP.

Countries and regions that have joined the FOIP vision have their own motives and aims, some of which are converging while others are diverging. The converging factors behind the FOIP are the perception that the Indo-Pacific covers roughly half of the global economy supported by secured sea lanes of communication. Also, the Indo-Pacific is a center of geostrategic gravity with rising powers. Another converging factor is values Japan's FOIP has identified to be shared by the like-minded such as democracy, human rights, rule of law, and free trade. The FOIP has offered a platform for bilateral, minilateral, and multilateral cooperation for quality infrastructure development, vaccine supply, and maritime security.

The logic for multilateralism along this path is based on individual initiatives from similar but not identical perspectives. Members vary by agenda. The logic that connects participants is the perceived national interest that can be attained by cooperation. Whether this form of multilateral cooperation will be sustained or not is yet to be seen. Nevertheless, it has certainly paved a new avenue for multilateralism, avoiding a difficult entry point of membership, treaties, and institution building. Along with it has come a versatile geometry of bilateral, minilateral, and multilateral cooperation.

A New Logic of Multilateralism on Demand

The logic of multilateralism has so far been based on pro forma equality among members that are sovereign. Non-intervention has been the key principle. Multilateral institutions were membership-driven and most often based on consensus (Fukushima 1999). However, in practice, multilateralism has been initiated and led by hegemon(s) or by the victorious powers of a war that enjoy privileged positions in multilateral institutions. The explicit or implied use of veto has affected their functioning. They had more say in deciding members and in running the institutions.

Today's rivalry between the United States and China has made numerous institutions difficult to manage. Rising powers have become increasingly dissatisfied with the existing institutions. When their grievances were not heard, some powers opted to grab leadership roles in existing multilateral institutions or to create new parallel institutions more to their liking. This trend has invited more competition than cooperation among members, occasionally demanding that member states take sides. A new logic is necessary.

The above analysis offers possible steps to be taken in developing a new logic. It must evolve around like-minded members who are keen to promote cooperation as in the case of Alliance for Multilateralism. Moreover, it is time to rectify the structure of multilateral institutions, starting with the UN, and to identify a new diffuse reciprocity of the kind argued by Keohane (1986, 1–11). Reciprocal benefits in the twenty-first century should reflect advances in science and technology.

A new logic should also shed light on the entry points of multilateralism. Cooperation does not need to start from preexisting formal members but may also do so from members who share concerns, principles, and values. In this sense, the logic should be inclusive. The way that participants look at an agenda does not need to be identical but can be at the least converging. Also multilateralism does not need to start from institution building. Thus, a new logic demands a comprehensive and integrated approach in terms of what issues to work on. Moreover, the world should find a logic strong enough to enforce rules with penalties. Or a logic should clearly show the downside risks of breaching agreed principles. The only alternative is chaos and war.

References and Further Reading

Asahi Shimbun. 2022. "Shinko Watashitachi Zenin no Ayamachi (We Have All Failed in Preventing the Aggression)," May 6.
Association of Southeast Asian Nations (ASEAN). 2019. "ASEAN Outlook on the Indo-Pacific," June.
Diebold, W., Jr. 1988. "The History and the Issues." In *Bilateralism, Multilateralism and Canada in U.S. Trade Policy*, ed. W. Diebold Jr. Cambridge, MA: Ballinger.
European Union (EU). 2021. *Strategy for Cooperation in the Indo-Pacific*, September.
Fukushima, A. 1999. *Japanese Foreign Policy: The Emerging Logic of Multilateralism*. Houndmills: Palgrave.
———. 2017. "Multilateralism Recalibrated." In *Postwar Japan*, eds. M.J. Green and Z. Cooper. Washington, D.C.: Center for Strategic and International Studies.
Guterres, A. 2022. "This Conflict Must Stop Now," February. https://unric.org/en/statement-by-the-secretary-general-on-ukraine/.
Jervis, R. 1982. "Security Regimes." *International Organization* 36 (2): 357–78.
Johns Hopkins University. 2022. COVID-19 Dashboard. https://coronavirus.jhu.edu/map.html.
Karns, M.P. 1988. "Multilateralism Matters Even More." *SAIS Review of International Affairs* 28 (2): 3–15.
Kelland, K., and J. Mason. 2021. "WHO Reform Needed in Wake of Pandemic, Public Health Experts Say." Reuters, January 13.
Keohane, R.O. 1986. "Reciprocity in International Relations." *International Organization* 40 (1): 1–27.
———. 1990. "Multilateralism: An Agenda for Research." *International Journal* 45 (4): 731–64.
Koerber Foundation. 2021. "Making It Matter: Thought Experiments for Meaningful Multilateralism." https://www.koerber-stiftung.de/fileadmin/user_upload/koerber-stiftung/redaktion/paris-peace-forum/pdf/2021/Broschuere_MultilateralismLab-2021_Make-it-Matter.pdf.
Kupchan, C., and C. Kupchan. 1986. "Concerts, Collective Security and Future of Europe." *Review of International Studies* 16 (2): 114–64.
Maull, H.W. 2019. "The Once and Future Liberal Order." *Survival* 61 (2): 7–32.
Ministry of Foreign Affairs (Japan). 2020. *Diplomatic Blue Book 2020*. https://www.mofa.go.jp/policy/other/bluebook/2020/html/feature/f0104.html.
Newman, E. 2006. "Multilateral Crises in Historical Perspective." In *Multilateralism under Challenge?: Power, International Order, and Structural Change*, eds. E. Newman, R. Chandra Thakur, and J. Tirman. Tokyo and New York: United Nations University Press.
Permanent Mission of Ukraine to the United Nations. 2022. Statement by the Permanent Representative of Ukraine to the UN, Ambassador Sergiy Kyslytsya at the UN Security Council Meeting on Maintenance of Peace and Security of Ukraine, May 5. https://ukraineun.org/en/press-center/556-statement-by-the-permanent-representative-of-ukraine-to-the-u-n-ambassador-sergiy-kyslytsya-at-

the-un-security-council-meeting-on-maintenance-of-peace-and-security-of-ukraine/.

Ruggie, J.G., ed. 1993. *Multilateralism Matters*. New York: Columbia University Press.

Simon, L. 2021. "The Geopolitics of Multilateralism: What Role for the EU in the Indo-Pacific." *CSDS Policy Brief* 2021/14. https://brussels-school.be/sites/default/files/CSDS %20Policy %20brief_2114_0.pdf.

UN News. 2022a. "'The World Sees You' UN Chief Tells Ukrainians, Pledging to Boost Support," April 28. https://news.un.org/en/story/2022/04/1117202.

———. 2022b. "Security Council Speaks with One Voice for Peace in Ukraine," May 6. https://news.un.org/en/story/2022/05/1117742.

United Nations (UN). 2022. "UN GA Overwhelmingly Adopts Resolution to Demand the Russian Federation Immediately End Illegal Use of Force in Ukraine, Withdraw All Troops," March 2. https://www.un.org/press/en/2022/ga12407.doc.htm.

White House. 2021. "Fact Sheet: Quad Leaders' Summit," September 24. https://www.gr.emb-japan.go.jp/files/100239762.pdf.

———. 2022. *Indo-Pacific Strategy*, February. https://www.whitehouse.gov/wp-content/uploads/2022/02/U.S.-Indo-Pacific-Strategy.pdf.

World Trade Organization (WTO). 2021. "DG Okonjo-Iweala: WTO Can Deliver Results if Members 'Accept We Can Do Things Differently,'" March 1. https://www.wto.org/english/news_e/spno_e/spno1_e.htm.

WTO Public Forum. 2021. "Climate, Pandemic, E-commerce, Inclusivity – Public Forum Addresses Priorities for Reform," September 29. https://www.wto.org/english/news_e/news21_e/pf21_29sep21_e.htm.

Zelikow, P. 2017. "Is the World Slouching Toward a Grave Systemic Crisis?" *Atlantic*, August 11. https://www.theatlantic.com/international/archive/2017/08/zelikow-system-crisis/536205/.

23

About Spheres of Influence

Chas W. Freeman Jr.

Security is a prerequisite for the prosperity, welfare, and economy of any society. Throughout history, nations have sought security through the establishment of empires, no-go zones (*cordons sanitaires*), buffer states, as well as military, economic, political, or cultural spheres of declared strategic interest or dominant influence. There are alternatives to these safeguards, among them systems based on the shifting coalitions of balances of power. But it is natural for states to want to have friends rather than enemies on their borders and for great powers to expect deference rather than challenges to their security from the collusion of lesser states with great power rivals.[1]

Both nations and empires wax and wane. As they do, they shape political, economic, and military interactions in the regions around them or dependent upon them. Some states seek the protection of greater powers. Others reject and resist others' hegemony.[2] Spheres of influence are creations of statecraft intended to fend off potential competitors.

U.S. secretaries of state have recently taken to declaring that "the United States does not recognize spheres of influence" (Removska 2021). In light of

---

[1] Consider the cautious approaches to relations with the United States of Canada and Mexico, both targets of past U.S. aggression.
[2] Hegemony generates its own antibodies.

C. W. Freeman Jr. (✉)
Watson Institute for International and Public Affairs, Brown University, Providence, RI, USA

Americans' continued insistence on the validity of the Monroe Doctrine, this is more than ironic (Fuller 2022). The United States may refuse to recognize or respect other nation's spheres of influence or their right to establish them, but it insists on enforcing its own, which, though officially undeclared, is no longer limited to the Western Hemisphere but worldwide.[3]

The 2022 war in Ukraine is at heart a struggle over spheres of influence. This makes it timely as well as important to review them, their origins, their purposes, and their intensity, all of which vary from case to case. Understanding and coping with great power rivalry demands recognition of the interests that spheres of influence serve as well as the degrees of deference, subordination, or exclusiveness they seek to enforce.

Why Are Spheres of Influence Established?

Spheres of influence are assertions of an exclusive right to supervise or participate in deciding the alignments and affairs of another nation or nations in relation to still others either in general or in specific domains.[4] As such they are manifestations of international contention between peers.[5] They can be

---

[3] The United States continues to attempt to bring Cuba and other countries in Latin America, like Venezuela, to heel. Yet it rejects any effort by Russia to incorporate Georgia or Ukraine into a Russian sphere of influence as illegitimate, while insisting on its right to include both countries in its own sphere by admitting them to NATO. In Africa, Asia, Australia, Europe, and North and South America, the United States is currently engaged in coercive diplomacy and economic warfare to exclude Chinese companies from any role in telecommunications or infrastructure investment. U.S. policies in the Indo-Pacific seek to sustain American military primacy and the hub-and-spoke alliance system that implemented policies of "containment" in the Cold War. In the Middle East, where American influence is visibly in retreat, the U.S. focus is on rolling back the sphere of influence it and its security partners' bungled military interventions in Afghanistan, Iran, Lebanon, Syria, and Yemen enabled Iran to create.

[4] For example, politico-military, economic, technological, etc.

[5] The concept of spheres of influence, like so many other elements of modern statecraft, emerged from the projection of power abroad by the many competitive powers that made up the European state system. Imperial China's position as the center of gravity in the "tributary state system" did not give it a sphere of influence in the modern sense. The tributary system might best be described as a "circle of deference." Unlike a sphere of influence, it was not part of a competition for hegemony with a peer competitor of China because there was none. Nor, despite insistence on deference to its court rituals by foreigners seeking the favor of the emperor, did China usually seek to regulate the behavior of so-called tributary states toward each other. Much like the nominal allegiance of European princes to the Pope, the sycophantic deference of lesser rulers to the Chinese emperor was a matter of self-interest as well as tradition. The emperor's recognition conferred trade advantages and prestige upon them and provided them with a measure of diplomatic, if not military protection from each other. It also encouraged China to leave them alone, rather than to attempt to make them outright vassals (as it did, with varying degrees of success, with Korea, Tibet, and Vietnam). In Asia, the sphere of influence was an artifact introduced by European, American, and, later, Japanese—not Chinese—imperialism and applied *to* China, not *by* it.

formal[6] or informal and defensive or domineering. Elites in the societies within them may see them as necessary protection or resent them as disrespecting their sovereign autonomy. Whatever their attitude, they tend to learn the language of their sphere's dominant nation, to assimilate its industrial and military standards as well as its cultural and commercial practices, to send their children to study in its educational institutions, and to prefer its goods and services over those of its rivals.

The term "sphere of influence" first appeared in the division of Africa at the Berlin Conference of 1884–85, which apportioned dominance of the continent between Britain, Belgium, France, Germany, Italy, Portugal, and Spain. In 1885, a bilateral agreement between Great Britain and Germany divided control of the Gulf of Guinea between them. Each undertook not to interfere in the interests of the other in its designated sphere. In 1890, the two concluded a similar division of spheres of influence in East Africa.

The concept of spheres of influence inspired the organization of the United Nations Security Council, whose permanent members each brought with them dominance of distinct groups of other countries.[7] The General Assembly, by contrast, enshrines the principle of the sovereign equality of states.

History suggests that great powers establish spheres of influence to limit the autonomy of lesser states and thereby:

---

[6] The "Monroe Doctrine" was the first formal declaration of a sphere of influence by any country, though the term itself was not used in diplomacy until 1885. In its original form, it was an effort to deny extra-hemispheric powers spheres of influence that might threaten U.S. security. (The 1904 Roosevelt Corollary transformed it from an instrument of strategic denial into an active assertion of U.S. dominance of the Hemisphere.) Proclaimed by U.S. President James Monroe December 2, 1823, on the advice of Secretary of State John Quincy Adams, the Monroe Doctrine demanded the respect of European colonial powers for the independence of states in the Western Hemisphere and declared that any effort on their part to "extend their system to any portion of [the] hemisphere [would be seen] as dangerous to [U.S.] peace and safety." In 1864, as the United States was preoccupied with its civil war, France installed Archduke Ferdinand Maximilian Joseph von Hapsburg-Lorraine as the emperor of Mexico. In 1865, with the civil war behind it, the United States massed 40,000 troops on the Mexican border and demanded that the French remove him. The French withdrew their forces from Mexico. Maximilian was then captured and executed by the forces of Benito Juárez. In 1895, the United States threatened to go to war with Britain if it intervened in Venezuela. In 1917, a German proposal of an alliance with Mexico helped persuade the United States to enter World War I.

[7] As early as 1942, President Franklin D. Roosevelt envisaged a post-World War II world managed by what he called "the four policemen" or "four sheriffs," each of which would be responsible for maintaining peace in its sphere of influence. In his naïve conception, Britain would be in charge in its empire and Western Europe, the Soviet Union in eastern Europe and the central Eurasian landmass, China in East Asia and the western Pacific, and the United States in the Western Hemisphere. At the insistence of British Prime Minister, Winston Churchill, France was later added and recognized as responsible for the affairs of its empire.

- exclude competitors from markets they wish to dominate with mercantilist policies,
- deny other powers influence in a region while enhancing their own,
- deny the strategic use of territory or resources to potential adversaries,
- forestall the incorporation of potential buffer states into others' spheres of influence,
- assure the ideological conformity or allegiance of client states and their elites,
- gain or maintain access to territory and facilities from which to project power, and
- subordinate and exercise quasi-imperial control over lesser states.

In the absence of an international system based on shifting coalitions to balance hegemonic ambitions[8] and the creation of buffer and neutral states, spheres of influence are inextricable from the rivalries between great powers like China, India,[9] Iran,[10] Russia, and the United States. They are instruments of statecraft and diplomacy designed to distance, deter, and counter prospective adversaries by measures short of war. They presume a relatively stable distribution of power in the international state system as opposed to one in which relations are fluid.

Great powers trying to project their power or deflect that of potential adversaries seldom find it difficult to secure the deference of those whose autonomy they seek to limit. Still, a few less powerful states or groupings of them have been able to preserve their national identities and autonomy through a combination of armed neutrality, studied inoffensiveness, and recognition or acknowledgment of their status by potentially predatory powers.[11]

---

[8] In a system based on balances of power, a state that seeks hegemony will be balanced by coalitions among its rivals for hegemony. The classic exposition of such a system is Kissinger (1957).

[9] See note 14.

[10] Iran has created a politico-military sphere of influence in the Fertile Crescent (Iraq, Lebanon, occupied Palestine, Syria) and Yemen at the expense of Saudi Arabia and the United States. See also note 28.

[11] For example, Switzerland has remained independent by virtue of the strategic convenience this offers the great powers that surround it, a tough citizen army trained to exploit its difficult topography for defense, and its scrupulous neutrality in times of peace as well as war. Its neutrality was recognized at the Congress of Vienna in 1815. Austria was freed from great power occupation and exempted from their spheres of influence by the Austrian State Treaty of May 15, 1955. Finland severed its union with Russia in 1917. It lost 10 percent of its territory in the Winter War of 1939–40, the Continuation War of 1941–44, and the War of Lapland of 1944–45. Thereafter, it refused to compromise its independence and distinctive democratic social order while prudently maintaining cordial relations with Moscow and avoiding obvious challenges to core Russian interests. Finland's conduct proves that there is nothing ideologically pernicious about prudent self-restraint that recognizes the potential perils of offending more powerful neighbors. In 2022, in the wake of the Russian invasion of Ukraine, Finland felt free to abandon neutrality in favor of NATO membership. See also the discussion of the Association of Southeast Asian Nations (ASEAN), below, and at note 36.

These stances both deter and mitigate threats by others to subordinate or subjugate them. Spheres of influence demand deference and restrict the geopolitical or geoeconomic freedom of maneuver of the countries or regions within them. As such, they are inherently hegemonic.

They fall into two broad categories: (1) passive, defensive efforts to deny influence to other potential other competitors, and (2) active, assertive efforts to dominate the strategic choices of the nations within them, usually to bar and counter the influence of a single rather than multiple adversaries.[12] Each has different implications for competing powers, and each requires a distinct response from them.

The Origins of Spheres of Influence

Just as Rome and Carthage competed in the third and second centuries BCE to control peripheral areas of the western Mediterranean,[13] in the eighteenth and nineteenth centuries, Britain, France, and other European imperialist powers competed to divide areas far from home, like India,[14] China,[15]

---

[12] Spheres of influence are not the same as colonial empires, communities of settler states, or linguistic communities. Spheres of influence preserve but constrain sovereignty; colonialism extinguishes it. The age of European global ascendancy that began with the sixteenth century and ended in the twentieth included the establishment of new states through migration from other countries and created settler states. The primary example of a community of sibling settler states is the Anglosphere (Britain plus Australia, Canada, New Zealand, and the United States), but there are others (e.g., France and Québec, Portugal and Brazil.) Linguistic communities are a legacy of imperial expansion, for example, the Anglophone countries of the British Commonwealth plus the Philippines, the Arab world, the *Francophonie*, the Lusophone countries of Africa plus Timor Leste, and the twenty-plus countries where Spanish is the official language.

[13] The three Punic Wars were fought from 264 BCE to 146 BCE and culminated in Rome's destruction of Carthage.

[14] The eighteenth-century military struggle between the British East India Company and the French *Compagnie Française des Indes* for direct control in India continued until the British victory at Plassey in the Seven Years War (1756–63) ended it. The French, having been denied empire, then cultivated a sphere of influence with warring Indian states by supplying them with advisers and trainers, turning them against the British, and thus indirectly imperiling the British presence in India while Britain and France contested control in Europe. In response, the British cultivated and conquered Indian states, ultimately achieving imperial control of the subcontinent.

[15] Foreign nations initially competed for trade with China by establishing "treaty ports" within which their law, rather than Chinese law, applied. They then sought to divide the Chinese hinterland into mercantilist spheres of influence within which only they enjoyed the right to trade, invest, and proselytize. On the eve of the Chinese revolution of 1911, Russia claimed the largest such sphere, followed by Britain, France, Japan, Germany, and Italy. The United States, under the "Open Door" policy it adopted after its conquest of the Philippines, abjured the establishment of its own sphere of influence in China but claimed equal access and commercial rights in others' spheres. In 1895, Japan annexed Taiwan from China, while removing Korea from the Chinese sphere of influence. In 1905, it annexed Korea.

Southeast Asia,[16] and Africa,[17] between them. The initial impulse for these divisions was mercantilist,[18] but they evolved into primarily military contests aimed at geopolitical dominance. They persisted as political demarcations until overwhelmed by World War II and the subsequent end of the colonial era.

Formally declared primacy in a defined area, like the U.S. Monroe Doctrine's assertion of a unique right to exclude the Western Hemisphere from expanded influence by extra-regional powers or the proactive partition of China, the Middle East, and Africa between European great powers, was a feature of the nineteenth-century colonial world order. As the century ended, spheres of influence constituted proto-imperial impositions of exclusive politico-military and ideological control on the societies within them.

Consistent with this, the 1904 Roosevelt Corollary to the Monroe Doctrine amended it to proclaim a U.S. right to intervene militarily to correct "flagrant and chronic wrongdoing by a Latin American nation." The new policy, which actively asserted U.S. hegemony in the Western Hemisphere, was implemented with vigor.[19] In the 1930s, when Germany and Japan attempted to erode American primacy in countries like Brazil and Peru, the United States tempered its unabashed interventionism by adopting what it called a "Good Neighbor Policy." Still, during World War II, Washington felt free to kidnap and intern thousands of Latin Americans of German, Japanese, and Italian descent (German-American Internee Coalition n.d.; Warren 2014).

World War II, the Cold War, and Decolonization

The defeat of Germany in World War II and the subsequent Communist victory in the civil war on the Chinese mainland enabled the Soviet Union to

---

[16] By the beginning of the twentieth century, Southeast Asia other than Thailand (which had been divided into British and French spheres of influence) had been subjected to the colonial rule of Britain, France, the Netherlands, Portugal, and the United States.

[17] This process culminated in the Berlin Conference (also known as the "Congo Conference") of 1884–85.

[18] Mercantilism is an economic policy designed to maximize the exports and minimize the imports for an economy. The states that practice it use all elements of state power, including the military, to protect home markets and defend their privileges in markets abroad from competition by others.

[19] By 1904, the United States had already seized Cuba and Puerto Rico from Spain, threatened to go to war with Great Britain over Venezuela, and intervened to detach Panama from Colombia. It subsequently invaded Nicaragua, Honduras, Mexico, Haiti, the Dominican Republic, Guatemala, Cuba, Panama, Costa Rica, and Grenada, and engaged in covert regime-change operations in many of these countries as well as in Chile, Venezuela, and Bolivia. The first version of the Monroe Doctrine had been passive and defensive. The second was active and domineering.

install subservient regimes in central and eastern Europe,[20] as well as Korea north of the 38th parallel. In the first decade after the 1949 proclamation of the People's Republic of China, Moscow appeared to have gained paramount influence in China and North Vietnam.[21]

The United States had previously restricted its aspirations to overlordship of the Western Hemisphere under the Monroe Doctrine. But, once engaged in a global struggle with the USSR for global strategic and ideological hegemony, it began to build new, extra-hemispheric spheres of influence based on treaties offering protection from the USSR to an expanding inventory of states in Europe and Asia. Within these spheres, America demanded varying degrees of allegiance from those it had offered to protect. In the context of the Cold War's static bipolar world order, they were an important stabilizing factor.

In Europe in 1949, the United States sponsored the North Atlantic Treaty Organization (NATO) to hold the USSR and its ideology at bay, submerge the traditional antagonisms of western Europe's great powers (France, Germany, Italy, and the United Kingdom) in an American-led alliance structure, and facilitate the economic and political recovery of western Europe. As a purely defensive alliance of democratic states led by the United States, NATO very effectively served all three purposes throughout the Cold War.

In maritime Asia and the Pacific, having defeated Japan, Washington fell heir to Tokyo's wartime sphere of influence. To secure this sphere and thereby protect its new Asian client states, the United States began to build a series of bilateral alliances[22] to contain China, the USSR, North Korea, and North Vietnam.

America called the areas of the world in which it exercised dominant influence "the free world."[23] In the four-decade-long "Cold War" (1948–91),[24]

---

[20] Meeting with Joseph Stalin in Moscow, in October 1944, British Prime Minister Winston Churchill, a committed imperialist, privately proposed specific percentages of influence to be exercised by each party in the countries of eastern Europe and the Balkans. Stalin agreed, but the subsequent imposition of what Churchill called "the iron curtain" ensured that, except in Greece and Yugoslavia, Soviet influence excluded any influential role for the British or other Western powers.

[21] The division of Korea and Vietnam laid the basis for subsequent wars to reunite them. In Korea, the North Korean invasion of South Korea failed. In Vietnam, the North Vietnamese were able to conquer south Vietnam.

[22] These protective U.S. alliances included Australia and New Zealand (1951), the Philippines (1951), the Republic of Korea (1853), the Southeast Asian Treaty Organization (SEATO, including Australia, France, New Zealand, Philippines, Thailand, and the United Kingdom, 1954), and Japan (1960).

[23] "Free" appears to have meant little more than "not subordinate to the USSR or China." The term was an appealing but inaccurate description of an agglomeration of democracies, dictatorships, military regimes, monarchies, and kleptocracies whose only thing in common was their affiliation with the United States rather than its adversaries.

[24] The Cold War began with the 1948–49 Berlin airlift and ended with the 1989 fall of the Berlin Wall and the 1991 dissolution of the Soviet Union.

Soviet and American-led ideological and geopolitical blocs each sought to achieve dominant ideological and political influence everywhere they could and to prevent the other from doing so. The withering away of Euro-Atlantic nations' empires in Asia, the Middle East, and Africa, with which this struggle coincided, created both independent states and apparent power vacuums. The newly independent states of the so-called Third World were fertile ground for both overt and covert U.S.-Soviet proxy wars, notably in Indochina, West Asia and North Africa, the Congo, Lusophone Africa,[25] the Horn of Africa, and Afghanistan.

In 1961–62, the USSR took advantage of a recent (1959) regime change in Cuba to establish a strategic outpost ninety miles from the United States.[26] Cuba's defection to the Soviet bloc triggered a violent U.S. reaction to the challenge this posed to Washington's Monroe Doctrine assertion of hegemony in the Americas. The Soviets, in partnership with Cuba, looked for openings to entrench their ideological, if not their military, influence in Nicaragua, Chile, and Grenada. In each case, the United States forcefully intervened to uphold its strategic paramountcy in the Western Hemisphere.[27] More recently, Washington has relied on economic warfare plus covert action to challenge and overthrow ideologically heterodox regimes in Latin American countries like Bolivia and Venezuela.

In the 1960s, Britain's need to reduce its overseas commitments "east of Suez" led it to concede its sphere of influence in the Persian Gulf[28] to the United States. By 1967, countries in this region were independent but drawn to the United States by their need for protection from each other as well as from Iran, which became acute after the 1979 Islamic revolution there. In the early 1970s, the United States buttressed China's exit from the Soviet bloc by

---

[25] The 1975 revolution in Portugal led to the dissolution of the Portuguese Empire and to the emergence of pro-Soviet regimes in Lusophone Africa (Angola, Cabo Verde, Guinea-Bissau, Mozambique, and São Tome e Principe). With the demise of the USSR, these countries left the Soviet orbit and were increasingly connected to post-*apartheid* South Africa.

[26] This was an ill-considered response by the USSR to the U.S. emplacement of nuclear-armed missiles aimed at it from Turkey.

[27] These U.S. reactions included the 1961 Bay of Pigs invasion and other efforts to produce regime change in Cuba, the Cuban missile crisis of 1962, the 1973 overthrow of the government of Chile, the 1981–88 Contra war in Nicaragua, and the 1983 U.S. invasion of Grenada.

[28] Britain had dominated what is now the United Arab Emirates as well as Bahrain, Kuwait, Oman, and Qatar since the early nineteenth century, when the British rulers of India intervened to eliminate piracy and secure lines of communication between India and the British Isles. Similar strategic concerns about lines of communication between Asia and Europe have driven the informal U.S. security commitments to Saudi Arabia and other Persian Gulf states. The fall of the Shah of Iran and his replacement by Shiite Islamists hostile to the United States and the Sunni Arab monarchies of the Gulf encouraged them to place themselves under American influence and protection.

offering it politico-military protection from the USSR. Later in the decade, Washington took advantage of Egypt's desire to make peace with Israel to remove it from the Soviet sphere of influence in the Middle East.[29]

Spheres of influence do not necessarily disappear as colonial empires contract or are abandoned, though allegiances sometimes change. Since granting independence to its African colonies in 1960, France has maintained an internationally acknowledged politico-military and monetary sphere of influence in them, sometimes called *Françafrique*.[30] In 1968, the USSR retroactively justified its invasions of Hungary and Czechoslovakia by formally claiming a right to reverse any effort to dislodge its version of "socialism" in central and eastern Europe.[31] When applied to the "Communist bloc," this Soviet parallel to the Monroe Doctrine produced a definitive rupture in Sino-Soviet relations and opened the way for the United States to court China as a partner in the containment of the USSR.

Contemporary Spheres of Influence

Today, with the notable continuing exception of the Monroe Doctrine, spheres of influence are usually neither formally declared nor negotiated between great powers. India's sphere of influence in sub-Himalayan Asia[32]; Iran's in Iraq, Lebanon, Syria, and Yemen[33]; Australia's in the south Pacific[34];

---

[29] The 1979 "Camp David Accords" were accompanied by an Egyptian shift away from Moscow to allegiance to and dependence on Washington. Since then, Egypt has received substantial annual subventions from the United States.

[30] The French continue to police their African sphere of influence and to sustain a monetary union with them. The Euro-pegged currency known as the CFA franc is used in Benin, Burkina Faso, Côte d'Ivoire, Guinea-Bissau, Mali, Niger, Senegal, and Togo. France requires these countries to maintain 65 percent of their hard currency reserves in the French Treasury.

[31] The USSR intervened in Hungary on November 4, 1956, and in Czechoslovakia on August 20, 1968. On November 13, 1968, in what became known as the Brezhnev Doctrine, Leonid Brezhnev, the General Secretary of the Soviet Communist Party, declared that no member country could leave the Soviet-dominated Warsaw Pact or disturb a ruling Communist party's monopoly on power.

[32] No external great power has ever attempted to interfere with coercive policies by India in its region. None challenges Indian suzerainty in Bhutan. None actively opposed the Indian annexation of Goa or Sikkim, separation of Bangladesh from West Pakistan, prolonged occupation of Sri Lanka, blockade of Nepal, or counter-coup intervention in the Maldives. On the other hand, no other naval power has accepted India's intermittent claims that it is entitled to primacy in the Indian Ocean.

[33] Bungled American policies in the Levant and the Arabian Peninsula set the stage for a major expansion of Iranian politico-military influence in the Levant and the Arabian Peninsula. Both Israel and Saudi Arabia now feel strategically encircled by an Iranian sphere of influence.

[34] See White (2019).

and South Africa's in southern Africa[35] are informal. To formalize them would pose an obvious challenge to the Westphalian principles of state independence, immunity from military intervention, and sovereign equality on which the United Nations system and the post-colonial world order are grounded. But the fact that spheres of influence are undeclared should not obscure their continuing relevance.[36] They are assertions of military, economic, technological, and political dominance that are as likely to evoke challenge as acquiescence from others, especially in periods of major shifts in balances of power and prestige.

Spheres of influence both constrain and stimulate great power strategic interactions. As such they are a factor that statecraft and diplomacy cannot ignore.

Post-Soviet Europe

Beginning in 1989, the Soviet empire and then the Soviet Union itself imploded, disappearing as a security threat to the rest of Europe, China, the Middle East, and the world. NATO's "Partnership for Peace"[37] briefly held out the promise of a Europe-wide cooperative security architecture in which the reconstituted Russian Federation as well as the United States would both participate and play a stabilizing role. But instead of dismantling the alliances and protective arrangements it had established to deal with now vanished Cold War threats, as the 1990s proceeded, Washington embraced the Russophobia of central and eastern European countries and their American diasporas by reemphasizing NATO as a defense against possible threats from

---

[35] South Africa is now at the politico-economic center of the sphere of influence defined by the Southern African Development Community (SADC), originally established to coordinate efforts by its neighbors to end its *apartheid* and colonial control of Namibia. SADC now consists of Angola, Botswana, Comoros, the Democratic Republic of the Congo, Eswatini, Lesotho, Madagascar, Malawi, Mauritius, Mozambique, Namibia, Seychelles, Tanzania, Zambia, and Zimbabwe, in addition to South Africa.

[36] A negative case in point is the Association of Southeast Asian Nations (ASEAN). The governments of Indonesia, Malaysia, the Philippines, Singapore, and Thailand established ASEAN in 1967. Its purpose was to promote peace and security in Southeast Asia and to accelerate economic development despite the ongoing wars between the United States and Chinese and Soviet-aided forces in Indochina. After the 1975 Communist victories there, ASEAN helped its members adjust to the changed balance of power and expanded to include Brunei, Vietnam, Laos, Myanmar, and Cambodia. Today, ASEAN is a means by which its members can avoid incorporation into the spheres of influence of any of the great powers contending for strategic primacy in Asia. It enables them to speak collectively to external great powers about their shared security, economic, and political concerns. Such powers recognize "ASEAN centrality," accept that ASEAN is non-aligned between them, and seek to cooperate with it rather than antagonize it. Like Switzerland, ASEAN balances its relationships with those most likely to limit its independence and leaves ideology to ideologues.

[37] Proposed by the United States in October 1993 and formally launched by NATO in January 1994.

a revived Russia. The United States undertook to expand NATO not just to the frontiers of the former USSR but beyond them.[38] This was an impulse born of America's so-called unipolar moment, in which it sought universal deference to its values and interests and began to launch massive interventions to change regimes that refused to comply. In doing so, it set aside the UN Charter and other foundational elements of international law.

Belying its original purely defensive *raison d'être*, NATO then vivisected Serbia (ripping Kosovo from it), joined the post-9/11 American effort to pacify and transform Afghanistan, and helped overthrow the government of Libya. Russia and other great powers came to see NATO as a threateningly offensive tool of American foreign policy. Meanwhile, the alliance, which was coterminous with an American sphere of politico-military influence in Europe and the Mediterranean, resumed justifying its continued existence by reference to the threats from Russia it had helped to resurrect.[39] Eventually, Russia resorted to shows of force followed by military intervention in Ukraine to block any further expansion of the American military sphere of influence in Europe.[40]

In its long history, Europe has been at peace only when its major powers have all been included in a cooperative security system. The Concert of Europe moderated warfare and enabled a broad European peace for a century. The exclusion of Germany and the USSR from the councils of Europe in the 1920s and 1930s catalyzed World War II and the Cold War. The attempted

---

[38] As early as the U.S. midterm elections of 1994, both the Republican Party and the Clinton administration were courting ethnic Slavic and Baltic voters by suggesting early membership in NATO for their ancestral homelands. By December 1994, Russia, which professed to have been seeking partnership with the United States, angrily declared that it felt threatened and betrayed (see NSA 2018). The Czech Republic, Hungary, and Poland were admitted to NATO in 1999; Bulgaria, Estonia, Latvia, Lithuania (all formerly part of the USSR), Romania, Slovakia, and Slovenia in 2004; Albania and Croatia in 2009; Montenegro in 2017; and North Macedonia in 2020. In 2008, when NATO declared it would be prepared to admit Georgia and Ukraine to membership, Russia warned that it would regard this as "a direct threat" to its security. Meanwhile, the United States briefly attempted to establish its influence in Central Asia before ceasing to contest the dominant politico-military influence of Russia and the economic influence of China there.

[39] In 2020, when the United States and other NATO countries, citing election fraud, refused to recognize the Lukashenko government, Belarus placed itself under Russian protection, thus confirming its position as part of a residual Russian sphere of influence in eastern Europe.

[40] By 2021–22, Russia had built enough military strength to mount a diplomatic challenge to the continued expansion of NATO. Moscow demonstrated an apparent ability to overwhelm Ukraine, signaled that admitting it to NATO membership might trigger a nuclear confrontation with the United States, and demanded that the United States and NATO end the menace such expansion posed to its peace of mind. Russia consistently denied that it had any intention of invading Ukraine. But when it received no U.S. or NATO answer to its demands, it nonetheless attacked, changing its apparent objective from strategic denial of Ukraine to the U.S. sphere of influence to the incorporation of Ukraine into a reestablished sphere of influence of its own.

exclusion of Russia from a role in the maintenance of peace and security in Europe in the twenty-first century has deprived it of diplomatic alternatives to a relapse into belligerent behavior.

The Middle East

In the Middle East, the collapse of the USSR orphaned Iraq and Syria, both of which had remained part of the shrunken Soviet sphere of influence that followed Egypt's defection to America. No longer constrained by Moscow, Iraq gambled that it could alleviate the financial exhaustion of its eight-year war with Iran[41] by seizing Kuwait and its oil riches. In response, a UN-authorized coalition of forces led by the United States and Saudi Arabia liberated Kuwait.[42] Syria joined this coalition, signaling a willingness to explore relations with the United States as a partial substitute for the support of the vanished USSR, but was rebuffed due to its hostility to Israel.

In 2003, the United States invaded Iraq, ousted its government, and attempted to incorporate it into the American politico-military sphere of influence. The United States achieved military dominance in Iraq only to see Iran gain a paramount position in its politics. The concurrent U.S. effort to engineer regime change in Syria failed, entrenching Iranian influence there and providing an unexpected opportunity for a resurgence of Russian influence in the Assad government (Yacoubian 2021). The destabilization of Iraq and Syria provoked a backlash by Islamist extremists, who briefly erased the border between the two and established an "Islamic state." Turkey incorporated parts of northern Iraq and Syria into its military and economic spheres. The United States established a blatantly illegal military presence in Syria. After the withdrawal of all but a residual U.S. military training mission (Tritten 2021), China became the preeminent foreign participant in the Iraqi economy (Bonesh 2021). Meanwhile, "fracking" enabled the United States to resume its historic status as a major energy exporter and made it the swing producer in global energy markets. This reduced the centrality of the Persian Gulf in U.S. global policy. The American commitment to Persian Gulf security diminished concomitantly.

As the twenty-first century proceeded, U.S. dominance of the affairs of the "Middle East" eroded. Despite the resurgence in Russian influence and intermittent French attempts to reassert a leading role in Lebanon, regional rather

---

[41] 1980–88.
[42] Iraq invaded Kuwait on August 4, 1990. It agreed to a ceasefire with U.S. and Saudi-led forces at Safwan on March 3, 1991.

than external powers began to drive politico-military rivalries and dynamics there. China is displacing other great powers as the region's largest economic partner, but the Middle East is no longer in the sphere of influence of any great power or divided between several, as in the past.

The U.S. "Pivot" to East Asia

In Asia, the disappearance of the USSR as a shared Sino-American adversary eliminated the major rationale for strategic cooperation between Beijing and Washington. The U.S.-China diplomatic finesse that had set the Taiwan issue aside to cooperate in the containment of Soviet ambitions began to break down. Ideological differences reemerged to estrange the United States from China.[43] The return of China to wealth and power after its two-century-long eclipse by the West and Japan began to erode the primacy the United States had exercised in the Asia-Pacific since the defeat of Japan in 1945. Alarmed American strategists and military planners began to view China as a potential "near peer competitor"[44] of the United States. America reaffirmed its post-Cold War determination to prevent the rise of any power anywhere that might rival it (Tyler 1992). The U.S. military progressively diverted reconnaissance and other resources previously devoted to Russia to targets in China, stepped up aggressive military activities along China's borders, and attempted to enlist NATO members in support of efforts to balance rising Chinese power. But the United States proved unable to develop or implement a strategy to retain its previous economic leadership in the region, which became steadily more centered on China.

Sino-Russian Entente

NATO's expansion and what the United States called its "pivot to Asia" produced a growing, openly hostile presence, headed by senior U.S. combatant commanders, on the peripheries of both Russia and China that aimed at

---

[43] The brutal military suppression of the 1989 student and worker uprisings in Beijing's Tiananmen Square and elsewhere in China put human rights issues at the center of the relationship at a time when the end of the Cold War had made America feel omnipotent. Meanwhile, Taiwan, which had been a dictatorship, democratized, endearing it to American proponents of democracy promotion abroad.

[44] The U.S. Department of Defense's Office of Net Assessment invented the "peer competitor" concept as a means of modeling force structure and guiding the development of military capabilities in the absence of a real-world high-tech enemy like the USSR. The enemy it posited would be able to match and counter any capability the U.S. armed forces might field. Such a "peer competitor" was a maximally challenging enemy in war games and the perfect driver of weapons procurement. In time, defense planners settled on China as the real-world "peer competitor."

militarily containing both. Not surprisingly, both pushed back. Moscow escalated its objections to further expansion of the American sphere of influence represented by NATO and warned that it would have to react militarily if this were not halted.

Beijing renewed its drive to end the division of China produced by U.S. military intervention in the Taiwan Strait to separate the combatants in the Chinese civil war. Sino-American hostility grew apace.

As the twenty-first century began, Russia had no acknowledged sphere of influence in Europe other than the former Soviet republic of Belarus, though its European neighbors (other than the newly established state of Ukraine) remained careful not to provoke it.[45] But, as the newly globalized American sphere of influence (represented in Europe by NATO) neared its borders, Moscow became obsessed with strategic denial of neighboring countries to dominant American influence. Meanwhile, long-standing objections by China to continuing U.S. support of Taiwan (the Chinese island province to which the U.S.-supported losing side in the Chinese civil war had retreated) intensified. China sought to remove Taiwan from the U.S. sphere of influence in Asia and to deny it status as an independent polity. Despite having no claims of its own, the United States challenged China's territorial claims in the East and South China Seas.

Washington's labeling of both Russia and China as ideological and geopolitical adversaries and its treatment of them as such gave their partnership a common focus and helped to consolidate it. Escalating U.S. pressure pushed these two formerly estranged great powers into an increasingly open and comprehensive anti-American entente, committed to coordination of policies and actions directed at reducing the menacing military presence and hostile political influence of the United States on their respective peripheries.

NATO, the EU, Turkey, and Russia

By 2020, five post-Cold War enlargement rounds had extended NATO to all of Europe other than its officially neutral states[46] and expanded the alliance to thirty members. For most of these, especially the new members, NATO was

---

[45] For example, Norway, the only founding member of NATO to border Russia, has long barred the peacetime stationing of troops and offensive weapons from other NATO countries on its territory. See also the discussion of the armed neutrality of Finland, above.

[46] Austria and Switzerland are officially neutral and internationally recognized as such. Finland, Ireland, and Sweden remained until recently outside alliance structures, though all three have long been part of the American politico-economic sphere of influence in Europe. Bosnia and Herzegovina, and Ukraine aspire to join NATO. Moldova is constitutionally neutral. Serbia seeks to join the EU but not NATO.

still a purely defensive alliance. They had no significant ability to contribute to expeditionary military operations and sought dependence on the United States, NATO, and its larger member states for their defense.

But the post-Cold War era saw NATO cease to emphasize its defensive character and to become a platform for offensive military operations in the Balkans and "out of area" interventions by "à la carte" coalitions led or backed by the United States.[47] Efforts to include Russia in consultations with the United States and NATO about European security issues foundered. Meanwhile, Turkey both distanced itself from the United States and, like Russia, set aside its centuries-old aspiration to be recognized as part of the European community of nations centered on Berlin, London, Paris, and Rome. And, as Sino-American relations turned adversarial, U.S. efforts to enlist NATO and its members in operations directed at countering Chinese naval power in the South China Sea helped convince China that it should share Russian opposition to further NATO enlargement.

Post-Soviet Central Asia

The United States and the European Union (EU) briefly challenged China and Russia for influence in post-Soviet Central Asia, but it soon became obvious to them that they were at best marginal players in the region. Russia and China did not have to do much to deny them significant roles in its governance, economic development, and foreign relations. An effort by Turkey to assert a pan-Turkic sphere of influence has yet to succeed.

In Central Asia, the newly reconstituted Russian Federation has worked out a de facto division of influence domains with China. The Shanghai Cooperation Organisation (SCO)[48] provides a forum and mechanism in which the two countries can cooperate with the countries of the region to deny the region to Islamist extremism, terrorism, separatist movements, and regime change through "color revolutions." Meanwhile, given Beijing's insistence on Westphalian norms of non-intervention, China seems content to

---

[47] Fourteen of NATO's then-nineteen members participated in the U.S.-led 1999 air war with Serbia. NATO commanded the International Security Assistance Force (ISAF) in Afghanistan in which a total of fifty nations took part, many of them not NATO members, but most NATO members declined to join the U.S. invasion and occupation of Iraq. Nine NATO member states spearheaded the 2011 intervention in Libya, which was joined by two non-NATO members. The majority of member states did not take part in the conflict.

[48] Established in 1996, the SCO has become the world's largest regional security organization in geographic scope and population, covering three-fifths of the Eurasian continent, two-fifths of the world population, and about one-fourth of global GDP. Its current members are China, India, Iran, Kazakhstan, Kyrgyzstan, Pakistan, Russia, Tajikistan, and Uzbekistan.

leave military intervention in Central Asia to Russia and its partners in the Russian-sponsored Collective Security Treaty Organization (CSTO).[49] The CSTO, which took its current form in 1999,[50] has defined a military sphere of influence for Russia in Central Asia,[51] where it is the universally acknowledged "first responder."

On a visit to Kazakhstan in 2013, Chinese president Xi Jinping announced what has become known as the "Belt and Road Initiative" (BRI). This began as a framework by which to build infrastructure, facilitate trade and transit, and connect all points in the Eurasian landmass, maritime Southeast Asia, and East Africa to China, but has since expanded to encompass the globe. Moscow has linked its Eurasian Economic Union (EAEU) to the BRI. Russia is ruled by realists who recognize that they do not have the capacity to compete with Beijing in trade and investment in the lands between them, which are unlikely to be able to resist the attractions of China's huge and expanding market.

Central Asia illustrates a likely global future in which worldwide and regional orders are both multipolar and multidimensional in terms of the domains they cover. There are already four overlaid spheres of influence there:

- A post-colonial Russian sphere of linguistic and cultural influence with its center of gravity in Moscow.
- Dominant Russian politico-military influence through the CSTO, which protects the region's regimes from "color revolutions."
- A shared Sino-Russian antiterrorist sphere of influence embodied in the SCO, which is directed at neutralizing extremist and separatist movements and preventing them from penetrating China's or Russia's borders.
- An emerging Chinese sphere of economic influence.
- The absence of effective military, economic, technological, or political competition from the United States or the EU.

---

[49] China registered no objection to the CSTO intervention in Kazakhstan. The "Five Principles of Peaceful Coexistence," which have been central tenets of Chinese foreign relations since 1954, are a succinct restatement of Westphalianism and hence the principles of the United Nations Charter. They are "mutual respect for each other's territorial integrity and sovereignty, mutual non-aggression, mutual non-interference in each other's internal affairs, equality and cooperation for mutual benefit, and peaceful co-existence."

[50] Current CSTO members are Armenia, Belarus, Kazakhstan, Kyrgyzstan, Russia, and Tajikistan. In January 2022, the CSTO sent troops to restore order and protect the government from an insurrection in Kazakhstan. This was its first such intervention.

[51] The CSTO bars its members from joining any other military alliance.

The "Indo-Pacific"

In the Indo-Pacific[52] too, multipolarity and multidimensionality are becoming the norm, with different great powers now engaged in competition for dominant roles in an expanding variety of military, economic, technological, and political domains. In this region, as in others, the United States is perceived to be progressively less engaged than it was in the last century, given its erratic attendance at regional gatherings and withdrawal from trade and investment agreements. China's economic size gives it influence, but the rules for trade and investment are being made plurilaterally, not by China, and without participation from external powers like the United States.[53] Meanwhile geographic propinquity gives China military advantages that the United States lacks. Politically, China currently inspires more anxiety in its neighbors than emulation.

Japan remains the most trusted power in East Asia and the Pacific. Despite India's inclusion in the concept of the "Indo-Pacific" geopolitical zone, it remains largely sidelined. The Indo-Pacific region, which coincides with the area of responsibility of the former U.S. Pacific Command,[54] now encompasses:

* An intensifying Sino-American contest for strategic control of Taiwan,[55] which China seeks to wrest from the U.S. sphere of influence and bring under its renewed control.
* An increasingly Sinocentric Asian regional economy, in which Asians make the rules for trade and investment without the participation of the formerly dominant United States (or the EU).
* Vehemently asserted but slowly eroding American region-wide politico-military leadership.
* ASEAN determination to avoid having to choose between China and the United States even as some ASEAN member states begin to make such choices in favor of China.

---

[52] As a strategic concept, the "Indo-Pacific" combines East and South Asia. It originated as a Japanese formula to justify including India in efforts to balance Chinese influence in Southeast Asia.

[53] Key institutions include the Comprehensive and Progressive Agreement for Trans-Pacific Partnership (CPTPP), which Japan rescued from U.S. withdrawal and which China as well as the United Kingdom aspire to join, and the Regional Comprehensive Economic Partnership (RCEP), a free trade agreement between fifteen Asia-Pacific countries, including Australia, Brunei, Cambodia, China, Indonesia, Japan, South Korea, Laos, Malaysia, Myanmar, New Zealand, the Philippines, Singapore, Thailand, and Vietnam.

[54] Renamed the Indo-Pacific Command in 2018.

[55] See Freeman (2020) and (2021); Kritenbrink and Ratner (2021).

- Troubled relations between a neutral Myanmar and its neighbors, fellow ASEAN member states, Bangladesh, China, India, and the West.
- Australian confirmation of military dependence on the United States and cooperation with a rearming Japan in the context of deteriorating Sino-Australian relations.
- An U.S.-aligned Australian sphere of influence in the South Pacific that appears to be eroding as China establishes a competitive presence.[56]
- Strategic hedging, self-strengthening activity, and increasing regional outreach by formerly submissive U.S. allies in northeast Asia.[57]
- Indian politico-military hegemony in South Asia (countered only by Pakistan).
- Independent buffer states between China and India (Nepal) and China, South Korea, and Japan (North Korea).
- A strengthening Chinese military presence in the South China Sea.
- A restive, nonaligned, potential great power in Indonesia.

China's "Belt and Road Initiative"

The BRI began as an effort to extend China's domestic industrial policies[58] to countries beyond its borders. It was framed as a means of exporting surplus Chinese industrial capacity to build infrastructure[59] that could connect all the countries of the Eurasian "world island" and East Africa to China. But as other countries have sought to tap Chinese capital and construction expertise, the BRI has expanded to include partner states on every continent, including Africa and the Americas. In Africa, BRI-related investment has become the largest source of funding for economic uplift, dwarfing financial support from institutions like the World Bank. China's domestic savings are being channeled into foreign investment in development, not just through the BRI, but

---

[56] France and New Zealand also hold sway in parts of the Pacific.

[57] U.S. forces occupied Japan after World War II and never left. The U.S. troop presence there and in South Korea has long been unpopular. Japanese and Koreans tolerated it because of the Soviet threat to their independence and the perceived military superiority of North Korea to South Korea. With the end of the Cold War and the remarkable ascendancy of the Republic of Korea (ROK) over its northern rival, this tolerance is increasingly fragile. Meanwhile, Washington's stridently anti-Chinese posture has fed concern that Japan and the ROK could be dragged willy-nilly into a Sino-American war, and erratic American foreign policy behavior has raised doubts about the reliability of U.S. security guarantees.

[58] In China, the state sets strategic development objectives, which it supports with project finance from its banks. Projects are conceived by entrepreneurs (both state-owned and private) to respond to market conditions and designed to be profitable. Officials are rated on how well they support the creation of enterprises and jobs consistent with these objectives. The combination encourages strong public-private partnership that is supportive of national objectives.

[59] Roads, railroads, pipelines, fiber optic cables, ports, airports, industrial and free trade zones.

through new institutions[60] that are compatible with and complement the Bretton Woods framework.

The BRI finances investment in infrastructure to raise economic efficiency and bring into being a worldwide logistics network that is connected to China but available to others. It emphasizes market opening and includes the negotiation of free trade agreements and standardized arrangements to speed customs clearance, bonded storage, and the transit of goods. It imposes no requirement for Chinese partners to exclude relationships with other countries. So, it has little if anything in common with mercantilism.[61]

Nevertheless, linking other countries' economies to China undercuts their previous dependence on the United States and its allies. Even if the BRI continues to avoid efforts to exclude others from trade and investment in the countries that participate in it, it gives them an incremental stake in good relations with Beijing to balance their interest in cooperating with other great powers. This makes it likely to create a politico-economic circle of deference for China, if not dependence on it or an exclusionary sphere of influence.

Although the BRI is geoeconomic, rather than geopolitical, in nature, and has no unified planning apparatus or oversight of the projects it fosters, it is viewed with alarm by the United States, which sees it as a threat to its previous global primacy and as a potential Chinese sphere of influence. So far, U.S. opposition to the BRI has taken the form of coercive diplomacy and hostile information campaigns. This approach has registered few if any successes because it misconstrues the geoeconomic nature of the BRI as geopolitical. Fiscal and other constraints make it difficult, if not impossible for the United States to offer attractive alternatives to cooperation by BRI member countries with China. Neither the United States nor its European allies now have the financial or engineering capacity to compete effectively with Chinese policy banks or construction companies.[62] The adage, "you can't beat something with nothing" applies.

---

[60] For example, the Silk Road Fund (established 2014), the 105-member Asian Infrastructure Investment Bank (established 2015), and the New Development Bank (formerly the BRICS Bank, established 2017).

[61] See note 18.

[62] Lacking the capacity to carry out a politico-economic strategy to counter rising Chinese influence, the United States has sought to answer it with increased military spending and deployments, accompanied by coercive diplomacy through financial sanctions. But this approach does not provide alternative financing or a substitute for Chinese investment and construction projects, and therefore does nothing to reduce the BRI's appeal.

Neo-Mercantilism and Technological Spheres of Influence

Under the Trump administration, the United States responded to the challenge of China's growing economic strength and technological competence by adopting neo-mercantilist[63] policies. These policies have been continued by the Biden administration. While they pay lip service to the need for the reinvigoration of the American political economy, they aim at hamstringing the Chinese economy and retarding its technological advance. They have so far galvanized rather than curbed efforts by China to reduce its long-standing dependence on the United States for imports of food and high-tech components for manufacturing.[64] Meanwhile, Washington's and Beijing's efforts to decouple high-tech supply chains is leading to the emergence of new technological spheres of influence with incompatible industrial and consumer standards.[65]

The Global American Sphere of Influence

Washington no longer frames its arguments for and against policies in terms of the provisions of the UN Charter or major international legal conventions. Instead, it promotes the idea of a worldwide "rules-based order" in which liberal internationalism serves as a thin cover for U.S. primacy.[66] The "rules-based order" amounts to the assertion of a global sphere of influence in which the United States, assisted by the Anglosphere and a few former colonial powers,[67] sets and enforces the rules. American primacy and overlordship are

---

[63] Neo-mercantilism is a revived theory of mercantilism emphasizing trade restriction policies justified by "national security" concerns. It seeks to increase domestic employment through protectionist measures, while using export controls and restrictive immigration policies to limit foreign access to scientific knowledge and technology with military applications.

[64] China is no longer the fastest growing market for U.S. exports, as it once was. The imposition of tariffs has exacerbated supply chain problems resulting from the COVID-19 epidemic and fed inflation in the U.S. economy. There has been no significant "reshoring" of industrial jobs from China to the United States.

[65] The U.S. campaign against Chinese telecommunications companies like Huawei and ZTE and its efforts to choke off Chinese access to extreme ultraviolet lithography (EUV) technology and equipment exemplify this effort to divide the global technology market. The irony is that, in many instances, the United States cannot itself produce alternatives to Chinese products.

[66] The new "rules-based order" omits references to the United Nations Charter and international law. Due to domestic political gridlock, the United States is no longer able to ratify international treaties and conventions, but it insists on its right to interpret them without regard to the views of others. The "rules-based order" presumes that the United States and its key allies (in the G-7) have the authority to make the rules, determine when and how to apply them, and exempt themselves from them while imposing and enforcing them on others.

[67] The "G-7," whose members are Britain, Canada, France, Germany, Italy, Japan, and the United States.

symbolized by the unique,[68] comprehensive set of U.S. regional military commands. These span the globe and are headed by quasi-viceregal four-star flag officers. The U.S.-directed "rules-based order" is institutionalized and reinforced:

- Militarily, by a network of some 800 bases beyond U.S. borders,[69] the world's widest ranging (if no longer the world's largest) navy, counterterrorism operations in much of the world,[70] and the world's greatest volume of arms sales.
- Economically, through use of dollar sovereignty and dominance of key multilateral institutions[71] to impose a bewilderingly complex set of financial and other sanctions on other countries.[72]
- Technologically, through the extraterritorial application of U.S. export and retransfer controls.[73]
- Informationally, by the dominant role of U.S. media and digital communication platforms.
- Politically, by regime-change operations, selective democracy promotion,[74] adjustments in levels of foreign assistance,[75] the enforcement of the Roosevelt

---

[68] No other country defines defense in global terms rather than by reference to its homeland.

[69] Of which 170 reportedly have golf courses!

[70] According to the Cost of War project sponsored by the Watson Institute at Brown University, in 2021, the U.S. military was engaged in such operations in eighty-five countries (Watson Institute 2021).

[71] For example, the Society for Worldwide Interbank Financial Telecommunication (SWIFT).

[72] Countries or regions subject to direct U.S. sanctions (either unilaterally or in part unilaterally) include (but are not limited to) the Balkans, Belarus, Burma, Burundi, Central African Republic, China, Cuba, Democratic Republic of Congo, Hong Kong, Iran, Iraq, Lebanon, Libya, Mali, Nicaragua, North Korea, Somalia, Sudan, South Sudan, Syria, Ukraine/Russia, Venezuela, Yemen, and Zimbabwe. U.S. secondary sanctions target normal arms-length commercial activity that does not involve a U.S. nexus and may be legal in the jurisdictions of the transacting parties. While U.S. individuals and entities must adhere to primary sanctions as a matter of U.S. law or face potential criminal/civil penalties, secondary sanctions present non-U.S. targets with a choice: do business with the United States or with the sanctioned target, but not both. Targeted sanctions prohibit U.S. persons from transactions with an individual or entity designated by the State or Treasury Departments under a specific sanctions regime.

[73] The United States now gives export controls and economic boycotts extraterritorial application. As a result, persons and companies in other states are prevented from exporting to or investing in the states targeted by the United States The United States previously argued (e.g., in the case of the Arab boycott of Israel) that this was illegal under international law.

[74] It is instructive to contrast the U.S. reaction to the 2013 military coup in Egypt and the 2021coup in Myanmar. Egypt is in the U.S. sphere of influence while Myanmar is outside it.

[75] For example, adjustments in aid policy toward El Salvador after its August 2018 switch in diplomatic relations from Taipei to Beijing and similar moves after anti-Chinese riots in the Solomon Islands in 2021.

Corollary to the Monroe Doctrine,[76] and the denial of technology and arms sales to countries that cooperate with designated U.S. adversaries.[77]

In effect, Washington now claims and seeks to exercise a right to help determine the policies and international alignments of all the world's countries other than China, Iran, the Democratic People's Republic of Korea, and the Russian Federation, all of which it regards and has designated for military planning purposes as implacable adversaries. In what some have called "a contest for the allegiance of humanity," countries in the spheres of influence of other great powers or not yet incorporated into the U.S. sphere are either courted[78] or subjected to coercive diplomacy through sanctions[79] or thrown into anarchy by regime-change operations.[80]

But in a period of major global power shifts, as formerly eclipsed civilization states like China, India, and (in their own views) Russia and Turkey resurge to wealth and power, the partitions of legacy spheres of influence deter less than they invite challenge. This defeats their purpose, which is to protect the security, political culture, and domestic tranquility of the states that establish them. The once-unchallenged U.S. global sphere of influence is under widening attack as other nations seek to deny territories and activities to American dominance and to compete in domains other than the politico-military. What seems to be replacing the once-unified world order is a congeries of regional, overlapping, multidimensional, political, economic, informational, technological,[81] and military spheres of influence.

Conclusion

In the beginning, there were military empires forged through conquest. Then there were trading empires that evolved into political control of areas like India and Indonesia. Some spheres of influence were devoted to denying other

---

[76] See note 19.

[77] For example, the termination of previously agreed cooperation in developing and building the F-35 "Lightning II" with Turkey after it bought the Russian S-400 air defense system. Also, threatened sanctions on India for the same transgression.

[78] For example, Ukraine.

[79] For example, Cuba, Myanmar, Nicaragua, and Venezuela.

[80] For example, Libya and Syria.

[81] The exchange of technology may be regulated by governments, but it takes place without much reference to them through companies, universities, and research institutes. Non-state actors play a significant role, as illustrated by the cyber-attacks on Russia by "Anonymous" following the Russian invasion of Ukraine.

powers influence in areas of strategic interest to those proclaiming them. Now the norm is spheres of influence that seek a measure of exclusivity through demands for deference and the power to veto the decisions of the countries they incorporate about military, economic, technological, informational, or political matters. The global U.S. sphere of influence is comprehensive but of this kind. It is now being challenged in various regions of the world and globally, through the rise of other innovative economies and information systems. Rivalry between the world's greatest powers directed at defending or expanding the arenas in which they exercise primacy may still drive their strategic decisions, but regional powers have their own ideas about this, and their views are gaining ground.

As the world traverses the third decade of the twenty-first century, the worldwide ascendancy and global sphere of influence of the United States is under challenge from its designated adversaries, particularly Russia and China:

- Latin America is building new relationships with China, Russia, Iran, and Turkey in defiance of the Monroe Doctrine.
- In the Asia-Pacific, China proposes the negotiation of a "new type of great power relations" that would give it a significant role in the management of the region. In the absence of such an agreement, it is exploring the possible use of force to remove Taiwan from the U.S. sphere of influence and integrate it with the Chinese mainland.[82]
- In Europe, viewing NATO as an American sphere of influence, Russia initially demanded negotiations to achieve strategic denial of Ukraine to the United States but then went to war to roll back U.S. influence and to incorporate at least part of Ukraine into its own sphere of influence while neutralizing the rest.
- The resulting effort by the United States and its allies to isolate and weaken Russia is driving it toward dependence on China (as well as India) and

---

[82] The Taiwan issue—the question of what political relationship Taiwan should have with the rest of China—is not just an issue of Chinese nationalism. For China (and less convincingly for the United States) it is a geostrategic issue. On the eve of Japan's surrender, the State Department published a note on Taiwan (cited in Iriye 1992, 221), which remarked: "Strategic factors greatly influence the problem of Formosa [Taiwan]. With the exception of Singapore, no location in the Far East occupies such a controlling position. Formosa is separated from the continent of Asia by one hundred miles, from the main island of the Philippines by two hundred miles, and from Kyushu, the nearest home island of Japan, by seven hundred miles. Flying distance from military airports in Formosa is 559 miles to Canton, 438 miles to Shanghai, 1290 miles to Tokyo. Formosa, larger than the State of Maryland, stands in a strategic relation to the China coast comparable for the United States to an imaginary island of such size one hundred miles off the coast of North Carolina, four hundred miles from New York City. Every point off the entire coast of China falls within a radius of 1100 miles. A radius of 2000 miles includes Burma, Singapore, Borneo, Guam, and Japan, including Hokkaido."

raising concerns that it may become part of a Chinese sphere of influence on the borders of Europe.
- In the Middle East, previous great power spheres of influence, including the six-decade-long primacy of the United States, are challenged by Islamism and nationalism, and are giving way to regional dynamics driven by local religious and geopolitical rivalries. Turkey has sought to establish preeminent influence in parts of Syria, the Persian Gulf, and northeast Africa.
- In Africa, new regional alignments are emerging, as the French retreat from Islamist attacks in *Françafrique*, Nigeria establishes a regional order through the Economic Community of West African States (ECOWAS), South Africa exercises dominant influence in its neighbors, and other local spheres of influence emerge.
- The global dominance of U.S. media has been greatly eroded by the emergence of foreign competitors,[83] unattractive parochialism, corporate censorship, and increasing domestic focus. U.S. information dominance is challenged by locally sponsored social media and the emergence of sequestered national media zones in places like China and Iran.

These are strategic developments with enormous implications for global peace and development. Denying the validity and role of spheres of influence neither erases them nor helps deal with them or the process of their demise. Understanding what is at stake is essential to dealing effectively with contemporary conflicts between great powers.

Spheres of influence are an integral part of great power competition. They differ in their purposes and consequences in the varying domains they affect. They are now generating more instability and conflict than they confine.

Spheres of influence have been an abiding phenomenon of statecraft and diplomacy that deserves a great deal more study than it has so far received. It is time both to research them as a strategic phenomenon and to consider alternatives to them like the agreed establishment of neutral and buffer states or cooperative security systems.

---

[83] U.S. media are now grossly ill-equipped and staffed to cover events abroad. The vacuum is being filled by state-owned foreign news services like the BBC, Al Jazeera, Sputnik, Xinhua, and the like. The United States, which once commanded the global information domain, is no longer able to dominate it. Domestic media designed to appeal to partisan audiences at home alienate, rather than engage audiences abroad. Great powers are being driven to recognize the need for information strategies. The United States, having euthanized the U.S. Information Agency after the end of the Cold War, is, however, a holdout but has exploited social media and used information warfare to establish powerful narratives in support of Ukraine against Russian aggression and against China in support of its efforts to retain global primacy.

References and Further Reading

Bonesh, F.R. 2021. "China-Iraq Economic Relations." *MIRUPlus*, May 24. https://plus.iru-miru.com/en/article/42718.

Freeman, C.W., Jr. 2020. "War with China over Taiwan?" December 17. https://chasfreeman.net/war-with-china-over-taiwan/.

———. 2021. "Will the Chinese Civil War End with a Bang or a Whimper?" November 18. https://chasfreeman.net/will-the-chinese-civil-war-end-with-a-bang-or-with-a-whimper/.

Fuller, G. 2022. "Washington Denies Reality of 'Spheres of Influence' – A New Pinnacle of Hypocrisy," February 7. https://grahamefuller.com/washington-denies-reality-of-spheres-of-influence-a-new-pinnacle-of-hypocrisy/.

German American Internee Coalition. n.d. Latin American Internment Program. https://gaic.info/history/the-world-war-ii-latin-american-internment-program/.

Iriye, A. 1992. *Across the Pacific: An Inner History of American-East Asian Relations.* Chicago: Imprint.

Kissinger, H.A. 1957. *A World Restored: Metternich, Castlereagh, and the Problems of Peace, 1812–22.* Boston: Houghton Mifflin.

Kritenbrink, D., and E. Ratner 2021. Testimony on the U.S. Partnership with Taiwan, December 8. https://china.usc.edu/daniel-kritenbrink-and-ely-ratner-testimony-us-partnership-taiwan-dec-8-2021.

National Security Archive. 2018. "What Yeltsin Heard." https://nsarchive.gwu.edu/briefing-book/russia-programs/2018-03-16/nato-expansion-what-yeltsin-heard.

Removska, O. 2021. "U.S. Doesn't Accept 'Spheres of Influence,' Blinken Says in Comments Aimed at Russia." RFE/RL, May 6. https://www.rferl.org/a/u-s-doesn-t-accept-spheres-of-influence-blinken-says-in-comments-aimed-at-russia/31241682.html.

Tritten, T. 2021. "The U.S. Just Ended Combat in Iraq, but Thousands of Troops Will Stay Put for Now." *Military.com*, December 9. https://www.military.com/daily-news/2021/12/09/us-just-ended-combat-iraq-thousands-of-troops-will-stay-put-now.html.

Tyler, P.E. 1992. "U.S. Strategy Calls for Insuring No Rivals to Develop." *New York Times*, March 8.

Warren, M. 2014. "Sabiduría: A Japanese-Peruvian Born at U.S. Internment Camps in WWII," June 13. https://www.latinousa.org/2014/06/13/japanese-peruvian-internment-camps/.

Watson Institute, Brown University. 2021. "United States Counterterrorism Operations, 2018–2020." Costs of War Project. https://watson.brown.edu/costsofwar/files/cow/imce/papers/2021/US%20Counterterrorism %20Operations %202018-2020 %2C %20Costs %20of %20War.pdf.

White, H. 2019. "Our Sphere of Influence." *Australian Foreign Affairs*. https://www.australianforeignaffairs.com/essay/2019/07/our-sphere-of-influence.

Yacoubian, M. 2021. "What Is Russia's Endgame in Syria?" United States Institute of Peace, February 16. https://www.usip.org/publications/2021/02/what-russias-endgame-syria.

24

Regional Diplomacy and Its Variations: Change and Innovation

Rajiv Bhatia and Kishan S. Rana

Introduction

Regional diplomacy refers to cooperation and communication among the states of a geographic region or a group of states linked together through a geopolitical, geo-economic, or some other shared construct. This equation is also depicted as regionalism in international affairs studies. It is a type of multilateralism, but different from the universal multilateralism of the UN variety (or of the World Trade Organization, for instance), where most world states are members. In contrast, a regional grouping may vary from tiny, with three or four members, to those with many dozens.

Regional multilateralism is also distinguishable from bilateralism, that is, the interaction between two states, or unilateralism, where a state acts on its own and is responsible for the consequences of its actions.

Although existent earlier, regionalism gained salience in world affairs after the Second World War. Europe, devastated by two world wars and determined to learn from history, led the way. To address the challenges of building confidence and security, western Europe, the United States, and Canada formed the North Atlantic Treaty Organization (NATO), based on a concept of collective security, linking North America with western Europe. In parallel,

R. Bhatia
Gateway House, Mumbai, India

K. S. Rana (✉)
DiploFoundation, Gurugram, India

to confront the challenges of economic development, France and (the then) West Germany initiated a process of measured industrial cooperation, anchored on coal and steel, which in 1952 became the European Coal and Steel Community (ECSC), later transforming into the European Economic Community (EEC), the European Communities (EC), and eventually in 1993, the European Union (EU). This is considered the most successful experiment in regional cooperation and integration, though Jean Monnet's dream of a United States of Europe was a bridge too far. The tiny Organisation of East Caribbean States (OECS), composed of eight small states as full members, is the only other single market outside of Europe.

To complete that Second World War legacy story, the ensuing Cold War (1945–90) witnessed rival organizations: the Warsaw Pact as an adversary to NATO and the Council for Mutual Economic Assistance (COMECON) as the competitor to the EEC/EC/EU. The 1990 collapse of the Soviet Union ended both COMECON and the Warsaw Pact. However, since 2021 an escalating crisis over Ukraine—whether it should be barred from joining NATO and EU and what shape the European security order should take—amply shows that even seven decades after the Second World War, several intra-European issues of critical importance remain unresolved. Regional diplomacy faces complex challenges.

Regional organizations (ROs) have witnessed growth in virtually all parts of the world. We should note that some regional organizations may consist of states that are not contiguous, but nevertheless belong to the same region.[1] When clusters of countries base their cooperation on elements other than geographic proximity, we scramble for words to describe such entities. Examples: the International Coffee Organization (ICO) consists of 42 coffee-producing countries and 7 importing entities, which includes the EU (composed of 27 states). The Commonwealth has been an association of former British colonies and dominions, but has widened a little in recent years.[2] Plurilateral is one word applied to such entities, but "functional diplomacy" could be an alternate term.

---

[1] Two examples are the Pacific Alliance in Latin America and BIMSTEC that covers states in South and South-East Asia; trans-regional organizations cover countries in two regions, such as ASEM, which is a biennial meeting forum between leaders of Asia and Europe, with a small secretariat that pursues trans-regional cooperation. See below for more details.

[2] In 1995, Mozambique, which had no constitutional links to any Commonwealth member, was admitted, and in 2009, so was Rwanda on the grounds of exceptional circumstances, taking the membership to 54. The 26th Commonwealth Summit was held in Rwanda in June 2022.

But regional and plurilateral entities are typically small- to medium-sized groups, within which countries pursue mutually beneficial activities. The difference: the former is a geographically determined cluster of states, while the latter group of countries pursues a particular theme. Thus, the Gulf Cooperation Council (GCC) and the Southern Africa Development Community (SADC) are groups of 6 and 16 countries, respectively, the former based in the Arabian Peninsula and the latter in Southern Africa. In contrast, members of OIC (Organisation of the Islamic Conference) and OPEC (Organization of Petroleum Exporting Countries) are bound together, respectively, by religion and by shared interests in oil and gas exports. Functional groups can also take a global role: for example, the Non-Aligned Movement (NAM), with its 120 members, and the G-77 group of developing states that now extends to 140 countries.[3]

Regionalism: Driving Impulses

At the most essential level, diplomacy seeks to avoid and resolve conflict between and among nations. Peace-making and peacekeeping are part of the raison d'etre of a diplomat's work. But peace is not merely a negation of war. Its positive manifestation lies in the nurturing and cultivation of friendly and cooperative relations among neighbors and other nations in all relevant domains, including people-to-people relations. This is attempted at the global, continental, regional, and sub-regional levels. The focus of this chapter is on the last two levels. It goes without saying that the results of these endeavors are shaped as much by the objective conditions prevalent within a region or a sub-region, as by global and continental developments.

Geographical contiguity plays a key role in the formation of regional groupings. Like individuals, nations located in a specific geographic neighborhood find it easy and natural to share much with each other, facing similar situations or challenges on the path toward peace, security, and development. Through gradually enhancing mutual cooperation, they search for opportunity to grow together. Location in the same geography enables them to leverage the benefits arising from other common factors: shared history, ethnic affinity, cultural heritage, and economic complementarity. Thus, the creation of regional organizations like the Association of Southeast Asian Nations

---

[3] See https://www.g77.org/doc/. The phrase used at the UN is "G-77 and China," as Beijing chooses to identify itself with G-77, though China is no longer a developing state.

(ASEAN), South Asian Association for Regional Cooperation (SAARC), and the Gulf Cooperation Council (GCC) was seminally influenced by geography. Another form of the influence of geography may be seen in the establishment of the Indian Ocean Rim Association (IORA), earlier known as IOR-ARC, where membership is determined by the fact that member states as widely dispersed as Australia and Mauritius or UAE or Indonesia, all are littorals of the Indian Ocean.

But geography alone cannot explain the birth and development of regional groupings. Different regions such as Central Asia and South Asia agreed to work together in the Shanghai Cooperation Organization (SCO). A few states of South Asia and of Southeast Asia experimented with the idea of forging sectoral cooperation under the aegis of the Bay of Bengal Initiative for Multi-Sectoral Technical and Economic Cooperation (BIMSTEC) before they began to acquire a new identity as the Bay of Bengal community. On the other hand, cooperation through unity at the continental level, a rare phenomenon, was envisaged when the African continent united first under the flag of the Organization of African Unity (OAU) in 1963, transforming itself later into the African Union (AU) in 2002. There are no equivalents of such widespread integration in Asia and Europe.

Another interesting example of a geo-economic idea triggering a regional grouping covering different continents is provided by BRICS. That four emerging economies of Brazil, Russia, India, and China might jointly promote their common interests came from Jim O'Neill, chairman of Goldman Sachs, in his 2001 paper "Building Better Global Economic BRICs." Like many bright ideas emanating from thought leaders and think tanks, this proposal may have remained just a sparkling suggestion, but the concerned governments bought into the notion of a trans-continental cooperative entity, even a variation on the Western G7 group. After exploratory talks at their permanent missions at the UN, they launched a new formation called BRIC in June 2009. In 2010, South Africa joined as the fifth member and the group was renamed BRICS.

This has had two outcomes, one indirect. In 2012, the BRICS countries proposed the establishment of the New Development Bank (NDB), headquartered in Shanghai, with subscribed capital of $50 billion. That perhaps prompted China to take the initiative in 2013 to propose the Asian Infrastructure Investment Bank (AIIB), which came into existence in 2016, with 104 members, with a starting capital of $100 billion (equal to the initial capital of the Asian Development Bank). These actions have widened funding options for developing countries, plus added to China's international clout.[4] Some will assert, especially in the West, that BRICS is not relevant now, after the Russian attack on Ukraine in February 2022 and the continuing war there. But another perspective would be that the very fact of stronger Western unity after these events makes this group of states, all outside the G7, all the more relevant.

A different large country group is RIC, an acronym for Russia, India, and China. It started in 1999 as forum for think tanks of the three countries, exchanging views on international affairs. In 2002 the foreign ministers of the three countries met at New York on the margins of the UN General Assembly. Subsequently, they have held intermittent meetings at different locations, and the leaders of the three have also held summit meetings, on the margins of other summit events. The underlying motivation is a shared interest in countering U.S. and Western domination in world affairs, even while India and China have manifested sharp differences among themselves, especially in the past decade.

A contrast to the above is the Quadrilateral Security Dialogue, now formally known as the Quad, composed of Australia, India, Japan, and the United States, formed specifically to address the impact of China's challenge in the Indo-Pacific region. After a slow start, it became active in 2020, with virtual and in person meetings, including a live summit held in Washington D.C. in September 2021. In the wake of Russia's 2022 attack on Ukraine, India's refusal to join the West in criticizing Moscow has drawn media attention, but Quad members appear to understand India's reluctance to condemn Russia, while upholding the territorial integrity of all states.

In short, factors and motivations behind the origin and development of regional groupings are diverse. Often multiple driving impulses lie behind their work and explain their achievements and failures. A scholar (Kols 2019) has noted:

> Regional organizations do not represent an end in themselves: they are tools to serve political, ideational, economic and strategic interests. Furthermore, they allow states to enhance and influence by binding themselves to institutions, while at the same time providing the means to increase their own internal cohesion by spreading prosperity more evenly within their societies.

---

[4] China controls half of AIIB's voting shares. The United States and Japan have stayed away, but half of NATO's members are contributors.

These studied observations make complete sense. ROs follow their own trajectory, some performing better than others. In the final analysis, they mirror their membership. What should interest us is that they are a vehicle for cooperation.

Case Studies

African Union (AU)

Africa's experiments in creating regional institutions imbued with pan-African goals or purely regional objectives are relevant to any analysis of regionalism. Since the liberation of African states, beginning in 1957, the continent has worked to address its massive political and socio-economy challenges through continental and regional routes to cooperation.

It is widely recognized that more than Europe or Asia, Africa "engenders a strong sense of unity and solidarity among Africans molded by a history of humiliation and exploitation by others" (Bhatia 2022, 88). Kwame Nkrumah, Ghana's first prime minister and president, spoke for every African's aspirations when he observed, "I am not African because I was born in Africa but because Africa was born in me" (quoted in ibid.).

That emotional bond prevailed over diversities, differences, and disputation, leading to the formation of the Organization of African Unity (OAU) in May 1963. When Africa entered the twenty-first century and was fired by a vision of renaissance, the OAU was replaced by the African Union (AU). It was tasked with safeguarding the independence and sovereignty of African states, while also promoting unity, political and economic integration, improved international cooperation, and a stronger place for Africa in world affairs. The AU's new institutions include its Peace and Security Council (PSC), Pan-African Parliament (PAP), New Partnership for Africa's Development (NEPAD) with its vital component—the African Peer Review Mechanism (APRM).[5]

A dispassionate assessment of AU's functioning shows partial success in achieving its goals. It also faces enormous challenges, but it has been striving continuously to invent practical solutions for them. Robert Malley (2019),

---

[5] The APRM is unique as an all-African effort, to improve governance, using former African leaders to informally advise countries facing problems to convincing current leaders in countries facing problems to improve their methods. Another effort, on the same lines, is the Mo Ibrahim Prize, that offers $5 million (given out five installments of $1 million), to encourage African leaders to uphold democratic norms.

24 Regional Diplomacy and Its Variations: Change and Innovation 487

the former president of International Crisis Group, noted, "From reforming institutions, to safely and credibly steering political transitions, to tackling festering conflicts and crises, the list of AU challenges is long." Another observer has noted, "Power asymmetry in world politics as well as within Africa do affect its functioning where stronger states set the terms of debate while weaker ones remain at the receiving end" (Harshé 2019, 64).

Africa faces a range of divisions, born of geography, history, ethnicity, culture, tribes, and languages. It is often divided into five regions—north, east, southern, central, and west. Within these regions, diversities of social and economic development and neighborhood rivalries abound. That explains a multitude of regional and sub-regional groupings.

The AU recognizes eight regional economic communities (RECs). The Arab Maghreb Union (AMU), founded in 1989, links five North African states. The Economic Community of Central African States (ECCAS) has 11 member states. The Common Market of Eastern and Southern Africa (COMESA), founded in 1994, is an association of 21 member states, while the Southern African Development Community (SADC), created in 1992, promotes peace and security as well as economic growth among its 16 members. COMESA, EAC, and SADC overlap significantly.[6] The Intergovernmental Authority on for Development (IGAD) has been engaged in the task to develop "a regional identity" for the people of its eight states. The Economic Community of West African States (ECOWAS) seeks to serve as a Customs Union and a Common Market and now promote economic integration among its 15 member states. The East African Community (EAC) styles itself as the regional governmental organization of six member states, serving as a Customs Union and a Common Market and now seeks to elevate itself to a Monetary Union.[7] Finally, the Community of Sahel-Saharan States (CEN-SAD) has had a checkered record, moving from the original treaty in 1998 to the new one signed in 2013 that awaited ratification by an adequate number of states. It wants to focus on regional security and sustainable development.

Three observations: First, four RECs have been successful: EAC, COMESA, SADC, and ECOWAS. Second, the AU has worked to analyze the success of integration efforts. In 2016 the Africa Regional Integration Index (ARII) was advanced. It has been replaced by a more comprehensive Africa Multidimensional Regional Integration Index (AMRII), with 7 dimensions and 29 qualitative and quantitative indicators.[8] Third, the Agreement on the

---

[6] There has been talk of merging COMESA, EAC, and SADC, but this idea has not moved forward.
[7] "Common Market" is distinguished here from "Single Market" mentioned above with reference to the EU.
[8] For details, see African Union (2019).

African Continental Free Trade Area (AfCFTA) was signed in 2018, but its implementation was delayed due to COVID-19. Several building blocks are missing, but it is likely that AfCFTA could move forward.

AU's unifying actions resemble the proverbial half-full glass. But consider: Africa is a 54-nation continent, divided by its cultural and linguistic characteristics, the Arab North and "Africa South of the Sahara" binary. On top of that, Africa faces a multiplicity of colonial legacies and artificial borders that split tribal nations, plus a multiplicity of communication languages. That was further compounded by a long-term liberation struggle that has stretched from 1957 (when Ghana was the first to taste freedom) to 1990 (when Namibia won its independence from *Apartheid*-led South Africa). Yet, one should consider that there also exists no notion, even a rough plan, for pan-Asian unity; even the definition of Asia poses challenges. In Latin America, brave attempts at unity have often withered on the vine. The continent of Africa should be saluted for what it has achieved, despite all its challenges.

BIMSTEC

This entity was formed in 1997 by seven states of South Asia (India, Bangladesh, Sri Lanka, Nepal, and Bhutan) and Southeast Asia (Thailand and Myanmar). After a slow start, in 2022 it has taken on the aspiration to become a major instrument for trans-regional cooperation, anchored on the Bay of Bengal. Its 2018 summit held in Nepal signaled this new ambition, in its joint declaration, "Towards a Peaceful, Prosperous and Sustainable Bay of Bengal Region."

To nurture bold ambition is one thing, but to face the reality is another. Its 1997 Bangkok Declaration covered eight areas: trade, investment and industry, technology, human resource development, tourism, agriculture, energy, and infrastructure and transportation. Its first two decades saw modest progress, as noted by a former secretary-general of the grouping. In 2016 India, the largest member state, decided to give high priority to BIMSTEC, realizing that the bigger grouping in South Asia—SAARC—faced a bleak future.

At the Leaders' Retreat in 2016 some decisions were taken to institute reform, drafting a new Charter, strengthening the Secretariat, and creating a development fund. But ironically, the fifth summit due in 2020 has been repeatedly deferred due to the COVID pandemic and Sri Lanka's hesitations. The summit was rescheduled for March 2022, but uncertainty lingers over Myanmar's participation after its military coup.

BIMSTEC's record shows progress in counter-terrorism, intelligence sharing cyber security and coastal security, plus disaster risk management and humanitarian assistance. But it has encountered serious difficulties over trade, investment, and industrial cooperation. It is far from its goal for a free trade agreement. A major transport connectivity plan has identified 264 projects requiring an investment of $126 billion during 2018–28. Official sources indicated that projects worth $55.2 billion are already at different stages of implementation, through a variety of other partnerships and funding sources.

The future will show if BIMSTEC manages to emulate the successful ASEAN model. Problems may arise over the fact that many of the above are major projects, funded by China, follow a North-South axis, whereas long-standing plans for trans-Asian road and rail routes follow an East-West axis. Consequently, linking connections will be needed.

Pacific Alliance

Created in 2011, this four-member Pacific Alliance (PA) group has built on existing affinities between Chile, Colombia, Peru, and Mexico, all countries strongly orientated toward the Asia Pacific region; three are contiguous in geography. Unusually, this small group has 61 observer countries. They have also carried out three rounds of negotiations with several countries that want a higher status with PA, as "associated states." They have special working arrangements with ASEAN, APEC, MERCOSUR, and the EU. PA views itself as a "strategic platform," favoring open trade and multilateralism. They swiftly moved to eliminate tariffs on 96 percent of their traded merchandise goods.[9]

This is practical, focused on simple actions like collective business promotion activities in foreign countries, trade fair participation via shared regional booths, a $40 million fund to boost entrepreneurship, and sharing of embassy space at over a dozen capitals around the world—though they are yet to take the next step, joint embassies that fly all the four flags. Consular assistance is provided at locations where a member state may not be represented.

Hitherto, the Organisation of East Caribbean States (OECS) is the only RO to implement such "unified" representation, at Brussels, London, and Rabat. OECS is an 11-member group with 8 that now share a common market and single passport, and 4 that are associate members: the British Virgin Islands, Anguilla, Martinique, and Guadeloupe.[10] They all depend on foreign tourists and have suffered since early 2020 owing to the COVID-19 pandemic.

---

[9] See: https://alianzapacifico.net/en/what-is-the-pacific-alliance/#:~:text=The%20Pacific%20Alliance%20is%20an,established%20on%20April%2028th%2C%202011

[10] Like the EU, OECS countries have a single passport and are pioneers in small state neighborhood joint actions. See https://www.oecs.org/en/who-we-are/about-us

PA also works on promoting academic, student exchanges, and cultural activities. As part of a work style that is lean and focused on deliverables, they do not have a secretariat; the country holding the annual rotating chairmanship handles coordination and administration tasks. The PA also has 22 working groups to handle specific tasks. Some scholars have called this a form of "modular regionalism" in Latin America (Gardini 2013). PA is a breath of fresh air in a vast continental region that has seen many regional initiatives that failed to deliver.

> **Box 24.1 Novel Actions**
>
> Sometimes, ROs are formed in unusual ways, working across regions, overcoming historical legacy, or pursuing unusual opportunities. Examples:
>
> First, the Asia-Europe Foundation (ASEF) is a dialogue between the two continents, with the lead taken by the EU. It produces biennial summits, called ASEM between the leaders of 21 Asian states (evidently selected by the EU, including India, Bangladesh, and Pakistan, but no Asian country to its west) and the EU member states. A small ASEF secretariat exists in Singapore, funded entirely by the EU, with an Asian heading it, representing "the civil society outreach of the Asia-Europe Meeting."[11] A comparable EU mechanism exists for Latin America and the Caribbean.[12]
>
> Second, ASEAN has always seen a special vocation for itself in reaching out beyond Southeast Asia, offering a platform for wider Asian intra-regional dialogue and cooperation. The ASEAN Regional Forum (ARF) was established in 1967, nearly three decades later. Initially limited to the dominant powers active in SE Asia at the time, it now extends to many more countries, on the basis of its 1996 criteria. The non-ASEAN countries are: Australia, Bangladesh, Canada, China, Democratic People's Republic of Korea, European Union, India, Japan, Mongolia, New Zealand, Pakistan, Papua New Guinea, Republic of Korea, Russia, Sri Lanka, Timor-Leste, and the United States. The focus is on preventive diplomacy, to discuss issues before they become sharp disputes; it is the only such instance of wide conflict-prevention outreach by any RO.
>
> Third, in 1997 ASEAN launched its ASEAN-Plus Three (APT) initiative, to improve economic cooperation between its ten member states, with China, Japan, and the Republic of Korea (ROK). (It has evolved ever since, first by bringing into the process Australia, India, and New Zealand, and then widening it further to include Russia and the United States.) The three East Asian countries have a complex history that goes back to the past millennia, of cultural and linguistic assimilation, conflict, and political contestation. In 2011, the ROK took the initiative to create a new mechanism for mutual consultation, the Trilateral Cooperation Secretariat (TCS).[13]

---

[11] ASEF acts as a public diplomacy outreach effort for the EU. See https://asef.org/about-us/who-we-are/

[12] For a detailed description of this EU-LAC action, see https://eulacfoundation.org/system/files/web-version-revisiting-relations-eu-lac-dialogue_end.pdf

[13] Perhaps this Secretariat is not very active now; its website is not accessible. See Korea Herald (2011).

RO Typology

Several approaches can be taken to establish a taxonomy of ROs. One method is descriptive, based on the characteristics of regional and plurilateral institutions. Another approach places them in functional clusters based on their activities and the degree of integration effectiveness. Both these are inexact, subjective forms of analysis, open to interpretation, because they depend on perceptions. One can also consider a third method, based on an objective criterion, which is indicative, sometimes used for comparison. But it only measures one dimension of integration and has its own problems.

First: consider the objectives of ROs and of functional entities, and classify them accordingly.
Geographic: Feature: neighborhood cooperation.
Examples: Gulf Cooperation Council (GCC); South Pacific Forum.
Thematic: Feature: Narrow focus on specific subjects.
Examples: North Atlantic Council; Coffee Producers Association.
Geopolitical: Political cooperation is the main driver.
Examples: NATO; G-7; UN Security Council Permanent Members (P-5)
Geo-economic: The focus is on economic cooperation.
Examples: Organization for Economic Cooperation and Development (OECD)[14]; free trade agreements such as the 15-member Regional Cooperation and Economic Partnership (RCEP) that went into force on January 1, 2022.
Cultural or linguistic: United by linguistic or cultural affinity.
Examples: Francophonie[15]; Ibero-American Partnership.[16]
Religious: Brings together countries that mainly practice the same religion.
Example: Organisation of the Islamic Conference (OIC).
Second: another subjective, and consequently inaccurate way to classify ROs is in terms of their profile and performance. Here is a possible taxonomy.

---

[14] OECD, with 38 members in early 2022, was long viewed as a rich countries' club; in January 2022 it initiated action to give full membership to six states, Argentina, Brazil, Bulgaria, Croatia, Peru, and Romania. It also works closely with several large economy countries it calls key partners, which are Brazil, China, India, Indonesia, and South Africa.

[15] Headquartered in Paris, linking France with its former colonies, Francophonie has widened its appeal to include countries such as Greece and the United Arab Emirates, countries that admire French culture, but do not have a special historical connection with France.

[16] This intergovernmental body established in 1991 (well after counterparts such as the Commonwealth and Francophonie) is headquartered in Madrid, Spain, works in "the field of education, science, technology and culture in the context of integral development, democracy and regional integration." See https://www.devex.com/organizations/organization-of-ibero-american-states-oei-70324

Well integrated: (EU)

- The EU, with 27 member states (after UK's 2021 exit), demonstrates strong political integration. A significant portion of sovereign power stands transferred to the collective entity, which decides on a wide swathe of legislation and rules. Thus, the EU bears some resemblance to a state, even while many Europeans resist further integration; some, or perhaps many among the EU publics, want only a federation of nation states. In any event, further EU integration is not feasible now.
- Solid economic cooperation is the EU's foundation (a single market), buttressed by political vision. But each major country handles its own trade and FDI promotion activities.
- The EU legislates for its members on many issues; with a parliament and a court of justice, it is in effect a quasi-government. It also runs delegation offices in about 140 non-member states, which coordinate EU actions in the assignment country, playing the role of embassies.[17]
- A Common Foreign and Security Policy mechanism (CFSP) coordinates foreign policy. This works well on secondary issues. On matters of core concern, member states usually opt to go their own ways.
- Member states remain the key actors. Brussels, headquarters of the EU Commission and its large, expensive bureaucracy, is ahead of the public in member states, which retain their rivalries and key differences among themselves. The EU's high tide has passed.

Advanced: (G20, ASEAN, Caribbean Community [CARICOM], OECD, OECS, Pacific Alliance)

- G20 began as a gathering of 19 large economy finance ministers in and has morphed into a 20-member political-economic group with the inclusion of the EU, with rotating summits, G20 "chairmanships," and *sherpas* that meet to prepare meetings, but no fixed secretariat. In effect it is a global version of the Western group, G7.
- Cooperation extends to multiple areas, with a roadmap for future growth, often with limited success at real integration.

---

[17] The European External Action Service (EEAS) functions like a diplomatic service, but major EU states have resisted calling it a diplomatic service. At the UN, the EU is now treated as a member state, elevated from its earlier observer status. See https://eeas.europa.eu/headquarters/headquarters-homepage/area/geo_en. It was initially expected that these delegations might jointly and singly represent the EU at some far-flung locations, but that has not happened in the sense of a single entity representing the entire collective group. On the ground, some competition exists, especially in that promotion of economic objectives, including inward FDI and tourism, is mostly handled individually by EU member state embassies.

24 Regional Diplomacy and Its Variations: Change and Innovation

- Serious bilateral dispute among members was contained, even in a large and diverse group like G20, but after the February Russian invasion of Ukraine, that will need reassessment.
- Outsiders want membership or other forms of association.
- ASEAN adopted a new charter in December 2008, aiming at a single market by 2015, emulating the EU model, but without surrender of sovereignty to the collective entity. But this is far from reality. The target date for a single market has been pushed back to 2025, but this may be delayed further.[18]
- The other entities are discussed elsewhere in this chapter.

Medium intensity: (AU, ECOWAS, GCC, Mercosur, Cairns Group)

- Some have a long history, but have not fulfilled expectations, often due to unresolved differences among member states or inadequate political will.
- A solid basis for economic cooperation is not fully mobilized, despite good intentions.
- Non-members attend as observers, but arrangements with other organizations may have a pro-forma character.

Nascent or aspirational: (BIMSTEC, Community of Democracies, IORA)

- Some are at the starting blocks; their promise is greater than actual performance, either because the organization is evolving or because there are internal roadblocks.
- A vision of mutual gains exists but is not usually sufficient to become a driving force.

Dormant: (G15)

- Weak unifying force: the initial vision was offset by other factors.
- No strong drivers, members disinterested. Some are outdated, like G15 which was an inner grouping within the Non-Aligned Movement.

Third: a different and objective way of determining the level of integration within a regional group is to compare the percentage of total foreign trade of

---

[18] AEC2025 seems unattainable (Ishikawa 2021). The key challenge is the economic disparity between the original six members and the "CLMV" Group of four later entrants, though Vietnam is now more or less the equal of the original six.

member states that is conducted among the group's members. This figure is around 50 percent for the EU, about 25 percent for ASEAN, around 12 percent among the Caribbean Community (CARICOM) states, and barely 4 percent among the members of the South Asian Association of Regional Cooperation (SAARC). Two decades back the World Bank had called South Asia the least integrated region in the world, and this situation has not changed in substantive terms, even while India's trade with Bangladesh, Nepal, and Sri Lanka has grown, and official trade with Pakistan has declined.[19]

In regions where economies are comparable, trade intensity within the RO is useful. But with a marked difference in the economy size and development, this argument falls apart. In South Asia, the total trade between the eight countries is barely $21 billion, and even if it were to triple to $63 billion, and would only represent about 8 percent of their total foreign trade. The small economies of Bhutan and Nepal almost completely depend on India, just as the Maldives depends on Sri Lanka. While the exports of Bangladesh and Sri Lanka have grown dramatically in the past 20 years, they go to the EU, enjoying special access for their textiles. They have little interest in the Indian market, which points in turn to the fallacy of simple numerical analysis.[20]

Innovation and Adaptation

The explosion in the number of regional and functional organizations, especially the geographic clusters, has accelerated innovation. Economies of scale, trading advantages, shared human resource development, sectoral and functional cooperation among subsidiary entities, cultural and people exchanges are among the drivers in this process. What is sometimes missed is the information exchange and the mutual learning that ROs promote. We also see innovative actions, like the annual report that the African Union (AU) produces on the competitive efficiency of different sub-regional organizations, applying clear, open criteria. This is but one example of the African Union's actions that do not seem to attract the attention that they deserve.

---

[19] It is estimated that besides the officially recorded India-Pakistan trade, sizable quantities of Indian equipment, such as pumps, electric motors, and industrial machinery travel to Pakistan, after re-labeling in Dubai and elsewhere. Of course, this results in profits for third parties and a loss of revenue for both countries.

[20] See CUTS International (2013); Herrera Dappe and Kunaka (2021).

24 Regional Diplomacy and Its Variations: Change and Innovation

Governance: A delicate task for any RO is to help errant states toward improved domestic governance. This is difficult given that ROs typically insulate the internal policy of member states from discussion at the RO. But since the home policy of members has direct impact on their cooperation in the group, that distinction is difficult to sustain, the more so when a member state regime engages in harsh domestic repression through dictatorial actions. ASEAN offers an interesting example. Another instance: the AU's peer review mechanism through which eminent African personalities visit countries that open themselves to this process. These visiting African statesmen help to persuade countries to improve their governance through gentle persuasion. Those results are not publicized.

For many, tackling the internal governance within a member state is delicate and potentially hazardous. Myanmar is a case in point in the past two decades. That country's military leaders are not easily amenable to persuasion-pressure from fellow members of ASEAN. This is an instance where the ASEAN does not deliver viable results. But on the flipside there is no other soft, sustained way of guiding errant states toward better governance. One marvels at the story of sanctions and other forms of overt external pressure, which have a relatively poor record of efficacy. Worse, sanctions tend to hurt the weakest sections of the targeted country, which are already victims of poor domestic governance.

Security: Mutual security, even when not listed in the goals, is always implicit in good neighborhood cooperation. Countries that work together seldom let potential disputes escalate into real crisis. In addition, the group ethic also works in favor of easing bilateral tensions and exploring acceptable solutions. When ASEAN was created in 1967, all but one of its initial five members had territorial claims on one another. The Organization of American States (OAS) came into existence as a Pan-American entity premised on mutual security. And then of course there are the regional organizations dedicated to sharing or pooling armed forces and engaging in joint defense.

The Soviet counterpart to NATO during the Cold War was the Warsaw Pact. It was succeeded in part by a Russia-led entity, the Collective Security Treaty Organization (CSTO), with Armenia, Belarus, Kazakhstan, Kyrgyzstan, Russia, and Tajikistan as charter members; Uzbekistan joined in 2006 but withdrew in 2012. There is also a different kind of soft security initiative in the shape of the Conference on Interaction and Confidence Building Measures in Asia (CICA), which first met in 1992, at the initiative of Kazakhstan. Its 27 member states include Afghanistan, India, Russia, Palestine, and Vietnam (Indonesia, Malaysia, Japan, and the United States are observers). Then there is the China-led Shanghai Cooperation Organization (SCO), established in

2001, successor to the Shanghai Five that first met in 1996.[21] Its members are China, Kazakhstan, Kyrgyzstan, Russia, Tajikistan, and Uzbekistan, with India and Pakistan having joined in 2017 (Afghanistan, Belarus, Iran, and Mongolia are observers, and unusually, attend summit meetings at Heads of State or Government level). Other regional security organizations which have disappeared include CENTO and SEATO, which once covered Central and Southeast Asia.

Organizational morphing: The 15-member ECOWAS in West Africa is an interesting example of an entity created for economic cooperation, which has taken on major peacekeeping, peace-building, and conflict-prevention functions. Through innovative collective actions it has mobilized the collective entity against errant members. The presence of the heavyweight Nigeria in that group has been an important success factor. In contrast, SADC, which includes Zimbabwe among its 16 members, could do rather little to improve conditions during the darkest period of President Robert Mugabe's regime, including the rigged elections of 2002 and 2008. It kept the dialogue open with the Mugabe government when it was confronted with targeted UN sanctions, commencing 2002.[22]

Country size and leadership: Among countries of comparable size and capabilities, cooperation is usually easier. In contrast, a large state has to take care to avoid an impression of domination. That also applies to a country that has pulled ahead in economic performance; perhaps that's one reason that Singapore, a strong ASEAN member, as also a fully developed country by any criterion (per capita income of over U.S. $70,000), opts not to join the OECD. Singapore also at times opts for a low profile in other groups.

Sometimes, founding countries which are often large powers tend to continue with a major role, which is served by the principles of sharing high offices and of rotation, plus the usual large number of small states. But overall, no hard and fast rule applies.

Secretariat: Often, a secretariat becomes a player in the RO with its own agenda. Examples show that prudence in creating this permanent body is worthwhile. If created before activities have expanded to an optimal level, it can push the RO toward an over-ambitious agenda, more than some members want. ASEAN, created in 1967, embarked on multi-sided actions from the outset but waited for over 14 years to establish an independent permanent

---

[21] See http://eng.sectsco.org/
[22] See Saunders and Melbert (2017).

secretariat in Jakarta.[23] The Non-Aligned Movement (NAM), in contrast, resisted this option throughout its active existence—NAM remains in existence, but it has lost its élan, according to some popular accounts: "One of the challenges of the Non-Aligned Movement in the 21st century has been to reassess its identity and purpose in the post-Cold War era. The movement has continued to advocate for international cooperation, multilateralism, and national self-determination, but it has also been increasingly vocal against the inequities of the world economic order" (*Encyclopedia Britannica* 2022).

Vision: Statements setting out long-term goals are important, but only when these are rooted in reality. Grandiose words are not sufficient; it is far better to have a treaty or major document that is negotiated through an intense, open, and candid fashion. Visions that are unrealistic only lead to disenchantment and eventual decline of interest in the RO. What counts above all is a sense of shared purpose and ideas that are shared by all members.

> **Box 24.2 CARICOM: A Joint Negotiator**
>
> CARICOM is based in the Caribbean, with 15 members, plus 5 associated states. It views itself as a unique integration RO in the developing world. It established a novel method in 1990s, in anticipation of achieving a single market and economy (which is part of its formal title CSME) by designating a single external trade negotiator for all its full member states. While the single market goal has been delayed for a range of practical issues, having just one negotiator for all its members has given it a degree of strength in dealings at the EU, WTO, and elsewhere, which has been watched with envy by other ROs. The single negotiator method has also been applied since 2018 to climate change negotiations, giving the group substantial clout (*Caricom Today* 2018).

The UN and Regionalism

An important dimension of the role of regional organizations in contemporary world affairs is reflected in their contribution to resolving political crises and preventing and resolving conflicts. In contrast to the colonial or even the post-colonial era when the responsibility seems to rest largely with the Western capitals or the UN that essentially functioned under the control of P5 in the Security Council, the prevalent thinking favors regional solutions to regional problems, secured through regional groupings.

---

[23] The ASEAN Secretariat was initially set up in the Indonesian Foreign Ministry in February 1976. It was established as an independent entity, in Jakarta, in 1981: https://asean.org/asean-secretariat-and-eria-pay-tribute-to-dr-surin-pitsuwan/

During a debate on improving collective security and maintenance of peace in April 2021, António Guterres, UN secretary-general, observed that collaborative effort with regional and sub-regional organizations has grown exponentially since 1945.

After an extensive debate in the Security Council on this important theme, a presidential statement was issued on April 19, 2021. It highlighted the agreed view that regional and sub-regional organizations are in a good position to appreciate "the root causes of armed conflicts owing to their knowledge of the region" and can thus help in contributing to their prevention and resolution. The statement went on to stress: "The Council underlines the importance of utilizing the existing and potential capabilities of regional and subregional organizations in this regard, including encouraging countries in the region to resolve differences peacefully through dialogue, reconciliation, consultation, negotiation, good offices, mediation and judicial settlement of disputes" (UN Security Council 2021).

Conclusions

Several further diagnoses of regional organizations and their behavior are offered here as an invitation to think creatively about the future of these bodies.

An Excess of ROs

Even the smallest countries find themselves engaged in a dozen or more ROs. Larger countries are members of 30 and more ROs, which have a financial cost and stretch the manpower in foreign ministries that must track key events. The lead role at each is distributed among several ministries, but the foreign ministry needs to work with these leads, to ensure consistent, so-called whole of government actions at each entity. This has become a challenge for many countries: to pursue consistent actions, actively using membership to serve the country's interests.

Calculated Focus

The group Small Island Developing States (SIDS) was formed out of climate change necessity, by microstates that face inundation and extinction owing to rising sea levels. It consists of 38 UN members and 20 small entities that are not either UN members or associate members.[24] With the Maldives taking the lead, they attracted significant attention to their existential plight in the face of rising sea levels. It remains to be seen how the international community finds solutions which may involve major migration to new lands when projections on rising sea levels come to reality.

A different kind of example is provided by the Pacific Alliance (PA), which is a four-nation cluster, evidently not keen on taking new members. It works on realistic, actionable ideas that advance the interests of Chile, Columbia, Mexico, and Peru.

Political Targeting

In 1951, Prime Minister Jawaharlal Nehru had hosted the first India-Africa meeting, at a time when no African country had gained independence, but vigorous liberation movements were rampant on that continent. This tradition was revived in April 2008 when the leaders of 14 countries chosen by OAU met with Indian counterparts. The second summit took place in May 2011 and the third met in October 2015.

China launched its first Forum on China-Africa Cooperation (FOCAC), held in Beijing at the ministerial level, in October 2000. China has alternated between Africa and Asia with subsequent conferences, some the summit level. The eighth meeting, at the ministerial level, took place in Dakar, Senegal, in November 2021 (*The Diplomat* 2018). That can be seen as a high point of China's African diplomacy, focused heavily on its Belt and Road Initiative (BRI) of 2011, as a global effort to promote Chinese investment in infrastructure projects across the world. A key point: with the COVID-19 pandemic and the emergence of loan repayment issues, in Africa and elsewhere, one analysis suggests: "Quantity-wise, China is significantly scaling back its planned activities in Africa" (Brookings Institution 2021).

As part of that same ambitious BRI project, Beijing came up with the notion of its 17+1 project, reaching out into the backyard of the EU. This calculated political lobbying, in effect challenged major EU countries that do not support that influx of China's investments but could not block member states from taking advantage of what appeared to be attractive investments. That has now largely unraveled, because of over-ambition. "In 2012, China

---

[24] See https://www.un.org/ohrlls/content/about-small-island-developing-states#:~:text=Small%20Island%20Developing%20States%20(SIDS,social%2C%20economic%20and%20environmental%20vulnerabilities.

was received with wide open arms in central and eastern Europe, as it put forth its 16+1 mechanism, which was later expanded to the 17+1 with the addition of Greece. Almost 10 years later, what was probably China's biggest disappointment in Europe paradoxically happened right in these 17 countries" (*The Diplomat* 2021).

Both China and India have also held similar conferences with the small island states of the South Pacific region, on a smaller scale.

Mutual Learning

In different regions, especially in the Global South, a culture and habit of studying the international affairs experiences of other countries and regions are not widespread. This blocks the migration of good practices across different parts of the world. ASEAN and CARICOM are two entities that are exceptions.

It is almost as if regional organizations in the Global South are determined not to look around and profit from positive experiences in different parts of the world. This is one more example of a near-complete absence of any institutional or sustained machinery for countries of the Global South to even learn from, much less to listen to, the experiences of others. This is part of a deeper absence of any mechanism for mutual learning among foreign ministries and an absence of comparative studies of diplomatic practices.

ROs and Inclusivity

G8 became G7 when Russia was excluded from this forum of the world's top economies. Yet, these two entities had always co-existed, with the G7 as a political group and G8 more an economic entity. After Moscow's February 2022 Ukraine invasion, prospect of Russia being invited back to that group has receded into the far distance. But neither heavy national and personal, nor targeted sanctions, nor other ostracization efforts can be productive. The road to negotiation and diplomacy is the only viable method to a sustainable solution. And that includes joint actions in regional and functional groups. A global community must be able to socialize and negotiate across tables, rather than strike-up threatening postures against one another, or worse, resort to armed conflict. The short point offered here is that Russia has long harbored a grievance over its loss of status after the collapse of the Soviet Union in 1990. Both the eastward expansion of NATO and Russia's exclusion from what used to be the G8 group have fed Russia's sense of grievance. That spectacular failure of regional diplomacy has carried a high cost.

In South Asia this may be seen in a different context, but the same principles apply. Because of blockages in the functioning of SAARC, South Asian cooperation has been in a frozen state for about a decade, weighed down by the long persisting India and Pakistan contradictions.[25] This has produced unexpected outcomes. First, Bangladesh, Bhutan, India, and Nepal (through a group called BBIN) have developed new logistics and transport connections in the eastern region of India, using rail links, roads, and waterways to find mutually accommodative solutions. For example, the shortest route between Kolkata, a major logistics hub and port, and India's North-East states, is through Bangladesh. These connections are currently under activation. For the first time in recent memory, the four countries are using rivers as inland waterways. The Asian Development Bank has promoted this sub-regional cooperation. The truly remarkable feature is that civil society organizations and think tanks have been instrumental in building this cooperative momentum in all the four countries, including persuading their own governments. An Indian think tank, CUTS, based in Jaipur has played the notable role in this effort, working closely with a range of think tank and other counterparts in the three countries.[26] This has helped overcome doubts and create a groundswell of civil society support. This is an important learning experience, relevant for other ROs.

Second, through small steps India and Pakistan have recently worked out some trade facilitation. Since early 2021, direct trade between India and Afghanistan via the land route across Pakistan has commenced. Islamabad had blocked this transit trade for over two decades. It is too early to assess if these moves are significant, given the very checked history of past efforts to improve this bilateral relationship. A possible straw in the wind is renewed interest in Pakistan in expanding direct trade between India and Pakistan, which currently stagnates at barely $2 billion per annum, against a real potential that is many multiples of that number.[27] Some de-escalation in India-Pakistan border tensions after 2021 has also helped. If sustained, these trends will strengthen the case for regional diplomacy.

---

[25] It is easily forgotten that the Narendra Modi government that took office in May 2014 for the first time ever, invited the leaders of South Asian countries, and all of them attended (including Pakistan PM, Nawaz Sharif). Given South Asian complexities, that effort at improving relations also failed.

[26] For comprehensive narrative, please see CUTS International (n.d.).

[27] From the time of creation of WTO in 1996, Pakistan denied Most Favored Nation trade treatment to India. In 2019, after a major Pakistan-led terrorist attack at Phulwana that killed 40 members of the paramilitary force CRPF, India withdrew MFN treatment it had unilaterally given to Pakistan since 1996. See Suneja (2019).

Overall, regionalism is an active force in international affairs, traversing varied paths and engaging clusters of states, both in relation to overarching political issues as also narrow themes that are of interest to special, functional groups. It offers rich potential for further development, along both time-tested and new innovative paths, but it cannot in itself become a path to new solutions for complex problems, global, regional, or bilateral. At the UN and at global conferences, ROs give added strength to small states, even if the great powers see them as a hindrance. They have a potential to advance the interests of their member states, which is not always mobilized.

It may be asked, has the international system placed too much faith in ROs? One should remember that ROs are a fairly recent innovation, and outside of Europe, Latin America, and then Asia and Africa really experimented with this form of group diplomacy, commencing in the 1960s, with a major surge after the end of the Cold War. The right question might be, why do countries in different regions experiment with ROs over time? Is that simply part of a normal human trait to work with neighbors?

Perhaps the answer may be found most clearly in Latin America, which has seen a profusion of new ROs that have come and sometimes just faded away. One should also not overlook the Pacific Alliance, a four-member group that has done especially well since its inception in 2011. The Caribbean region seems to have done better, with greater stability and continuity. Africa has done even better with its ROs, and the African Union carries out a ranking of the best among its eight ROs—the only continental organization to do this. Asia has seen much greater stability with its ROs, with ASEAN as an exemplar. Europe has also done well with the EU.

Overall, however, regional integration still gives a mixed bag, with some great results and much work in progress. Given the ossification of the multilateral process at the UN—or rather, the inability to show much result either over the C-19 pandemic since early 2020 or over the war that broke out in Ukraine after Russia's invasion of its neighbor in February 2022—many will surely be inclined to place greater hope on regional organizations.

References and Further Reading

Acharya, A. 2021. *ASEAN and Regional Order: Revisiting Security Community in Southeast Asia*. London: Routledge.

Adluri Subramanyam, R., ed. 2021. *Bilateral and Multilateral Cooperation in South Asia*. London: Routledge.

African Union. 2019. "African Union Commission Rolls Out a Tool for Monitoring and Evaluating African Regional Integration," September 20. https://au.int/en/articles/au-rolls-out-framework-monitoring-and-evaluating-status-african-regional-integration.

Bayne, N., and S. Woolcock. 2003. *The New Economic Diplomacy: Decision-making and Negotiation in International Economic Relations*. London: Ashgate.

Bhatia, R. 2022. *India-Africa Relations: Changing Horizons*. London: Routledge.

Bow, B., and G. Anderson. 2016. *Regional Governance in Post-NAFTA North America: Building without Architecture*. New York: Routledge.

Briceño-Ruiz, J., and A. Rivarola, eds. 2020. *Regionalism in Latin America: Agents, Systems and Resilience*. London: Routledge.

Brookings Institution. 2021. "Africa in Focus: China's Retrenchment from Africa," December 6. https://www.brookings.edu/blog/africa-in-focus/2021/12/06/focac-2021-chinas-retrenchment-from-africa/.

Calleya, S.C., ed. 2000. *Regionalism in the Post-Cold War World*. London: Ashgate.

Caricom Today. 2018. "CARICOM Negotiating with 'One Voice' in Global Climate Change Talks," December 4. https://today.caricom.org/2018/12/04/caricom-negotiating-with-one-voice-in-global-climate-change-talks/.

CUTS International. 2013. *Reforming Non-tariff Barriers: Case for a Participatory Approach in South Asia*. Jaipur: CUTS International.

———. n.d. "Enabling a Political Economy Discourse for Multi-modal Connectivity in the BBIN (Bangladesh, Bhutan, India, Nepal) Sub-region (M-Connect)." https://cuts-citee.org/enabling-a-political-economy-discourse-for-multi-modal-connectivity-in-the-bbin-bangladesh-bhutan-india-nepal-sub-region/.

Datta, S., ed. 2021. *BIMSTEC: The Journey and the Way Ahead*. New Delhi: Pentagon Press.

Dent, C.M. 2008. *East Asian Regionalism*. London and New York: Routledge.

The Diplomat. 2018. "Rebranding China in Africa," September 5. https://thediplomat.com/2018/09/focac-2018-rebranding-china-in-africa/.

Encyclopedia Britannica. 2022. "Non-aligned Movement." https://www.britannica.com/topic/Non-Aligned-Movement.

Gardini, G. 2013. *The Added Value of the Pacific Alliance and 'Modular Regionalism' in Latin America*. London: London School of Economics. http://eprints.lse.ac.uk/81601/.

Harshé, R. 2019. *Africa in World Affairs: Politics of Imperialism, the Cold War and Globalisation*. New York: Routledge.

Herrera Dappe, M., and C. Kunaka, eds. 2021. *Connecting to Thrive: Challenges and Opportunities of Transport Integration in Eastern South Asia*. Washington, D.C.: The World Bank Group.

Hettne, B., A. Inotai, and O. Sunkel, eds. 1999. *Globalism and the New Regionalism*. London: Macmillan.

Ishikawa, K. 2021. "The ASEAN Economic Community and ASEAN Economic Integration." *Journal of Contemporary East Asia Studies* 10 (1): 24–41.

Kols, R. 2019. "Rising Regionalism: A New Trend or an Old Idea in Need of Better Understanding?" Atlantic Council, September 4. https://www.atlanticcouncil.org/blogs/new-atlanticist/rising-regionalism-a-new-trend-or-an-old-idea-in-need-of-better-understanding/.

Korea Herald. 2011. "Trilateral Secretariat Officially Opens in Seoul," September 27. http://www.koreaherald.com/view.php?ud=20110927000898.

Malley, R. 2019. "Comment: Eight Priorities for the African Union in 2019." International Crisis Group, February 11. https://mg.co.za/article/2019-02-11-eight-priorities-for-the-african-union-in-2019.

Murithi, T., and T. Karbo, eds. 2017. *The African Union: Autocracy, Diplomacy and Peacebuilding in Africa.* London: I.B. Tauris.

Saunders, C., and H. Melbert. 2017. "What Southern Africa Can Learn from West Africa about Dealing with Despots." *The Conversation*, January 23. https://theconversation.com/what-southern-africa-can-learn-from-west-africa-about-dealing-with-despots-71722.

Suneja, K. 2019. "Pakistan's Most-favoured Nation Status Scrapped." *Economic Times*, February 16. https://economictimes.indiatimes.com/news/politics-and-nation/pakistans-most-favoured-nation-status-crapped/articleshow/68018002.cms?from=mdr.

———. 2021. "How China's 17+1 Became a Zombie Mechanism," February 10. https://thediplomat.com/2021/02/how-chinas-171-became-a-zombie-mechanism/.

UN Security Council. 2021. Statement by the President of the Security Council, April 19. https://www.securitycouncilreport.org/atf/cf/%7B65BFCF9B-6D27-4E9C-8CD3-CF6E4FF96FF9%7D/s_prst_2021_9.

Yeo, A. 2019. *Asia's Regional Architecture: Alliances and Institutions in the Pacific Century.* Stanford: Stanford University Press.

Youngs, R. 2021. *The European Union and Global Politics.* London: Macmillan Education.

25

Why Collective Diplomacy Needs to Embrace Innovation

Martin Wählisch

Introduction

"We need more innovation, more inclusion and more foresight, investing in the global public goods that sustain us all," emphasized the UN Secretary-General in his landmark report *Our Common Agenda* (UN 2021). With the aim to advance toward a United Nations 2.0, he promoted a "quintet of change," including data, analytics, and communications; innovation and digital transformation; strategic foresight; behavioral science; and performance and results orientation to make the organization more effective (ibid.). He also underlined the UN Charter's focus on value of "collective efforts" to achieve a better world, stressing that "cooperation and solidarity are the only solutions, within societies and between nations" (ibid.). *Our Common Agenda* is a reminder of the need of a surge of collective action to overcome the vast range of globalized social, economic, and security challenges.

Tackling the many new challenges to international conflict management and diplomacy, the UN is increasingly using modern technologies and other innovative methods to advance diplomacy and collective responses (Druet 2021; Hirblinger 2020; Panic 2020; Duursma and Karlsrud 2019; UN 2019a; Perera 2017; Firchow et al. 2017; Karlsrud 2014; Dorn 2009). Complex data analysis, artificial intelligence (AI), virtual reality (VR), and behavioral and

M. Wählisch (✉)
United Nations, New York, NY, USA

future research are now part of the steadily growing repertoire in the field of peace and security. The COVID-19 pandemic has in many ways promoted and accelerated new approaches to diplomacy, including the use of new technologies, digital dialogues, and other innovation. Multilateral affairs have increasingly adapted to the era of digital transformation, including the omnipresence of social media for public diplomacy, artificial intelligence, big data for strategic decision-making, and other advancements (Bjola 2019; National Research Council 2015; FCO 2012).

UN Member States have grown to pay attention to both the positive and negative effects of technological innovation, including the dark side of cyber issues, challenges to digital cooperation, and global digital disparities. Following a series of Security Council meetings on cyber security over the last years, the United States hosted a Council session on the use of digital technologies in maintaining international peace and security in May 2022. U.S. Representative to the United Nations, Ambassador Linda Thomas-Greenfield, noted in her remarks in the session that "to effectively maintain peace and security in the 21st century, we need to respond to 21st century threats and deploy 21st century tools" (Thomas-Greenfield 2022). The Permanent Representative of the Russian Federation, Ambassador Vassily Nebenzia, raised deep concerns about the "information battlefield" and cyberattacks, including related to the Ukraine, while calling for "professional dialogue, aimed at elaboration of concrete practical solutions" (Nebenzia 2022). China's Ambassador, Zhang Jun, underlined that it is important to "vigorously advocate for scientific and technological innovation," while stressing that "technological innovation should not produce only one champion" but serve the collective interests of all countries (Zhang 2022). The Security Council debate stands symbol for the tendency that new ways of advancing collective diplomacy are carefully approached, especially in the context of peace and security.[1] Although the UN Charter is generally understood to be a living document that is flexible enough to address changing challenges, new practices and themes take time to become mainstreamed. This makes the opportunity for innovation of collective diplomacy limited but possible.

This chapter looks at the changing landscape of international diplomacy in the context of new technologies and innovation at large, taking stock of recent developments and capturing emerging trends. Written from a practitioner

---

[1] I am mindful that the term "collective diplomacy" (often also called "collective engagement") has found a plethora of interpretations in the literature over decades and admit that I use it more broadly here as a frame to address how UN Member States and the UN Secretariat try to maintain peace and security, including prevention, mediation, and peacebuilding initiatives. For a helpful overview on the terminology, see Wiseman (2015), 316.

perspective, it focuses on the recent experience in the United Nations responding to innovation in the peace context, including through new evidence-driven approaches to international relations, creative forms of diplomatic communication and conversations, and non-tech approaches such as cognitive and behavioral science in diplomatic practice. These are ways the UN Secretariat has tried to create value and win over some Member States to cherish innovation as a chance to strengthen multilateral responses.

Reflecting on those emerging trends leads to the belief that diplomacy needs to embrace innovation as an opportunity to co-create new solutions, nurture collective progress, and expand the greater common good of the international community. Universal and all-embracing organizations like the United Nations had to constantly reinvent themselves, in parts, throughout history to stay relevant and fit-for-purpose. For its very survival, innovation and change are essential for the UN, despite the usual drive of public institutions to rather preserve the status quo and bureaucratic resistance to transformative change (Juma 2016).

The UN Secretariat in Upheaval and Departure

When UN Secretary-General António Guterres took office in January 2017, he promised the international community that he would reform the venerable world organization. Guterres reiterated that the UN must be willing to change (Guterres 2016). In September 2018, the Secretary-General presented his "Strategy on New Technologies," in which he underlined new opportunities but also the dangers of emerging tech (Guterres 2018). In the same year, he appointed the High-Level Panel for Digital Cooperation, which was tasked with raising awareness of the transformative effects of digital technologies on society and the economy (UN 2022a). But the Secretary-General's reform agenda should go even further. Innovation became one of the leitmotifs of the United Nations 2.0, with the aim of capturing and recalibrating the institutional organizational culture as a whole. The aim was and is to make the United Nations more imaginative, daring and future-oriented. "We can do things differently and we can do different things ... Innovation isn't just about advanced technologies, sometimes it's about the simplest things. Be bold, be revolutionary ... and disrupt ... because without innovation, there is no way we can overcome the challenges of our time," Guterres declared (UN 2019b).

Motivated by the internal will to change, the Policy and Peacebuilding Department (DPPA) in the UN Secretariat founded an interdisciplinary team, the "Innovation Cell," which took on new technologies, instruments, and practices in the areas of conflict prevention, mediation, and peacebuilding (UN 2022b). As part of the Policy and Mediation Division, the DPPA Innovation Team was entrusted with exploring innovative methods, expanding pilot projects and finding new approaches to problem solving through human-centered design. The areas and initiatives of the DPPA Innovation Team now include the use of AI-supported digital dialogues to strengthen inclusive peace efforts, the use of social media as a resource for information evaluation and a channel for advocacy, virtual reality (VR) to improve the situational awareness of diplomats and decision-makers, the use of geospatial data analysis to improve early warning of possible conflicts, the application of behavioral sciences and cognitive science in the field of international cooperation and peace, as well as the topics of strategic foresight and futures research (UN 2022c). Innovation in the field of peace was included as a reorientation in DPPA's Strategic Plan with the overall ambition to become a more forward-looking and future-leaning member of the UN family (UN 2022d). Partnerships with academia, technology pioneers, and other innovators were acknowledged as essential to this vision. Political and financial support has been given from UN Member States, including Germany, Japan, Qatar, China, Finland, Norway, Ireland, Turkey, the Netherlands, and others.

Creating a dedicated capacity for innovation at the UN is not new. The UN Innovation Network (UNIN) was founded in 2015 and now has more than 65 separate United Nations innovation units (UN 2022e). The establishment of a specialized unit for innovation in the field of peacemaking and peacekeeping was therefore probably only a matter of time. The developments fit into the series of professionalization and specialization tendencies in the UN Secretariat that have already found their expression with the establishment of the Mediation Support Unit (MSU) in 2006 and the Unit for Gender, Peace and Security (GPS) in 2016 (UN 2022f, 2022g).

New Challenges and Opportunities in the Digital Era

Since its inception, the United Nations has been a motor for innovative ideas and new approaches to global problems, especially in the area of peace and security (Schechter 2016). The establishment of peacekeeping missions, creative initiatives as part of the good offices of the UN Secretary-General, and new thematic angles, such as climate security, are an expression of the constant attempt to seek progress and advance collective diplomacy. Even if the

UN often reaches its limits in serving as an effective global institution and community due to global political circumstances, there has still been space for new vantage points during the past few decades (Weiss 2010, 3).

With the digital revolution, challenges for the peace and security architecture of the United Nations and thus the need for other solutions have again multiplied. Digital technologies are influencing all facets of today's private and public life. One example of this is the spectacular growth and influence of social media, including its use for malicious purposes. In recent years, parties to the conflict have increasingly used digital disinformation campaigns to manipulate public opinion, and so-called hate in the web has opened up new fronts. This dynamic is accentuated by the algorithmic engineering of social media channels, which are designed to reinforce existing preferences, and therefore biases, to maximize user engagement.

New technologies are a double-edged sword for peace. The internet has created new freedoms, but the dark web has also provided new avenues for terrorists and violent extremist groups to aid recruitment, plan attacks, and fund operations. Cybercrime poses new challenges for law enforcement agencies, particularly in view of the possibility of remote actions and the ephemeral nature of electronic evidence. In view of the rapid technological progress, existing regulatory frameworks, social norms, and ethical standards also require a new assessment. All these were and are reasons for the UN to explore new tools for conflict management through innovation, but also to systematically assess the role and impact of new technologies on the global security architecture.

"Without increased, intelligent, and responsible use of technology, we will fall short of the SDGs and miss opportunities to prevent conflict and keep peace. And with greater reliance on innovation using new technologies, the management culture of the United Nations can become more efficient, agile and proactive – and deliver better results for our members," stressed the UN Secretary-General in his strategy on new technologies (Guterres 2018). The COVID-19 pandemic has accelerated digitization for the UN as an organization on a large scale, as for many other parts of the public and private sector, but has also helped to modernize diplomacy on a particularly small scale. Online meetings of the Security Council, virtual visits to conflict regions, and science and data-based debates on peace and security are now more part of the UN's repertoire than before (Wählisch 2020). It has arrived at a time when new technologies and innovation are taking a greater place in UN practice (*The Economist* 2021). Even if there are still critics who rightly emphasize the limits of technologies for interpersonal and intergovernmental dialogue, the digital revolution in international relations seems unstoppable.

New Solutions in the Area of Peace

AI Support of Digital Dialogues

An example of the use of new technologies in peace processes is digital dialogues. The overall goal is to increase the inclusiveness of peace processes through public participation, whereby various digital applications can be useful. Computer-aided analysis can help to make conflicting public views more visible or to find common ground, based on linguistic argumentation patterns and the large-scale evaluation of public opinions.

In 2020, for example, the Office of the Secretary-General's Special Envoy for Yemen (OSESGY) conducted the first-ever large-scale virtual consultation with Yemeni citizens on the opportunities and challenges of the ongoing peace process (OSESGY 2020). During the interactive live online dialogue in Yemeni Arabic dialect, over 500 Yemeni participants, a third of them women, shared their thoughts on the prospect of a nationwide ceasefire, the future of the peace process, and the main humanitarian and economic measures. The deployed application used machine learning, commonly referred to as artificial intelligence (AI), to conduct consultations with a large group of people in local dialects, enabling real-time analysis of responses and segmentation by demographic interest. The advantage of digital consultations is that sentiments of public opinion can be quickly evaluated and the anonymity of those involved is guaranteed. It provides similar flexibility as focus groups, but with the quantitative scope of respondents in an opinion poll. Similar digital dialogues have been conducted in Libya, Iraq, Bolivia, Haiti, and Lebanon in support of existing peace efforts.

As follow-up projects, efforts have been initiated with a focus on machine-aided text analysis to develop language resources and tools for conflict-relevant local dialects. At the same time, UN DPPA is working on applications that enable easier transcription and translations from speech to text, which allows further points of contact for linguistic data processing. Among other issues, this is relevant for the timely evaluation of radio and television information, YouTube, and other audiovisual media that provide insights into the course of conflicts.

Geodata Analysis for Conflict Prevention

A second example from the work in the DPPA on the subject of innovation is the use of spatial data analysis for peacekeeping and conflict prevention

(Puccioni 2021). For example, undergoing testing are earth observation-based open-source approaches using new satellite technologies to enable data-based and computer-aided predictions of conflict-relevant regions. Interdisciplinary approaches such as remote sensing and machine learning are also used to develop more sophisticated early warning systems.

One application is the evaluation of geodata and satellite images in connection with the area of water security in the Middle East. A combination of geospatial assessment, conflict modeling, and machine-based analysis is used to assess different causes of conflict, providing insight into statistical correlations and providing the basis for assessing future trends in conflict risk indicators. Specifically, this is about observing water scarcity with the help of geospatial satellite analysis. Although aerospace technology is often used in the military field, similar methods can be used here to support peacebuilding initiatives. The advantage of new technologies is that they enable a new level of epistemic certainty, whereas traditional methods, for example, for pattern recognition and data correlation, would be more time-consuming.

Together with partners from the civil private sector, the UN is expanding further applications in the field of geodata analysis, which includes testing the use of so-called nanosatellites (CubeSat) in the field of peacebuilding. The denser satellite network and the rapid availability of commercial satellite images enable more efficient observation not only of front lines but also of other relevant conflict aspects such as transhumance, climatic factors, and economic circumstances (e.g. oil and gas production).

Using Virtual Reality

A third example of innovation in the UN to strengthen collective diplomacy is the use of virtual reality (VR) for briefing decision-makers, particularly members of the UN Security Council (DPPA 2021). VR can help raise awareness of conflict issues through the immersive experience. This allows UN officials and Member State delegations to experience the situations they are discussing without security and logistical concerns. Through the feeling of being there, immersive environments can help to increase emotional reactions and strengthen the sense of responsibility for decisions.

The first VR film was used by the DPPA during the German Presidency of the UN Security Council in April 2019 for a briefing on the situation in Iraq. More VR films followed to illustrate the work of the United Nations Integrated Transition Assistance Mission in Sudan (UNITAMS) and the UN Verification Mission in Colombia in 2021 (Futuring Peace 2022a, 2022b). In January

2022, for the first time under the Norwegian presidency, the Security Council was held directly in the Security Council Chamber taught in VR (Norway UN 2022). In May 2022, together with Japan, UN DPPA launched a VR experience on climate security in the Asia Pacific region with the aim to advance policy action. In June 2022 under the Albanian Presidency of the Security Council, a UN-produced VR experience on Yemen was shown in the Council's chamber to strengthen empathy and mutual understanding.

In the future, VR films are to be expanded to include more interactive experiences in order to simulate the consequences of different solutions. The three-dimensional space in VR also gives the possibility to visualize complex data sets. A first attempt was made with the UN Secretary-General's report on the state of global peace and security, which was rendered as an interactive VR experience (DPPA 2022).

Challenges and Opportunities of Innovating Collective Diplomacy

"The United Nations is a last-ditch, hard-core affair, and it is not surprising that the organization should often be blamed for failing to solve problems which have already been found to be insoluble by governments," noted U Thant (1971), then-Secretary-General of the United Nations. He added: "There are times when action, dynamism and innovation are in demand, and other times when governments shun them like the plague" (ibid.). His words are a reminder of multilateral diplomacy's need for constant innovation. Institutional advancements are key to tackling new challenges and staying competitive. However, novel approaches must be carefully calibrated for them to work. This is especially complex in organizations like the UN where minimal changes are often countered with maximum resistance as the status quo is a result hard-won compromise (Nagelhus Schia 2017, 55).

Innovation in the public sector is difficult as the common organizational culture tends to be risk-averse and cautious (Slack and Singh 2018, 361). Although institutional practices are changing in the public sector of some places of the world, the common mantra remains one of preserving the state of affairs instead of being adventurousness and daring, which is required for achieving progress (Al Noaimi et al. 2022, 201; Bozeman and Kingsley 1998, 109). As Sandford Borins (2001, 310–11) has pointed out, "the public sector is characterized by asymmetric incentives that punish unsuccessful innovations much more severely than they reward successful ones," and another disadvantage is that there is "no share ownership" in the public sector. As he goes on to observe, there is a certain eagerness "to expose public sector failures and pillory the public servants involved, with potentially disastrous effects on their careers," and that "stringent central agency controls put in place to minimize corruption and ensure due process also constrain the innovativeness of public servants" (ibid.). He concludes that "these asymmetric incentives make the public sector a far less fertile ground for innovation than the private sector" (ibid.). All this explains why thematic or structural change in public institutions like the UN is complicated (Bauer et al. 2017, 239).

Meanwhile, the public sector is under growing pressure to create renewed value through various types of innovations, including improved organizational efficiency, economic performance, and new operational methods (Alves 2012, 671). Public institutions have to provide "service satisfaction" to maintain commitment to and confidence in them (Heintzman and Marson 2005, 549). The same applies to international organizations, including the UN. "The people we serve and represent may lose faith not only in their governments and institutions – but in the values that have animated the work of the United Nations for over 75 years," stressed UN Secretary-General Guterres in his opening address to the UN General Assembly in September 2021 (Guterres 2021). He emphasized: "Like never before, core values are in the crosshairs. A breakdown in trust is leading to a breakdown in values. Promises, after all, are worthless if people do not see results in their daily lives" (ibid.). In the context of collective diplomacy, innovation needs to bring to the forefront why the UN matters and why powerful Member States should care about multilateralism.

Innovation spaces and entities have mushroomed over the last two decades in the UN (Bloom and Faulkner 2016, 1371). Different parts of the UN organization have made "innovation" part of their operational principles, including through introducing dedicated innovation labs, hubs, cells, teams, and other capacities. Public sector innovation capacities are safe spaces to address difficult problems through design-thinking and rapid prototyping of new ideas (McGann et al. 2018, 249). They allow the bringing together of science, technology, art, design, and other multi-disciplinary perspectives to attempt addressing unusual solutions to impossible problems (Cole 2022, 164). Their overall aim is to integrate a culture of user-led solution-making, build spaces for experimentation and exploration, and co-create innovations. The drive to postulate and push for innovation as a more explicit principle in the organizational culture of the UN has been encouraging and promising, even if the long-terms effects might not be fully visible yet to many skeptics (Saarelainen et al. 2019). Innovation is not free of failure and it is hard to overcome the status quo bias in organizations, but distinct innovation spaces allow for a safe spot to test out boundaries and unusual ideas. They can absorb enthusiasm of motivated staff members in a delineated setting to bring new approaches into the organizational practice once they have been tested and are ready for scaling.

The COVID-19 pandemic has given rise to the digital transformations of diplomacy, and, indeed, this has equally posed new challenges for international relations, including questions about risks and effectiveness of virtual means (Hedling and Bremberg 2021, 1595). Ultimately, the recent digital revolution of diplomacy is a collective learning process because of jointly experienced errors and failures (Al Jazeera 2020). In the best case, this dose of innovation and disruptive change can be new oxygen for collective diplomacy with effects that are only beginning to be addressed (Hare 2017, 235).

Final Considerations

Kofi Annan wrote in the second year of his tenure in 1998: "Despite the setbacks of the last decade, it has become apparent to all that the United Nations remains as much in demand as in need of change. That is our momentous challenge but also our great promise. In our efforts to fulfil that promise, we are leaning new ways to do what we do better, and we are finding new strategies to suit a changed environment" (Annan 1998, 123). His observations spotlight that the UN needs to innovate to progress which is indispensable in an ever-changing world. As the parameters for peace and security will constantly in flux, so must our collective response remain imaginative, flexible, and regenerative.

During the UN Security Council session on the use of digital technologies in maintaining international peace and security in May 2022, the Permanent Representative of Gabon, Ambassador Michel Xavier Biang, emphasized that the maintenance of peace depends on a solid system of technologies and innovation (UN 2022h). The UK Deputy Permanent Representative to the UN, Ambassador James Roscoe, called on the Security Council "to work together, including with civil society organisations, the private sector and other communities, to realise the benefits of, but also to counter the risks associated with, digital technologies" (Roscoe 2022). UN Under-Secretary-General for Political and Peacebuilding Affairs, Rosemary DiCarlo, highlighted in her briefing to the Council how technological developments have "improved our ability to detect crises, to better pre-position our humanitarian stocks, and to design data-driven peacebuilding programming" (DiCarlo 2022). She stressed that "we must fully embrace the opportunities offered by digital technologies to advance peace," but also need to "mitigate the risks that such technologies pose, and promote their responsible use by all actors" (ibid.). DiCarlo underlined that "collective action by Member States remains essential towards this goal" (ibid.). This debate in the Security Council is a testimony to the ongoing pursuit in the United Nations to find new instruments and approaches to foster peace and security.

While emerging technologies play a key role, they represent only a fraction of the spectrum of innovation. The UN Secretary-General's *Our Common Agenda* highlights other issues such as strategic foresight and behavioral science, which are seeing new momentum as instruments to advance multilateral diplomacy (UN 2021). Innovation means creating space for cross-cutting ideas, allowing measured experimentation, and integrating new practices, such as through digital dialogues in support of ongoing peace processes or geospatial remote sensing to advance conflict prevention in the context of climate security, as the DPPA Innovation Cell has explored over the last years (DPPA 2022; Alavi et al. 2022). It also means working with more evidence-based and developing new data sources in the area of peace and security. In order to succeed, this must be a joint effort of all, the UN Secretariat and Member States, individually and collectively, to promote new approaches and means with the aim to expand the greater common good of the international community.

Note

The views in the article are solely those of the author and do not necessarily reflect those of the United Nations or its Member States.

References and Further Reading

Al Jazeera. 2020. "UN Holds Virtual Meetings, Technical Problems Ensue," April 27. https://www.aljazeera.com/program/newsfeed/2020/4/27/un-holds-virtual-meetings-technical-problems-ensue.

Al Noaimi, H.A., C.M. Durugbo, and O.R. Al-Jayyousi. 2022. "Between Dogma and Doubt: A Meta-synthesis of Innovation in the Public Sector." *Australian Journal of Public Administration* 81 (1): 201–23.

Alavi, D.M., M. Wählisch, C. Irwin, and A. Konya. 2022. "Using Artificial Intelligence for Peacebuilding." *Journal of Peacebuilding & Development*, May. https://journals.sagepub.com/doi/full/10.1177/15423166221102757.

Alves, H. 2012. "Co-creation and Innovation in Public Services." *Service Industries Journal* 33 (7–8): 671–82.

Annan, K. 1998. "The Quiet Revolution." *Global Governance* 4 (2): 123–38.

Bauer, M., H. Jörgens, and C. Knill Bauer. 2017. "Organizational Change in International Bureaucracies." In *The Management of UN Peacekeeping: Coordination, Learning, and Leadership in Peace Operations*, eds. J. Junk, F. Mancini, W. Seibel, and T. Blume, 239–64. Lynne Rienner: Boulder.

Bjola, C. 2019. "Trends and Counter-Trends in Digital Diplomacy." In *New Realities in Foreign Affairs: Diplomacy in the 21st Century*, ed. V. Stanzel, 51–62. Nomos: Baden-Baden.

Bloom, L., and R. Faulkner. 2016. "Innovation Spaces: Lessons from the United Nations." *Third World Quarterly* 37 (8): 1371–87.

Borins, S. 2001. "Encouraging Innovation in the Public Sector." *Journal of Intellectual Capital* 2 (3): 310–19.

Bozeman, B., and G. Kingsley. 1998. "Risk Culture in Public and Private Organizations." *Public Administration Review* 58 (2): 109–18.

Cole, L. 2022. "A Framework to Conceptualize Innovation Purpose in Public Sector Innovation Labs." *Policy Design and Practice* 5 (2): 164–82.

DiCarlo, R. 2022. Remarks to the Security Council on Technology and Conflict, May 23. https://dppa.un.org/en/remarks-under-secretary-general-rosemary-dicarlo-to-security-council-technology-and-conflict.

Dorn, W. 2009. "Intelligence-led Peacekeeping: The United Nations Stabilization Mission in Haiti (MINU.S.TAH), 2006–07." *Intelligence and National Security* 24 (6): 805–35.

DPPA. 2021. "Virtual Reality Bites: Using Technology to Bring Post-conflict Situations to Life." *DPPA Politically Speaking*, July 12. https://dppa.medium.com/virtual-reality-bites-using-technology-to-bring-post-conflict-situations-to-life-bd5cb98ce3f6.

———. 2022. https://vimeo.com/672124404.

Druet, D. 2021. *Enhancing the Use of Digital Technology for Integrated Situational Awareness and Peacekeeping-intelligence*. Montreal: McGill University Press.

Duursma, A., and J. Karlsrud. 2019. "Predictive Peacekeeping: Strengthening Predictive Analysis in UN Peace Operations." *Stability: International Journal of Security and Development* 8 (1): 1–19.

The Economist. 2021. "Diplomacy Has Changed More than Most Professions During the Pandemic," April 29. https://www.economist.com/international/2021/04/29/diplomacy-has-changed-more-than-most-professions-during-the-pandemic.

Firchow, P., C. Martin-Shields, A. Omer, and R. Mac Ginty. 2017. "PeaceTech: The Liminal Spaces of Digital Technology in Peacebuilding." *International Studies Perspectives* 18 (1): 4–42.

Foreign and Commonwealth Office. (FCO) 2012. Digital Strategy. https://www.gov.uk/government/publications/the-fco-digital-strategy.
Futuring Peace. 2022a. Sudan Now. https://futuringpeace.org/VR/Sudannow/.
———. 2022b. Pathways Colombia. https://futuringpeace.org/VR/Pathwayscolombia/.
Guterres, A. 2016. Remarks to the General Assembly on Taking the Oath of Office, December 12.
———. 2018. "UN Secretary-General's Strategy on New Technologies." https://www.un.org/en/newtechnologies/.
———. 2021. Secretary-General's Address to the 76th Session of the UN General Assembly, September 21. https://www.un.org/sg/en/content/sg/speeches/2021-09-21/address-the-76th-session-of-general-assembly.
Hare, P. W. 2017. *Making Diplomacy Work: Intelligent Innovation for the Modern World*. Washington, D.C.: CQ Press.
Hedling, E., and N. Bremberg. 2021. "Practice Approaches to the Digital Transformations of Diplomacy: Toward a New Research Agenda." *International Studies Review* 23 (4): 1595–618.
Heintzman, R., and B. Marson. 2005. "People, Service and Trust: Is There a Public Sector Service Value Chain?" *International Review of Administrative Sciences* 71 (4): 549–75.
Hirblinger, A. 2020. "Digital Inclusion in Mediated Peace Processes: How Technology Can Enhance Participation." *Peaceworks* 168: 1–45.
Juma, C. 2016. *Innovation and Its Enemies: Why People Resist New Technologies*. Oxford: Oxford University Press.
Karlsrud, J. 2014. "Peacekeeping 4.0: Harnessing the Potential of Big Data, Social Media, and Cyber Technologies." In *Cyberspace and International Relations: Theory, Prospects and Challenges*, eds. J.-F. Kremer and B. Müller, 141–60. Cham: Springer.
McGann, M., E. Blomkamp, and J.M. Lewis. 2018. "The Rise of Public Sector Innovation Labs: Experiments in Design Thinking for Policy." *Policy Sciences* 51 (1): 249–67.
Nagelhus Schia, N. 2017. "Horseshoe and Catwalk: Power, Complexity, and Consensus-making in the United Nations Security Council." In *Palaces of Hope: The Anthropology of Global Organizations*, eds. R. Niezen and M. Sapignoli, 55–77. Cambridge: Cambridge University Press.
National Research Council. 2015. "Diplomacy for the 21st Century: Embedding a Culture of Science and Technology Throughout the Department of State." https://nap.nationalacademies.org/catalog/21730/diplomacy-for-the-21st-century-embedding-a-culture-of-science.
Nebenzia, V. 2022. Statement at UNSC Briefing on Technology and Security in the Context of Maintaining International Peace and Security, May 23. https://russiaun.ru/en/news/230522n.
Norway UN (@NorwayUN). 2022. Twitter, January 20. https://twitter.com/NorwayUN/status/1484187692372008961.

OSESGY. 2020. "Cutting-Edge Tech in the Service of Inclusive Peace in Yemen, Office of the Special Envoy of the Secretary-General for Yemen," August 3. https://osesgy.unmissions.org/cutting-edge-tech-service-inclusive-peace-yemen.

Panic, B. 2020. *Data for Peacebuilding and Prevention Ecosystem Mapping: The State of Play and the Path to Creating a Community of Practice*. New York: Center on International Cooperation, New York University.

Perera, S. 2017. "To Boldly Know: Knowledge, Peacekeeping and Remote Data Gathering in Conflict-affected States." *International Peacekeeping* 24 (5): 803–22.

Puccioni, A. 2021. "How to Change the World from Space." *Medium*. (Futuring Peace), July 9. https://medium.com/futuring-peace/how-to-change-the-world-from-space-d4186e76da43.

Roscoe, J. 2022. Statement at the UN Security Council Briefing on Technology and Peace and Security, May 23. https://www.gov.uk/government/speeches/technology-is-changing-how-we-monitor-understand-and-respond-to-conflict-and-to-humanitarian-crises.

Saarelainen, E., D. Zyadeh, and I. Núñez Ferrera. 2019. "Creating a Culture of Innovation in the Humanitarian Sector." *Stanford Social Innovation Review*, October 9. https://ssir.org/articles/entry/creating_a_culture_of_innovation_in_the_humanitarian_sector.

Schechter, M.G., ed. 2016. *Innovation in Multilateralism*. Houndmills: Palgrave Macmillan.

Slack, N.J., and G. Singh. 2018. "Diagnosis of Organizational Culture in Public Sector Undertakings Undergoing Reforms." *Public Organization Review* 18 (3): 361–80.

Thant, U. 1971. "In This I Believe." *New York Times*, September 21. https://www.nytimes.com/1971/09/21/archives/in-this-i-believe.html.

Thomas-Greenfield, L. 2022. Remarks at a UN Security Council Meeting on the Use of Digital Technologies in Maintaining International Peace and Security, May 23. https://usun.usmission.gov/remarks-by-ambassador-linda-thomas-greenfield-at-a-un-security-council-meeting-on-the-use-of-digital-technologies-in-maintaining-international-peace-a/.

United Nations. 2019a. "E-analytics Guide: Using Data and New Technology for Peacemaking, Preventive Diplomacy and Peacebuilding." New York: United Nations.

———. 2019b. UN Innovation Toolkit. https://www.uninnovation.network/un-innovation-toolkit.

———. 2021. *Our Common Agenda*. https://www.un.org/en/content/common-agenda-report/assets/pdf/Common_Agenda_Report_English.pdf.

———. 2022a. Secretary-General's High-Level Panel on Digital Cooperation. https://www.un.org/en/civil-society/secretary-general%E2%80%99s-high-level-panel-digital-cooperation.

———. 2022b. DPPA Innovation. https://dppa.un.org/en/innovation.

———. 2022c. Futuring Peace. https://futuringpeace.org/.

———. 2022d *UN DPPA Strategic Plan 2020–2022*. https://dppa.un.org/en/strategic-plan-2020-2022.

———. 2022e. UN Innovation Network. https://www.uninnovation.network/.

———. 2022f. DPPA Prevention and Mediation. https://dppa.un.org/en/prevention-and-mediation.

———. 2022g. DPPA Women Peace and Security. https://dppa.un.org/en/women-peace-and-security.

———. 2022h. UN Doc. SC/14899, May 23. https://www.un.org/press/en/2022/sc14899.doc.htm/.

Wählisch, M. 2020. "How to Hack Dystopia in Our Current Global Mess." *Medium* (Futuring Peace), July 24. https://medium.com/futuring-peace/how-to-hack-dystopia-in-our-current-global-mess-139ff85bbbd6.

Weiss, T.G. 2010. "How United Nations Ideas Change History." *Review of International Studies* 36 (1): 3–23.

Wiseman, G. 2015. "Diplomatic Practices at the United Nations." *Cooperation and Conflict* 50 (3): 316–33.

Zhang, J. 2022. Remarks at the UN Security Council Briefing on Technology and Security, May 23. http://un.china-mission.gov.cn/eng/hyyfy/202205/t20220524_10691574.htm.

26

Innovating International Cooperation for Development: A New Model for Partnerships Between Developed and Middle-Income Countries

José Antonio Zabalgoitia and Antonio Tenorio

Middle-Income Countries' Development Bottlenecks

The United Nations Millennium Declaration, adopted on September 8, 2000, set the reduction of poverty as its first and foremost objective (UN 2000).[1] This is undoubtedly the achievement that will most fundamentally impact the

---

[1] The Millennium Declaration dedicates its third section to "Development and Poverty Eradication." It categorically commits to "spare no effort to free our fellow men, women and children from the abject and dehumanizing conditions of extreme poverty" and to create an environment conducive to its elimination. It specifically focuses on Least Developed countries, rewarding those who make demonstrable commitments to poverty reduction with debt relief, and calling donors "To grant more generous development assistance, especially to countries that are genuinely making an effort to apply their resources to poverty reduction."

This chapter is the sole responsibility of its authors and does not necessarily reflect the viewpoints or policies of the Secretariat of External Relations of Mexico.

J. A. Zabalgoitia (✉)
Embassy of Mexico to the Netherlands, Amsterdam, The Netherlands

A. Tenorio
Universidad Iberoamericana, Mexico City, Mexico

greatest number of individuals at a global scale. In accordance with that decision, basic paradigms and guidelines for official development assistance (ODA) have also been reoriented to fulfill that aspiration.

However, when ODA donor countries follow the Millennium Declaration and concentrate resources on reducing poverty, alleviating hunger, and improving health for the poorest, they naturally lean toward helping least-developed and lower-income countries.[2] Thus, the 92 middle-income countries (MICs) currently included in the OECD's Development Assistance Committee list have witnessed a decline in overall available ODA resources even though a majority (62 percent) of the total world population under the poverty line lives in this group of countries (WBG 2020).

Along with this paradox of poverty demographics in developing countries, ODA has been experiencing profound changes in the past two decades stemming from at least two additional factors that constrain developing nations' access to aid for development: insufficient donor budgets (OECD 2001)[3] and an increasing number of countries ranked as MICs.

These factors are signs that the traditional development assistance model is reaching its limits. The increasing number of middle-income countries is undoubtedly the result of their relative success and advances in their own development processes, but at the same time, it makes competition among them to obtain scarce ODA and other resources much more intense.

This traditional model where developed countries provide "development aid" funding to projects in developing nations is becoming widely questioned, and recipient countries are also facing increasing donor requirements and controls that they find difficult to comply with. Thus, the scope of this traditional cooperation model is shrinking: only a limited number of projects meet the strict criteria applied by donors.

There is an underlying misconception that explains this: both donors and recipients used to understand their relationship to promote development as "aid" rather than cooperation. This established an asymmetrical relationship between donor and recipient, both in terms of resources and on the capacity for decision-making regarding the projects.

Middle-income or emerging market nations find themselves ineligible from receiving bilateral cooperation grants for development projects under this

---

[2] The World Bank income classification categories are followed here as applied by the OECD in its Development Assistance Committee's List of ODA Recipients for 2022 and 2023.

[3] According to OECD's DAC official ODA statistics, donors are still very far from achieving the UN benchmark of allocating 0.7 percent of Gross National Income (GNI) to foreign aid. DAC members donated an average of 0.33 percent of GDI in 2021. Despite that, total ODA to developing countries has grown since 2006.

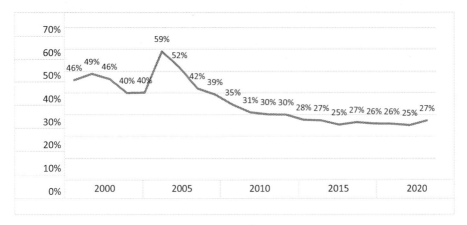

Fig. 26.1 Middle-income countries' share of total ODA 2000–20. Source: OECD 2022

model. These issues, among others, are reflected by a sharp decline in their access to ODA resources. In 2020 MICs' share of total ODA fell to less than half of what it was at its peak in 2005 (Fig. 26.1).

In fact, their relatively higher development level has meant a double disadvantage for MICs: on the one hand, they are excluded from funding by donor government sources, and on the other hand, they still face, to a significant extent, development challenges similar to those of low-income nations.

MICs in fact confront several development bottlenecks or, as specialists call them, "middle income development traps." One of these experts (Alonso 2013, 3) identifies some of the structural imbalances that obstruct their paths to development: governance factors—weak social cohesion or ineffective institutional framework, for example; persistent poverty and extreme inequality that lead to social fragmentation; macroeconomic vulnerabilities and unfavorable access to international financial sources; new environmental protection responsibilities that require the allocation of financial, technical, and human resources besides modernizing production processes and the energy matrix.

However, there is an upside to this situation: most middle-income countries have developed well-educated, technology-proficient human resources and also possess the necessary bureaucratic sophistication and economic complexity that allow them to allocate public and private funds to their own high priority development projects. These two assets, while not enough to overcome "development traps," do provide an opportunity for collaboration with developed nations that may provide technical expertise and best practices that may help to address them, even when giving grants or project funding does

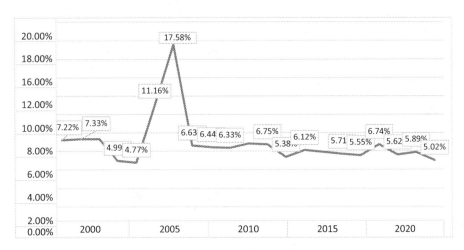

Fig. 26.2 Select middle-income countries' share of total ODA 2000–20. Source: OECD 2022

not result as attractive to donor countries due to their international cooperation rules and policies.

The next chart shows that a select group of seven MICs[4] with big, relatively industrialized economies, and above average capabilities to engage in national development policies, have received, despite an atypical surge around 2007, a rather stable share of total ODA funding in the last two decades. However, these seven countries have also concentrated about a third of all ODA destined to MICs in this period. This shows that high poverty levels aside, being able to carry out sophisticated and complex development projects on their own has also allowed them to attract ODA to complement their own resources (Fig. 26.2).

However, a second paradox is present on ODA received by MICs: despite the MICs' share of total ODA decreasing as shown above, the group of seven selected larger economies have been attracting an increasing share of the ODA received by all MICs. This may indicate that possessing a larger economy and stronger institutional capabilities provides distinctive advantages to attract ODA, as is shown in the next graph (Fig. 26.3).

In those cases where developed donor nations join MICs to design and execute development projects, the parties engage in a partnership among equals and the asymmetry in their cooperation relationship is reduced. Furthermore, the development gap between donors and middle-income partners in human resources on knowledge-based and technical disciplines is not

---

[4] Brazil, China, India, Mexico, Nigeria, South Africa, and Turkey.

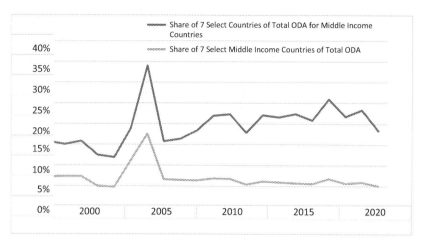

Fig. 26.3 Select middle-income countries' share of total ODA and of ODA to middle-income countries 2000–20. Source: OECD 2022

as wide as in other areas. Thus, science, technology, and innovation-related projects become the most suitable for cooperation and partnerships between developed and middle-income countries.

Strengths of Middle-Income Countries for Development Partnerships with Donors

This chapter is written with the fundamental assumption that the traditional international assistance for development model is not the best way either to reach very significant portions of the world's population living in poverty as is the goal of most developed, donor countries; nor does it allow to take full advantage of the capabilities of MICs to carry out development projects. There is enormous potential to advance development in these countries through new partnership relationships with donors.

In order to move forward to a new partnership model for development, donor countries should realize that their most valuable assets are not of a financial nature. Beyond assigning an ODA chapter on their budget, some of the most valuable features of a developed donor country are possessing a strong, knowledge-based economy and a deep pool of well-educated human resources in scientific and technical fields. Along with a strong, diversified, and decentralized higher education and scientific research institutional network, and competitive and innovative manufacturing and services sectors of their economies, they provide essential elements to engage in international cooperation partnerships. Providing knowledge and sharing best practices and innovation can have a deeper and longer lasting impact on the success of international development projects than exclusively allocating fiscal funds or making preferential financing available.

Likewise, as was mentioned, most ODA recipient, emerging market economies display a dual development reality: they possess modern, competitive, technologically sophisticated, export-oriented industries and sectors on parts of their territories, while other areas of their countries lag behind, surviving on more traditional, self-enclosed, and inefficient production methods. As a result, there is an increasing domestic income gap, and large portions of the population subsist below poverty lines. Middle-income countries thus show very large-income distribution inequalities: they are middle income on a national average, but in reality they are poor countries with a small, high-income, well-educated elite. It is precisely in this dichotomy where the opportunities for new international development partnerships lie.

Given this dichotomy, the main objective for MICs should be to identify potential partners among donor countries according to their comparative advantages in relation to any specific project they intend to carry out. In this regard, it is essential that MICs' international cooperation areas get involved in project planning from the earliest stage possible. This will allow foreign ministries to instruct their outposts to first explore the relative strengths of developed nations that may complement domestic capabilities and then to approach the relevant public or private sector institutions to interest them on the project.

The main diplomatic task is to design partnerships in which the developed country government understands that traditional "aid" is not being requested but rather the involvement and participation of its best knowledge-based businesses and academic institutions. It is possible that the initial diplomatic approach needs to be established through a research center or an expert firm in a specific field, rather than through the donor foreign ministry or international cooperation agency.

Middle-income country diplomacy needs to be sufficiently creative and persuasive so as to attract the interest in the projects of its potential partners, without their perceiving it either as a traditional aid request or as a mere business opportunity to sell technology. In this task, understanding their own country's strengths and resources, as well as being able to relay the shortcomings that the potential partnership may help to solve, is essential.

To show the capabilities of MICs to engage in development partnerships with developed ODA donors, we will once again rely on a set of economic and social indicators using the group of seven larger and relatively more developed countries as an example. This set of indicators will help us demonstrate that MICs can be attractive partners for donors in development projects, but we must also be aware that there are significant differences among them as well. This group of seven nations is also illustrative of the great diversity and heterogeneity that characterizes MICs.

Size

Our group of selected MICs are big countries with large economies and populations. The largest are the People's Republic of China and India. They are currently the world's second and sixth largest economies respectively, measured by their GDP. In terms of population, each has over 1.4 billion people living in their territories.

Brazil, Mexico, and Turkey have also significant GDPs. They are the 12th, 15th, and 20th largest economies in the world. Nigeria and South Africa follow them at 28th and 41st. The seven countries are all within the group of 50 largest economies in the planet, regardless of their income level or their stage of development. By population size, Nigeria and Brazil are close to each other, with slightly over 200 million inhabitants each. Turkey and South Africa have significantly less population, with 85 and 61 million people, respectively. Mexico is positioned somewhat halfway between both subgroups, with 130 million inhabitants.

These first, very general indicators provide a broad perspective on the size of our group of selected MICs, as shown in Table 26.1.

Table 26.1 Size of economies

	Economy size	World ranking by GDP	Population
	GDP		Million people
	Current $Bn		
Brazil	1445	12	213,911
China	14,723	2	1,412,547
India	2660	6	1,405,221
Mexico	1074	15	130,118
Nigeria	0.432	28	216,747
South Africa	0.335	41	61,060
Turkey	0.720	20	85,682

Source: (WBG 2022; IMF 2022; Statistics Times 2021)

Development Challenges

These very broad indicators provide us with a general idea of our select group of seven nations' economic and demographic size. We will now provide a similarly wide panorama of their poverty and other social challenges, and afterward some indicators of the assets they rely on to confront them.

As is the case with developing nations, our group of seven selected larger MICs struggle with large segments of their population living below poverty lines[5] and are extremely unequal in both economic and social terms. To illustrate this, we will provide the latest available Gini index[6] data for them.

Poverty is undoubtedly the main concern for all developing nations, and our seven selected countries are no exception. India and Nigeria, even when taking into account their condition as Lower MICs which implies a less severe poverty threshold, have very large portions of their populations under poverty conditions. One in two Indians and three out of four Nigerians qualify as poor.

Of the Upper MICs in the group, South Africa has almost 57 percent of its population in poverty, exactly twice the percentage of Mexico, who is next with 28.1 percent. Turkey, Brazil, and China are much better off, with 10.2 percent, 13.1 percent, and 15.1 percent, respectively. It should be noted that China has been the most effective country in the world in reducing the share of its population living in poverty over the past two decades.

In absolute terms, 629 million poor inhabit India, followed by 223 million in China, and 154 in Nigeria. Demographic conditions are the most significant factors related to poverty. Even after dramatic achievements in their economic and social development, China still has over 200 million poor. By itself, China has almost twice the poor that live in all the other four Higher MICs in our group: 27.9 million in Brazil; 36.2 in Mexico; 31 in South Africa; and 8.5 in Turkey.

Alongside poverty, inequality is a most unfavorable feature of underdeveloped countries. The world's most unequal economy is part of our group of selected large MICs. With a Gini index of 63, there is no other country that deviates as much as South Africa from a perfectly equal distribution of income.

---

[5] To illustrate the magnitude of the challenge posed by poverty, we will rely on the U.S. Dollar $5.50/day (Purchasing Power Parity in 2011) threshold established by the World Bank poverty calculator on October 2017 based on poverty lines from upper middle-income economies. For India and Nigeria, the corresponding U.S. Dollar $3.20/day is applied (WBG 2022b).

[6] The Gini index compares the degree in which an actual income distribution between individuals in an economy deviates from a theoretical perfect distribution curve for that economy. Perfect distribution is represented by "0" and total inequality is represented by "100." The higher the index figure, the more unequal is a country (WBG 2022c).

Table 26.2 Inequality

	Poverty	Poverty	Inequality
	Million people	Percentage of total population	Gini index
Brazil	27.9	13.1	48.9
China	223.0	15.1	38.2
India	629.2	47.0	35.4
Mexico	36.2	28.1	45.4
Nigeria	156.9	71.0	35.1
South Africa	31	56.9	63.0
Turkey	8.5	10.2	41.9

Source: World Bank, Poverty and Equity Brief, April 2022. National Profiles for all countries shown. India's figures are for 2020 (WBG 2022c)

Brazil, Mexico, and Turkey have also very unequal societies, with their Gini index figures in the 40s. China, India, and Nigeria fare slightly better, with Gini index markings in the 30s. Table 26.2 expresses poverty and inequality indicators for our group of seven large MICs.

Social Policies

No sensible government can avoid the responsibility of putting public policies in place to alleviate and correct this situation. To a different extent and following their own paths, the governments of the seven selected MICs have pursued specific actions to provide for the most essential needs of the poorest segments of their societies while attempting to move out of poverty as many people as possible, as quickly as possible. These seven selected countries are fortunate in having relatively big economies and strong public institutions. Thus, the government sector has, in most cases, been the main driver of social programs and of education as the most effective vehicle for social mobility.

All seven countries in our sample have general government expenditures that fluctuate between 10 and 20 percent of GDP. This level of public resources is never enough, but by no means negligible. China (16.7 percent), Turkey (15.2 percent), Mexico (12.8 percent), and India (12.5 percent) stand close to each other on relatively tight budgets. South Africa (20.7 percent) and Brazil (20.5 percent) are relatively better off. In all cases, governments would welcome additional income, given the magnitude of poverty and other social challenges.

MICs build their government budgets with development as their main overall goal. While they cannot ignore the need to provide social programs to the impoverished sectors of their population, they must also invest in education and infrastructure projects. It goes without saying that with a few exceptions and for limited periods due to exceptional circumstances, their resources are never enough to move forward as fast as necessary to eradicate poverty and reach a higher stage of development.

Keeping in mind that significant portion of their populations live in poverty, it is not surprising that members of our seven country sample finance social safety net programs to the largest extent possible. Since social programs are destined for the underprivileged, there is a direct correlation between the size of the population in poverty and the percentage of the population covered by these programs. Thus, 93 percent of the population in India benefitted from social welfare (2011), while 79 percent of South African poor were in the same situation (2014). China reported a figure of 44 percent of its inhabitants (2013), Mexico of 27 percent (2018), Brazil 22 percent (2019), Nigeria 17 percent (2018), and Turkey 14 percent (2019) (WBG 2022d).

Since social programs need to be combined with other public policies to become sustainable and contribute to reduce poverty, MICs' governments consider important amounts on their budgets for education and to build and maintain infrastructure. Our group of seven countries scores important achievements in this regard. Except for Nigeria, who spends scarcely 5.7 percent of its total budget on education, all other members of the group invest twice or even three times as much on this essential component of any development strategy. South Africa spends most (18.4 percent), followed closely by Mexico (16.6 percent), and Brazil (16.1 percent). India (12.8 percent), Turkey (12.4 percent), and China (11.5 percent) do not fall too far behind (WBG 2022e).

Infrastructure

According to a recent study by the Office of the Chief Economist at the World Bank, governments finance between 87 percent and 91 percent of construction and maintenance of infrastructure (Fay et al. 2019, 46) in Lower and MICs. With the exceptional and outstanding case of China, where investments on infrastructure reach two digits as a percentage of GDP (16 percent) and are the result of sustained double digit growth rates as well, the other countries perform more modestly: Mexico invests 4.99 percent, Turkey (4.0 percent), South Africa (3.34 percent), Brazil (3.06 percent), and Nigeria (2.79 percent). There was no data available for India (Fay et al. 2019, 47–49) (Table 26.3).[7]

---

[7] Of the different alternatives provided by these authors, we have chosen the indicator built by combining Gross Fixed Capital Formation and Private Participation in Infrastructure data.

Table 26.3 Public expenditure

	Government expenditure	Social programs coverage	Education expenditures	Investment in infrastructure
	Percentage of GDP 2020	Percentage of total population	Percentage of total budget 2018	Percentage of GDP 2011
Brazil	20.5	22	16.11	3.06
China	16.7	44	11.5	16.0
India	12.5	93	12.8	N/A
Mexico	12.8	27	16.6	4.99
Nigeria	8.7	17	5.7	2.79
South Africa	20.7	79	18.4	3.34
Turkey	15.2	14	12.4	4.0

Sources: WBG (2022d); Fay et al. (2019), 46–49

Strengths for Partnerships

The relatively higher capabilities of MICs in fiscal, administrative, and social policy have already been established here. We can now move on to illustrate their relative strengths to partner with donor countries to carry out development projects on equal terms.

The modern sectors of MICs with emerging market economies are as competitive and as well-versed in scientific and technological advances, as their counterparts in high-income countries. These modern sectors of middle-income economies are equally suited for innovation and entrepreneurship as the equivalent ones in developed nations.

Education and Human Capital

Consistent fiscal efforts to provide education to the general population, and to some extent the availability of high-quality education for members of the elite, have resulted in the formation of the most valuable human capital in MICs. This is one of the strongest assets of these societies and can be used to sustain longer term development strategies.

To illustrate the potential of MICs as reliable and equal partners of donors in complex development projects, we will now examine some indicators for education and human capital. Given that education is one of the main factors that allow for social mobility, access to university education is fundamental to create and consolidate a middle class, which in turn means reducing poverty, and constitutes a valuable resource to carry out development projects.

The main indicator is the "gross enrollment ratio," defined as the share of the population enrolled at a university in relation to the total population from the same age expected to pursue higher education programs. According to this definition, three of the countries in our sample achieve a university coverage of about half the potential students in their societies: China has a 58 percent coverage, whereas Brazil has 55 percent and Mexico has 43 percent. The next three countries in the group fluctuate at a coverage of around a quarter of potential university students: India has 29 percent, and both South Africa and Turkey have 24 percent, although in Turkey's case the last figure available is for 1999. Finally, Nigeria only achieves a coverage of 10 percent of the total (WBG 2022f).

Only four of the seven countries in our sample have higher education institutions that rank with the top 200 universities in the world. China has seven universities in the top 200, while India has 3, Mexico 2, and Brazil just 1 (QS 2022). Regardless of their occupying positions in global rankings of excellence, all seven countries finance and maintain a network of higher education institutions that cover almost any field of knowledge and are located in the diverse sub-regions of each country.

Resulting from the thematic and geographical coverage of these networks, MICs are able to produce a significant number of graduates in key disciplines for development. For instance, according to the World Health Organization, four of the seven countries in our group of MICs graduate an important number of physicians: Mexico graduates every year 24.25 doctors per 10,000 inhabitants; Brazil 23.11; China 22.27; and Turkey 19.28. These figures are significantly reduced for the rest of the countries in our group: South Africa 7.92; India 7.35; and Nigeria 3.81 (WHO 2022).

Just as important as medical doctors are for, poverty eradication programs are engineers for infrastructure projects. Our group of seven countries also plays a significant role in educating their nationals on the diverse fields of engineering. According to the World Bank's "Availability of Scientists and Engineers Ranking,"[8] most of the countries in our sample occupy places on the top third of the list. China is the best positioned among the members of our group of selected nations, occupying position 29 on this list of 137 countries. India follows closely at position 32; Turkey is next at 49; and Mexico closely behind on 53. Nigeria (79), Brazil (90), and South Africa (100) lag further away, close to the bottom third of the list (WBG 2022g) (Table 26.4).

---

[8] The ranking considers the number of engineering graduates per 10,000 inhabitants.

Table 26.4 Education rankings

	QS World universities ranking	Gross university enrollment	Medical doctors graduated	Scientists and engineers ranking
	Position	Share of eligible population	Per 10,000 inhabitants per year	Position
Brazil	1	55	23.11	90
China	7	58	22.27	29
India	3	29	7.35	32
Mexico	2	43	24.25	53
Nigeria	–	10	3.81	79
South Africa	–	24	7.92	100
Turkey	–	24[a]	19.28	49

Sources: QS (2022), WHO (2022), WBG (2022g)
[a] Latest figure listed by the World Bank: 1999

Science, Technology, and Innovation

Higher education capabilities should also reflect strengths in science, technology, and innovation. The group of selected MICs does not invest significantly in research and development, with the exception of China, which devotes 2.14 percent of its GDP to them. Only Brazil, with 1.16 percent, and Turkey, with 1.09 percent, place themselves above the one percentage point mark. South Africa invests 0.83 percent, India 0.65 percent, Mexico 0.30 percent, and Nigeria 0.13 percent (WBG 2022e; OECD 2022).

Larger MICs tend to place themselves around the top quarter of the World Intellectual Property Organization's World Innovation Index. Again, the best placed within our group of selected countries is China, at position 12. Turkey and India follow the Chinese from a significant distance, at positions 41 and 46, respectively. Not too far from there are Mexico (55), Brazil (57), and South Africa (61). Nigeria places itself near the bottom of the 132 countries on the list, at position 118 (Dutta et al. 2021). Table 26.5 shows figures for these two indicators.

Private Sector Capabilities

Just as the public sector is the most relevant promoter of infrastructure projects, as shown by Marianne Fay and her coauthors (2019), the private sector is the fundamental engine of economic activity, growth, and employment. As

Table 26.5 Investment

	Investment in R&D	Global innovation index 2021
	Percentage of GDP	Position
Brazil	1.16	57
China	2.14	12
India	0.65	46
Mexico	0.30	55
Nigeria	0.13	118
South Africa	0.83	61
Turkey	1.09	41

Sources: Dutta et al. (2021), *Fortune* (2022)

will be seen in the next section, private sector involvement in development projects has become essential, for both donors and MICs.

Many middle-income economies now host their own multinational corporations, even among the list of Fortune's 500 (*Fortune* 2022).[9] Many of those entities are not only among the largest in the world by revenue, but their main activities also take place in strategic sectors with global relevance. These companies are perfectly capable and well-positioned to engage with their counterparts from donor countries in development projects.

Private sector size, level of diversification, degree of efficiency, among other factors, are extremely unequal among MICs. China, for example, is home to 134 corporations listed by *Fortune* among the world's 500 largest. This includes three firms in the top ten of this list. India has seven companies, Brazil has six corporations, and Mexico has two.[10] However, it must be acknowledged that not all corporations strictly belong to the private sector, since several of them, particularly in China, might be government-owned or controlled. Nevertheless, this indicator helps to illustrate the relevance and the potential of the private sector for development projects.

The New Knowledge, Complementarity-Based Partnership Model (the "Triple Helix")

Collaboration between equal partners from developed and middle-income economies in a development project is not only possible but desirable. Funding and/or financing may be sourced mostly from the "host country"

---

[9] See Annex 1 for the list of Fortune 500 Companies incorporated in sample of seven middle-income countries.
[10] Ibid.

(where the project is located) and not the "recipient country." The developed-economy partner may provide technical knowledge or experience that enhances the effectiveness and soundness of the project.

Many MICs benefit from ancient cultures whose traditional knowledge persists in their current societies. This is an additional asset in the context of a global environment where Western paradigms and the knowledge patterns associated with them are being questioned. The world's environmental crisis has produced a social awareness that questions traditional paths to progress and development. Societies across the planet now underscore the need to reconcile scientific and technological advances with a healthy environment, and the deep cultural roots of MICs thus acquire new value.

Their ancient cultural reservoir has been a source of knowledge that in many cases is closer to nature and better related to the conditions necessary to protect and preserve the environment. In this regard, the traditional idea of "community" as a cultural concept, which is very strong in these societies, nurtures traditional practices and experiences that constitute forms of knowledge that in turn suit the purposes of eradicating poverty and promoting growth and development, and doing so in a sustainable way.

Hence, the world is rediscovering nature-based solutions to development problems. These solutions are rooted in the way communities relate to their environment or in traditional knowledge preserved in their collective memory. Since scientists and professionals in MICs share this traditional knowledge, this cultural factor contributes to further reduce the asymmetry between developed and middle-income partners, and becomes the cornerstone of a new cooperation model that is built upon the notions of partnership and complementarity.

The Complementarity-based Cooperation Partnership should also recognize the value of host country nature-based solutions that enhance the scientific and technical capabilities of all participants, as well as place host country communities at the center of gravity of these exercises.

Diplomats must help these countries transition to a new partnership model that is agile, sustainable, effective, circular, and dynamic, in which all parties complement each other. Such a framework not only is an excellent cooperation structure, but it can also have an impact beyond the individual development projects and contribute to:

- engagement with global transitions, trends, and transformations;
- multi-dimensional cooperation experiences that foster innovation;
- groundbreaking arrangements with maximum social impact; and
- development partnerships to achieving the Sustainable Development Goals.

In this context, the point of departure for the partnership model proposed in this chapter is the "Triple Helix" (Etzkowitz 2008) approach developed in the Netherlands. This Dutch public policy strategy brings together the private sector, specialized knowledge and research institutions, and government authorities, to devise a solution to any given problem and to design feasible projects to attain common objectives.

The Triple Helix is a domestic cooperation model that rests on the strengths and comparative advantages of the three sectors involved: the government may provide the seed capital to start working on the project and explain the limits set by the regulatory framework within which it must be developed and carried out. Environmental and circular economy national goals may establish the overall nature and scope of any given project. Academic or knowledge institutions may provide the scientific support and latest technological advances not only to make the project comply with the regulatory framework but, among other things, also to ensure solutions will not become anachronistic or otherwise technologically dated after a short time. The private sector guarantees the economic feasibility of projects and, when possible, develops business models that allow to profit from applying the envisaged solutions to similar questions in the future.

The Triple Helix being essentially a Dutch domestic collaborative model between partners from government, academia, and business, it contains all the required components of an international cooperation exercise. A middle-income country can thus envisage any given project it is under its consideration, as suitable to integrate any or all three Triple Helix sectors onto its design or execution.

However, this Triple Helix "fusion" into a development project in any middle-income country needs to include a fourth and essential element in order to be attractive for developed-nation counterparts willing to allocate resources and actively engage with it. The proposed project should be designed to have a significant social impact that contributes to the middle-income nation's efforts to surmount its development traps, to reduce its regional development and income gaps, or to improve its environmental standards.

However, a partnership for development model based on complementarity transcends the single objective of guaranteeing that positive social impact be the fundamental result of any given project. That should be granted. The new partnership blueprint improves from the previous model by turning host country communities from "passive objects" of aid into active participants in the design and implementation of development solutions that will impact their lives. In this regard, the asymmetry present in traditional cooperation between donor and host countries is further reduced.

26 Innovating International Cooperation for Development: A New...

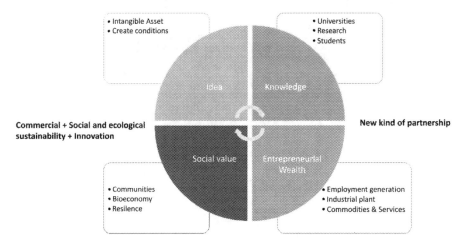

Fig. 26.4 Optimus4 helix cycle

Hence, the proposed Complementarity-based Cooperation Partnership should integrate a fourth pillar to the Triple Helix model that has been so successful for Dutch public policies: social impact and nature-based social knowledge and experiences (Fig. 26.4). The new model would also introduce circularity into the development partnership by including a double track by means of which all parties will provide and receive profit, but also by placing communities on the same institutional level as universities, business firms, and government authorities, as illustrated below.

Each of the pillars on this new "four-quadrant helix" adds new elements to enhance economic growth opportunities with social equity and to encourage innovation that positively impacts communities. It consists of a business and social arrangement deeply rooted in strong collective commitments to respect nature and promote environmentally sound and sustainable economics and favor solutions to mitigate, adapt to, and build resilience against climate change.

Additionally, following the previous chart and superimposing on it a roadmap designed by UNDP's Mexico office to form some sort of an "inner circle," four strategic and two cross-cutting lines of action should be considered as shown in the next graph (Fig. 26.5).

The four strategic courses of action are:

- Prosperity and innovation
- Green economy and climate change

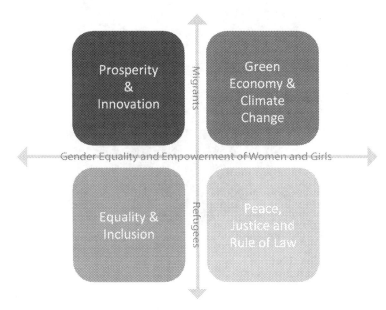

Fig. 26.5 Partners. Four strategic lines and two cross-cutting areas. Source: Sistema de Naciones Unidas México 2020

- Equality and inclusion
- Peace, justice, and rule of law

The cross-cutting criteria are:

- Gender equality and empowering women
- Migrants and refugees

Implications for Diplomatic Innovation

This new international partnership model implies the need for a new diplomatic approach by MICs. On the domestic front, ministries of foreign relations need to make themselves part of the decision-making in charge of designing and funding landmark development projects. As has been stated, the earlier their involvement takes place, the more valuable and effective the input of various contributors is to the projects.

The most difficult diplomatic task will be to convince governments from developed countries to partner on projects undertaken with this innovative modality of ODA. MICs' diplomats will need to promote their projects with very solid scientific and technical arguments that address four principal sets of questions:

- How will the project help the host country to advance their development goals? How is the government funding the project and, as has always been the case, show that it is technically well-supported?
- What will be the role of the donor nation in the project and what counterparts will be invited to participate, and why? What will be the approximate cost to the donor government?
- What global social or development benefits are expected from the project? For example, is it going to have a positive effect on reverting climate change? Will it contribute to reduce migration flows?
- What will be the expected social impact on the host country and how much will it be the result of the donor nation's participation?

In the diplomatic sphere, specialists on scientific and technological disciplines will be needed to carry out the identification of suitable counterparts for the projects and to provide a solid basis to the arguments with which diplomats approach them. Adding these science and technology experts will help establish a direct, results-oriented dialogue between partners, putting an end to the asymmetrical relationships of the past.

An additional advantage for developed donor countries of encouraging these innovative partnerships is that projects will automatically turn into capacity-building exercises for the MICs. In the medium term, these partnerships will produce experiences that can be replicated in triangular or even South-South cooperation projects.

It is also likely that the ever-present tension between technical considerations and political or ideological imperatives will make itself present within this model when MICs decide which partnerships to seek and which counterparts to invite to any given project. Foreign policy decisions are essentially political, after all. However, as MICs increasingly rely on the most relevant technical aspects to plan a project and de-politicize the nature of these partnerships, they will be showing advances in their degree of development. By approaching development projects as partnerships under this new model, and by integrating scientific and technology specialists, MICs will strengthen their foreign services and innovate their diplomacy.

Conclusions

MICs are affected by two great disadvantages that reduce their possibilities to receive official development assistance: their relative success in improving their economic and social conditions and, on the other hand, the persistence of poverty and inequality, and of economic inefficiencies at the subnational level. In fact they are poor countries with relative small, high-income, well-educated elites. It is precisely in this dichotomy, along with their deep sense of community and their strong cultural roots expressed by nature-based solutions, where their comparative advantages for new international development partnerships reside.

An analysis of these comparative strengths reveals that relatively larger, administratively more sophisticated MICs are better equipped to engage in cooperation with donors from developed economies. Studying a sample of seven such countries has shown that even though ODA destined to MICs has been shrinking, these countries have captured a growing share of ODA granted to all nations at their income level.

In order to take full advantage of MICs comparative advantages to cooperate with developed counterparts, a new, Complementarity-based Cooperation Partnership is proposed. This new framework is based on the successful strategy applied in the Netherlands to design and implement public policy. The so-called Triple Helix formula integrates academic, business, and government institutions in a concerted effort driven by the characteristic Dutch "polder mentality" that incentives consensus-building.

By incorporating deep social considerations into this structure and applying it as a partnership among equals, an international "Four Quadrant Helix" model is thus configured. By not limiting the developed-nation participation to financial assistance, the main obstacle to international cooperation between developed and middle-income countries is thus surmounted. The relationship among the partners under this new scheme reduces the former asymmetries between "donor" and "recipient."

The partnerships that follow this "Four Quadrant Helix" model favor knowledge-based collaborations, where the gap between countries is narrower, and produce processes and experiences that can be applied to less developed nations by all participants either as triangular or even as South-South cooperation projects.

By following the "Four Quadrant Helix" model, a stronger participation by the private sector is encouraged, contributing to reduce dependence on governments' almost exclusive prerogative in launching development projects.

The most relevant innovation put forward in this new Complementarity-based Cooperation Partnership, however, is that projects will be designed with community participation and deep social impact at their core. Such projects will help narrow the domestic development gap in middle-income nations by reducing poverty, raising living standards, and creating economic opportunities in their least favored sectors and regions.

Finally, a new diplomatic approach by MICs is needed to put in place these partnerships. Besides including international cooperation options from the drawing board stage of development projects, branches of scientific and technological specialists are needed within MICs' foreign services. These experts will help identify the most suitable counterparts for specific projects and will provide the facts and technical considerations needed to support efforts to build partnerships with the governments of developed countries—which is essentially a diplomatic task.

Methodological Disclosure

The international debate regarding ODA is held at different international organizations, from the United Nations to regional integration mechanisms across the globe. In particular, the World Bank and the OECD have engaged in discussing the flows and trends of aid resources, and in establishing common criteria and guidelines on the subject. This chapter relies mostly on information from the Development Assistance Committee at the OECD, and it follows its definition of Official Development Assistance (OECD 2001).

References and Further Reading

Alonso, J.A. 2013. *Cooperación con países de renta media: un enfoque basado en incentivos*. Madrid: AECID, Documentos de Trabajo No. 1.

Dutta, S., et al. 2021. *Global Innovation Index 2021; Tracking Innovation Through the COVID 19 Crisis*. Geneva: World Intellectual Property Organization and Portulans Institute.

Etzkowitz, H. 2008. *The Triple Helix: University-Industry-Government Innovation in Action*. London and New York: Routledge.

Fay, M., et al. 2019. *Hitting the Trillion Mark; a Look at How Much Countries Are Spending on Infrastructure*. Washington, D.C.: World Bank Group, Sustainable Development Practice Group, Policy Research Working Paper 8730.

Fortune. 2022. *Fortune* 500. https://fortune.com/fortune500/.

International Monetary Fund (IMF). 2022. IMF Country Information. https://www.imf.org/en/countries#B.

OECD Secretariat. 2001. *Is It ODA?* Paris: Official Document DCD/DAC/STAT.

OECD. 2022. *Official Development Aid (ODA) Disbursements to Countries and Regions [DAC2a]*. https://stats.oecd.org/Index.aspx?DataSetCode=TABLE2A https://stats.oecd.org/Index.aspx?DataSetCode=TABLE2A.

QS Quacquarelli Symonds. 2022. QS World University Rankings 2022. https://www.topuniversities.com/qs-world-university-rankings.

Sistema de Naciones Unidas en México. 2020. *Marco de cooperación de las Naciones Unidas para el desarrollo sostenible de México 2020–2025*. https://mexico.un.org/sites/default/files/2021-11/ONU-Mexico-Marco-de-Cooperacion-2020-2025.pdf.

Statistics Times. 2021. "Projected GDP Ranking." https://statisticstimes.com/economy/projected-world-gdp-ranking.php.

UN General Assembly. 2000. "United Nations Millennium Declaration." Resolution Adopted by the General Assembly. https://digitallibrary.un.org/record/422015?ln=en.

World Bank Group (WBG). 2020. *The World Bank in Middle Income Countries, Overview*, October 5. https://www.worldbank.org/en/country/mic/overview#1.

———. 2022. National Accounts Data, and OECD National Accounts Data Files. https://data.worldbank.org/indicator/NY.GDP.MKTP.CD.

———. 2022b. "People Lived Below the $1.90 Per Day Poverty Line in 2018." *Poverty and Inequality Platform*. https://pip.worldbank.org/#.

———. 2022c. Poverty Calculator. *Poverty and Inequality Platform*. https://pip.worldbank.org/poverty-calculator.

———. 2022d. "Coverages of Social Safety Net Programs." *Data Bank*. https://data.worldbank.org/indicator/per_sa_allsa.cov_pop_tot?locations=CN-BR-IN-MX-NG-ZA-TR.

———. 2022e. "Government Expenditure on Education." *Data Bank*. https://data.worldbank.org/indicator/SE.XPD.TOTL.GB.ZS?locations=CN-BR-IN-MX-NG-ZA-TR.

———. 2022f. "School Enrollment, Tertiary." *Data Bank*. https://data.worldbank.org/indicator/SE.TER.ENRR.

———. 2022g. "Availability of Scientists and Engineers Ranking, 2017." *TC Data 360*. https://tcdata360.worldbank.org/indicators/h7c08e10f?country=MEX&indicator=608&countries=BRA,CHN,IND,NGA,TUR,ZAF&viz=line_chart&years=2016,2017.

WHO World Health Organization. 2022. *The Global Health Observatory*. https://www.who.int/data/gho/data/indicators/indicator-details/GHO/medical-doctors-(per-10-000-population).

27

The UAE's Innovative Diplomacy: How the Abraham Accords Changed (or Did Not Change) Emirati Foreign Policy

William Guéraiche

Innovation has been a buzzword in the United Arab Emirates (UAE). Associated with entrepreneurship, incubators, and other startups, it has entered the realm of governance, public policy, and, not least, diplomacy. However, the contrast is striking between a conservative country, proud of its Bedouin, Muslim heritage, and a country with a visible and adamant drive to acquire the contemporary features of modernity. In the long run, very little has changed in diplomacy since the independence of the Trucial States in 1971. The face-to-face interpersonal relations with a preference for dealing with the neighboring countries of the Gulf Cooperation Council (GCC, with Bahrain, Kuwait, Oman, Qatar, and Saudi Arabia), or at least Arab and Muslim states, seem to have prevailed until the signing of the Abraham Accords in August 2020. While the world was struggling with the management of the COVID-19 crisis, the normalization between a major Arab state and Israel had the same long-term effect as the Camp David Accords between Egypt and Israel in 1978. Nonetheless, on the surface, no major landslide was visible. "The day after" will never be like the day before.

How can we explain this rapprochement? Was it an "innovation" or the result of innovative diplomacy? If the structures of the UAE foreign policy have been long delineated, the recent evolutions—innovations?—have put them into question. The legacy of Sheikh Zayed, the "founding father" and

W. Guéraiche (✉)
University of Wollongong, Dubai, United Arab Emirates

president of the Federation from 1971 to 2004, strictly applied until the Arab Spring. In 2011, the intervention in Bahrain and in Libya marked a shift in the generally peaceful and cautious foreign policy. The UAE economy had become globalized and inevitably the Federation had become entwined in the global world, let alone regional affairs. Innovations could therefore be associated with the adjustments to an ever-changing international environment. Although the Emiratis aspire to sustain their traditional lifestyle, their rulers[1] have never hidden the ambition to transform the country into one of the dominant powers in the region and the world. Economy and diplomacy have merged into economic diplomacy, the contemporary solid pillar of Emirati external action. But there is more. The expression, the UAE is the "Switzerland of the Middle East," has been more used as well.[2] Like its European counterpart and perhaps its model, the economic ambition is undeniable. However, what does it mean for diplomacy? Global diplomacy or the diplomacy of global events may bring insights to the mapping and comprehension of UAE international cooperation and its causes.

The Switzerland of the Middle East?

Once used to praise Lebanon, the UAE has been lately described as the "Switzerland of the Middle East," an expression that the Emirati officials also use now. The Federation and especially Dubai have been lauded for their economic openness in terms of trade, investment, and free enterprise. But in diplomacy as well, the expression evokes neutrality and the willingness to act as a peace broker.

The Abraham Accords: A New Camp David?

If scattered information suggested a forecast of changing relations between the UAE and Israel, for security reasons in general and intelligence in particular, no clear signals were sent to announce a quick rapprochement between

---

[1] The seven rulers of the Emirates are under the leadership of Sheikh Mohamed bin Zayed Al Nahyan, ruler of Abu Dhabi, de facto leader of the country, and Sheikh Mohammed bin Rashid Al Maktoum, ruler of Dubai and Prime Minister. However, the federal constitution allows them to keep local power. Especially in the Northern Emirates, the local sheikhs have remained the most prominent political figures.

[2] In an interview given to CNN, Omar Al Olama, Minister of Artificial Intelligence, described the UAE as such. https://www.youtube.com/watch?v=KrUk2fM5eVo.

the two states.[3] If we compare this development with the Camp David Accords, the Abraham Accords followed a different pattern. Instead of practicing a policy of small steps, Emirati and Israeli diplomats adopted a strategy of a big leap forward. On August 23, 2020, Bahrain, Israel, the United Arab Emirates, and the United States signed an agreement to normalize their relations. The final document, *Abraham Accords Peace Agreement: Treaty of Peace, Diplomatic Relations and Full Normalization Between the United Arab Emirates and the State of Israel*, was signed in the White House on September 15, 2020. With a domino effect, Sudan and Morocco followed the footpath of the four first partners by the end of the year, while Oman and Jordan did so in 2021.

The Accords have altered the nature of UAE foreign policy. First, until then, although major changes had occurred in the wake of the Arab Spring (Guéraiche 2018), Emirati external action remained in line with the principles established under Sheikh Zayed Al Nahyan from 1971 to his death in 2004. The implication in international politics corresponded to the Emirati perception of the world. Abdul Monem Al Mashat described it as a nested configuration of concentric circles, "the external setting, both regional and international" (Al Mashat 2008, 461). Abu Dhabi, Dubai, Sharjah, and the Northern Emirates formed the center of gravity of the Great Arab Nation (the Arabs of the Peninsula)—gathered in the Gulf Cooperation Council but also incorporating Yemen, the cradle of Arab culture. The authorities or the peoples in the Peninsula could be considered a "family," eternally close in spite of tensions, for instance, with Qatar between 2017 and 2021. The third circle encompassed the Arab world following, more or less, the geography of the 22 Arab League states. Beyond the *ummah*, made up of states and Islamic communities worldwide such as in the Horn of Africa, outsiders had been put on an equal footing. It meant that the relations with the United States were equivalent to relations with China or India. This representation of the world helped explain the priorities of the Emirati foreign policy for half a century. The GCC and the Arab League have been the preferred multilateral partners. For its security, Abu Dhabi could easily replace outsider states like Britain or France with others such as India or China. The Abraham Accords blur this long-standing diplomatic pattern.

Second, the recent recognition of Israel raises parallels with the Camp David Accords primarily because it questions the commitment of the UAE to its Arab "family." Arab solidarity, until August 2020, has been the backbone of diplomacy. Cooperation with the Arabs of the Peninsula or with the

---

[3] Interestingly, there were no leaks from the Israeli side. Israelis have the reputation of not being able to keep a secret. The Accords demonstrated otherwise.

members of the Arab League has structured foreign policy since 1971. The competition for the role of leader of the Arab and Muslim world was a powerful driver in regional action as well as bilateral relations (Al Ketbi 2020, 395). The traditional patron-client relationship was a good framework to understand the dynamic between the different stakeholders, be they states, groups (communities like the Sunnis in Lebanon or the Palestinian Liberation Organization), or individuals. In addition, beyond Muslim solidarity, the Palestinian cause was the common denominator between Arabs (Almezaini 2012). The cornerstone, already cracked in 1978, has quaked and threatened the unity of the Arabs. Even if on the surface the Abraham Accords paved the way for the creation of a Palestinian state, it sends the "cause" to the background. The price to pay could be the weakening of the traditional network of concertation, the GCC and of the Arab League. If the UAE sets aside its ambition to lead the Arab world and seeks legitimacy in global international organizations and fora, the role of these regional organizations will consequently decrease. Other major players, first and foremost Saudi Arabia, followed by Qatar, could be tempted to do the same. The GCC and the Arab League would become empty shells. One might argue that it is already the case for the Arab League. In addition, if the GCC is no longer a major decision-making body, it eases the reintegration of Qatar, which was ostracized in June 2017 until the Al-Ula Declaration in January 2021 (re-establishment of political and economic ties).

In an era of post-truth politics where words could mean exactly their contrary, the insistence on "peace" in the Accords hints perhaps at "war." Iran epitomizes an existential threat for the UAE as well as for Israel. One way to read the Accords could be a realist partnership to contain Iranian nuclear ambitions. The drone attack in Abu Dhabi airport on January 22, 2022, followed by a missile attack on ARAMCO's facilities on March 25, 2022, reminded regional leaders that their "Switzerland" may not be the safe haven they aim it to be without necessary measures. The Accords could therefore be a way to alleviate this existential threat.

Talking to Everyone

Talking to all kinds of regimes (democratic or not), regardless of their nature, has been an argument used to legitimize the Accords. It could be seen as a normal evolution for the UAE whose ambition is to become a major actor in the globalized world. In parallel to the Abraham Accords, the UAE had already been practicing a policy of engagement.

Although Emirati diplomacy showed certain preferences, new types of bilateral relations took place before 2020. The relations with South Asia illustrate their evolution. Faithful to Muslim solidarity, the Federation has maintained close and friendly relations not only with Pakistan but also with India. As major economic partners and suppliers of labor in the Emirates, the two countries have become over time closer to the UAE. After reciprocal state visits, India has reached a new status. It has been not only an economic but also a strategic partner in the security architecture of the Indian Ocean (Janardhan 2022). The UAE has been seen and treated as a major partner in both Pakistan and India. The same could be said with the United States and China. Instead of taking sides, the Emiratis have tried to keep an open mind with the two main rivals. This "agility," the term often used in the UAE (in the business world), has helped the Emirates reach a new stage during the COVID crisis. While the international community pointed at China for the outbreak of the pandemic or to Italy for the spread of the virus, Sheikh Mohamed bin Zayed al Nahyan, crown prince of Abu Dhabi and de facto ruler of the country, called Xi Jinping and Giuseppe Conte. He did the same with Bashar Al Assad in Syria to supply assistance. The pandemic became an opportunity to strengthen collaboration with some UN agencies (see below) and to reach out to new regions like sub-Saharan Africa (Guéraiche 2022a, b, 271–85). Therefore, UAE foreign policy had already begun to follow new guidelines before the breakthrough of the Abraham Accords.

The appetite for a more efficient, more "modern" foreign policy results from the legacy of the past, from more recent evolutions, and, perhaps, from the influence of other countries, namely Oman and China. On the Peninsula, Oman has been for centuries a crossroads of many cultures, from India to the Southern rim of Africa. As Jeremy Jones and Nicholas Ridout have written, the culture of diplomacy is deeply entrenched in Omani society (Jones and Ridout 2012). Oman is also sometimes described as the Switzerland of the Middle East or Switzerland of Arabia (Worrall 2021). While antagonism has been widespread in recent decades (Iran/Iraq during the 1980–86 war, Iran/Saudi Arabia or Yemen and the Coalition led by Saudi Arabia), Sultan Qaboos tried as much as he could to apply a simple diplomatic statement. Oman had been "friend to all, enemy to none" (Worrall 2021, 138). Against the backdrop of U.S. disengagement, Qaboos' strategy has achieved security through mediation, as in 2022 when Oman was a key partner in peace discussions with regard to Yemen. The UAE has shared most of the diplomatic features of its neighbor such as deepening economic and security interests or cooperation, seeking consensus rather than conflict. But the Federation has been more involved in multilateralism (from the UN to the Arab League and the GCC) than Oman, which has always been reluctant to share its "omanibalancing" (O'Reilly 1998) with other states. The UAE, like Saudi Arabia, grounded their security in seeking an alliance with the United States and other European allies (Britain and France). The dislocation of Libya in 2011, Daesh in 2014, and the Houthi threat in 2015 drove the UAE into international coalitions with mixed results. Being described as a Little Sparta (*The Economist* 2017) harmed the reputation of the UAE as a "good" country (Anholt 2020). Although a preference for open diplomacy may still be found, geopolitical considerations (priority to the GCC states, Arab leadership, etc.) have led to a rebalancing between multilateral and bilateral relations on the Chinese model. Since the 1990s, the UAE has used Joint Committees to deepen the "friendship" with economic partners (Guéraiche 2017, 125–28), but bilateral relations are fine-tuned like in the way the Chinese have done with 47 countries since 2004. With the ambition to create a new world order, China has defined its own diplomatic toolkit. After 2017, "comprehensive" and "strategic" partnerships emerged in its official discourse. The former implied that the cooperation "should be all-dimensional, wide-ranging and multi-layered" while the latter, that "strategic" partnership is "used in the field of economy and politics … with overarching, comprehensive, and decisive implications" (Zhongping and Jing 2014, 7). In 2019, the UAE signed comprehensive partnerships with Singapore (WAM 2019) and China (Fulton 2019), and upgraded them to strategic partnerships two years later (WAM 2021).

This does not mean that Oman and China have exerted undue influence over UAE diplomacy, but instead that the latter, especially, has flouted Western models. Accordingly, open to good practices and ideas—the meaning of agility—UAE diplomacy is a blend of its tradition merged with pragmatic solutions found elsewhere—and one of the structural causes that led to the Abraham Accords.

Global Diplomacy or Diplomacy of Global Events?

The UAE was one of the first countries in the world to use nation-branding for its promotion. The government of Dubai defined a model that Abu Dhabi, the UAE as whole, and many Arab countries like Qatar and Saudi Arabia adopted afterward (Guéraiche 2017, 11–31). Nation-branding inspired diplomats. Following in the footsteps of Joseph Nye, not only scholars in International Relations but also decision-makers have integrated "soft power" as a key element of a country's foreign policy. The UAE has been no exception in planning international events (Guéraiche 2019, 100–1) such as the Expo 2020 or the annual meeting of climate change (Conference of the Parties, COP, 28th meeting in 2023).

Making Good Use of "Soft Power"

In November 2017, Sheikh Mohammed bin Rashid Al Maktoum, prime minister of the UAE and ruler of Dubai, launched a UAE Soft Power Council with the purpose of enhancing the country's reputation based on the promotion of science, culture, technology, humanitarian, and economic sectors. The prime minister stated that the country was already a military and an economic power, but needed to build "diplomatic relationships and systems in order to pursue his vision of making the UAE a global example of prestige and excellence" (WAM April 29, 2017). In September 2017, a strategy for "integrated diplomatic action" was officially presented to the media. The main objective was to establish the Federation as a regional capital for culture, art, and tourism, and to strengthen its reputation as a "modern and tolerant country." Therefore, public diplomacy was intended to cover all new domains: "humanitarian diplomacy, scientific and academic diplomacy, national representatives' diplomacy, people diplomacy, cultural and media diplomacy, economic diplomacy" (WAM September 27, 2017). The cabinet approved this new strategy on October 15, 2017. Although the Council has not been active since then, the debate around it has popularized the use of "soft power."

Emirati "soft power" has been overused in the media but also in scholarly literature, blurring its content. Since 2017, strategic analyses have shifted to more subjective explanations neglecting military and security data (military balance, illegal migrations, etc.). Thus, the expression may justify all kinds of information or sectors involved in foreign policy. Using the Soft Power Index 30, Osman Antwi-Boateng and Amira Ali Alhashmi identified "power tools and elements" used in UAE foreign policy (Antwi-Boateng and Alhashmi 2021, 5). "Global engagement" is one of the six items broken down into subsections: diplomatic missions with the embassy and the consular network; hosting international events with an emphasis on world-class sports events; philanthropy; foreign aid; peacekeeping contributions; and conflict resolution (Antwi-Boateng and Alhashmi 2021, 12–14). Among the traditional tools of diplomacy, only the organization of events is new. If event organization cannot be assimilated into other categories, it is because it denotes a different way of nation-branding. This latter concept overlaps with soft power but can also be used in a more rigorous way (Gienow-Hecht 2019), as Simon

Anholt, who coined the expression in 1998, has described (Anholt 1998) in deconstructing the concept of reputation. He has also described how "Good Countries" can be defined and perceived (Anholt 2020). In a nutshell, nation-branding uses marketing tools to advertise political entities (states but also regions) like Dubai, which pioneered branding in this domain with the Dubai Commerce and Tourism Board (DCTB) in 1983 (Guéraiche 2017, 16–18). Its main endeavor was to project abroad a good image of the merchant city to attract selected (rich) tourists and Foreign Direct Investments (Guéraiche 2017, 16–20). It worked so well that it expanded to Abu Dhabi and affected other domains, such as diplomacy. Comparing Qatar and the UAE, Steffen Hartog noted the development: "A quest to acquire post-oil statehood that would give the rentier monarchies an international identity" (Hertog 2017, 20). Dubai's nation-branding certainly created a good international identity, but a very effective international identity would be a more accurate way to describe it.

From the Expo 2020 to the COP 28

Expo 2020, postponed to 2021, was for a while a perfect window display of Dubai and of the UAE. The timing was good in terms of nation-branding. The financial depression of 2009–10 struck Dubai; and after the inauguration of the Burj Khalifa, the highest tower in the world, the city and the Federation needed a new narrative to showcase their global ambitions. On November 26–27, 2013, the 153rd session of the International Bureau of Expositions had to select the laureate for the Universal Fair. São Paulo competed with the theme, "Power of Diversity, Harmony to Growth"; Izmir with "New Roads to a Better World, Health for All"; Yekaterinburg with "The Global Mind"; and Dubai with "Connecting Minds, Creating the Future." Dubai won.

Expo 2020 carried out the diplomatic ambition of the country. From October 2021 to March 2022, 191 countries used their pavilions to showcase their interpretation of the future. Twenty-four million visitors made the event a success.[4] In her closing speech, Reem Al Hashemi, Director-General of the Expo and minister of State for International Cooperation, underlined that the country leadership had "promised an Expo that would amaze the world" and that the promise was fulfilled. "We have shared our cultures and ideas, and we have sought solutions to some of our greatest global challenges. And this is

---

[4] The COVID-19 crisis jeopardized the Expo. Before the crisis, the government of Dubai expected between 25 and 100 million visitors. However, reaching the lowest estimate while the pandemic was not over was still regarded as a success.

just the beginning of the new world we have started making together" (WAM April 2, 2022). To illustrate such official discourse, the World Governments Summit and the first World Humanitarian Summit were organized in the last days of the Expo. In addition, one of the aims of the Expo was to become the most sustainable World Expo in history. Meeting this challenge made a good transition toward organization of the COP 28 in the UAE.

In Emirati media and official discourse, environmental diplomacy justified the organization of the Conference of the Parties (COP) 28 in the UAE. Like soft power, the concept of "environmental diplomacy" is pervasive yet elusive. Initially conceived as a subset of international law, gaining momentum after the summit of Rio in 1992, it aimed to elaborate treaties and other international rules (mostly restrictions) to protect the earth or to limit the consequences of pollution (Susskind and Ali 1994, xi). Because of its implications on various domains such as conflict resolution or management of local resources (Ali and Vladich 2016, 601), it has encompassed many aspects of Global Environmental Politics (GEP) and Global Environmental Governance (GNG). It does not follow the same pattern as other top-level negotiations. Unlike disarmament, peace, or international trade, environmental diplomacy involves states and numerous non-state actors (NGOs, activists, transnational corporations, etc.) with necessary—but not always accepted—interventions of scientists (Chasek 2001, 2). In line with its communication strategy, the UAE always points out its eco-friendly policies. During the COP 26 in Glasgow in November 2021, the Federation sided with Canada, India, Germany, and the UK on the Industrial Deep Decarbonization Initiative.[5] Dr. Sultan Al Jaber, minister of Industry and Special Envoy for Climate in Glasgow, reiterated that development aid and "climate action" are "powerful catalysts for economic growth, both domestically and internationally" (MOFAIC 2021). Emirati environmental diplomacy would use the Abu Dhabi Fund for Development (ADFD) and the International Renewable Energy Agency (IRENA), also located in the capital, to raise intervention funds ($400 million in Glasgow for the Energy Transition Accelerator Financing Platform, or ETAF, for instance).

The organization of the COP 28 will shed light on the paradox between a country whose economy and lifestyle cause a high carbon footprint per capita and its ambition to reduce it domestically and globally. The UAE affirms that public policies are already aligned since 2017 on the Sustainable Development Goals (SDG) (Guéraiche 2019, 104–5). Environmental issues already impact the UAE. Water scarcity, loss of biodiversity, land and marine pollution,

---

[5] By 2025, for all major public construction projects, the carbon footprint will be revealed.

wastes, and overfishing all pose the question of sustainability. Since 2016, environmental projects became a high priority under local agencies and the creation of a Ministry of Climate Change and Environment (Luomi, 2022, 41–42). At the COP 26 in Glasgow, the UAE and the United States announced a $4-billion project for "Climate Initiative to Invest in Agricultural Innovation and Climate Action" as well as a $1 billion platform for "Renewable Energy Projects in Developing Countries."[6]

The Blurred Borders Between Humanitarian Diplomacy and International Cooperation

"International Cooperation" is an expression broadly used and it encompasses many sub-groups such as humanitarianism, development, foreign aid, assistance, and so on, which may be discussed equally (Ali and Zeb, 2016). In 2013, the Ministry of International Cooperation and Development merged with the Ministry of Foreign Affairs to become the Ministry of Foreign Affairs and International Cooperation (MOFAIC) (Almezaini 2018, 583). The following year, the UAE became a member of the Organization for Economic Cooperation and Development's Development Assistance Committee (OECD-DAC) (Almezaini 2017, 232). Since then, MOFAIC has used the OECD criteria, notably the new Official Development Assistance (ODA) methodology, to clarify and classify its external operations. As Logan Cochrane rightly points out, since 2009, the transparency of the ODA helps delineate the structure of such international cooperation (Cochrane 2021).

Tolerance: a Political and Diplomatic Project

Islamic solidarity and charity are at the root level of international cooperation for the UAE and exist as a shared conception of prosperity among the Emiratis (Guéraiche 2019, 93–97). This question of Islamic solidarity may challenge the new orientation of the Federation's foreign policy.

Dubai and the UAE have developed a concept of tolerance that is used in many domains, for instance, security (Guéraiche 2022b, 292–93) as well as foreign policy. Tolerance is a political project, making the link between tradition and modernity. Since the Umayyads, in the abode of Islam, the Islamic

---

[6] "Collaborating for Climate Action: the UAE at the COP26." https://uaeun.org/collaborating-for-climate-action-the-uae-at-cop26/.

rulers have maintained peace and order as the protectors of other religious communities. Jews and Christians paid the *dhimmi* in exchange for this protection. Tolerance has therefore been perceived as the source of harmony, or mutual respect, between the three monotheistic religions. A Ministry of Tolerance was created in 2016, and in February 2019, the visit to Abu Dhabi by Pope Francis was the highlight of the "Year of Tolerance."

Promoting the spirit of tolerance by the Federation presented a double advantage for the Emirati authorities. First, as the Ministry of Tolerance points out on its website, the concept of Tolerance is "derived from the moderation of the True Islam, the noble Arab customs and traditions" (UAE Ministry of Tolerance 2022). Some Western scholars express criticism of moderate Islam defined as a "by-product of this small power's geopolitical transformation into an international actor that aspires to lead the Arab world" (Kourgiotis 2020, 2). Others also point out that what really matters is how the religious discourse is entangled with political considerations (Shushan and Marcoux 2011, 1973–75; Tittensor et al. 2018, 294). Second, in light of the Abraham Accords tolerance could be used as the adjustment variable in sensitive and historically uncharted areas. Instead of considering the creation of a Jewish state in the Middle East as a major disruption, the tolerance spirit reshuffles the narrative of Muslims and Jews living together in the region. If the tradition of the three monotheistic religions is mutual respect, why not apply it in the realm of interstate relations? This discourse, valid for communities anchored in history, could easily be adjusted to states. In communication strategy, local public opinion, that is, the variations of the "Arab street," remains the main target. After generations of Arabs have been educated to develop empathy with the Palestinian cause, the shift toward rapprochement with the Israelis may look surprising; it has not been set aside by the Israeli-Emirati alliance against Iran, one of the main geopolitical rationales for the Accord.

The COVID-19 Crisis: a Game-Changer?

In its five-year strategic plan for Promoting Global Peace and Prosperity, MOFAIC explained in 2017 its ambitions regarding Multilateral Institutions and International Partnerships. The UAE wanted to be an active participant and contributor to the multilateral system. It wanted to create a partnership, in line with the SDG no. 17, with international organizations, international NGOs, and other stakeholders (MOFAIC 2017, 28–29). As a matter of fact, during the past five years, the UAE has built up an efficient network. The perception has been positive mainly because, for nine years in a row, the UAE was among the world's top 20 donors of Official Development Assistance as a proportion of Gross National Income (ODA/GNI) (MOFAIC 2020, 9). Since 2018, the UAE has established good relations with the UN agencies (Guéraiche 2019, 102–3). Some agencies became closer partners. In 2019, the UAE tripled its contribution to the Central Emergency Relief Fund (CERF) to $5 million. Typhoon Ida was an opportunity to support the World Food Program (WFP) at $3 million. The UAE finally teamed up with the High Commissioner for Refugee (HCR) on many projects, notably what MOFAIC calls "forgotten emergencies" (MOFAIC 2017, 21). Interestingly, during the pandemic, the last two agencies and the World Health Organization received "generous support" from the UAE (WAM April 15, 2021).

The COVID-19 crisis reinforced and enhanced the partnerships that the UAE had already established (Guéraiche 2022a, 281), showing new preferences for UN agencies. Their close cooperation resulted from different factors such as effectiveness, previous collaboration, and the logistical use of the International Humanitarian City in Dubai. From a communication perspective, the UN label enhanced the reputation of the Federation in the international media—more than entities identified as Arab or Muslim did. The focus on such entities underscores the weakness of such regional organizations, namely the GCC and the Arab League, in striking contrast with the period before 2020. The rift with Qatar in June 2017 inevitably undermined the operations of the Gulf Council, whereas the Al Ula Accord on January 5, 2021, marked an end of Qatari ostracism. The Arab League has not recovered from its failure to stabilize the Arab Spring and notably the civil war in Syria. Other organizations like the Organization for the Islamic Conference have barely worked with the Federation.

The Abraham Accords have not altered UAE foreign policy and diplomacy because major changes had already occurred before then. In this regard, they are not so much an achievement, but rather the genesis of a new relationship with the outside world—different from the traditional perception of the Bedouins, and beyond the Arab and Muslim circles of solidarity. Yet, the accords also reveal the global ambition of a "small state" which intends to lead not only the Arab world but also a geopolitical block stretching from South Asia to Africa. Regarding the means to achieve this goal, the UAE has never hesitated to use innovative solutions or practices. Nation-branding (a more accurate term than "soft power") is the best illustration of using a marketing tool for a state's personal promotion, be it humanitarian aid or promoting the SDGs. This agility can be confusing for Westerners, and especially Western diplomats, who believe that Western diplomacy should remain the benchmark. Emirati leadership showed an ability to adopt new efficient practices overnight during the COVID-19 crisis (Guéraiche 2022a, 277–78). Emirati diplomacy does not precisely fit a traditional model. It is more a blend of different influences rather than a genuine product of a single tradition.

References and Further Reading

Al Ketbi, E. 2020. "Contemporary Shifts in UAE Foreign Policy: From the Liberation of Kuwait to the Abraham Accords." *Israel Journal of Foreign Affairs* 14 (3): 391–98.

Ali, M., and A. Zeb. 2016. "Foreign Aid: Origin, Evolution and its Effectiveness in Poverty Alleviation." *Dialogue* 11 (1): 107–25.

Ali, S., and H. Vladich. 2016. "Environmental Diplomacy." In *The SAGE Handbook of Diplomacy*, eds. C. Constantinou, P. Kerr, and P. Sharp, 601–16. London: SAGE.

Al-Mashat, A.M. 2008. "Politics of Constructive Engagement: The Foreign Policy of the United Arab Emirates." In *Foreign Policies of Arab States: The Challenge of Globalization*, eds. B.D. Korany and A.E. Hillal Dessouki, 457–80. Cairo: Cairo University Press.

Almezaini, K.S. 2012. *The UAE and Foreign Policy: Foreign Aid, Identities and Interests*. London: Routledge.

———. 2017. "From Identities to Politics: UAE Foreign Aid." In *South-South Cooperation Beyond the Myths*, 225–44. London: Palgrave Macmillan.

Almezaini, K. 2018. "Implementing Global Strategy in the UAE Foreign Aid: From Arab Solidarity to South-South Cooperation." *International Relations* 18 (3): 579–94.

Anholt, S. 1998. "Nation-brands of the Twenty-first Century." *Journal of Brand Management* 5 (6): 395–406.

———. 2020. *The Good Country Equation: How We Can Repair the World in One Generation*. Oakland: Berrett-Koehler.

Antwi-Boateng, O., and A.A. Alhashmi. 2021. "The Emergence of the United Arab Emirates as a Global Soft Power: Current Strategies and Future Challenges." *Economic and Political Studies*: 1–20.

Chasek, P.S. 2001. *Earth Negotiations: Analyzing Thirty Years of Environmental Diplomacy*. Tokyo: United Nations University Press.

Cochrane, L. 2021. "The United Arab Emirates as a Global Donor: What a Decade of Foreign Aid Data Transparency Reveals." *Development Studies Research* 8 (1): 49–62.

Fulton, J. 2019. "China-UAE Relations in the Belt and Road Era." *Journal of Arabian Studies* 9 (2): 253–68.

The Economist. 2017. "The Gulf's Little Sparta: The United Arab Emirates," April 8.

Gienow-Hecht, J. 2019. "Nation Branding: A Useful Category for International History." *Diplomacy & Statecraft* 30 (4): 755–79.

Guéraiche, W. 2017. *The UAE. Geopolitics. Modernity and Tradition*. London: I.B. Tauris.

———. 2018. "The UAE and the Arab Spring: Rethinking Foreign Policy." In *Foreign Policy Analysis of the Arab Spring: How the International Community Responded to the Popular Uprisings in the Middle East*, eds. C. Çakmak and A.O. Özçelik, 395–416. London: Palgrave-Macmillan.

———. 2019. "International Cooperation, the UAE Soft Power?" In *Pratiques du soft power*, eds. R. Gura and G. Rouet, 96–110. Paris: L'Harmattan.

———. 2022a. "The Securitization of the Covid 19 Crisis in the UAE." In *Facets of Security in the United Arab Emirates*, ed. W. Guéraiche, 271–84. London: Routledge.

———. 2022b. "Security, Peace and Tolerance in a Post-modern Yet Traditional State." In *Facets of Security in the United Arab Emirates*, ed. W. Guéraiche, 286–94. London: Routledge.

Hertog, S. 2017. *A Quest for Significance: Gulf Oil Monarchies' International 'Soft Power' Strategies and Their Local Urban Dimensions*. LSE Kuwait Programme Paper Series, no. 42. London: The London School of Economics and Political Science, LSE Kuwait Programme.

Janardhan, N. 2022. "The UAE and India's Unconventional Security Strategies." In *Facets of Security in the United Arab Emirates*, ed. W. Guéraiche, 133–42. London: Routledge.

Jones, J., and N. Ridout. 2012. *Oman, Culture and Diplomacy*. Edinburgh: Edinburgh University Press.

Kourgiotis, P. 2020. "'Moderate Islam' Made in the United Arab Emirates: Public Diplomacy and the Politics of Containment." *Religions* 11 (1): 1–18.

Luomi, M. 2022. "Environmental Change and Security." In *Facets of Security in the United Arab Emirates*, ed. W. Guéraiche, 36–49. London: Routledge.

MOFAIC. 2017. *Promoting Global Peace and Prosperity UAE Policy for Foreign Assistance 2017–2021*, January. Abu Dhabi.

———. 2020. *2020 Aid Report*. Abu Dhabi.

O'Reilly, M. 1998. "Omanibalancing: Oman Confronts an Uncertain Future." *Middle East Journal* 52 (1): 70–84.

Shushan, D., and D. Marcoux. 2011. "The Rise (and Decline?) of Arab Aid: Generosity and Allocation in the Oil Era." *World Development* 39 (11): 1969–80.

Susskind, L.E., and S.H. Ali. 1994. *Environmental Diplomacy: Negotiating More Effective Global Agreements*. Oxford: Oxford University Press.

Tittensor, D., M. Clarke, and T. Gümüş. 2018. "Understanding Islamic Aid Flows to Enhance Global Humanitarian Assistance." *Contemporary Islam* 12 (2): 193–210.

Worrall, J. 2021. "'Switzerland of Arabia': Omani Foreign Policy and Mediation Efforts in the Middle East." *International Spectator: Italian Journal of International Affairs* 56 (4): 134–50.

Zhongping, F., and H. Jing. 2014. "China's Strategic Partnership Diplomacy." European Strategic Partnerships Observatory, Working Paper, June 8.

Internet Resources

MOFAIC. 2021. "AE, IRENA Launch $1 Billion Global Platform to Accelerate Renewable Energy at COP26," November 3. https://www.mofaic.gov.ae/en/mediahub/news/2021/11/3/03-11-2021-uae-cop-26.

Ministry of Tolerance. 2022. "Tolerance in UAE: Fruit of Wise Leadership's Support."

WAM/Majok. 2017. "Mohammed bin Rashid Launches UAE Soft Power Council," April 29.

WAM. Tariq Alfaham. 2017. "People of UAE Are a Valuable Part of Our Soft Power Strategy to Build a Strong Reputation for the Nation, says Mansour bin Zayed," September 26. http://www.tolerance.gov.ae/en/tolerance.aspx.

———. Nour Salman, MOHD AAMIR. 2019. "UAE, Singapore Sign Comprehensive Partnership Agreements," February 28.

———. 2020. "UN Praises UAE's Support for African Countries during Coronavirus Crisis," April 15.

———. Tariq Alfaham. 2021 "The UAE-China Relationship in 2021: A Golden Year, a Golden Future: UAE Ambassador to China," December 2.

———. Tariq Alfaham. Amjad Saleh. 2022. "Dubai Delivers on Promise Recording over 24 Million Visits at Expo 2020 Dubai," April 2.

28

Small States: From Intuitive to Smart Diplomacy

Vesko Garčević

Small States: "Lump of Weakness"?

There is not a good time for the smalls in global affairs. From a legal point of view, all sovereign states, great or small, are equal before the law. From a stance of realpolitik, however, they are far from being equal. Small states are commonly seen as second-class citizens in the international system. They are often defined as a "lump of weakness," which does not recognize their ability to exercise power, even if limited to specific issues, geographies, or relationships (Vital 1971).

The example of Montenegro, whose existence as a modern independent state is the result of big power politics, can prove that postulate. The Berlin Congress (June–July 1878) is seen as one of the milestones in Montenegrin state history. By revising the Treaty of San Stefano (March 1878), the big powers granted independence to Montenegro, Serbia, and Romania. The Principality of Montenegro sent two representatives to Berlin, but they were not able to participate in the event (Andrijašević 2006, 202–12). The Congress reconfirmed that neither Montenegro nor any other Balkan state, at the time, can independently decide about its future. Many changes that were introduced in Berlin were imposed on the regional actors (ibid.).

V. Garčević (✉)
Boston University, Boston, MA, USA

Is not the history of international politics the history of great powers? Following the same logic, one may conclude that "the strong would do as they could, and the weak would suffer what they must" (*Thucydides, The Peloponnesian War*). The invasion of Ukraine is, regrettably, confirmation of that assertion. Even the second largest country in Europe can easily be targeted by a larger, more powerful, and extremely assertive power.

For many, small states remain "fragile creatures in the rough sea of international relations" (Goetschel 1998, 13–31). While, due to their size, they may be more suitable for the creation of an inclusive political system, externally, they are perceived as "helpless and constantly threatened by extinction" (ibid.). Their power can be understood as a variable contingent on the interests of big and middle powers as Carsten Holbraad (1971) posits. For Jeanne A. K. Hey (2003, 1–13), the post-cold war has narrowed space for small actors in the international arena for they "are no longer able to play the superpowers off one another and have fewer policy options" than before.

The Montenegrin referendum in 2016 may serve as another proof how little has changed since the time of the nineteenth-century congress diplomacy.

In the months preceding the referendum of independence, practitioners (particularly diplomatic representatives of the EU members) and scholars alike were on a stance that Montenegrin independence would not be an economically and politically viable project. This opinion comes from a deeply instilled view that equates smallness with weakness. It is common to believe that smalls are vulnerable because of (1) their limited territory, natural and human resources; (2) their modest administrative capacity (the management of the state's policy operations and the stability of its decision-making); (3) and their high economic vulnerability. Nonetheless, the lack of administrative cohesion and social stability that provide the conditions for long-term stable economic growth is not a function of size (Lewis 2009, vii–xvi).

Yet, the success of Montenegro to convince its European partners not only to accept the idea of a referendum but also to get closely involved in its organization, observation, and verification, speaks that small states may fulfill their goals despite the initial objection by "the rule setters."

How to Define States: Small, Smaller, and Micro?

When in 2007 permanent representatives of Cyprus, the Holy See, Iceland, Lichtenstein, Malta, and Montenegro at the Organization of Security and Cooperation in Europe (OSCE) launched an informal platform of cooperation, they had a modest ambition to keep one another informed and increase their visibility in the organization.[1] One of the first issues that they had to address was how to define which OSCE participating state qualified to become a member of this informal (regrettably, short-lived) club of microstates. Soon they realized that the criteria to define smallness are fluid and the subject of various interpretations.

The literature lacks a common definition or set of criteria to define which states count as "small." Indeed, who is small and who is big? As Erling Bjol (1971, 29–39) explains, "by itself the concept of small state means nothing. A state is only small in relation to a greater one."

Size perception is a subjective category. Bahldur Thorhallsson (2009, 119–43) distinguishes "preference size that includes three features: ambition, prioritization and the ideas regarding the international system." On the other hand, "Perceptual size includes how the size of a particular small state is perceived comparing to other states." Both categories reveal the ambition of the governing political elites in that state as political elites' preferences and perception of the role of their state in international order determines the way how diplomatic activities are conducted.

Iver B. Neumann and Sieglinde Gstöhl (2004) use resources as criteria to distinguish small from macrostates. "Lack of capacity means capacity that is seen to be beyond a minimum; what this minimum is, is a question of continuous negotiation. We stress that, for a state to be micro ... The perceived reason has to be a lack of resources."

Conversely, examining a larger group of small states from different corners of the world, Naren Prasad argues that small and microstates have developed a set of unique, unorthodox, strategies to cope with their vulnerabilities or comparative disadvantages at the global level. These strategies involve a mix of economic and political approaches and the development of niche capabilities, products, and services. According to it, small states are capable to use their sovereignty, geographical location, state branding as *intrinsic (soft) power* in global affairs to advance their cause (Prasad 2013, 41–65).

The Global Competitive Report 2019 ranks many small and microstates as very competitive (Schwab 2019). According to the 2021 World Competitiveness Yearbook (IMD 2021), Luxembourg is the 12th most competitive country in the world and outstrips its direct competitors Germany (15th), Belgium (24th), and France (29st).

---

[1] Andorra, San Marino, and Monaco did not have permanent representatives at the Organization for Security and Cooperation in Europe (OSCE), and their diplomats did not take part in the informal gathering co-organized by the group of small participating states.

Keeping resources in mind, it is commonly understood that factors like size, population, economic strength, or military capabilities determine smallness. In literature, small states are often defined by population thresholds of 10–15 million (Herbert Armstrong and Robert Read, quoted in Thorhallsson 2012).

If 10 million inhabitants is taken as a threshold, there are 110 United Nations (UN) members that can be categorized as small, which is the majority of the global organization.[2] But, almost 70 percent of these small UN members have less than 5 million inhabitants: 45 countries have less than 1.5 million citizens and can be described as microstates, while 30 members have a population less or around 5 million[3] and can be placed in the category between micro and small states.

The Commonwealth[4] and the World Bank usually use the threshold of 1.5 million people although there is no theoretical justification why this is used as a threshold.[5] On the other hand, the study that discusses the economies of the European Union (EU) Small Member and Candidate States perceives the states with a population of three million or less as small states (Briguglio 2018).

When it comes to the Balkans, for the purpose of this chapter, we consider small those states that have less than five million citizens—Albania, Bosnia and Herzegovina, North Macedonia, Kosovo, and Montenegro (Western Balkan-5 or WB5). The scope of their global involvement is shaped by inherent challenges pertinent to administrative capacities, democratic deficit, structural political and economic problems exacerbated by the COVID-19 pandemic, and bilateral outstanding issues. Montenegro is a microstate with a population of less than a million. Kosovo is not a member of the UN and is yet to be recognized by all the EU members and the UN Security Council (UNSC) permanent members. North Macedonia had been caught in a 27-year-long name dispute with Greece (BBC News 2019). The very existence of Bosnia and Herzegovina is challenged from inside (AFP/France 2021).

---

[2] Members States of the UN, World Data. https://www.worlddata.info/alliances/un-united-nations.php.
[3] Members States of the UN, World Data. https://www.worlddata.info/alliances/un-united-nations.php.
[4] The Commonwealth: Small States. https://thecommonwealth.org/our-work/small-states.
[5] The World Bank in Small States. https://www.worldbank.org/en/country/smallstates/overview#1.

Diplomacy Matters

Since small states lack more traditional forms of power, they must specialize in how they employ their resources and relationships. According to Tom Long (2017), the power of small nations originates in three categories: "derivative, collective and particular-intrinsic." Derivative power relies upon the relationship with great power. Collective power involves building coalitions of supportive states, often through institutions. Particular-intrinsic power relies on the assets of the small state trying to do the influencing (ibid.).

Diplomacy can serve as a facilitator or inhibitor of how countries utilize their resources in global affairs. One of the main questions for every state, particularly for the small one, is what type of diplomatic service they should develop to be able to keep control over issues of their interest?

Taking examples of the WB5[6] and their diplomatic networks—this chapter argues that if the smalls want to adapt to new global trends, they need to create professional, cost-effective, non-orthodox diplomacy—also known as "smart" diplomacy. Although all the five countries have made several diplomatic successes, they are often the result of "intuitive diplomacy" that relies on the expertise, skills, and knowledge of several professionals rather than a well-thought-out strategy. The case of Montenegro is taken as an example of "intuitive diplomacy" while the elements of "smart, non-orthodox" diplomacy are discussed in the closing section.

Multilateralism Paved the Way for Small States: The WB5 Made Some Success

In relative terms, this has been one of the best times in history to be a small state. Their integrity is protected by international legal norms better than ever, and the power of the world's strongest nations seems to be institutionalized more than before. Legal norms of sovereign equality give small states a voice in many international organizations (IOs) (Long 2017). With the increasing importance of global cooperation, "the status and prestige of small powers have risen, while their relative strength in the traditional elements of power has actually declined" (Rothstein 1968, x, 381).

Although the Russian aggression proves again the vulnerability of smaller states in confrontation (hegemonic) systems, regardless of its limitations,

---

[6] This research is based on primary and secondary sources (in English and local languages) and interviews with former or current career diplomats from the WB5.

international institutions and multilateralism create a better opportunity for less powerful actors. In more restrictive environments, they will have fewer foreign policy options and less successful outcomes.

Small states aspire to join IOs to receive official approval and international recognition of their independence and sovereignty (Thorhallsson 2012). IOs and consensus-based organizations like North Atlantic Treaty Organization (NATO) or the OSCE, in particular, appeal to small countries for, at least, four attributes: (1) their formal equality; (2) the potential security of membership; (3) the possible capacity of the organizations to restrain Great Powers (Keohane 1969); (4) possibility to project their power by employing the strength of an IO on issues of national importance for them.

Even the smallest among smalls see the merit of being involved in global cooperation and aspire to gain membership to IOs. Liechtenstein, San Marino, and Monaco can be used as examples. In 1920, Liechtenstein's application for membership in the League of Nations was rejected because it had "chosen to depute to others some of the attributes of sovereignty" (Gunter 1974). Decades later, in 1990, Liechtenstein became the smallest UN member, when there was a turn toward acceptance of microstate claims to equal sovereignty within international society (*Los Angeles Times* 1990). San Marino joined the global organization in 1992, and Monaco did it in 1993.

From 1991 to 2010, 25 states with a population of less than five million were elected to the UN Security Council (UNSC) (Thorhallsson 2012). Currently, three countries with less or around five million citizens serve on the UNSC—Albania, Gabon, and Norway. But, it was St. Vincent and Grenadines that broke the record as the smallest nation ever in UN history to be elected as a UNSC non-permanent member (UN News 2019b).

A more prominent role of small states cannot be limited only to the UN system. Regional organizations offer even more opportunities to small countries to demonstrate their ability to govern much bigger systems.

Brunei Darussalam, a country with less than 500,000 citizens, took the chairmanship of the Association of Southeast Asian Nations (ASEAN) in 2021. In the last ten years, it has been for the second time that Brunei governs the organization that covers a total population of over 662 million people and has a combined gross domestic product (GDP) of $3.2 trillion.[7] Likewise, in 2012, the Republic of Djibouti assumed the chairmanship of the Council of Foreign Ministers of the Organization of Islamic Cooperation (OIC), the

---

[7] Association of Southeast Asian Nations: ASEAN Chairmanship. https://asean.org/category/chairmanship/.

second-largest organization after the UN with a membership of 57 states spread over four continents (Kazinform 2012).

The Presidency of the Council of the European Union (EU) was held by Slovenia in 2021. Likewise, the chairmanship of the Arctic Council was in the hands of Iceland, while Montenegro assumed the Presidency of the Central European Initiative (CEI) in January 2021.[8]

When it comes to the WB5, they have made several diplomatic successes and proved that participation in IOs is perceived as the way to confirm their administrative capacity, build international visibility, and, besides Albania, reinforce their newly gained sovereignty.

Kosovo exemplifies how membership in the UN and other IOs is intrinsic to sovereignty recognition in global affairs. Since the declaration of independence in 2008, the country has been recognized by 117 countries, established a separate diplomatic service, opened 32 embassies and 14 consulates, but it has not yet been admitted to the UN.[9] According to the UN Charter, for this to happen a country needs the recommendation of the UNSC and the support of a two-third majority in the UN General Assembly (UNGA). Having not been recognized by China and the Russian Federation and given their firm non-recognition stance, Kosovo's UN membership seems almost impossible in the foreseeable future. Notwithstanding its de-jure sovereign status, the lack of UN membership is often taken as the argument against Kosovo's full sovereignty. However, the declaration of independence and diplomatic relations with more than 100 states is seen by Kosovo's diplomats as the key diplomatic achievement so far.

Since its independence, North Macedonia has been facing numerous challenges related to identity politics. Their neighbors have either disputed its name (Greece), its national identity and language (Bulgaria), or the existence of its autocephalous Orthodox Church (Serbia). Given the gravity of its problems with the neighbors, even membership in the UN with an acceptable state name was a daunting task for a fledgling diplomatic service in the 1990s (Lewis 1993).

Before the UN-brokered Prespa Agreement that settled the 27-year-long dispute between Athens and Skopje and formally recognized the Former Yugoslav Republic of Macedonia as the Republic of North Macedonia, Greece had for decades vetoed North Macedonian NATO membership and its accession to the EU (UN News 2019a). With the Greek veto lifted, the country

---

[8] Central European Initiative, official website: Montenegro's Presidency 2021. https://www.cei.int/presidency.

[9] The Ministry of Foreign Affairs of the Republic of Kosovo and Diaspora, official website: https://www.mfa-ks.net/en/.

joined the Alliance and finally fulfilled the criteria to open accession negotiation talks with the EU. Suddenly, Bulgaria, another neighbor, blocked the opening of Skopje's accession talks with the EU, asking North Macedonia to fulfill its six demands (Marušić 2021).

While this case underscores the vulnerability of small states in global affairs, the Greeks' veto at the NATO Summit in Bucharest in 2008, despite the U.S. support to Skopje, confirms how a consensus-based organization (NATO) may empower a relatively small nation (Gallis et al. 2008). Both countries, Bulgaria and Greece, have utilized their memberships in globally relevant IOs to transform the nature of their bilateral disputes and elevate them to the level of significant importance for the organizations of which they are members.

Bosnia and Herzegovina was the first small country from the region to serve as a non-permanent member of the UNSC in 2010 and 2011 (UN News 2009). Bosnian's election did not go without controversy as some Western states believed that its election could create an unusual situation in the Council. (Something similar had happened before with another small state—Lebanon.) At the time when the country was serving as a non-permanent member, it hosted an EU-led peacekeeping mission, the European Union Force Bosnia and Herzegovina,[10] and was subject to UNSC scrutiny and discussion about the implementation of the Dayton Agreement.

It had a tiny diplomatic team of only seven diplomats in New York backed by a group of professionals in the capital. Due to a perplexing political system created by the Dayton Agreement, the presidency of the country had to be involved in the work of the Mission almost on a daily basis. The head of the Mission during the two-year term in the UNSC was a political appointee, and the Ministry appointed a career diplomat as his deputy to facilitate the Mission's work.

In the meantime, the country has chaired several regional initiatives, but to many Bosnian diplomats and politicians, the election to serve in the UNSC is still "the biggest achievement of the country's foreign policy since independence in 1992."

Albania seems to be the leader of proactive diplomacy among the WB5. The Government has prioritized regional cooperation and recognized opportunities existing in international affairs. Tirana took over the chairmanship of the OSCE during a challenging 2020. As Albanian Prime Minister Edi Rama described, chairing the OSCE marks the highlight of the Albanian

---

[10] European Union Force in Bosnia and Herzegovina, official website: https://www.euforbih.org/.

transformation from the communist regime that opposed the Helsinki spirit to a country that leads the same Organization (OSCE Newsroom 2020).

The country is currently serving as a non-permanent member of the UNSC.[11] Under the motto "Finding Solution Through Partnership," Albanian diplomats see the UNSC membership as good for exposure and the visibility of the country. Around 20 diplomats currently work at the Albanian Mission to the UN, which makes this office the largest in the Albanian diplomatic network. The Albanian involvement in the work of the UNSC is based on three pillars: (1) realistic expectations as to their influence in global affairs; (2) an "honest broker" approach to addressing global challenges since "the country has no hidden agenda and is sincerely committed to global peace and security"; (3) niche capabilities: Albania keeps a European and particularly regional agenda in focus. At the beginning of the aggression against Ukraine, Albania co-authored a UN resolution on ending the Ukrainian crisis (UN News 2022).

It is the common understanding in Albania, North Macedonia, and Montenegro that NATO membership is their major diplomatic achievement. While chairmanships of regional IOs or participation in the UNSC showcase a country's capacity to successfully coordinate complex systems, NATO membership is unequivocally seen as a long-term, strategic accomplishment that allows small states from the region to become "contributors to global security" and actors involved in the decision-making process of the European and global importance. With the ongoing crisis in Ukraine, the membership serves as a "platinum insurance policy" for their territorial integrity and sovereignty.

The self-perception of the WB5 role in global affairs has been determined by their "preference size," or how they have prioritized their foreign policy goals and utilized opportunities existing in international affairs. From that perspective, participation in the work of IOs may not only increase administrative competence but can enhance the political relevance of the smalls. As the case of North Macedonia proves, IOs not only provide practical benefits to small states in the form of information, but also serve as an avenue of influence (Novosad and Werker 2019). Greece and Bulgaria have been able to develop "issue-specific power" to make up for what they lack in aggregate structural power. IOs allow small and micro-states to possess power disproportionate relative to their size on issues of utmost importance to them (Steinsson and Thorhallsson 2019). Small countries are not only manipulated

---

[11] The Dag Hammarskjöld Library, official website: *Security Council Membership*. https://research.un.org/en/unmembers/scmembers.

by big(ger) powers as it happens often, but they may successfully exploit their membership to enforce their will to (consensus-based) organizations in disputes of their national interests. "The power of powerlessness" manifests itself in a variety of ways, and the "ability of small states to exploit their smaller size to achieve their indented, even if unlikely, policy outcomes" (Baldacchino 2013, 21–41).

Montenegro: An Example of "Intuitive" Diplomacy

Many small states rely on what we can define as intuitive diplomacy. This type of service is built on the expertise, skills, knowledge, and engagement of several accomplished diplomats rather than on a systematic, well-thought-through strategy. Diplomatic activities, therefore, become overly personalized and individualistic. Habitually, the success of diplomatic initiatives depends on a few people involved in it. While flexible and successful in some cases, intuitive diplomacy is mostly responsive, short-term oriented, and often opportunistic.

Diplomats of small states like Montenegro can develop great versatility. They make a wide array of decisions and perform many of the duties that tend to be distributed among multiple officials and even ministries in large states. Freedom that prominent diplomats in a small service enjoy is both rewarding and restraining. It is rewarding as they are entitled to make decisions or shape the foreign policy of their states to a level incomparable to their colleagues working in larger diplomatic systems. Yet, the lack of systematic approach, the absence of information, vague or non-existing instructions from the capital, or overly politicized service make the system vulnerable and restrain its ability to conduct a coherent foreign policy. While Montenegro is taken as an example, "intuitive" diplomacy is pervasive among small countries, and not only in the Balkans.

Montenegro's diplomatic achievements since its independence have exceeded expectations. The country was blessed to have several seasoned and accomplished diplomats who had served in Yugoslav diplomacy before Montenegro created its Ministry. They played a critical role in a smooth transition toward an independent diplomatic service and global diplomatic engagement of the country.

Montenegro acknowledged that a proactive regional agenda, involvement in regional initiatives, and membership in other IOs would reaffirm its international sovereignty. Soon after the independence, Montenegro joined the OSCE (OSCE Newsroom 2006) and the UN (UN News 2006). Membership in IOs does not provide only a place at the table or a vote, it gives an opportunity to nurture contacts with representatives of other states. The country has effectively used its mission to the UN to establish diplomatic relations with countries where it is not represented on a permanent basis.

The strategic priority—integration into Euro-Atlantic structures—was defined at the early stage, which made the country's foreign policy look coherent (Djurović 2009). Not only was the participation in the International Security Assistance Force Mission (ISAF) and the Resolute Support Mission (RSM) seen as a way to show the country's solidarity with NATO members, but it also increased the country's outreach and allowed Podgorica to be involved in the decision-making process reserved only for contributing states. Subsequently, it was granted EU candidate country status in 2010 and opened accession talks with the EU in 2012.[12] Joining NATO in 2017 is considered the major diplomatic success (NATO Press 2017). Yet, Montenegro has not drafted a comprehensive strategy about how to implement its strategic priorities or how to make the country's niche capabilities known to its foreign partners.

Intuitive diplomacy may produce a short-term success, for it is goal-oriented. But, it cannot guarantee a consistent, sustainable, and recognizable international engagement because of its malleable, spontaneous nature. To paraphrase Friedrich Hayek—the success of this type of diplomacy is often the result of human action, but not necessarily of the execution of the human design.

Toward Smart Diplomacy

"Smart" diplomacy emphasizes individual distinctiveness, prioritizes efforts, and focuses on policy sectors of great importance and/or where direct benefits can likely be gained. Those are its essential elements. It entails the development of a two-pronged service: a network capable to promote a country's interests, and the concept that can be a soft tool by itself, a specific niche capability in the world of diplomacy. The term "niche diplomacy" was used by Gareth Evans, Australia's foreign affairs and trade minister in the late 1980s and early 1990s. To him it meant "concentrating resources in specific areas

---

[12] European Council: *Montenegro—Status of Negotiation*. https://www.consilium.europa.eu/en/policies/enlargement/montenegro/.

best able to generate returns worth having, rather than trying to cover the field."

In practical terms, besides group diplomacy which has been extensively discussed, "smart" diplomacy implies steps that small states should take to overcome unique constraints and make their diplomacies cost-effective, but more impactful. The idea of "smart," "clever," or "focused" (Henrikson 2017, 1–17) diplomacy is not new. Several authors, including Baldur Thorhallsson and Sverrir Steinsson (2017), Dietrich Kappeler (2007), Alan K. Henrikson (2017), and Milan Jazbec, have discussed how to improve diplomacy of small states. Henrikson distinguishes ten types of diplomacy that can be employed by small states, including "enterprise," "niche," "group," "diasporic," and "cyber" diplomacy (2017, 1–17).

The proposed five pillars of smart diplomacy comprise many of their viewpoints and suggestions. While discussing each of them, we shall provide a succinct examination of the state of play among the WB5 in each of the five areas.

1. The creation of a flexible, professional, cost-effective, and depoliticized service is by far the most daunting challenge for small diplomatic systems. Almost every diplomacy is susceptible to political influence, but small systems are particularly vulnerable since the diplomatic forces that small states can muster are far smaller, less skillful, and less diverse.

    While big systems may afford to have a number of political appointees as ambassadors because of the large number of professionals working in diplomacy, in the case of small states this may cause a functional paralysis of the network. A small embassy with two or three diplomats will likely get dysfunctional if the ambassador is a political appointee.

    As Milan Jazbec (2010) illustrates in cases of Slovenia, Estonia, Latvia, and Lithuania, with more robust global engagement, diplomatic services of small states rapidly grow. Due to the lack of qualified professionals, they have a penchant for recruiting diplomats among non-professionals, mostly politicians.

    Besides obvious negative effects on the functionality of diplomatic services, this practice makes a lasting negative impact on the workplace culture at ministries and relations among employees, creating latent or open conflicts between professionals and non-professionals. In ministries captured by politics, there is no room for innovation, reform, and adaptation; young professionals become apathetic and unmotivated, while senior professionals are indifferent and unconcerned. It often results in a diplomatic service that consists of a few dozen senior diplomats, mostly political appointees, and many junior diplomats lacking experience and skills.

Conversely, a modern diplomatic service implies a new organizational structure that does not shy away from experiences from small and medium-sized enterprises when it can be usefully transferred to diplomatic organizations (ibid.). This structure should nurture a functional diplomatic concept focused on areas of great importance for a small country and the development of niche capability or issue-specific power (Steinsson and Thorhallsson 2019). It means that the diplomacy of small states should focus on policy sectors of great importance for them, where they can make a distinctive contribution and/or where they can gain political and other benefits.

Sadly, none of the WB5 has embarked on fundamental reform of their services. The ministries are heavily politicized and often characterized by political opportunism. In several cases, countries create diplomatic offices to suit the interests of party leaders or do staffing of embassies according to the popularity of the destination. Very often ambassadorial positions in key countries and IOs (the United States, Russia, and NATO) are vacant due to political feuds at home.

Bosnia and Herzegovina, with the Dayton formula of ethnic representations in the state institutions, is the primary example. The country has no law on foreign policy, nor has it a rule (bylaw) that regulates personnel promotion and appointments in the Ministry. Montenegro or Kosovo, for example, have laws that limit the number of political appointees to 30 percent and 50 percent, but the number of non-professionals at senior diplomatic positions surpasses the limit imposed by the law.

Despite financial constraints and limited human capital, the idea of pooling and sharing resources has never been genuinely considered. There have been sporadic examples of it, Montenegro and North Macedonia were sharing a building in Paris for three years, but they are perceived as temporary solutions caused by financial problems rather than an innovative approach that enables cost-effective representation abroad.

2. The creation of smart ministries and embassies: New technology and twenty-first-century innovation can facilitate small countries to overcome vulnerabilities related to their administrative capacity (Kurbalija 2016). Yet, the question is "how new technological capabilities can enhance the ability of small states' decision-makers to match complex systems in respect of particular objectives or challenges to their growth or their maintenance of viability" (Lewis 2009).

Digital diplomacy requires at least a twofold action: (a) the creation of smart, digitized ministries, virtual embassies, and consulates. As diplomacy depends on human interaction and networking, smart embassies and consulates are not designed to completely replace diplomatic offices abroad. Their goal is to make diplomacy more impactful and cost-effective, and to expand the coverage of issues/regions of interest for small states; (b) digital connectivity: smart diplomacy uses social media ad networks to build countries' visibility, enhance their connectivity, share information about their achievements, and spread influence (Sandre 2013).

All five countries have invested considerable efforts to enhance digital connectivity and outreach using social media. To a lesser extent, their activities focus on image building and country branding. They rarely support or participate in online activities of other countries, IOs, or international non-governmental organizations (INGOs), if those activities are not closely linked to the national interests of the WB5. By using social media platforms to advocate global initiatives in areas such as climate change, human rights, humanitarian efforts, south-south cooperation, and so on, small states from the region would get a chance to increase the scope of their activities.

The creation of smart ministries and virtual embassies is in the rudimental phase. None of the WB5 has created a comprehensive digitalization strategy, envisaging a gradual "smart" transformation of their diplomacy. Albania has recently developed some digital consular services, but other states lag significantly behind other small countries like Malta or Iceland (Henrikson 2017).

There are no plans to create virtual interactive embassies (websites) oriented toward specific countries. In the case of virtual embassies, the desk officer administering the site may also act as chargé d'affaires for that country. In the case of most important embassies and IOs, a host state's smart diplomatic service may provide virtual support in real-time to a small diplomatic team abroad. This concept enables the situation in a particular place to be monitored and interpreted by knowledgeable, experienced persons physically far removed from the scene. Diplomats who have been shifted to new posts or rotated home, or even retired, can be brought electronically into detailed deliberation of problems that may require a country's statement or action.

3. Outsourcing diplomatic activities and cooperation with INGOs cannot substitute for a domestic diplomatic network, but INGOs with recognized issue-based global capabilities, renowned advisory groups, and field

experts, politicians, or the private sector can be an advocate of particular national interests of small states.

The scope of external involvement shall depend on the field of cooperation and its goals. It either can be developed on an ad-hoc basis with foreign and domestic experts or is built upon a broad or interest-centered partnership with non-state international actors. While consultants can provide thorough expertise in form of detailed analyses, advice, and recommendations, INGOs can draw international attention to important issues for small states, strengthening their voice in global affairs or becoming their goodwill advocates. In some cases, non-state actors may be involved in capacity building of a diplomatic network.[13] In other circumstances, external consultants may be strategic partners or official advocates/representatives of small countries in particular matters.

The experience of the WB5 confirms some benefits of this approach despite sporadic comments that "ideas proposed by foreign consultants don't always meet a country's expectations." In the years preceding independence and during the negotiation, Kosovo hired an independent advisory group, Independent Diplomat.[14] Independent Diplomat was offering legal expertise about the status of Kosovo and practical advice during the negotiating process. During UNSC membership, Bosnia and Herzegovina closely cooperated with *the Security Council Report.*[15] The Security Council Report was providing valuable and objective information to Bosnian diplomats that otherwise would not be available due to the lack of personnel.

4. The importance of group diplomacy is extensively covered in the works of scholars and practitioners. Even if security is not fully achieved and great powers are often not effectively restrained, grouping is the most effective leverage in global affairs that small states can rely on. The leaders of small states have realized that although they may be able to do little together, they can do virtually nothing separately (Keohane 1969).

There are numerous examples used in publications about small states to illustrate how they "punched above their weight" because of group diplomacy. The most actual example is how the group of small island states "have played a leading role in raising awareness of climate change" through the Alliance of Small Island States (AOSIS) (Ourbak and Magnan 2018).

---

[13] DAI, the official website: Kosovo—Ministry of Foreign Affairs Support (KMFAS). https://www.dai.com/our-work/projects/kosovo-ministry-foreign-affairs-support-kmfas.

[14] The Diplomatic Advisory Group, Independent Diplomat, official website *Kosovo—the First Ever Project.* https://independentdiplomat.org/project/kosovo/.

[15] The Security Council Report, official website: https://www.securitycouncilreport.org/.

The example of AOSIS reinforces the idea that modern networking should be interest-driven, flexible, asymmetric, and organized horizontally (by way of non-institutional associations). Ad-hoc forums can be created around one issue to serve the interests of group members. Simply, holding a group together on one issue is more feasible than across a broad agenda. They may have smaller subgroups within the core group and enable states to fluctuate from one to another group following their national interests.

Smaller in size and less institutionalized regional organizations, on the other hand, can allow small states to identify a set of common interests, develop mutually supportive action plans, and shape regional agendas. Regional cooperation or ad-hoc forums can serve small states better as platforms for policy coordination and joint mechanisms for engagement in global affairs.

Notwithstanding common understanding that for these groups "to gain significance, they would have to be so large that each state has minimal influence," the amount of collective power does not depend on a sheer number of small states summoned in an IO (Keohane 1969). It depends more on their organizational capacity, competence, and knowledge, cooperation with non-state actors who can advance their agenda, and negotiating strategies that minimize the existing power asymmetry in global affairs.

The common foreign policy goals of EU and NATO membership have served as a catalyst for change of the region after the traumatic experience caused by the conflicts in the 1990s. The WB5 have been involved in regional cooperation, participating in or chairing regional initiatives and organizations such as the South-East European Cooperation Process (SEECP),[16] the Central European Initiative (CEI),[17] the Adriatic Ionian Initiative,[18] the Regional Cooperation Council,[19] the Berlin Process,[20] to mention some of them. The Adriatic Charter—A5 initiative[21] has confirmed itself as instrumental for regional cooperation in the security field. Nevertheless, most if not all of the existing regional cooperative mechanisms have been created by external actors, the EU and the United States, to facilitate post-conflict reconciliation, trust-building, and cross-border cooperation.

The regional actors have shown little enthusiasm for homegrown initiatives and ideas. While there have been examples of ad-hoc cooperation and

---

[16] The South East European Cooperation Process—SEECP, official website: https://www.seecp.info/.
[17] Central European Initiative, official website: https://www.cei.int/.
[18] The Adriatic Ionian Initiative, official website: https://www.aii-ps.org/.
[19] Regional Cooperation Council, official website: https://www.rcc.int/.
[20] The Berlin Process, official website: https://berlinprocess.info/.
[21] U.S. Department of State Archive: Adriatic Charter. https://2001-2009.state.gov/p/eur/rls/fs/112766.htm.

support, sharing resources, knowledge, and experience is yet to be developed. With a few exceptions in the domain of Euro-Atlantic integrations, the WB5 have not acted as a group in relations with much stronger global actors.

5. Smart Diaspora—empower your citizens through diasporic diplomacy. Diasporas can be of critical importance for the advancement of small countries' foreign policy agendas. Through their connections and potential influence, expatriates are sometimes more impactful in the host country. Henrikson (2017) highlights diasporic diplomacy as one of the ten most important diplomatic features of small states' diplomacies.

The traditional outreach to the diaspora is often exploitative, based on interest to attract investments and remittances, exert control, and generate political support. Immigration is perceived stereotypically, as passive, politically malleable, and dependent on the host country and the country of origin. Due to limited human resources, the consular diplomacy of small states is mostly focused on accommodation of citizens' immediate needs, while the consistent work on networking is often neglected.[22]

Robin Cohen (2008, 1–21, 159–72) was among the first to introduce a distinctive, modern view on the role of diaspora in the contemporary world. Similarly, Rima Berns-McGown argues that a new definition and approach to diaspora should keep in mind factors like globalization and changed international circumstances (Berns-McGown 2007). The novelty in a modern diplomatic approach to diaspora lies in the perspective adopted toward the country's emigrants not merely as a source of remittances and unwavering political and financial support to its (former) country (Henrikson 2017). Instead of a top-down relationship, it nurtures inclusiveness, equality, and understanding of specific interests of the diaspora.

Diverse political, social, and economic factors throughout the twentieth century have shaped events that forced citizens of the WB5 to leave their countries. The brain drain is another big challenge for the region. The World Economic Forum's Global Competitiveness Report from 2019 ranks Bosnia and Herzegovina and North Macedonia among the countries most affected by the brain drain (Schwab 2019, 102–5, 434–37).

The WB5 have made certain progress in this area, but regional diaspora diplomacy is shaped to large extent by the consequences of recent wars, the post-Yugoslav transition, economic and political challenges, and the lack of trust among countries in the Western Balkans (Murgatroyd et al. 2020).

---

[22] DiploFoundation, official website: *Consular and Diaspora Diplomacy*. https://www.diplomacy.edu/topics/consular-and-diaspora-diplomacy/.

They have adopted legal frameworks, established institutions, endorsed projects related to their diaspora, or developed projects with representatives of their communities abroad (ibid.). As part of intuitive diplomacy, occasional successes are contingent on a few energetic individuals and their initiatives.

The WB5 have not created a detailed central database with information about their distinguished citizens living abroad, whereas representatives of diaspora rarely take part in formulation of national policies in this field. The practice of goodwill ambassadors is almost non-existent; the countries rarely cooperate with distinguished diaspora members or celebrities on well-designed projects with a more significant impact (Cartwright 2020; Al Jazeera 2019). Montenegro, for example, has missed the opportunity to deepen cooperation with Marina Abramovich after her involvement in a Montenegrin cultural project supported by UNESCO (UNESCO 2012; Montenegro Government 2012).

Conclusion

Departing from the premise that behavior of small states varies considerably according to the types of international systems in which they operate—hegemonic systems, confrontation systems, integration systems, and security communities—according to the geographic parameters which condition their foreign policy and according to their domestic structures, this chapter highlights that the current geopolitical context is more beneficial for small states (Erling 1971).

Thorhallsson (2012) defines two categories of qualitative factors that determine the ability of small states to influence the UNSC, but a similar analogy can apply to global affairs as a whole. The first is administrative competence; the second is the image of the state in the international system, with specific regard to its perceived neutrality or reputation as a norm entrepreneur in particular policy fields.

The improvements in communication, technological innovations, and digitalization; increasing integration of world economies; and better connectivity have created a system that can empower smaller actors. Global challenges ask for a new type of multilateralism that can be labeled as the fourth generation of cooperation. If congress diplomacy marks the beginning of contemporary multilateralism, the second generation of global cooperation is embodied in the League of Nations, while the third "upgraded" version was created with the post-World War II liberal order. The new type of global cooperation must be more inclusive, multidimensional, and decentralized (Stuart and Samman 2017). Imagining a post-COVID 19 world implies a new UN where partnership should be expanded to non-state actors and the role of small states should be further enhanced (Carayannis and Weiss 2021).

As the global environment changes so grows the need for modernization of diplomatic services of small countries like the WB5. This chapter argues that while small states are unable to field a large and diverse diplomatic force, which limits the skills and human resources that can be put into forming foreign policies and taking part in negotiations (Steinsson and Thorhallsson 2019), to be able to play a relatively significant role in global affairs, they should nurture "smart," functional, and focused diplomacy (Henrikson 2017).

As seen from a small countries' perspective, including the WB5, the creation of a flexible, professional, cost-effective, depoliticized, and digitalized diplomatic service is a necessity rather than a policy luxury.

References and Further Reading

AFP/France 24. 2021. "Bosnia's Serb Leader Dodik Unveils Plans to Dismantle 'Failed Country,'" October 22. https://www.france24.com/en/live-news/20211022-bosnia-s-serb-leader-dodik-unveils-plans-to-dismantle-failed-country.

Al Jazeera. 2019. "Pop Stars Rally for Albania Following Deadly Earthquake," November 29. https://www.aljazeera.com/features/2019/11/29/pop-stars-rally-for-albania-following-deadly-earthquake.

Andrijašević, Ž. 2006. *Montenegrin History.* Podgorica: Pobjeda.

Baldacchino, G. 2013 "Thucydides or Kissinger? A Critical Review of Smaller State Diplomacy." In *The Diplomacies of Small States: Between Vulnerability and Resilience*, eds. A.F. Cooper and T.M. Shaw, 21–41. London: Palgrave Macmillan

BBC News. 2019. "Macedonia and Greece: Vote Settles 27-year Name Dispute," January 25. https://www.bbc.com/news/world-europe-47002865.

Berns-McGown, R. 2007. "Redefining 'Diaspora': The Challenge of Connection and Inclusion." *International Journal* 63 (1): 3–20.

Briguglio, L. 2018. *Small States and the European Union.* London: Routledge.

Carayannis, T., and T.G. Weiss. 2021. "The 'Third' UN: Imagining Post-COVID-19 Multilateralism." *Global Policy* 12 (1): 5–14.

Cartwright, C. 2020. "Kosovo's Influence on British Pop," *The New European,* August.

Cohen, R. 2008. *Global Diasporas: An Introduction.* London: Routledge.

Djurović, G. 2009. "Montenegro's Strategic Priorities on the Path of Euro-Atlantic Integration." *Connections* 9 (1): 93–112.

Erling, B. 1971. "Small States in International Politics." In *Small States in International Relations*, eds. A. Schou and A.O. Brundtland, 29–39. Stockholm: Almqvist and Wiksell.

Gallis, P., P. Belkin, C. Ek, J. Kim, J. Nichol, and S. Woehrel. 2008. *CRS Report for Congress, Enlargement Issues at NATO's Bucharest Summit*, April. https://news.un.org/en/story/2019/06/1040071.

Goetschel, L., ed. 1998. *Small States Inside and Outside the European Union*. Boston/Dordrecht/London: Kluwer Academic.

Gunter, M. 1974. "Liechtenstein and the League of Nations: A Precedent for the UN's Ministate Problem?" *American Journal of International Law* 68 (3): 496–501.

Henrikson, A.K. 2017. *Ten Types of Small State Diplomacy*. Medford: The Fletcher School of Law and Diplomacy, Tufts University. https://is.muni.cz/el/1423/podzim2008/MVZ157/um/TEN_TYPES_OF_SMALL_STATE_DIPLOMACY.pdf.

Hey, J. 2003. *Introducing Small State Foreign Policy; Small States in World Politics—Explaining Foreign Policy Behavior*. Boulder: Lynne Rienner.

Holbraad, C. 1971. *Middle Powers in International Politics*. Houndmills: Palgrave Macmillan.

IMD World Competitiveness Center. 2021. *The World Competitiveness Yearbook*.

Jazbec, M. 2010. "Small States and Diplomacy: An Indispensable, Though Much Diversified Relationship." *Halduskultuur—Administrative Culture* 11 (1): 66–83.

Kappeler, D. 2007. "The Role of Diplomats from Small States." International Conference: Diplomacy of Small States. Malta, January.

Kazinform. 2012. "Kazakhstan to Hand Over Its OIC Foreign Ministers' Council Chairmanship to Djibouti," November 13. https://www.inform.kz/en/kazakhstan-to-hand-over-its-oic-foreign-ministers-council-chairmanship-to-djibouti_a2509735.

Keohane, R.O. 1969. "Lilliputians' Dilemmas: Small States in International Politics." *International Organization* 23 (2): 291–310.

Kurbalija, J. 2016. "An Introduction to Internet Governance." Malta: DiploFoundation, November 8. https://www.diplomacy.edu/topics/internet-governance-and-digital-policy/#geopolitics.

Lewis, P. 1993. "U.N. Compromise Lets Macedonia Be a Member." *New York Times*, April 8.

Lewis, V.A. 2009. "Studying Small States over the Twentieth into the Twenty-first Centuries." In *The Diplomacies of Small States: Between Vulnerability and Resilience*, eds. A.F. Cooper and T.M. Shaw, vii–xvii. London: Palgrave Macmillan.

Long, T. 2017. "Small States, Great Power? Gaining Influence through Intrinsic, Derivative, and Collective Power." *International Studies Review* 19: 185–205.

Los Angeles Times. 1990. "Principality of Lichtenstein Becomes 160th, and the Smallest, Member of UN," September 20.

Marušić, S. J. 2021. "Can North Macedonia Meet Bulgaria's Six Demands for Breakthrough?" *Balkan Insight*, October 19.

Montenegro Government 2012. "PM Luksic: Marina Abramovich Community Center Obod Cetinje New Montenegro's Development Reality," October 1. https://www.gov.me/en/article/116711%2D%2Dmarina-abramovic-community-center-obod-cetinje-new-montenegro-s-development-reality.

Murgatroyd, B., S. Krenar, and R. Gresa. 2020. *Western Balkans Diaspora: Opportunities for the Region*, 1–30. Briefing: The Balkan Forum.

NATO Press. 2017. "Montenegro Joins NATO as 29th Ally," June 5. https://www.nato.int/cps/en/natohq/news_144647.htm.

Neumann, I.B., and S. Gstöhl. 2004. *Lilliputians in Gulliver's World? Small States in International Relations*. Centre for Small State Studies Institute of International Affairs, Reykjavik: University of Iceland.

Novosad, P., and E. Werker. 2019. "Who Runs the International System? Nationality and Leadership in the United Nations (UN) Secretariat." *Review of International Organizations* 14 (4): 1–33.

OSCE Newsroom. 2006. "Montenegro Welcomed onto OSCE Permanent Council as 56th Participating State," June 22. https://www.osce.org/cio/47461.

———. 2020. "OSCE Chairmanship: Implementing Political Commitments Together, Making a Difference on the Ground Continuing to Strengthen Dialogue to Define Albania's 2020 OSCE Chair," January 1. https://www.osce.org/chairmanship/443215.

Ourbak, T., and A.K. Magnan. 2018. "The Paris Agreement and Climate Change Negotiations: Small Islands, Big Players." *Regional Environmental Change* 18: 2201–7.

Prasad, N. 2013. "Small but Smart: Small States in the Global System." In *The Diplomacies of Small States: Between Vulnerability and Resilience*, eds. A.F. Cooper and T.M. Shaw, 41–65. London: Palgrave Macmillan.

Rothstein, R.L. 1968. *Alliances and Small Powers*. New York: Columbia University Press.

Sandre, A. 2013. "Twitter for Diplomats." Geneva and Rome: Istituto Diplomatico and Diplo Foundation. https://www.diplomacy.edu/topics/digital-diplomacy/#toolfordiplo.

Schwab, K. 2019. *The Global Competitiveness Report 2019*. World Economic Forum. https://www3.weforum.org/docs/WEF_TheGlobalCompetitivenessReport2019.pdf.

Steinsson, S., and B. Thorhallsson. 2019. *Small State Foreign Policy*. OSF Preprints. Oxford: Oxford University Press.

Stuart, E., and E. Samman. 2017. "Defining 'Leave No One Behind.'" Briefing Note, Overseas Development Institute, October.

Thorhallsson, B. 2009. "Can Small States Choose Their Own Size? The Case of a Nordic State—Iceland." In *The Diplomacies of Small States: Between Vulnerability and Resilience*, eds. A.F. Cooper and T.M. Shaw, 119–43. London: Palgrave Macmillan.

———. 2012. "Small States in the UN Security Council: Means of Influence?" *The Hague Journal of Diplomacy* 7: 135–60.

Thorhallsson, B., and S. Steinsson. 2017. "The Small-State Survival Guide to Foreign Policy Success." *National Interest,* September 28. https://nationalinterest.org/feature/the-small-state-survival-guide-foreign-policy-success-22526?nopaging=1.

UN News. 2006. "Annan, General Assembly Welcome Montenegro as 192nd UN Member State," June 28. https://news.un.org/en/story/2006/06/184172-annan-general-assembly-welcome-montenegro-192nd-un-member-state.

———. 2009. "Next Five Non-Permanent Members of Security Council Chosen," October 15. https://news.un.org/en/story/2009/10/317512.

———. 2019a. "UN Chief Hails Victory of 'Political Will' in Historic Republic of North Macedonia Accord," February. https://news.un.org/en/story/2019/02/1032731.

———. 2019b. "St. Vincent and the Grenadines Breaks a Record, as Smallest Ever Security Council Seat Holder," June 7. https://news.un.org/en/story/2019/06/1040071.

———. 2022. "Security Council Fails to Adopt Draft Resolution on Ending Ukraine Crisis, as Russian Federation Wields Veto," February 25. https://www.un.org/press/en/2022/sc14808.doc.htm.

UNESCO. 2012. "Diversity of Cultural Expressions: MACCOC—Project of Marina Abramovic." https://en.unesco.org/creativity/policy-monitoring-platform/maccoc-project-marina-abramovic.

Vital, D. 1971. *The Survival of Small States: Studies in Small Power-Great Power Conflict.* Oxford: Oxford University Press.

29

Urban Diplomacy: How Cities Will Leverage Multilateralism

Juan Luis Manfredi-Sánchez ⓘ

The Urban Planet

The "urban age" (Burdett and Rode 2018) and "planetary urbanization" (Brenner 2014) are terms that describe how the populations, economic initiative, and wealth of cities and urban hinterlands have increased, including the development of multimodal transport and high-speed rail systems. Economic globalization is reflected in those cities concentrating inputs, population, capital, technology, and knowledge (Toly 2017). There are currently around three dozen cities driving global economic growth and attracting migrants, which has resulted in an ever-widening gap between urban and rural areas (Balland et al. 2020). "Superstar cities" (Gyourko et al. 2013) accumulate complex economic activities that require investment and scientific production, in addition to public and private knowledge institutions. New York, London, Paris, Tokyo, Singapore, Beijing, Dubai, and Hong Kong are the "Big Eight" as regards corporate connectivity and globalization (Beaverstock et al. 2017). Global cities are calling for autonomy and decision-making power in a multitude of international activities, thus creating tensions over the exercise of authority and the responsibility for public policy. This group is attempting to set standards in a wide range of fields of public policy, which are eventually adopted by similar cities and then followed by countries. Cities' request for a

J. L. Manfredi-Sánchez (✉)
School of Foreign Service, Georgetown University, Washington, D.C., USA

voice in the global arena is driven by the fact that these cities can address global issues at a local level (climate change and immigration, mobility, migrant integration, waste management, among other key policies) and internationalize domestic issues (city networks, cultural issues, and response to pandemics).

The literature on city diplomacy has revolved around these examples (Friedman 1986; Sassen 2004; Taylor Buck and While 2017; Barber 2017). The novelty lies in the fact that city diplomacy is no longer exclusive to the wealthy cities of the Global North. All cities, irrespective of their size and capabilities, have access to the global agenda and can participate in the globalization/de-globalization process (Haselmayer 2018). That is when the qualitative transition from city to urban diplomacy occurs. They are not isolated cities, but urban territories that participate actively in the management of international affairs and which aspire to cause a splash on the global stage. The metropolitan approach is the consequence of multiple jurisdictions and government levels working on urban issues and sharing responsibility, as well as a symbol of spatial and functional interdependencies materializing public policies or their absence (Trejo Nieto 2022). The dynamics of such metropolitanization highlight the paradoxes of globalization with a plethora of shadow cities (Neuwirth 2016) and the inequalities existing in global cities themselves. Istanbul, Madrid, Jakarta, Tel Aviv, São Paulo, Medellín, Lima, and Manila are good examples of cities with a global agenda (inequality, informal economy, ecological impact, etc.). The urban answer to global problems is learned and copied through networks and informal systems of exchange, regardless of whether they be of a diplomatic or merely political nature (Clerc 2021).

In sum, the leading role played by cities in global issues is one of the most dynamic aspects of diplomatic studies, with three direct consequences. Firstly, the phenomenon has led to an increase in the number of geographical centers of power. Not only do states act and exert influence, but in different parts of the world cities redound to the diversity of actors, opinions, and policies with the wherewithal to change the course of a global issue.

Secondly, cities are currently responding to new demands for power and activism. For both social mobilizations, which channel protests in urban centers, and political leaders, cities are the ideal place for people making themselves heard. The interests of a city, its citizenry, and its political leaders are not expressed in a national context, but in that of local reality: a "city is a far more concrete space for politics than the nation" (Sassen 2004, 655). In other words, cities lead protests against their own country's foreign policy, such as that on immigration and the signing of trade agreements, or in favor of global movements (feminism, anti-racism, etc.).

Thirdly, political geography and demographic change ultimately precede shifts in diplomatic practice. It is difficult to accept that the weakness of states and international organizations represents a real opportunity for cities to increase their power and legitimacy on the international stage. The COVID-19 pandemic, however, has promoted collaboration between cities as prime examples of horizontal and networked structures (Pipa and Bouchet 2020). This is not a zero-sum game against states (vaccinations, travel permits, etc.), but a local response to a global problem.

What Is Urban Diplomacy?

Urban diplomacy contributes to the reform of diplomatic institutions and practices by providing new sources of legitimacy (political power close to the citizen), facilitating the fulfillment of a political agenda (local power with the capacity to solve real, proximate problems), and broadening the actors involved in foreign policy. Urban diplomacy can also serve to recover spaces of trust, bringing international issues closer to public opinion and facilitating cooperation between public and private actors who wish to improve global governance.

City diplomacy, on the other hand, is defined as a "formal strategy in dealing with other governmental and non-governmental actors on the international stage" (Curtis and Acuto 2018, 1). This definition is the most appropriate of all, as it is not limited to legal systems or international agreements, but instead aims to produce a change in the international sphere, together with other public and private actors. Amiri and Sevin (2020, 2) acknowledge the role of cities in international relations, especially in the field of public diplomacy, because "cities are the first physical spaces where foreign publics come to interact with a country, and its people." While Marchetti (2021) considers that cities are playing a significant role in cooperating/competing in an increasingly more decentralized form of globalization.

In their pioneering study, Van der Pluijm and Melissen (2007, 6) narrow the definition of city diplomacy as follows: "The institutions and processes by which cities engage in relations with actors on an international political stage with the aim of representing themselves and their interests to one another." The authors identify six dimensions or areas of activity in this respect: security, development, economy, culture, networks, and representation. For their part, Lefèvre and d'Albergo (2007, 317) have coined the term "political internationalization" to describe how cities started to participate in environmental agenda setting.

The transition from city to urban diplomacy occurs when at least one of the political actors promoting an international strategy is a city located in a dynamic territory, when the agenda is global (technology, gender, employment, immigration, and housing) and has the support of civil society (civic activism, the business community, and local leaders) and when it has a recognizable political leader (normally a mayor with a strong social media presence).

Urban diplomacy is a new object of analysis in the field of international studies. As against a city diplomacy model (i.e., the actions that are planned by major cities in their own interests, in the shape of investments, influence, tourism, and events), its urban counterpart results from the citizenry's demands for a global approach to local problems, a sort of extension of citizenship above and beyond the nation-state. The expression of identity, the gender perspective and the impact of climate change, plus policies on migration, mobility, and digital transformation are just some of the issues at stake. New citizen rights and demands, plus new habits and agendas, thus emerge. All this connects with the principles of cosmopolitanism which ignore political borders, passports, and nationalities. Urban diplomacy has an impact on the ordinary practice of international relations, even though the results are to date not that spectacular.

Urban diplomacy is by nature public. It is deliberated on and exercised in the public sphere, because it emerges when individuals and social initiatives connect with other global currents. Whereby the relevance of public and symbolic communication which allows them to classify themselves as "sanctuary cities" (Bauder 2016), "age-friendly cities" (WHO Age-Friendly Cities Framework), and "gender equal cities" or "feminist cities," and to identify with these transversal demands, among others. Transversality comes from the incorporation of groups (social and neighborhood movements, NGOs, etc.) to the construction of political proposals. The groups are not organized along traditional political lines (progressive-conservative), but around a particular public issue and, for this reason, are known to integrate different groups across political lines.

Urban diplomacy is also replicable, contributes to improve the quality of life of the citizenry, and does not depend on a city's size, economic strength, resources, or capital status. City diplomacy, which is based on the third-party recognition of the powerful influence and impact of major cities, is a centrifugal phenomenon: from globalization to the city. In contrast, urban diplomacy is completely the opposite: from local to global issues, urban centers promote a culture of collective online work. Neither sovereignty nor ideology is at stake, but the resolution of specific problems, usually involving the externalities of globalization.

This is why urban diplomacy is based on specific and applicable solutions on an urban scale. It involves public policies that require planning and management, not international political ambition (Burke 2021). This perspective makes a relevant contribution (although neither ideological nor argumentative) to global governance. The political connotations of urban solutions have nothing to do with traditional standards or the left-right dichotomy, but with others associated with the post-pandemic world: open or closed international flows, globalizing or de-globalizing, identity- or citizen-oriented. Urban diplomacy requires its own global political culture, because it is not a by-product of the external action of states.

Nonetheless, there are a number of risks. Urban diplomacy causes a rift in pursuit of the interests of the citizenry, according to geography, and exploits differences (Schragger 2016; Rodden 2019; Fukuyama 2020; Dijkstra et al. 2019). The convergence between the urban agenda and the challenges of globalization promotes the phenomenon known as "new localism" (Katz and Nowak 2018). This concept points to the need to leverage the power of cities for resolving global problems with tangible, less biased, multi-stakeholder solutions, namely a sort of practical, non-ideological management. The real power be connected not only to traditional structures but also to the capacity to address social and political challenges such as climate change. Localism reclaims the space for cities, networks, and civic actors to solve contemporary problems, and innovating governance institutions in the process.

Political and Legal Development Differs According to Setting

In the United States, urban diplomacy has gained ground over the past few years. Progress is being made in the "City and State Diplomacy Act" (Lieu and Wilson 2019), whose aim is to coordinate the external action of state governors and mayors with that of their international colleagues, with an eye to addressing issues inherent or exclusive to the territories that they represent (AFSA 2022). By the same token, the act foresees the creation of a "State Department office of subnational diplomacy" as a direct communication channel with the federal government. This piece of legislation chimes with the post-Donald Trump administration vision of "foreign policy that works for middle-class Americans." It is thus a multifaceted project (Pipa and Bouchet 2021) with the following objectives: to drum up support for economic promotion, to regain the credibility of the United States, to explore new approaches to soft power, and to promote cooperation and measures aimed at resolving problems relating to global public goods. At present, the act has an economic and commercial goal, while avoiding any criticism of federal foreign policy, whose affects are unequal depending on the state (energy, commerce, climate change, environmental protection, migration, and public healthcare). In short, these legislative developments attempt to provide local international departments in New York, Los Angeles, and Austin, among others, which are already developing their own global action agendas, with legal coverage.

In the European Union, the local and sub-state dimensions form part of the subsidiary nature of the European institutions. Here, cities design different strategies aimed at influencing the political and legal spheres, beyond the conventional institutions, in order to obtain funding, to become involved in institutional development, and to coordinate requests for action or community services (Terruso 2016; Trobiani 2016). They have been recognized by the Urban Agenda for the EU since 2016, an approach that adapts European policies and legislation to the urban space (Armondi 2020).

The agenda has 14 priority themes managed by four partnerships: "Urban Poverty; Inclusion of Migrants and Refugees; Air Quality; Housing; Digital Transition; Urban Mobility; Jobs and Skills in the Local Economy; Circular Economy; Sustainable Use of Land; Climate Adaptation; Public Procurement; Energy Transition; Culture/Cultural Heritage; and Security in Public Spaces." Each partnership is independent and participation is on a voluntary basis. Urban diplomacy is under the aegis of the Committee of the Regions as a multilateral instrument (Conference of Regional and Local Authorities for the Eastern Partnership and the Euro-Mediterranean Regional and Local Assembly). But the arrangement is insufficient. European cities lack mechanisms for cooperation in institutions, because precedence is given to the state dimension, a situation that city networks have been incapable of altering. The limited interpretation of global action frames cities in an internal or intra-European context, but not as international agents (Parkes 2020). The tendency toward the centralization of policy-making and the de-Europeanization of agendas (Müller et al. 2021) at the expense of the European Commission and Parliament reduces their real capacity for action. In practice, this state-centric vision limits the European Union's effectiveness.

In Latin America, special mention should go to the Mercociudades (founded in 1995) initiative of Mercosur (Argentina, Brazil, Paraguay, and Uruguay 1991), with 11 founding cities. The process of regional integration focuses on investments, infrastructures, migration, employment, environmental protection, public healthcare, mobility, and the impact on two dimensions of cooperation (Juste and Oddone 2020). At a regional level, these cities lead projects and territorial development, while at an international level, they symbolize new spaces for social participation and democratic quality in the region. At present, Mercociudades is formed by 364 cities from 10 Latin American countries (with Venezuela, Chile, Bolivia, Ecuador, Peru, and Colombia joining the founders), organized in 15 units and 7 working groups.

In the Association of Southeast Asian Nations (ASEAN), urban diplomacy operates in the technological (Smart Cities Network) and environmental dimensions (Initiative on Environmentally Sustainable Cities), with a view to allowing for the participation of local and corporate actors in agenda setting.

In the African Union (AU), for its part, the urban issue is addressed in the Specialized Technical Committee on Public Service, Local Government, Urban Development, and Decentralization. It does not foresee specialized initiatives, but actions at an interstate level. The most noteworthy aspect is its interest in the impact of climate change on territorial development.

As a response to the dwindling power of states, cities are gaining authority to act in the international sphere, either individually or in networks, and to take specific actions linked to their own interests. Cities operate on the international stage as a legitimate, effective source of power for the transformation of political realities and for connecting citizens with global politics.

Based on these political and legislative developments, a different definition is proposed here:

> Urban diplomacy consists of the systematic and politically motivated management of international affairs for the defense of local interests. It puts diplomatic tools to an innovative use, with special emphasis on political and symbolic communication. The success of initiatives depends on the extent to which the citizenry want to become involved in international affairs to express their own opinions, rather than on a city's size, national context or own resources.

Urban Diplomacy in Action

It is often contended that urban diplomatic initiatives are the result of a crisis of a state or multilateral institutions. However, this is not the case. States continue to be the main players in international relations, providing security and solid institutions, as well as border control and hard power. Consequently, urban diplomacy will never replace relations between states. The challenge for conventional diplomacy is to incorporate the advantages of urban diplomacy into foreign policy operations. Cities can leverage political action agendas, mobilize public opinion, identify new problems or social demands, legitimize decisions and deliver new results, outside traditional channels. Traditional diplomatic institutions (ministries of foreign affairs, embassies, consulates, treaties, agreements, etc.) follow a state-centric pattern of international relations. Cities have not created new institutions or norms that vie with them, but have extended their use, have promoted new mechanisms of cooperation, and have signed local agreements. The expression "city foreign policy" frequently appears in the literature, but it poses an epistemological problem insofar as the citizenry tend to view it in terms of its similarities and differences as regards state foreign policy and the practice of diplomacy. It is important to avoid drawing parallels between theoretical constructs. The approach "is not intended to diminish the still considerable diplomatic skills required but may better capture their focus on the connectivity of people, goods and services, and ideas" (Hutzler 2019, 15). Cities are where real coordinated global governance is applied (Rosenau and Czempiel 1992).

Urban diplomacy extends global governance (Roberts 2016) and places local decisions at the top of the growing agenda of global issues (see Table 29.2). Urban diplomacy involves a range of activities aimed at exerting an influence on the international stage with an agenda of its own. The external projects implemented by cities are unique, depending on their geographical location, political tradition, economic activity, or cultural strength (see Tables 29.1 and 29.2).

The success of urban diplomacy depends on the capacity of mayors to lead proposals aligned with the interests of citizenry: Beall and Adam (2017, 23) describe success as rooted in a program which is "organic and consistent with the reality and interests of a city's citizens." The urban diplomacy agenda responds to concrete interests and is built through participation and accountability. Thus, although the mayor's role is central, neighborhood movements,

Table 29.1 City diplomacy (Acuto et al. 2018)

City diplomacy	Key characteristics
Place-based global engagement	Cities as international actors engaging with local markets, politics, and cultures
Local foreign policy	International engagement and a more explicit and modern foreign policy
City twinning and bilateral relations	City-to-city bilateral relations and engagement. Long track record
City networks	A mix of place-based global engagement and growing local foreign policy connected with national and international actors
Non-local city networking	Globalizing connections between city councils and the world

Table 29.2 Urban diplomacy

Urban diplomacy	Key characteristics
The quest for an urban agenda	Global issues need local response. From climate change to immigration, all these issues impact local agenda, despite the diversity of government levels
Innovation	Cities improve global governance. Diplomacy by advocacy, not by passing rules or contesting sovereignty
Tools	Communication and symbolic proposals. They refer to non-regulatory action, but they affect decision-making, compromise political positions, and coordinate civil society action
Limitation	Refers to the legitimacy of the political project, the resources. State unity in the field of external action and foreign policy
Diplomatic theory impact	The city cohesively responds to globalization. Despite its limited executive capacity, the city manages in a more agile way, responds concretely to the problems of citizenship, and does not deal with problems of nationality, territory, or borders. This practical vision facilitates the incorporation of plural voices under the political leadership of the mayor, often empowered in social media

business groups, civil society actors, and local leaders also shape urban diplomacy. It is not a closed phenomenon, organized through the chancellery or professional diplomats, but is open to collective action.

Therefore, it is not a question of internationalizing the agenda by any means, but of understanding local concerns and giving them a global perspective. Woods (2015, 62) explains that the success of urban diplomacy initiatives lies in the selection of undertakings and priorities, for which reason they "should narrow their focus while deepening their engagement. They should tackle only the serious, collective-action problems, and they need to tackle these with their full concentration." However, there are some consequences for theoretical development in this field. As already observed, urban diplomacy is developed by practice.

Wang and Amiri (2019) have completed the practical analysis by identifying the roles developed by cities with a global perspective. Urban economic development influences the tourism industry, foreign investment, and business opportunities. In the field of diplomatic representation, consulates attend to the needs of the already established migrant population and diasporas (Alejo 2022). Diplomatic institutions connect with local activity in cultural life, schools, and decision-making centers. Collaboration expands networks and alliances, settings in which cities share best practices and bring pressure to bear on governments in relation to issues in which they have a stake. The fourth role is social empowerment, an issue of interest to populations with a strong presence of foreigners. Learning to coexist with other cultures, religions, and customs enriches social life. Lastly, cities take center stage when they organize and host international events (Olympic Games, cultural festivals, congresses, encounters, etc.).

A Practical Orientation Allows for Identifying Outcomes

In the case of place-oriented global engagement, place-branding initiatives, heritage management, and recognition of the value of a territory stand out. Urban diplomacy aspires to surpass fast-food policy models and marketing campaigns to attract tourists and investors (Vanolo 2020). The objective is to transform local activity with global proposals that redefine the attributes of a city.

Paris has promoted "The 15-minute City" model, whose purpose is to transform urban planning in order that basic services (education, culture, healthcare, etc.) are close at hand. Fostering the use of bicycles and reorganizing communal spaces are specific measures for reducing traffic, promoting local businesses, and countering speculation in city centers. Still in the process of being defined, the model is currently being discussed in Melbourne, Barcelona, Milan, and London, above all owing to the drive of collectives of citizens interested in reviewing the basic principles of urban planning.

Place-oriented global engagement allows for transferring universal values to a territory. The Hay Festivals initiative is a cultural diplomacy benchmark organized by cities. Arequipa, Segovia, and Querétaro, to name but a few, have leveraged the initiative to renew their cultural offerings and, during one week, to become the epicenter of the global literary scene. Although it has the institutional support of British diplomacy, it is a charity with public and private backing, organized in nine chapters and four local forums with an independent agenda and activities. Public debate, the participation of prominent artists and writers, as well as a supplementary agenda, enable cities organizing the festival to attract tourists and, at the same time, to activate their cultural economy (bookshops, concert halls, universities, etc.). In this category, the Davos Forum, the Perugia International Journalism Festival, and the Aspen Ideas Festival are also good examples.

Reputation attracts tourists, non-permanent residents, and investments. Dubai has committed itself to the internationalization of its educational services through the promotion of the Dubai International Academic City (DIAC). It touts itself as "MENA's largest educational hub," with 30 institutions offering undergraduate and postgraduate programs and around 27,000 students from all over the world. With local delegations from British, French, U.S., Indian, and Swiss universities, this educational initiative has reinforced the diplomacy of the United Arab Emirates, which aims to consolidate its position as a partner open to economic development based on science and industry.

In the field of local foreign policy, climate change appears in most of the literature (Bäckstrand et al. 2017). The UN Climate Change Conferences (COP) have been expanded to make room for local initiatives (e.g., the Cities Race to Zero campaign under the C40 leadership, which calls for a "healthy, resilient, zero carbon recovery") and citizen participation. Cities link national political decisions to everyday life, revealing the consequences of acting to reduce global warming and emissions. In practice, cities provide the data for nationally determined contributions (NDC), which are the aggregate of local data. By aggregation, transparent local data improve national policies. While, for its part, local accountability increases the quality and capacity of monitoring, along with the sharing of best practices with other stakeholders, private partners, and voters, inasmuch as the local scale requires *sui generis* metrics and indicators.

In the political sphere, the Pact of Free Cities is a local political initiative with a European impact (2019). The mayors of Budapest, Warsaw, Prague, and Bratislava are conveying an inclusive, pro-European message to counter ultra-nationalist and populist discourses contrary to the principles of the European Union. Leading the Visegrad Group, these mayors defend a "progressive network of dynamic cities," with proposals based on freedom, human dignity, democracy, sustainability, equality, the rule of law, social justice, tolerance, and cultural diversity. The urban defense of the community acquis breaks with the rhetorical unity of the member states of the Visegrad Group, frequently portrayed as a conservative bloc contrary to the European Union. It is not a question of symbolic positioning. The aim of the pact is to enable cities themselves to receive European resources and funds without needing the approval of their national governments. While they do not want to pay the price of the diplomatic pressures of political conditionality, these cities do indeed embrace European values and want to manage their own funds, without having to obtain the prior authorization of the states to which they belong. So, the case of Free Cities chimes with the proposal of Amiri and Kihlgren (2021) for cities that combine moral principles with their own interests, above and beyond state institutions.

Another city, Barcelona, is a good example of how to expand international activities. With over 100 diplomatic missions, the city hosts the headquarters of the Union for the Mediterranean, plus the regional offices of relevant international organizations including the WHO Office for Health Systems Strengthening (WHO/Europe), the UN-HABITAT City Resilience Profiling Programme (UN-Habitat/CRPP), the Global Water Operators' Partnerships Alliance (UN-Habitat/GWOPA), the United Nations University Institute on Globalization, Culture, and Mobility (UNU-GCM), the Global University Network for Innovation (GUNI), and the European Forest Institute (EFI). In addition, as one of the leading cities in global municipalism, it hosts the headquarters of the main international city networks, such as United Cities and Local Governments (UCLG), Metropolis, and MedCities (Roig 2018).

Security issues are reflected on the urban agenda by the development of mediation capabilities, for cities play a diplomatic role when they facilitate encounters between groups in conflict in their different phases. Both cities and networks can become involved in the prevention and resolution of conflicts and rebuilding relations following them. The Mayors for Peace initiative currently involves 8063 cities promoting the abolition of nuclear weapons and a global conflict-resolution agenda (hunger and poverty, refugees, human rights, and environmental protection).

In the multilateral sphere, the opinions of cities make logical sense at UN conferences, the meetings of multilateral organizations, and public diplomacy events (Barnett and Parnell 2016). However, cities are not systematically involved in international policy-making, with the exception of the UN-Habitat conferences. According to the New Urban Agenda, which was adopted in Quito in 2016, the development of local authorities aims to increase the implementation of long-term projects with the power to plan, fund, and have an impact on the development of sustainability policies. In this respect, mention should go to the "pro-urban consensus" (Abdullah 2019, 10) in the adoption of Sustainable Development Goals (hereinafter SDGs) 10 and 11. SDGs represent the model of implementation of global decisions, promoted by states in the international community, at a local level. The recognition of these local capabilities ought to involve the explicit recognition of the constraints of the current model of global governance.

Urban diplomacy creates its own multilateral institutions, the most relevant of which is the Global Parliament of Mayors (GPM), which brings together mayors, national representatives, and those of multilateral institutions with a view to promoting the role of cities in global issues. It is defined as a "city rights movement," an advocacy initiative aimed "at creating a platform, an assembly of the political leaders of cities (the mayors), to become a voice in the global debate, as global leaders to defend the urban solutions to planetary challenges" (Global Parliament of Mayors 2022).

Bilateral relations allow for connecting two territories sharing geographical, sectoral, or functional interests. The traditional "sister cities" have given way to other types of inter-territorial relations. The Trade and Services Desk between California and Mexico is a new tool to discuss common interests in jobs, investment, capacities, and commercial services. The bureau creates new spaces for public and private collaboration and for dialogue between political representatives, as well as leveraging its own economic promotion agenda by mixing official jurisdictions. In open markets, cities make the most of their assets to improve their competitive edge. London is making good use of the post-Brexit period to revamp its financial services, to promote initiatives for attracting global talent (visas), and to digitize its activities. Although its economic activity has fallen by around 10 percent, the city continues to be appealing in terms of reputation, business-friendliness, services, and infrastructure. On the other side of the English Channel, Amsterdam is expanding its global financial services in order to attract those financial institutions and businesses that have decided to leave London following Brexit.

At an operational level, urban diplomacy implements its repertoire of action through networks in which actors engage in dialogue and negotiations, facilitate public diplomacy, share best practices, encourage collaboration between international private and public entities, and, ultimately, influence world politics (Acuto and Leffel 2021). As noted by Dan Koon-gong Chan (2016, 138), "Non-state actors can organize into transnational networks more readily than state actors." These same concerns can be approached from a local perspective. Acuto and Rayner (2016, 1149–50) define city networks "as formalized organizations with cities as their main members and characterized by reciprocal and established patterns of communications, policy-making and exchange," offering more than 200 examples with distinctive organizational profiles, capabilities, or political aims. The competitive edge of city networks lies in the scalability of their proposals and solutions. The application of real, specific solutions adapted to a territory allows for the inclusion of a growing number of cities. City networks have also gained traction, with examples such as C40 Cities or the Global Covenant of Mayors for Climate and Energy (GCoM). The first has innovated with the creation of "Urban 20." This space coordinates the action of the cities in the G20 group, so that urban demands have continuity over and above the specific interests of each member state. The second facilitates the exchange of data, knowledge, and best practices in the management and mitigation of climate change. Regardless of the commitment of each national government, cities can implement public policies, with an international vocation, but on a local scale.

The "non-municipal city networking" category includes those social, corporate, and citizen initiatives that have an international echo. The resolution of migratory issues on the urban agenda takes the shape of non-discriminatory access to public services and advocacy campaigns for social and economic integration (Thouez 2020). The political benchmark in this respect is the Marrakech Mayors Declaration (2018), signed by more than 80 cities, in favor of the UN Global Compact for Migration (GCM), plus policy frameworks like the Global Forum on Migration and Development (GFMD) (Oomen 2020). Cities do not dispute the monopoly of states in migration policy. The interest of these urban initiatives lies in the recognition of the city's role in managing the consequences of international migration, so that its voice must be heard in the search for practical solutions, oriented toward the care of people arriving in cities, regardless of their legal status. In the same vein, there is a growing interest in diasporas as catalysts of local-international connections, above all in border cities (Bravo and De Moya 2021).

In light of the increase in migration, connecting with communities can accelerate regulation processes, identify problems and expectations, foster integration, broaden cultural life, and reduce health problems. The incorporation of civil society actors (clubs, churches, non-governmental organizations, neighborhood associations, etc.) is fundamental for the success of such initiatives. This category includes promoting gender equality policies. The aim of the City Hub and Network for Gender Equity (CHANGE) (2020) initiative is to create cities that allow for the public expression of identities. Mexico DF, Barcelona, Tokyo, Freetown, London, and Los Angeles are sharing good practices, data, and indicators so as to achieve their objectives.

In sum, urban diplomacy is about more than identifying global issues than defining the concept of city or major city. This perspective allows for identifying geographical spaces of political action that combine representation, legitimacy, and capabilities. In cities, global issues interest the local authorities, the citizenry, multinationals, and minorities. For this reason, urban diplomacy fosters international political action.

Conclusions

The aim of this chapter has been to define urban diplomacy in the post-COVID-19 world (Florida et al. 2021). Global debates on climate change, public healthcare, science and innovation, continuing education, migration, tourism, mobility, political identity/citizenship, and economic development are all issues with a place on urban agendas, insofar as cities ultimately suffer their consequences. The expansion of urban agendas and action plans has repercussions for the practice of diplomacy and involves some aspects that should be considered in these conclusions. Cities are one of the driving forces behind innovation in diplomatic theory and practice, whose two core tenets remain unchanged, namely negotiation and the representation of interests in accordance with a set of political principles of action and relations with foreign actors. Nowadays, it is hard to accept that those actors are only nation-states.

The implications that the foregoing has for diplomatic theory are as follows:

As to political philosophy, cities represent one of the first experiments in hybrid governance in the post-Westphalian and post-liberal world. Their political and representative nature allows for reviewing the legitimacy of decisions and for promoting new agreements, not necessarily rooted in the rigidness of international law or national electoral cycles. The defense of the liberal order needs new support beyond sovereignty, nationality, and territory. The political space of the city has encouraged debate on how we should approach an orderly exit from the chaos in the midst of the de-globalization process. Cities will probably be the keystone of post-liberal cosmopolitanism. In contrast to traditional studies, based on cleavage politics or global governance, urban diplomacy allows for interpreting the global agenda from a different perspective. The political and institutional leadership of cities connects the demands of social movements with local interests. Ultimately, mayors with a global projection are fundamental. Their ability to understand global problems and to offer local solutions to them will make it possible to advance in a shared agenda. It is not a question of coming up with an alternative to nation-states—a sort of macro republic of cities—but to make room for urban institutions in international political agenda setting. In practice, urban diplomacy is a counterweight to anti-diplomatic practices that have become established in the international community and to the deinstitutionalizing current of diplomacy. The value of mayors in urban diplomacy is emphasized because they are the individuals who legitimize local decisions, provide cohesive messages, and facilitate international recognition. Mayors represent the pluralism of voices, although their policy proposals require political vision and operational capacity. Mayors' efforts do not operate in a vacuum, but require the express support of economic initiatives, neighborhood movements, and other council colleagues. The friendly face of urban diplomacy is the mayor, but the legitimacy of his or her proposals and their long-term sustainability depend on his or her ability to connect with citizen and business interests, with public and private actors, and with other sources of power.

The second relevant question has to do with the effectiveness of the measures adopted by cities. Urban diplomacy does not pursue the substitution of the existing international legal framework or the creation of new norms. The success of urban diplomacy lies in the management of global issues from a local perspective and operates with de facto efforts (declarations, non-regulatory agreements, the sharing of best practices, etc.). Willingness to cooperate and to participate in common projects is more relevant than adapting to an international legal system. Multilateral governance, through the incorporation of cities, should not make the practice of diplomacy more difficult, but should encourage the subsidiary implementation of the decisions of the international community. Future research on urban diplomacy should inquire more deeply into the mechanisms employed so as to make sure that decisions are lasting and assessable, and to contribute to the creation of legal certainty. In this connection, urban diplomacy develops as an epistemic and practical community through networks of collective action. This perspective offers hope for a structural review of multilateral diplomacy. During the pandemic, the concept of "national interest" blocked initiatives, joint projects, and best practices with ominous consequences.

The third aspect is the professionalization of urban diplomacy. The consolidation of global cities makes it necessary to reconsider the professional role of diplomats and ministries of foreign affairs in the future. On the one hand, the institutions of nation-states ought to incorporate cities in the decision-making process and not only in the implementation stage. Mayors and local public workers should have a greater say in the design and prioritization of foreign policy. On the other hand, cities ought to professionalize their international activities with career diplomats, who can work in both these institutions and ministries of foreign affairs. It is not a question of creating a new professional body within the administration, but to facilitate the transition from the state to the local sphere. Together with career diplomats, cities should also bring on board professionals from other fields (business and social leaders, university professors, journalists and artists, etc.). The incorporation of professionals from other areas of knowledge and fields impacts the ethical framework of traditional diplomacy. This aspect of urban diplomacy is a promising avenue for research on training, negotiating styles, risk relationships, corporate and institutional culture, and professional careers.

Fourthly, the urban perspective allows for incorporating non-Western cities in diplomatic studies and for broadening the corpus of case studies and practices. In the race to understand the global world, the international action of Jakarta, Rio de Janeiro, Manila, and Cape Town will help to introduce globalization in other regions and to create new research agendas. Cities as units of social science facilitate the analysis of political action and diplomatic and communication practices in a more uniform and comprehensive manner.

In conclusion, urban diplomacy is a laboratory of innovation and change in the uses and purposes of conventional diplomacy. In diplomatic management, it places new social and citizen demands on the agenda more swiftly. It allows for identifying the specific challenges and unintended consequences of globalization/de-globalization. As to professional aspects, it facilitates the incorporation of new profiles in executive positions, without the need for resorting to the centrality of ministries of foreign affairs. This new blood revamps procedures and lays the foundations for a new corporate culture more open to change and accountability. In the organizational dimension, cities can generate a multiplier effect and contribute to build a bridge between global challenges and ordinary life, while defending political and institutional pluralism. As problem resolution and practical orientation are good management principles, the multiplication of levels or red tape should be avoided. The role of urban diplomacy is to resolve problems—not to contest nation-states—to coordinate agendas and to renew foreign policy instruments. In sum, the phenomenon is good news for the profession, academia, and citizenry as a whole.

References and Further Reading

Abdullah, H., ed. 2019. *Cities in World Politics. Local Responses to Global Challenges*. Barcelona: CIDOB Centre Barcelona Centre for International Affairs.

Acuto, M., H. Decramer, J. Kerr, I. Klaus, and S. Tabory. 2018. "Toward City Diplomacy: Assessing Capacity in Select Global Cities." Chicago Council on Global Affairs, February 7. https://www.thechicagocouncil.org/publication/toward-city-diplomacy-assessing-capacity-select-global-cities.

Acuto, M., and B. Leffel. 2021. "Understanding the Global Ecosystem of City Networks." *Urban Studies* 59 (9): 1758–74.

Acuto, M., and S. Rayner. 2016. "City Networks: Breaking Gridlocks or Forging (New) Lock-ins?" *International Affairs* 92: 1147–66.

American Foreign Service Association (AFSA). 2022. "On a New Approach to City and State Diplomacy." *Foreign Service Journal* 99 (1): 20–21.

Alejo, A. 2022. "Diasporas as Actors in Urban Diplomacy." *The Hague Journal of Diplomacy* 17 (1): 138–50.

Amiri, S., and L. Kihlgren Grandi. 2021. "Cities as Public Diplomacy Actors. Combining Moral 'Good' with Self-interest." In *The Frontiers of Public Diplomacy: Hegemony, Morality, and Power in the International Sphere*, ed. C.B. Alexander, 146–58. London: Routledge.

Amiri, S., and E. Sevin, eds. 2020. *City Diplomacy: Current Trends and Future Prospects*. Cham: Palgrave Macmillan.

Armondi, S. 2020. *The Urban Agenda for the European Union: EU Governmentality and Urban Sovereignty in New EU-City Relations?* The Urban Book Series. Cham: Springer.

Bäckstrand, K., J.W. Kuyper, B.-O. Linnér, and E. Lövbrand. 2017. "Non-State Actors in Global Climate Governance: From Copenhagen to Paris and Beyond." *Environmental Politics* 26 (4): 561–79.

Balland, P.A., C.I. Jara-Figueroa, S. Petralia, M. Steijn, D.L. Rigby, and C. Hidalgo. 2020. "Complex Economic Activities Concentrate in Large Cities." *SSRN Electronic Journal* 4: 248–54.

Barber, B. 2017. *Cool Cities: Urban Sovereignty and the Fix for Global Warming*. New Haven: Yale University Press.

Barnett, C., and S. Parnell. 2016. "Ideas, Implementation, and Indicators: Epistemologies of the Post-2015 Urban Agenda." *Environment Urbanization* 28 (1): 87–98.

Bauder, H. 2016. "Sanctuary Cities: Policies and Practices in International Perspective." *International Migration* 55 (2): 174–87.

Beall, J., and D. Adam. 2017. *Cities, Prosperity and Influence: The Role of City Diplomacy in Shaping Soft Power in the 21st Century*. London: The British Council.

Beaverstock, J.V., R.G. Smith, and P.J. Taylor. 2017. *The World According to GaWC 2016*. Loughborough: Loughborough University. http://www.lboro.ac.uk/gawc/world2016t.html.

Bravo, V., and M. De Moya. 2021. "Introduction: Diasporas from Latin America and Their Role in Public Diplomacy." In *Latin American Diasporas in Public Diplomacy*, eds. V. Bravo and M. De Moya, 1–24. Cham: Palgrave Macmillan.

Brenner, N., ed. 2014. *Implosions/Explosions: Towards a Study of Planetary Urbanization*. Berlin: Jovis Verlag.

Burdett, R., and P. Rode, eds. 2018. *Shaping Cities in an Urban Age*. London: Phaidon Press.

Burke, L. 2021. "Threats to Democracy: City Edition." German Marshall Foundation, August 12. https://www.gmfus.org/news/threats-democracy-city-edition.

Clerc, L. 2021. "A Different View on City Diplomacy: Mid-sized Baltic Towns and Their International Contacts." *Diplomatica* 3 (1): 180–86.

Curtis, S., and M. Acuto. 2018. "The Foreign Policy of Cities." *RUSI Journal* 163 (6): 8–17.

Dijkstra, L., H. Poelman, and A. Rodríguez-Pose. 2019. "The Geography of EU Discontent." *Regional Studies* 54 (6): 737–53.

Florida, R., A. Rodríguez-Pose, and M. Storper. 2021. "Cities in a Post-COVID World." *Urban Studies*: 1–23.

Friedman, J. 1986. "The World City Hypothesis." *Development and Change* 17 (1): 69–83.

Fukuyama, F. 2020. "30 Years of World Politics: What Has Changed?" *Journal of Democracy* 31 (1): 11–21.

Global Parliament of Mayors. 2022. "Why Join the GPM?" https://globalparliamentofmayors.org/faqs/.

Gyourko, J., C. Mayer, and T. Sinai. 2013. "Superstar Cities." *American Economic Journal: Economic Policy* 5 (4): 167–99.

Haselmayer, S. 2018. "The De-Globalized City." *New Global Studies* 12 (1): 65–73.

Hutzler, K. 2019. *America's Cities on the World Stage. A Report on How U.S. Cities Are Deepening Their International Engagement*. Los Angeles: Figueroa Press. https://uscpublicdiplomacy.org/sites/uscpublicdiplomacy.org/files/America%27s_Cities_on_the_World_Stage_Web_12.17.19.pdf.

Juste, S., and N. Oddone. 2020. "Aportes teóricos para el estudio de la cooperación transfronteriza de unidades subestatales de doble periferia." *Cuadernos de Política Exterior Argentina* 132: 63–78.

Katz, B., and J. Nowak. 2018. *The New Localism. How Cities Can Thrive in the Age of Populism*. Washington, D.C.: Brookings Institution Press.

Koon-hong Chan, D. 2016. "City Diplomacy and 'Glocal' Governance: Revitalizing Cosmopolitan Democracy." *Innovation: The European Journal of Social Science Research* 29 (2): 134–60.

Lefèvre, C., and E. d'Albergo. 2007. "Why Cities Are Looking Abroad and How They Go About It." *Environment and Planning C: Government and Policy* 25 (3): 317–26.

Lieu, T., and J. Wilson. 2019. H.R. 3571—City and State Diplomacy Act. U.S. Congress.

Marchetti, R. 2021. *City Diplomacy. From City-States to Global Cities*. Ann Arbor: University of Michigan Press.

Müller, P., K. Pomorska, and B. Tonra. 2021. "The Domestic Challenge to EU Foreign Policy-making: From Europeanisation to de-Europeanisation?" *Journal of European Integration* 43 (5): 519–34.

Neuwirth, R. 2016. *Shadow Cities: A Billion Squatters, a New Urban World*. London: Routledge.

Oomen, B. 2020. "Decoupling and Teaming Up: The Rise and Proliferation of Transnational Municipal Networks in the Field of Migration." *International Migration Review* 54 (3): 913–39.

Parkes, R. 2020. *City Diplomacy: The EU's Hidden Capacity to Act*. Berlin: DGAP Policy Brief.

Pipa, A.F., and M. Bouchet. 2020. "Multilateralism Restored? City Diplomacy in the COVID-19 Era." *The Hague Journal of Diplomacy* 15 (4): 599–610.

———. 2021. "Partnership Among Cities, States, and the Federal Government: Creating an Office of Subnational Diplomacy at the U.S. Department of State." Washington, D.C.: Brookings Institution. https://www.brookings.edu/research/partnership-among-cities-states-and-the-federal-government-creating-an-office-of-subnational-diplomacy-at-the-us-department-of-state/.

Roberts, B.H. 2016. "The New Urban Agenda Needs to Recognize a Future of City-to-City Networks and Trade." *Citiscope*, June 14. http://citiscope.org/

habitatIII/commentary/2016/06/new-urbanagenda-needs-recognize-future-city-city-networks-and-trade.

Rodden, J.A. 2019. *Why Cities Lose: The Deep Roots of the Urban-Rural Political Divide*. New York: Basic.

Roig, A. 2018. *Towards a City-led Science Diplomacy: The Rise of Cities in a Multilateral World and Their Role in a Science-driven Global Governance*. Barcelona: United Nations Institute for Training and Research.

Rosenau, J.N., and E.-O. Czempiel, eds. 1992. *Governance without Government: Order and Change in World Politics*. Cambridge: Cambridge University Press.

Sassen, S. 2004. "Local Actors in Global Politics." *Current Sociology* 52 (4): 649–70.

Schragger, R. 2016. *City Power. Urban Governance in a Global Age*. Oxford: Oxford University Press.

Taylor Buck, N., and A. While. 2017. "Competitive Urbanism and the Limits to Smart City Innovation: The UK Future Cities Initiative." *Urban Studies* 54 (2): 501–19.

Terruso, F. 2016. "Complementing Traditional Diplomacy: Regional and Local Authorities Going International." *European View* 15 (2): 325–34.

Thouez, C. 2020. "Cities as Emergent International Actors in the Field of Migration Evidence from the Lead-up and Adoption of the UN Global Compacts on Migration and Refugees." *Global Governance* 26 (4): 650–72.

Toly, N. 2017. "Brexit, Global Cities, and the Future of the Global Order." *Globalizations* 14 (1): 142–49.

Trejo-Nieto, A. 2022. "A Framework for Contextualizing Metropolitan Governance in Latin America." In *Metropolitan Governance in Latin America*, eds. A. Trejo-Nieto and J.L. Niño Amézquita, 23–48. London: Routledge.

Trobbiani, R. 2016. *European Regions in Brussels: Towards Functional Interest Representation?* Bruges: Bruges Political Research Papers, no. 53.

Van der Pluijm, R., and J. Melissen. 2007. *City Diplomacy. The Expanding Role of Cities in International Politics*. The Hague: Netherlands Institute of International Relations.

Vanolo, A. 2020. "Cities Are Not Products." *Tijdschrift voor Economische en Sociale Geografie* 111 (1): 10–17.

Wang, J., and S. Amiri. 2019. *Building a Capacity Framework for U.S. City Diplomacy*. Los Angeles: U.S.C. Center on Public Diplomacy.

Woods, N. 2015. "New Governance Architecture." In *Outlook on the Global Agenda 2015*, eds. Klaus Schwabe et al., 60–63. Geneva: World Economic Forum. https://www3.weforum.org/docs/GAC14/WEF_GAC14_OutlookGlobalAgenda_Report.pdf.

30

Reforming Global Health Diplomacy in the Wake of COVID-19

Mark C. Storella

Introduction

There is no good time for a pandemic. But the SARS-CoV-2 virus hit in a particularly inopportune period of broad global disruptions—the rise of China, climate change, large levels of migration, an American lurch toward isolationism, and the Russian invasion of Ukraine. All this fed gaps in trust of both intentions and institutions. Global instruments developed over decades of health diplomacy underperformed as trust deficits complicated construction of new instruments to meet the challenge.

When the world needed enlightened self-interest, it instead got heavy doses of unenlightened competition in the form of "vaccine diplomacy" and "vaccine nationalism" that exacerbated underlying inequities in global health. COVID-19, the disease SARS-CoV-2 causes, resulted in over 15 million excess deaths worldwide (as of December 2021) (UN News 2022b) and destruction of an estimated $22 trillion in lost global economic output (Independent Panel for Pandemic Preparedness and Response 2021).

The great challenge of reforming global health diplomacy will be to develop better modes of cooperation to build forward-looking global systems despite the persistence of disruption and eroded trust. The sheer magnitude of the pandemic has provoked soul searching among international leaders but also

M. C. Storella (✉)
Boston University, Boston, MA, USA

the potential for political will to sustain broad reform. This reform, in turn, requires a balance between competing goals of health diplomacy—the use of diplomatic tools to produce enhanced global health outcomes and the use of health tools as a means to advance other national interests. Effective reform must reconcile both idealistic and realist views of global health diplomacy. New measures will need to advance both global health and national objectives.

This chapter examines the record of health diplomacy, draws conclusions about strengths and weaknesses in global health diplomatic efforts, and suggests the following areas for reform:

* Ensuring Consistent Political Engagement and Scientific Integrity;
* Reforming Health Financing;
* Strengthening Global Health Surveillance, Reporting and Investigation;
* Enhancing Global Health Equity;
* Preparing Health Diplomats;
* Maintaining Diversity of Health Diplomacy Architecture;
* Working toward a Broader Entente among Great Powers on Health Diplomacy; and
* Addressing the Impact of Technological Advancements and Public Trust.

A principal conclusion of this chapter is that global health diplomacy reform will require diverse tools and methods since current disruptions and distrust will complicate any single overarching global effort to provide the health protections the world needs.

What Is Global Health Diplomacy?[1]

Global health diplomacy is a relatively new term for a practice that has been going on for centuries but that came into broader use only in the 1990s (Almeida 2020). Rebecca Katz et al. (ibid.) label the following categories of health diplomacy:

(1) core diplomacy, formal negotiations between and among nations; (2) multi-stakeholder diplomacy, negotiations between or among nations and other actors, not necessarily intended to lead to binding agreements; and (3) informal diplomacy, interactions between international public health actors

---

[1] This section draws heavily on research conducted by the author's graduate assistant, Shamim Butt-Garcia, which is reflected in Ms. Butt-Garcia's unpublished master's thesis: "The Future of American Leadership in Global Health Diplomacy: Lessons from the COVID-19 Pandemic" (2022). It appears here in modified form with her permission.

and their counterparts in the field, including host country officials, nongovernmental organizations, private-sector companies, and the public.

While the most widely accepted definition refers to the use of the tools of diplomacy and statecraft (Brown et al. 2014) to produce beneficial public health outcomes, there is another valid perspective:

> Health diplomacy can be understood through two interconnected perspectives; first, advocacy for health objectives through non-health policy means like foreign policy; and second, the use of global health initiatives and policies to achieve *non-health objectives* such as preserving strategic national interests, such as Switzerland does. Global health diplomacy is not a one-size-fits-all policy approach however and needs a variety of approaches for different levels and degrees of engagement. (Conway 2021)

Kickbusch et al. (2021) note that these elements of global health diplomacy can pull in different directions: "Tensions can arise—also within national delegations—between the national interest that diplomats are expected to uphold and the solidarity at the heart of the concept of 'common goods for health,' which should be the prime concern of global public health action."

Cuba was one of the first countries to pursue global health diplomacy explicitly by sending medical brigades around the world to aid countries facing conflict or natural disasters (Kirk 2009). The European Union (EU) has recently reinforced its global health role (European Commission 2020). The 2010 report "The EU Role in Global Health" recommended the EU "build up a collective expertise on capacity in global health analysis and policy dialogue…" (ibid.). This report also explained that "the EU Health Strategy states that sustained collective leadership in global health is needed for better health outcomes in Europe and beyond" (ibid., 4).

Chancellor Angela Merkel used Germany's G7 presidency to hold the Gavi Vaccine Alliance funding replenishment conference as the first G7 event and launched a plan to strengthen global preparedness for international health emergencies (ibid., 20).

China and Russia also use global health diplomacy to advance their broader national interests (Kevany 2014). China recently elevated the "Health Silk Road" initiative within China's broader Belt and Road agenda. China increasingly sees health assistance as a tool in its broader competition with the United States (Habibi and Zhu 2021).

Beginnings and Early Achievements of Health Diplomacy

Health is inherently global since pathogens know no borders. To protect both public health and commerce from the Black Death, the Venetian Republic from 1347 to 1350 imposed restrictions on ships and their cargoes, first for 30 days—"il trentino"—and then for 40 days—"il quarantino"—the origins of the modern term quarantine. Ottoman Sultan Mahmud II established the Conseil Superieur de Sante de Constantinople on June 10, 1839, so Ottoman health officials could cooperate with maritime commercial states since the Sultan's quarantine "would be in conflict with certain rights that (European powers) had enjoyed as a result of earlier treaties" (World Health Organization 1958). This may have been the first international health organization.

With the further growth of commerce, the threat of global disease burgeoned. France hosted the 1851 International Sanitary Conference to set international health standards to address the threat posed by plague and cholera. This first in a series of 14 International Sanitary Conferences into the mid-twentieth century included delegations made up of one diplomat and one medical doctor—with each allowed to vote according to their individual best assessments. Even at this early date, the necessity of balancing policy and science was evident.

In the early 1900s, the sanitary conferences agreed on a series of conventions with basic principles still relevant today: states parties must notify partners of disease outbreaks, must provide specified types of information, should convey notifications via diplomatic or consular offices, and must restrict movement and commerce from contaminated areas. The conventions also established in 1907 an *Office International d'Hygiene Publique* in Paris to further global health cooperation.

When the Great Influenza struck in 1918 during another period of profound international disruption, killing perhaps 50 million people worldwide, the international community failed to mobilize its embryonic global health structure to mount any concerted international response whatsoever.

International health diplomacy did have some early success. The International Sanitary Bureau, launched in 1902—subsequently named the Pan American Health Organization (PAHO) in 1923—helped tame the threat of yellow fever that had impeded construction of the Panama Canal (Kiernan 2002). In the wake of the First World War, the League of Nations established a Permanent Health Committee in 1923, which scored modest progress in controlling typhoid outbreaks (Fitzgerald 1933).

Delegates from American states at the 1945 San Francisco Conference that established the United Nations pressed for a global version of PAHO and, on April 7, 1948, the World Health Organization (WHO) began its work as the central international organization pillar devoted to global health. Its constitution makes clear WHO is a member-state organization with the expansive mission of "the attainment by all peoples of the highest possible level of health" (World Health Organization 1946). WHO leaned toward the technical side urging that member states send delegations composed of "persons most qualified by their technical competence in the field of health, preferably representing the national health administration of the Member." WHO's central body, the World Health Assembly (WHA), sought to make decisions by consensus on the premise that health decisions should be primarily matters of science. WHO's founding document—including the primacy of member states but also deference to objective science—effectively enshrined the tension between policy and science.

WHO's signal achievement came at the height of the Cold War as the United States and the Soviet Union jointly supported a global campaign to eradicate smallpox. With strong political backing, a technically led team of doctors at WHO mounted a global effort that even today seems extraordinary—reaching every household needed around the world to administer smallpox vaccines. With WHO's declaration of the eradication of smallpox in 1980—and the conviction that the dreaded killer would never again strike humans since it no longer existed in any human host—the world body seemed poised for a series of technical breakthroughs in global health.

Financing of Global Public Health

At this stage, it is important to introduce how nations and other donors fund global health. In 2020, the World Health Organization received about 17 percent of its funding through assessed contributions, which are dues paid by UN member states based on an agreed formula that factors in such elements as gross domestic product, per capita GDP, and debt burden. The formula also sets a cap at 22 percent paid by the United States. However, 80 percent of WHO funding comes from voluntary contributions by states and large philanthropies, with those donors often earmarking funding for select programs and purposes. In fact, while the three of the largest individual donors to WHO in the 2020–21 biennium were Germany, the United States, and Japan, among the top ten donors were three foundations and organizations, including the Bill and Melinda Gates Foundation (#2), the Gavi Alliance

(#6), and Rotary International (#9) (World Health Organization 2022b). Other important players in global health such as Gavi itself and the Global Fund rely principally on voluntary contributions for their funding.

A great deal of global health spending—which totaled $1.7 trillion—comes from national budgets but also passes through or is generated by private enterprises, particularly large pharmaceutical companies, sometimes known as Big Pharma. Big Pharma also has a decisive role in determining research investment, which in turn helps define the universe of tools available to address global health needs.

There are several important implications of this funding structure. First, while each institution has its own governing structures, rich nations inherently have a larger role in setting the global health diplomacy agenda than do poorer countries. Moreover, institutions like the Bill and Melinda Gates Foundation, which does not have a vote in the World Health Assembly, nevertheless has a permanent seat on the board of Gavi Alliance and sits on the board of the Global Fund as well. As such, nongovernmental actors play an important role in global health governance and help determine global health priorities, strategies, and programs.

While the funding mechanisms are complex and diverse, one key implication is that global health priorities are often "supply driven," that is, determined by the main funders, rather than "demand driven," that is, based on the needs of constituencies whose wellbeing global health diplomacy serves. Reducing the degree to which donors set the global health agenda could help ensure that the affected populations themselves have more say identifying their own needs.

Lessons from Recent Global Efforts in Response to Global Health Crises

In the years since smallpox eradication, patterns emerged in global health diplomacy that demonstrated strengths, but also critical and predictable weaknesses. The most important were the stigmatization of peoples and countries due to disease, a boom and bust cycle of international engagements, and attendant rises and drops in global health funding. To understand the evolution of health diplomacy, one can review key disease outbreaks and international response.

HIV/AIDS: Stigmatization and Intellectual Property Issues

The human immunodeficiency virus (HIV)—which causes acquired immunodeficiency syndrome (AIDS)—struck the world as the HIV/AIDS pandemic in 1981. American and French teams identified the virus in 1983. However, due largely to stigmatization of the populations most affected, the international community responded with appalling tardiness. It was not until 1994 that the UN and its member states acted to establish UNAIDS, the UN's own AIDS office. In the first UN Security Council meeting of the new millennium, on January 10, 2000, with U.S. Vice President Al Gore presiding as Council president, UN Secretary General Kofi Annan declared that "the impact of AIDS in that region (Africa) is no less destructive than that of warfare itself. Indeed, by some measures it is far worse. Last year, AIDS killed about ten times more people in Africa than did armed conflict" (Annan 2000).

In UNSC (UN Security Council) Resolution 1308 of July 7, 2000, the Security Council took what seemed a fateful step and declared that the HIV/AIDS pandemic "may pose a risk to stability and security" (UNSC 2000). For the first time, the UN Security Council established disease as central to the functions of the UN's most powerful body. It may have seemed that the UNSC had crossed a diplomatic Rubicon in terms of its engagement on global health. But that step would turn out to be a halting one, with several missteps to come. In 2002, with seed money from the Bill and Melinda Gates Foundation, the Global Fund to Fight AIDS, Tuberculosis and Malaria began operations as a pool of donor resources to fight HIV/AIDS and other diseases (FGATM 2022). The Global Fund became itself a focus of health diplomacy. However, the decisive response to HIV/AIDS would in fact be a largely unilateral—not global—action, albeit with significant partner support. U.S. President George W. Bush launched the President's Emergency Plan for AIDS Relief (PEPFAR) in a State of the Union speech in 2003. Through PEPFAR, the United States has led the fight against HIV/AIDS with a cumulative over $100 billion in U.S. investments and done so with enormous positive impact.

The fight to control the AIDS pandemic quickly ran directly into the issue of health equity, as the South African government and civil society groups led a successful campaign to win concessions on intellectual property protections for antiretroviral drugs that could save lives but were too costly on the open market. The World Trade Organization Doha Declaration introduced flexibility in the application of Trade Related Aspects of Intellectual Property Rights (TRIPS) that constituted a signal success for equity, without impairing the financial incentives needed to promote private investment in drug research (World Trade Organization 2001). However, the international community did not institutionalize the Doha Declaration flexibilities in a manner that would provide for automaticity in case of another dangerous pandemic (Colvin and Heywood 2012). The issue of how, when, and under what conditions TRIPS protections should be waived remained hotly debated during the COVID pandemic 20 years later, and would prove a stumbling block to providing rapid access to COVID vaccines for poor countries (Thrasher 2021).

Gavi, CEPI, and Public-Private Models

Two important elements of global health architecture emerged to address the need for widespread immunization. In 1999, the Bill and Melinda Gates Foundation pledged $750 million to help establish Gavi, the Vaccine Alliance (formerly GAVI Alliance and the Global Alliance for Vaccines and Immunizations), which began work in 2000 with the goal of expanding vaccination, especially for children. Gavi, which now supports vaccination of about half the world's children, is a public-private partnership that brings together the World Health Organization, UNICEF, the World Bank, and the Bill and Melinda Gates Foundation, along with governments, corporations, vaccine manufactures, and research institutions. Gavi seeks to work with the market for vaccines to help develop vaccines and provide access to vaccination for low- and middle-income countries (Kaiser Family Foundation 2022).

Gavi's market-based approach also influenced the formation of CEPI (the Coalition for Epidemic Preparedness Innovations), launched in 2017 at the Davos World Economic Forum. Focused on promoting innovation in development of vaccines, CEPI also is a public-private partnership. Gavi and CEPI have done exceptional work. However, their public-private partnership model helped shape global response to COVID—with market mechanisms ultimately frustrating equity in vaccine access.

SARS and IHR Revision: Sovereignty and Surveillance

The outbreak in China in 2002 of Severe Acute Respiratory Syndrome (SARS)—caused by SARS-CoV-1, related to the COVID-19 virus—spread panic in Southeast Asia and caused significant economic damage, although there were only 8096 confirmed cases and 774 confirmed deaths (Michaud et al. 2021). Chinese officials were aware of the outbreak as early as November

2002, but did not report the disease to WHO until February 7, 2003, and did not permit WHO access to Guangdong province until April 7, 2003. China's slow reporting undermined confidence in the existing International Health Regulations (IHR; World Health Organization 2016), the WHO-led agreement that governed surveillance and reporting of certain dangerous pathogen outbreaks (and that were the successor rules to the original International Sanitary Conventions of the late nineteenth and early twentieth centuries). Many recognized that the IHR in force in 2003 was anachronistic. WHO's World Health Assembly had even called for revision in WHA resolution 48.7 of 1995, but little had been done (World Health Assembly 1995).

Under the threat of the SARS outbreak, the IHR revision agreed in 2005 was one of the most important and forward-looking breakthroughs in global health diplomacy in the past 50 years (World Health Organization 2016). Through intense intergovernmental working group meetings, as documented in Katz and Muldoon (2012), technical experts and government officials pressed through a series of controversial issues—non-state reporting, sovereignty, Taiwan, reference to chemical, biological, radiological, and nuclear events, and travel restrictions—to produce the revised IHR in 2005. It included among its most important provisions:

(a) a scope not limited to any specific disease or manner of transmission, but covering "illness or medical condition, irrespective of origin or source, that presents or could present significant harm to humans";
(b) State Party obligations to develop certain minimum core public health capacities;
(c) obligations on States Parties to notify WHO within 24 h of events that may constitute a public health emergency of international concern according to defined criteria;
(d) provisions authorizing WHO to take into consideration unofficial reports of public health events and to obtain verification from States Parties concerning such events;
(e) procedures for the determination by the Director General of a "public health emergency of international concern" and issuance of corresponding temporary recommendations, after taking into account the views of an Emergency Committee;
(f) protection of the human rights of persons and travelers; and
(g) the establishment of National IHR Focal Points and WHO IHR Contact Points for urgent communications between States Parties and WHO (ibid.).

The great achievement of IHR revision should not obscure some shortcomings. It was a legally binding instrument that called on 196 countries to conduct surveillance and reporting and provided for international investigations, but had no enforcement mechanism. IHR 2005 set criteria for announcing a "Public Health Emergency of International Concern," but did not envision any intermediate steps. And the IHR's call for minimum core public health capacities had no funding attached.

H5N1 and the PIP Framework: Equity at Center Stage

Although the main impetus for IHR revision had been the spread of the SARS CoV-1 virus, many global health experts were much more concerned about the pandemic potential of influenza (flu) virus, which had been the cause of the world's deadliest pandemic, the 1918–20 Great Influenza. In order to establish an effective global influenza surveillance network, starting in 1952, the World Health Organization's Global Influenza Surveillance Network (GISN—later GISRS) provided for the free sharing of virus samples among National Influenza Centers and WHO Collaborating Centers in Australia, Japan, the United Kingdom, and the United States. GISN permitted health experts to evaluate potential pandemic threats and plan strain selections for seasonal flu vaccines.

Persistent cases of H5N1 avian influenza (also called "bird flu") beginning in 1997 set the stage for an eruption in global health diplomacy. In December 2006, Indonesia abruptly halted sharing of its influenza samples with GISN. Indonesian Health Minister Siti Fadilah Supari said that Indonesia would refuse to share its influenza samples unless Indonesia received equitable access to influenza vaccines. The argument was simple and compelling: Indonesia shared its influenza samples, which pharmaceutical companies in developed countries then turned into vaccines, and which less developed countries like Indonesia could not afford—putting its citizens at the back of the line for vaccine protection (Gelling 2007). Supari declared at WHO in March 2007 that "We must work together to change the perverse incentives that have resulted in developing countries being disadvantaged" (ibid.).

It is hard to overstate the level of international consternation at Minister Supari's assertion of what came to be called "viral sovereignty," linked to the otherwise unrelated Convention on Biological Diversity. Richard Holbrooke, the U.S. Ambassador to the UN in New York, and health journalist Laurie Garrett declared, "the failure to share potentially pandemic viral strains with world health agencies is morally reprehensible" (Holbrooke and Garrett).

Nongovernmental organizations, particularly the Third World Network, also played an important advocacy role.

Although tough negotiations proceeded for three years, the outbreak of a new influenza strain, H1N1 in 2009 along the U.S.-Mexico border, injected considerable urgency. Under the careful management of Mexican Permanent Representative to the UN in Geneva Ambassador Juan Jose Gomez-Camacho and Norwegian Permanent Representative Ambassador Bente Engell-Hansen, negotiators hammered out an agreement two years later for the Pandemic Influenza Preparedness Framework for the Sharing of Influenza Viruses and Access to Vaccines and Other Benefits, also known as the PIP Framework (World Health Organization 2022e).

The PIP Framework broke new ground in global health diplomacy by expressly linking the willingness of countries to provide samples of pathogens with pandemic potential to the international surveillance regime in return for specified benefits, including early access to vaccines. This link was possible thanks to the conclusion of a "standard material transfer agreement 2" (SMTA 2) with participating pharmaceutical companies, which in turn promised 10 percent of future vaccines for developing countries up front. In effect, the PIP Framework addressed the equity issue by constructing a kind of "user fee" so that the pharmaceutical industry would provide benefits for less developed nations in return for full cooperation with the influenza surveillance network.

The PIP Framework was a significant achievement in health diplomacy. PIP, however, extended provisions for equity in global health benefit sharing only to influenza viruses. And it remains dependent on SMTA 2 agreements with private industry that are feasible only because of the need at this time for pharmaceutical makers to have access to actual physical samples. The PIP Framework does not cover other pathogen strains, including the SARS, Ebola, Zika, HIV, or COVID viruses. While poor countries should have early access to pandemic flu vaccines, when COVID struck those nations found themselves at the back of the line for COVID vaccines. Moreover, it is unclear at this writing what the potential impact of advances in vaccine technologies might be on the functioning of the PIP Framework.

H1N1: Stigmatization Redux

The 2009 H1N1 outbreak had other repercussions. WHO Director General Margaret Chan invoked the International Health Regulations in declaring the first Public Health Emergency of International Concern on April 25, 2009, which triggered international efforts to develop vaccines against the emerging pathogen.

The H1N1 virus was also called "swine flu" due to its possible zoonotic origins in pigs. Some majority Muslim countries did not want to be associated with a vaccine that might have any connection to swine. The European Union invested heavily in swine flu vaccine, only to learn that the pathogen was not nearly as virulent as feared and the vaccine, as a result, was not urgently needed. Members of the European parliament condemned what they deemed a "disproportionate" EU response to the swine flu outbreak (European Parliament 2011), which in the end caused 284,000 deaths worldwide (Michaud et al. 2021). In a resolution adopted by the EU Parliament's public health committee, members criticized the expense of the vaccine program (European Parliament 2011). In effect, some in the EU condemned the WHO for crying wolf.

While the response to swine flu was actually impressively quick and effective, a relatively weak communications strategy permitted stigmatization to rear its ugly head again and also led some to draw the unfortunate conclusion that big investments in vaccines may not be justified.

Ebola: Politics, Capabilities, and the WHO's Health Emergencies Programme

The 2013–15 outbreak of Ebola in West African countries, particularly Liberia, Guinea, and Sierra Leone, provided another IHR stress test that the world sputtered to confront. The outbreak raged on as health and political leaders delayed, fear obstructed international response and affected countries became increasingly isolated in their moment of greatest need. U.S. Health and Human Services Assistant Secretary for Global Affairs Ambassador Jimmy Kolker said in 2015 to the WHO Executive Board, "the WHO we had was not the WHO we needed" (Kolker 2017).

A number of blue ribbon reports suggested both serious shortcomings in the international response system and recommended broad reforms. Among the weaknesses experts cited: slow detection of the outbreak in remote locations in Guinea; disincentives at a local level to report cases for fear of panic and economic consequences; weakness in WHO's local capacity in the field; political failures that led WHO officials to downplay the outbreak and late declaration of a Public Health Emergency of International Concern by WHO Director General Margaret Chan—only on August 8, 2014; and attendant slow mobilization of resources to respond (Moon et al. 2015);

30 Reforming Global Health Diplomacy in the Wake of COVID-19

In time, the world mobilized. The UN Security Council adopted UNSC resolution 2177: "Urging Immediate Action, End to Isolation of Affected States" on September 18, 2014, which invoked the Council's primary responsibility for international peace and security in the health field for only the second time: "*Determining* that the unprecedented extent of the Ebola outbreak in Africa constitutes a threat to international peace and security" (United Nations Department of Public Information 2014). The United States, the UK, and France deployed their own national resources to the affected countries with significant assistance from nongovernmental organizations.

The blizzard of post mortem reports on the global response focused on the weakness of global response capacity, particularly in WHO. While these critiques identified a giant lacuna in the global response framework, in fairness, WHO was a technical agency, not a first responder. Lacking any clear alternative, the international community moved to strengthen WHO's response capability by launching WHO's World Health Emergencies Programme (HEP) with a mandate including helping countries to strengthen capacities to detect, prevent, and respond to health emergencies; mitigating the risk of high threat diseases and infectious hazards; detecting and assessing emergency health threats and informing public health decision-making; responding rapidly and effectively to emergencies under a coordinated incident management system; and ensuring WHO's work in emergencies is effectively managed, sustainably financed, adequately staffed, and operationally ready to fulfill its mission (World Health Organization 2022d).

The global response to the Ebola crisis underlined the need to create systems that would minimize the chances of politically motivated delay in pandemic response—but little was done to overcome this obstacle. While the development of the WHO's Health Emergencies Programme, often under strong leadership, was a welcome development, HEP would suffer from chronic under funding and staffing shortfalls.

Global Health Security Agenda: A Mutual Assistance Ad Hoc Group

In the midst of the Ebola crisis, in February 2014 the United States helped launch an initiative to strengthen national capacities to respond to health emergencies called the Global Health Security Agenda (GHSA). GHSA would bring together over 70 countries, international organizations, and nongovernmental organizations, as well as private sector companies to conduct evaluations of health security capacity and then work to fill gaps through "action packages" aimed at common standards of health preparedness in several specified areas (Global Health Security Agenda 2022).

The GHSA had a consciously practical approach aimed at reinforcing capacities directly related to IHR 2005 national commitments. The G7 endorsed the GHSA, and WHO offered a loose affiliation that conferred legitimacy without cumbersome bureaucratic requirements. The GHSA was in many ways a coalition of the willing in global health that fostered mutual assistance and aid to those most in need of support (Michaud et al. 2021).

COVID: Politics, Nationalism, and Vaccine Diplomacy

Against this background of diverse diplomatic efforts on global health, in 2019 the SARS CoV-2 virus emerged from China to toss the world into its most destructive pandemic since the Great Influenza a century earlier. As of mid-2022, COVID-19 has killed over 15 million people worldwide (UN News 2022a, b). The disruption to trade and normal life made the world economy shrink by 4.3 percent in 2020, and the Independent Panel for Pandemic Preparedness (2021) has estimated that COVID-19 has wiped out $22 trillion in global economic output. While the global economy bounced back somewhat in 2021, the IMF (2022) forecast a slowing down of expected global growth in 2022 of 1.5 percent, due largely to COVID. Diplomatic energy over COVID went in at least four different directions.

First, senior government officials played the blame game. U.S. President Donald Trump and Chinese President Xi Jinping initially downplayed the severity of the outbreak. Once the seriousness of the disease became manifest, Trump sought to place responsibility on China including through derogatory name-calling. Trump also raised doubts about Chinese candor on the origins of the disease. Chinese officials sought to duck responsibility and even suggested that the virus might have originated in U.S. military activities, despite no supporting evidence (Davidson 2021). Trump then blamed WHO and, in a shocking abdication of America's traditional leadership in global health, announced the intention to pull out of WHO, which his successor, Joe Biden, quickly reversed.

Second, COVID-19 stress-tested IHR, again with poor results. China delayed notification of the virus and its characteristics, but did provide genetic sequences if not biological samples. When many criticized an initial WHO investigation of the virus' origins in China, WHO Director General Dr. Tedros Adhanom Ghebreyesus said further investigation was needed. China responded that claims that the virus could have emerged from a lab leak in the city of Wuhan were a "political farce," and obstructed further cooperation (Felter 2021).

Third, rather than finding a collective approach to focus vaccine doses where they were most needed, rich nations engaged in "vaccine nationalism"—the hoarding of available vaccine doses—to support their own populations. Canada quickly sealed contracts to obtain more than seven doses per Canadian, while poor countries went almost completely without (Kirk et al. 2021). When India confronted a deadly COVID-19 wave, Delhi broke its commitments to provide vaccines for poorer nations and halted exports of the AstraZeneca vaccine from the Serum Institute of India (Paravicini 2021). The inequity of vaccine distribution was stark. In early 2022, the UN reported that only 1 percent of the world's COVID vaccines had been administered in low-income countries (UN News 2022a, b).

As anger mounted, South African President Cyril Ramaphosa decried what he called "vaccine apartheid" (*The Economist* 2021). But Ramaphosa went further, arguing that there was a global common interest in ensuring that people in all corners of the world had vaccine protection, asserting that, "(the pandemic) has challenged the notion that richer nations can successfully insulate themselves from the plight of the developing world ... The inequitable distribution of these vaccines means that the recovery will be uneven and, potentially, short-lived" (ibid.).

Ramaphosa built on the argument made more broadly that, in a pandemic, "no one is safe until everyone is safe." Gavi argued that "To end the pandemic, the virus needs to be stamped out simultaneously across the world, but government hoarding and export restrictions are getting in the way of making this happen" (Berkley 2021). As long as a virus could be transmitted freely among unvaccinated populations somewhere in the world, it would continue to morph into new and potentially dangerous variants that would pose a threat to the whole world. But rich countries did not seem convinced and were driven to demonstrate that they spared no effort to protect their own citizens and constituents. In the end, market forces, not scientific analysis, dictated early vaccine distribution.

Fourth, several countries sought to take advantage of the challenge to advance interests beyond health. China pressed ahead with its "Health Silk Road" to enhance its public image over its initial handling of COVID through a campaign of vaccine diplomacy—using promises of Chinese vaccine contributions to win friends. In the end, this effort won some positive recognition. But in time it became clear that the vast majority of Chinese vaccine exports were actually sold, not donated (Wee 2021; Bridge 2022). Donations often came with strings—requirements for public shows of gratitude and even support on political issues including the status of Taiwan.

Russia's efforts to leverage its "Sputnik V" vaccine—reminiscent of the USSR's achievements in space—fell fairly flat as the Russian vaccine's efficacy came under question.

Under President Trump, as already mentioned, the United States abdicated its leadership role, announcing its withdrawal from WHO and curtailment of funding for WHO.

In a sign of just how much disruption in the international system had stymied cooperation, the UNSC took eight months to produce a resolution on COVID-19. UNSC Resolution 2532 of July 1, 2020 (UN 2020), was a toothless response to the pandemic which even failed to identify COVID as a threat to international peace and security. With a change in U.S. administrations, the UNSC would later muster a more forward leaning resolution, UNSC 2565 of February 26, 2021—15 months after the original outbreak—which acknowledged that "the unprecedented extent of the COVID-19 pandemic is likely to endanger the maintenance of international peace and security" (UN 2021). The resolution called for support for global vaccine equity, but it set no specific goals and failed to invoke any mandatory actions. The UNSC response was initially embarrassing and subsequently inadequate. In the face of these daunting setbacks, health diplomacy pushed forward in two ambitious directions, neither fully successful yet.

ACT Accelerator

In a sense, in the COVID-19 pandemic, health changed diplomacy. Middle powers, and especially France and its partners, took the lead. French President Emmanuel Macron led a G7 meeting in March 2020 on the crisis. The EU hosted a fundraising summit on May 4, 2020. The UK hosted another meeting to raise funds for the Gavi Vaccine Alliance (Jones 2020).

In April, 2020, WHO Director General Tedros, the President of France, the President of the European Commission, and the Bill and Melinda Gates Foundation led a meeting to launch the ACT Accelerator (Global Collaboration to accelerate the Development, Production, and Equitable Access to New COVID-19 diagnostics, therapeutics, and vaccines) (World Health Organization 2022a). According to WHO, the ACT Accelerator "brings together governments, scientists, businesses, civil society, and philanthropists and global health organizations (the Bill and Melinda Gates Foundation, CEPI, FIND, Gavi, The Global Fund, Unitaid, Wellcome, the WHO, and the World Bank)," with UNICEF and PAHO later becoming delivery partners (ibid). The ACT Accelerator comprises four pillars: diagnostics, treatment, vaccines, and health system strengthening—and sought to make ACT a player in the global market, rather than a charity waiting for handouts. As of early 2022, various donors had committed a gargantuan $18.7 billion toward the Act Accelerator—although even these staggering sums fell short of the global need (Agarwal et al. 2022).

Despite this huge commitment, the ACT Accelerator underperformed in its key task, equitable delivery of affordable vaccines to the poorest countries. Rich countries moved faster than COVAX could to buy up the vast majority of available vaccine doses before COVAX—the vaccine arm of ACT—could move. Other disruptions grew out of COVAX's reliance on Indian manufacturers as a supplier when India halted its own deliveries. Populations in upper- and middle-income countries were nearly ten times more likely to be vaccinated than those in low-income countries (Our World in Data 2020). Nevertheless, in late 2021, donated doses began to pour into COVAX, although some of these doses were too close to expiration to be useful. Even when it was available, many Africans—and others—declined vaccination due to distrust of the science and the officials who touted vaccines.

Pandemic Treaty: Diplomacy to the Rescue or Politics Over Science?

The COVID pandemic prompted a series of high-level assessments of global health systems. The most important of these were:

* The Report of the Independent Panel for Pandemic Preparedness and Response headed by former New Zealand Prime Minister Helen Clark and Former Liberian President Ellen Johnson Sirleaf (Independent Panel 2021);
* The WHO International Health Regulations Review Committees established by the Director General of the World Health Organization (2022f);
* The Report of the Global Preparedness Monitoring Board (GPMB) co-convened by the Director General of the World Health Organization and the President of the World Bank: the GPMB (2021) comprises political leaders, agency principals, and world-class experts tasked with providing an independent and comprehensive appraisal about progress toward increased preparedness and response capacity for disease outbreaks and other emergencies with health consequences; and

* The Report of the Independent Oversight and Advisory Committee for the WHO Health Emergencies Programme established by WHO to provide oversight and monitoring of the development and performance of the Programme and to guide the Programme's activities (World Health Organization 2021a).

With the COVID pandemic raging and a menu of proposed reforms to draw from, political leaders felt the need—but also the opportunity—to propose a bold initiative. Twenty-six global leaders, including European Union Council President Charles Michel and French President Emmanuel Macron—but with the notable absence of officials from China, Russia, or the United States—published an article on March 30, 2021, calling for a pandemic treaty, "to foster an all-of-government and all-of-society approach, strengthening national, regional and global capacities and resilience to future pandemics." They said such a treaty would greatly enhance "international cooperation to improve, for example, alert systems, data-sharing, research, and local, regional and global production and distribution of medical and public health counter measures, such as vaccines, medicines, diagnostics and personal protective equipment" (World Health Organization 2021b).

In only its second special session ever, the World Health Assembly met from November 29–December 1, 2021, and established a mandate for an Intergovernmental Negotiating Body (INB) to begin talks on such an international instrument (World Health Assembly 2021). The INB was to report to the WHA at its May 2024 session. A key unresolved question was what form this instrument would take, whether a binding treaty, a regulation, or simply a hortatory resolution.

The table was set for broad reform of global health architecture through a diplomatic process. But the form this reform would take was yet to be seen.

Tackling the Challenges: The Axes of Reform in an Era of Disruption

The track record of health diplomacy and lessons from the COVID-19 pandemic point to several critical avenues of reform needed to make global health diplomacy more effective. This urgent reform must play out at a time of general disruption in the international order in which leading countries—especially China, Russia, and the United States—find it particularly difficult to mount joint action due to political differences. Global trends have also tended

30 Reforming Global Health Diplomacy in the Wake of COVID-19

to diminish trust in leaders and institutions. Health diplomacy will need to demonstrate concrete progress on key issues. This progress, in turn, can help rebuild trust. That can start with eight areas of reform.

Ensuring Consistent Political Engagement and Scientific Integrity

Health diplomacy needs to help overcome the "boom and bust" cycle of global engagement on health. This will require keeping senior political leaders engaged while preserving the integrity of science in determining most aspects of global health response. The challenge of achieving a sustainable balance is sometimes called the fight between New York (UN HQ, UNSC, UNGA) and Geneva (home of the top global health technical agencies). The following diplomatic steps can help. First, elevate global health issues as a permanent agenda item for key organizations such as the G7 and the G20 to ensure that senior political leaders will engage health issues on a regular basis. Second, establish a stronger health role for New York institutions while not relying on action of the UN Security Council where political differences may block effective action. This could take the form of establishment of a health advisor role to the Secretary General and a Global Health Threats Council which would assemble political leaders to focus on health crises. Third, maintain WHO as the central clearinghouse for consideration of ongoing health challenges and response.

Reforming Health Financing

The current financing model relies excessively on voluntary contributions by states and mega-donors like the Gates Foundation. This funding structure is too clearly subject to political vagaries and even the whims of individuals (World Health Organization 2022g). The challenge is to find ways to preserve the funding that comes with often earmarked voluntary contributions while ensuring that key global health institutions have predictable and adequate funding for core activities.

In May 2022, the World Health Assembly approved a decision to adopt the recommendations of the Working Group on Sustainable Financing. These recommendations included a series of proposed budgetary reforms, largely aimed at improving transparency as well as a stated aspiration to progressively step up assessed contributions with the goal of those assessed contributions covering 50 percent of the WHO base budget by the 2030–31 biennial budget. While not explicitly tying the increase in assessed contributions to specific reforms, member states will have the option of considering the proposed steps toward 50 percent in light of progress on reforms. The recommendations also include the idea of an additional replenishment funding mechanism that would presumably offer even greater reliability in WHO financing (World Health Organization 2022h).

While this decision is a dramatic step forward by WHO member states, it is essential that diplomats working in the health field keep the pressure up to follow through on these goals. This will require maximum support for budgetary reforms that will in turn support movement up the steps to 50 percent funding by assessed contributions. Reform of WHO's budget should include full transparency on distinctions between core functions and other priorities, with a view to eventually increasing the 50 percent goal to cover all core functions, and especially all the costs of WHO's Health Emergencies Programme. Moreover, health diplomacy should stress good donorship principles to ensure that WHO retains maximum flexibility in its use of voluntary contributions and that those contributions come wherever possible with multiyear commitments.

While other global health organizations such the Global Fund, Gavi, and CEPI will continue to rely on voluntary contributions to cover costs, donors should commit to increased flexibility and multiyear funding for these organizations as well.

Strengthening Global Health Surveillance, Reporting, and Investigation

SARS, Ebola, and COVID-19 have all demonstrated the dangers of politicization of disease surveillance and reporting. While it is impossible to eliminate political bias, health diplomacy should work through the ongoing reform of the International Health Regulations to minimize the opportunities for political concerns to obstruct proper operation of international systems. A first step would be to build in as much automaticity as possible into IHR systems for surveillance, reporting, and investigation of disease, to include thresholds which would trigger technical investigations by groups of previously identified experts in cases of disease outbreaks. Second, diplomats should move to replace the existing system in which the WHO Director General has only one level of determination of health threats—declaring a "Public Health Emergency of International Concern"—with a tiered system of alerts tied to objective criteria that can advise international actors of emerging health threats at early stages.

Enhancing Global Health Equity

The construction of the ACT Accelerator in the midst of the COVID-19 pandemic was a remarkable achievement, even though market forces and vaccine nationalism undermined its effectiveness. This predicament highlighted the need to have systems in place that work with the market for vaccines and therapeutics, but also ensure that poor countries will not fall to the back of the line.

Health diplomats should work to win agreement in advance of future health threats for triggers that will ensure limited waivers of intellectual property protections for vital health resources while still offering private companies international property rights protection in lucrative rich country markets. The World Trade Organization took a step in this direction at its June 2022 ministerial meeting to strengthen the commitments under the 2001 Doha Declaration to facilitate waivers of certain procedural obligations under the TRIPS agreement (Trade Related Aspects of Intellectual Property Rights) with regard to COVID-19 vaccines (World Trade Organization 2022a). This is a positive step, but remains too narrow in its scope and could still slow poor countries' access to vaccines in a future pandemic (World Trade Organization 2022b).

To strengthen these commitments, health diplomacy should first broaden this decision to cover vaccines and therapeutics for any future global pandemic. Second, diplomats should work toward development of a mechanism by which rich countries will pledge up front some percentage of their national vaccine, therapeutic, and other health product manufacturing for distribution to poor countries in the case of a health emergency. Third, governments should work through a global health alliance involving Big Pharma to diversify the locations of vaccine production to ensure that there is greater capacity housed in developing countries themselves.

Preparing Health Diplomats

There is considerable debate over who should lead global health diplomacy—diplomats or scientists. Some have suggested creating a cadre of "scientist diplomats" or "diplomat scientists" by training each side deeply in the profession of the other. As Kickbusch et al. commented, "The function of a foreign ministry has shifted from that of a gatekeeper overseeing all official contacts in the official level toward being the coordinator and enabler of a whole-of-government and whole-of-society approach … As one saying puts it, 'Nowadays everyone is a diplomat'" (Kickbush et al., 36).

A more practical approach is not to create a new species of diplomats or scientists, but rather to ensure that diplomats and scientists can easily communicate with one another and understand the fundamentals of the other profession. A promising path would be to develop collaboration among WHO, other global health agencies, and UNITAR (the United Nations Institute for Training and Research) to produce courses that would bring diplomats and technical experts together to study the fundamentals of each profession to increase fluency on both sides of the political-science divide.

Maintaining Diversity of Health Diplomacy Architecture

The impulse to develop a "pandemic treaty" or some other international instrument on pandemic preparedness and response may result in negotiations over several years. Both the agenda of this new overarching framework and its actual form—treaty, regulation, or resolution—are still not set and may be subject to complicated and prolonged political tradeoffs. Negotiators may find themselves stuck on the horns of a dilemma: if health diplomats design an instrument with important and binding obligations, it may lose many adherents; if they push for a widely acceptable formula, they may have to settle for an instrument that lacks teeth. Therefore, while those negotiations proceed, global health diplomacy needs to reinforce its diversity of health diplomacy fora focusing on a variety of aspects of global health.

(a) Encourage health diplomacy "coalitions of the willing" like the Global Health Security Agenda to ensure that those willing to take practical steps at international cooperation can find venues to do so outside of formal UN structures.
(b) Continue to encourage activism by middle powers such as France and South Africa in leading health diplomacy efforts in cases where larger powers will not or have not.
(c) Support groups like the Foreign Policy and Global Health Initiative created in 2006 by France and Norway that brings together seven countries from Europe, Africa, Asia, and the Americans to promote global health (Government of France 2022).

The New Health Diplomacy Entente

While differences between China and the United States over the COVID-19 pandemic will play out over years, health diplomats will need to find ways to repair the fabric of cooperation between the two largest global powers. This new "health diplomacy entente" may now seem a distant goal. However, enlightened self-interest can be a guiding principle to help harness competition among leading powers to find new areas of cooperation.

Diplomats should encourage cooperation among great powers on local health projects in the developing world that exploit each nation's competitive advantage while still fostering cooperation to build health systems and surveillance, reporting, and health product production capacity in less developed countries. A way to accelerate this entente might be to foster a race to the top in assisting the development of national health system capacities in low-income countries to support more effective surveillance and response at a local level.

Addressing the Impact of Technological Advancement and Public Trust

A signal feature of the COVID-19 pandemic was the humbling process of adaptation to an emerging and unknown pathogen and its variants. The rapid evolution of technical understanding and attendant changing modes of response eroded the trust in science, political leaders, and global health institutions, and witnessed a broadening of vaccine hesitancy around the world. Technology also performed at an astonishingly high level in meeting the COVID-19 pandemic. mRNA technology has opened new vistas for rapid scale up of vaccines, with G20 leaders committing to develop systems that can produce targeted vaccines at scale within 100 days from the identification of a pathogen. The success of health diplomacy will require adaptation to new technologies but also a global effort to explain, as follows:

(a) Develop global plans to support basic education of national populations in the fundamentals of global health technologies to encourage understanding of the potential and limits of technologies using both educational curricula and accessible social media platforms that are understandable to diverse populations.
(b) Adapt global health diplomatic efforts to focus increasingly on surveillance based on information—such as DNA sequencing—as opposed to reliance on physical samples.

Conclusion

The COVID-19 pandemic has included tragic loss of life, erosion of economic wellbeing, and depleted trust in global leadership and institutions. While COVID-19 is sometimes referred to as a once-in-a-century health event, one cannot rule out that an even more virulent pathogen may be in store for humanity as the interface between humans and animals grows steadily closer in an ever more crowded and climate stressed world. These challenges underscore the importance of effective health diplomacy reform and illuminate the avenues reform could take.

The greatest danger would be if the world repeats past errors and permits urgency on health diplomacy to dissipate as the COVID-19 health crisis recedes. Complacency—not disease—is the greatest threat.

References and Further Reading

Agarwal, R., J. Farrar, G. Gopinath, R. Hatchett, and P. Sands. 2022. "A Global Strategy to Manage the Long-term Risks of COVID-19." International Monetary Fund, April.

Almeida, C. "Global Health Diplomacy: A Theoretical and Analytical Review." *Oxford Research Encyclopedia of Global Public Health*, February 28.

Annan, K. 2000. Address by Kofi Annan to the Security Council on the Situation in Africa: The Impact of AIDS on Peace and Security. United Nations, January 10. https://www.un.org/sg/en/content/sg/speeches/2000-01-10/address-kofi-annan-security-council-situation-africa-impact-aids.

Berkley, S. 2021. "No One Is Safe Until Everyone is Safe." Gavi, the Vaccine Alliance, October 29. https://www.gavi.org/vaccineswork/no-one-safe-until-everyone-safe.

Bridge. 2022. "China COVID-19 Vaccines Tracker." https://bridgebeijing.com/our-publications/our-publications-1/china-covid-19-vaccines-tracker/.

Brown, M.D., T.K. Mackey, C.N. Shapiro, J. Kolker, and T.E. Novotny. 2014. "Bridging Public Health and Foreign Affairs: The Tradecraft of Global Health Diplomacy and the Role of Health Attachés." *Science & Diplomacy* 3 (3). http://www.sciencediplomacy.org/article/2014/bridging-public-health-and-foreign-affairs.

Colvin, C.J., and M. Heywood. 2012. "Negotiating ARV Prices with Pharmaceutical Companies and the South African Government." In E. Rosskam and I. Kickbusch, eds. *Negotiating and Navigating Global Health: Case Studies in Global Health Diplomacy*. Singapore: World Scientific Publishing.

Conway, A. 2021. "Global Public Health Diplomacy: An Opportunity for Ireland?" *Global Europe*, June. https://www.iiea.com/images/uploads/resources/Global-Public-Health-Diplomacy.pdf.

Davidson, H. 2021. "China Revives Conspiracy Theory of US Army Link to Covid." *Guardian*, January 20. https://www.theguardian.com/world/2021/jan/20/china-revives-conspiracy-theory-of-us-army-link-to-covid.

The Economist. 2021. "Cyril Ramaphosa Says the World Must End Vaccine Apartheid," November 8. https://www.economist.com/the-world-ahead/2021/11/08/cyril-ramaphosa-says-the-world-must-end-vaccine-apartheid.

European Commission. 2020. Communication from the Commission to the Council, the European Parliament, the European Economic and Social Committee, and the Committee of the Regions. "Building a European Health Union: Reinforcing the EU's Resilience for Cross-border Health Threats," November 11. https://ec.europa.eu/info/sites/default/files/communication-european-health-union-resilience_en.pdf.

———. 2010. Communication from the Commission to the Council, the European Parliament, the European Economic and Social Committee, and the Committee of the Regions. "The EU Role in Global Health," March 31. https://eurlex.europa.eu/LexUriServ/LexUriServ.do?uri=COM:2010:0128:FIN:EN:PDF.

European Parliament. 2011. "Swine Flu: Lessons to Learn from 'Disproportionate' EU Response," January 25. https://www.europarl.europa.eu/news/en/press-room/20110125IPR12478/swine-flu-lessons-to-learn-from-disproportionate-eu-response.

Felter, C. 2021. "Will the World Ever Solve the Mystery of COVID-19's Origin?" Council on Foreign Relations, November 3. https://www.cfr.org/backgrounder/will-world-ever-solve-mystery-covid-19s-origin.

Fitzgerald, J.G. 1933. "The Work of the Health Organization of the League of Nations." *Canadian Journal of Public Health*, August 3, https://www.jstor.org/stable/41979240?seq=5.

France, Government of. 2022. Foreign Policy and Global Health Initiative. https://www.diplomatie.gouv.fr/en/french-foreign-policy/development-assistance/priority-sectors/health/news/article/foreign-policy-and-global-health-initiative-22-08-19.

Gelling, P. 2007. "Indonesia Defiant on Refusal to Share Bird Flu Samples." *New York Times*, March 26. https://www.nytimes.com/2007/03/26/world/asia/26cnd-flu.html.

Global Fund to Fight AIDS, Tuberculosis and Malaria (FGATM). 2022. *Devex*. https://www.devex.com/organizations/the-global-fund-to-fight-aids-tuberculosis-and-malaria-gfatm-30677.

Global Health Security Agenda. 2022. "A Partnership Against Global Health Threats." https://ghsagenda.org/.

Global Preparedness Monitoring Board. 2021. *Global Preparedness Monitoring Board Strategic Plan 2021–2023*. https://www.gpmb.org/annual-reports/overview/item/gpmb-strategic-plan-2021-2023.

Habibi, N., and H.Y. Zhu. 2021. "The Health Silk Road as a New Direction in China's Belt and Road Strategy in Africa," February 16, Brandeis Scholar Works. https://scholarworks.brandeis.edu/esploro/outputs/workingPaper/The-Health-Silk-Road-as-a/9924131522401921.

Holbrooke, R., and L. Garrett. 2008. "'Sovereignty' that Risks Global Health." *Washington Post*, August 10. https://www.washingtonpost.com/wp-dyn/content/article/2008/08/08/AR2008080802919.html.

Independent Panel for Pandemic Preparedness and Response. 2021. "COVID 19: Make It the Last Pandemic." https://theindependentpanel.org/.

Jones, B. 2020. "Can Middle Powers Lead the World Out of the Pandemic?" *Foreign Affairs*, June 18. https://www.foreignaffairs.com/articles/france/2020-06-18/can-middle-powers-lead-world-out-pandemic.

Kaiser Family Foundation. 2022. "The U.S. Government & Gavi, the Vaccine Alliance," January 19. https://www.kff.org/global-health-policy/fact-sheet/the-u-s-government-gavi-the-vaccine-alliance/.

Katz, R., and A. Muldoon. 2012. "Negotiating the Revised International Health Regulations (IHR)." In E. Rosskam and I. Kickbusch, eds. *Negotiating and Navigating Global Health: Case Studies in Global Health Diplomacy*. Singapore: World Scientific Publishing.

Kevany, S. 2014. "Global Health Diplomacy, 'Smart Power,' and the New World Order." *Global Public Health* 9 (7): 787–807.

Kickbusch, I., H. Nikogosian, M. Kazatchkine, and M. Kökény. 2021. *A Guide to Global Health Diplomacy*. Graduate Institute of Geneva: Global Health Centre, February 18. https://www.graduateinstitute.ch/sites/internet/files/2021-02/GHC-Guide.pdf.

Kiernan, J.P. 2002. "1902–2002: 100 Years of Pan-Americanism." Pan American Health Organization (PAHO). https://www.paho.org/en/who-we-are/history-paho/1902-2002-100-years-pan-americanism.

Kirk, A., F. Sheehy, and C. Levett. 2021. "Canada and UK Among Countries with Most Vaccine Doses Ordered per Person." *Guardian*, January 29. https://www.theguardian.com/world/2021/jan/29/canada-and-uk-among-countries-with-most-vaccine-doses-ordered-per-person.

Kirk, J.M. 2009. "Cuba's Medical Internationalism: Development and Rationale." *Bulletin of Latin American Research* 28 (4): 497–511.

Kolker, J. 2017. "HHS and Global Health in the Second Obama Administration." Center for Strategic and International Studies: Global Health Policy Center, April. https://csis-website-prod.s3.amazonaws.com/s3fs-public/publication/170410_Kolker_HHSObama_Web.pdf.

Kümmel, B. 2017. "Germany: Putting Health on the G7 Agenda." In *Health Diplomacy: European Perspectives*, ed. World Health Organization Regional Office for Europe. https://www.euro.who.int/__data/assets/pdf_file/0009/347688/Health_Diplomacy_European_Perspectives.pdf.

Lin, S., L. Gao, M. Reyes, F. Cheng, J. Kaufman, and W.M. El-Sadr. 2016. "China's Health Assistance to Africa: Opportunism or Altruism?" *Globalization and Health* 12 (1): 83.

Michaud, J., K. Moss, and J. Kates. 2021. "The U.S. Government and Global Health Security." Kaiser Family Foundation (KFF), May 21. https://www.kff.org/global-health-policy/issue-brief/the-u-s-government-and-global-health-security/.

Our World in Data. 2020. Coronavirus Pandemic (COVID-19). https://ourworldindata.org/coronavirus.

Moon, S., D. Sridhar, M.A. Pate, A.K. Jha, C. Clinton, S. Delaunay, et al. 2015. "Will Ebola Change the Game? Ten Essential Reforms before the Next Pandemic. The Report of the Harvard-LSHTM Independent Panel on the Global Response to Ebola." *Lancet* 386 (10009): 2204–21.

Paravicini, G. 2021. "India's Halt to Vaccine Exports 'Very Problematic' for Africa." Reuters, May 18. https://www.reuters.com/business/healthcare-pharmaceuticals/indias-halt-vaccine-exports-very-problematic-africa-2021-05-18/.

Rosskam, E., and I. Kickbusch, eds. 2012. *Negotiating and Navigating Global Health: Case Studies in Global Health Diplomacy.* Singapore: World Scientific Publishing.

Thrasher, R. 2021. "Why the TRIPS Waiver Should Include More than Just Vaccines." Boston University Global Development Policy Center, June 7. https://www.bu.edu/gdp/2021/06/07/why-the-trips-waiver-should-include-more-than-just-vaccines/.

United Nations Department of Public Information. 2014. "With Spread of Ebola Outpacing Response, Security Council Adopts Resolution 2177 (2014) Urging Immediate Action, End to Isolation of Affected States," September 18. https://www.un.org/press/en/2014/sc11566.doc.htm#:~:text=Resolution%202177%20(2014)%20was%20adopted,Chan%2C%20and%20a%20M%C3%A9decins%20Sans.

UN News. 2022a. "UN Analysis Shows Link between Lack of Vaccine Equity and Widening Poverty Gap," March 28. https://news.un.org/en/story/2022/03/1114762#:~:text=The%20overall%20number%20of%20vaccines,administered%20in%20low%2Dincome%20countries.

———. 2022b. "Nearly 15 Million Deaths Directly or Indirectly Linked to COVID-19," May 5. https://news.un.org/en/story/2022/05/1117582.

United Nations Security Council. 2000. UN Security Council Resolution 1308, July 27. https://www.refworld.org/docid/3b00efd10.html.

———. 2020. Resolution 2532. S/RES/2532. https://documents-dds-ny.un.org/doc/UNDOC/LTD/N20/169/84/PDF/N2016984.pdf?OpenElement.

———. 2021. Resolution 2565. S/RES/2565. https://documents-ddsny.un.org/doc/UNDOC/GEN/N21/053/90/PDF/N2105390.pdf?OpenElement.

Wee, S.-l. 2021. "They Relied on Chinese Vaccines. Now They Are Battling Outbreaks," *New York Times*, June 22.

World Health Assembly. 1995. "Revision and Updating of the International Health Regulations." Document WHA84.7, 12 May. https://apps.who.int/iris/bitstream/handle/10665/178403/WHA48_R7_eng.pdf?sequence=1&isAllowed=y.

———. 2021. "The World Together: Establishment of an Intergovernmental Negotiating Body to Strengthen Pandemic Prevention, Preparedness and Response." Document SSA2(5), December 1. https://apps.who.int/gb/ebwha/pdf_files/WHASSA2/SSA2(5)-en.pdf.

World Health Organization. 1946. "Constitution of the World Health Organization," Adopted by the International Health Conference, New York, July 22, 1946, entry into force on April 7, 1948. https://www.who.int/about/governance/constitution.

———. 1958. "The First Ten Years of the World Health Organization." https://apps.who.int/iris/bitstream/handle/10665/37089/a38153_eng_LR_part1.pdf.

———. 2016. *International Health Regulations*. 3rd ed., January 1. https://www.who.int/publications/i/item/9789241580496.

———. 2021a. Independent Oversight and Advisory Committee. https://www.who.int/groups/independent-oversight-and-advisory-committee.

———. 2021b. "COVID-19 Shows Why United Action Is Needed for More Robust International Health Architecture," March 30. https://www.who.int/news-room/commentaries/detail/op-ed%2D%2D-covid-19-shows-why-united-action-is-needed-for-more-robust-international-health-architecture.

———. 2022a. "What Is the ACT-Accelerator." https://www.who.int/initiatives/act-accelerator/about.

———. 2022b. "How WHO Is Funded." https://www.who.int/about/funding.

———. 2022c. WHO Coronavirus (COVID-19) Dashboard. https://covid19.who.int/.

———. 2022d. WHO Health Emergencies Programme. https://www.who.int/westernpacific/about/how-we-work/programmes/who-health-emergencies-programme.

———. 2022e. *Pandemic Influenza Preparedness Framework for the Sharing of Influenza Viruses and Access to Vaccines and Other Benefits*. 2nd ed., January 25. https://www.who.int/publications/i/item/9789240024854.

———. 2022f. https://www.who.int/teams/ihr/ihr-review-committees.

———. 2022g Deliberations of the Bureau of the Working Group on Sustainable Financing on Options for an Increase in Assessed Contributions, April 21. https://apps.who.int/gb/wgsf/pdf_files/wgsf7/WGSF_7_INF2-en.pdf.

———. 2022h. "Sustainable Financing: Report of the Working Group, A75/9," May 13. https://apps.who.int/gb/ebwha/pdf_files/WHA75/A75_9-en.pdf.

World Trade Organization, 2001. "Doha WTO Ministerial 2001, Ministerial Declaration," adopted November 14. https://www.wto.org/english/thewto_e/minist_e/min01_e/mindecl_e.htm#trips.

———. 2022a Draft Ministerial Decision on the TRIPS Agreement, June 17. https://docs.wto.org/dol2fe/Pages/SS/directdoc.aspx?filename=q:/WT/MIN22/W15R2.pdf.

———. 2022b. "COVID-19 WTO Ministerial Decision on TRIPS Agreement Fails to Set Rules that Could Save Lives," June 17. https://reliefweb.int/report/world/covid-19-wto-ministerial-decision-trips-agreement-fails-set-rules-could-save-lives.

31

The Reform of Humanitarian Diplomacy

Gregory Simons and Anna A. Velikaya

Introduction

At present, relations between many countries are far from friendly, and the contradictions are only growing. There is a dangerous militarization of the humanitarian agenda that can lead the world to the edge of the same abyss as did the most dramatic moments of the twentieth century. Humanity is entering a period when humanitarian aspects of diplomacy will be increasingly important. At the same time in the early 2020s there is uncertainty and global fragility, when the whole range of threats requires urgent, collective, and more determined responses.

Nowadays political, economic, and cultural influence in the international arena is shifting toward humanitarian issues, and there is a public desire for the humanization of international relations. There are worsening humanitarian consequences of conflicts for civilians, women, children, and elderly people; increased targeted violence against them is used by armed groups. The attention to the humanitarian aspects of armed conflicts and the importance of the problems of humanitarian support and protection of civilians in urban conflicts is growing. This is the task of humanitarian diplomacy (HD).

G. Simons
Uppsala University, Uppsala, Sweden

A. A. Velikaya (✉)
Russian Presidential Academy of National Economy and Public Administration, Moscow, Russia

Modern trends have significantly expanded the boundaries of diplomacy. The current research covers humanitarian diplomacy (government-to-people or people-to-people) tools, highlighting its similarities and differences with the traditional diplomacy (government-to-government) (Kireçci 2015). Humanitarian diplomacy can be used as an innovative tool to bring nations closer together despite the current upsurge in armed conflicts worldwide and the significant global challenges nowadays. That use includes various national models of humanitarian diplomacy and its audiences, the role of international institutions and NGOs, and the ways to improve their effectiveness. Humanitarian diplomacy's positive impact remains underestimated and not fully utilized; the holistic and systematic approach in this regard is lacking, which often substitutes by fragmentary activities with no tangible long-lasting results. Strengthening the humanitarian aspects of diplomacy depends on active, interregional cooperation. This chapter indicates potentially useful applications for such comparative, cross-cutting, and meaningful analysis of these perspectives interconnected within the broader context of the humanitarian aspects of diplomacy.

Establishing the Priorities of Humanitarian Diplomacy

Humanitarian diplomacy (HD) includes the strengthening of public administration, building infrastructure, maintaining security and stability, ensuring the educational process, developing healthcare, and promoting international dialogue through confidence-building measures. The very concept of HD is understood by scientific schools in different ways. U.S. and European researchers interpret it as the provision of humanitarian assistance during conflicts, in the post-conflict period, during crisis and emergency situations; that is, they analyze its political aspects.

However, humanitarian diplomacy is not only about humanitarian assistance; it also includes cooperation in the sphere of arts, science, sports, tourism, confidence-building measures—that is, public diplomacy. It has two dimensions: to help those in need and to promote an engagement in international dialogue. According to Nicholas Cull, humanitarian outreach by international actors is an important part of public diplomacy. Cull notes that the final intersection of public and humanitarian diplomacy is the need for public diplomacy to mobilize international action on the great issues of today: climate, migration, political extremism, and so forth.

These "problems without passports," as Kofi Annan termed them, can only be addressed collectively and the necessary partnerships require the public articulation of a vision, the selling of a "win-win," and careful public management of inevitable tensions within the partnership. The rewards for success in this endeavor are infinite. Being part of the solution to the humanitarian crises of our era promised to be the ultimate soft power play even as it is the ultimate investment in the tangible security of the state. Conversely, without such investment, humanity seems headed for a rough future (Cull 2022). These quotations suggest that humanitarian diplomacy is all about establishing bridges and creating positive relational dynamics among and between peoples.

Various states and regions have established models of humanitarian diplomacy. States are taking these steps not only for the sake of humane motives of providing assistance to those in need, but also for the goals of nation branding and public diplomacy priority regions (Komleva 2020), as well as for other, related political and economic reasons.

Sustainable peace depends on confidence-building measures, which involve the engagement of different official and unofficial global, national, and local actors. Track II efforts are also sustainable parts of humanitarian diplomacy. The "second track" of diplomacy is a humanitarian diplomacy tool for creating confidence aimed at resolving a certain international conflict or reducing tension through informal negotiations. The experts who initially coined this term, W. Davidson and J. Montville, considered it to be both humanitarian and public diplomacy: as "strategically optimistic" steps to prevent war, identify common interests, and level mutual fears (Davidson and Montville 1981–82, 153–57).

Nowadays the "second track" is understood as a preliminary humanitarian diplomacy discussion preceding the official negotiations where participants in the dialogue formats are close to the decision-making process, being unofficial representatives of their countries: politicians and other leaders, retired military personnel, experts with political weight, or scientific authority. It is necessary that the participants of the "second track" have the opportunity to transfer the ideas developed at such meetings to the official sphere; they should be trusted in the official environment, but being able to apply innovative thinking to complex problems.

Being part of humanitarian diplomacy, track two diplomacy had helped to lay the groundwork for formal attempts to stop the Tajikistan Civil War of 1992–97 or to sign the Iran nuclear deal in 2015. It was also used to try and resolve deadlocks in Korea, the Armenian-Azerbaijani conflict, the Indo-Pakistani conflict, in various Middle East conflicts, and in Cyprus. Sometimes such dialogue formats are implemented through the mediation of an impartial "third party" that finances the cost of air tickets and such. These processes, if successful, can lead to significant results, including a change in the perception of the conflict and a deeper understanding of the complexities, internal logic, and "red lines" of the other side. New channels of communication can be established between the warring parties.

Humanitarian diplomacy is very diverse in its forms, motives, and scale. Its practice is based on the Universal Declaration of Human Rights, the UN Charter, the Final Act of the Helsinki Conference on Security and Cooperation in Europe, the Fourth Geneva Convention; the Additional Protocol I of 1977 Relating to the Protection of Victims of International Armed Conflicts (Articles 51–53); and the Additional Protocol II Relating to the Protection of Victims of Non-International Armed Conflict. In the UN Charter, one of the main goals is "the implementation of international cooperation in resolving international problems of an economic, social, cultural and humanitarian nature." Humanitarian diplomacy is interconnected with international human rights law, international humanitarian law, and international refugee law.

If one considers humanitarian diplomacy on a larger scale, then its history includes religious missions. For example, in 1810, the American Board of Commissioners for Foreign Missions (ABCFM) was founded and its Palestine Mission was established in 1819, renamed the "Mission to Syria and the Holy Land" in 1928, and the "Syria Mission" in 1842. Presbyterian missionaries Eli and Sarah L. Smith arrived in Lebanon in 1835 (Zeuge-Buberl 2017), and upon noticing the prevalent illiteracy among girls in Beirut, they decided to offer classes to the local population—the *American School of Girls*, which in 1994 would become the *Lebanese American University (LAU)*. One of the key events for U.S. humanitarian diplomacy in the Middle East took place on April 24, 1863, when the State of New York granted a charter for the establishment of a new school in Beirut, which was to be known as the *Syrian Protestant College*. After the First World War, the SPC was renamed the *American University of Beirut* (AUB). The new countries of Lebanon, Syria, Iraq, Palestine, and Transjordan looked to the University to train leaders in every field of public life. AUB graduates reside in more than 115 countries worldwide. Thanks to the activities of religious communities, residents of developed countries realized the importance of this humanitarian assistance and began to provide them with financial support.

Today's humanitarian diplomacy can be also interconnected with the religious goals of its conceptual foundations. To illustrate the point, at the heart of Turkey's humanitarian policy is an effective combination of work with Turkic-speaking peoples within the framework of the policy of pan-Turkism (educational and religious policy, tourism, rallying the "Turkic world"), of support for Islam, as well as of the promotion of Turkish business, primarily construction, in carrying out numerous projects to create facilities infrastructure in the recipient countries of Turkish economic assistance, and of Turkish Airlines in turning Istanbul into the main hub of air traffic with African and Central Asian countries (Çevik 2020). In recent years, Turkey has come out on top in the world in terms of humanitarian aid in GDP (one percent). This policy has already allowed Turkey reportedly to become the center of power of the first magnitude in Transcaucasia and Central Asia, whose influence is comparable to that of Russia and China, and significantly superior to Europe; and a significant player in Northern Africa, creating tangible competition for China and the United States. The main reason for such success is not being associated with a major center of world but instead with a clear ideological foundation, be it pan-Turkism, pan-Islam, or neo-Ottomanism. Turkey has broadcast an image of the future that appeals to relevant audiences, which explains why cooperation with Ankara is beneficial. Indian humanitarian work in the Southeast and Central Asia is similarly based on religious and cultural assets.

Humanitarian Diplomacy as a Concept

The term was coined by the U.S. diplomat Oscar Straus, who sought to separate this type of diplomacy from traditional diplomacy after World War II. The most widely used definition is the one offered by the International Federation of Red Cross and Red Crescent Societies (IFRC), suggesting that humanitarian diplomacy involves "persuading decision makers and opinion leaders to act, at all times, in the interests of vulnerable people, and with full respect for fundamental humanitarian principle. This definition has been critiqued due to its being based on the IFRC's work and its broadness in lacking distinction 'between advocacy or communication and diplomacy itself'" (IFRC 2017). The ICRC's humanitarian diplomacy is a strategy for influencing the parties to armed conflicts and others—states, non-state actors, and members of civil society.

In the period 2010–11, as the IFRC prepared a strategic concept on humanitarian diplomacy, it discovered some 89 different definitions (Regnier 2011, 1213). There is a significant risk with this lack of conceptual clarity, which in turn has exerted negative implications for operational implementation. As noted, the concept falls within a subset of public diplomacy as a politicized relational activity in the wider sphere of international relations and politics. Veuthey (2012, 195) defines humanitarian diplomacy "as a dialogue (private or public) between governments and/or humanitarian organizations, inter-governmental organizations and non-governmental organizations or other non-state actors. Representatives from civil society are also playing an increasingly significant role in the processes of humanitarian diplomacy." The aims of humanitarian diplomacy are linked to another definition, which is to facilitate and negotiate the alleviation of harm to victims of a humanitarian crisis (Veuthey 2012, 195–96). Egeland (2013, 354) uses the Red Cross definition of "humanitarian diplomacy is persuading decision makers and opinion leaders to act, at all times, in the interests of vulnerable people, and with the full respect for fundamental humanitarian principles."

These various visions and interactions are also seen in other definitions of humanitarian diplomacy:

Regnier (2011, 1211–12) states that the concept and practice of humanitarian diplomacy is generally fashionable; however, it is also controversial as the term is imprecise and contested and its operational application is unclear. Turunen (2020, 459, 460) states that humanitarian diplomacy is a new term, however, it is also "an old practice that has received relatively little academic attention." The countries pursuing it brand themselves as leaders in the fields of education, science, and economy in order to demonstrate the attractiveness of a chosen state model. Again, according to Regnier (2011, 1211), humanitarian diplomacy focuses on "maximizing support for humanitarian peacekeeping operations and programs, as well as building the partnerships needed to humanitarian goals." While, according to Rousseau and Pende (2020, 254), it is a type of negotiation carried out by state and non-state actors in order to intervene in situations in which humanity is in danger.

The relationship between the theory and practice of HD are generally clear and logical, however. Jan Egeland notes that humanitarian diplomacy differs from other types of diplomacy as it is narrower in focus and "is done on behalf of people in humanitarian need, either specific groups or general groups, and it seeks specific objectives" (quoted in Turunen 2020, 468). It is also a very case specific form of diplomacy, where operations are linked to the prevailing conditions in the field of operations. Turunen (2020, 459) advances her own similar vision of the nuances of humanitarian diplomacy as Egeland: "humanitarian diplomacy covers humanitarian action and its intricacies in catering for humanitarian needs, which sets it distinctly apart from other forms of diplomacy." She also notes a link between humanitarian diplomacy with humanitarianism and humanitarian aims, as HD "strives to follow idealistic logics of neutrality, impartiality and independence in the name of shared humanity" (ibid., 467). The conceptualization of humanitarian diplomacy at an academic level allows for a clear categorization and visualization of a pragmatic political activity. However, this balance and harmony between theory and practice holds during what may be considered as essentially ordinary situations for key stakeholders and especially those engaged in rendering assistance to victims. Kireçci (2015) points out, in extraordinary times, when the scale of the crisis can overwhelm the capability and capacity to effectively assist, then the relationship can become strained.

Humanitarian Diplomacy as Practice

The practical aspects and concerns with envisaging and implementing humanitarian diplomacy and intervention have grown of late. In 2014, the President of the ICRC, Peter Maurer (2016, 446), observed that "over U.S.$20 billion are invested each year in responding to the essential needs of populations affected by humanitarian crises, including natural disasters, armed conflicts and other similar situations of violence. An estimated 250,000 humanitarian workers are engaged in these operations."

In the UN system humanitarian assistance is provided by the UN High Commissioner for Human Rights (UNCHR), the UN Children's Fund (UNICEF), the United Nations Development Program (UNDP), the World Food Program (WFP), and the World Health Organization (WHO), whose staff can indeed be called "humanitarian diplomats" because they have diplomatic immunity and can negotiate with political figures. In 1991, the organization of humanitarian activities within the UN was institutionalized through the creation of the Office for the Coordination of Humanitarian Affairs (OCHA). OCHA's mission is to mobilize and coordinate effective and principled humanitarian action in partnership with national and international actors in order to alleviate human suffering in disasters and emergencies; to advocate for the rights of people in need; to promote preparedness and prevention; and facilitate sustainable solutions to urgent and complex humanitarian problems.

The range of humanitarian issues discussed by the UN Security Council has also expanded. By the early 2000s, the Security Council began to consider a large amount of requests from member states of a humanitarian nature.

> First, there are security issues for individuals in armed conflicts (civilians, children, women, UN and other humanitarian personnel). Secondly, these are the civilian aspects of conflict management and peacebuilding. Thirdly, these are separate "soft security" issues (issues of humanitarian assistance and such "soft threats" security, such as HIV/AIDS epidemics, food crises and climate change).

Besides, in its resolutions, the Security Council also touches upon the problems of human rights violations. (Lebedeva and Ustinova 2020, 136)

Yet, the systematic discussion of humanitarian diplomacy is still lacking at the UN.

Activities in the humanitarian field are related to foreign policy tasks and many of the efforts in this area are carried out by governmental and semi-governmental institutions, albeit with the involvement of civil society. At the same time, this tool is not a panacea: it brings results in the long-run, and only in combination with attractive domestic and foreign policies. Economic aid to different countries that be a positive story does not guarantee loyalty; for example, Pakistan annually received $500 million in humanitarian aid from the United States, while 75 percent of its population perceive the United States as a rival in 2012, compared to 64 percent in 2009 (Rugh 2014).

There have been several limitations to humanitarian diplomacy, namely, the manipulation by certain actors that are pursuing political interests (for themselves or for another entity); institutional interests that are prioritized ahead of the actual interests of victims; cultural misunderstandings; human error; significant security concerns for various stakeholders; skewed or no media coverage of a humanitarian crisis; and, paradoxically, a lack of confidentiality due to media exposure at times when confidentiality is required for negotiations to effectively progress (Veuthey 2012, 203). According to Bowden and Metcalfe-Hough (2020), the practice of humanitarian diplomacy is entering an "age of caution" that is driven by such factors as changing public opinion and an increasing scarcity of funds. This perhaps creates an environment of greater pragmatism and the willingness to permit a deeper level of compromise. Meanwhile, Egeland (2013, 367) notes the factors of politics and communication as important to either supporting or ignoring humanitarian diplomacy action, if there is not sufficient political attention and will among the political elite or public or the event is ignored or misrepresented in the media there is unlikely to be a rally around justice, security, and so forth, to alleviate the situation for the victims. Maurer (2016, 446) indicates similarly that there are "dilemmas of priority-setting in situations of overwhelming needs and limited resources; dilemmas between fulfilling our commitment to humanity and taking into account the stark realities of power, justice and discrimination in many areas of operations; between access to populations and security and safety of humanitarian personnel, and many more dilemmas." There are also dilemmas and opportunity costs to consider for national governments in terms of weighing foreign policy and of supporting national interests or supporting the principled action of humanitarian diplomacy.

Humanitarian diplomacy is now global. States such as the Arab monarchies of the Gulf are actively involved in humanitarian activities both at the global and national levels, and consider it as one of the key elements of their foreign policy. The humanitarian activities of these states are multifaceted and coordinated by Ministries of Foreign Affairs. They do not generally delimit humanitarian aid and development assistance, so they consider development funds as one of the components of humanitarian activity in the broad sense of the word. Funds for assistance in the economic development of developing countries are used actively by all the Gulf countries. The United Arab Emirates (UAE) in 2016 became the third largest global donor of humanitarian aid relative to gross national income (Gökalp 2020, 3). In addition to supporting the country's overall foreign policy ambitions, it is also used to create and maintain alliances, business contacts, and economic partnerships in their area of interest (Africa, Arabian Peninsula, and the Indian Ocean, mainly). The UAE has tended to embrace and borrow Western-style rhetoric and international norms that surround the logic and use of humanitarian diplomacy (ibid., 6). The security concerns raised by the 9/11 attacks in the United States, and the Arab Spring unrest, prompted the UAE to associate their humanitarian diplomacy with the nation's brand (ibid., 9), which gives a neat delineation between national and humanitarian interests. In Latin American countries as well, the cooperation of Latin American states, UNHCR, NGOs, and the scientific community can be defined as multilateral humanitarian diplomacy aimed at protecting the rights of refugees and displaced persons (Albro 2019).

One of the regions in most need of humanitarian diplomacy attention is the Middle East, which has continued to bear some of the most adverse and prolonged humanitarian crises (Hodynskaya-Golenishcheva 2018). The Syrian conflict remains one of the largest humanitarian and refugee crisis in the world with 6.1 million Syrians remaining internally displaced. Throughout the region, according to the UNHCR, there are about 13.5 million internally displaced people and refugees. Nearly half of the population in the Middle East is aged under 24; these adolescents and youth have great potential, but to unleash that potential, they need access to opportunities to learn and develop the skills needed to earn a dignified living. However, currently most education systems are failing, leaving learners without the skills they need for a prosperous future, and that, in turn, threatens the stability of the entire region.

Weaponization of HD

The practice of recent conflicts has shown that NGOs are gradually delegating many of their roles to the armed forces involved in their resolution. In the process of implementing humanitarian policy, this includes humanitarian organizations. Their employees must adhere to the principles of impartiality and neutrality, and provide timely assistance to victims of a conflict. It must be remembered that even insignificant (by Western standards) material assistance or political support to one of the parties to the conflict may lead to a violation of the fragile balance of power that restrains outbursts of violence in traditional societies.

Of course, the leading international non-governmental organizations play a crucial role in the process of providing assistance to post-conflict societies, but often the military-political interests of the leading powers have a significant influence on the activities of NGOs during humanitarian operations. As noted, the main feature of the action of NGOs in world processes is their strong social and humanitarian influence on politics in various ways, from creating public opinion regarding humanitarian crisis to assisting in Track II talks.

Many NGOs are concerned with maintaining independence from military forces when they occupy the same physical operational space. The 2007 publication, "Guidelines for Relations Between U.S. Armed Forces and Non-Governmental Humanitarian Organizations in Hostile or Potentially Hostile Environments," which was adopted by U.S. Department of Defense (DoD) and the group of NGOs under the Inter Action umbrella, identifies U.S. Agency for International Development (USAID) as a potential bridge between the U.S. military and NGOs in the field (USAID 2015). As appropriate, USAID may serve as a liaison between DoD and USAID's implementing partners. In its engagements, USAID will seek suitable opportunities to provide information to DoD about the mission of NGOs; principles, roles, and best practices of humanitarian and development organizations; and USAID's important liaison role between the military and the broader NGO community.

According to Howard Roy Williams, ex-director of the U.S. Center for Humanitarian Cooperation, the initial reaction of non-governmental organizations to the U.S. military operation in Afghanistan was negative, but later it turned to the opposite (Williams n.d.). Then the U.S. military involved the so-called provincial reconstruction teams, performing de facto functions of humanitarian organizations and civil authorities, the priority activity of which was the restoration of transport infrastructure, water supply systems, the implementation of projects in the field of education and health, the construction of schools, hospitals, and power plants. Russia's first humanitarian aid experience to European countries during the COVID pandemic in March of 2020 to Italy and Serbia was delivered through Ministry of Defense and Emergency Ministry channels following the model of civil-military cooperation in HD.

Practice shows that along with numerous examples of providing humanitarian assistance to post-conflict societies and the important public function of protecting human rights that many NGOs perform—for example, in Haiti, Sudan, and Somalia—the real formats of humanitarian diplomacy have increasingly changed and evolved. From an element of "soft power" they become a factor of "hard" power. The introduction of external institutions of power into a country that recently was plunged into chaos makes these institutions more of an imitation of those that should have been created, since, being placed in difficult conditions, the alien reformers objectively underestimate the requirements for their strength and effectiveness and at the same time do not allow the local society to develop its own internal need for (new) institutions (Zeuge-Buberl 2017).

Politicization of HD

Humanitarian diplomacy today is highly politicized. The politicization of humanitarian diplomacy can be direct, targeted, or indirect and based on imitation (Baykov 2022). Since the 1990s humanitarian intervention has been justified by the concept of the "responsibility to protect," which is the interference in the affairs of a state if it does not protect its own population from genocide, war crimes, ethnic cleansing, and crimes against humanity. Researchers have noted a greater importance of political considerations when making decisions about the provision of assistance, which has increased the likelihood of manipulation of the humanitarian system. Also notable is the risk that humanitarianism itself can justify military action (Gromoglasova 2018; Suchkov 2020). Such an approach creates a dangerous precedent and contributes to the delusion that humanitarianism underwrites such ambitious forms of protection (Chandler 2001, 681; Macrae 1998, 309–17; Rieff 2002; see also Gordon and Donini 2015, 107–8).

Unfortunately, humanitarian diplomacy, based on the principles originally formulated by the ICRC and the Charter of the United Nations, has therefore become highly politicized. Its focus has shifted from addressing the root causes of crises (chronic poverty; heightened vulnerability to natural and man-made disasters; and their consequences, including war, disease, famine, and forced displacement) toward a more political form of engagement. Meanwhile, most conflicts are being managed instead of solved.

In the process of implementing humanitarian policy, humanitarian organizations play a key role because humanitarian actors must adhere to the so-called principle of impartiality. It must be remembered that even insignificant (by Western standards) material assistance or political support to one of the parties in a conflict could lead to a violation of the fragile circumstances that restrain outbursts of violence. Of course, generally recognized international non-governmental organizations play a crucial role in the process of providing assistance to post-conflict societies, but often the military-political interests of the leading powers have a significant influence on the activities of NGOs during such humanitarian operations (Borishpolets 2021).

The politicization of humanitarian diplomacy is interconnected with the humanitarian influence of hundreds of intermediaries: partners and subcontractors in the form of government agencies, international organizations, private foundations, NGOs, and individual actors. Politicians can deny access to territory, as well as regulate the legal conditions for the presence in its jurisdiction of cross-border humanitarian infrastructure, which, in turn, is also influenced by the local context: from political conditions to staffing. For example, departments, foundations, and NGOs that run humanitarian programs have become powerful lobbyists fighting for government funding through media and political parties.

Intergovernmental organizations (EU, ASEAN, SCO, African Union, and others) are becoming the coordinators of what is happening in the region, while they are increasingly including a humanitarian component in their activities. Regional cooperation in the sphere of HD is based on two main components: first, an open, inclusive dialogue between governments, civil society, including academia, international and regional organizations; and secondly, the ability of regional actors to generate innovative ideas and effective own solutions based on the principles of regional solidarity and responsibility. All this turns the process of HD into a dynamic situation of interaction—with the aim of finding solutions to complex problems.

Localization

There are different actors and levels of humanitarian diplomacy. Regnier (2011, 1219–21) argues that the practice operates at the (1) international and

(2) at the national and local levels. HD can be international, from country to country, or it can be provided to individual entities, state authorities or local governments, legal entities, and individuals. All this is necessary to solve global problems, for example, the restoration and restitution of cultural heritage, the disposal of life-threatening substances after military operations or disasters, and much more. The most common, especially during a pandemic, is cooperation in the field of medicine. In military conflicts, this is the arrangement of medical camps or support for local hospitals, as well as medical examinations after an emergency or humanitarian assistance.

The problem is the head office of UN agencies and international NGOs often have the power of veto over local field officers. For example, the calls for investigations by the WHO into the reasons for very high incidence of cancer among local residents in Southern Iraq were blocked by the United States (owing to the use of depleted uranium rounds against large concentrations of Iraqi armor). In the field, the programs are adjusted to local conditions. Each country has special regulations, different aspects of working with government bodies, specific conditions for the activities of foreign organizations. Those activities are formulated on a needs assessment, which is initiated on requests by an external actor, and then creating solutions that meet those assessed needs.

There are three strategies for humanitarian diplomacy: standardization, localization, and adaptation. For most cases, some standardization of HD is inevitable. Localization involves adjusting HD programs in accordance with national regulations and local conditions. Adaptation involves changing the program depending on the audience. Adaptation is necessary when in different countries there is a large differentiation in the foreign policy needs of the population. The standard HD program does not have to be adapted to people's preferences, but still needs to be localized. The development of an international standard of humanitarian diplomacy requires data analysis, intensive work of local branches of NGOs and deep knowledge in making foreign policy decisions in this area. The benefits of developing a certain level of adaptation, a targeted approach are obvious.

Although it may seem that the process of pursuing humanitarian diplomacy can be standardized as far as there are "humanitarian universals"—universal human needs and rights of people in need, processes that do not vary much across globe, culture similarities—in the field the programs should be adjusted to local conditions. Each country has special regulations, different aspects of working with government bodies, specific conditions for the activities of foreign organizations. It is based on needs assessment, on the requests of an external audience, and creating solutions that meet them. International humanitarian financing, however, remains oriented to international humanitarian agencies and NGOs, with only a small proportion of reported funding being channeled directly to local and national NGOs.

Proposals

Recent years have seen a series of events that will shape global strategies across the development and humanitarian spheres for some time to come. It is essential that a coherent approach emerges from these various processes. The COVID-19 pandemic reversed decades of progress toward achieving the UN's Sustainable Development Goals and led to financial challenges in nearly all countries. Between 2019 and 2020 an estimated 50 million more people were forced into extreme poverty, and by 2021 an estimated 698 million people, or nine percent of the global population, were still living in extreme poverty. The full impact of humanitarian diplomacy will also be felt for years to come, but the pandemic has exposed deeper problems (Sucklin et al. 2021).

There is no unified theory of HD but some generalizations may be useful for the purpose of offering policy recommendations (Gromoglasova 2018). A broadened international discussion on HD should be launched by international organizations such as the International Studies Association or the International Communication Association. There should be both scholars and practitioners, representatives of international organizations, and of international and local humanitarian NGOs. For example, according to Nicholas Cull, "our humanitarian diplomacy would be better supported if the surrounding language spoke of 'people seeking asylum,' 'people migrating' or 'people seeking refuge' rather than the impersonal categories of asylum seeker, migrant and refugee. We might even ask people how they wish to be referred to, which has also been transformative in domestic disability rights work" (Cull 2022). In conflict resolution there is also a growing consensus that peace agreements can no longer be exclusively or even primarily made on an official level. Sustainable peace depends on the engagement of different official and non-official global, national, and local actors.

People affected by humanitarian emergencies want to be more involved in the evaluation of the response. Knowing exactly who and where people in need are, what resources are reaching them, and with what results, is a long-standing challenge across development and environmental as well as humanitarian communities (Clark 2018). This not only concerns the tangible aspects of HD operations in the field, but also the intangible aspects, such as cultural specificities and identities of those both giving and receiving assistance.

In particular, the wider involvement of women in solving significant problems and challenges of our time is urgently needed. Although 20 years ago the UN Security Council adopted resolution (S/RES/1325) on women and peace and security reaffirming the important role of women in the "prevention and resolution of conflicts, peace negotiations, peace-building, peacekeeping, humanitarian response and in post-conflict reconstruction and stressing the importance of their equal participation and full involvement in all efforts for the maintenance and promotion of peace and security," there has been little serious progress in this sphere, and implementation of this resolution has been faulty. So far, it cannot be said that a radical change in the status of women has occurred everywhere in the world. Women, more than men, suffer from poverty, lack of access to education, medical services, violence, and discrimination in its most diverse forms.

Current conflicts result in higher levels of gender-based violence against women and girls, including arbitrary killings, torture, sexual violence, and forced marriage. Women and girls are primarily and increasingly targeted by the use of sexual violence, including as a tactic of war. While states bear primary responsibility for addressing sexual violence, the international community, and the United Nations system in particular, can provide much-needed development assistance, capacity-building, technical support, and training. Sexual violence prevention and response should be incorporated in peacekeeping mandates and more women should be deployed in peacekeeping missions to work closely with communities on the ground. Women also suffer not only from armed groups, but also from international institutions and humanitarian NGO employees—that is, from the people who are supposed to help them.

So-called feminine qualities—empathy, flexibility, modesty, willingness to compromise—can be used more actively in promoting dialogue and settling conflicts. It is natural for women to participate in solving the most important socio-economic problems and working toward advancing sustainable global development. Women leaders should seize the initiative in matters ranging from climate change to combating common threats and counteracting social engineering. At the same time, all these common challenges can be a chance for countries to develop mechanisms of effective cooperation. Projects should be ambitious in partner-engagement, large-scale in resources, and long-term in vision in keeping with the familiar slogan, "progress for women is progress for all."

Beyond furthering better gender relations, the personalization and diversification of HD should be diverse enough to include various values, lifestyles, and ethnicities. Humanitarian diplomacy should meet unique demands of multiple cultures by expanding outreach: every person should feel it is addressing him/her. This is often not the case. Intercultural competences are needed for and by the practitioners. It is necessary to know what diagnoses and prescriptions the counterpart staff and institutions accept and what they reject, what needs they articulate, what problems they want to solve, how they perceive the impact of a particular problem, and how resources and culture influence the capacity of local actors and institutions.

Developing country actors disagree over the right structure for providing and coordinating aid to these most vulnerable groups of people instead of uniting joint efforts to achieve goals including sustainable economic growth, effective social services, responsible governance, and timely humanitarian relief. For all this to be achieved, international resources are needed to complete community projects with quick impact: to construct schools, clinics, and governance facilities, and to implement projects designed to revitalize agricultural productivity and economic growth.

Conclusion

As Turunen (2020, 481) has observed, "humanitarian diplomacy mediates between the apolitical and political, between ideals and pragmatism." This observation is the basis for this chapter. Cooperation between states at the diplomatic and intergovernmental level continues, but at the same time so do national egoism and its motives. Meanwhile, humanitarian diplomacy also continues in search of specific objectives aimed at humanitarian needs. Those are closely related with national interests, national security, and foreign policy goals, which makes HD a more powerful instrument of foreign policy.

The main problem for HD in many countries is a lack of strategic planning. Its structural apparatus is amorphous, and its practitioners are overburdened with additional functions. While recognition of the importance of humanitarian diplomacy and advocacy has grown, the international humanitarian system still lacks focus, strategy, and multi-agency coordination. In other words, according to Clark (2018, 46), "in humanitarian emergencies, humanitarian effectiveness is dependent on prompt diplomacy and advocacy. One of the challenges to aid effectiveness is the decentralization of the humanitarian system that is made up of a myriad of independent, professional, and informal actors."

HD needs to undergo a thorough audit by the UN or another multilateral organization to reveal what ideas that have been tried in the past, and what negative and positive impacts they have had, as well as what the reasons were for failures and successes in implementation. In particular, the wider involvement of women in solving significant problems and challenges in humanitarian diplomacy is urgently needed. It is no exaggeration to say that the attention to the humanitarian aspects of armed conflicts and the importance of the problems of humanitarian support and protection of civilians, including in conflicts and in post-conflict zones, are mounting.

The abovementioned audit should be accompanied by a broad international discussion on HD involving scholars and practitioners, representatives of international organizations, and international and local humanitarian NGOs. Citizens of developing countries should play an important role, of course. Finally, it is important to bear in mind that humanitarian diplomacy includes not only crisis and emergency response, but also cooperation in the sphere of arts, science, sports, tourism, and more generally in public diplomacy. These efforts help those in need and build the confidence necessary to promote engagement and international dialogue.

References and Further Reading

Albro, R. 2019. "Normative Accounts of International Environmental Migration in Latin America and the Religious Component of Intangible Loss." *Center for Latin American & Latino Studies*, Working Paper Series, No. 20, May.

Baykov, A.A. 2022. "Glava 1 Megatrendy i Global'nye Problemy: Konstanty i Novelly Predmetnogo Polya." In *Megatrendy: Osnovnye Traektorii Evolyucii Mirovogo Poryadka v XXI Veke*, eds. A.A. Baykov, A.D. Bogaturov, and T.A. Shakleina, 11–20. Moscow: Obshchestvo s ogranichennoj otvetstvennost'yu Izdatel'stvo "Aspekt Press."

Borishpolets, K.P. 2021. "Politika Vedushchih Gosudarstv v Oblasti Zdravoohraneniya i ih Vzaimodejstvie na Ploshchadkah." In *Social'no-gumanitarnaya Transformaciya Sovremennogo Mira*, ed. K.P. Borishpolec, 117–48. Moscow: Moskovskij Gosudarstvennyj Institut Mezhdunarodnyh Otnoshenij (Universitet).

Bowden, M., and V. Metcalfe-Hough. 2020. *Humanitarian Diplomacy and Protection: Advocacy in an Age of Caution*. Briefing Note, Humanitarian Policy Group, November.

Çevik, S.B. 2020. "Turkey's Public Diplomacy in Flux: From Proactive to Reactive Communication." In *Routledge Handbook of Public Diplomacy*, eds. N. Snow and N.J. Cull, 350–59. New York: Routledge.

Chandler, D. 2001. "The Road to Military Humanitarianism: How the Human Rights NGOs Shaped a New Humanitarian Agenda." *Human Rights Quarterly* 23 (3): 678–700.

Clark, M.D. 2018. *Humanitarian Multi-track Diplomacy: Conceptualizing the Definitive, Particular, and Critical Role of Diplomatic Function in Humanitarian Action*. Groningen: University of Groningen.

Cull, N.J. 2022. University of Southern California's Center for Public Diplomacy Blog. https://uscpublicdiplomacy.org/newswire/cpdblog_main.

Davidson, W.D., and J.V. Montville. 1981–82. "Foreign Policy According to Freud." *Foreign Policy* 45: 145–57.

Dus', Y.P. 2006. "Osnovnye Principy Regulirovaniya Mezhdunarodnoj Trudovoj Migracii." *Vestnik Omskogo Universiteta, Seriya: Mezhdunarodnyj Biznes* 1 (2): 100–5.

Egeland, J. 2013. "Humanitarian Diplomacy." In *The Oxford Handbook on Modern Diplomacy*, eds. A.F. Cooper, J. Heine, and R. Thakur, 352–68. Oxford: Oxford University Press.

Entman, R.M. 2004. *Projections of Power: Framing News, Public Opinion, and U.S. Foreign Policy*. Chicago: University of Chicago Press.

Fereday, J., and E. Muir-Cochrane. 2006. "Demonstrating Rigor Using Thematic Analysis: A Hybrid Approach of Inductive and Deductive Coding and Theme Development." *International Journal of Qualitative Methods* 5 (1): 80–92.

Gelev, I., and B. Popovska. 2020. "Humanitarian Diplomacy and Its Impact in Times of Pandemics and Health Crises." *International Scientific Journal* 20 (39): 163–78.

Gökalp, D. 2020. *The UAE's Humanitarian Diplomacy: Claiming State Sovereignty, Regional Leverage and International Recognition*. CMI Working Paper No. 1, February.

Gordon, S., and A. Donini. 2015. "Romancing Principles and Human Rights: Are Humanitarian Principles Salvageable?" *International Review of the Red Cross* 97 (897/898): 77–109.

Gromoglasova, E.S. 2018. *Gumanitarnaya diplomatiya v sovremennyh mezhdunarodnyh otnosheniya: opyt sistemnogo issledovaniya*. Moscow: IMEMO RAN.

Hodynskaya-Golenishcheva, M.S. 2018. "Sirijskij Krizis v Transformiruyushchemsya Miroporyadke: Rol' Emigrantskih Oppozicionnyh Struktur" (2011–2015—Sirijskij Nacional'nyj Sovet, Nacional'naya Koaliciya). *Aziya i Afrika Segodnya* 1 (726): 17–25.

Hyett, N., A. Kenny, and V. Dickson-Swift. 2014. "Methodology or Method? A Critical Review of Qualitative Case Study Reports." *International Journal of Qualitative Studies on Health and Well-Being* 9 (1): 23606.

IFRC. 2017. *Humanitarian Diplomacy Policy*. https://www.ifrc.org/sites/default/files/Humanitarian-Diplomacy-Policy_EN.pdf.

Kireçci, M.A. 2015. "Humanitarian Diplomacy in Theory and Practice." *Perceptions* 20 (1): 1–6.

Komleva, V.V. 2020. "Mezhdunarodnoe Gumanitarnoe Sotrudnichestvo: K Voprosu o Ponimanii Sushchnosti i Opredelenii Ponyatiya." In *V sbornike: Rossiya i Mir: Dialogi*, 56–67. Moscow: Materialy Mezhdunarodnoj Nauchno-Prakticheskoj Konferencii.

Krasnyak, O., and P-B. Ruffini. 2020. "Science Diplomacy." In *Oxford Bibliographies in International Relations*, ed. P. James. New York: Oxford University Press.

Lebedeva, O.V. 2019. *Instituty Mnogostoronnej Diplomatiii: Uchebnoe Posobie Dlya Vuzov*. Moscow: Obshchestvo s ogranichennoj otvetstvennost'yu Izdatel'stvo "Aspekt Press."

Lebedeva, M.M., and M.I. Ustinova. 2020. "Gumanitarnye i Social'nye Voprosy v Sovete Bezopasnosti OON." *Vestnik Mezhdunarodnyh Organizacij* 15 (1): 135–54.

Macrae, J. 1998. "The Death of Humanitarianism?: An Anatomy of the Attack." *Disasters* 22 (4): 309–17.

Maurer, P. 2016. "Humanitarian Diplomacy and Principled Humanitarian Action." *International Review of the Red Cross* 97 (897/898): 445–52.

Minear, L., and H. Smith, eds. 2007. *Humanitarian Diplomacy: Practitioners and Their Craft*. Tokyo: United Nations University Press.

Prohorenko, I.L. 2020. "Gruppa Dvadcati." In *Problemy Global'noj Cifrovizacii. Politika Razvitiya v Usloviyah Cifrovizacii Obshchestva: Materialy Vserossijskoj Nauchnoj Konferencii s Mezhdunarodnym Uchastiem*, ed. I.L. Prohorenko, 242–46. Krasnodar: Vika-Print.

Regnier, P. 2011. "The Emerging Concept of Humanitarian Diplomacy: Identification of a Community of Practice and Prospects for International Recognition." *International Review of the Red Cross* 93 (884): 1211–37.

Rieff, D. 2002. "Humanitarianism in Crisis." *Foreign Affairs* 81 (6): 111–21.

Rousseau, E., and A.S. Pende. 2020. "Humanitarian Diplomacy." In *Global Diplomacy. The Sciences Po Series in International Relations and Political Economy*, eds. T. Balzacq, F. Charillon, and F. Ramel. Cham: Palgrave Macmillan.

Rugh, W. 2014. *Front Line Public Diplomacy. How U.S. Embassies Communicate with Foreign Publics*. New York: Palgrave.

Schutz, A. 1967 [1932]. *The Phenomenology of the Social World*, trans. G. Walsh and F. Lehnert. Evanston: Northwestern University Press.

Simons, G. 2020a. "Russian Foreign Policy and Public Diplomacy: Meeting 21st Century Challenges." *Vestnik RUDN: International Relations* 20 (3): 491–503.

———. 2020b. "The Corona Virus Pandemic and Global Transformations: Making or Breaking International Orders?" *Outlines of Global Transformations: Politics, Economics, Law* 13 (5): 20–37.

Solana, J. 2020. "The Case for 'Human Diplomacy.'" *The Hague Journal of Diplomacy* 15 (4): 670–80.

Straus, O.S., E.P. Wheeler, T.P. Ion, C.L. Lange, T. Marburg, and J. Wheless. 1912. "Humanitarian Diplomacy of the United States." In *Proceedings of the American Society of International Law at Its Annual Meeting*, April 6: 45–59.

Suchkov, M. 2020. "Liderstvo i Prinyatie Yneshnepoliticheskih Reshenij v Epohu Novogo Tekhnologicheskogo Uklada." *Mezhdunarodnye Processy* T. 18. 4 (63): 62–80.

Sucklin E., Z. Christensen, and D. Woltun. 2021. *Poverty Trends: Global, Regional and National*, November 10. https://devinit.org/resources/poverty-trends-global-regional-and-national.

Turunen, S. 2020. "Humanitarian Diplomatic Processes." *The Hague Journal of Diplomacy* 15 (4): 459–87.

USAID. 2015. *Policy on Cooperation With the Department of Defense*. Washington, D.C., June. https://www.usaid.gov/sites/default/files/documents/1866/USAIDPolicyCooperationDoD.pdf.

Velikaya, A. 2022. "Soviet Public Diplomacy." *Place Branding and Public Diplomacy* 18: 77–92.

Velikaya, A., and G. Simons, eds. 2019. *Russia's Public Diplomacy: Evolution and Practice*. London: Palgrave Macmillan.

Veuthey, M. 2012. "Humanitarian Diplomacy: Saving It When It Is Needed Most." In *Humanitarian Space*, eds. A. Vautravers and Y. Fox, 195–208. Geneva: Webster University.

Williams, H.R. n.d. *International Humanitarian Cooperation and International Humanitarian Law*. New York: Center for Humanitarian Cooperation.

Zeuge-Buberl, U. 2017. *The Mission of the American Board in Syria: Implications of a Transcultural Dialog*. Stuttgart: Franz Steiner Verlag.

Zonova, T.V. 2018. "Diplomatiya Svyatogo Prestola." In *Diplomaticheskaya Sluzhba Zarubezhnyh Stran*, eds. A.V. Torkunova and A.N. Panova, 134–57. Moscow: Obshchestvo s Ogranichennoj Otvetstvennost'yu Izdatel'stvo "Aspekt Press."

32

Geoeconomic Diplomacy: Reforming the Instrumentalization of Economic Interdependencies and Power

Kim B. Olsen

In the hours and days after President Vladimir Putin, in late February 2022, announced Russia's recognition of the independence of the Ukrainian oblasts Donetsk and Luhansk and launched a weaponized assault on Ukraine's territory, the primary response of the European Union (EU) and its international partners to this blatant demonstration of brute military power came to be a geoeconomic one. Watching in real-time how Russian troops and tanks crossed the border of a sovereign European state, political leaders from the EU and the G7 univocally agreed to launch a series of financial and economic sanctions targeted to undermine Russia's political and economic leadership and, ultimately, socio-economic fabric. Although Western governments also pledged lethal and non-lethal support to Ukraine's army and armed resistance, this predominantly geoeconomic response to a military attack on the European continent came to emphasize the importance that EU governments are giving to their abilities for "weaponizing" their economic wealth and resources as integral parts of their foreign and security policy-making.

A few months into the Russian aggression against Ukraine, at the time of writing, Russia has become the target of substantial financial and economic sanctions from the EU, the United States, the United Kingdom, Canada, Japan, Singapore, and others. Together, they establish one of the most complex and encompassing sanctions regimes ever directed against a major

K. B. Olsen (✉)
Danish Institute for International Studies, Copenhagen, Denmark

© The Author(s), under exclusive license to Springer Nature Switzerland AG 2023
P. W. Hare et al. (eds.), *The Palgrave Handbook of Diplomatic Reform and Innovation*, Studies in Diplomacy and International Relations, https://doi.org/10.1007/978-3-031-10971-3_32

military and economic power in modern times. Particularly for the EU, the comprehensive move to sever economic ties with Russia has been a remarkable one. Many of its member states had either held strong trade relations with Russia or made much of their energy consumption dependent on the import from Russian, such as coal, oil, and, most important, natural gas. Such dependencies also soon proved to be main drivers for disagreements between member states in terms of how far-reaching the Russia sanctions should be and which economic losses should be accepted on the European side. But in light of the Putin government's barefaced violation of Ukrainian territorial sovereignty, and its disregard of the human and humanitarian consequences hereof, EU member states on balance managed to agree on substantial individual and sectoral sanctions aimed at containing and, ultimately, changing Russia's aggressive behavior.

Seen in the broader picture, the EU's response to Russia's military aggression is emblematic of a more general trend in EU foreign and security policy, where instruments of economic power have come to play an increasingly important role (Olsen 2022a). From the viewpoint of diplomats, this development comes with opportunities and challenges. Most importantly, this is because any governmental use of geoeconomic instruments, or instruments of economic statecraft, implies a certain degree of state-led interference with and manipulation of market structures and global value chains (Blackwill and Harris 2016). This could be through sanctions, embargoes, or defensive trade instruments against political "foes" or through the support or subvention of specific actors or structures such as tariff reductions or direct economic assistance for political "friends." Yet, all the while the appetite of policymakers to reach geostrategic ends through economic means is only growing, the diplomatic structures to support these ambitions are rarely reforming at the same pace. Be it at the domestic, European, or international level, emerging disconnects between states' geoeconomic policy aims and their diplomatic capabilities for implementing them in manageable and conflict-reducing ways are only becoming more apparent. An additional challenge—particularly in countries with governance traditions that underpin liberal market capitalism, for example, found in Europe, North America, and most parts of East Asia—a closer integration of state and market spheres in the realm of foreign and security policy might be hindered by ideological traditions for guarding a strong independence of markets from overt state influence.

This chapter will focus on the distinct diplomatic practice of geoeconomic diplomacy that governments can use to reduce the challenges they might face when seeking to realize their ambitions for instrumentalizing state-market relations to their geostrategic advantage. After explaining how geoeconomic diplomacy distinguishes itself from other types of diplomatic actions, this chapter will take departure in the two recent geoeconomic cases—the EU sanctions against Russia and the deliberations around the EU's new instrument to counter economic coercion by major strategic rivals like China—to discuss the challenges, demands, and possibilities for organizational and norm-oriented reforms in rethinking European diplomatic capabilities in the geoeconomic field. Inside the EU, this chapter argues that organizational reforms should focus on ensuring a stronger integration of private market logics, actors, and structures in the state-driven arena of geoeconomic power politics, which has often been impeded at both the level of domestic diplomatic services and the level of international and multilateral diplomatic engagement on geoeconomic issues. Possible reform measures should focus on a stronger cross-integration of security policy and economic pillars at both the national and EU institutional level, including the creation of "geoeconomic committees" to integrate private sector and civil society actors in foreign and security policy deliberations and decision-making. In terms of the EU's engagement with international partners, this chapter discusses how the EU should critically assess to what degree the increasing, unregulated instrumentalization of market forces is in its own self-interests and what it would take to build the foundations for future multilateral governance structures beyond the G20, the United Nations Security Council (UNSC), and the World Trade Organization (WTO), whose relevance in giving order to the geoeconomic field has become increasingly challenged over the past decades.

What is Geoeconomic Diplomacy and Why is It Important?

Governments' use of power resources, be they military or economic, has traditionally been seen as an antidote to engaging in the international realm through means of diplomacy (Baldwin 1985). In this classical understanding of diplomacy, the fostering of intra-state relations is understood as means for building alliances or reducing tensions and mediating agreements between conflicting parties. Scholars of diplomacy, such as those contributing to this volume, have for decades nuanced this view and called for attention to the broad span of activities that diplomats engage in as representatives of a given polity.

Seen from the level of diplomatic practitioners, operating at the intersection of states and markets is, of course, far from being a novel phenomenon.

Arguably, the active interference by governmental representatives into the functioning of markets constitutes one of the most traditional spheres of diplomatic work (Badel 2010). In the post-Cold War era, and particularly in light of the growing competition so-called non-Western emerging economies in the early 2000s and the financial and economic crises of 2008–9, diplomatic practitioners of both EU institutions and member states gradually strengthened their understanding and capacities for how governmental representatives might support European business interests in international markets and for ensuring advantageous trade conditions for domestic market actors through the establishment of free trade agreements. This area of diplomatic engagement, commonly described as economic diplomacy, is conducted with an ultimate view to use political means for supporting ends of economic prosperity (Okano-Heijmans 2011).

One area of diplomatic activity in the state-market nexus that has so far received less conceptual attention is when diplomats work toward ends that are not intrinsically economic but geostrategic. Whereas a state's use of economic coercion vis-à-vis other states is a well-described area of economic statecraft (Baldwin 1985), the engagement of diplomatic practitioners that is necessary for putting geoeconomic policies into practice has been less acknowledged in academic literature as a distinct practice of diplomatic activity. This chapter highlights the field of geoeconomic diplomacy is a unique form of diplomatic engagement in that it describes the particular realm in which governments pursue the ability to employ national economic capabilities to realize specific geostrategic objectives in the conduct of their relationships with other international actors.

Based on the observation that geoeconomic instruments, such as sanctions and defensive trade measures, are utilized by governments in attempts to steer market forces in certain directions that ultimately should underpin their geostrategic aims, the concept of geoeconomic diplomacy not only describes the engagement between diplomatic representatives with non-state and private market actors but particularly puts spotlight on the limits of governmental control over such actors who—at the same time—might influence the practical implementation of geoeconomic policies. Whereas the prerogative of formulating and interpreting legal rules and regulations rests with governments, parliaments, and judicial systems, the complexities of putting geoeconomic policies into practice in a highly integrated and interdependent global economy should not be underestimated. A state's or multiple states' decision to embark on a specific geoeconomic policy is one thing. To successfully implement this policy in the global state-market nexus is another (Lohmann and Vorrath 2021). Investigating a given government's or group of governments' geoeconomic diplomacy implies looking for the means, actors, and processes with and through which they seek to ensure that relevant stakeholders—be they national or international, public or private—understand, accept, and, possibly, support the foreign and security policy objectives behind a certain geoeconomic intervention. In other words, geoeconomic diplomacy is the human-centric mechanism through which governments might be able to gain additional governance influence over potentially uncontrollable market actors and structures for foreign and security policy purposes. Particularly in times where structures of global governance are challenged by rising great power conflicts and antagonisms, and the mutual non-benign use of economic power resources becomes more likely at a significant scale, understanding how and why diplomats engage with various actors that influence the functioning of state-market relations in security-sensitive areas is as critical as ever.

The EU: A Geoeconomic Contender with Governance Challenges

The EU's choice to counter Russia's military aggression through geoeconomic means was significant, but not unexpected. Leaders of the EU, the United States, and allied countries had long made clear that a Russian military aggression toward Ukraine—or other partner countries in eastern Europe—would be met with "the most severe sanctions that have ever been imposed" (White House 2022). In the months of lead up to Russia's intervention, some of the most forceful sanctions provisions, such as the blockade of Russia's central bank from access to large parts of its foreign exchange reserves, had been prepared through a substantial diplomatic groundwork (Pop et al. 2022). This groundwork was not in the least possible because it built on a more general development in EU foreign and security policy-making, namely its increasing willingness to utilize its substantial wealth and wide-spanning trade relations as key geostrategic leverages. In what has been described as the EU's "geoeconomic pivot," European policymakers are more frequently and more thoroughly than before reverting to economic-based power instruments to counter behavior from international competitors deemed as detrimental to European interests (Olsen 2022a). Besides the enhanced use of financial and economic sanctions, this pivot, for example, also materializes in recent EU plans to design a new anti-coercion instrument (ACI) to counter coercive trade practices of third states. As explicitly stated by EU officials, the timing and scope for launching such an instrument has not least been informed by actions of another key strategic rival, China. Such was, for example, the case when China announced to cut its trade relations with EU member state Lithuania after the latter had allowed for the opening of a Taiwanese representative office in Vilnius—a decision that Beijing assessed as a direct challenge to its one-China policy that forbids any international recognition of Taiwan as an independent state and actor (Hackenbroich and Zerka 2021).

All the while the EU's use of its economic clout in foreign and security policy is not new, the EU's enhanced engagement in the field of geoeconomics has in recent years led to renewed attention to the matter both in academic literature and at the practitioners' level. Throughout the 2010s, the growing literature on the EU's role and capabilities in the realm of economic power politics was predominantly concerned with the strategic objectives and actual political will with which European policymakers would be ready to advance the use of economic power instruments. In a slow, yet steady, reckoning of how the twenty-first century's hyper-globalizing economy not only promised to provide for unprecedented levels of market access and the integration of global value chains, but that such economic interdependences could also pave the way for an increasing of "weaponization" of states' economic resources in geostrategic disputes or conflicts (Drezner et al. 2021), observers also called for the need to both strengthen the EU's political will of engaging in this developing geoeconomic reality and reform the organizational capabilities that could underpin such ambitions.

The calls were heard by president of the European Commission, Ursula von der Leyen, who shortly after her appointment in mid-2019 emphasized her aim to build a "geopolitical Commission." In von der Leyen's vision, the EU needed to reinforce its capabilities for defending its "open strategic autonomy and resilience" in a global economy that had become "increasingly multipolar" and where "the short-term pursuit of unilateral interests by specific actors can undermine effective multilateral cooperation" (European Commission 2021a, 1). The imperative for strengthening the EU's position could only be realized through reforming central pillars of the EU's macroeconomic and financial organization. In a first round of proposals of early 2021, the Commission specifically aimed at solidifying the euro in international currency markets to reduce its reliance on other major currencies, reinforcing EU financial market infrastructures, and improving the EU's use and implementation of economic and financial sanctions. A few months later the Commission, together with other EU institutions, followed up by disseminating plans for strengthening the EU's use of defensive trade measures to respond to the use of economic coercion by third parties to undermine or interfere in "legitimate sovereign choices by the Union or a Member State" (Crochet 2022, 4).

While recent developments pertaining to two of the EU's announced reform measures with clearest geoeconomic characteristics—the use of financial and economic sanctions and the still emerging ACI—will be discussed in greater detail below, it is important to note that they can be seen as response to the same symptom: the persistence of inadequate EU governance structures to solidify links between the realms of trade and economy with those of foreign and security policy. As will be shown, such insufficiencies have had a direct negative impact on the EU's abilities for conducting a successful and reliant geoeconomic diplomacy. Looking at the possible root causes behind the insufficient governance structures that are to underpin the EU's geoeconomic diplomacy, several ideational, organizational, and cultural factors are to be considered, both individually and in relation to each other. It should here be noted that while the below points relate to the contextual circumstances of diplomatic practitioners operating in the EU context, similar factors might be met in other countries and regions, especially where state-market cooperation is characterized by governance models of liberal market capitalism. Other factors would most likely need to be considered when scrutinizing the geoeconomic abilities of more state capitalistic countries such as China and India. State-owned enterprises here play a large role in economic activity, which, arguably, could lead to other types of possibilities and challenges for their geoeconomic diplomatic practitioners (Olsen 2022b).

Ideationally, even in times of crisis and upheaval, the EU has proven to be largely resistant to international developments with the potential of challenging its adherence to the principles of open, liberal, and free trade. Even after the external shocks emanating from the financial and economic crises of 2008–9, and despite opposition from mainly eastern and southern European member states preferring a more protectionist course, the EU as such remained committed to trade practices that would "epitomise the prioritisation of liberalisation over protection" (Bollen et al. 2016, 290). As a consequence of this overarching ideational commitment to liberal trade measures, which entailed a strong focus on the expansion of free trade agreements and enhanced economic partnerships between the EU with established (the United States, Canada, and Japan) or emerging (China, India, and South Korea) global economic powers, the EU's primary focus was to enhance global market integration and trade. It was only during the 2010s where EU policymakers increased their appetite for exploring the coercive potentials of the Union's economic weight in global trade relations. This development was not least fostered by the hardening geoeconomics strategies and increasing protectionist tendencies among the EU's greatest global contenders, China and the United States. Looking east, the EU found itself confronted with large-scale Chinese investments in inter-regional infrastructure with geostrategic importance (i.e., the Belt and Road Initiative) or alternative financial investment structures (i.e., the Asian Infrastructure Investment Bank), as well as Beijing's attempts to use its economic clout to drive a wedge between EU member states (e.g., through the 17+1 cooperation between China and central and eastern European countries). Looking West, the Trumpian "America First" agenda included not only threats of imposing wide-scale tariffs against European economic interests but also the use of so-called secondary sanctions as part of the "maximum pressure" campaign against Iran, meaning that unilateral sanctions initiated by the United States would also have effects on European banks and companies with engagements in Iran. This gave important indications to EU policymakers that also supposed allies could—and would—utilize market interdependencies in coercive ways. Such developments helped to catalyze debates around the EU's own geoeconomics capacities and operational resources, meaning that fundamental questions about the instrumentalization of global market structures and value chains would become a more central part of the broader European discourse (Moraes and Wigell 2020).

Organizationally, the EU's geoeconomic sway was long hampered by a deficient linkage between the realms of trade and economy with those of foreign and security policy. The clear distinction between the Common Commercial Policy (CCP), in which the European Commission holds exclusive institutional responsibility to represent the EU in trade-related matters, and the Common Foreign and Security Policy (CFSP), governed by the intergovernmental, unanimity-demanding decision-making procedures among member states in the Council of the EU, did for long not invite for cross-silo thinking. And even if the Foreign Affairs Council (FAC), established with the Treaty of Lisbon in 2009 to oversee the EU's external relations, would also have special minister meeting formats focusing on defense, development, and trade, direct and operational links between the EU's foreign and security policy experts with those focusing on trade and commercial interests would consistently be at a limited level.

Culturally, following the above, diplomats covering the Council's regional working groups would generally not be in possession of a detailed technical understanding and expertise for analyzing the scope and usability of various specialized geoeconomic measures at the EU's disposal, such as sanctions and defensive trade instruments. Many CFSP diplomats would not be schooled to engage deeply in geoeconomic issues, leaving them somehow technically exposed in circumstances were the EU was to react decisively to geostrategic events, such as when the Union responded using large-scale individual and sectoral sanctions to the assault of the Syrian government on its own citizens in 2011 and Russia's annexation of Crimea in 2014 (Olsen 2022b).

Recent years have, however, shown signs of change to the working procedures and practices within the EU's structures. Not least exemplified by the clear geoeconomic framing of the von der Leyen Commission's reform drive, EU institutions and member states have been shifting gears toward a more assertive use of economic power instruments, especially against two other geoeconomic powers, Russia and China, who, albeit in different ways, have transformed from the role as the EU's strategic partners to becoming its geostrategic rivals. The remainder of this chapter will take a closer look at most recent developments in the EU's use of financial and economic sanctions against Russia and the development of the ACI in light of the intensification of coercive practices by China. This is to both identify some of the changes that European geoeconomic diplomacy is currently undergoing and suggest some longer-term reform measures that could further strengthen geoeconomic diplomatic governance, in Europe and beyond.

Facing Russia through Sanctions: Nascent Signs of European Reforms and Strengthened Transatlantic Cooperation

Russia's invasion of Ukraine on February 24, 2022 not only marked a historical moment for Europe's security architecture but also became the beginning of an unprecedented geoeconomic stand-off between some of the world's major economies. Over the first six week after the Russian crossing into Ukrainian territory—beyond Crimea and parts of the Donbass, which had already been forcefully occupied by pro-Russian separatists in 2014—the EU adopted five sanctions packages targeting visa bans and asset freezes against hundreds of Russian individuals and entities, deemed to be direct enablers or in other ways supporters of the Kremlin's war efforts, as well as a long range of sectoral sanctions against key Russian infrastructure, financial frameworks, and economic sectors. The EU sanctions were furthermore closely coordinated with those of the United States, the United Kingdom, and other allies. Particularly because Russia's warfare and atrocities, Ukraine's armed resistance, and, therefore, the international community's response are under daily development, the present chapter cannot speak to the overall direction that this defining development will take the EU, Ukraine, Russia, and others. It will limit its scope to draw out three preliminary learnings about the state-of-play in the EU's use of sanctions as a geoeconomic instrument and how its approach to geoeconomic diplomacy is developing in this context.

First, EU policymakers and diplomats would spend the initial weeks of the Russian warfare to develop a clearer, yet not conclusive, understanding of the strategic aims behind and, to some degree, the broader consequences of the EU's historical sanctions packages. Whereas the initial rounds of sanctions adopted in the war's first days had the characteristic of being purely reactive measures of punishment of the Russian government and the inner circle around president Putin, as well as the aim to cut of the Russian access to strategically important goods and assets, the subsequent weeks animated a renewed debate and, ultimately, consensus among EU institutions and member states about the necessity for Europe to enhance its political and economic independence of Russia, not least with a view to some member states' heavy dependence on Russian energy and fossil fuels. At the same time, heated debates between member state representatives about the EU sanctions' aim and scope also revealed a lack of comprehensive deliberations about how the sanctions might affect other geostrategic objectives outside of the situation in Ukraine. As a matter of example, it soon became clear that the combination of Russia's aggressive warfare in Ukraine and its blockade of non-sanctioned trade routes, in combination with the West's broad sanctioning of Russia would lead to large-scale disruptions of trade in key agriculture commodities, such as wheat and barley, not only to Europe but also to countries in the Middle East and Africa with major dependencies on these imports in terms of their food security. Although European policymakers would argue that any policy response that could help to halt Russia's forceful and violent invasion of another European country should be used, no matter the second-order consequences on the EU's relations with or the domestic situation in third countries, and that humanitarian exemptions in the sanctions regimes explicitly allow for the continuation of trade and food products, it could also be argued that the case illustrates a lack of EU governance structures to embed strategic deliberations about the use of economic power weapons: how are they to achieve their goals, and, particularly, which kind of intended and unintended effects would they have for other aspects of the EU's broader geostrategic environment. Were EU member states or other Western allies to consider the direct use of military weaponry, such strategic questions would likely be addressed prior to the execution of an executive decision. Even if the uses of military and economic warfare are incomparable in nature and possible consequences, the processes around the EU's utilization of sanctions against Russia nonetheless exposed a certain lack of strategic culture within the EU geoeconomic governance structures, consequently reducing the ability of diplomatic actors to continuously evaluate whether sanctions, once implemented, are helping to achieve a range of geostrategic objectives.

Second, realizing the necessity of keeping Europe's business community adequately informed about the rapidly developing sanctions provisions, the Commission spent significant resources to publish elaborated communication products about the sanctions measures possible scope and reach for private and non-governmental actors. If done properly, such types of public communication can form an important component of helpful geoeconomic diplomatic practice as the success of any attempt to economically coerce another state hinges on the exhaustive and precise implementation of the chosen measures. When implementing financial and economic sanctions, undermining primarily happens either through the mal-intended violation or circumvention and the search for legal loopholes by private actors or third-party countries, or because such actors fail to insufficiently comprehend the sanctions regulations and their legal consequences. Only days into the conflict EU institutions recognized that the rapidly evolving sanctions regimes—comprehensively targeting the EU's fifth largest trading partner (5.8 percent of total EU goods trade)—would leave many European companies, financial institutions, and other commercial actors with numerous unanswered questions at the level of practical implementation, such as the exact limits of specific export and import restrictions or the level to which listed Russian individuals were to have their assets frozen. To counter the risk that private actors could either unintendedly misinterpret or intentionally violate the sanctions' provisions, EU institutions ramped up their coordination mechanisms with other sanctions stakeholders as well as their public outreach to a hitherto unparalleled level. In terms of formal coordination, EU diplomats soon established various new institutional structures to ensure the sanctions' effective implementation. One of those was the so-called Freeze and Seize task force, responsible for coordinating efforts by EU institutions and member states to enforce sanctions against the more than 1000 listed individuals under the Russia sanctions regime. Another was the "Russian Elites, Proxies, and Oligarchs (REPO)" task force, established between the EU, the G7 members, as well as Australia to coordinate the sanctions enforcement between like-minded partners having established sanctions regimes against Russia (European Commission 2022a). In terms of public outreach to non-state and market actors, the Commission had in recent years already increased its publication of FAQs, guidelines, and legal opinions concerning the implementation of the more than 30 active EU sanctions regimes (European Commission 2022b). Such communication products were however often criticized by the receiving actors for being published too late and in a complicated language that would not give answers with sufficient clarity (Olsen 2022b). And even if the numerous FAQs and guidance notes published by the Commission throughout the first weeks after the adoption of the first updated EU sanctions package against Russia in late February 2022 were still characterized by instances of overtly legalistic formulations, the mere attempt to enhance public outreach to private and non-governmental actors could be seen as clear indicators for a stronger understanding among the EU's geoeconomic diplomatic practitioners for the value added to include such actors in their thinking.

Third, the EU's Russia sanctions were subject to a high level of coordination with international partners, most importantly the United States. Whereas transatlantic coordination has traditionally been part of the preparation, execution, and adjustment of unilateral—as opposed to the UNSC-mandated multilateral—sanctions regimes, observers have noted that the non-existence of formalized meeting formats between diplomatic practitioners from both sides of the Atlantic have previously reduced the comprehensiveness and viability of such international coordination efforts (Nephew 2017; Zarate 2013). In the case of the comprehensive and wide-spanning Russia sanctions packages, the first of which were released only hours after Russia's invasion into Ukrainian territory, these coordination efforts however reached previously unseen levels (Pop et al. 2022). Following closely the Russian military build-ups along the Ukrainian border, which had already intensified in late 2021, trade and sanctions experts from primarily the EU and the United States, but also from allies such as Canada and the United Kingdom, had used the time to investigate and coordinate possible geoeconomic responses. The geostrategic imperative for responding forcefully to Russia's aggression, short of involving their own military troops in the armed conflict, furthermore brought together high-level decision makers from both sides of the Atlantic. The most critical aspects of the sanctions packages, such as the unprecedented step to sanction the central bank of a G20 member, would be sorted out directly at the level of heads of states and governments.

Reverting to such ad hoc formats in a time of acute crisis does, however, not resolve the more fundamental challenge of international sanctions coordination. This challenge already begins at the intra-EU level. Some member states will, depending on the case in question, be more inclined than others to propose the use of the EU's sanctions instruments. Even if it is the EU institutions, that is, the Commission and the European External Action Service (EEAS) that formally presents sanctions proposals to the Council, preparations of such proposals are normally not possible without the input from member states, who generally hold a greater access to relevant information and intelligence sources concerning the state or states to be sanctioned. In practice, this means that non-EU sanctions representatives are constantly forced to reassess which EU member state is particularly important to coordinate with over each sanctions question. Furthermore, because no formalized sanctions coordination formats exist between like-minded allies, diplomatic representatives run the risk of losing precious time in establishing the right transatlantic relations at the right time. And even if the Commission and the EEAS have taken a greater role in preparing the Russia sanctions packages than has previously been the case, the challenge of coordination will prevail as member states, over time, are unlikely to accept that international sanctions coordination is handled without their direct involvement. As discussed below, such diplomatic redundancies could be alleviated through organizational reform measures at the international level.

Facing China through Anti-coercion Measures: Innovative Bridges over the Trade-Security Gap

In the years before the EU was forced to concentrate much of its economic power resources on confronting Russia's military advances in eastern Europe, it was another major economic power, and geostrategic rival, that had been the key catalyzer of the EU's diplomatic reorientation and organizational reform in the geoeconomic field: China. Whereas China, from the early 2000s onward, had positioned itself as one of the most profitable non-European export and trade markets for many EU member states, its increasingly coercive trade practices during the 2010s would become a source of growing political concern among EU institutions, governments, and business representatives, who would agree that "economic coercion [from China and elsewhere] is a growing and pressing problem that needs to be addressed by a dedicated legislative instrument" (Szczepański 2022, 6).

A recent and noticeable example of China's coercive trade practices was its punishment, in late 2021, of Lithuania due to the latter's acceptance of the opening of a Representative Office by Taiwan, and not by its capital Taipei, which until then had been a common way for EU member states to reduce the risk of possible confrontations with Beijing. Interpreted by the Chinese government as an overt challenge to its one-China policy, Beijing began to halt trade with Lithuania by removing the country from its customs clearing system. Furthermore, Beijing allegedly started threatening companies from other EU member states that their access to the Chinese market would be blocked if they were to continue trade relations in and with Lithuania (Hackenbroich et al. 2022). The Chinese-Lithuanian stand-off soon came to symbolize a prime example of a more general point of caution raised by European policymakers for some years, namely that China—and other powerful economic actors—could be capable of instrumentalizing their economic weight to coerce EU institutions and member states into political and economic concessions against their own interests. Even if China's de facto capacity for successfully applying economic coercive measures has been put into question by observers (Patey 2021), the Commission and others have in recent years emphasized the need for the EU to advance geoeconomic instruments to counter such coercive measures.

Such was the case in Spring 2021, when EU trade commissioner Valdis Dombrovskis argued for the necessity to establish a new legal framework for a redefined approach to European trade, which would allow EU institutions and member to being "more assertive in defending our interests" (European Commission 2021e). One specific policy action to be derived from this standpoint was the Commission's legislative proposal to create a so-called anti-coercion instrument, formally presented in December 2021. In its legislative proposal, which is still to be negotiated with the European Parliament and the Council, the Commission outlines how it should ultimately be granted the institutional mandate to respond to third countries economically coercive behavior with instruments such as restrictions on EU trade, foreign direct investments, access to capital markets, the suspension of tariff concessions and the imposition of new custom duties, the exclusion of from EU services and programs, and other similar tools (European Commission 2021d). In other words, the Commission, as the holder of the EU's joint trade mandate, is now seeking new formal capabilities, which will make it capable of responding to the coercive trade measures of third states with its own coercive trade measures.

While such an enhancement of the Commission's trade-related instruments could be seen as a pure expansion of its existing mandate in the trade realm, the lens of geoeconomic diplomacy suggests that there is more at play. Namely because the EU might become the target of a coercive trade behavior by countries who are seeking to advance their broader geostrategic ends outside the realm of trade, the ACI holds the inherent potential of bringing the realms of EU trade and security closer together. The example of the Chinese-Lithuanian confrontation again illustrates the point: Beijing used trade-centered measures to respond to what it deemed as Lithuania's political support of Taiwan's territorial status, a question over which China has persistently signaled its willingness to engage in via military terms. In other words, whenever assessing whether coercive trade measures against the EU should be retaliated with other coercive trade measures, broader geostrategic considerations should soon come into play. EU diplomats should comprehensively consider whether possible EU countermeasures against China in the realm of trade and sanctions could lead to unintended consequences in terms of a further conflict escalation. Recent experiences show that the Chinese willingness to retaliate sanctioning measures should not be underestimated: when the EU and United States in 2021 sanctioned a number of specific Chinese individuals and entities for their complicity in human rights violations or the circumvention of economic sanctions against Iran and North Korea, China responded not only by directly sanctioning a number of Western individuals but also by initiating a legal provision that would make it possible for Beijing to generally target foreign actors, accused for implementing coercive measures against Chinese interests, with entry bans to or expulsions from China (Tian 2021). To limit the scope of such unintended tit-for-tat dynamics that could become a de facto part of a new trade-related instrument such as the ACI, EU diplomatic practitioners will need to further enhance their understanding of possible escalatory measures on behalf of the targeted state, either within or outside the realm of direct trade relationships.

For practitioners of EU geoeconomic diplomacy, the organizational reforms that would be embedded in the ACI—and ultimately bridge the trade-security gap in the EU's governance structures—therefore both hold possibilities and challenges. In terms of possibilities, debates on the ACI as a policy initiative have already forced a stronger dialogue across the trade-security gap, both externally with representatives from the private sector and civil society but also internally among diplomats and civil servants working within the EU system and at the member state level. Externally, in the preparation of the legislative proposal, the Commission had organized an unusually extensive stakeholder engagement and public consultation process. More than 120 public, academic, commercial, and civil society actors were included in several rounds of dialogue about the instrument's design and scope (European Commission 2021b).

Such stakeholder engagements are, however, likewise important once a geoeconomic instrument is to be put into practice, although formats for ensuring such inputs are less structured. These concerns were, for example, reflected by the EU's largest private sector interest organization, the Confederation of European Business, which emphasized that the ACI's future use should be "proportionate and targeted" to maximize its effects while minimizing its impact on European operators and interests, adding that the "involvement of stakeholders, including business, in this process is critical" (BusinessEurope 2022, 2). The inherent duality in the confederation's answer reflects a broader point in geoeconomic decision-making: the need for weighing out concerns on all sides of the trade-security gap carefully against each other. Translating such concerns into the EU's diplomatic machinery therefore also requires a similar willingness of diplomatic practitioners and civil servants, who have so far worked in either the trade-dominated CCP or the security-focused CFSP, to forge new institutional linkages. While it remains to be seen to what degree the creation of the ACI can help to stimulate novel forms of cross-silo interaction, it can serve as a platform for forcing dialogues for how to integrate structures and policies in a way that better serves the EU's interests of bringing the realms of trade and security closer to each other.

Looking Ahead: Ensuring Stakeholder Involvement in the Geoeconomic Field

When assessing the geostrategic landscape within which Europe finds itself at the beginning of the 2020s, much suggests that EU institutions and governments will only face an increasing demand for being able to operate in geoeconomic terms in the years to come. Be it offensively, using sanctions or other economically coercive measures to engage in international conflicts or crises, or defensively, when fending off coercive market attacks by third-party actors, the EU will need to enhance its capacities at all levels, not least in terms of its abilities to engage successful forms of geoeconomic diplomacy. Consequently, it should be assumed that demands for further organizational integration across the trade-security gap will only grow in importance. In other words, diplomats operating in the EU's geoeconomic realm are confronted with the demand to both ensure state-market stakeholder involvement at the domestic, European, and international levels, all the while they need to maintain a clear focus on often security-related objectives that are the primary reasons for applying EU geoeconomic instruments in the first place. Considering this major challenge, this chapter concludes with a series of reflections on how EU diplomats could enhance their abilities for operating in the geoeconomic realm through internal and external institutional reforms and innovations.

Internally, it is important to note that diplomatic reforms and integration should happen not only within and between institutions at the EU level but also at the domestic level within EU member states, whose national approaches to cross-sectoral efforts in the geoeconomic field vary in both width and depth. Recent research has, for example, demonstrated how inter-ministerial cooperation between ministries of foreign affairs and ministries of economic affairs are by no means conducted in equal manners across member state capitals. The EU's two major economies, Germany and France, here serve as diverging examples: Whereas the cooperation between Germany's Federal Foreign Office and its Federal Ministry of Economic Affairs is generally embedded in heavily institutionalized coordination mechanisms, collaboration between their counterparts in France has traditionally been characterized by greater levels of intra-governmental frictions and disagreement over respective mandates and responsibilities. But the German and French cases also demonstrate how domestic reforms in the geoeconomic realm are possible. During the 2010s, both countries launched a series of reform initiatives which, even if not directly targeted at their individual geoeconomic capabilities, helped to advance certain aspects of inter-ministerial cooperation (Badel 2014; Olsen 2020). And while it would be up to individual EU member states to engage in similar reform processes to enhance their domestic abilities in the geoeconomic realm, it could be assumed that the maintained focus on geoeconomic questions at the EU level could help to initiate such developments across the Union.

At the EU level, the strengthened engagement between security-oriented diplomatic practitioners, normally found within the CFSP structures, with private and civil society stakeholders, traditionally operating outside the structures of foreign and security policy, should be another key concern for diplomatic reform. Collective EU actions in the geoeconomic realm will often require inputs from those actors in the state-market nexus who might become directly impacted by them. Here it is essential to note that the Union's founding fathers, when creating the EU's predecessor—the European Economic Community (ECC)—in 1957, understood the necessity for policy-making input from Europe's civil society actors. In an institutional attempt for ensuring regular and structured consultations between lawmakers and civil society representatives, they created the Economic and Social Committee (EESC) as an advisory body, which has since been institutionally strengthened. Currently consisting of 329 members representing European employers and trade unions as well as social, occupational, economic, and cultural organizations, the EESC is organized in six sections, one of which focuses on the EU's external policies, including trade and CFSP policies (EESC 2020). In this capacity it provides the EU institutions with opinions on various policy areas and initiatives with relevance to the EU's external actions. The actual impact of such opinions on EU policy-making processes has, however, been put into question, not least due to the EESC's burdensome and time-consuming internal processes (Abels 2021).

All the while retaining the idea of including voices outside the traditional realms of foreign and security policy, alternative institutional measures could be considered. So far, successes for ensuring broad stakeholder engagements in geoeconomic decision-making and policy implementation have been limited, even if intentions for improving the dialogue can occasionally be observed. In its proposal for strengthening the implementation of EU sanctions, the Commission, for example, suggested the need for establishing a sanctions expert group with representatives from EU institutions and member states, adding—in a non-committing way—that NGO's and civil society "may be invited as appropriate to ensure that humanitarian aspects are to the fore" (European Commission 2021a, 16). These viable intentions notwithstanding, the question of stakeholder engagement in the agile world of geoeconomic diplomacy should be addressed in a more systematic way. EU diplomats could consider the creation of formalized, but ad hoc, consultation forums in the form of "geoeconomic committees," tailored to each major geoeconomic decision in the making. Even if discretion in the decision-making process leading up to the launch of any geoeconomic intervention is key to enhance the instrument's effectiveness, it would be in the interests of geoeconomic diplomats to find new modes of interaction that allows for a more structured and confidential dialogue with and—just as important—among implied state and non-state actors.

Turning to its relations and cooperation with its international partners, EU decision makers are likewise faced with the need to reconsider how to embed geoeconomic decisions in broader bi- or multilateral frameworks. The deteriorating relationships with two geoeconomic powers, Russia and China, will in all likelihood negatively affect diplomatic cooperation in existing multilateral forums such as the G20, the UNSC, and the WTO. All the while these institutions will remain in place for the foreseeable future, Western antagonisms with Russia and China, as well as their partners and allies, will not cease to propagate. Whereas European lawmakers are adamant about confirming their adherence to a rules-based order (European Commission 2021c; Gehrke 2022), observers are questioning whether the EU and like-minded partners are moving in the direction of "departing from universal, global institutions in favor of a new arrangement based on rules set within likeminded clubs" (Leonard 2021). As this encroaching breakdown of multilateral structures will continue in parallel to the increasing global malign instrumentalization of economic power resources, practitioners of EU geoeconomic diplomacy will soon need to critically assess whether it is in the EU's interest to engage in a looming "geoeconomic arms race," in which states catalyze state-driven weaponization of market forces against each other.

In the geoeconomic sphere, the movement from larger multilateral structures to cooperation in like-minded clubs already seems to be underway. Here, the Western-led sanctions response against Russia again proves to be a case in point: Whereas transatlantic coordination in terms of a military posture and response to the Russian aggression was primarily discussed in within the structures of the North Atlantic Treaty Organization (NATO), the geoeconomic response was coordinated in ad hoc consultation within the G7. But these geoeconomic deliberations did, at least in the first weeks of the war, not transcend from this small club to a larger format such as the G20, which, since the financial and economic crises of 2008–9, had evolved into a key forum for global economic coordination (Cooper 2019). But the G20's positive development might soon be in reverse. Given the discontentment numerous G20 members—including China, India, Indonesia, Mexico, Saudi Arabia, South Africa, and Turkey—of the sanctions use of the G7 members, as well as the uncertain future of Russia's G20 membership, which the United States and others have called to revoke, it would be unsurprising to see certain disruptions of yet another key diplomatic forum to discuss global state-market relations. A foretaste hereof could already be observed at a G20 finance ministers' gathering in April 2022, the first meeting in the format after the Russian invasion into Ukraine: when the Russian finance minister took the floor, numerous—mostly Western—members walked out in protest, while others—mostly non-Western—members stayed (Rajghatta 2022). Officials from both the EU and the United States have actively sought to sway particularly non-Western democracies, such as India, to join a harsher stance against Russia, including political pressure on India to not purchase Russian fossil fuels. India, on the other hand, early after the Russian invasion, signaled its wish to remain neutral, not least due to its well-established political and economic ties with Moscow (Siddiqui 2022).

For practitioners and observers of geoeconomic diplomacy, both in Europe and beyond, the rapid developments that are currently being observed will continue to call for critical thinking about reforms of existing or the establishment of new structures for dialogue and compromises. Geoeconomic practitioners will here need to foster a more horizontal understanding of the causes, effects, and limitations of economic power measures. If the West's coordinated sanctions response to the Russian invasion of Ukraine showed surprising levels of transatlantic unity and willingness to leverage their economic sway, the situation also demonstrated a widespread hesitation among many non-Western countries to openly support the weaponization of economic interdependencies in the realm of foreign and security policy. And all the while Western diplomats might feel empowered to see that encompassing sanctions can be of fruitful use in a direct confrontation with a geopolitical adversary, it likewise remains a diplomatic task to ensure that geoeconomic governance structures that help to uphold a minimum of global cooperation. Without institutional innovations to replace declining ones, the bridge between the world's geoeconomic powers will only become more fragile, meaning that the practice of geoeconomic diplomacy runs the risk of becoming an inward-looking exercise without the adequate means to counter the slowly, but steadily, emerging contours of an increasingly confrontational and hostile international geoeconomic order.

References and Further Reading

Abels, G. 2021. "The European Economic and Social Committee and the Committee of the Regions: Consultative Institutions in a Multichannel Democracy." In *The Institutions of the European Union*, eds. D. Hodson, U. Puetter, S. Saurugger, and J. Peterson, 5th ed., 369–90. Oxford: Oxford University Press.

Badel, L. 2010. *Diplomatie et grands contrats: L'Etat français et les marchés extérieurs au XXe siècle*. Paris: Publications de la Sorbonne.

———. 2014. "Conflicting Identities: French Economic Diplomacy between the State and Companies in the Twentieth Century." *Diplomacy & Statecraft* 25 (3): 432–52.

Baldwin, D.A. 1985. *Economic Statecraft*. Princeton: Princeton University Press.

Blackwill, R.D., and J.M. Harris. 2016. *War by Other Means: Geoeconomics and Statecraft*. Cambridge, MA: Harvard University Press.

Bollen, Y., F. De Ville, and J. Orbie. 2016. "EU Trade Policy: Persistent Liberalisation, Contentious Protectionism." *Journal of European Integration* 38 (3): 279–94.

BusinessEurope. 2022. *Towards an EU Anti-coercion Instrument—Feedback on the European Commission Proposal for a Regulation on the Protection of the Union and Its Member States from Economic Coercion by Third Countries*. https://www.businesseurope.eu/sites/buseur/files/media/position_papers/rex/2022-03-31_towards_an_eu_anti-coercion_instrument-feedback_on_european_commission_proposal.pdf.

Cooper, A.F. 2019. "The G20 Is Dead as a Crisis or Steering Committee: Long Live the G20 as Hybrid Focal Point." *South African Journal of International Affairs* 26 (4): 505–20.

Crochet, V. 2022. "The EU Anti-Coercion Proposal: Legitimate Trade Instrument or Hidden 'Economic' Sanctions?" *EU Law Live*. https://issuu.com/eulawlive/docs/weekend_edition_96.

Drezner, D.W., H. Farrell, and A.L. Newman, eds. 2021. *The Uses and Abuses of Weaponized Interdependence*. Washington, D.C.: Brookings Institution Press.

EESC. 2020. REX Work Programme (October 2020–April 2023). https://www.eesc.europa.eu/sites/default/files/files/eesc-2020-05848-00-02-tcd-tra-en.docx.

European Commission. 2021a. Communication from the Commission to the European Parliament, the Council, the European Central Bank, the EuropeanEconomic and Social Committee and the Committeeof the Regions. "The European Economic and Financial System: Fostering Openness, Strength and Resilience" (COM/2021/32 final). EUR-Lex. https://eur-lex.europa.eu/legal-content/EN/TXT/?uri=CELEX:52021DC0032.

———. 2021b. "Inception Impact Assessment: Instrument to Deter and Counteract Coercive Actions by Third Countries." https://ec.europa.eu/info/law/better-regulation/have-your-say/initiatives/12803-Trade-mechanism-to-deter-&-counteract-coercive-action-by-non-EU-countries_en.

———. 2021c. Joint Communication to the European Parliament and the Council on Strengthening the EU's Contribution to Rules-based Multilateralism (JOIN(2021) 3 final). EUR-Lex. https://eur-lex.europa.eu/legal-content/EN/ALL/?uri=CELEX:52021JC0003.

———. 2021d. Proposal for a Regulation of the European Parliament and of the Council on the Protection of the Union and its Member States from Economic Coercion by Third Countries (COM(2021) 775 final). EUR-Lex. https://eur-lex.europa.eu/legal-content/EN/TXT/?uri=celex%3A52021PC0775.

———. 2021e. "Strengthening the EU's Autonomy—Commission Seeks Input on a New Anti-coercion Instrument [Press Release]," March 23. https://ec.europa.eu/commission/presscorner/detail/en/IP_21_1325.

———. 2022a. "Enforcing Sanctions against Listed Russian and Belarussian Oligarchs: Commission's 'Freeze and Seize' Task Force Steps Up Work with International Partners [Press Release]," March 17. https://ec.europa.eu/commission/presscorner/detail/en/IP_22_1828.

———. 2022b. Overview of Sanctions and Related Tools. https://ec.europa.eu/info/business-economy-euro/banking-and-finance/international-relations/restrictive-measures-sanctions/what-are-restrictive-measures-sanctions_en#guidance.

Gehrke, T. 2022. "EU Open Strategic Autonomy and the Trappings of Geoeconomics." *European Foreign Affairs Review* 27 (2): 61–78.

Hackenbroich, J., and P. Zerka. 2021. "Economic Arm-twisting Is On the Rise. Europe Must Learn How to Resist It." *European Council on Foreign Relations*, November 25. https://ecfr.eu/article/economic-arm-twisting-is-on-the-rise-europe-must-learn-how-to-resist-it/.

Hackenbroich, J., F. Medunic, and P. Zerka. 2022. "Tough Trade: The Hidden Costs of Economic Coercion." European Council on Foreign Relations, February 1. https://ecfr.eu/publication/tough-trade-the-hidden-costs-of-economic-coercion/.

Leonard, M. 2021. "The Rule Maker Race." *Project Syndicate*, December 31. https://www.project-syndicate.org/commentary/us-eu-china-who-decides-global-rules-by-mark-leonard-2021-12.

Lohmann, S., and J. Vorrath, eds. 2021. *International Sanctions: Improving Implementation through Better Interface Management*. German Institute for International and Security Affairs, Working Paper. https://www.swp-berlin.org/publications/products/arbeitspapiere/WP_International_Sanctions.pdf.

Moraes, H. C., and M. Wigell. 2020. *The Emergence of Strategic Capitalism: Geoeconomics, Corporate Statecraft and the Repurposing of the Global Economy*. Finnish Institute of International Affairs, Working Paper. https://www.fiia.fi/wp-content/uploads/2020/09/wp117_the-emergence-of-strategic-capitalism_final30092020.pdf.

Nephew, R. 2017. *The Art of Sanctions: A View from the Field*. New York: Columbia University Press.

Okano-Heijmans, M. 2011. "Conceptualizing Economic Diplomacy: The Crossroads of International Relations, Economics, IPE and Diplomatic Studies." *The Hague Journal of Diplomacy* 6 (1–2): 7–36.

Olsen, K.B. 2020. "Diplomats, Domestic Agency and the Implementation of Sanctions: The MFAs of France and Germany in the Age of Geoeconomic Diplomacy." *The Hague Journal of Diplomacy* 15 (1–2): 126–54.

———. 2022a. "Diplomatic Realisation of the EU's 'Geoeconomic Pivot': Sanctions, Trade, and Development Policy Reform." *Politics and Governance* 10 (1): 5–15.

———. 2022b. *The Geoeconomic Diplomacy of Economic Sanctions: Networked Practices and Sanctions Implementation*. Leiden/Boston: Brill.

Patey, L. 2021. *How China Loses: The Pushback against Chinese Global Ambitions*. Oxford: Oxford University Press.

Pop, V., S. Fleming, and J. Politi. 2022. "Weaponisation of Finance: How the West Unleashed 'Shock and Awe' on Russia." *Financial Times*, April 6. https://www.ft.com/content/5b397d6b-bde4-4a8c-b9a4-080485d6c64a.

Rajghatta, C. 2022. "G20 = G10 + G10: India and U.S. Diverge on Russia Again." *Times of India*, April 21. https://timesofindia.indiatimes.com/india/g20-g10-g10-india-and-us-diverge-on-russia-again/articleshow/90982557.cms.

Siddiqui, S. 2022. "Biden Meets Modi as U.S. Presses India over Russia." *Wall Street Journal*, April 11. https://www.wsj.com/articles/biden-meets-modi-as-u-s-presses-india-over-russia-11649697111.

Szczepański, M. 2022. Proposed Anti-coercion Instrument. European Parliamentary Research Service. https://www.europarl.europa.eu/RegData/etudes/BRIE/2022/729299/EPRS_BRI(2022)729299_EN.pdf.

Tian, Y.L. 2021. "China Passes Law to Counter Foreign Sanctions." Reuters, June 10. https://www.reuters.com/world/china/china-passes-law-counter-foreign-sanctions-2021-06-10/.

White House. 2022. Remarks by President Biden and Chancellor Scholz of the Federal Republic of Germany at Press Conference, February 7. https://www.whitehouse.gov/briefing-room/statements-releases/2022/02/07/remarks-by-president-biden-and-chancellor-scholz-of-the-federal-republic-of-germany-at-press-conference/.

Zarate, J. 2013. *Treasury's War: The Unleashing of a New Era of Financial Warfare.* New York: PublicAffairs.

33

Science Diplomacy with Diplomatic Relations to Facilitate Common-Interest Building

Paul Arthur Berkman

Considering Diplomatic Reform

This discourse considers the text of the Vienna Convention on Diplomatic Relations (1961) as a straw man to identify the diplomatic challenges for humanity to evolve as a globally interconnected civilization, recognizing that 193 nations are parties to this framework agreement from last century after the Second World War. The words about diplomatic relations that have been negotiated by diplomats carry lessons and wisdom, which are important to preserve, reflecting national interests and in rare cases common interests with survival as the umbrella consideration for humanity across time. The concept of time is at the heart of science—natural sciences, social science, and Indigenous knowledge—all of which characterize patterns and trends that have become the bases for decisions to address change, requiring diplomacy (Berkman et al. 2017, 2022a; Young et al. 2020).

Concepts in the first preambular phrases of the Vienna Convention on Diplomatic Relations (Box 33.1) reflect the course for humanity, which is across time, "ancient" into the future. Having in mind the purposes and principles of the Charter of the United Nations (United Nations 1945) further

---

P. A. Berkman (✉)
Science Diplomacy Center™ / United Nations Institute for Training and Research (UNITAR) / Program on Negotiation at Harvard Law School, Falmouth, MA, USA

amplifies the notion of time, considering the first half of the twentieth century when nations collided on a planetary scale, requiring international solutions forever after (Fig. 33.1).

> **Box 33.1 Vienna Convention on Diplomatic Relations (1961)**
>
> **Preamble**
> *Recalling* that peoples of all nations from ancient times have recognized the status of diplomatic agents,
> *Having in mind* the purposes and principles of the Charter of the United Nations concerning the sovereign equality of States, the maintenance of international peace and security, and the promotion of friendly relations among nations…

The Vienna Convention on Diplomatic Relations also identifies fundamental responsibilities at local-global levels to nurture the diplomatic agents (Box 33.1) who will contribute to the maintenance of international peace and

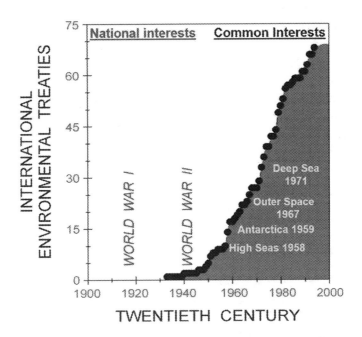

Fig. 33.1 Balancing national interests and common interests on a planetary scale began during the twentieth century, illustrated with international environmental treaties to address sustainability questions at local-global levels. Adapted from Berkman (2002), including legal establishment of areas beyond national jurisdictions (yellow), international spaces (Kish 1973; Berkman et al. 2011; Berkman 2020a) to build common interests and minimize risks of conflict over jurisdictional boundaries across the Earth on a planetary scale (Berkman 2009)

security and the promotion of friendly relations among nations across our world (Box 33.1). This challenge exists despite the sovereign equality of states, which will always look after national interests first and foremost, asserting national prerogatives however interpreted often without global consideration. While the promotion of friendly relations among nations may be necessary, such efforts are insufficient unless they also prevent conflict, recognizing the persistent planetary risk of mutually assured destruction (MAD) for humankind.

Considering the context of ancient times (Box 33.1), the oldest continuous calendars on Earth have been recording time annually with human populations across nearly 6000 years, sixty centuries. The simple fact is we are just in our infancy as a globally interconnected civilization, recognizing last century was the first in all of human history with "world" war (Fig. 33.1). The questions below are designed to awaken consideration about the global transformations since the Vienna Convention on Diplomatic Relations was signed, within heartbeats of the Second World War.

- Considering the persistent global risks of nationalism (Fig. 33.1), is it reasonable to leave diplomacy solely in the hands of states?
- What types of diplomatic relations are necessary for humankind to mature as a globally interconnected civilization?

If there is a singular lesson of the twentieth century—it is nationalism in our world with billions of people, advanced technologies, and industrial capacities is a recipe for global conflict. In this context, the acceleration of nationalism (Weiss et al. 2019; Bieber 2022; Ashford and Shifrinson 2022) suggests that diplomatic relations can be greatly improved "to balance national interests and common interests for the benefit of all on Earth across generations" (Fig. 33.1), which is a defined goal of science diplomacy (Berkman et al. 2011, 2022a; Berkman and Vylegzhanin 2012).

Diplomatic Relations and Missions

It is clear from reviewing the Vienna Convention on Diplomatic Relations (1961) that its focus is on the mechanics of diplomatic intercourse, especially with privileges and immunities that are conferred between states to diplomatic agents (Box 33.1) and diplomatic missions (Box 33.2). While the development of friendly relations among nations (Boxes 33.1 and 33.2) is an explicit objective of this Convention from sixty years ago, its national focus seems incomplete in our world with eight billion people this decade.

> **Box 33.2 Vienna Convention on Diplomatic Relations (1961)**
>
> **Preamble**
> *Believing* that an international convention on diplomatic intercourse, privileges and immunities would contribute to the development of friendly relations among nations, irrespective of their differing constitutional and social systems.
> **Article 2**
> The establishment of diplomatic relations between States, and of permanent diplomatic missions, takes place by mutual consent.

Well beyond the national-international dynamics of the twentieth century (Fig. 33.1), humankind now has diverse linkages on a planetary scale. Exponential impacts at local-global levels—across diverse time scales (Fig. 33.2a–d)—underscore the arenas of diplomacy and even the characteristics of next-generation diplomats in the twenty-first century and beyond. We each can see exponential change with the COVID-19 pandemic as a powerful illustration, across orders of magnitude during months-years with the first reported death in the United States in January 2020 (Mueller 2021); past 10, 100, 1000, 10,000, 100,000 and reaching 1,000,000 deaths on 17 May 2022 (Donovan 2022). The idea of "bending the curve" with COVID-19 is exactly what is anticipated over decades-centuries with carbon that has been increasing exponentially in the Earth's atmosphere in relation to climate change, for example (Fig. 33.2).

Looking across the twenty-first century and beyond on a planetary scale (Fig. 33.2a–d)—the challenges and the solutions for humankind will involve holistic (international, interdisciplinary, and inclusive) considerations among people in digital world when dis- and mis-information are easy to convey with social media. Enhancing research abilities inclusively with science as the "study of change" (Berkman 2020a; Berkman et al. 2022a)—revealing patterns, trends, and processes that underlie decisions—is a path for all to apply in their quest of truth.

- Who are the diplomatic agents (Boxes 33.1 and 33.3)?
- What are the characteristics and skills of next-generation diplomatic agents (Boxes 33.1 and 33.3)?
- What is the purpose of diplomacy in the twenty-first century, in contrast to ancient times (Box 33.1)?

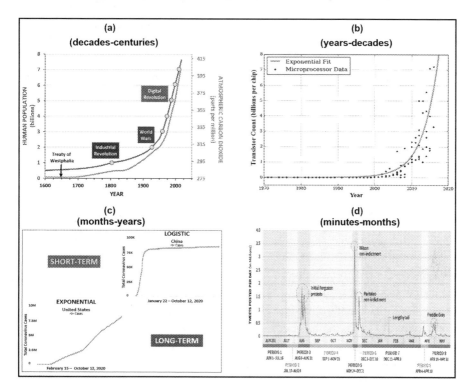

Fig. 33.2 a–d Globally interconnected civilization time scales revealed by exponential changes with **(a)** climate and human-population size over decades to centuries in view of global events; **(b)** high-technology change over years to decades illustrated by "Moore's Law" with transistors on a chip; **(c)** global pandemic over months to years with COVID-19 cases; and **(d)** social-media interactions over minutes to months, illustrated by 2014–15 tweets about "Black Lives Matter." Adapted from Berkman (2020b), which has references to data sources with elaboration

Certainly, one of the enduring diplomatic skills in our globally interconnected civilization (Figs. 33.1 and 33.2)—across differing constitutional and social systems (Box 33.2)—will be to interact with people, optimally among friends with trusted relations, building common interests. Whether between states, permanent diplomatic missions, or other entities, the concept of mutual consent also will remain as a boundary condition of diplomacy with respect for the decision-makers and the institutions they represent.

The difference between 1961 and today, operating into the future, involves the capacities for inclusive dialogues on a planetary scale to address questions of common concern over diverse time scales. The concept of permanent diplomatic missions presumably was to address issues across all of these time scales. Distinguishing these tempos of our world, now raises questions about impermanent diplomatic missions to enhance diplomatic relations across jurisdictions today into the future.

- What types of diplomatic relations are necessary for humankind to build sustainable local-global connections inclusively short-to-long term (Fig. 33.2a–d)?

Answering this question benefits from a historical perspective over the same period, across decades-centuries, considering the origin of the nation-state with the 1648 Treaties of Westphalia (Croxton 1999) as the starting point across a diplomatic threshold (Box 33.1).

In the twentieth century (Fig. 33.1), as human population size continued accelerating globally (Fig. 33.2a), nations bumped into each other, necessitating national-international governance with the League of Nations after the First World War and the United Nations after the Second World War, crossing a new diplomatic threshold. Two billion humans were alive at the time of the First World War and the last global pandemic around 1920. One century later, there are eight billion people living on Earth—when the intricacies of diplomatic relations have expanded exponentially across diverse time scales (Fig. 33.2a–d)—awakening the next threshold to cross, which again will require diplomatic relations at new levels in our world of the 21st century.

Today, nations are appointing ambassadors to the technology industry (Satariano 2019; Clarke 2021), which is then hiring these diplomatic agents (Boxes 33.1 and 33.3) and creating ambassadorial training, as in the case with Microsoft (2020, 2022), resulting in new types of diplomatic relations. Cities are operating on a planetary scale, independent of nations, to address global challenges such as climate change (C40 2022) and subnational jurisdictions surpass the economic capacities of many nations, noting that California has the fifth largest economy in the world (Cooper 2018). In effect, to be inclusive, there is a spectrum of subnational-national-international jurisdictions (Fig. 33.3), recognizing the nation is the central jurisdictional unit (like meters with kilometers larger and centimeters smaller) with public-private and other partnerships that are involved with diplomatic relations.

Additionally, across the jurisdictional spectrum for sustainability (Fig. 33.3), non-state actors are connecting with international law (Noortmann 2001) but operating without specific addresses for diplomatic relations. In effect, the diversity of connections that are involved with diplomatic relations are as broad and deep as the United Nations Sustainable Development Goals (United Nations 2015), with implementation at local-global levels across generations.

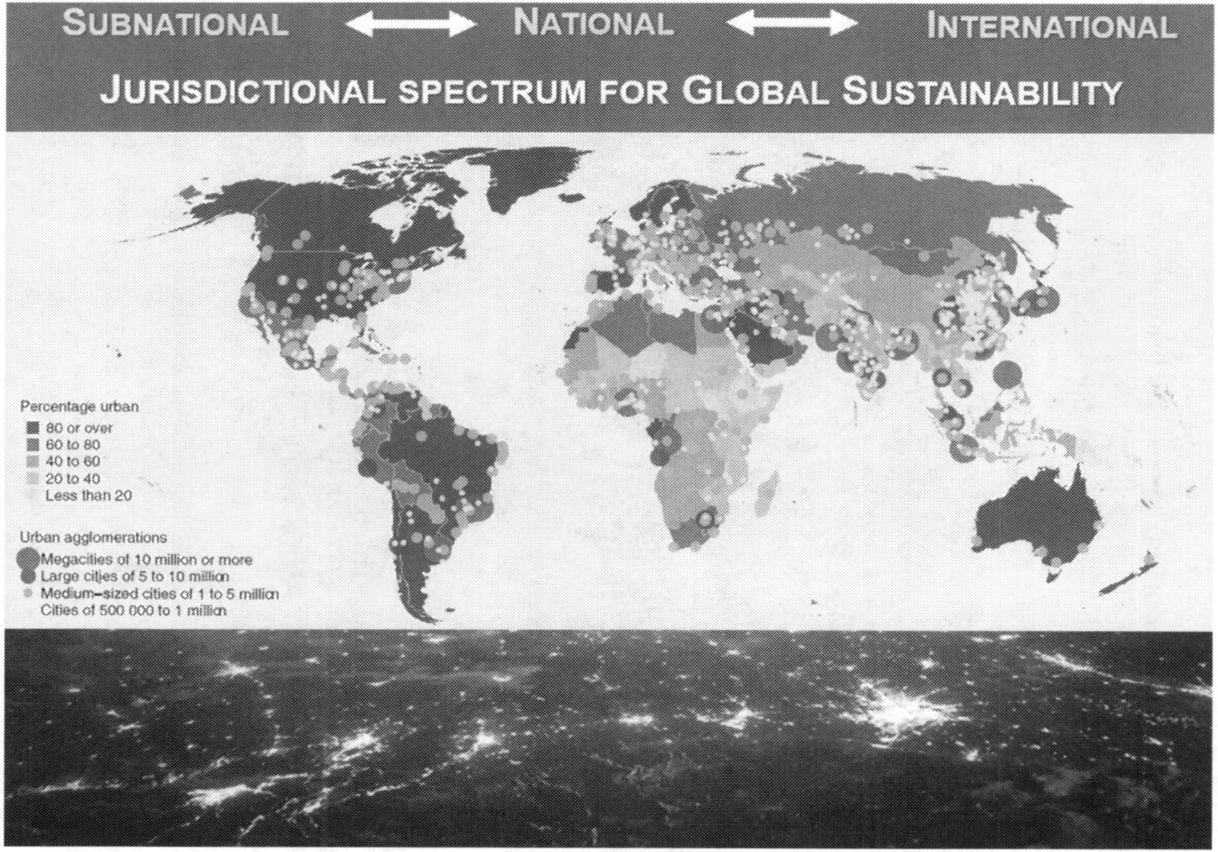

Fig. 33.3 Spectrum of jurisdictions on Earth, illustrated by megacities with capacities of states at subnational levels, representing an inclusive framework for humankind to address impacts, issues, and resources in our globally interconnected civilization (Fig. 33.1) with diplomacy across diverse time scales (Fig. 33.2a–d). Adapted from Berkman et al. (2022a)

National Security and Armed Conflict

Despite the vision to operate across a jurisdictional spectrum (Fig. 33.3) for the maintenance of international peace and security (Box 33.1)—the reality is nations will consider their security individually first and foremost. National security broadly and social security in the context of tax exemption (Box 33.3) are specifically mentioned in the Vienna Convention on Diplomatic Relations (Box 33.3), noting many additional forms of security have entered into the regulatory arenas of nations since 1961: climate security, cyber security, environmental security, food security, health security, and other security types inclusively. With greater precision about the types of security also comes enhanced resolution of the diplomatic agents (Boxes 33.1 and 33.3) who are involved with implementation, indicating that diplomatic relations have become increasingly complicated.

> **Box 33.3 Vienna Convention on Diplomatic Relations (1961)**
>
> **Article 26**
> Subject to its laws and regulations concerning zones entry into which is prohibited or regulated for reasons of national security, the receiving State shall ensure to all members of the mission freedom of movement and travel in its territory.

Importantly, across all of the types above, a common feature of security is to address risks of instabilities that are immediate (Berkman and Vylegzhanin 2012), whether actual or perceived, as with Russia during a future Cold War (Berkman 2013). The immediacy also represents time with issues, impacts, and resources connected to the present. Subsequent diplomatic relations operate across diverse time scales (Fig. 33.2a–d). This diplomatic complexity across time also has a common feature, noting there is an inflection point when exponential change decelerates (Fig. 33.4). Understanding inflection points and the surrounding circumstances is a fundamental skill required for diplomatic agents (Boxes 33.1 and 33.3) to exert leverage, especially to be transformational, as happened during the Second World War.

The Second World War, which ended in August 1945, is a critical example of diplomatic relations before-through-after an inflection point. In 1943, despite being in the middle of a world war, plans were laid for the United Nations Food and Agriculture Organization to ensure humanity's freedom

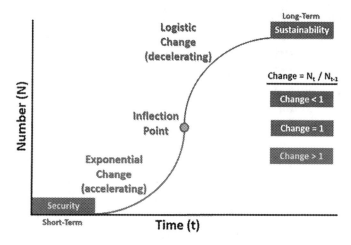

Fig. 33.4 Short- to long-term features of diplomatic relations, highlighting exponential change across an inflection point toward logistic (S-shaped, sigmoid) change, as described by numbers (N) changing per unit of time (t). Diplomatic relations are required before-through-after inflection points with scalability across embedded time scales in our globally interconnected civilization (Fig. 33.2a–d). Adapted from Berkman (2020b, 2020c)

from hunger, contributing also to an expanding world economy (OECD/FAO 2016). The Bretton Woods Conference in New Hampshire in July 1944 initiated a worldwide economic regime with a vision of the International Monetary Fund and the International Bank for Reconstruction and Development that would become the World Bank (Steil 2013). The United Nations Conference on International Organization in San Francisco, from April to June 1945, produced the Charter of the United Nations and Statute of the International Court of Justice to govern human activities on a planetary scale (United Nations 1945).

After the 1945 inflection point of armed conflict (Box 33.4) with atomic bombs—human interactions were transformed on a planetary scale by strategies conceived during the period when there was a common interest in survival among humans across the Earth (Fig. 33.1). We are living during such a moment now, when there is a common interest in survival once again at local-global levels, due to diverse causes at different time scales (Fig. 33.2a–d).

Box 33.4 Vienna Convention on Diplomatic Relations (1961)

Article 45

If diplomatic relations are broken off between two States, or if a mission is permanently or temporarily recalled:

(a) the receiving State must, even in case of armed conflict, respect and protect the premises of the mission, together with its property and archives;…

With emphasis, armed conflict (Box 33.4) is mentioned three times in the Vienna Convention on Diplomatic Relations, displacing all other security (Boxes 33.1 and 33.3) considerations. In this context, it is noteworthy that COVID-19 was the "most challenging crisis we have faced since the Second World War" (Guterres 2020) until the Russian invasion of Ukraine.

With hope, the diplomatic opportunity remains to operate before-through-after the inflection point of the COVID-19 pandemic (Fig. 33.2c), which will happen with certainty as with all plagues, although when and how are the questions with the latter determined by diplomatic missions. Importantly, operating in the short-to-long term is to recall the global acceleration of intrastate armed conflicts (Box 33.4) throughout the Cold War (Tillema 1991; Center for Systemic Peace 2022), further reflecting the need for subnational-national diplomacy (Fig. 33.3). The challenge is to recognize the inflection points (Fig. 33.4), which are few and far between, and then to capitalize on those rare moments as levers for transformation, which could be considered as a successful outcome of diplomatic relations that are inclusive.

Science Diplomacy to Negotiate Transformation

The goal of this chapter is to introduce questions about diplomatic reform, exploring the utility of the 1961 Vienna Convention on Diplomatic Relations (Boxes 33.1, 33.2, 33.3, and 33.4) after the twentieth century, when humankind unambiguously became interconnected across the Earth (Fig. 33.1) at both:

- Security Time Scales (mitigating risks of political, economic, cultural, and environmental instabilities that are immediate); and
- Sustainability Time Scales (balancing economic prosperity, environmental protection, and societal well-being across generations).

To be inclusive, these different time scales represent a "continuum of urgencies" (Fig. 33.4), operating from minutes-centuries (Fig. 33.2a–d) at the levels of peoples, nations, and our world (Fig. 33.3).

To be transformational is to be brave, if not humble, introducing options (without advocacy), which can be used or ignored explicitly with respect for the decision-makers and their institutions, which operate across subnational-national-international jurisdictions inclusively (Fig. 33.3). Across a globally interconnected civilization (Figs. 33.1, 33.2, and 33.3), another way of interpreting inclusion is in view of scalability (does this work for me and you?),

Fig. 33.5 Informed decisions operate across a "continuum of urgencies," illustrated for peoples, nations, and our world from security to sustainability time scales (Figs. 33.1, 33.2, 33.3, and 33.4). Negotiation strategies that contribute to the decision-making with diplomatic agents (Boxes 33.1 and 33.3) also exist short term in view of conflicts to resolve and long term in view of common interests to build—balancing societal, economic, and environmental considerations across generations. Adapted from Vienna Dialogue Team (2017); Young et al. (2020); Berkman et al. (2022a)

involving all humanity with stewardship responsibilities on a planetary scale. The diplomatic agents (Boxes 33.1 and 33.3) are each of us.

For example, without plenipotentiary credentials, I co-convened and chaired the first formal dialogue between the North Atlantic Treaty Organization (NATO) and Russia regarding security in the Arctic (Berkman and Vylegzhanin 2012). The option (without advocacy) simply was for allies and adversaries to consider their common interests, starting with questions (Fig. 33.6) rather than asserting prerogatives to resolve conflicts. Such common-interest building opened the doors to translate all of the Russian Arctic laws into English from the early nineteenth century to the present (Berkman et al. 2019), enabling rare legal transparency for user-defined assessment to generate informed decisions (Fig. 33.5). This history led to the Science Diplomacy Center at MGIMO University in Moscow with me as the Director from Boston (MGIMO 2021), being brave to convene inclusive dialogues (Berkman et al. 2022b), protecting and enhancing open science (United Nations 2021) that will enable humanity to operate short-to-long term (Figs. 33.1, 33.2, and 33.4) across a "continuum of urgencies" (Fig. 33.5).

The transdisciplinary process, starting with questions (Arthur et al. 1989), is represented in Fig. 33.6 as the foundational feature to build common interests inclusively. When questions of common concern arise, the diversity of science methods (natural science, social sciences, and Indigenous knowledge) to study change also is revealed, generating necessary data as stages of research. However, data to answer questions is fundamentally different from evidence

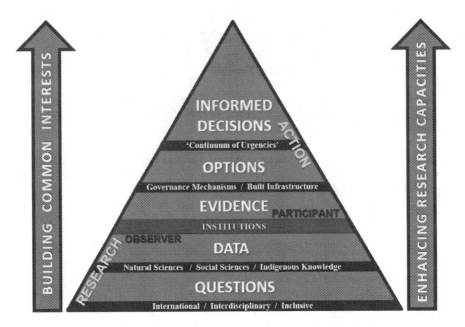

Fig. 33.6 Pyramid of informed decision-making with science diplomacy to apply, train, and refine across a "continuum of urgencies" (Vienna Dialogue Team 2017), characterizing the scope of an informed decision (Fig. 33.5) as the apex goal of an holistic process that begins at the stage of questions to build common interests among allies and adversaries alike. Enhancing research capacities is a positive feedback that results from common-interest building. Adapted from Berkman et al. (2022a)

for decisions, which involves institutions that take action. The data-evidence interface is where the science diplomat sits, contributing as both an observer and participant in the process to generate informed decisions (Fig. 33.5).

Across the data-evidence interface with research into action (Fig. 33.6), the diplomacy with science simply is in revealing options (without advocacy), which can be used or ignored explicitly, respecting the institutions. Options (without advocacy) underlie diplomacy as a process with science, empowering diplomatic agents (Boxes 33.1 and 33.3) to navigate dialogues without making recommendations that would engender political dynamics with perceived or actual agendas.

The challenge with diplomatic relations is to be eminently practical, recognizing that sustainable development at local-global levels involves close coupling of:

- Governance Mechanisms (laws, agreements, and policies as well as regulatory strategies, including insurance, at diverse jurisdictional levels); and

- Built Infrastructure (fixed, mobile, and other assets, including communication, research, observing, information, and other systems that require technology plus investment).

The two generalized arenas of decision-making (Fig. 33.6) to achieve progress with sustainable development (United Nations 1987, 2015) also represent the public and private institutions involved with diplomatic relations, as observed above with the technology industry.

Conclusion

The rationale for science diplomacy to balance national interests and common interests (Fig. 33.1) recognizes such capacity is only possible if nations have common interests. The lesson of the 1959 Antarctic Treaty is that a common interest in survival does exist at local-global levels with compassion for the future, even among superpower adversaries. The future operates across diverse time scales (Fig. 33.2), each with its own exponential trajectory and all converging with challenges for humanity together as part of a globally interconnected civilization with planetary dynamics across a spectrum of jurisdictions (Fig. 33.3).

Understanding there will be inflection points (Fig. 33.4) is an opportunity for all diplomats—especially those who study change—to build common interests before-through-after the global inflection point that is happening now across a "continuum of urgencies" (Fig. 33.5), writing the future of all on Earth inclusively. The gift of science diplomacy is to build common interests so that balance can be achieved short-to-long term, as illustrated with the concept of sustainable development, with methodology that simply starts from questions, leading to informed decisions (Fig. 33.6): not good decisions or bad decisions; right decisions or wrong decisions; but decisions that optimize the questions and available information inclusively.

Informed decision-making is like driving a car, constantly adjusting to the immediacies on the left and right while maneuvering in view of future urgencies with red lights ahead and circumstances to consider in the rear. As the engine of science diplomacy (Berkman 2020c), informed decision-making is available for humankind inclusively, recognizing that reading, writing, and arithmetic are necessary, but no longer sufficient when each of us has effectively infinite and instantaneous access to digital information. The sufficiency comes with being able to operate across a "continuum of urgencies" (Figs. 33.5 and 33.6), which is something that can be trained at K-12 with basic education, starting with questions, enhanced with research skills in universities, and polished with leadership through the professions.

This local-global journey is underway with science diplomacy and informed decision-making as reflected in training the diplomatic corps of nations through their foreign ministries, including Algeria, Armenia, Canada, Costa Rica, Ethiopia, and Indonesia among others, as described in the *Informed Decisionmaking for Sustainability* book series (Young et al. 2020; Berkman et al. 2022a). The scope of this science diplomacy training with informed decision-making extends across the United Nations with the United Nations Institute for Training and Research (UNITAR). Informed decision-making also is being introduced at the level of universities as with the joint course between Tufts University and MGIMO University (Berkman and Vylegzhanin 2020), recognizing science diplomacy courses are emerging around the world more broadly.

The science diplomats are the brokers of dialogues, starting with questions that contribute to informed decisions (Figs. 33.5 and 33.6), which operate short-to-long term (Figs. 33.1, 33.2, and 33.4), at local-global levels across generations (Fig. 33.3), which will take generations to test as a proposition, triangulating education-research-leadership with lifelong learning (Fig. 33.6). Transforming diplomatic relations with science diplomacy as a common language—involving diverse diplomatic agents (Boxes 33.1 and 33.3) who can contribute inclusively—is an option (without advocacy) for all nations.

With informed decision-making, science diplomacy becomes a language of hope "for the benefit of all on Earth across generations." The opportunity is to turn science fiction into science reality, like traveling from the Earth to the Moon (Verne 1865) across the next century.

Acknowledgments This essay is a product of the Science Diplomacy Center™ with support from the United States National Science Foundation (Award Nos. NSF-OPP 1263819, NSF-ICER 1660449 and NSF-OPP 1917434). I thank the Multilateral Diplomacy Programme at the United Nations Institute for Training and Research (UNITAR) and Program on Negotiation at Harvard Law School for their institutional support as well as the United States Department of State and Norwegian Ministry of Foreign Affairs for their award of the Fulbright Arctic Chair 2021–22.

References and Further Reading

Arthur, M.B., D.T. Hall, and B.S. Lawrence. 1989. "Generating New Directions in Career Theory: The Case for a Transdisciplinary Approach." In *Handbook of Career Theory*, eds. M.B. Arthur, D.T. Hall, and B.S. Lawrence, 7–25. Cambridge: Cambridge University Press.

Ashford, E., and J. Shifrinson. 2022. "How the War in Ukraine Could Get Much Worse: Russia and the West Risk Falling into a Deadly Spiral." *Foreign Affairs*, March 8.

Berkman, P.A. 2002. *Science into Policy: Global Lessons from Antarctica*. San Diego: Academic Press.

———. 2009. "International Spaces Promote Peace." *Nature* 462: 412–13.

———. 2013. "Preventing an Arctic Cold War." *New York Times*, March 12.

———. 2020a. "Polar Science Diplomacy." In *Research Handbook on Polar Law*, eds. K.N. Scott and D. Vander Zwaag, 105–23. London: Edward Elgar.

———. 2020b. "'The Pandemic Lens': Focusing Across Time Scales for Local-Global Sustainability." *Patterns* 1 (8).

———. 2020c. "Science Diplomacy and Its Engine of Informed Decisionmaking: Operating Through Our Global Pandemic with Humanity." *The Hague Journal of Diplomacy* 15: 435–50.

Berkman, P.A., and A.N. Vylegzhanin, eds. 2012. *Environmental Security in the Arctic Ocean*. NATO Science for Peace and Security Series. Brussels: NATO.

———. 2020. "Training Skills with Common-Interest Building." *Science Diplomacy Action* 4: 1–68.

Berkman, P.A., M.A. Lang, D.W.H. Walton, and O.R. Young, eds. 2011. *Science Diplomacy: Antarctica, Science and the Governance of International Spaces*. Washington, D.C.: Smithsonian Institution Scholarly Press.

Berkman, P.A., L. Kullerud, A. Pope, A.N. Vylegzhanin, and O.R. Young. 2017. "The Arctic Science Agreement Propels Science Diplomacy." *Science* 358: 596–98.

Berkman, P.A., A.N. Vylegzhanin, and O.R. Young. 2019. *Baseline of Russian Arctic Laws*. Dordrecht: Springer.

Berkman, P.A., A.N. Vylegzhanin, O.R. Young, D.A. Balton, and O. Øvretveit, eds. 2022a. *Building Common Interests in the Arctic Ocean with Global Inclusion. Volume 2. Informed Decisionmaking for Sustainability*. Dordrecht: Springer.

Berkman, P.A., J. Baeseman, and A. Shibata. 2022b. "Arctic Science Diplomacy Maintains Russia Co-operation." *Nature* 604: 625.

Bieber, F. 2022. "Global Nationalism in Times of the COVID-19 Pandemic." *Nationalities Papers* 50 (1): 13–25.

C40. 2022. C40 Network of Worldwide Leading Cities. https://www.c40.org/.

Center for Systemic Peace. 2022. *Global Trends in Armed Conflicts: 1946–2019*. http://www.systemicpeace.org/conflicttrends.html.

Clarke, L. 2021. "Tech Ambassadors Are Redefining Diplomacy for the Digital Era." *Tech Monitor,* February 16.

Cooper, J.J. 2018. "California Now World's 5th Largest Economy, Surpassing UK." Associated Press, May 4.

Croxton, D. 1999. "The Peace of Westphalia of 1648 and the Origins of Sovereignty." *International History Review* 21 (3): 569–91.

Donovan, D. 2022. "U.S. Officially Surpasses 1 Million Covid-19 Deaths." Johns Hopkins University Coronavirus Resource Center, May 17.

Guterres, A. 2020. Transcript of UN Secretary-General's Virtual Press Encounter to Launch the Report on the Socio-Economic Impacts of COVID-19, March 31. https://www.un.org/sg/en/content/sg/press-encounter/2020-03-31/transcript-of-un-secretary-general%E2%80%99s-virtual-press-encounter-launch-the-report-the-socio-economic-impacts-of-covid-19.

Kish, J. 1973. *The Law of International Spaces.* Leiden: A. W. Sijthoff.

MGIMO. 2021. "MGIMO Opens Center for Science Diplomacy." Moscow: MGIMO University. https://english.mgimo.ru/news/center-for-science-diplomacy.

Microsoft. 2020. Casper Klynge – Official Microsoft Blog. https://blogs.microsoft.com/wp-content/uploads/prod/sites/73/2020/01/casper-klynge-biog.pdf.

———. 2022. Student-Ambassadors. https://studentambassadors.microsoft.com/.

Mueller, B. 2021. "When Was the First U.S. Covid Death? C.D.C. Investigates 4 Early Cases." *New York Times,* September 9.

Noortmann, M. 2001. "Non-State Actors in International Law." In *Non-State Actors in International Relations,* eds. B. Arts, M. Noortmann, and B. Reinalda, 59–78. Aldershot: Ashgate.

OECD/FAO. 2016. *International Regulatory Co-operation and International Organisations: The Case of the Food and Agriculture Organization of the United Nations (FAO).* Paris: Organisation for Economic Co-operation and Development (OECD) and Food and Agriculture Organization (FAO). https://www.oecd.org/gov/regulatory-policy/FAO_Full-Report.pdf.

Satariano, A. 2019. "The World's First Ambassador to the Tech Industry." *New York Times,* September 3.

Steil, B. 2013. *The Battle of Bretton Woods: John Maynard Keynes, Harry Dexter White, and the Making of a New World Order.* Princeton: Princeton University Press.

Tillema, H.K. 1991. *International Armed Conflict Since 1945: A Bibliographic Handbook of Wars and Military Interventions.* New York: Routledge.

United Nations. 1945. United Nations Archive: United Nations Conference on International Organization (UNCIO) (1945) – AG-012. https://search.archives.un.org/united-nations-conference-on-international-organization-uncio-1945.

———. 1987. *Our Common Future: From One Earth to One World.* Report Transmitted to the General Assembly as an Annex to Resolution A/RES/42/187. New York: World Commission on Environment and Development. https://sustainabledevelopment.un.org/content/documents/5987our-common-future.pdf.

———. 2015. *Transforming Our World: The 2030 Agenda for Sustainable Development*. Resolution Adopted by the General Assembly, September 25. A/RES/70/1. https://www.un.org/ga/search/view_doc.asp?symbol=A/RES/70/1&Lang=E.

———. 2021. UNESCO Recommendation on Open Science. Paris: United Nations Educational and Scientific Cultural Organization. https://en.unesco.org/science-sustainable-future/open-science/recommendation.

Verne, J. 1865. *De la Terre á la Lune*. Paris: Pierre-Jules Hetze.

Vienna Convention on Diplomatic Relations. 1961. Signed Vienna, April 18. Entry into Force: April 24, 1964. https://legal.un.org/ilc/texts/instruments/english/conventions/9_1_1961.pdf.

Vienna Dialogue Team. 2017. "A Global Network of Science and Technology Advice in Foreign Ministries." *Science Diplomacy Action* 1: 1–20. https://scidiplo.org/wp-content/uploads/2020/11/Synthesis_1.pdf.

Weiss, T.G., D.P. Forsythe, and R.A. Coate. 2019. "The United States, the UN, and New Nationalisms: Old Truths, New Developments." *Global Governance: A Review of Multilateralism and International Organizations* 25 (4): 499–508.

Young, O.R., P.A. Berkman, and A.N. Vylegzhanin, eds. 2020. *Governing Arctic Seas: Regional Lessons from the Bering Strait and Barents Sea. Volume 1. Informed Decisionmaking for Sustainability*. Dordrecht: Springer.

34

Climate Diplomacy for a 1.5 Degree World

Olivia Rumble and Andrew Gilder

The world has already warmed by 1.1°C compared to 1990 levels. It has witnessed record-breaking annual heat waves, wildfires, hurricanes, droughts, and floods, year after year, with devastating results. This year, more than 400 people died in national floods in South Africa. It is estimated that a further 90 died in India and Pakistan after a spell of heatwaves, assessed to have been 30 times more likely as a result of climate change (World Weather Attribution Network 2022). These events follow on from last year's calamitous floods in Jakarta, and apocalyptic fires in Australia in 2020.

Notwithstanding the increased frequency and intensity of these impacts, nations have collectively failed to take action at the requisite scale. Recent estimates indicate that the full implementation of current national climate mitigation commitments under the Paris Agreement will only fractionally reduce emissions by 7.5 percent by 2030, putting the world on track for a temperature increase of 2.7°C by the end of the century (United Nations Environment Programme 2021). What is needed is a reduction of up to 30 percent if warming is to remain at 2°C and a 55 percent reduction in emissions is needed to achieve 1.5°C (ibid.).

In order to maintain a 1.5 degree future, unprecedented changes will be required across society, transforming and redefining financial, trade, and

O. Rumble (✉)
Climate Legal, Cape Town, South Africa

A. Gilder
Climate Legal, Durban, South Africa

production systems. For many years climate change was conceived of as an environmental issue, but as the scale and scope of required responses have become clearer, it is evident that climate change must be mainstreamed across all society's sectors and government ministries, such as trade, health, agriculture, economic development, energy, and international relations. Macroeconomic considerations will increasingly be impacted by climate change, and macroeconomic policies will, in turn, be part of climate responses. The challenge for twenty-first century diplomacy is that, within this and a fragmented multi-scalar context, it must raise climate ambition, mold transformative systems change, and promote and facilitate new modes of multilateral collaboration (Carius and Risi 2021).

In this chapter we explore the current global climate architecture under the Paris Agreement and United Nations Framework Convention on Climate Change (UNFCCC), including some of the most topical issues for negotiators. We then turn to how climate change issues are being addressed in other forums and key institutions. We argue that the UNFCCC and Paris Agreement, while important, are no longer the locus of decision-making for key climate issues, and that climate diplomacy, if it is to be effective, needs to actively and collaboratively engage within all of these forums working in trans-disciplinary manner that promotes higher levels of participation and ambition.

The Multilateral Negotiations

The multilateral regime, while achieving some degree of momentum in Paris in 2015, has continued to stutter both in terms of ambition and effectiveness. To be fair, the Paris Agreement is only in its early years of implementation, however these have not proven to be particularly fruitful. It was hoped that the novel structure of the Paris Agreement that gives parties autonomy to determine the extent of their emission reduction targets under Nationally Determined Contributions (NDCs), but which imposes a ratcheting mechanism requiring successive NDCs to reflect higher levels of ambition, coupled with transparency "name and shame" provisions, would overcome the inertia that had settled into the regime in the preceding decade. The initial round of NDCs gave little hope though, with the synthesis report preceding last year's Conference of the Parties (COP) concluding that the current round of NDCs will actually see emissions rise in the period leading up to 2030.[1] For this

---

[1] By 13.7 percent above the 2010 level; see United Nations (2021).

reason, the Glasgow Climate Pact from 2021 requests parties to revise and strengthen their 2030 targets in their NDCs before the end of this year.

Focusing solely on emissions targets as the sole measure of success of the global diplomatic effort is misleading. Developing countries are righty pushing for adaptation to be recognized, funded, and supported through capacity building and technology transfer, as they are more vulnerable to the impacts of climate change but lack the adaptive capacity to respond. For this reason, the issue of climate finance became a central feature of the negotiations in 2021, particularly the failure of developed countries to meet their climate finance pledge of U.S.$100 billion/year up until 2025 (Rumble et al. 2021). Moreover, developing countries took issue with the significantly skewed allocation of finance toward mitigation projects over adaptation, the procedural difficulties in getting adaptation projects funded through global climate funds, the cost of climate finance, and its lack of predictability.

In addition, many emerging economies harbor concerns over the push by developed countries for them to adopt net-zero targets within their NDCs. It is felt that this would unfairly hamper their development trajectories and have inequitable socio-economic impacts. As a recent submission by the African Group of Negotiators (AGN) demonstrated, fossil fuels are approximately 40 percent of Africa's exports (Republic of Zambia 2022). Their position is that "the case for African economies to [achieve net-zero] sensibly… is less clear. There are growing concerns that an abrupt devaluation of asset classes could constitute a systemic risk, create large amounts of stranded assets and set back progress made by African countries in achieving the sustainable development goals (SDGs)" (ibid.). They also cite equity concerns that it would cost lower income countries more to decarbonize their assets than it would for developed countries. In this context, not only is the AGN asking for more climate finance, but they are seeking finance targeted toward Just Transition support (see below), in the form of new predictable grant and concessional finance to buy down risks and create new asset classes for clean investments.

While these developments give little room for hope of a consensus on key issues, there is comfort that some progress is being achieved in bilateral discussions that preceded the 2021 COP. For instance, a Just Energy Transition Partnership (JETP) was agreed between South Africa and the United Kingdom, the United States, France, Germany, and the European Union. The partnership is supported by a pledge of $8.5 billion to finance South Africa's Just Transition process to reduce the carbon intensity in its electricity system and to develop new sectors such as green hydrogen and electric vehicles. Similar finance is under discussion within G7 which is seeking to conclude financially supported Just Energy Transition Partnerships with Indonesia,

India, Senegal, and Vietnam (*Nikkei Asia* 2022). Interestingly, this initiative is touted as the alternative to China's Belt and Road initiative, and opens up new pathways for multilateral cooperation in the global effort to decarbonize. These initiatives are building trust and hopefully will go some way to repairing governmental relations arising from fractious history of the climate finance negotiations. A longer path however needs to be travelled in order to meet developing country demands for at least $1.3 trillion in climate finance per year by 2030, of which 50 percent is for adaptation.

Developing countries are also looking for better recognition, support, and finance for loss and damage that are already being sustained as a result of climate impacts. Loss and damage are broadly understood as impacts that "go beyond" what a country is able to adapt to. This issue also became a highly contested topic at the negotiations last year. During discussions, the G77 plus China made a formal submission, asking for the establishment of a dedicated Loss and Damage Finance Facility, to bolster overall volumes of and overcome some of the barriers encountered in accessing finance for loss and damage. This call was rejected by developed countries, notably the EU and the United States, with the final outcome being an agreement to a two-year dialogue on the topic.

These are some of the main debates at the international level, but they are by no means the only ones. Negotiators are also gripped with talks on the global goal on adaptation, carbon markets, the global stock take, and reporting under the transparency framework. The regime has now evolved to such levels of complexity, that many negotiators do not know or follow what was discussed and agreed upon by their negotiation team counterparts in the room next door.

But key decisions on climate are increasingly happening outside of the UNFCCC and the Paris Agreement. Climate and questions around decarbonization feature strongly across negotiation platforms traditionally focused on other sectoral concerns, most notably global trade, intellectual property, and debt relief. This is unsurprising as climate change and the global architecture and means to respond to it are already impacting on countries' future economic trajectories, causing them to explore innovative and novel ways of using existing instruments or repurposing them for climate objectives. In the sections which follow we explore a few of these developments, including how carbon border tariffs are being developed and how this may influence bilateral relations and the creation of climate clubs; the potential for intellectual property rights to play a catalytic role in innovation and technology transfer; and how developments within the IMF and debt for climate swaps may provide some relief to developing countries in their quest for financial support.

Carbon Clubs and Trade

The Paris Agreement does not contain any punitive mechanisms to penalize countries for failing to impose and achieve ambitious mitigation targets, nor does it solve the free rider problem in the case of countries that do not have such targets. Countries that impose strong targets, and seek to achieve these through ambitious carbon pricing and other instruments, face the risk of carbon leakage and their domestic industries becoming relatively less competitive compared to countries that do not impose carbon prices. In response to this challenge the European Union (EU) is imposing a carbon border adjustment mechanism (CBAM) on its borders. Under this mechanism, a border tariff is imposed on emission-intensive goods such as iron, cement, and steel imported into the EU. The purpose is to "level the playing field," so that EU producers who are subject to carbon pricing are not unfairly competing against lower cost imports that do not have to pay a carbon price in their country of origin. In its current form there are no waivers for goods originating from LDCs although one of the recommendations provides for financial support for LDC decarbonization projects.

A number of developing countries have expressed "grave concern" about the CBAM (Government of South Africa 2021). It is perceived to be a discriminatory trade barrier and against principles of international environmental law, with China and India complaining that the mechanism runs afoul of WTO rules against protectionism. Notwithstanding these objections, the EU remains on track to implement the mechanism with the transitional phase having commenced on January 1, 2023.

The Democrats in the United States have also put forward a proposal on a polluter import fee that would target imports from nations lacking progressive climate policies. It was announced on the same day the EU introduced the CBAM. In furtherance of this proposal, in June this year, Democrats introduced a bill called the "Clean Competition Act" that would apply a levy on a large selection of energy-intensive imports, including fossil fuels, petrochemicals, steel, cement, fertilizer, and hydrogen. When introducing the bill, Senator Sheldon Whitehouse commented that "[t]here's a real prospect that Canada, EU, and UK all basically bind together on a common carbon border adjustment. And if we haven't joined up with them, we're just sort of deliberate losers" (*Scientific American* 2022).

These fears are stoking discussions about the potential creation of "carbon clubs." Originally conceived of by Nobel Prize-winning economist William Nordhaus, carbon clubs are groups of countries that agree to achieve a higher emissions reduction target between them through technological change that supports rapid decarbonization, with associated tariff penalties for its members. In doing so these (at present theoretical) clubs overcome the challenge of free-riding under the global regime, while also fostering green growth between club members. As Nordhaus described it, under the Paris Agreement, nations speak loudly but carry the tiniest of sticks (Nordhaus 2021). A carbon club effectively allows the erection of carbon borders in a coordinated manner that hedges against industries moving to regions with lower climate ambitions (World Economic Forum 2021), indirectly encouraging those outside the club to take on similarly ambitious measures in order to participate.

The topic of climate clubs was raised by the UK when it led the G7 in 2021, and it has become topical again under Germany as 2022s G7 leader that has expressed the wish to make a "cooperative and open climate club" a signature of its presidency. The notion may well gain more traction in the context of the unprecedented global energy crisis, together with the structural shake-up of global relations from Russia's war in Ukraine. It has been suggested that these dynamics will force countries to approach national security for energy and food far more carefully, and that climate policy may be a tool to justify national energy security needs (Principles for Responsible Investment 2022). It may well be that as countries turn away from now untrusted energy partners, they will seek to restructure their energy supply chains, and invest heavily in industries (including renewable energy) at a scale and pace not witnessed previously. A benefit of this geostrategic shift may be that renewable energy accelerates dramatically because of the energy independence it offers (although this remains to be seen, as demand for fossil fuel imports has also spiked in mid-2022). For countries wishing to use this opportunity to foster rapid green energy deployment, they may wish to do so within the protection of a carbon club to achieve joint geostrategic objectives. In this sense carbon pricing can be used as a stick to incentivize alignments that also achieve national objectives, including national security, climate goals as well as industry protectionism.

The risk of carbon clubs, the rapid shifts in energy geopolitics, and the voluntary pursuit of net-zero targets create a powerful incentive to compel countries to claim a stake in the global investment surge in decarbonized technology innovation and infrastructure. Countries that do not do so risk being left behind.

Clean Energy Innovation and Intellectual Property

However, to join and effectively participate within any carbon club, many emerging economies and developed countries will need to significantly invest in clean energy technologies. In the coming decades it is anticipated that the clean technology sector will grow exponentially. The Intergovernmental Panel on Climate Change (IPCC) has observed that, to stay within a temperature goal of 1.5°C, renewable energy output must grow to 52–62 percent of global primary energy supply by 2050 (Rogelj et al. 2018). In 2020, the world spent $501.3 billion on renewable power, electric vehicles, and other technologies (Saul and Mathis 2021). To remain competitive (either within or outside of any carbon club), countries will need to increase their budgets for research and development (R&D) in low-carbon technologies. To this end the Paris Agreement specifically recognizes that accelerating, encouraging, and enabling innovation is critical for an effective, long-term global response to climate change, through new collaborative approaches to climate technology research, development, and demonstration; the creation and promotion of relevant enabling policies; and the active engagement of the private sector and closer collaboration between the public and private sectors.[2]

While the global regime acknowledges the importance of scaled up innovation, there has been a longstanding debate within climate negotiations and discussions on Sustainable Development Goal 17,[3] regarding intellectual property, technology transfer, and climate change. During the 2007 negotiations under the UNFCCC, developing countries had argued for the creation of a multilateral acquisition fund to buy intellectual property rights, a demand that was ultimately unsuccessful. In the 2015 Paris Agreement negotiations, the BASIC (Brazil, South Africa, India, and China) group advocated for wider forms of technology transfer, and the G77 pushed for the adoption of intellectual property flexibilities. Ultimately these issues were not expressly addressed within the Paris Agreement, and instead, parties agreed to a Technology Framework to support the implementation of the existing Technology Mechanism of the UNFCCC. The latest version of the Framework, agreed to in 2019, does not create an intellectual property acquisition fund nor does it speak to intellectual property at all. Rather, it focuses on enhancing innovation through various collaborative and support actions, including

---

[2] UNFCCC Decision -/CMA.1 Technology framework under Article 10, paragraph 4, of the Paris Agreement.
[3] Relating to strengthening the means of implementation and revitalizing the global partnership for sustainable development.

actions that promote the deployment and dissemination of existing innovative technologies and accelerating the scale up and diffusion of emerging climate technologies.

While the issue of intellectual property has not gained much traction under the Paris Agreement, it still remains within the purview of the WTO and the Agreement on Trade-related Aspects of Intellectual Property Rights (TRIPS). The latter governs how intellectual property rights are granted, regulated, and exercised. If technology transfer and innovation are to be fostered and encouraged across borders, climate diplomacy needs to go beyond negotiations at successive COPs for the UNFCCC, and to interrogate the equity, effectiveness, and appropriateness of the current TRIPS regime.

For example, some developing country delegations have argued that the "flexibilities" in the TRIPS Agreement are significant for ensuring access to green technology. These flexibilities enable governments to relax some basic obligations of intellectual property protection, such as patent rights, subject to certain conditions being met. This issue was raised on a few occasions by Ecuador in 2013, but does not appear to have been addressed since (World Trade Organization 2022).

It may well be that developing countries are focusing their attentions elsewhere, including TRIPs waivers for vaccines to respond to the COVID-19 pandemic. Moreover, developing countries also rightly need to focus their attention on developing national R&D systems, dedicating budgets and developing cross-border partnerships for innovation and technology transfer. However, if these systems are to be meaningfully scaled, and in the context of the current energy crisis, it would be important for climate negotiators to consider the role of TRIPs waivers in "essential" goods, which could be meaningfully defined to include renewable energy technologies, particularly for low-income countries.

Debt, Climate Finance, and the Finance Sector

The pandemic and ensuing debt distress, coupled with volatile fuel prices, have also placed many developing countries in precarious economic positions. Moreover climate change poses heightened macro-financial risks to highly vulnerable countries as a result of the physical and transition risks it brings about, which in turn threatens debt sustainability, worsens sovereign risk, and harms investment and development prospects (Vulnerable 20 2020). These factors have prompted calls by developing countries for the International Monetary Fund (IMF) and related international financial institutions to intervene. The group of Vulnerable 20 (V20), for example, have made numerous overtures to the IMF asking for it to reform its support, technical assistance, and emergency lending functions. They have been calling on the IMF to support the re-channeling of Special Drawing Rights (SDRs) to vulnerable countries to enhance their liquidity and, in turn, their ability to respond to climate change. The Global Centre on Adaptation has made similar calls, asking for more collaboration on debt relief, and the channeling of funds to ensure sustainable recoveries, including through debt for climate swaps (Richmond, Choi, Rosane, et al. 2021). These are considered useful both for debt and climate reasons insofar as they operate as instruments to increase fiscal space for multiple reasons, but in particular to undertake climate investments, and they have the benefit of being attractive to private creditors.

In August 2021, the IMF issued $650 billion in SDRs—more than double the total number of SDRs it has ever issued and equivalent to approximately 5 percent of total global reserves. The reason for doing so was to give immediate additional liquidity and to support global economic resilience in response to the pandemic. Because of the quota system, most of the new SDRs issued were allocated to high-income countries, which did not face the same liquidity challenges as developing countries. In response to this inequity the IMF called on developed countries to re-channel some of the SDRs to developing countries. The G7 pledged to channel $100 billion worth of SDRs last year, an amount equivalent to the disputed amount of annual climate finance that was pledged under the UNFCCC almost a decade ago. Some of this has gone to the IMF's Poverty Reduction and Growth Trust (PRGT), which provides zero-interest loans to low-income countries. But the IMF has also established a $40 billion Resilience and Sustainability Trust (RST), which will re-channel SDRs to countries that would not qualify for the PRGT. The RST took effect in May 2022 and provides help to countries to build resilience to external shocks and ensure sustainable growth, with a view to long-term balance of payments stability. It will focus on longer term structural challenges, including climate change,[4] and it is anticipated that part of the loan conditionality will include climate change requirements.

The inclusion of climate as a major component of the RST is reflective of the IMF's wider acknowledgment that climate risks are impacting the global economic system and national economies, and that these impacts and the potential to shape global and national responses are now being incorporated into its work and mandate (Rumble and Sidiropoulos 2022). The IMF is not

---

[4] It is a loan-based trust with access based on the countries' reforms strength and debt sustainability considerations.

alone in this regard, and with climate change now increasingly acknowledged as both a risk and a major driver of long-term strategy across multiple financial institutions. Climate change is no longer a peripheral issue in global economics and financial matters, and global institutions are increasingly being called to repurpose their processes and existing instruments to respond to climate change in a manner that directly responds to evolving national and global trends and needs. Policymakers are starting to recognize the dramatic implications of climate change for financial stability and the importance of accelerated decarbonization. For example, an increasing number of central banks and financial regulators such as those within the Network for the Greening of the Financial System (NGFS) are acknowledging the importance of these issues and are seeking to integrate climate-related risks into financial stability oversight. Many financial institutions are also setting net-zero targets and incorporating climate change considerations into their management and lending policies. To be effective, a new order of climate diplomacy must support international cooperation in sustainable finance, working with non-state actors, such as global and regional financial institutions to increase finance and to mobilize ambition and partnerships at all levels.

Conclusion

The climate landscape is complex and varied. Climate diplomacy has an important role to play, but it must do so in a manner that frames climate as more than an environmental concern and embraces it across all sectors of intergovernmental relations. Partnerships between foreign policy stakeholders, such as humanitarian, trade, economic, development, and security communities, are critical to facilitating synergies and revitalizing multilateral and plurilateral approaches to climate action.

This chapter has sought to demonstrate that climate is already being discussed within multiple forums and institutions; and the UNFCCC and Paris Agreement, while central, are no longer the locus of climate decision-making. If the trends of the past few years are anything to go by, it is within the G7 and G20 meetings, the World Economic Forum, the IMF, the WTO, voluntary initiatives in the financial sector, and within key bilateral meetings that climate policy is being forged. This is in addition to the critical role that civil society, NGOs, and youth activism are playing in framing policy and challenging governments to respond both in the streets and in the courtrooms.

While a global response is the only means to effectively stem the crisis, the energy security crises, industry protectionism, rising debt levels, and to some degree, populism and nationalism, are undermining this response. Novel approaches outside of the Paris Agreement, such as border carbon adjustments, the potential evolution of climate clubs, new approaches to innovation and intellectual property, and debt relief and debt for climate swaps, may offer a means to overcome some of the inertia within the UNFCCC and the poor beginnings of the Paris Agreement. This requires diligent and ongoing diplomatic effort sustained consistently over time and across multiple platforms, and not at annual COPs, in a manner that is all encompassing and cuts across portfolios.

References and Further Reading

Carius, A., and L. Herzer Risi. 2021. "Editorial." In *Century Diplomacy: Foreign Policy Is Climate Policy*, eds. A. Carius, N. Gordan, and L. Herzer Risi, 1. Washington, D.C.: The Wilson Center.

Nikkei Asia. 2022. "G7 Infrastructure Investment to Target Indo Pacific's Clean Energy Transition," June 27.

Nordhaus, W. 2021. "Dynamic Climate Clubs: On the Effectiveness of Incentives in Global Climate Agreements." *Proceedings of the National Academy of Sciences*, 118.

Principles for Responsible Investment. 2022. "Global Carbon Pricing: Assessing the Potential of the EU CBAM and Climate Clubs," May.

Richmond, M., J. Choi, P. Rosane, et al. 2021. *Adaptation Finance in the Context of Covid-19*. N.p.: Global Centre on Adaptation.

Rogelj, J., et al. 2018. "Mitigation Pathways Compatible with 1.5°C in the Context of Sustainable Development." In *Global Warming of 1.5°C, An IPCC Special Report on the Impacts of Global Warming of 1.5°C Above Pre-industrial Levels and Related Global Greenhouse Gas Emission Pathways, in the Context of Strengthening the Global Response to the Threat of Climate Change, Sustainable Development, and Efforts to Eradicate Poverty*, eds. V. Masson-Delmotte et al., 93–174. N.p.: Intergovernmental Panel on Climate Change.

Rumble, O., and E. Sidiropoulos. 2022. "Exploring the Potential Role of the IMF in South Africa's Just Transition." In *SAIIA Special Report*. Cape Town: South African Institute of International Affairs.

Rumble, O., E. Sidiropoulos, and S. Fakir. 2021. "A New South African Climate Diplomacy: G7; G20 and Beyond," October 22. Cape Town: South African Institute of International Affairs.

Saul, J., and W. Mathis. 2021. "Spending on Global Energy Transition Hits Record $500 Billion." *Bloomberg*, January 19.

Scientific American. 2022. "How the U.S. Is Preparing for Europe's Carbon Tariffs," June 16.

South Africa. 2021. Government of, Joint Statement issued at the Conclusion of the 30th BASIC Ministerial Meeting on Climate Change, April 8.

United Nations. 2021. "Nationally Determined Contributions Under the Paris Agreement." Revised Note by the Secretariat. UN Document FCCC/PA/CMA/2021/8/Rev.1. New York: United Nations.

United Nations Environment Programme. 2021. *Emissions Gap Report 2021: The Heat Is On – A World of Climate Promises Not Yet Delivered.* Nairobi: UNEP.

Vulnerable 20. 2020. *Macrofinancial Risks in Climate Vulnerable Countries.* N.p.

World Economic Forum. 2021. "Why the EU's Proposed CBAM Must Not be Used to Launch a Carbon Club," June 2. Davos: World Economic Forum.

World Trade Organization. 2022. Meeting Minutes of the Trade-Related Aspects of Intellectual Property Rights, 2013–22. https://docs.wto.org/.

World Weather Attribution Network. 2022. "Climate Change Made Devastating Early Heat in India and Pakistan 30 Times More Likely," May 23. N.p.

Zambia, Republic of. 2022. "Views on the New Collective Mobilization Goal on Climate Finance." Lusaka.

35

Global Diplomacy and Multi-stakeholderism: Does the Promise of the 2030 Agenda Hold?

Felicitas Fritzsche and Karin Bäckstrand

In 2015, all 193 Member States of the United Nations (UN) adopted the 2030 Agenda and its 17 Sustainable Development Goals (SDGs) as a "comprehensive, far-reaching and people-centered set of universal and transformative Goals and targets" (UNGA 2015, para. 2). UN Member States recognized that implementing these ambitious aspirations requires "bringing together Governments, the private sector, civil society, the United Nations system and other actors" (UNGA 2015, para. 39). The involvement of non-state actors and partnerships is not a new feature of global governance for sustainable development. Fifty years of environmental and sustainable development diplomacy from the 1972 UN Conference of Human Environment in Stockholm to the "Stockholm+50" UN summit in June 2022 have consolidated a model of multi-stakeholder or public-private multilateralism, with institutionalized participation of non-state actors such as civil society and businesses, as well as the establishment of partnerships as implementation mechanisms. Raymond and DeNardis (2015, 573) define multi-stakeholderism "as two or more classes of actors engaged in a common governance enterprise concerning issues they regard as public in nature, and characterized by polyarchic authority relations constituted by procedural rules." As an essential part of virtually all UN summits on sustainable development and a new domain of

F. Fritzsche • K. Bäckstrand (✉)
Department of Political Science, Stockholm University, Stockholm, Sweden

national foreign policy, multi-stakeholderism has become a distinct form of global diplomacy. This chapter takes stock of multi-stakeholderism in global diplomacy for sustainable development with a focus on the 2030 Agenda and the SDGs, which raised many expectations for a more inclusive, integrative, and accountable global sustainable development governance. It asks whether multi-stakeholderism can live up to these promises—both as a result and as a way of practicing diplomacy. To this end, it assesses existing literature while also highlighting normative aspects of multi-stakeholder diplomacy.

The first section discusses the historical context of multi-stakeholderism up to the 2030 Agenda and the SDGs and provides a definition. Thereafter, the expectations the 2030 Agenda and the SDGs raised for a more inclusive, integrated, and accountable global sustainable development governance are clarified. In previous scholarship, these are benchmarks for assessing whether innovative reforms occurred. The third section analyzes emerging studies on multi-stakeholderism and whether it has become more inclusive, adopting a "whole of society" approach and focusing upon those left behind. The fourth section presents findings on changes in multi-stakeholderism related to the integrative and holistic nature of the 2030 Agenda and the SDGs, calling for cooperation and implementation across policy areas. The fifth section engages with research on the emerging accountability frameworks at the global, regional, and national level. The last section highlights continued contestations and challenges ahead. Altogether a mixed picture emerges which calls for more systematic research on multi-stakeholderism for the 2030 Agenda, as well as a better awareness, institutional safeguards, and capabilities among diplomatic practitioners.

Multi-stakeholderism in Global Diplomacy of Sustainable Development and Beyond

Since the 1992 United Nations Conference on Environment and Development in Rio de Janeiro, global sustainable development diplomacy has been a laboratory for innovations such as multi-stakeholder dialogues, partnerships, collaborations, and the inclusion of stakeholders. For example, the 2002 World Summit on Sustainable Development (WSSD) in Johannesburg not only focused upon intergovernmental negotiations and agreement between UN Member States. It also made partnerships, framed as voluntary agreements between governments, international organizations, businesses, and civil society, an official outcome of the summit (Pattberg et al. 2012). As an example, the Renewable Energy and Energy Efficiency Partnership (REEEP), which has the aim to advance markets for clean energy and accelerate energy efficiency in developed and developing countries, was established in 2002 to implement WSSD commitments.

This is a distinct mode of global diplomacy—multi-stakeholderism or multi-stakeholder and private-public multilateralism (Gleckman 2018). Multi-stakeholderism goes beyond earlier state-centric views on multilateralism, such as Keohane's (1990, 731) definition of multilateralism as "the practice of co-ordinating national policies in groups of three or more states" or Ruggie's (1992) more normative account as "an institutional form which coordinates relations among three or more states on the basis of 'generalized' principles of conduct—that is, principles which specify appropriate conduct for a class of actions, without regard to the particularistic interests of the parties or the strategic exigencies that may exist in any specific occurrence." Barnett et al. (2021) emphasize that global governance and multilateralism have become messier and more complex as three modes of governance exist in parallel and overlap—hierarchy, markets, and networks. Multi-stakeholderism is strongly linked to multi-sectoral networks. Recent research has focused upon the role of the UN in leveraging such networks in connection to multilateral summits, conferences, or platforms (Andonova 2017; Sapatnekar 2022). This resonates with accounts of UN Secretary General's "Our Common Agenda" (Guterres 2021), where inclusive, accountable, and networked multilateralism is highlighted. New mechanisms for deliberation and participation have emerged at multilateral summits or forums on sustainable development, such as the High-level Political Forum on Sustainable Development (HLPF), which includes platforms with registered commitments by states and non-state actors, and spaces for exchanging best practices or learning sessions on multi-stakeholderism. International organizations have also granted widespread access to non-state actors, as for example the World Bank which increased civil society participation in funded projects from 21 percent in 1990 to 72 percent in 2006 (Tallberg et al. 2013). In climate change, Sapatnekar (2022, 2) refers to this as the "collective choreography of cooperation" and finds that the convening power, autonomy, and organizational skills of the UN organization matter for the effectiveness of partnerships.

Focusing on national governments, Scheler (2022) highlights that foreign policy in the twenty-first century will "largely be about whether states manage to harness and catalyze the power of private actors in tackling the great global challenges that humanity is faced with." Scheler (2022) builds her argument on the fact that the power of private entities has in fact increased. Global Justice Now (2018) finds that 69 out of 100 of the richest entities worldwide are private corporations, with governments only being the clear majority among the top ten. Manulak and Snidal (2021) highlight larger shifts in today's diplomacy. The advent of new communication technologies has made the turn toward informal forms of international cooperation more feasible. National executives do not have to rely upon formal intergovernmental organizations and diplomatic missions anymore. They get together informally to formulate broad aspirations, to be implemented by national ministries and agencies in different forms of multi-stakeholderism. Therefore, the role of foreign ministries and diplomatic missions is changing, from a central node and gatekeeper, to a more coordinative and flexible role. And in the realm of sustainable development, the number of multi-stakeholder initiatives or commitments registered with the UN has indeed increased—from about 300 in 2002 to 6248 in 2022 (United Nations 2022b).

In official policy rhetoric, multi-stakeholderism has been conceived as a means to increase the legitimacy and reduce implementation deficits simultaneously in global governance. UN diplomacy for sustainable development during the past 50 years is underpinned by normative ideals of what has been framed as global stakeholder democracy (Bäckstrand 2006; Gleckman 2018; Macdonald 2008). For instance, the 2012 UN "Rio-20" summit in Brazil was conceived as a "global expression of democracy" by the then-Brazilian President Dilma Rousseff (Earth Negotiations Bulletin 2012, 1). As a central practice in multilateral summitry of sustainable development, multi-stakeholderism has been questioned by researchers and practitioners as an innovative form of global diplomacy that can shape more legitimate and effective global governance (Gleckman 2018). Advocates of participatory or deliberative democracy argue that the critical force of an autonomous civil society is tamed as they become collaborative partners with governments and business actors (Bäckstrand 2013). Multi-stakeholderism can easily lapse into symbolic or "simulative" participation, reinforce power asymmetries between different types of non-state actors, and consolidate global neo-corporativism (Cerny 2021; Nasiritousi et al. 2016; Willetts 2000).

Earlier research on partnerships in global sustainable development governance, building upon functionalist assumptions, shows for example that these have been highly dominated by Northern countries and international organizations, while affected and vulnerable stakeholders such as indigenous people and women are rarely represented (Bäckstrand 2006; Beisheim and Liese 2014; Chan and Müller 2012). Scholars have also questioned their effectiveness, as they do not fill governance gaps or promote the implementation of existing agreements (e.g. Pattberg et al. 2012). It is on this basis that some authors have outlined success factors (Pattberg and Widerberg 2016). Despite these criticisms, the 2030 Agenda and the SDGs re-legitimized multi-stakeholderism as a form of global diplomacy for sustainable development.

Expectations of Innovation from the 2030 Agenda

Within the 2030 Agenda and the SDGs, multi-stakeholderism is closely tied to funding and means of implementation. SDG 17 aspires to "strengthen the means of implementation and revitalize the Global Partnership for Sustainable Development" (UNGA 2015, 26). The broad and partially diametrical 19 targets of SDG 17 reflect different perspectives among UN Member States and stakeholders, as some aim for traditional state-centered development assistance, or trade and capacity-building, while others focus on the involvement of non-state actors, such as businesses. Target 17.16 states the need to "enhance the *Global Partnership* for sustainable development, complemented by *multi-stakeholder partnerships*," while target 17.17 focuses on the need to "encourage and promote effective *public, public-private and civil society partnerships*" (UNGA 2015, 27; emphasis added). Contestations along the Global North-South divide revolving around different perspectives on the role of the state and the sources of funding persisted throughout the negotiation of SDG 17 (Beisheim et al. 2022b, 25–26). The Global Partnership, a historically well-established term in UN history, refers to existing commitments and efforts to decrease international inequalities between countries (Ocampo and Gómez-Arteaga 2016, 5). The G77 and China have downplayed partnerships, stressing that the Global Partnership should remain intergovernmental in nature, with donor countries taking the lead in funding (Thérien and Pouliot 2020, 16). They also highlighted the need for better representation and equality in global economic governance (Fukuda-Parr and Muchhala 2020, 7–8). Another UN negotiation group consisting of the Western European as well other States focused on enhancing participation of the private sector, emerging economies, and multiple stakeholders, such as the nine "major groups."[1] The NGO Major Group, in turn, criticized this as an attempt to privatize multilateralism to big corporations (Thérien and Pouliot 2020, 16). Bernstein (2017, 233–34) feared that the focus of SDG 17 on partnerships diverts

---
[1] The nine major groups are business, farmers, indigenous people, local governments and municipalities, NGOs, science and technology, trade unions, women, and youth.

attention from development finance, trade rules, or market access for developing countries.

Altogether, scholars emphasize that multi-stakeholderism related to the 2030 Agenda and the SDGs should learn from earlier experiences of transnational partnerships (Abbott and Bernstein 2015, 7; Beisheim 2015, 32; Biermann et al. 2017, 28). The universal, but flexible as well as aspirational approach of the 2030 Agenda and the SDGs has been described as "governance by goals" in much of the academic literature. Despite the different perspectives outlined above, practitioners and scholars alike have highlighted several aspects of the 2030 Agenda and the SDGs as innovative modes of governance for a different kind of global diplomacy for sustainable development (see e.g. Biermann et al. 2017; Kanie and Biermann 2017; Vijge et al. 2020). These are based on both the negotiations and mandate of the 2030 Agenda (see UNGA 2015). Consequently, they serve as natural benchmarks for determining whether multi-stakeholderism in the age of the 2030 Agenda has been reformed and constitutes an innovation in global diplomacy.

Firstly, the 2030 Agenda and its 17 SDGs formulate universal aspirations for all UN Member States and are not limited to the donor-recipient logic advanced by their predecessor, the Millennium Development Goals (MDGs). Also, the negotiation process was more participatory compared to the top-down process of the MDGs. A common stocktaking process and a system of sharing seats loosened traditionally opposing negotiating blocs. Civil society was involved regularly in the intergovernmental negotiations, while citizens were consulted through broad online consultations and surveys (Chasek et al. 2018; Chasek and Wagner 2016; Dodds et al. 2017). Even though these participatory innovations only had moderate influence on the policy-making outcomes (Sénit 2020), compared to the MDGs, it is notable, again, that the SDGs were created in a more bottom-up and participatory manner (Fox and Stoett 2016). Additionally, UN Member States pledged to leave no one behind in the implementation of the 2030 Agenda (UNGA 2015, para. 4). Some hoped that this would make multi-stakeholderism more inclusive, also including the most vulnerable (for an overview see Sénit et al. 2022) as well as emerging actors (Independent Group of Scientists appointed by the Secretary-General 2019, 6). This accounts for our first benchmark.

Secondly, the 2030 Agenda and the SDGs address all three dimensions of sustainable development (social, environmental, economic) and are very broad in their scope, ranging from SDG 1 on ending poverty in all its forms everywhere, or SDG 12 on responsible consumption and production, to SDG

16 on peace, justice, and strong institutions. The 2030 Agenda itself states that a "balanced and integrated" implementation of the SDGs is crucial (UNGA 2015, para. 2). Many scholarly contributions focus upon how the goals affect each other (for an overview see Nilsson et al. 2022). These interlinkages between the SDGs are frequently referred to as synergies (positive interactions) or trade-offs (negative interactions) (Pradhan et al. 2017) and are linked to transformative pathways and leverage points (Independent Group of Scientists appointed by the Secretary-General 2019, xxi). The 2030 Agenda and the SDGs have, according to Bornemann and Weiland (2021), advanced a new notion of policy integration. From early on scholars have stressed the importance of coherent institutional arrangements (Bernstein 2017). Boas et al. (2016, 460), for example, propose a nexus approach for the global institutional setting, where multi-stakeholderism and transnational partnerships address synergies and trade-offs between SDGs. As multiple pathways toward transformation might exist, scholars stress that networks need to collaborate, exchange, and promote learning in this regard (Macaspac Hernandez and Vogel 2022). This has also created new aspects for assessing the effectiveness of multi-stakeholderism, referring to its transformative potential (e.g. Horan 2019; Li et al. 2020). This serves as our second benchmark.

Thirdly, there was recognition among scholars that the integrated and holistic nature of the 2030 Agenda and the SDGs requires different accountability mechanisms (e.g. Karlsson-Vinkhuyzen et al. 2018). Ocampo and Gómez-Arteaga (2016) emphasized that the focus upon multi-stakeholderism requires accountability mechanisms exercised by civil society, such as shadow reports, but also frameworks which hold civil society and the private sector accountable, for example via strong monitoring processes at the global level. In the end, the accountability mechanisms for the 2030 Agenda across governance levels and jurisdictions have been negotiated by UN Member States as rather weak, due to fear of prescriptive mechanisms (Beisheim 2015). Some argued that this could yield benefits due to "bottom-up, non-confrontational, country-driven, and stakeholder-oriented aspects of governance through goals" (Biermann et al. 2017, 27). There have, however, also been staunch critics of such a voluntarist, flexible system, in particular in light of accountability needs for partnerships and means of implementation, and transformative pathways required (e.g. Cooper and French 2018; Spangenberg 2017). These discussions serve as our third benchmark.

Innovative Seeds for Inclusivity

Diplomatic practices play a crucial role in ensuring that multi-stakeholderism as a means and an outcome of global diplomacy is inclusive and reaches those left behind. New research on multi-stakeholderism in the 2030 Agenda shows that the private sector and universities play a central role, as Duran y Lalguna and Dorodnykh (2018) highlight in their analysis of the newly created UN SDG Fund. While the private sector was only marginally involved in partnerships created at the WSSD (see e.g. Andonova and Levy 2003), an initial analysis of partnerships for the 2030 Agenda and the SDGs shows an increase in its involvement (Bäckstrand et al. 2022). Researchers have highlighted how the private sector can contribute to achieving the 2030 Agenda and the SDGs (e.g. Murillo et al. 2019; Ordonez-Ponce et al. 2021; Pfisterer and Van Tulder 2020). Despite this potential, Fowler and Biekart (2020) find that businesses are still not broadly represented in multi-stakeholder dialogues for national SDG implementation. Others argue that incentives for private sector participation in partnerships at the national level are better than those at the global level (Pérez-Pineda and Wehrmann 2021). An analysis of UN-registered partnerships involving business actors indicates that these are still numerically dominated by companies from the United States or the EU. Chinese and other emerging and developing countries are, however, increasing their involvement (Bull and McNeill 2019, 483). Altogether the increased participation of businesses remains contested amongst practitioners and scholars, and has led to recurrent critique of privatization of multilateralism (Adams 2016; Spangenberg 2017). This constitutes a balancing act for diplomatic practices, and critical engagement by diplomats is necessary.

Universities and research institutes also collaborate with industry actors (Castillo-Villar 2020). For example, the Triple and Quadruple Helix approach sheds light on how research is transferred through interactions for innovation in European regions (Committee of the Regions et al. 2016). Universities are involved in co-production with public administrations on the national level, for example in Sweden's Innovation Lab 2030, which aims to support Swedish authorities in developing their innovation capacity to implement the 2030 Agenda (Palm and Lilja 2021). Mago (2017), however, highlights the challenges for stronger North-South collaboration between research institutes. In addition, scholars call for stronger citizen science (e.g. Shulla et al. 2020) and engaging community-based organizations in data gathering for the 2030 Agenda and the SDGs (e.g. Thinyane et al. 2018). Nevertheless, a case study of Ireland demonstrates that general awareness of the 2030 Agenda and the

SDGs among non-state actors is still low, which is exacerbated by a historical lack of knowledge about partnerships (Banerjee et al. 2020). A recent empirical survey in Brazil, the UK, and the United States illustrates this lack of knowledge on global partnerships among the general public (Koliev and Bäckstrand forthcoming).

In light of the transformative aspirations of the 2030 Agenda and the SDGs, therefore, scholars have stressed the importance of involving those negatively affected and left behind by transformative change (e.g. Horan 2019). Wakely (2020) for example highlights the need to include the urban poor in local government-community partnerships for sustainable urban housing. The 2030 Agenda and the SDGs are criticized for not reflecting indigenous preferences (e.g. Movono and Hughes 2020); and government reporting on the implementation of the 2030 Agenda and the SDGs indeed neglects them (see Gilbert and Lennox 2019). Multi-stakeholderism needs to be based on meaningful and responsive participation of vulnerable groups. Sondermann and Ulbert (2021) operationalize this as attendance and active engagement, as well as a minimum threshold of responsiveness, and find that merely informal participation is not meaningful. Structural factors in inter-institutional arrangements of partnerships can benefit the normative views and interests of certain actors, which prevail over others (see Breitmeier et al. 2021). This concurs with previous findings on the importance of institutional designs of partnerships (e.g. Beisheim and Liese 2014; for an overview see Pattberg and Widerberg 2016).

As the implementation of the 2030 Agenda and the SDGs is left to the preferences of national governments, scholars find that governmental support and structures play a crucial role in promoting multi-stakeholderism (e.g. Almeida and Davey 2018; Banerjee et al. 2020). It has generally been argued that the closure of civic space will have a negative impact on the implementation of all SDGs (Hossain et al. 2019). Legal and regulatory frameworks matter crucially in this regard (Fowler and Biekart 2020). Changes therein can also have adverse effects, as an analysis of collaborative water governance partnerships in Ecuador highlights (Cisneros 2019). Generally, barriers to partnerships need to be reduced, as for example Haywood et al. (2019) highlight in the case of South Africa. However, Almeida and Davey (2018) find that stakeholders themselves do not always agree upon the barriers to implementation of SDG 11 on cities in Brazil, while funding is a key concern. As resources are also a challenge for international agencies, Sondermann and Ulbert (2021, 160) suggest prioritizing those left behind. Additionally, concurring with previous research, local realities and ownership are considered to be crucial (Fowler and Biekart 2017; Movono and Hughes 2020), while some argue that particular challenges in dealing with complexity and interrelations exist at this level (Herrera 2019). Beisheim and Ellersiek (2018, 71) find that some donors and funders have adjusted their practices to promote partnerships in light of the 2030 Agenda and the SDGs, for example by enhancing local and national ownership in programs on market development.

In sum, there are indications that new actors are involved, while those most vulnerable continue to be left behind. Systematic assessments of the inclusiveness of multi-stakeholderism related to the 2030 Agenda and the SDGs are, however, still lacking. Global diplomacy, practiced by both national diplomats and international bureaucrats, must keep these challenges and the importance of institutional aspects and local ownership in mind when leveraging multi-stakeholderism for the 2030 Agenda. The integrated nature of the 2030 Agenda and the SDGs makes inclusiveness particularly crucial, which leads us to our second benchmark.

Innovative Seeds for Integrated Policy-making

Many scholars emphasize that multi-stakeholderism should promote more integrated and transformative policies, rooted in a "whole of society" approach. Diplomats and international bureaucrats can play a crucial role as brokers in this regard. Awareness about some of the success factors the emerging literature identifies should be also promoted, even though Clarke and Crane (2018) find that scholars refer to different concepts of systemic change when analyzing cross-sector partnerships. Broader and more systematic assessments linking transformative potential to research on effectiveness of multi-stakeholderism are still lacking (e.g. Andonova et al. 2022), but some factors that could make multi-stakeholderism more suitable for transformation can be deduced from policy literature and case studies. Li et al. (2020) examine 41 partnerships from a delimited partnership ecosystem and conclude that four factors were particularly relevant for enhancing the transformative potential of partnerships. This includes firstly a good grasp of the system to be transformed and the policies needed; secondly, an inclusive agreement on a vision for transformation; thirdly, strong monitoring tools which integrate systems thinking; fourthly, strong links and the advocacy involvement of external stakeholders and affected communities. In a single case study, Moreno-Serna et al. (2020) highlight that flexibility and facilitation by all partners are crucial for transformative partnerships to be effective. Fowler and Biekart (2017) find that interlocutors, in the forms of secretariats, focal points, platforms, and hosts, crucially matter for performance. This has often been connected to orchestration, a soft and indirect mode of governance (e.g. Abbott and Bernstein 2015; Horan 2019; Pérez-Pineda and Wehrmann 2021) as well as meta-governance, referring to the overarching guiding rules and frameworks. Meta-governance, coupled with participatory innovations and capacity-building efforts, has been found crucial for cross-sectoral and transformative partnerships (e.g. Al Sabbagh and Copeland 2019; Eweje et al. 2020). Here again, diplomats and international bureaucrats can act as brokers, and play a role by advocating for stronger frameworks.

Bull and McNeill (2019, 484), however, propose that the Agenda 2030 and the SDGs have only had discursive impacts and raised incentives for registration of partnerships so far (for a broader assessment see Biermann et al. 2022). They warn that indicators of SDG 17 have been formulated in a weak manner and their impact on practices in multi-stakeholderism and partnerships remains relatively weak or at best questionable. This preliminary assessment speaks to earlier warnings that SDG 17 lacks guidance on how to implement partnerships for the SDGs and upholds a voluntarist framework for the achievement of sustainable development (Cooper and French 2018). Horan (2019) holds that the voluntary framework pursued by the UN will fail to leverage effective transformative partnerships, as these are unlikely to provide what it is needed—the involvement of winners and losers, partners with low capacities, long time horizons, mechanisms for coordination, and aligned incentives and policies suitable for transformations. Strengthening diplomatic practices around these aspects could address such shortcomings. Informal fora could be used by diplomats to uphold stronger principles in this regard, for example by engaging with resources provided by the Partnering Initiative and the Partnership Accelerator provided by UN entities (see United Nations 2022a).

There are, however, also researchers who stress that at the heart of the 2030 Agenda and the SDGs are conflicting and enduring, and so fundamentally incompatible political interests and priorities that continue to shape global development and cannot be managed or wished away. In the end, negotiation processes (and embedded power structures) are at the heart of these issues (Brand et al. 2021). Bull and McNeill (2019) also find that the type of partnership a company engages in depends on the form of capitalism of their home base, which might have very different views on what transformation entails. Despite this, Breitmeier et al. (2021) find in their analysis of SDG 2 that inter-institutional arrangements related to partnerships can promote a common normative understanding of sustainability related to ending hunger and ensuring food security. The design of partnerships in this respect matters (MacDonald et al. 2018), and diversity has been identified as a crucial factor in this regard (Beyers and Leventon 2021). Hedlund et al. (2022) find that on the local level, actors avoid collaboration in case of synergies and do not engage with trade-offs. Florini (2018) highlights that cross-sector partnering requires a specific skill set (Florini 2018, 114). External partnership mediators, internal entrepreneurs, and secretarial staff must be educated to not only understand cross-sectoral incentives and practices, but also how to approach the integrative nature of the SDGs, as well as complex systems and the non-linearity and unpredictability of global developments (Florini 2018, 115). This crucially applies to diplomats and international bureaucrats as well. In sum, broader conceptual and empirical assessments on the integrated features and transformative potential for multi-stakeholderism are still lacking, which remains a challenge. Strong accountability mechanisms could provide much needed guidance, which brings us to our third benchmark.

Innovative Seeds for Accountability

New or at least refurbished accountability mechanisms were established for the 2030 Agenda and the SDGs across all governance levels and these have implications for diplomatic practices and modes of engagement. At the global level, the HLPF is the central UN forum for leadership and guidance, as well as follow-up and review of the 2030 Agenda and the SDGs, with universal participation from Member States and major groups (UNGA 2015, para. 47). Early scholarly contributions agreed that the authority and resources of the HLPF are limited. Abbott and Bernstein (2015), however, propose that it could rely upon orchestration, a soft and indirect mode of governance by enlisting intermediaries, such as partnerships and action networks. Scholars suggest that the HLPF could offer an enhanced accountability framework for partnerships, provide spaces for exchange and learning, and highlight areas left behind by partnerships as well as advice other UN agencies (Abbott and Bernstein 2015, 7–8; Boas et al. 2016, 45). The HLPF comes together annually under the auspices of the UN Economic and Social Council (ECOSOC) and every four years on the level of heads of state and government under the auspices of the UN General Assembly (UNGA). Its review functions, related to the annual HLPF, are indeed mandated to provide a platform for partnerships; however, the provisions remain very weak and open (UNGA 2013, para. 8c). This has negatively affected both its leadership and its more informal orchestrating role to scale up partnerships (see e.g. Beisheim et al. 2022b; Beisheim and Fritzsche 2022).

A stronger mandate for UN meta-governance of partnerships has been heavily contested in the past (Beisheim and Simon 2018), which has led the secretariat of the HLPF, located with the UN Department of Economic and Social Affairs (DESA), to organize more informal events related to partnerships alongside the official HLPF program. From 2016 to 2018 UN DESA, together with the UN Office for Partnerships (UNOP) and the UN Global Compact, put together a Partnership Exchange. From 2019 onwards the annual ECOSOC Partnership Forum was moved to take place in the margins of the HLPF. Since 2022 it has taken place at the beginning of the year, in combination with an ECOSOC coordination segment, as an annual start to the work of ECOSOC and leading up to the HLPF (Beisheim 2021). A 2019 survey among HLPF participants, conducted by UN DESA (United Nations 2019) in preparation for the first HLPF reform, indicates that 26 percent agree strongly that the HLPF has mobilized partnerships, while 40 percent somewhat agree, 20 percent neither agree nor disagree, only 9 percent somewhat disagree and 5 percent strongly disagree.

To ensure some accountability, UN DESA also (re-)developed an online platform for self-registering partnerships and co-launched the Partnership Accelerator. However, the only new features introduced are that proposals need to follow the SMART (specific, measurable, achievable, resource-based, and time-bound) criteria, while reporting is still voluntary, with only its status being now indicated via a traffic light system (Bäckstrand and Kylsäter 2014; Beisheim and Ellersiek 2018). In general, the follow-up of partnerships registered with the UN DESA platform remains weak. Initial assessments show that the formal procedures of the HLPF do not provide strong accountability mechanisms for partnerships (Beisheim et al. 2022b). Innovation is more feasible in the many more informal side-events during the HLPF, which create more space for learning and exchange. Orchestration efforts by the UN DESA come to more fruition in these areas. The same holds for the voluntary peer-review mechanism introduced for the 2030 Agenda and the SDGs, the so-called Voluntary National Reviews (VNRs), which are presented annually at the HLPF. Official presentations are often showcased, while the smaller, less formalized VNR labs offer more space for exchange and learning. These formats, however, are not connected to the official proceedings and their outcomes remain unclear, as follow-up is lacking (Beisheim and Fritzsche 2022). Negotiations on a reform of the HLPF only made small changes, but did not strengthen the overall leadership of the HLPF, as political conflicts made agreement on more far-reaching reforms impossible (Beisheim 2021).

Aside from that, the UN Development System (UNDS) has undergone significant reforms since the adoption of the 2030 Agenda (see e.g. Weinlich

2021). However, altogether the UN system was not able to develop stronger accountability frameworks for multi-stakeholderism. An internal evaluation of the UN found that "the lack of a comprehensive framework to guide how these partnerships operate has created risks of ineffectiveness and inefficiency" (Office of Internal Oversight Services 2019, 16). Similarly, there have been demands for improving rules and operational guidelines for partnerships with the private sector, in order to ensure due diligence (Adams 2021; Dumitriu 2017). However, UN frameworks for partnerships focus more on quantity than quality. Also, rules and guiding frameworks remain detached from coherent and concrete implementation (Beisheim and Ellersiek 2018, 73). Even though this is an area often sought-after to make partnerships successful or enhance their transformative potential (e.g. Horan 2019; Pattberg and Widerberg 2016), scholars find a lack of political will and leadership to improve this area, as contestations and turf battles continue (Beisheim and Ellersiek 2018; Beisheim and Simon 2018).

On the regional level, the UN Regional Economic Commissions have organized annual sustainable development forums, also in preparation of the HLPF. They are, however, very different in their membership and focus (Beisheim 2015, 2020). Civil society mechanisms exist to organize the involvement of stakeholders, while accountability and monitoring of partnerships have not been a focus area so far (see e.g. Surasky 2021).

At the national level, the VNRs, an entirely voluntary and soft global peer-review mechanism, have proven successful in terms of improving participation by UN Member States. So far 176 countries have delivered one or more VNR, with 247 VNRs in total until including 2021 (Partners for Review 2021). Stakeholder-engagement and a whole-of-society approach are aspects UN Member States report upon in this regard. These reports indicate that the private sector and research institutes could be more integrated. Also, COVID-19 contributed to an increase in the establishment of tools and platforms for partnerships (Partners for Review 2021). Shadow reports by NGOs, however, often offer better accountability measures and space for peer-learning (Oosterhof 2020). Nevertheless, horizontal accountability measures prevail over vertical ones (Bexell and Jönsson 2021). There are some positive signs, as research demonstrates that national development planning has become more collaborative following the 2030 Agenda and the SDGs (Chimhowu et al. 2019). Nevertheless, Forestier and Kim (2020) show that some SDGs receive more attention than others in reporting practices, highlighting the danger of cherry-picking based on previous development trajectories. Also, Brolan et al. (2019), for example, find that in Australia the views by stakeholders on SDG3 were disconnected from the VNR presentation of the government. SDG 17 is generally still rarely reported upon (Committee for Development Policy 2020). Voluntary local reviews (VLRs) have become more popular, also among cities and metropolitan areas (see e.g. Pipa and Bouchet 2020; Trejo Nieto and Niño Amézquita 2022), but reporting on stakeholder engagement processes at the local level is still low (Ortiz-Moya et al. 2020). Diplomats could provide know-how and advocate for more ambitious and principle-guided national or local reporting practices.

Altogether, accountability frameworks for multi-stakeholderism related to the 2030 Agenda and the SDGs remain relatively weak and fragmented, and political will to strengthen them seems to be lacking (Beisheim 2021; Bexell and Jönsson 2021). Substantive shifts are needed to harvest some of the innovative seeds the 2030 Agenda and the SDGs have planted.

Persistent Contestations

Harvesting the innovative seeds the 2030 Agenda and the SDGs have planted for multi-stakeholderism is complicated by the fact that the multi-stakeholderism advanced by the 2030 Agenda and the SDGs has been interpreted in a broader manner. While previously a certain organizational form of partnerships was advanced, the 2030 Agenda and the SDG partnership registry also includes voluntary commitments by single organizations (Bäckstrand and Kylsäter 2014). As with other SDGs, the interpretation, measurement, and implementation of SDG 17 and the kind of multi-stakeholderism advanced therein continue to be contested (on other SDGs, see Fukuda-Parr and McNeill 2019). Reporting practices by UN Member States seem to confirm the concerns raised regarding the diversion of attention from more structural issues. Reporting on commitments toward least-developed countries in SDG 17 remains very scarce (Committee for Development Policy 2020, 14). Scholars highlight that the level of funding provided to developing countries is insufficient to implement the 2030 Agenda and the SDGs (e.g. Barua 2020), which has been further exacerbated by the COVID-19 pandemic (Kharas and Dooley 2021). In negotiations on the reform of HLPF, UN Member States could not even agree on a new name for the ECOSOC Partnership Forum (Beisheim 2021). Similar contestations have made reforms of stronger UN leadership for partnerships impossible (Beisheim and Simon 2018). In their response to the "Our Common Agenda" report, the Civil Society Financing for Development Group (2021) has argued that the UN should not focus on multi-stakeholder forums or networks, but instead ensure greater intergovernmental decision-making about global challenges.

The Way Forward

The 2030 Agenda and the SDGs have yet again re-legitimized multi-stakeholderism as a distinct form of global sustainable development diplomacy. Representation, inclusion, and participation of the nine major groups in the intergovernmental processes, a new generation with thousands of partnerships to implement the 2030 Agenda, a discourse around more integrative policies, and the establishment of new accountability mechanisms were supposed to reinvigorate a new type of multi-stakeholderism. Yet almost midway through the implementation of the 17 SDGs, there is weak or mixed evidence that these promises for a new type of multi-stakeholderism will become a reality. This worry is exacerbated by insufficient financing for the implementation of the 2030 Agenda at the present time, especially in developing countries. The COVID-19 pandemic was a major set-back for the achievement of the SDGs in terms of poverty eradication, protection of public health, gender equality, environmental protection, and development assistance. As global efforts to "build back better" were marshalled in the run up to the UN Stockholm+50 summit, intergovernmental global diplomacy is facing a deadlock in light of Russia's invasion of Ukraine. This makes a shift toward more transformative practices of multi-stakeholderism even more pressing (Beisheim et al. 2022a).

Diplomacy can contribute to improving multi-stakeholderism in manifold ways, primarily by catalyzing more innovative forms and learning from past mistakes. It is crucial that the strengths and weaknesses are first acknowledged among practitioners, not only diplomats and international bureaucrats, but also those in other sectors and at other governance levels. This also requires more systematic research on multi-stakeholderism in general and in light of the 2030 Agenda and the SDGs specifically. Lessons learned should be integrated into existing and emerging partnerships for the 2030 Agenda and the SDGs on all levels. Secondly, accountability frameworks should be strengthened by following the example of the 2023 global stocktaking of the Paris Agreement that formalized a transparency framework to assess progress of greenhouse gas emissions reductions. National governments should improve monitoring and knowledge management of how past and present multi-stakeholderism functions on the ground (Scheler 2022). Existing monitoring, accountability, and evaluation frameworks need to be improved and be made more accountable to whether impacts were achieved as the result of specific investments alongside more long-term transformative effects of multi-stakeholderism (see e.g. Habbel et al. 2021). A UN hub for partnerships, as suggested in the "Our Common Agenda" report, should be supported by UN Member States (Beisheim et al. 2022a). The 2030 Agenda and its 17 SDGs can serve well in this regard. Thirdly, a more networked and hub-based approach could be pursued in multilateral diplomacy. Multilateral embassies could serve in this manner (Scheler 2022; Beisheim and Fritzsche 2021a, 60). Also, cooperation among governments is necessary so as to avoid duplication of efforts. Multilateral fora and platforms, such as the HLPF, should be used more to exchange best practices, and follow-up on commitments for multi-stakeholderism, linking them more strongly to intergovernmental discussions (Beisheim and Fritzsche 2021b). To this end, fifthly, diplomatic training programs may need to be adjusted. As Slaughter (2017) indicates, understanding and connecting with private actors is a crucial aspect of today's diplomacy, especially in the realm of global sustainable development governance (see also Manfredi-Sánchez 2022; Scheler 2022). Diplomacy labs already exist to this end (e.g. Global Diplomacy Lab 2022). Diplomats need to become partnership-literate, for example by being able to communicate across sectors, in order to safeguard multilateral processes and account for power imbalances and structural inequalities in multi-stakeholderism for the 2030 Agenda.

References and Further Reading

Abbott, K.W., and S. Bernstein. 2015. "The High-Level Political Forum on Sustainable Development: Orchestration by Default and Design." *Global Policy* 6 (3): 222–33.

Adams, B. 2016. "United Nations and Business Community: Out-Sourcing Or Crowding In?" *Development* 59 (1): 21–28.

———. 2021. "Private Finance and Partnerships at the UN." In *Routledge Handbook on the UN and Development*, eds. S. Browne and T.G. Weiss, 165–83. London: Routledge.

Al Sabbagh, S., and E. Copeland. 2019. "Partnering for Sustainable Development: Case Study of a 10-Year Donor–Recipient Partnership." *Development in Practice* 29 (5): 651–61.

Almeida, A., and P. Davey. 2018. "Environmental Sustainability Partnerships for SDG 11 Implementation in Brazil Understanding the Vulnerabilities and Common Interests from a Multi-Stakeholder Perspective." *International Journal of Environmental Sustainability* 14 (2): 1–17.

Andonova, L.B. 2017. *Governance Entrepreneurs: International Organizations and the Rise of Global Public-Private Partnerships*. Cambridge: Cambridge University Press.

Andonova, L.B., and M.A. Levy. 2003. "Franchising Global Governance: Making Sense of the Johannesburg Type II Partnerships." In *Yearbook of International Cooperation on Environment and Development 2003/2004*, eds. O.S. Stocke and O.B. Thomessen, 19–31. London: Earthscan.

Andonova, L.B., M.V. Faul, and D. Piselli, eds. 2022. *Partnerships for Sustainability in Contemporary Global Governance: Pathways to Effectiveness*. Routledge Research in Environmental Policy and Politics. New York: Routledge.

Bäckstrand, K. 2006. "Multi-Stakeholder Partnerships for Sustainable Development: Rethinking Legitimacy, Accountability and Effectiveness." *European Environment* 16 (5): 290–306.

———. 2013. "Civil Society Participation in Sustainable Development Diplomacy. Towards Global Stakeholder Democracy?" The 8th Pan-European Conference on International Relations. Warsaw.

Bäckstrand, K., and M. Kylsäter. 2014. "Old Wine in New Bottles? The Legitimation and Delegitimation of UN Public–Private Partnerships for Sustainable Development from the Johannesburg Summit to the Rio+20 Summit." *Globalizations* 11 (3): 331–47.

Bäckstrand, K., F. Koliev, and A. Mert. 2022. "Governing SDG Partnerships. The Role of Institutional Capacity, Transparency and Inclusion." In *Partnerships and the Sustainable Development Goals*, eds. E. Murphy, P. Walsh, and A. Banerjee, 41–58. Cham: Springer.

Banerjee, A., E. Murphy, and P.P. Walsh. 2020. "Perceptions of Multistakeholder Partnerships for the Sustainable Development Goals: A Case Study of Irish Non-State Actors." *Sustainability* 12 (21): 8872.

Barnett, M.N., J.C.W. Pevehouse, and K. Raustiala. 2021. "Introduction: The Modes of Governance." In *Global Governance in a World of Change*, eds. M.N. Barnett, J.C.W. Pevehouse, and K. Raustiala, 1–47. Cambridge: Cambridge University Press.

Barua, S. 2020. "Financing Sustainable Development Goals: A Review of Challenges and Mitigation Strategies." *Business Strategy and Development* 3 (3): 277–93.

Beisheim, M. 2015. "Reviewing the Post-2015 Sustainable Development Goals and Partnerships: A Proposal for a Multi-Level Review at the High-Level Political Forum." Research Paper 01. Berlin: Stiftung Wissenschaft und Politik.

———. 2020. "Reviewing the HLPF's 'Format and Organizational Aspects'–What's Being Discussed? Assessing Current Proposals under Debate." Working Paper 01. Berlin: Stiftung Wissenschaft und Politik.

———. 2021. "Conflicts in UN Reform Negotiations: Insights into and from the Review of the High-Level Political Forum on Sustainable Development." SWP Research Paper 09. Berlin: Stiftung Wissenschaft und Politik.

Beisheim, M., and A. Ellersiek. 2018. "Towards Quality Partnerships for the SDGs." *Annual Review of Social Partnerships* 13: 70–73.

Beisheim, M., and F. Fritzsche. 2021a. "German Foreign Policy in Transition – Foreign Sustainability Policy." SWP Research Paper 10. Berlin: Stiftung Wissenschaft und Politik.

———. 2021b. "Networked Multilateralism: ECOSOC and HLPF Reviews as Window of Opportunity." International Institute for Sustainable Development, January 20.

———. 2022. "The UN High-Level Political Forum on Sustainable Development: An Orchestrator, More or Less?" *Global Policy*.

Beisheim, M., and A. Liese, eds. 2014. *Transnational Partnerships: Effectively Providing for Sustainable Development?* Governance and Limited Statehood Series. Basingstoke: Palgrave.

Beisheim, M., and N. Simon. 2018. "Multistakeholder Partnerships for the SDGs: Actors' Views on UN Metagovernance." *Global Governance: A Review of Multilateralism and International Organizations* 24 (4): 497–515.

Beisheim, M., A. Berger, L. Brozus, A. Kloke-Lesche, R. Scheler, and S. Weinlich. 2022a. "The G7 and Multilateralism in Times of Aggression: Maintaining and Strengthening Cooperative and Inclusive Approaches for the Global Common Good." Policy Brief. Berlin: Global Solutions Initiative.

Beisheim, M., S. Bernstein, F. Biermann, P.S. Chasek, M. van Driel, F. Fritzsche, C.-A. Sénit, and S. Weinlich. 2022b. "Global Governance." In *The Political Impact of the Sustainable Development Goals: Transforming Governance Through Global Goals?* eds. F. Biermann, T. Hickmann, and C.-A. Sénit, 22–58. Cambridge: Cambridge University Press.

Bernstein, S. 2017. "The United Nations and the Governance of Sustainable Development Goals." In *Governing Through Goals: Sustainable Development Goals as Governance Innovation*, eds. N. Kanie and F. Biermann, 213–40. Cambridge, MA: MIT Press.

Bexell, M., and K. Jönsson. 2021. *The Politics of the Sustainable Development Goals: Legitimacy, Responsibility, and Accountability*. Routledge Studies in Sustainable Development. New York: Routledge.

Beyers, F., and J. Leventon. 2021. "Learning Spaces in Multi-Stakeholder Initiatives: The German Partnership for Sustainable Textiles as a Platform for Dialogue and Learning?" *Earth System Governance* 9: 100113.

Biermann, F., N. Kanie, and R.E. Kim. 2017. "Global Governance by Goal-Setting: The Novel Approach of the UN Sustainable Development Goals." *Current Opinion in Environmental Sustainability* 26/27: 26–31.

Biermann, F., T. Hickmann, C.-A. Sénit, M. Beisheim, S. Bernstein, P. Chasek, L. Grob, et al. 2022. "Scientific Evidence on the Political Impact of the Sustainable Development Goals." *Nature Sustainability* 5: 795–800.

Boas, I., F. Biermann, and N. Kanie. 2016. "Cross-Sectoral Strategies in Global Sustainability Governance: Towards a Nexus Approach." *International Environmental Agreements: Politics, Law and Economics* 16 (3): 449–64.

Bornemann, B., and S. Weiland. 2021. "The UN 2030 Agenda and the Quest for Policy Integration: A Literature Review." *Politics and Governance* 9 (1): 96–107.

Brand, A., M. Furness, and N. Keijzer. 2021. "Promoting Policy Coherence Within the 2030 Agenda Framework: Externalities, Trade-Offs and Politics." *Politics and Governance* 9 (1): 108–18.

Breitmeier, H., S. Schwindenhammer, A. Checa, J. Manderbach, and M. Tanzer. 2021. "Aligned Sustainability Understandings? Global Inter-Institutional Arrangements and the Implementation of SDG 2." *Politics and Governance* 9 (1): 141–51.

Brolan, C.E., C.A. McEwan, and P.S. Hill. 2019. "Australia's Overseas Development Aid Commitment to Health Through the Sustainable Development Goals: A Multi-Stakeholder Perspective." *Globalization and Health* 15 (1): 1–19.

Bull, B., and D. McNeill. 2019. "From Market Multilateralism to Governance by Goal Setting: SDGs and the Changing Role of Partnerships in a New Global Order." *Business and Politics* 21 (4): 464–86.

Castillo-Villar, R.G. 2020. "Identifying Determinants of CSR Implementation on SDG 17 Partnerships for the Goals," ed. L.T. Wright. *Cogent Business & Management* 7 (1): 1847989.

Cerny, P.G. 2021. "Business and Politics in an Age of Intangibles and Financialization." In *Handbook of Business and Public Policy*, eds. A. Kellow, T. Porter, and K. Ronit, 193–214. Cheltenham: Edward Elgar.

Chan, S., and C. Müller. 2012. "Explaining the Geographic, Thematic and Organizational Differentiation of Partnerships for Sustainable Development." In *Public–Private Partnerships for Sustainable Development Emergence, Influence and Legitimacy*, eds. P. Pattberg, F. Biermann, S. Chan, and A. Mert, 44–66. Cheltenham: Edward Elgar.

Chasek, P.S., and L.M. Wagner. 2016. "Breaking the Mold: A New Type of Multilateral Sustainable Development Negotiation." *International Environmental Agreements: Politics, Law and Economics* 16 (3): 397–413.

Chasek, P.S., D. Chadwick O'Connor, and M. Kamau. 2018. *Transforming Multilateral Diplomacy: The Inside Story of the Sustainable Development Goals*. London: Routledge.

Chimhowu, A.O., D. Hulme, and L.T. Munro. 2019. "The 'New' National Development Planning and Global Development Goals: Processes and Partnerships." *World Development* 120: 76–89.

Cisneros, P. 2019. "What Makes Collaborative Water Governance Partnerships Resilient to Policy Change? A Comparative Study of Two Cases in Ecuador." *Ecology and Society* 24 (1): 29.

Civil Society Financing for Development Group. 2021."Civil Society Financing for Development (FfD) Group Response to SG's 'Our Common Agenda' Report." https://csoforffd.org/2022/01/19/response-to-un-secretary-generals-our-common-agenda-report/.

Clarke, A., and A. Crane. 2018. "Cross-Sector Partnerships for Systemic Change: Systematized Literature Review and Agenda for Further Research." *Journal of Business Ethics* 150 (2): 303–13.

Committee for Development Policy. 2020. "Voluntary National Reviews Reports: What Do They (Not) Reveal?" Background Paper 50. New York: United Nations Department of Economic and Social Affairs. https://www.un.org/development/desa/dpad/publication/voluntary-national-reviews-reports-what-do-they-not-reveal/.

Committee of the Regions, Progress Consulting S.r.l., and Fondazione FORMIT, Italy. 2016. *Using the Quadruple Helix Approach to Accelerate the Transfer of Research and Innovation Results to Regional Growth*. LU: Publications Office. https://data.europa.eu/doi/10.2863/408040.

Cooper, N., and D. French. 2018. "SDG 17: Partnerships for the Goals – Cooperation within the Context of a Voluntarist Framework." In *Sustainable Development: Law, Theory and Implementation*, eds. D. French and L.J. Kotzé, 271–304. Cheltenham: Edward Elgar Publishing.

Dodds, F., D. Donoghue, and J. Leiva Roesch. 2017. *Negotiating the Sustainable Development Goals: A Transformational Agenda for an Insecure World*. London: Routledge.

Dumitriu, P. 2017. *The United Nations System – Private Sector Partnerships Arrangements in the Context of the 2030 Agenda for Sustainable Development*. Geneva: Joint Inspection Unit.

Duran y Lalaguna, P., and E. Dorodnykh. 2018. "The Role of Private–Public Partnerships in the Implementation of Sustainable Development Goals: Experience from the SDG Fund." In *Handbook of Sustainability Science and Research*, ed. W. Leal Filho, 969–82. World Sustainability Series. Cham: Springer.

Earth Negotiations Bulletin. 2012. *Summary Report UNCSD (Rio+20)*. https://enb.iisd.org/events/uncsd-rio20/summary-report-13-22-june-2012.

Eweje, G., A. Sajjad, S. Deba Nath, and K. Kobayashi. 2020. "Multi-Stakeholder Partnerships: A Catalyst to Achieve Sustainable Development Goals." *Marketing Intelligence & Planning* 39 (2): 186–212.

Florini, A. 2018. "Professionalizing Cross-Sector Collaboration to Implement the SDGs." In *From Summits to Solutions*, eds. R.M. Desai, H. Kato, H. Kharas, and J.W. McArthur, 106–25. Innovations in Implementing the Sustainable Development Goals. Brookings Institution Press. http://www.jstor.org.ezp.sub.su.se/stable/10.7864/j.ctt21h4xhs.8.

Forestier, O., and R.E. Kim. 2020. "Cherry-picking the Sustainable Development Goals: Goal Prioritization by National Governments and Implications for Global Governance." *Sustainable Development* 28 (5): 1269–78.

Fowler, A., and K. Biekart. 2017. "Multi-Stakeholder Initiatives for Sustainable Development Goals: The Importance of Interlocutors: Multi-Stakeholder Initiatives for Sustainable Development Goals." *Public Administration and Development* 37 (2): 81–93.

———. 2020. "Activating Civic Space for Sustainable Development: Helping and Hindering Factors for Effective CSO Engagement in the SDGs." Synthesis Report. The Hague: International Institute of Social Studies.

Fox, O., and P. Stoett. 2016. "Citizen Participation in the UN Sustainable Development Goals Consultation Process: Toward Global Democratic Governance?" *Global Governance: A Review of Multilateralism and International Organizations* 22 (4): 555–73.

Fukuda-Parr, S., and D. McNeill. 2019. "Knowledge and Politics in Setting and Measuring the SDGs. Introduction to Special Issue." *Global Policy* 10 (1): 5–15.

Fukuda-Parr, S., and B. Muchhala. 2020. "The Southern Origins of Sustainable Development Goals: Ideas, Actors, Aspirations." *World Development* 126: 104706.

Gilbert, J., and C. Lennox. 2019. "Towards New Development Paradigms: The United Nations Declaration on the Rights of Indigenous Peoples as a Tool to Support Self-Determined Development." *International Journal of Human Rights* 23 (1–2): 104–24.

Gleckman, H. 2018. *Multistakeholder Governance and Democracy: A Global Challenge*. 1st ed. New York: Routledge.

Global Diplomacy Lab. 2022. Global Diplomacy Lab. https://global-diplomacy-lab.org/home/.

Global Justice Now. 2018. "69 of the Richest 100 Entities on the Planet Are Corporations, Not Governments, Figures Show." https://www.globaljustice.org.uk/news/69-richest-100-entities-planet-are-corporations-not-governments-figures-show/.

Guterres, A. 2021. *Our Common Agenda*. New York: United Nations. https://www.un.org/en/content/common-agenda-report/#download.

Habbel, V., M. Orth, J. Richter, and S. Schimko. 2021. *Evaluierungssynthese Zusammenarbeit mit der Privatwirtschaft*. Bonn: Deutsches Evaluierungsinstitut der Entwicklungszusammenarbeit.

Haywood, L.K., N. Funke, M. Audouin, C. Musvoto, and A. Nahman. 2019. "The Sustainable Development Goals in South Africa: Investigating the Need for Multi-Stakeholder Partnerships." *Development Southern Africa* 36 (5): 555–69.

Hedlund, J., D. Nohrstedt, T. Morrison, M.-L. Moore, and Ö. Bodin. 2022. "Challenges for Environmental Governance: Policy Issue Interdependencies Might Not Lead to Collaboration." *Sustainability Science*, May.

Herrera, V. 2019. "Reconciling Global Aspirations and Local Realities: Challenges Facing the Sustainable Development Goals for Water and Sanitation." *World Development* 118: 106–17.

Horan, D. 2019. "A New Approach to Partnerships for SDG Transformations." *Sustainability* 11 (18): 4947.

Hossain, N., N. Khurana, S. Nazneen, M. Oosterom, P. Schröder, and A. Shankland. 2019. "Development Needs Civil Society: The Implications of Civic Space for the SDGs." Synthesis Report. Geneva: ACT Alliance. https://opendocs.ids.ac.uk/opendocs/handle/20.500.12413/14541.

Independent Group of Scientists appointed by the Secretary-General. 2019. *Global Sustainable Development Report: The Future Is Now: Science for Achieving Sustainable Development*. New York: United Nations. https://sustainabledevelopment.un.org/gsdr2019.

Kanie, N., and F. Biermann, eds. 2017. *Governing Through Goals: Sustainable Development Goals as Governance Innovation*. Earth System Governance. Cambridge, MA: MIT Press.

Karlsson-Vinkhuyzen, S., A.L. Dahl, and Å. Persson. 2018. "The Emerging Accountability Regimes for the Sustainable Development Goals and Policy Integration: Friend or Foe?" *Environment and Planning C: Politics and Space* 36 (8): 1371–90.

Keohane, R.O. 1990. "Multilateralism: An Agenda for Research." *International Journal* 45 (4): 731–64.

Kharas, H., and M. Dooley. 2021. "International Financing of the Sustainable Development Goals." In *Financing the UN Development System: Time to Meet the Moment*, 87–96. Uppsala: Dag Hammarskjöld Foundation / MPTF Office.

Koliev, F., and K. Bäckstrand. Forthcoming. "Public Legitimacy of Global Multistakeholder Partnerships: Evidence from Survey Experiments in Brazil, UK, and the US." Unpublished Paper.

Li, S., E. Gray, and M. Dennis. 2020. *A Time For Transformative Partnerships: How Multistakeholder Partnerships Can Accelerate the UN Sustainable Development Goals*. World Resources Institute. https://www.wri.org/research/time-transformative-partnerships.

Macaspac Hernandez, A., and J. Vogel. 2022. "Transnational Networks as Relational Governance Infrastructure." Future of Globalisation (blog). https://blogs.die-gdi.de/2022/02/09/transnational-networks-as-relational-governance-infrastructure/.

Macdonald, T. 2008. *Global Stakeholder Democracy*. Oxford: Oxford University Press.

MacDonald, A., A. Clarke, L. Huang, M. Roseland, and M.M. Seitanidi. 2018. "Multi-Stakeholder Partnerships (SDG #17) as a Means of Achieving Sustainable Communities and Cities (SDG #11)." In *Handbook of Sustainability Science and Research*, ed. W. Leal Filho, 193–209. World Sustainability Series. Cham: Springer.

Mago, S. 2017. "North–South Research Collaboration and the Sustainable Development Goals: Challenges and Opportunities for Academics." In *Knowledge for Justice: Critical Perspectives from Southern African-Nordic Research Partnerships*, eds. T. Halvorsen, H. Ibsen, H.-C. Evans, and S. Penderis, 163–74. Cape Town: African Minds.

Manfredi-Sánchez, J.L. 2022. "Corporate Diplomacy in a Post-COVID-19 World." In *Diplomacy, Organisations and Citizens*, eds. S. Pedro Sebastião and S. de Carvalho Spínola, 125–37. Cham: Springer.

Manulak, M.W., and D. Snidal. 2021. "The Supply of Informal International Governance: Hierarchy Plus Networks in Global Governance." In *Global Governance in a World of Change*, eds. M.N. Barnett, J.C.W. Pevehouse, and K. Raustiala, 182–213. Cambridge: Cambridge University Press.

Moreno-Serna, J., T. Sánchez-Chaparro, J. Mazorra, A. Arzamendi, L. Stott, and C. Mataix. 2020. "Transformational Collaboration for the SDGs: The Alianza Shire's Work to Provide Energy Access in Refugee Camps and Host Communities." *Sustainability* 12 (2): 539.

Movono, A., and E. Hughes. 2020. "Tourism Partnerships: Localizing the SDG Agenda in Fiji." *Journal of Sustainable Tourism*: 1–15.

Murillo, F., E. Charvet, K. Konya, I. Ohno, and H. Shiga. 2019. "Scaling Up Business Impact on the SDGs." *G20 Insights*. https://www.g20-insights.org/policy_briefs/scaling-up-business-impact-on-the-sdgs/.

Nasiritousi, N., M. Hjerpe, and K. Bäckstrand. 2016. "Normative Arguments for Non-State Actor Participation in International Policymaking Processes: Functionalism, Neocorporatism or Democratic Pluralism?" *European Journal of International Relations* 22 (4): 920–43.

Nilsson, M., J. Marjanneke, I. Vijge, A. Lobos, B. Bornemann, K. Fernando, T. Hickmann, M. Scobie, and S. Weiland. 2022. "Interlinkages, Integration and Coherence." In *The Political Impact of the Sustainable Development Goals: Transforming Governance Through Global Goals?*, eds. F. Biermann, T. Hickmann, and C.-A. Sénit, 92–115. Cambridge: Cambridge University Press.

Ocampo, J.A., and N. Gómez-Arteaga. 2016. "Accountability in International Governance and the 2030 Development Agenda." *Global Policy* 7 (3): 305–14.

Office of Internal Oversight Services. 2019. "Evaluation of United Nations Entities' Preparedness, Policy Coherence, and Early Results Associated with Their Support to Sustainable Development Goals." New York: United Nations.

Oosterhof, P. 2020. *SDG16 in VNRs and Spotlight Reports*. Eschborn: Deutsche Gesellschaft für internationale Zusammenarbeit; TAP Network.

Ordonez-Ponce, E., A. Clarke, and A. MacDonald. 2021. "Business Contributions to the Sustainable Development Goals Through Community Sustainability Partnerships." *Sustainability Accounting, Management and Policy Journal* 12 (6): 1239–67.

Ortiz-Moya, F., H. Koike, J. Ota, Y. Kataoka, and J. Fujino. 2020. *State of the Voluntary Local Reviews: Local Action for Global Impact in Achieving the SDGs*. Hayama: Institute for Global Environmental Strategies. https://www.iges.or.jp/en/pub/vlrs-2020/en.

Palm, K., and J. Lilja. 2021. "On the Road to Agenda 2030 Together in a Complex Alliance of Swedish Public Authorities." *Environment, Development and Sustainability* 23 (6): 9564–80.

Partners for Review. 2021. *2021 Voluntary National Reviews – A Snapshot of Trends in SDG Reporting*. Bonn: Deutsche Gesellschaft für internationale Zusammenarbeit.

Pattberg, P., and O. Widerberg. 2016. "Transnational Multistakeholder Partnerships for Sustainable Development: Conditions for Success." *Ambio* 45 (1): 42–51.

Pattberg, P., F. Biermann, S. Chan, and A. Mert. 2012. "Introduction: Partnerships for Sustainable Development." In *Public–Private Partnerships for Sustainable Development Emergence, Influence and Legitimacy*, eds. P. Pattberg, F. Biermann, S. Chan, and A. Mert, 1–18. Cheltenham: Edward Elgar.

Pérez-Pineda, J.A., and D. Wehrmann. 2021. "Partnerships with the Private Sector: Success Factors and Levels of Engagement in Development Cooperation." In *The Palgrave Handbook of Development Cooperation for Achieving the 2030 Agenda*, eds. S. Chaturvedi, H. Janus, S. Klingebiel, X. Li, A. de Mello e Souza, E. Sidiropoulos, and D. Wehrmann, 649–70. Cham: Springer.

Pfisterer, S., and R. Van Tulder. 2020. "Navigating Governance Tensions to Enhance the Impact of Partnerships with the Private Sector for the SDGs." *Sustainability* 13 (1): 111.

Pipa, A.F., and M. Bouchet. 2020. *Next Generation Urban Planning: Enabling Sustainable Development at the Local Level through Voluntary Local Reviews (VLRs)*. Washington, D.C.: Brookings Institution.

Pradhan, P., L. Costa, D. Rybski, W. Lucht, and J.P. Kropp. 2017. "A Systematic Study of Sustainable Development Goal (SDG) Interactions." *Earth's Future* 5 (11): 1169–79.

Raymond, M., and L. DeNardis. 2015. "Multistakeholderism: Anatomy of an Inchoate Global Institution." *International Theory* 7 (3): 572–616.

Ruggie, J.G. 1992. "Multilateralism: The Anatomy of an Institution." *International Organization* 46 (3): 561–98.

Sapatnekar, P. 2022. *Global Governance 2.0: The Collective Choreography of Cooperation*. Center for International & Security Studies at Maryland. https://spp.umd.edu/research-impact/publications/global-governance-20-collective-choreography-cooperation.

Scheler, R. 2022. *Multilateralism 2.0: Why International Cooperation Needs a Makeover and How This Can Be Achieved*. Multilateralismus Weiter | Denken. Frankfurt am Main: Goethe-Universität Frankfurt. https://multilateralismus.com/en/blog/scheler-multilateralism-2-why-international-cooperation-needs-a-makeover#foot2.

Sénit, C.-A. 2020. "Leaving No One Behind? The Influence of Civil Society Participation on the Sustainable Development Goals." *Environment and Planning C: Politics and Space* 38 (4): 693–712.

Sénit, C.-A., C. Okereke, L. Alcázar, D. Banik, M. Bastos Lima, F. Biermann, R. Fambasayi, et al. 2022. "Inclusiveness." In *The Political Impact of the Sustainable Development Goals: Transforming Governance Through Global Goals?* eds. F. Biermann, T. Hickmann, and C.-A. Sénit, 116–39. Cambridge: Cambridge University Press.

Shulla, K., W. Leal Filho, J.H. Sommer, A.L. Salvia, and C. Borgemeister. 2020. "Channels of Collaboration for Citizen Science and the Sustainable Development Goals." *Journal of Cleaner Production* 264: 121735.

Slaughter, A.-M. 2017. *The Chessboard and the Web: Strategies of Connection in a Networked World*. The Henry L. Stimson Lectures Series. New Haven: Yale University Press.

Sondermann, E., and C. Ulbert. 2021. "Transformation Through 'Meaningful' Partnership? SDG 17 as Metagovernance Norm and Its Global Health Implementation." *Politics and Governance* 9 (1): 152–63.

Spangenberg, J.H. 2017. "Hot Air or Comprehensive Progress? A Critical Assessment of the SDGs." *Sustainable Development* 25 (4): 311–21.

Surasky, J. 2021. *Report on the 2021 Regional Forums on Sustainable Development*. Bogota: CEPEI.

Tallberg, J., T. Sommerer, T. Squatrito, and C. Jonsson. 2013. *The Opening Up of International Organizations: Transnational Access in Global Governance*. Cambridge: Cambridge University Press.

Thérien, J.-P., and V. Pouliot. 2020. "Global Governance as Patchwork: The Making of the Sustainable Development Goals." *Review of International Political Economy* 27 (3): 612–36.

Thinyane, M., L. Goldkind, and H.I. Lam. 2018. "Data Collaboration and Participation for Sustainable Development Goals – A Case for Engaging Community-Based Organizations." *Journal of Human Rights and Social Work* 3 (1): 44–51.

Trejo Nieto, A., and J.L. Niño Amézquita, eds. 2022. *Metropolitan Governance in Latin America*. London: Routledge.

UNGA. 2013. Format and Organizational Aspects of the High-Level Political Forum on Sustainable Development. A/RES/67/290. New York: United Nations.

———. 2015. *Transforming Our World: The 2030 Agenda for Sustainable Development*. A/RES/70/1. New York: United Nations.

United Nations. 2019. *Comprehensive HLPF Survey Results: Evaluation of the HLPF after 4 Years*. UN: DESA. https://sustainabledevelopment.un.org/content/documents/24802Comprehensive_HLPF_Survey_Results_FINAL.pdf.

———. 2022a. 2030 Agenda Partnership Accelerator. http://partnershipaccelerator.org/.

———. 2022b. The Partnership Platform. UN: DESA. https://sdgs.un.org/partnerships.

Vijge, M.J., F. Biermann, R.E. Kim, M. Bogers, M. Van Driel, F.S. Montesano, A. Yunita, and N. Kanie. 2020. "Governance through Global Goals." In *Architectures of Earth System Governance*, eds. F. Biermann and R.E. Kim, 254–74. Cambridge: Cambridge University Press.

Wakely, P. 2020. "Partnership: A Strategic Paradigm for the Production & Management of Affordable Housing & Sustainable Urban Development." *International Journal of Urban Sustainable Development* 12 (1): 119–25.

Weinlich, S. 2021. "The Review of the Resident Coordinator System: Give UNDS Reform a Chance." *Deutsches Institut Für Entwicklungspolitik* (blog), July 21. https://blogs.die-gdi.de/2021/07/21/the-review-of-the-resident-coordinator-system-give-unds-reform-a-chance/.

Willetts, P. 2000. "From 'Consultative Arrangements' to 'Partnership': The Changing Status of NGOs in Diplomacy at the UN." *Global Governance: A Review of Multilateralism and International Organizations* 6 (2): 191–212.

36

Conclusions

Paul Webster Hare

This book has aimed to go beyond a critique of modern practices of diplomacy. Diplomacy, its methods and status, needs re-addressing by states and citizens if it is to confront the challenges they face.

Diplomacy, its methods, and its practitioners have been the subject of criticism throughout its history. For example, Charles de Gaulle said "Diplomats are useful only in fair weather. As soon as it rains they drown in every drop." Our critique though is not about diplomats, the diplomatic profession, or even particular institutions. It is about the activity of diplomacy and how far the methods used are proving detrimental to its core objective—to solve or alleviate international problems. The stereotype of the pampered envoy, with high-living and cocktail parties, has done much to damage diplomacy's image. That has affected the resources that states apply to the activity. And diplomacy is used to failures from the past. The record of wars, humanitarian crises, and hostility between states since the UN Charter was signed are evidence enough. Today, diplomacy faces many challenges to the key concepts that shape its activity—sovereignty, the respect for norms of behavior, the contentious role and prevailing arrangement of the UN Security Council, and the new evolving meanings of such concepts of allies and war. The Cold War is long past but the multipolar world has not yet given a new discipline to diplomatic endeavors.

P. W. Hare (✉)
Boston University, Boston, MA, USA

Diplomacy has always had to face up to rebuilding broken structures. It helped build the networks of a globalized economy. It has to contend now with de-globalization and with a fragmentation of power. In parts of the world the advantages of democracy are seen to be declining which reduces the accountability of leaders for their diplomacy. Extremism and divisiveness in the digital arena challenge diplomacy's capacity to smooth edges. And at the same time it needs to take account of the rise of Big Tech's influence and power over communications. Protectionism is again being widely promoted. States like individuals and organizations live hybrid lives. In this context we editors and authors have tried to examine how diplomacy can incorporate reform and innovation into a traditional and professional activity without losing the essence of its identity as a public good. The world is developing fast in forming relationships and networking which create new opportunities and vulnerabilities. Diplomacy has yet to catch up. Diplomacy has not developed sufficient capacity to anticipate and reduce the damage caused by crises and provide the shared perspectives where global issues cannot be solved by any one country.

Many of this handbook's chapters propose specific measures that diplomacy should take to become more effective or to innovate its methods in particular issue areas. The handbook has also looked at key aspects of the reform of the institutions of diplomacy, some of which are already being addressed. Competitive diplomacy, aiming to do it better than others in areas like trade and investment promotion, will continue to be a focus and that can provide incentives for all to do better. But collaborative diplomacy also needs attention. A sudden concerted effort at reform is unlikely but given the lead of the UN Secretary-General and perhaps some chairs of regional organizations there is a realistic possibility of progress. A coalition of interested NGOs would also be helpful. In any case where reform is possible the problem is how to initiate the process of reform.

Here are a few ideas which we editors believe might start a reconsideration of diplomatic methods and revive the mutual benefits that lie at the heart of its activity. They are relatively modest but are practical and could be implemented quickly. They would all be consistent with a renewed recognition of the values of diplomacy and a commitment to re-address how it is conducted. They include ideas for inter-state diplomacy—both bilateral and multilateral—and also some new initiatives from the existing non-state sector.

* Revision of the Vienna Conventions on Diplomatic and Consular Relations. Neither has been revised since the 1960s. The International Law Commission (ILC) was formed in 1947 by the UN General Assembly pur-

suant to the Charter of the UN. Its task is to help develop and systematize international law. Article 17 of the governing Statute of International Law Commission offers various routes to initiate this process and gives considerable powers to the United Nations itself. Its terms provide that "The Commission shall also consider proposals and draft multilateral conventions submitted by Members of the United Nations, the principal organs of the United Nations other than the General Assembly.…" The Secretariat of the United Nations is one of the "principal organs of the United Nations." The Secretary-General should therefore have the capacity to propose to the ILC consideration of revisions to the Vienna Conventions. The importance of these Conventions goes far beyond the central issues of diplomatic immunities and privileges. A conference of this nature would oblige states to reconsider the core concepts of sovereignty and diplomatic relations. And the impact of the digital communication and information revolution inserting itself into diplomacy's key activities. The existing Conventions were negotiated by less than a third in number of present UN member states. They were also negotiated in the context of the Cold War and bear the imprints of a Western model of diplomacy. The ILC could also propose discussing how non-state actors as citizens of member states need also to commit to the diplomatic norms their states recognize.

- Renewing Diplomacy's Vows. This may be a feasible way of formally reaffirming some of the key principles of the UN Charter such as respect for sovereignty and the renunciation of the use of force. In the absence of any realistic prospect of renegotiating the UN Charter, states might be asked to rededicate themselves to the framework ideals and commitments of 1945. The ILC might also play a role here in setting this as a work agenda.
- The P5 and the role of the United Nations Security Council. The erosion of authority and respect for the UN Security Council is a long-standing problem. The longer that this goes on the more likely that states, including some of the P5, will circumvent and marginalize the UN system. The problem remains how to reinvigorate the work of the Security Council. The United Nations General Assembly might call on the P5 to renew their commitments assumed as guardians of global security. In the seven decades' long history of the UNSC over 2600 Resolutions have been passed, even if many remain unimplemented. Nearly 300 however have been vetoed by one of the five powers. The P5 could be asked to make a new statement committing to limiting and eventually eliminating this power.
- Points of Contact on the Future Agenda of Diplomacy. Diplomacy is faced with collective discussions and problem solving on the key issues it must confront in the future—climate, energy, water, health, migration, refugees,

cyber vulnerabilities, and the role of the private sector in diplomacy. All of these issues are critical to domestic policies of states. In the area of small arms proliferation, an issue involving multiple domestic agencies of all states, those states participating in the UN Program of Action agreed to appoint a single Point of Contact. A single Point of Contact should be appointed in the governments of states—not UN missions in New York or Geneva—for the future diplomatic agenda. This would ameliorate the stovepipe problem and anticipate what the role of each state should be in future crises. Such Points of Contact could have a permanent virtual forum, which would be a new experiment in tele-diplomacy. Again the United Nations would have a central role in promoting the establishment of such Points of Contact.

* The Future Agenda of Diplomacy. The United Nations' *Our Common Agenda* is ambitious and appropriate. The activities in these areas of reform and innovation are underappreciated in the context of diplomacy. But there is a danger of overburdening the agenda for reform with too many ideas across the spectrum. By concentrating on the Global Digital Compact proposed within this agenda would enable states to integrate Big Tech for the first time in a norm-setting exercise for digital interaction.[1] The aims of the Compact are directly relevant to the future of diplomacy through promoting digital cooperation. "Complex digital issues that could be addressed may include: reaffirming the fundamental commitment to connecting the unconnected; avoiding fragmentation of the Internet; providing people with options as to how their data is used; application of human rights online; and promoting a trustworthy Internet by introducing accountability criteria for discrimination and misleading content. More broadly, the Compact could also promote regulation of artificial intelligence to ensure that this is aligned with shared global values." The United Nations should urge that this Compact be the basis of new activity and lobby hard for interested non-state parties to commit to a global cause. Non-state actors will need to coalesce to implant their views in the negotiations and assume commitments in this Compact, for example on privacy of information and the tackling of deliberate misinformation designed to undermine diplomacy.

* Restructuring of Foreign Ministries. A collective effort is needed here as well. Diplomacy has found it increasingly difficult to cope with the decline in status and coordinating role of Foreign Ministries. Much of the raw material that Foreign Ministries negotiate are the central concerns of

---
[1] See https://www.un.org/techenvoy/global-digital-compact.

domestic departments. Bilateral diplomacy could gain much by exchanges between states on how ministries are organized in functional and regional terms and comparing best practices. This could also be done within regional groupings. The reforms of bilateral diplomacy and the capacity of ministries to respond could be shared more and form part of the agenda alongside issues of mutual concern. New departments being created in ministries such as those on cyber-security could coordinate best practice and make national efforts at reform more effective.

- The G20. This group has done little to live up to its potential as a major stabilizing institution in world diplomacy with its key role in addressing global financial issues. The G20 was largely invisible in promoting collective diplomacy during the COVID pandemic. A future chair of the G20 might propose that all the members contribute to a joint development fund, based on funding formulae agreed in the UN budget. They would apply funding to projects agreed between states in non-member countries. Such projects would demonstrate the G20's recognition that prosperity and global financial stability are in the interests of all members of the G20. Funding would be modest—but the principle of some collaboration between the new power centers of this century would be symbolically important and could lead to further initiatives.
- The Nobel Foundation. A prize for diplomacy should be established. Nobel's famous Peace Prize has done much to highlight the value of peacemakers. This is awarded for "the best work for fraternity between nations, for the abolition or reduction of standing armies and for the holding and promotion of peace congresses." The Prize has rightly acknowledged those who have addressed contentious issues which arise in diplomacy and have contributed to establishing or preserving peace between states. But an additional Nobel Prize for Diplomacy would add much value in showing that what it rewards is the wider art of problem solving internationally.
- The Geneva Conventions. These remain the landmark achievements of diplomacy in preventing the world returning to a state of barbarism where wars randomly massacre civilians and there is little or no international accountability. Large-scale war has recently returned to Europe. The ICRC might now revive focus on the Conventions which have not been fully revised since 1949. In 2009 the ICRC proposed a reconvening of the conference but to no avail. The humanitarian focus of the Conventions now extends to intra-state conflicts. But they need reaffirmation and revision. Cyberattacks which target civilians in another state are now realistic threats, for example by poisoning water supplies and denying electricity. The Conventions need to address such non-kinetic, hybrid warfare.

These ideas we believe would give bilateral and multilateral diplomacy an opportunity for a new start. We hope those who read this book will contribute other ideas for its reform and innovation. All those interested in the cause of diplomacy will recognize that its benefits cannot be taken for granted.

Index[1]

Aachen, Treaty of (2019), 317, 318
Abe, Shinzo, 178, 450
Abraham Accords (2020), 543–555
Abu Dhabi, 544n1, 545–548, 550, 553
Abu Dhabi Fund for Development (ADFD), 551
Access to COVID-19 Tools (ACT) Accelerator, 616–617, 621
Adalet ve Kalkınma Partisi (AKP), 150
Adriatic Charter, 574
Adriatic Ionian Initiative, 574
Afghanistan, 49n23, 49n24, 57n65, 57n67, 257, 264, 304, 456n3, 462, 465, 469n47, 495, 496, 501, 638
African Development Bank (AfDB), 70, 71, 291
African Growth and Opportunity Act (AGOA), 201, 202, 286
African National Congress (ANC), 194, 195, 197–199, 201–206, 208
African Peer Review Mechanism (APRM), 278, 289, 486, 486n5
African Union (AU), 6, 17, 70, 71, 92n18, 200, 277–291, 330, 484, 486–488, 494, 495, 502, 587, 640
African Union Assembly, 279, 283, 287, 288
African Union Commission (AUC), 73, 278, 279, 281–284, 287, 289–291
Agenda 2063 (African Union), 70–73, 291
Air Defense Identification Zone, 175
Albanese, Anthony, 270
Albania, 465n38, 562, 564–567, 572
Aleph-Alpha Company, 343n1, 354, 362, 363
Algeria, 70, 71, 73, 101n45, 686
Alliance for Multilateralism, 436, 448, 449, 452
Alliance of Small Island States (AOSIS), 573, 574

---

[1] Note: Page numbers followed by 'n' refer to notes.

Alliot-Marie, Michèle, 318
Al-Ula Declaration (2021), 546
Annan, Kofi, 514, 607, 631
Anti-coercion instrument (ACI), 653, 655, 657, 662–664
Arab League, 545–547, 554
Arab Spring, 367, 544, 545, 554, 637
Araud, Gérard, 369
Araújo, Ernesto, 225, 226, 226n19
Arctic Council, 565
Argentina, 50n28, 94, 195, 198, 398, 399, 401, 404, 408, 412, 491n14, 586
Armenia, 100, 470n50, 495, 686
Armenian-Azerbaijani conflict, 631
Artificial Intelligence (AI), 16, 18, 340, 343–364, 390, 505, 506, 510, 734
ASEAN Plus Three (APT), 301, 311, 437, 490
Asia-Europe Meeting (ASEM), 299, 311, 482n1, 490
Asian Games, 296, 303
Asian Infrastructure Investment Bank (AIIB), 174, 179, 441, 473n60, 484, 485n4, 656
Asia-Pacific Development, Diplomacy and Defense Dialogue (AP4D), 252, 262, 265–269, 268n1
Asia-Pacific Economic Cooperation (APEC), 179, 251, 255, 257, 299, 311, 489
Assange, Julian, 5
Association of Southeast Asian Nations (ASEAN), 254, 255, 268n1, 301, 305, 397, 436n1, 438, 443, 451, 459n11, 464n36, 471, 472, 484, 489, 490, 492–496, 500, 502, 564, 587, 640
Australia, 17, 48n21, 57n66, 84, 87n11, 90, 93, 93n24, 95, 99, 99n41, 105, 112, 117, 118, 121, 121n4, 122, 122n5, 131–137, 251–270, 359, 437, 443, 450n6, 456n3, 459n12, 462n22, 463, 471n53, 484, 485, 490, 569, 659, 691, 716
Austria, 44n6, 84n3, 112, 128, 350–354, 359, 459n11, 469n46
Axis Powers, 47, 53n45

B

Bachelet, Michelle, 409
Bandung Conference (1955), 28
Bangladesh, 464n32, 472, 488, 490, 494, 501
Barbuda, 92
Barcelona, 590, 591, 594
al Bashir, Omar, 199
Bay of Bengal Initiative for Multi-Sectoral Technical and Economic Cooperation (BIMSTEC), 482n1, 484, 488–489, 493
Belarus, 384, 444, 465n39, 468, 470n50, 475n72, 495, 496
Belt and Road Initiative (BRI), 179, 441, 470, 472–473, 474n62, 499, 656, 694
Berlin Conference (1884–1885), 457, 460n17
Biang, Michel Xavier, 514
Biden, Joseph R., 11, 112, 120, 202, 263, 265, 436, 451, 474, 614
"Big Tech," 371, 372, 732, 734
Bildt, Carl, 368, 369
Bill and Melinda Gates Foundation, 605–608, 616
Blair, Tony, 369
Bloom, Allan, 32
Bolsonaro, Jair, 225, 226, 403
Borel, Suzanne, 318
Borins, Sandford, 512
Bosnia-Herzegovina, 469n46, 562, 566, 571, 573
Botha, P. W., 203

Botswana, 97, 97n36, 464n35
Boxer rebellion (1899–1901), 46n9
Brazil, 17, 87n9, 89, 98n37, 112, 213n1, 214, 214n2, 215, 217–219, 222, 224, 225n18, 227–229, 231, 356, 398, 399, 401–403, 408, 410, 412, 459n12, 460, 484, 491n14, 527–530, 532–534, 586, 706, 711
Brazil, Russia, India, China, South Africa (BRICS), 228, 484, 485
See also Brazil, South Africa, India, and China (BASIC) group
Brazil, South Africa, India, and China (BASIC) group, 697
Bretton Woods Conference (1944), 374, 681
"Brexit," 94, 308, 317, 380, 593
British Council, 77
Brunei, 464n36, 471n53, 564
Budapest Convention (2001), 355
Bulgaria, 465n38, 491n14, 565–567
Burns, William, 12, 13
Busan Asian Games, 299

C40 Cities Climate Leadership, 337
Cameroon, 70, 71
Camp David Accords (1978), 543, 545
Canada, 84, 90, 93, 99n41, 103, 253, 264, 338, 435, 459n12, 475n67, 481, 490, 551, 615, 649, 655, 660, 686, 695
Carbon border adjustment mechanism (CBAM), 695
Caribbean Community (CARICOM), 492, 494, 497, 500
Çavuşoğlu, Mevlüt, 153
Central Asia, 305, 307, 465n38, 469–470, 484, 633
Central European Initiative (CEI), 565, 574

CGTN-Africa (television network), 385
Chavez, Hugo, 197
Chile, 92n19, 262, 398, 401, 403–405, 407–409, 412, 413, 460n19, 462, 462n27, 489, 499, 587
Chile, Ministry of Foreign Affairs of, 399–403, 409, 411
China, 484, 491n14
China Central Foreign Affairs Commission (CFAC), 186
China, Communist Party of (CPC), 87n11, 177, 181, 184–187, 189, 385, 386
China, Department of Consular Affairs of, 176, 177
China, Ministry of Commerce of (MOC), 173, 179, 287, 385
China, Ministry of Foreign Affairs of, 167–168
China, People's Republic of (PRC), 8, 50n29, 169, 176, 181, 183, 287, 385, 461, 527
China, Republic of, *see* Taiwan
Chun Doo-hwan, 296
Churchill, Winston, 8, 47n12, 457n7, 461n20
Clark, Helen, 617
Clinton, Bill, 29, 368
Clinton, Hillary, 202, 203, 263, 368, 369, 465n38
Coalition for Epidemic Preparedness Innovations (CEPI), 608, 616, 620
Cohen, Raymond, 5, 6
Cold War, 9, 25–29, 33, 42n2, 44, 44n5, 47, 49n25, 53n45, 55n53, 55n55, 56n58, 57, 82, 148, 168, 176, 199, 213, 214, 216–230, 254, 255, 295, 296, 303, 384, 421, 436, 440, 447, 456n3, 460–465, 467n43, 472n57, 478n83, 482, 495, 502, 605, 680, 682, 731, 733

Collective Security Treaty Organization (CSTO), 470, 470n49, 470n50, 470n51, 495
Colonna, Catherine, 318
Comissão Nacional da Verdade, 216, 219
Common Market of Eastern and Southern Africa (COMESA), 487
Comprehensive and Progressive Agreement for the Trans-Pacific Partnership (CPTPP), 435, 471n53
Conference of the Parties (COP) 29, 422, 549–552, 591, 692–701
Confucius Institutes, 385
Congress of Vienna (1814–1815), 315, 374, 438, 459n11
Convention on the Law of the Sea (1982), 425
Cooper, Andrew, 59, 69, 115, 126, 137, 146, 183, 391, 408, 667
Copeland, Darryl, 85n7, 104, 713
Corbyn, Jeremy, 199
Costa Rica, 449, 460n19, 686
Council for Mutual Economic Assistance (COMECON), 482
Council of Europe, 355, 360
COVID-19 pandemic, 82, 208, 309, 323, 325–327, 329, 332, 334, 337, 397, 401, 413, 422, 441, 448, 449, 489, 499, 506, 509, 514, 562, 583, 616, 618, 621, 623, 624, 642, 676, 682, 698, 717, 718
COVID-19 Vaccines Global Access (COVAX), 443, 617
CPC-World Political Party High-Level Dialogue, 181
Crimea, 32, 199, 384, 388, 441, 445, 657
Cuba, 30, 98, 98n38, 199, 201, 398, 456n3, 460n19, 462, 462n27, 475n72, 603

CubeSat, 511
Cull, Nicholas, 326, 330, 386, 391, 398, 401, 630, 631, 642
Curtin, John, 254
Cyprus, 560, 631
Czechoslovakia, 32, 350–352, 354, 463, 463n31

D

Dahl, Robert A., 120
Dalai Lama, 199
Darroch, Kim, 369
Davos Forum, 590
Dayton Agreement (1995), 566
De Gaulle, Charles, 50n29, 315–319, 731
de Klerk, F. W., 203
"Digital diplomacy," 15, 18, 143–161, 323–340, 367, 369–373, 398–402, 404–410, 412, 413, 571
Democratic People's Republic of Korea (DPRK), 54n49, 57n68, 176, 181, 182, 440, 476, 490
See also North Korea
Department of Foreign Affairs and Trade, Australia (DFAT), 105, 112, 116, 118, 132, 134–136, 252–254, 257, 261, 262, 270
Department of International Relations and Co-Operation, South Africa (DIRCO), 194–196, 198, 204, 205
Diaoyu islands, 178
DiCarlo, Rosemary, 514, 515
Dickie, John, 96
DiploFoundation, 84, 84n4, 98n37
Djibouti, 52n35, 564
Doha round (World Trade Organization), 440
Dombrovski, Valdis, 662
Dominica, 92

Dorsey, Jack, 369
Duarte, Jessie, 205
Dubai, 494n19, 544, 544n1, 545, 548–550, 550n4, 552, 554, 581, 590
Dubai International Academic City (DIAC), 590

E

East StratCom Task Force, 388, 390
École Nationale d'Administration (ENA), 316
Economic Community of Central African States (ECCAS), 487
Economic Community of West African States (ECOWAS), 281–283, 290, 478, 487, 493, 496
Eisenhower, Dwight D., 25, 26
"English School" (International Relations), 145
Erdoğan, Recep Tayyip, 150
Estonia, 370, 465n38, 570
Ethiopia, 686
Eurasian Economic Union (EAEU), 470
European Coal and Steel Community (ECSC), 482
European Commission, 317, 329, 336, 389, 586, 603, 616, 654, 656, 659, 662, 663, 666
European External Action Service (EEAS), 92, 240, 316, 317, 319, 492n17, 660, 661
European Parliament, 389, 612, 662
European Union (EU), 6, 18, 28, 34, 49n22, 54n49, 71, 84n5, 92, 92n17, 101, 106, 129, 150, 202, 235, 237, 239, 240, 246, 283, 286, 301, 303, 305, 317, 318, 328, 329, 331, 332, 336, 338, 356–359, 372, 387–390, 428, 429, 436–438, 441, 443, 451, 468–471, 482, 487n7, 489, 490, 490n11, 492–494, 492n17, 497, 499, 502, 560, 562, 565, 566, 569, 574, 586, 591, 603, 612, 616, 640, 649–667, 693–695, 710
European Union Common Foreign and Security Policy (CFSP), 492, 656, 664, 665
European Union Emergency Response Coordination Centre, 329
Evans, Gareth, 569
EXPO 2020, *see* Conference of the Parties (COP)

F

Facebook, 222, 225, 348, 369, 370, 372, 401, 413
Ferguson, Niall, 223
Fernández, Cristina, 404, 409
Fielding, Leslie, 371
First World War, 27, 441, 604, 632, 678
Fletcher, Tom, 18, 99, 371
Forum on China-Africa Cooperation (FOCAC), 286, 385, 499
Four Quadrant Helix, 537, 540
Fourteen Points (Woodrow Wilson), 25, 27
France, 8, 44n6, 46n8, 46n11, 47n12, 47n14, 47n15, 48n16, 48n17, 52n35, 57n66, 116, 239, 317–319, 350–354, 436n1, 437, 444, 445, 451, 457, 457n6, 457n7, 459, 459n12, 460n14, 460n15, 460n16, 461, 462n22, 463, 463n30, 472n56, 475n67, 482, 491n15, 545, 548, 561, 562, 604, 613, 616, 622, 665, 693
Free and Open Indo-Pacific (FOIP), 436–438, 436n1, 450, 451
French Revolution, 315
Friedman, Thomas, 223

742   Index

G

Gabon, 283, 514, 564
Gates, Bill, 336
Gates, Robert, 263
Gavi Vaccine Alliance, 603, 616
Gaza, 205
Geneva Conventions (1951), 632
Geneva Protocol (1922), 350
Geneva Summit (1955), 28
German-Austrian Customs
    Union, 349–350
Germany, 32, 47, 47n12, 48n16,
    48n19, 53n45, 54n47, 71, 73, 92,
    96, 98, 101, 201, 204, 235–246,
    318, 328, 349–354, 358, 437,
    439, 451, 457, 460, 460n15, 461,
    465, 475n67, 508, 551, 561, 603,
    605, 665, 693, 696
Germany, Federal Foreign Office of,
    236, 237, 239, 240, 245, 665
Glasgow Climate Pact (2021), 693
Global Digital Compact, 13, 15, 734
Global Fund to Fight AIDS, 607
Global Health Security Agenda
    (GHSA), 613–614, 622
Global Justice Now, 706
Global Parliament of Mayors
    (GPM), 592
"Global South," 24, 26, 81–106, 227,
    398, 500
Good Neighbor Policy (U.S.), 460
Gorbachev, Mikhail, 32
Graham, Suzanne, 207
Greece, 262, 461n20, 491n15, 500,
    562, 565–567
Grenada, 92, 460n19, 462, 462n27
Group of Seven (G7), 9, 390, 441,
    443, 484, 485, 492, 500, 524,
    527–530, 532, 603, 614, 616,
    619, 649, 659, 667, 693, 696,
    699, 700

Group of Seventy-seven (G77), 694,
    697, 707
Group of Twenty (G20), 9, 135, 179,
    193, 251, 256, 262, 305, 332,
    334, 390, 404, 492, 493, 593,
    619, 623, 651, 660, 666, 667,
    700, 735
Guinea, 288, 612
Gulf Cooperation Council (GCC),
    483, 484, 491, 493, 543, 545,
    546, 548, 554
Gulf War (1990–91), 31
Guterres, António, 10–12, 419, 442,
    443, 446, 498, 507, 509,
    513, 682

H

Hague Conference (1907), 215
Hague, William, 370
Haiti, 460n19, 510, 639
Hamas, 199
Harris, Harry, 175
Hayek, Friedrich, 569
Heine, Jorge, 18, 143, 236, 399–401,
    406, 409
Helsinki Final Act (1975), 28
Henrikson, Alan, 570, 572, 575, 577
Hezbollah, 199
High-level Political Forum on
    Sustainable Development
    (HLPF), 705, 714–717, 719
HIV/AIDS, 442, 443, 607–608,
    611, 635
Holbrooke, Richard, 610
H1N1 virus (influenza), 611–612
Hong Kong, 170, 171
Hungary, 92n20, 93, 128n9, 463,
    463n31, 465n38
Hu Jintao, 185
Huntington, Samuel, 30, 31

Iceland, 560, 565, 572
IMF Poverty Reduction and Growth Trust (PRGT), 699
IMF Resilience and Sustainability Trust (RST), 699
Independent Diplomat, 573
India, 44n5, 51n33, 51n34, 52n39, 53n44, 54n50, 55n56, 56n58, 57n68, 71, 86, 87, 89, 89n12, 94, 96, 96n30, 98, 100, 102n47, 104, 112, 286, 356, 397, 437, 440, 443, 444, 451, 458, 459, 460n14, 463, 463n28, 464n32, 470n48, 471, 471n52, 472, 476, 476n77, 477, 484, 485, 488, 490, 494–496, 500, 501, 501n27, 527–530, 528n5, 532–534, 545, 547, 551, 615, 617, 655, 667, 694, 695
Indian Ocean Rim Association (IORA), 484, 493
Indian Pillai Committee, 95
Indonesia, 178, 257, 307, 310, 464n36, 471n53, 472, 476, 484, 491n14, 495, 610, 667, 686, 693
Indo-Pacific, 253, 256, 270, 438, 450, 450n6, 451, 456n3, 471–472, 485
See also Free and Open Indo-Pacific
Instituto Rio Branco, 215, 228n23
Integrated Review of Security, Defence, Development and Foreign Policy, 263
Intergovernmental Panel on Climate Change (IPCC), 697
International Academy (United Kingdom), 100
International Coffee Organization (ICO), 482
International Committee of the Red Cross (ICRC), 15, 446, 633, 635, 639, 735
International Court of Justice (ICJ), 408, 445, 681
International Criminal Court (ICC), 283, 445
International Department of the CPC (IDCPC), 175, 178, 181
International Federation of Red Cross and Red Crescent Societies (IFRC), 633
International Health Regulations (IHR), 608–611, 614, 620
International higher education and innovation (IHERI), 60, 61, 63–68, 70–78
International Law Commission (ILC), 15, 732, 733
International Monetary Fund (IMF), 90, 208, 614, 681, 694, 698–700
International Sanitary Conferences (1851–), 604
International Security Assistance Force Mission (ISAF), 264, 469n47, 569
Iran, 37, 52n39, 54n51, 174, 228n22, 235, 370, 456n3, 458, 458n10, 462, 463, 463n28, 466, 470n48, 475n72, 476–478, 496, 546, 547, 553, 631, 656, 663
Iraq, 46n10, 54n47, 54n51, 257, 458n10, 463, 466, 466n42, 469n47, 475n72, 510, 511, 547, 632
Ireland, 93, 94, 96, 469n46, 508, 710
Iron Curtain, 26, 461n20
ISIS, 149
Israel, 46n11, 51n33, 52n38, 52n40, 56n62, 57n68, 134, 199, 204, 205, 207, 227, 330, 334, 463, 464n33, 466, 476n73, 543–546
Italy, 47, 48n16, 48n19, 52n35, 53n45, 101, 102n46, 112, 128, 130, 239, 288, 318, 327, 331, 351, 457, 460n15, 461, 475n67, 547, 639
"Itamaraty," 213–226, 221n12, 223n15, 225n18, 228–231, 228n23, 402, 408, 410

Al Jaber, Sultan, 551
Jackson, Andrew, 169
Jamaica, 93
Japan, 29, 47, 47n14, 52n35, 53n45, 54n46, 54n47, 54n48, 56n57, 57n65, 71, 95, 96, 98, 100, 101n44, 174, 175, 178, 255, 286, 296, 299–301, 303, 305, 307, 308, 359, 435, 436n1, 437, 443, 449–451, 450n6, 460, 460n15, 461, 462n22, 467, 471, 471n53, 472, 472n57, 475n67, 478n82, 485, 485n4, 490, 495, 508, 512, 605, 610, 649, 655
Jiang Zemin, 185
Joint Comprehensive Plan of Action (JCPOA), 235
Joint United Nations Programme on HIV and AIDS (UNAIDS), 607
Jönsson, Christer, 344
Joseph, Nkosi, 197, 198
Just Energy Transition Partnership (JETP), 693

Kagame, Paul, 278, 290
Karns, Margaret, 435
Kazakhstan, 384, 470, 470n48, 470n49, 470n50, 495, 496
Kellogg-Briand Pact (1928), 438
Kennan, George, 31
Kenya, 70, 71, 86n8, 93, 97, 104n49, 206, 282, 283, 450
Keohane, Robert, 437, 452, 564, 573, 574, 705
Kerry, John, 369, 373
Kılıç, Serdar, 153
Kim Dae-jung, 296, 300–301, 310
Kim Jong-il, 176, 305
Kim Young-sam, 296, 298–299, 310

Kissinger, Henry, 118, 126, 126n8, 458n8
Koerber Foundation, 439, 440
Kolker, Jimmy, 612
Korea National Diplomatic Academy, 306
Korea, Republic of (ROK), 54n47, 54n49, 300, 308, 435, 437, 462n22, 472n57, 490
  See also South Korea
Koselleck, Reinhart, 34
Kosovo, 31, 32, 49n24, 370, 465, 562, 565, 571, 573
Kuwait, 31, 32, 46n10, 54n51, 440, 463n28, 466, 466n42, 543
Kyslytsya, Sergiy, 446

Lafer, Celso, 224
Lagarde, Christine, 317
Lampton, David, 167, 168, 180
Latin America, 18, 26, 217, 303, 305, 309, 336, 381, 387, 397–399, 408, 409, 413, 456n3, 477, 482n1, 488, 490, 502, 586
Lavrov, Sergei, 329
League of Nations, 350, 374, 398, 438, 447, 564, 576, 604, 678
League of Nations, Permanent Health Committee of, 604
Lebanon, 51n34, 367, 370, 456n3, 458n10, 463, 466, 475n72, 510, 544, 546, 566, 632
Le Drian, Jean-Yves, 448
Lee Myung-bak, 296, 303–306, 311
Liberia, 612
Libya, 46n8, 91n15, 198, 440, 465, 469n47, 475n72, 476n80, 510, 544, 548
Liechtenstein, 564
Lisbon, Treaty of (2007), 656

Lithuania, 465n38, 570, 654, 661, 662
Li Zhaoxing, 170
Louis XVI (France), 46n8
Lowy Institute, 95, 105, 256, 258, 261, 262
Lula da Silva, Luiz Inácio, 227–229, 231, 402
Luxembourg, 561

M

Maas, Heiko, 448
Macri, Mauricio, 404, 409
Macron, Emmanuel, 316–318, 616, 618
Maduro, Nicolás, 197–199
Magashule, Ace, 198
Al Maktoum, Sheikh Mohammed bin Rashid, 544n1, 549
Malcorra, Susanna, 409
Malta, 91, 93, 104, 560, 572
Mandela, Nelson, 195, 197, 201, 202
Mao Zedong, 384
Marrakech Mayors Declaration (2018), 594
Mashabane-Nkoana, Maite, 198
Maull, Hans W, 440, 441
McFaul, Michael, 369
Mercociudades Initiative (1995), 586
MERCOSUR (Southern Common Market), 220, 489, 493, 586
Merkel, Angela, 603
Mexico, 18, 84, 92n19, 94n25, 307, 398, 403, 413, 455n1, 457n6, 460n19, 489, 499, 527–530, 532–534, 537, 593, 667
Microsoft Corporation, 372, 378
Millennium Declaration, United Nations (2000), 521, 521n1, 522
Millennium Development Goals (MDGs), 708
Modi, Narendra, 451, 501n25
Molotov-Ribbentrop Pact (1939), 48n19

Monaco, 561n1, 564
Monnet, Jean, 26, 482
Monroe Doctrine (1823), 456, 457n6, 460–463, 460n19, 476, 477
Montenegro, 465n38, 559, 560, 562, 563, 565, 565n8, 567–569, 571, 576
Montserrat, 92
Moon Jae-in, 296, 308–311
Morrison, Scott, 256, 259, 265
Moynihan, Daniel Patrick, 30
Mugabe, Robert, 199, 496
Munmin government (South Korea), 298, 299
Muñoz, Heraldo, 409
Murrow, Edward R, 373
Myanmar, 464n36, 471n53, 472, 476n74, 476n79, 488, 495

N

Al Nahyan, Mohammed bin Zayed, 544n1, 545, 547
Namibia, 97, 102, 464n35, 488
NATO Membership Action Plans, 34
 See also North Atlantic Treaty Organization (NATO)
NATO StratCom Center of Excellence
 See also North Atlantic Treaty Organization (NATO)
Nebenzia, Vassily, 506
Netherlands, 94, 204, 253, 264, 437, 451, 460n16, 508, 536, 540
Network for the Greening of the Financial System (NGFS), 700
New Partnership for Africa's Development (NEPAD), 278, 284, 486
New Zealand, 90, 99, 99n41, 115, 121, 123, 459n12, 462n22, 471n53, 472n56, 490, 617
Nicolson, Harold, 25, 117, 168
Nigeria, 70, 71, 281, 478, 496, 527–530, 528n5, 532, 533

Nkosi, Joseph, 197
Nkrumah, Kwame, 486
Nobel Foundation, 15, 735
Non-Aligned Movement (NAM), 428, 483, 493, 497
Non-Proliferation Treaty (1968), 440
Nordhaus, William, 695, 696
North Atlantic Treaty Organization (NATO), 28, 31–33, 46n7, 46n8, 48n21, 49n22, 49n24, 54n47, 57n63, 106, 153, 186, 206, 317, 387, 436, 437, 441, 443, 456n3, 459n11, 461, 464, 465, 465n37, 465n38, 465n39, 466n40, 467–469, 469n47, 477, 481, 482, 485n4, 495, 500, 564, 566, 567, 569, 571, 574, 667, 683
North Korea, 50n27, 175–176, 181–182, 297, 300, 301, 303, 305–309, 311, 444, 461, 472, 472n57, 475n72, 663

See also Democratic People's Republic of Korea

North Macedonia, 465n38, 562, 565–567, 571
Norway, 86, 93, 468n45, 508, 564, 622
Nye, Joseph, 74–77, 146, 149, 195, 548

O

Obama, Barack, 185, 202, 263, 401
Office of the Secretary-General's Special Envoy for Yemen (OSESGY), 510
Official Development Assistance (ODA), 305, 522–527, 522n3, 539–541, 552, 554
Olympic Games, 408, 410, 590
Oman, 463n28, 543, 545, 547, 548
OpenAI, 354

See also Artificial Intelligence

Organization for Economic Cooperation and Development (OECD), 262, 299, 318, 491n14, 492, 522, 522n2, 522n3, 533, 541, 552
Organization for Security and Cooperation in Europe (OSCE), 29, 437, 560, 561n1, 564, 566, 569
Organization of African Unity (OAU), 277, 484, 486, 499
Organization of American States (OAS), 495
Organization of East Caribbean States (OECS), 91, 92, 92n16, 482, 489, 489n10
Organization of Islamic Cooperation (OIC), 483, 564
Our Common Agenda (United Nations), 705, 717, 719, 734

P

Pacific Alliance (PA), 92, 92n19, 482n1, 489–490, 499, 502
Pakistan, 50n27, 53n44, 56n58, 440, 470n48, 472, 490, 494, 494n19, 496, 501, 501n27, 547, 636, 691
Palestinian Liberation Organization (PLO), 546
Pan African Parliament (PAP), 278, 486
Pan African University (PAU), 70–73, 78
Pan American Health Organization (PAHO), 604, 605, 617
Pandor, Naledi, 206
Paris Agreement on Climate Change (2015), 691, 692, 694–698, 697n2, 700, 701, 718
Park Geun-hye, 296, 306–308, 311
Payne, Marise, 265, 268
Peace and Security Council (PSC), 282

See also African Union

People's Defense Units (YPG/PKK), 157
People's Liberation Army (PLA) (China), 174, 175, 180
Peru, 92n19, 98n37, 398, 399, 401, 403, 408, 412, 460, 489, 491n14, 499, 587
PIP Framework, 611
Plato, 323, 340
Plowden Report (1967), 95
Power, Samantha, 263
President's Emergency Plan for AIDS Relief (PEPFAR), 201, 607
Proliferation Security Initiative (PSI), 437
Putin, Vladimir, 11, 199, 206, 371, 387, 446, 649, 650, 658

Q

Qadaffi, Muammar, 198
Qatar, 52n39, 57n67, 463n28, 508, 543, 545, 546, 548, 554
Qi Yu, 187
Quadrilateral Security Dialogue (Australia, India, Japan, United States), 436, 437, 443, 485
Quai d'Orsay, 315, 319

R

Rachman, Gideon, 200
Ramaphosa, Cyril, 198, 200, 202–204, 206, 208, 615
Regional Cooperation and Economic Partnership (RCEP), 471n53, 491
Renewable Energy and Energy Efficiency Partnership (REEEP), 705
Republic of China, 8, 50n29
Republic of Korea (ROK), 54n47, 54n49, 300, 307, 308, 435, 437, 461n22, 472n57, 476, 490

Reykjavik Summit (1986), 28
Richelieu, Cardinal Jean du Plessis, 168
Rio de Janeiro, 213n1, 214, 214n2, 227, 230, 402, 596, 704
Roh Moo-hyun, 296, 301–303, 310
Roh Tae-woo, 297
Romania, 465n38, 491n14, 559
Roosevelt, Franklin D., 47n12, 52n37, 457n7
Roscoe, James, 514
Rotary International, 8, 606
Rousseff, Dilma, 225, 227, 231, 410, 706
RT (television network), 387–389
Ruggie, John Gerrard, 435, 437, 439, 705
Russia, 11, 12, 32, 33, 42n2, 47n14, 48n16, 48n17, 49n24, 50n27, 52n39, 53n42, 54n49, 87, 93n22, 145, 183, 193, 199, 201, 202, 205–207, 236, 258, 283, 300, 303, 307, 329, 343, 349, 350, 354–358, 360, 363, 371, 381, 387, 389–391, 441, 443–446, 456n3, 458, 459n11, 460n15, 464–470, 465n38, 466n40, 470n48, 470n50, 475n72, 476, 477, 477n81, 484, 485, 490, 495, 496, 500–502, 506, 565, 571, 603, 616, 618, 633, 639, 649–651, 653, 657–661, 666, 667, 680, 683, 696, 718
Russian Elites, Proxies, and Oligarchs (REPO), 659
Russian Federation, *see* Russia

S

St. Kitts and Nevis, 92
Saint Lucia, 92
St. Vincent and Grenadines, 94, 564
San Francisco Conference (1945), 7, 8, 255, 605

San Marino, 561n1, 564
San Stefano, Treaty of (1878), 559
Saudi Arabia, 52n35, 52n37, 52n39, 458n10, 463n28, 464n33, 466, 543, 546–548, 667
Schuman, Robert, 315
Science Diplomacy Center, MGIMO University, 683
Second World War, 4, 7, 25, 217, 254, 436, 438–441, 447, 448, 481, 482, 675, 678, 680, 682
Selimi, Petrit, 370
Senkaku islands, 178
Serbia, 49n24, 53n42, 370, 465, 469n46, 469n47, 559, 565, 639
Severe Acute Respiratory Syndrome (SARS), 608–611, 614, 620
See also COVID-19 pandemic
Shanghai Cooperation Organization (SCO), 484, 495
Sharjah, 545
Sharma, Dave, 134, 136
Sharp, Paul, 6, 116–117, 241
Shinawatra, Thaksin, 89
Sierra Leone, 612
Singapore, 91, 94, 99, 176, 464n36, 471n53, 478n82, 490, 496, 548, 581, 649
Sirleaf, Ellen Johnson, 617
Slovenia, 465n38, 565, 570
Small Island Developing States (SIDS), 498
Smart Traveler Enrolment Program (STEP), 327
Soft power, 76
Somalia, 282, 283, 475n72, 639
South Africa, 17, 19, 70, 88, 94, 96, 193–209, 281, 356, 462n25, 464, 464n35, 478, 484, 488, 491n14, 527–530, 532, 533, 622, 667, 691, 693, 697, 711
South African Council on International Relations (SACOIR), 196

South African Development Partnership Agency (SADPA), 196
South Asian Association for Regional Cooperation (SAARC), 484, 488, 494, 501
South China Sea, 175, 307, 468, 469, 472
South-East European Cooperation Process (SEECP), 574
Southern Africa Development Community (SADC), 464n35, 483, 487, 487n6, 496
South Korea, 94, 286, 295–312, 461n21, 471n53, 472, 472n57, 655
See also Republic of Korea
South Korea, Ministry of Foreign Affairs and Trade (MOFAT) of, 90, 297, 299–302, 304, 305
Soviet Union, 29, 30, 32, 33, 47, 47n12, 47n13, 49n24, 51n34, 53n45, 55n55, 56n58, 223, 297, 440, 441, 447, 457n7, 460, 462n24, 464, 482, 500, 605
See also Russia
Special Drawing Rights (SDRs), 699
Spicer, Sean, 129
Sputnik (satellite), 333, 336, 337, 388, 389, 478n83
Sputnik V vaccine, 616
Sri Lanka, 464n32, 488, 490, 494
Steinmeier, Frank-Walter, 238
Stettinius, Edward, 8
Stockholm+50 Conference (2022), 703, 718
Sudan, 199, 288, 475n72, 545, 639
Sudetenland, 32
Suez Canal, 46n11, 57n68, 444
Sultan Mahmud II, 604
Sunshine Policy (South Korea), 300, 301
Supari, Siti Fadilah, 610

Sustainable Development Goals (SDG), 372, 422, 425, 509, 535, 551, 553, 554, 592, 693, 703, 704, 707–718
  See also Millennium Development Goals
Switzerland, 44n5, 104, 204, 459n11, 464n36, 469n46, 544–546, 603
Sykes-Picot Agreement (1916), 48n19
Syria, 52n40, 157, 199, 440, 444, 456n3, 458n10, 463, 466, 475n72, 478, 547, 554, 632

T

Taiwan, 8, 50n29, 460n15, 467, 467n43, 468, 471, 477, 478n82, 609, 616, 654, 661, 662
  See also Republic of China
Tajikistan Civil War, 631
Talleyrand, Charles-Maurice de, 315, 373
Tanzania, 97, 464n35
Tedros, Adhanom Ghebreyesus, 614
Teilhard de Chardin, Pierre, 26
Terminal High Altitude Area Defense (THAAD), 308
Thant, U., 512
Thatcher, Margaret, 90
Thodey Review (Australia), 121
Thomas-Greenfield, Linda, 446, 506
Thorhallsson, B. Baldur, 561, 562, 564, 567, 570, 571, 576, 577
Tibet, 171, 456n5
TikTok, 406
Tillerson, Rex, 111
Timerman, Héctor, 409
Torre Tagle, 403, 408
Trade and Technology Council (European Union-United States), 37
Trade Related Aspects of Intellectual Property Rights (TRIPS), 607, 608, 621, 698

Trans-Pacific Partnership (TPP) Agreement (2016), 435
Triple Helix, 534–538, 540
Trump, Donald, 57n64, 111, 120, 128n9, 129–131, 176, 185, 201, 202, 225, 256, 308, 309, 330, 369, 371, 382, 435, 450, 474, 614, 616
Turkey, 17, 49n22, 85n6, 101n44, 144, 145, 150–153, 156–158, 160, 228n22, 286, 307, 462n26, 466, 468–469, 476–478, 476n77, 508, 527–530, 532, 533, 632, 633, 667
Twiplomacy, 145, 154–158, 367, 406, 412n2
  See also Twitter
Twitter, 34, 145, 151–154, 156–160, 222, 225, 256, 260, 330, 333, 336, 347, 368–371, 373, 400, 401, 404–407, 409–411
2030 Agenda (United Nations), 703–719

U

Ubuntu, 195
Ukraine, 3, 5, 32, 33, 55n49, 82, 106, 193, 199, 202, 205–207, 236, 258, 283, 307, 317, 331, 343, 363, 374, 382, 384, 391, 419, 436, 439, 441, 443–446, 456, 456n3, 458n11, 465, 465n38, 465n40, 468, 468n46, 475n72, 476n78, 476n81, 477, 478n83, 482, 485, 493, 500, 502, 506, 560, 567, 649, 653, 657, 658, 667, 682, 696, 718
UNAIDS, *see* Joint United Nations Programme on HIV and AIDS
UN-Habitat, 337, 592
Union of South American Nations (UNASUR), 228

750   Index

United Arab Emirates (UAE), 18, 85n6, 96, 100, 454, 462n28, 484, 491n15, 543–555, 591, 637
United Arab Emirates, Ministry of Foreign Affairs and International Cooperation (MOFAIC), 551–554
United Kingdom, 8, 46n11, 48n17, 50n28, 52n35, 239, 253, 254, 263, 318, 436, 444, 445, 461, 462n22, 471n53, 610, 649, 657, 660, 693
United Nations, Charter of, 4, 9, 639, 673, 674, 681, 733
United Nations Children's Fund (UNICEF), 608, 617, 635
United Nations Conference on Environment and Development (1992), 704
United Nations Department of Economic and Social Affairs (DESA), 715
United Nations Development Program (UNDP), 239, 537, 635
United Nations DPPA Innovation Team, *see* United Nations Policy and Peacebuilding Department
United Nations Economic and Social Council (ECOSOC), 714, 715
United Nations Educational, Scientific, and Cultural Organization (UNESCO), 221, 318, 390, 576
United Nations Emergency Force (UNEF), 445
United Nations Food and Agriculture Organization (FAO), 680, 681
United Nations Framework Convention on Climate Change (UNFCCC), 421, 692, 694, 697–701
United Nations General Assembly (UNGA), 355, 357, 359, 361, 390, 422, 442, 485, 513, 565, 619, 703, 707–709, 714, 732, 733
United Nations Global Compact for Migration (2018), 594
United Nations High Commissioner for Human Rights (UNCHR), 635
United Nations High Level Panel, 371
United Nations Innovation Network (UNIN), 508
United Nations Institute for Training and Research (UNITAR), 622, 686
United Nations Integrated Transition Assistance Mission in Sudan (UNITAMS), 511
United Nations Mediation Support Unit (MSU), 508
United Nations Office for Partnerships (UNOP), 715
United Nations Peacekeeping Operations, 305, 445, 447
United Nations Policy and Peacebuilding Department (DPPA), 507, 508, 510–512, 515
United Nations Program of Action on Small Arms, 734
United Nations Regional Economic Commission, 716
United Nations Secretariat, 424, 429, 506n1, 507–508, 515
United Nations Security Council (P5), 13, 46n10, 193, 227, 497, 651, 733
United Nations 2.0, 505, 507
United Nations Verification Mission in Colombia, 511
United States Agency for International Development (USAID), 263, 638
United States Center for Humanitarian Cooperation, 638
United States Department of Defense (DoD), 638

Index

United States Department of State, 263
United States of America, 8, 30, 50n29
United States Quadrennial Defense Review, 262
Uniting for Peace (1950), 444
Universal Declaration of Human Rights (1948), 632

V

Varghese, Peter, 126n8, 132, 133, 135, 270
Venezuela, 197–199, 388, 456n3, 457n6, 460n19, 462, 475n72, 587
Versailles, Treaty of (1919), 350
Vienna Conventions (1961, 1963), 10, 152, 402, 732, 733
Vietnam, 50n30, 51n34, 54n47, 54n50, 254, 368, 450, 456n5, 461n21, 464n36, 471n53, 493n18, 495, 694
Vietnam War, 439, 447
Vimont, Pierre, 317
Virtual Reality (VR), 505, 508, 511–512
Visegrad Group, 92n20, 591
Voluntary Local Reviews (VLRs), 717
Voluntary National Reviews (VNRs), 715, 716
Von der Leyen, Ursula, 654

W

Wang Yi, 185, 187, 188
"War on Terror," 36, 440
West African Science Center on Climate Change and Adapted Land Use, 73
Western Balkans 5 (WB5), 562–568, 563n6, 570–577
Western Sahara, 382

Westphalia, Peace of (1648), 32, 374, 678
WhatsApp, 222, 369, 374, 400
Wheeler, Tom, 196
Whitehouse, Sheldon, 695
Wilsonianism, 23, 30–33
Wilson, Woodrow, 23, 25–29, 169, 403, 585
Wiseman, Geoffrey, 60, 116, 117, 123, 127, 128n9, 506n1
World Bank, 70, 71, 90, 239, 437, 472, 494, 522n2, 528n5, 530, 532, 541, 562, 608, 617, 681, 705
World Competitiveness Yearbook, 561
World Economic Forum, 608, 696, 700
World Food Program (WFP), 554, 635
World Health Assembly (WHA), 422, 605, 606, 609, 618, 619
World Health Organization (WHO), 288, 310, 330–332, 337, 422, 439, 441–443, 447, 532, 554, 584, 592, 604–606, 608–614, 616–620, 635, 641
World Innovation Index (World Intellectual Property Organization), 533
World Summit on Sustainable Development (WSSD), 704, 705, 710
World Trade Organization (WTO), 82, 89, 89n12, 173, 286, 299, 439, 440, 447, 448, 481, 497, 501n27, 621, 622, 651, 666, 695, 698, 700
World War I, 54n50, 56n59, 169, 350
See also First World War
World War II, 48n19, 48n21, 53n45, 56n59, 169, 254, 460–463, 465, 472n57, 633
See also Second World War

X

Xi Jinping, 11, 174, 178, 184–188, 256, 258, 260, 470, 547, 614

Y

Yang Jiechi, 186
Yongxing Dao, 175
YouTube, 222, 226, 382, 510

Z

Zayed, Sheikh, 543, 544n1, 545, 547
Zelensky, Volodymyr, 206, 446
Zhao Lijian, 170
Zimbabwe, 199, 464n35, 475n72, 496
Zondo Commission (South Africa), 208
Zuckerberg, Mark, 371
Zuma, Jacob, 194, 203, 207–209